PUBLIC FINANCE

PUBLIC FINANCE
Public Choices and the Public Economy

John C. Winfrey

Washington and Lee University

HARPER & ROW, PUBLISHERS
New York, Evanston, San Francisco, London

TO BARBARA ANN

Sponsoring Editor: John Greenman
Project Editor: William Monroe
Designer: Gayle Jaeger
Production Supervisor: Valerie Klima

Public Finance: Public Choices and the Public Economy
Copyright © 1973 by John C. Winfrey

Library of Congress Cataloging in Publication Data
Winfrey, John C.
    Public finance.

    1. Finance, Public—United States. 2. Decision-
making. I. Title.
HJ243.W55   336.73   72-12139
ISBN 0-06-047156-5

CONTENTS

v

vii

PART IV: MACROECONOMICS AND THE PUBLIC SECTOR

PREFACE

By some odd scheme of things, a book's preface is the last part written. It is doubly odd since in the preface the author, although he is tired of his labor and desperately wants to put it down for awhile, nevertheless feels obliged to exhort the reader to diligent study.

Fortunately, the study of public finance is extremely interesting, and while at times the student may find the material difficult, he will never find it boring. *It was not always so.* Until the last few years texts were filled with laborious detail about budget procedures and tax and expenditure legislation. This approach has given way to questions such as: "Who benefits and who loses when taxes and expenditures are changed?" "How are the interests of various groups reconciled within public decision-making processes?" and "How do individuals and firms change their behavior in response to taxes and expenditures?"

Our basic approach will be to ask general questions and to present perspectives, concepts, and models useful for their analysis. It is a paradox that the more simple and abstract a model the more rigorous we must be about its assumptions and specifications. Yet being rigorous is well worth the effort since it allows the student to appraise critically the model's assumptions and value judgments and, of course, their implications for "real world" situations. This last step is crucial to the "learning experience." In order for the student to make this study his "own," he must not only learn the concepts and models but must relate them to his own feelings about the issues and policies.

The professor will find that there is maybe too much material here for a one-term course, especially if time is permitted to relate to the day-to-day unfolding of issues. Part IV may be deleted if the students have opportunity to study macroeconomic policy in another course. Moreover, Chapters 7 and 8 (outlining the growth of the public sector) may be assigned as outside reading and more class time spent on analyzing current, rather than past, issues.

Prefaces usually include an attempt to acknowledge the author's debt to others who have helped with the book. I find this task to be impossible. The economic theories in the text have been developed by innumerable economists through the years. I am particularly indebted to Professors Arrow, Buchanan, Musgrave, Tullock, and Samuelson. I have also received encouragement and aid from my colleagues and friends at Washington and Lee (particularly Lewis Adams and L. K. Johnson) and at Duke (particularly Frank deVyver and David Davies), as well as from my students (particularly Landon Lane). It is for students that this book is written, and I wish you rewarding learning experiences.

John C. Winfrey

I

**WELFARE ECONOMICS
AND PUBLIC CHOICES**

1
THE CASE FOR A PUBLIC SECTOR

How are we to study the public sector? Its economic activities take a variety of forms and there is more than one perspective we can use for analyzing them. In Part I we will use two basic approaches. The first approach is normative. We ask what norms or rules we can use for justifying public sector activities. This approach, which we elaborate in Chapters 1 and 2, is in the tradition of welfare economics. The central question is: How can we combine public and private sector activities so as to maximize our welfare? As economists we cannot expect to find "the" answer to such a question since it requires value judgments which we are not disposed to make.

The second perspective deals with the *how* of public choices. This approach is more in the tradition of positive economics and as such tries to avoid some of the difficulties of the normative approach. The emphasis here is on the nature of the decision-making processes we use in determining public finances.

Thus our approach may be described as eclectic or perhaps integrated. Our primary focus is on the process of making public choices. At the same time there are norms and value judgments inherent in those choices and we will attempt to make them explicit. We begin with the normative approach: Why is it necessary at all to have a public sector?

THE CLASSICAL LAISSEZ FAIRE MODEL REVISITED

Typically, we Americans are jealous of our economic freedom and are enamored of the way private market mechanisms seem to enhance the role of the individual in making economic choices. It is appropriate to ask whether the functions in question require *public* choice-making and implementation. If so, public sector activity is justified. We will tentatively agree that functions which can be carried on adequately by the private market should be left there. As the different functions of the public sector are examined we will also examine the arguments justifying them. These latter arguments necessarily include the explanation of why the private market cannot fulfill these functions. We will start with the familiar laissez faire[1] model of the market system and then move closer to our present "mixed" economy. The laissez faire model incorporates our

---

[1] The term *laissez faire* has come to mean a government economic policy of "hands off." The presumption is that the private sector can function best if left free of governmental interference.

value judgment that most economic functions are better left to the private sector. This was, of course, one of the major themes of Adam Smith, David Ricardo, and other classical economists writing in the eighteenth and early nineteenth centuries. Over the years, economists have embellished and added rigor to these arguments. The resulting classical laissez faire model demonstrates that, under certain assumptions, the free enterprise capitalistic system has self-contained incentives which, if allowed free play, make for maximum efficiency in the use of resources. Indeed, the model can be formulated to show (again under certain assumptions) that resources within this ideal economy are allocated so as to maximize the welfare of each citizen. The *classical laissez faire* model is an excellent starting point for our purposes. In the first place, we can develop a model economy with a minimum of public functions. These and additional public functions can be examined critically in the context of how they augment the private sector. Second, the *classical laissez faire* model (presenting as it does an "ideal economy") can be used as a norm with which to judge the efficiency of possible public sector activities.

It is necessary to begin by thinking of the economy as a system of interrelated economic units simultaneously carrying out their functions in response to market forces generated within the system. The genius of Adam Smith is that he saw the economy as a composite of interrelated units functioning together. Smith argued that capitalism operated according to natural law and, if left to follow its own course, would produce economic progress:

Projectors disturb nature in the course of her operations on human affairs, and it requires no more than to leave her alone and give her fair play in the pursuit of her ends that she may establish her own designs. . . . Little else is required to carry a state to the highest degree of affluence from the lowest barbarism but peace, easy taxes, and a tolerable administration of justice; all the rest being brought about by the natural course of things. All governments which thwart this natural course, which force things into another channel, or which endeavor to arrest the progress of society at a particular point are unnatural, and, to support themselves, are obliged to be oppressive and tyrannical.[2]

The underlying thesis of the classical model is that the interests of the community are simply the sum of the interests of its individual members; and each member, by seeking to maximize his own wealth, will maximize his neighbor's as well. The argument does not rest on the assumption that man is basically altruistic and therefore concerned about increasing his neighbor's wealth. Quite the contrary, the motives assumed to be central are those of self-interest and profit. The philosophical, theological, and scientific environment of eighteenth-century England and Europe was, of course, influential in shaping this concept of the economic system. The Renaissance emphasis on the individual; the rise of the merchant class; the naturalistic philosophy of Locke, Hume, and Hutcheson; and the theology of Scottish philosophers were all important in Adam Smith's formulation of the concept of a unified and naturally ordered economy. Accordingly, in his description of the "ideal" model Smith asserted the existence of an almost complete harmony between the general interests of the public and the particular interests of individuals:

Every individual is continually exerting himself to find out the most advantageous employment for whatever capital he can command. It is his own advantage, indeed, and not that of the society which he has in view. But the study of his own advantage naturally, or rather necessarily, leads him to prefer that employment which is most advantageous to the society.[3]

While the classical economists asserted that the competitive economic system functioned well in providing for increasing national wealth and a harmony of interests, they did not build a consistent model to prove their point. What was needed was an explanation of how the individual units within the system, by following their own goals, simultaneously worked toward a general equilibrium solution as well.

EXCHANGE IN THE OUTPUT MARKETS

Not until the introduction of the concept of maximizing by adjusting at the margin and the subsequent application of the equi-marginal rule at both the individual and firm level was it possible to incorporate the behavior of consumers and producers into a general equilibrium model. In the early 1870s, three works appeared in which the marginal principle was applied to utility.[4] All three writers, William Stanley Jevons of

[2] From a lecture given by the classical economist Adam Smith in 1749. Cited in John Rae, *Life of Adam Smith* (New York: A. M. Kelly, 1965), p. 62.
[3] Adam Smith, *Wealth of Nations*, ed. Edwin Cannan (New York: Modern Library, Random House, 1937) p. 421.
[4] William Stanley Jevons' *Theory* and Carl Menger's *Grundsätz* were published in 1871; Leon Walras's *Elements* was published in 1874. [Jevons, *Theory of Political Economy* (London and New York: Macmillan, 1871); Menger, *Grundsätz der Volkswirtshaftslehre*, 2nd ed. (Vienna: Holder-Pichler-Tempsky, 1923); and Walras, *Elements of Pure Economics*, trans. William Jaffé (Homewood, Ill.: Irwin, 1954).]

FIGURE 1-1

Long-run equilibrium of the
firm in perfect competition
(output market)

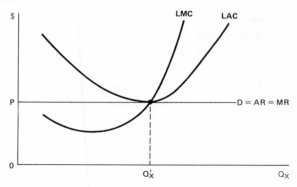

England, Carl Menger of Austria, and Leon Walras of France, had almost
simultaneously hit upon the same approach to analyzing the economic
system. They observed that each individual consumer maximized his utility
by comparing the benefits and costs of his purchases. He asks simply:
How much additional (marginal) utility per dollar will I get from purchasing a little more of good 1 and a little less of good 2?

It is assumed that the utility from each marginal unit purchased
diminishes as each additional unit is acquired. The consumer will purchase
additional units of a commodity only as long as its marginal utility per
dollar is greater than the marginal utility per dollar forthcoming from
other possible purchases. Hence the consumer will purchase additional
units of a particular commodity only to the point where the ratio of
marginal utility per price paid for the particular commodity is just equal
to the ratio of marginal utility per price paid for other commodities.
Carrying the consumption of the commodity in question further would
reduce total utility. The consumer's equilibrium position will be where the
ratio of marginal utility (MU) to price (P) is equal for all commodities
purchased:

$$\frac{MU_1}{P_1} = \frac{MU_2}{P_2} = \cdots = \frac{MU_m}{P_m}$$

EXCHANGE IN THE INPUT MARKETS

Although all three of the marginal " revolutionists " built their theoretical
systems with the aim of explaining marginal valuation for the economy as
a whole, only Carl Menger offered an explanation of how income distribution is related to the efficient allocation of resources by producers.

Menger conceived of the valuation process starting from consumers' judgments between commodities (lower-order goods) and extending to the factors used to produce these goods. Thus the value of productive factors was *imputed* from the value of the commodity produced. According to Menger this value could be ascertained by withdrawing one unit of the factor and observing the effect on total output. Menger's student, Friedrich von Wieser, improved this theory by explaining that it is the addition of the last marginal unit (rather than its withdrawal) that gives the correct value. More importantly, von Wieser demonstrated that this value could be expressed not merely in physical terms but also in terms of the economic value of the marginal product—that is, the monetary contribution of the factor in production.[5]

A similar approach had been begun by David Ricardo in his theory of rent. But whereas Ricardo had applied the concept only to rent, an American, John Bates Clark, and an Englishman, Philip Wicksteed, generalized this theory to explain the return to all factors of production.[6]

The producer also adjusts by the equi-marginal rule. It is assumed that within the relevant range of input combinations the marginal product of each input diminishes as more is added (the other inputs being held constant). The producer adds more of a particular input as long as its marginal product relative to its price is greater than the marginal product/price ratios of other inputs. When the marginal product/price ratios (MP/P) of all inputs are equal, the producer has attained the most efficient combination of inputs (say, inputs 1, 2, ..., m):

$$\frac{MP_1}{P_1} = \frac{MP_2}{P_2} = \cdots = \frac{MP_m}{P_m}$$

If the equilibria to which individual consumers and producers adjust are to reflect the most efficient use of resources, the output and input prices must reflect real opportunity costs. This condition is assured if perfect competition exists in all output and input markets. Consider Figure 1.1. The low point on the long-run average cost curve (LAC)

---

[5] See part I of Wieser's *Social Economics*, trans. A. Ford Hinrichs (New York: Adelphi, 1927).

[6] Wicksteed's presentation of the concept appeared in *An Essay on the Coordination of the Laws of Distribution* (London: Macmillan, 1894). Clark had outlined his thesis in "Possibility of a Scientific Law of Wages," *Publications of the American Economic Association*, vol. IV, no. 1 (1889).

FIGURE 1–2

Equilibrium of the firm in
perfect competition
(input market)

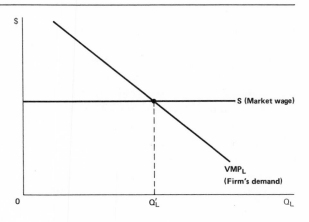

FIGURE 1–3

The firm's input demand
with more than one variable
input

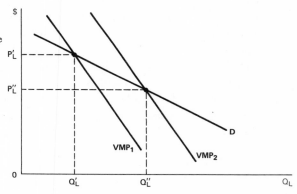

represents the optimum output for the firm. Q'_x is optimum in the sense
that it is the quantity at which present technology and the various
possible combinations of inputs make for the least possible average cost
per unit of output. With perfect competition firms will enter the market
until the market price, P, is driven down to the point where $LAC = P$
at Q'_x. The profit-maximizing condition of the firm is also met, since
$MR = LMC$.[7] If the firms in each output market adjust in this manner,
all market prices will reflect the costs of the inputs used in their production. Thus, the equilibrium combinations of goods to which consumers
adjust *will reflect utility maximization in the sense that the real costs of
producing the goods are implicit in their prices.*

Similar observations can be made concerning the input markets.

Consider Figure 1.2. The firm's demand for an input, say labor, is dependent on the marginal productivity of the input and is consequently downward sloping. The value of the marginal product (VMP) may be described in monetary terms as the marginal product, MP, multiplied by the price, P_X, of the product in question ($VMP_L = MP_L \cdot P_X$).[8] The supply of the input is assumed to be unlimited at the market price (since the firm is small relative to the market). The firm will maximize profit by adjusting the quantity of input units hired to the point Q'_L where additional revenue forthcoming is just offset by the additional costs incurred in hiring more units. At this point, VMP is equal to the market price, which in turn reflects the usefulness of the input to other firms as well.

GENERAL EQUILIBRIUM IN THE COMPETITIVE SYSTEM

But do all of the output and input markets hang together? More importantly, does the system operate in a way conducive to maximum social welfare? Although each had certain prescriptions for government intervention, Jevons, Menger, and Walras answered these questions affirmatively. Each thought his analysis demonstrated that a free exchange system was so ordered that individuals within it would behave so as to increase both individual and social welfare. Similarly Clark and the Swedish economist Knut Wicksell added strength to their argument by

---

[7] We recall from elementary economics that since the firm sells only at the market price, that price, P, becomes its demand, D, average revenue, AR, and marginal revenue, MR. We also recall that the firm maximizes profit by adjusting the quantity of output to the point, Q'_X, where the additional revenue forthcoming, MR, is just equal to the additional costs incurred in producing more output (long-run marginal costs, LMC).

[8] When several inputs, rather than one variable input, are being used in a productive process, the VMP curve of a particular input as described above does not exactly conform with the firm's demand for the input. In deriving the VMP curve, we assume that all other inputs are held constant. When several inputs are variable, however, a change in the price of one will change not only its quantity but the quantities of other inputs as well. Assume the price of the input in question is reduced. The composition of other inputs will be changed only if it augments the productivity of the first input. Hence, the VMP of the first input will shift to the right, as shown in Figure 1.3. The price of the input has fallen from P'_L to P''_L. Simultaneously the VMP has shifted from VMP_1 to VMP_2. In adjusting VMP to the lower price, the firm now employs quantity Q''_L. Thus the actual demand for the input is DD.

This addendum has not seriously affected our analysis, since the equilibrium to which the firm is shifting is still seen to be where $VMP = P_L$.

FIGURE 1-4

The circular flow model

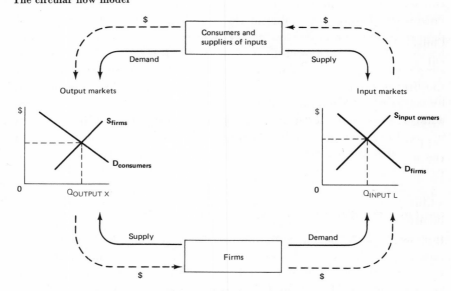

extending the equi-marginal principle to the behavior of producers as well as consumers.[9]

Let us briefly consider the way these markets are tied together. We will use the familiar "circular flow" model for our exposition. The system consists of economic units of two kinds, consumers (who are also suppliers of inputs) and producers. These two groups trade and set prices in two broadly defined types of markets: the output markets and the input or factor markets. Decisions made in markets of these two types determine (1) the composition of products manufactured, (2) the composition of resources going into the manufacture of various products, (3) the remuneration received by the owners of inputs, and (4) the provisions made for the maintenance and growth of the specific industries. These decisions are made effective by means of the prices set in the two types of markets.

This simple model is shown in Figure 1.4. The market price and quantity of a specific output are determined by the equilibrium of the amounts consumers *demand* (are willing to buy) at various prices and the amounts the firms *supply* (are willing to sell) at various prices. Simultaneously, the price and quantity of specific resources are determined by the equilibrium of the firms' *demand* for resources and the amounts of resources their owners are willing to *supply* in the specific occupation at various prices. Prices in all markets continually adjust towards the equilibrium between demand and supply.

In the output markets any temporary excess production of a particular market would require sellers to reduce their prices. At the same time producers would be reducing output and, as prices fell, consumers would increase their purchases. If a greater quantity were demanded than supplied, suppliers would respond by producing more, and, as prices rose, consumers would respond by reducing quantity demanded.

Correspondingly, prices in the input markets continually adjust to the equilibrium of the market demand (the summation of all firms' demand schedules) and the market supply (the summation of all resource owners' supply schedules). Thus, competition in the input markets insures that resources will be put to their most productive use and rewarded accordingly. The circular flow of money goes from consumers through the output markets to firms and from the firms through the input markets and back to the owners of inputs. Thus the organization of production is determined by "consumer sovereignty." The price system allows consumers to make known their willingness to buy certain products in the output markets; and firms, in turn, to adjust production to the changing tastes of consumers. The allocation of resources to those commodities which consumers value most highly turns out to be the allocation which promises the greatest profits to firms.

A rather esoteric question of the general equilibrium model is whether a unique solution exists for all of the behavioral functions making up the system. If one does exist, the argument that the internal relationships are consistent with maximum efficiency and welfare is strengthened. Walras, imposing the rigor of mathematics on his system, demonstrated that the system could be represented as a set of algebraic equations. In his model he included (1) m quantities of finished goods, (2) n quantities of factors of production, (3) specified techniques by which goods produced would require certain proportions of the factors, and (4) the marginal utility functions of consumers and owners of factors. The unknowns for this

[9] Clark had independently concluded that in equilibrium the exchange value of a commodity was reflected in its marginal utility to both individual and community. Hence, his theory of marginal productivity was an extension of this work. Wicksell's formulation derived primarily from the Austrians and Walras. See Wicksell's *Value, Capital, and Rent* (New York: Holt, Rinehart & Winston, 1954) and *Lectures on Political Economy* (London: Routledge & Kegan Paul, 1949).

system are *prices* for m finished goods and n factors, and *quantities* of m finished goods and n factors. One good can be designated the common denominator or *numeraire* and its price set equal to one. Thus the number of unknowns is $2_m + 2_n - 1$. Correspondingly, Walras demonstrates that precisely $2_m + 2_n - 1$ equations are given by the technical conditions and the utility functions. Hence a "determinate" solution is suggested.[10]

AN ASSESSMENT OF THE NECESSARY CONDITIONS OF THE PERFECTLY COMPETITIVE SYSTEM

Keeping in mind that we intend to justify public activity only on the basis of private sector inadequacies, let us assess conditions necessary for perfect competition in all markets. We begin by outlining the institutional framework within which the system is assumed to be operating: (1) self-interest as the driving motive, (2) freedom of enterprise and choice, (3) private property, (4) reliance upon the private price mechanism, and (5) a limited role of government. These characteristics need little further explanation. We have noted Smith's argument that the individual by following his own self-interest within the competitive system necessarily promotes the interests of others as well. In the process of maximizing profit, firms adjust the composition of output and input so as to use resources efficiently and in accordance with the maximum welfare for consumers.

We observe at the outset that one of the necessary functions of the public sector is to provide the legal framework under which private property may be obtained, controlled, and disposed of. This legal framework must include various restrictions on the freedom of enterprise and choice left open to the individuals within the system.

The basic assumptions regarding the behavior of consumers, input owners, and producers are as follows:

1. consistent behavior on the part of all buyers and sellers;
2. a large number of buyers and sellers in every market;
3. perfect mobility of all inputs;
4. perfect knowledge by all buyers and sellers; and
5. divisibility and assignability of all economic benefits and costs.

CONSISTENT BEHAVIOR

All consumers, input owners, and producers exhibit consistent behavior. More specifically: Individuals acting as consumers and/or input owners consistently use the equi-marginal rule to maximize the utility derived from purchases and sales of their economic goods and services. Similarly, producers consistently work to maximize profit by producing at that price-quantity combination where marginal revenue equals marginal cost, and by utilizing the equi-marginal rule with respect to the most efficient combination of inputs.

LARGE NUMBER OF BUYERS AND SELLERS

In order for the behavior of each consumer, input owner, and producer in each market to be consistent with efficiency and the maximization of utility by individuals there must be a large number of buyers and sellers in every market.

Consider the situation where there are only a small number of sellers in the output market. The actions of each seller now affect market price and hence the marginal revenue derived by the seller. The extreme case, pure monopoly, is illustrated in Figures 1.5 and 1.6. The producer maximizes profit by producing where marginal revenue, MR, equals long-run marginal cost, LMC. The most efficient use of resources would be at that output where long-run average costs per unit of output are lowest. In Figure 1.5 the profit-maximizing output is *less* than the optimum "least

---

[10] While the simple process of counting variables and equations is perhaps permissible for our expository purposes, it does not suffice as a complete proof that the system has a unique solution. The existence of an equal number of equations and unknowns does not guarantee that a solution exists, much less a unique solution. One difficulty with the general equilibrium analysis of the perfectly competitive system is in accounting for "free" goods, which are not accounted for by the pricing mechanism. Walras did not attempt to include in his system goods having zero or even negative values. The conditions under which the system may possess a meaningful solution (though not necessarily unique) were not rigorously outlined until 1935 by Wald. Since that time substantial refinement has taken place. For a discussion of Wald's existence proof see R. Dorfman et al., *Linear Programming and Economic Analysis* (New York: McGraw-Hill, 1958), chap. 13.

Walras did not merely count equations and unknowns to demonstrate the existence of general equilibrium in all markets. He attempted to show that the system was stable in that it contained automatic forces which brought it back towards equilibrium whenever it was disturbed. M. Blaug discusses the contribution of Walras in *Economic Theory in Retrospect* (Homewood, Ill.: Irwin, 1962), chap. 13. The stability question was, of course, inherent in our earlier discussion of the forces making for the equilibrium of market demand and supply. Walras and Marshall also discussed equilibrium in these terms and noted (though from different perspectives) the possibility of multiple equilibria when the long-run supply curve is negatively sloped. Since public financing is a relevant option when the market system breaks down, we will be concerned with this question at later stages in our study.

FIGURE 1–5

Profit maximization by the pure monopolist at a less than optimum size output

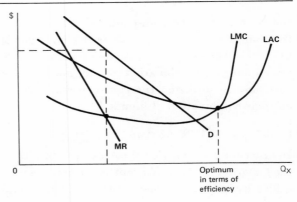

FIGURE 1–6

Profit maximization by the pure monopolist at a greater than optimum size output

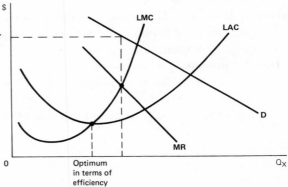

FIGURE 1–7

Demand of the pure monopolist for an input

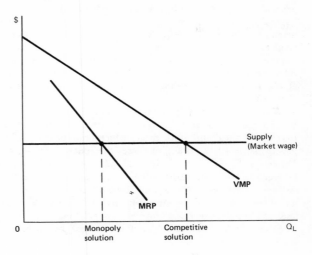

cost " solution; whereas in Figure 1.6 the profit-maximizing output is *greater* than the optimum "least cost " solution. These cases demonstrate that when output markets do not have a large number of sellers, the producers do not necessarily use the most efficient means of production, as they do in pure competition.

A second difficulty arises if monopoly is present. Note that in Figure 1.1 price equals long-run marginal costs. If all output prices reflect the marginal costs of producing particular goods, the utility-maximizing behavior of consumers will lead the economy to produce the composition of output consistent with the community's maximum welfare. This proposition will be discussed at length in Chapter 2. It is appropriate to note that when the number of sellers in a particular market is not sufficient to drive market price down to long-run marginal costs, the ratios of marginal utility to price will no longer reflect true opportunity costs and a misallocation of resources with respect to welfare maximization may occur.

Let us contemplate this aspect of resource misallocation by observing the effect of monopoly on the firm's demand for inputs. Firms operating in perfectly competitive markets apply the equi-marginal rule in terms of the value of the input's marginal product—the value being determined by the price of the output being produced: $VMP_L = P_X \cdot MP_L$ (see Figure 1.2). For a firm in a monopoly position, any addition of input *and resultant increase in the firm's output* has an effect on market price. Thus the value of the additional input's contribution declines not only because of its diminishing marginal product but also because of declining marginal revenue on the output produced. Input demand based on declining marginal revenue as well as declining marginal product is termed marginal revenue product: $MRP_L = MR_X \cdot MP_L$. The firm's demand based on marginal revenue product (MRP) will be lower than if based on the value of the marginal product (VMP). Consequently the firm will hire fewer inputs than it would if the market were purely competitive (see Figure 1.7).[11] The effect on prices paid for inputs will not be significant if

---

[11] The relationship between MRP and the firm's demand for a specific input *when several inputs are variable* is similar to that described between the VMP and the firm's demand (see footnote 6 for this chapter). If the employment of complementary inputs changes, say, increases in response to a decrease in the price of the input in question, the MRP will shift to the right, making the firm's demand for the good more elastic than the MRP curve. In each case the firm's demand curve will be more elastic than the VMP or MRP curves, respectively. However, except for the observation that the MRP curve does not accurately depict the elasticity of the firm's demand for an input when several inputs are variable, the analysis pictured in Figure 1.7 holds.

FIGURE 1–8

The monopsonistic input
market

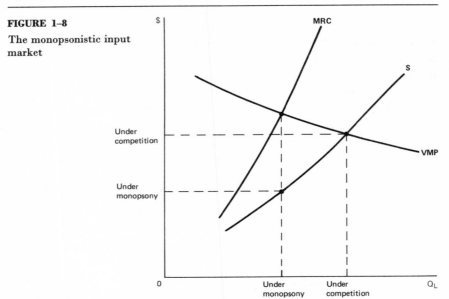

the firm is operating in a competitive input market. However, the quantity of the commodity produced will be smaller than in the competitive case, since fewer inputs are employed. Taking the perspective of the consumer who is maximizing welfare, we see that since the price of the commodity does not reflect the real costs of its production, use of the equi-marginal rule will no longer lead to the optimum combination of purchases. Hence the composition of output does not accord with that which maximizes welfare, as dictated by consumer preference in the general equilibrium model of perfect competition.

The point here is that the absence of the second necessary condition may lead to a misallocation of resources in the private market with regard to both efficiency and welfare maximization. Such a condition may warrant activity by the public sector.

PERFECT MOBILITY OF INPUTS

The third condition necessary for perfect competition is that all inputs possess perfect mobility. Each input must be capable of responding immediately to price changes in competitive input markets.

Efficient allocation of inputs necessarily depends on their being responsive to the price differentials which occur in the market. In a dynamic economy the composition of outputs desired is changing rapidly. In order to assume that the system is adequately accommodating to these changing tastes, one must assume that all inputs possess a high degree of geographical and occupational mobility. The assumption of complete geographical mobility implies that an input owner (for example a laborer) will have no reservations about moving from one locality to another provided there is a difference in wage rates. The related assumption of inter-industry mobility implies that labor is sufficiently homogeneous to insure rapid adaptation to changing skill and education requirements.

While the competitive model is useful as a starting point for our analysis, it is not an accurate picture of our current economic system. Perfect mobility is not consistent with the practices of labor unions or other organizations which attempt to monopolize the supply of a particular input. Moreover, individuals have many ties with their community and are often unwilling to move unless the wage differential is quite large.

Perfect mobility also implies that no barriers exist to the entry or exit of firms to or from any market. Hence, the existence of patent or copyright laws is not consistent with this condition nor is imperfect knowledge on the part of prospective entrants. Likewise, it must be assumed that the capital and administrative requirements for entering any particular industry pose no barrier to entry. Such conditions, of course, are not always present in real world markets, and their absence leads to an allocation of resources which may be undesirable and hence may call for economic activity through the public sector.

An input owner's lack of mobility may mean that the market for his services contains only a small number of potential buyers. The extreme case, monopsony, is pictured in Figure 1.8. When a firm employs a large proportion of the available units of an input (say a particular type of labor), hiring additional units has an effect on the market price (or wage). Raising wages to attract additional workers will also push up those paid to all workers currently employed. Thus the marginal costs of hiring additional workers are higher than the average costs. The firm, facing an upward-sloping supply curve, equates the value of marginal product with marginal resource costs (the latter now being different from the wage rate). As Figure 1.8 shows, the wage rate and quantity hired are lower under monopsony than they would be if the market were perfectly competitive. Here again the absence of enough buyers and sellers in the market (or the lack of input mobility) leads to an allocation of resources different from that foreseen in the general equilibrium model, where all markets are perfectly competitive.

The implications of these "imperfections" for public sector activity will be explored at length in later chapters. Our purpose now is to examine the conditions necessarily inherent in the perfectly competitive system and to briefly indicate the nature of possible departures from these conditions.

PERFECT KNOWLEDGE

The requirement of perfect knowledge has been made obvious by the foregoing discussion. Unless consumers, input owners, and producers have complete knowledge of all product and input prices as well as all productive techniques, resources will not be allocated correctly. Consumers might buy at higher prices than necessary, thereby neither maximizing satisfaction nor encouraging producers to produce the appropriate combination of goods. Producers, not having full knowledge of all input prices and production techniques, would also be in danger of choosing less than optimum combinations of resources.

Carried to its logical extreme, this condition would require that consumers, input owners, and producers have perfect knowledge of all future prices and technological breakthroughs. Otherwise their present actions would involve risk and the possibility of misallocation of resources. Here again we note that divergence of the real world from our model may make compensating activity by the public sector appropriate. For example, a major task of the governmental agricultural agencies is to disseminate information to farmers. The governmental employment agencies enhance the knowledge of firms and job seekers as to prospects in different labor markets. The New Deal's venture into producing electric power, the Tennessee Valley Authority, is often cited as an example of governmental intervention's overcoming imperfect knowledge on the part of private firms, who underestimated the potential demand for low-cost electric power. Currently, government intervention in the exploration of space and the development of large-scale transport jets is justified in part by the risk associated with imperfect knowledge.

DIVISIBILITY AND ASSIGNABILITY OF ALL ECONOMIC BENEFITS AND COSTS

If the price system is to provide the correct signals to individuals and firms, all benefits and costs must be accounted for in terms of prices, and

---

economic goods must be divisible into units which can be bought and sold. Most economic goods and services exhibit these characteristics. Consider a consumer's purchase of a refrigerator. Upon purchase, its benefits become his private property. These benefits are divisible in that they accrue not to everyone but only to the user. The institution of private property enhances the ability of the market system to assign prices to commodities which reflect the benefits accruing in their use. Hence the owner of the refrigerator has *exclusive* rights to its services.

Next consider the purchase of a machine by a firm. The price paid by the firm is based on the machine's services, which are the sole property of the firm. In order for the private sector to allocate resources effectively, all benefits and costs associated with the consumption and production of economic goods must be divisible and reflected in those prices assigned by the price mechanism. Otherwise the prices to which consumers, owners of inputs, and producers adjust will not represent the actual opportunity costs involved (in consumption and production), and welfare will not be maximized.

Our "real world" economic system does not comply fully with the requirement that all benefits and costs be completely divisible and assignable. Where the price system cannot assign appropriate values to goods and *exclude* nonowners from their use, public financing may be appropriate. The collective building of a lighthouse is often used to illustrate the absence of the "exclusion principle" in collective goods. We visualize a situation where local fishermen recognize the need for a lighthouse on a rocky portion of their coastline. Let us suppose in addition that it is not worthwhile for an individual fisherman to build the lighthouse if the only return he can expect is his own use of its light. Moreover, it is unlikely that the individual fisherman could hope to sell the light beams to those fishermen who desired them, since no means exist for excluding fishermen who do not pay. Consequently, community action is required if the lighthouse is to be built. Since the private market does not adequately provide for the production of goods whose benefits and costs are not fully divisible and assignable, it may be necessary to finance these goods through the public sector.

The question of divisibility and assignability of benefits and costs is crucial to our analysis of public finance. It behooves us to digress in order to develop these concepts further. We do so by developing the broader concept: "externalities."

EXTERNALITIES

Externalities exist, according to Buchanan and Stubblebine,[12] whenever the utility function of an individual (or the production function of a firm) includes a variable which is under the control of a second individual (or firm). Let us state the case in terms of an individual and his utility function. An externality is present when

$$u^A = u^A(X_1, X_2, \ldots, X_n, Y_1)$$

The utility of an individual A is a function not only of activities under his own control, $X_1, X_2, \ldots, X_n$, but also of another activity, Y_1, which is under the control of a second individual, B. Buchanan and Stubblebine define "activities" to include "any distinguishable human action that may be measured, such as eating bread, drinking milk, spewing smoke into the air, dumping litter on the highways, giving to the poor, etc."[13] The definition is obviously broad; there are an infinite number of ways our well-being can be affected by the actions of others. It behooves us to use some categories and ask what types of externality are important to our study. For example, externalities which may affect consumers or firms we categorize as consumption and production externalities. Secondly, we may wish to distinguish between the initiating agent (a producer or consumer) and the affected party (a producer or consumer). Thirdly, we may wish to differentiate between externalities which *benefit* the affected party (positive externalities) and those which *harm* him (negative externalities). Since we have already come up with eight possible categories let us give some examples:

Consumption activity creating a positive consumption externality. Many of us benefit from the "consumption" activities of others. Suppose my neighbor enjoys keeping a beautiful lawn and flowers. His enjoyment or "consumption" also creates enjoyment for me . . . a positive consumption externality.

Consumption activity creating a positive production externality. A producer may also gain from the consumption activity of others. Our broad definition of externality would cover even the changes in a buyer's tastes which increase the demand for a firm's product.

As we shall see, education creates several types of benefits. We may consider it a consumption activity since the student benefits directly. It also creates a positive production externality for the firm wishing to hire literate employees.

Consumption activity creating a negative consumption externality. If instead of keeping a beautiful lawn my neighbor preferred tinkering with junk cars which he kept in his front yard, his recreation would create a *negative* consumption externality for me. I would suffer from the noise and the unsightliness of his lawn.

Consumption activity creating a negative production externality. If a change in tastes *decreased* the demand for a firm's product, a *negative* production externality would result. Of course the market mechanisms will readily respond to such a change. But the market cannot accommodate all externalities. An example from this same category would be the negative production externality suffered by the owner of a fishing pier whose product is harmed by motor boats and water skiers.

Similar externalities can be created by production activities:

Production activity creating a positive consumption externality. Consumers experience positive externalities any time a firm lowers the price of a commodity they purchase. For example, if new technology allows a firm to maximize profit by selling a better product at a lower price his actions obviously benefit the consumer. Moreover if the market meets the competitive conditions, we would expect the externality to be appropriately resolved.

Here again we find externalities which cannot be resolved by the market. For example, new technology may make it profitable for a firm to adopt a process which reduces its pollution of a stream. Yet the market does not provide a process by which the firm can charge swimmers for the benefits they receive in the form of cleaner water.

Production activity creating a positive production externality. A model often used to describe externalities features a beekeeper located close to an apple orchardist. In the process of making honey, the bees naturally partake of the nectar of the apple blossoms. Assume that the beekeeper is operating at less than optimum size. Now suppose a new spray allows the orchardist to profit by increasing the size of his orchard: a positive production externality for the beekeeper.

Production activity creating a negative consumption externality. The literature on ecology is full of examples of production activities which harm various types of consumption. The consumption of air by city dwellers is

[12] J. M. Buchanan and W. C. Stubblebine, "Externality," *Economica* (November 1962), pp. 371–384.
[13] *Ibid.*, p. 372.

affected by smoke from factories, and the vacationer is confronted with polluted streams and omnipresent billboards.

Production activity creating a negative production externality. Firms may also create negative externalities for each other. A firm forced to pay a higher price for an input fits this category. A picturesque model is the "smokestack case." As usually contrived, the scene opens with a poor widow whose sole support comes from the hand laundry she washes and dries on her clothesline. Then the factory next door purchases new equipment which lowers its costs but blackens both the air and the poor little old lady's laundry. The pure air in the neighborhood had no price set on it although it was an input in the widow's business. Now, by expropriating this free good the factory imposes a negative externality.

PRIVATE SECTOR RESOLUTION OF EXTERNALITIES

Now we ask what types of externalities are important to our study. Our examples demonstrated that many types of externalities can be suitably resolved by the mechanics of the private sector markets described earlier. If the necessary conditions are fulfilled, these mechanics will lead to equilibria where no externalities remain. Recall that our definition of externality referred to an activity *under the control* of another individual. Recall also that in perfectly competitive markets *no one buyer or seller has any control over market price*. It follows that externalities disappear in the long run equilibrium of the perfectly competitive market.

In small number situations such as the washerwoman and the factory the externality will not disappear. However, it may be that both parties can gain by adjusting their activities. For example, the widow may find it beneficial to bribe the factory to filter its smoke. If so she could adjust her bribe so that the benefits received (which may be expressed in terms of marginal utility) are equal to the marginal costs of the bribe. Of course it is necessary that the firm also be able to gain. It would adjust its filtering activity to the point where its gains from the bribe were equal to the marginal costs of filtering. Thus *resolution is defined in terms of the equimarginal rules and occurs only when the activity has been adjusted in accord with the marginal benefits and costs of each party's other activities.*

If the highest bribe the widow could offer would not cover the cost of an adequate filter no trade would take place and the externality would remain "unresolved."[14] In both situations the solution qualifies as a Pareto optimum as described below. But whether the solution, whether resolved or unresolved, is *suitable* is another question. The word *suitable* reveals that if we wish to evaluate an externality in welfare terms, a value judgment is necessary. The "smokestack" case was described so that even if "resolved" it would seem *unjust*. Picture again the little old lady whose clean air had been expropriated by the factory. Is it just that she be required to pay the factory to filter its smoke? We cannot decide without making a judgment favoring the utility of one party at the expense of the other.

In Chapter 2 we will explore the difficulties in making judgments as to the utility of individual and public economic activities. We will find that our role *as economists* is quite restricted. Jevons, Menger, and Walras had assumed that the utility experienced by the individual could be measured. Moreover, as Walras explained:

> We need only assume that such a direct and measurable relationship does exist, and we shall find ourselves in a position to give an exact mathematical account of the respective influences on prices of extensive utility, intensive utility and the initial stock possessed.
>
> I shall, therefore, assume the existence of a standard measure of intensity of wants and intensive utility, which is applicable not only to similar units of the same kind of wealth, but also to different units of wealth.[15]

Armed with this information we could proceed to make interpersonal utility comparisons. If we also possessed knowledge of how *best* to distribute goods we could resolve all externalities in a "socially acceptable manner." But in the absence of a unique utility index no such prescriptions can be made. In fact, as the critics of Jevons, Menger, and Walras were quick to point out, the whole analysis fails if no index can be found.

Vilfredo Pareto (1848–1923), Walras' successor at the University of Lausanne, sought to avoid the difficulties of measuring utility and interpersonal utility comparisons by simply observing the individual's behavior as he traded certain goods or activities for others. Presumably trades would not take place unless the individual were made better off or were indifferent between his new and former positions. Trading would cease when further trading would make one of the traders worse off. In Chapter 2 we will consider the proposition that the freedom to trade leads to a

---

[14] In both cases, resolved and unresolved, the externality remains since the second party still has control over the activity which affects the first.

[15] Walras, *Elements of Pure Economics*, p. 11.

resource allocation which optimizes welfare. The Pareto criterion accepts as optimum any equilibrium where further gain by any individual could come only by making another worse off. But as our "smokestack" model illustrated the Pareto criterion has serious shortcomings if presumed to be a *norm*.

Earlier we asked what externalities may require public sector action. Our discussion has indicated that where one or more of the conditions of perfect competition are missing externalities may be created which can not be suitably resolved. Presumably if the externality cannot be suitably resolved in the private sector, *public* sector activity would be required. Unfortunately no criteria of suitability has yet been determined. However our general approach, which we will continue in the next chapter, is to evaluate the effects of an externality in terms of the perfectly competitive model; that is, how would resource allocation differ if perfect competition prevailed instead of the externality.

THE PRISONER'S DILEMMA

A concept closely related to "externality" which describes additional situations calling for public sector activity is the "prisoner's dilemma." In the prisoner's dilemma, as with an externality, the basic problem is reaching agreement where individuals are interdependent. If they could reach agreement and stick to it, all would be better off. Unfortunately, each individual has incentive to defect.

Let us explain this concept in terms of an example:[16] A robbery has been committed; two suspects have been apprehended and are being kept in separate cells. The district attorney is sure they are guilty but needs a confession to prove their guilt in court. He therefore attempts to get a confession by playing on their mutual mistrust and their inability to communicate with each other. He offers each the choice of confessing or not confessing. If neither individual confesses, each will receive punishment for a minor charge such as illegal possession of a weapon, resisting arrest, and receiving stolen goods; the penalty is one year each. If one individual confesses (and the other doesn't) the district attorney promises to let the confessor off with a light sentence, say three months, and "throw the book" at the other, say a sentence of five years. However, if both confess, each will have to serve four years. Obviously both would be better off if they could agree not to confess. Yet there is strong incentive for the individual prisoner to confess. If he confesses and the other doesn't, he is much better off; while if he doesn't confess and the other does, he gets the maximum sentence. The most likely outcome is that both prisoners will confess and receive the four-year sentence. Both would have been better off if they could have agreed not to confess.

The problem is not simply one of communication. For even if both prisoners had met beforehand and planned an alibi, there would be still good reason for each to defect on the prior agreement once the district attorney offered his alternatives. In order for the prisoners to insure that neither confesses, they must impose a penalty, say death, on the one who does. The dilemma can be overcome only by a reordering of incentives so that the most beneficial choice for each individual (not confessing) is also the one which is most beneficial for all.

The prisoner's dilemma is helpful in describing a large number of situations in which the incentive patterns of individual participants lead to results which are undesirable for the group as a whole. It would be beneficial, for example, for both the United States and Russia to limit the " arms race." Yet even if the difficulties of poor communication and unenlightened strategists could be overcome and agreement reached, there would still be incentive for each country to cheat, thereby gaining some military and political advantage.

In some situations involving interaction over time it is possible that the prisoner's dilemma will be resolved as the individuals change their behavior in response to each other. If, for example, there are only a few firms selling products which are very similar, each firm may capture a large part of the market simply by pricing its product slightly below the others. Such behavior, however, usually erupts in a price war which is undesirable for all. If repeated price wars occur, the individual firm will find that trying to underprice its competitors is not really advantageous. A market price will evolve that each firm honors. In other oligopoly situations, however, the incentive to undercut will still be great enough to cause frequent price wars.

The prisoner's dilemma also occurs in situations involving a large number of participants; in fact these are the situations where public

---

[16] We can gain further insight into the prisoner's dilemma by defining it in terms of the theory of games. In Chapter 3, where we utilize game theory perspectives for analyzing voting behavior, we elaborate on the prisoner's dilemma. The term is attributed to A. W. Tucker. A good explanation of the concept is presented in R. Duncan Luce and Howard Raiffa, *Games and Decisions* (New York: Wiley, 1957) pp. 94–113.

sector activity is more likely to be required if the dilemma is to be resolved. Consider the aforementioned "lighthouse" case, where fishermen must somehow agree to build a lighthouse. If the fishermen are few, they may be able to reach agreement on the building of the lighthouse. Moreover, they may be able to use community pressure to insure that everyone pays his share. This last step is important, since the benefits of the lighthouse—the light beams—are indivisible and unassignable, so that an individual fisherman can still gain them even if he does not contribute to their costs. Without some sort of coercion to make everyone contribute, each fisherman will attempt to "free-ride." Consequently, the "prisoner's dilemma" phenomenon will occur, and the lighthouse will not be built.

If the fishermen are numerous, several factors increase the difficulty of reaching a binding agreement. First, the logistics problem of getting everyone to participate in making the decision and in sharing the costs becomes more substantial. Second, the temptation to "free-ride" is increased, since the contribution of each individual is so small (relative to the whole cost) that its absence will have little effect on the quantity or quality of the lighthouse services.

The factors inhibiting socially favorable individual behavior in the "lighthouse" case are present in any situation which requires a decision to produce goods whose benefits are indivisible and unassignable. Each individual will have an incentive to "free-ride." Consequently, coercion by the public sector is usually necessary if individuals are to contribute their share of the costs.

Our illustrations demonstrate that the "prisoner's dilemma" phenomenon may occur in a wide variety of situations, and in some of these situations public sector activity may be appropriate to change the "rules of the game," so that individuals in pursuing their own interests will not at the same time produce socially undesirable results. As our study proceeds, we will examine additional examples and evaluate a variety of alternative responses by the public sector.

PURE VERSUS QUASI-PUBLIC GOODS

A "pure" public good may be defined as one whose consumption by one individual does not reduce the benefits received by another. Few activities fit this category. Classic illustrations are lighthouse beams and radio and television transmissions. Clearly these benefits are not divisible and assignable via the market price mechanism. Or consider the nature of the major federal expenditure: defense. The benefits of our defense system accrue to all our citizens, regardless of the amount of tax each pays. We observe that indivisibilities of production as well as consumption may be involved. If defense were not provided by government, no doubt certain wealthy individuals and corporations would acquire bombshelters, ICBM's, and the like for their own protection; however, the nature and level of defense expenditures would probably not be those desired by society.

Owing to the costs of producing an adequate defense system and the indivisibility of benefits in consumption, we may designate defense a pure public good. For most economic activities, however, the proportion of benefits and costs accounted for in the private market is higher. It often becomes a matter of judgment as to whether private financing alone will provide a " suitable " amount of the good. Activities which require such a judgment are termed " quasi-public " goods. From the standpoint of consumption the important difference between the " pure public good " and the " quasi-public good " is that the benefits of the former are completely indivisible and must be consumed equally by all, while the latter creates individual (divisible and assignable) benefits as well as public benefits.

In our economy, many quasi-public goods are publicly financed. The most important example is education. Many of the benefits from this activity are divisible and assignable, and one can in fact purchase education through the private sector. The reason is that obvious benefits accrue to the individual purchaser of education. However, educational activity also creates benefits that are indivisible and unassignable. The whole society benefits if the population is informed and well educated. Since these additional benefits would not be adequately reflected in competitive prices, it is appropriate that public financing be used to devote additional resources to education, so that the marginal benefits (including the social benefits) are more in accord with the marginal opportunity costs.

Another important quasi-public activity is the provision of medical care. One can hardly avoid debate on the "proper" way to finance medical care. Most medical doctors argue that further public financing of medical care will bring too much government control and bureaucratic inefficiency and waste. Americans in general and economists in particular are responsive to this argument. We have traditionally put much faith in the competitive price system as a means for allocating resources efficiently. Public financing can, of course, bring greater or lesser amounts of governmental decision making, depending on the way the spending is organized. But to the extent that decisions are made in government, rather than in the competitive market, the advantages of competition are lost. This may be reflected by patients' overindulgence in trips to the doctor or hospital, which needlessly crowds facilities. Or it may be reflected in the misallocation of resources by administrators who are uninformed or else unmotivated by resource prices that reflect market opportunity costs.

But the arguments one hears for increasing the public financing of medical care are also persuasive. In the first place, it is argued that the demand and supply of medical care do not exhibit the characteristics of the competitive market. It is asserted that the medical profession restricts the supply of new doctors—that many qualified applicants are refused entry to medical schools each year.[17] Therefore, monopoly elements are present in the market for medical services. To the extent that the prices of medical services do not reflect their real opportunity costs, some form of public financing and/or regulation may be the second-best solution.

Perhaps a more frequent argument for increased public financing stems from the externalities created. A healthy community offers its members certain indivisible benefits. These benefits may be purely economic—a healthier work force available to manufacturers. Or the benefits may be psychic—an individual may benefit by knowing that others, no matter how poor or underprivileged, can afford some minimum standard of medical care. Or perhaps one may benefit by knowing that all small children, the elderly, or the disabled are provided with publicly financed medical care. Such benefits obviously are not easily quantifiable.

To reiterate, the tasks of estimating these social benefits and of establishing an appropriate financing (so that benefits are in accord with costs) are difficult and subject to much debate. One's estimation of the relative magnitude of individual and social benefits accruing from a particular good or service will influence his ideas of the proper method of financing.

SOME OBSERVATIONS ON PUBLIC FINANCING IN THE COMPETITIVE MODEL

Let us pause to make observations stemming from our analysis thus far. We began by outlining the conditions under which the operation of the perfectly competitive model supposedly insures efficient allocation of resources and maximizes the welfare of society. Efficiency is generated because each perfectly competitive market contains the correct number of optimum-sized firms, each firm producing the quantity of output at which average costs are lowest and producing with the appropriate combination of inputs. Welfare maximization is insured because (1) individuals adjust their composition of purchases by the equimarginal rule, (2) the price mechanism communicates their desires to firms, and (3) the firms respond by adjusting the composition to meet consumer demands while utilizing resources as efficiently as possible.

In presenting the model we noted that several of the prerequisites and necessary conditions are quite unrealistic. Let us first reconsider the prerequisite that an " acceptable " distribution of wealth exists prior to the market adjustments leading to welfare maximization. Without the prior existence of an " acceptable " distribution of purchasing power, the signals transmitted through the price system to firms are erroneous and both the composition of output and its distribution among individuals are less than optimum. We note that there is nothing "built into" the model to insure movement towards an " acceptable " distribution of wealth. Moreover, the definition of an " acceptable " distribution involves a value judgment requiring considerable presumptivity on the part of the model builder. We observe that capitalism as it has operated in the real world has institutions which in fact encourage a high concentration of wealth through time. These institutions—such as private property and the right of inheritance—operating within capitalistic systems prior to the 1930s resulted in concentrations of wealth that were unacceptable to at least a majority of citizens in the United States and several other Western nations. Consequently, those nations which have retained a basically competitive system, have modified it so that the public sector performs the function of *redistribution*.

There are *positive externalities* to the redistribution activity. It cannot be assumed the "appropriate" amount of redistribution would occur simply by allowing the wealthy to redistribute as they choose. As Musgrave and Goldfarb point out, redistribution creates a collective benefit

---

[17] Unfortunately, most proposals to increase public financing of medical care are not directed to increasing the supply of doctors.

not subject to the *exclusion principle*.[18] That is, if one person gives to a poor person it benefits not only those two persons but any others who wish the poor person to be better off. Consequently a free rider problem exists even for such an "altruistic" activity. Of course, the number of persons in the group must be large for the free rider problem to be effective. However, if U.S. citizens are concerned about "the poor" of the entire country, public sector activity *to include involuntary participation* is required or the redistribution which takes place will be less than optimal.

Observation 1. The competitive system does not automatically insure an acceptable distribution of wealth. Moreover, there are positive externalities in redistribution. Hence one function of the public sector may be to redistribute wealth.

Our cursory examination also revealed various ways in which departures from the conditions necessary to the "perfectly competitive model" may make public financing appropriate. On the output side of the market, natural or man-made barriers to entry—such as economies of scale, ownership of key processes or materials, patents, licenses, or tariffs—may make for an allocation of resources inconsistent with the efficiency and welfare norms of the perfectly competitive model. Misallocation on the input side may result not only from the firm's output position but from a lack of input mobility caused by such factors as unions, family ties, or imperfect knowledge.

Finally we note that resource misallocation may occur because the benefits and costs associated with the production of certain goods are not divisible and assignable by means of price transactions in the private market. Hence, public financing may be used to augment or replace private sector activity when externalities which cannot be resolved suitably within the private market are present.

Observation 2. A second function of the public sector may be to influence the allocation of resources in cases of public or quasi-public goods or where other requirements for competitive markets are not fulfilled.

To complete our cursory comparison of the laissez faire model and our mixed economy we must consider the macroeconomic responsibilities of the public sector. Chronic unemployment is impossible in most depictions of the classical laissez faire model. The successors of Adam Smith illustrated that if prices were free to fluctuate, equilibrium would be attained in the markets for both outputs and inputs. Incentives within the economic system would insure that resources were efficiently employed as money flowed through the output and input markets and back again. In this ideal model of perfect competition, resource owners are paid in accord with their contribution to production; then, in turn, they use this income to purchase goods and services. Flexible prices insure that no surpluses or shortages occur and that unemployment is impossible.

It has become painfully obvious over the years, however, that our economic system does not function like the model, especially with respect to equating aggregate demand and supply at a full employment level of GNP. John Maynard Keynes's major contribution to economics is that he analyzed the departures of our system from the competitive model and made policy recommendations.

Briefly, our system differs from the classical model because prices do not fluctuate freely in the output and input markets and the circular flow of money is interrupted. In periods of inadequate aggregate demand, for example, this inflexibility causes decreased production rather than lower prices. In such a situation public monetary and fiscal policy is necessary in order to increase private and public spending. Alternatively, when aggregate demand[19] is increasing faster than the supply of real goods and services, public policy may be called for to curtail spending and avoid inflation. Macroeconomic policy, an important aspect of public financing, will be explored in detail in Part III. For the moment it is sufficient to observe that monetary and fiscal policy play an important part in providing for the stability and growth of our economic system.

Observation 3. A third function of the public sector may be to employ monetary and fiscal macroeconomic policy where the system does not automatically provide for full employment, stable prices, and economic growth.

In summary our normative approach to the economic rationale of the public sector has revealed three broad functions: enhancing resource allocation, redistributing income, and macroeconomic policy. The "norm" underlying our examination has been the ideal of the laissez faire economy complete with perfectly competitive markets. As we have observed, these

[18] For further discussion of the public nature of redistribution using the welfare approach see H. M. Hochman and J. D. Rodgers, "Pareto Optimal Redistribution," *American Economic Review*, vol. 59 (September 1969), R. S. Goldfarb, "Pareto Optimal Redistribution: Comment," *American Economic Review*, vol. 60 (December 1970), R. A. Musgrave, "Pareto Optimal Redistribution: Comment," *American Economic Review*, vol. 60 (December 1970), and G. M. von Furstenburg and D. C. Mueller, "The Pareto Optimal Approach to Income Redistribution," vol. 61 (September 1971).

[19] The term "aggregate demand" refers to the summation of all spending on final goods forthcoming from consumers, businesses, and government at different price levels.

functions—especially income redistribution—require a collective judgment involving interpersonal utility comparisons. We have outlined several types of "imperfection" in our economy which may result in misallocation of resources and thus warrant public sector intervention. In our discussion of externalities and the prisoner's dilemma we have introduced important questions concerning the ability of the decision-making processes of the private market to provide acceptable decisions. Undaunted by these questions we will continue our normative approach in Chapter 2.

2
THE SATISFACTION
OF PUBLIC WANTS

Let us explore in more detail the relationship between individual preferences and public economic activity. Our focus will be on the individual's welfare as it is affected by collective economic activity—specifically public financing. In Chapter 3 we will develop these criteria further by examining the question of how to best implement those wants of society which require public financing. In the remainder of Part I these criteria will be used to examine current and past governmental budgets.

There are two general approaches to the question of how individual wants for public goods may be satisfied through public financing. The *benefit approach* attempts to consider both benefits and costs of fiscal activity and is inherent in a concept we have used frequently—equating marginal benefits and costs. The *ability-to-pay* approach focuses only on the cost side of public financing, attempting to establish criteria for judging taxes in terms of the "sacrifice" they impose.

Both approaches are inherent in the following statement by Adam Smith:

The subjects of every state ought to contribute toward the support of the government, as nearly as possible, in proportion to their respective abilities; that is, in proportion to the revenue which they respectively enjoy under the protection of the state. The expense of government to the individuals of a nation is like the expense of management to the joint tenants of a great estate, who are obliged to contribute in proportion to their respective interests in the estate. In the observation or neglect of this maxim consists what is called the equality or inequality of taxation.[1]

Thus Smith adroitly linked the benefit approach to the ability to pay. The *benefit* derived by the individual is defined by Smith to be the revenue earned under the protection of the state. And since the individual's *ability* to earn revenue depends in part on the protection of the state, he can be expected to pay taxes accordingly.

Both approaches are with us today. The benefit approach has developed through the welfare economics of Antonio de Viti de Marco,[2] Knut Wicksell,[3] and the voluntary exchange theory of Erik Lindahl[4] to become

---

[1] Adam Smith, *Wealth of Nations*, ed. Edwin Cannan, (New York: Modern Library, Random House, 1937), p. 777.
[2] See Antonio de Viti de Marco, *First Principles of Public Finance*, trans. Edith Paolo Marget (New York: Harcourt Brace Jovanovich, 1936).
[3] See Knut Wicksell, "A New Principle of Just Taxation" in R. A. Musgrave and Alan T. Peacock, eds., *Classics in the Theory of Public Finance* (London: Macmillan,1958).
[4] See Erik Lindahl, "Just Taxation—A Positive Solution" and "Some Controversial Questions in the Theory of Taxation" in Musgrave and Peacock, *Classics in the Theory of Public Finance*. See also R. A. Musgrave, *The Theory of Public Finance* (New York: McGraw-Hill, 1959), pp. 73–78.

FIGURE 2–1

The "correct" quantity
of private good X

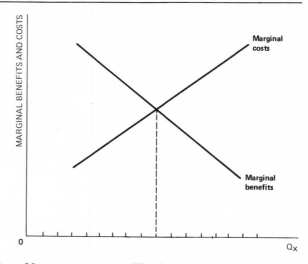

a part of the "new" welfare economics. The benefit approach views
government activity in terms of benefits (public goods and services) and
costs (taxes) to the individual citizen. The question is whether the composition of private and public goods may be adjusted so as to maximize
welfare. One starts from the familiar equi-marginal principle as used by
the individual when making purchases. Presumably the marginal benefits
derived from additional purchases of a particular good decrease as more
are purchased. That is, the second sport coat provides less marginal
utility than the first. One must also consider that in purchasing additional
units one gives up purchasing power which could have been used to
purchase other utility-producing goods. The individual maximizes his
satisfaction by purchasing enough of each good so that the marginal
benefits equal the marginal costs (in the form of other goods which must
be foregone). This adjustment, depicted in Figure 2.1, is made for all
goods. A question basic to the benefit approach is whether there is some
such unique equilibrium to which the individual may adjust both private
and public goods. The next question is whether the welfare of society as a
whole can be said to be maximized by the production of a particular
composition of private and public goods.

The ability-to-pay approach, which also is inherent in Adam Smith,
has more recently been expanded by Abba Lerner,[5] A. C. Pigou,[6] and
Hugh Dalton.[7] This approach emphasizes the revenue side of the ledger,
ignoring expenditures. The question becomes: How can public financing
be accomplished with the least sacrifice?

Both the benefit and ability-to-pay approaches are useful for evaluating fiscal policy. Yet both present serious difficulties. The benefit approach, in looking at both expenditures and taxes, must cope with the difficult task of deciphering individual wants. We have already perceived the problems attendant upon measuring and comparing individual preferences. Where preferences for public goods are to be deciphered, these problems are compounded by the absence of the exclusion principle and the reluctance of the potential taxpayer to reveal his preferences.[8]

The ability-to-pay approach ignores the question of wants (and the equating of marginal benefits and costs) and looks only at the costs or "sacrifices" entailed by a given tax bill. Consequently we are left with a rather limited view of the individual's "welfare." This approach is quite useful if one's task is to compare alternative tax plans—yet if alternative taxes are to be "evaluated" in terms of welfare, one again faces the task of obtaining knowledge of each individual's preference pattern; else how could the "sacrifice" of an individual be measured? Unfortunately, economists have had little success in discerning preference (utility) patterns of individuals; and without such knowledge, the "sacrifices" required of individuals by various taxes cannot be compared. As Richard Musgrave observes: "The ability-to-pay approach collapses completely if one accepts the hypothesis of the newer welfare economics, that interpersonal utility comparisons are inadmissible."[9]

THE ABILITY-TO-PAY APPROACH

The ability-to-pay argument could easily be traced into antiquity. No doubt the realization that one should tax those most willing and able to pay occurred simultaneously with the invention of taxes themselves.

But the argument as developed in recent periods is based on something more than the obvious fact that it is operationally efficacious to tax those able and willing to pay. Instead, like the benefit argument, it is derived from the notion of "justice."

---

[5] See A. P. Lerner, *The Economics of Control* (New York: Macmillan, 1944).

[6] See A. C. Pigou, *A Study of Public Finance*, 3rd ed. (London: Macmillan, 1951).

[7] See H. Dalton, *Principles of Public Finance*, 9th ed. (London: Routledge & Kegan Paul, 1936).

[8] The notion of the exclusion principle was introduced in Chapter 1.

[9] Musgrave, *The Theory of Public Finance*, p. 63.

FIGURE 2–2

Definitions of equal
sacrifice

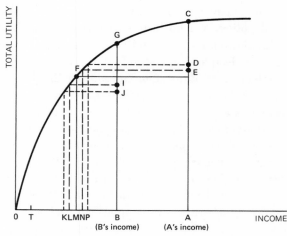

Equal absolute: CD = GJ

Equal proportional: $\dfrac{CE}{CA} = \dfrac{GI}{GB}$

Equal marginal: B's income after taxes = A's income after taxes

John Stuart Mill presented the classical economists' case for the ability-to-pay doctrine.[10] Mill had rejected the benefit approach. If the major function of government was protection of the citizenry, he felt that the benefit approach implied regressive taxation. If, however, "justice" were to be the basic criterion, the ability-to-pay doctrine could be argued strongly. To Mill, justice meant *equal treatment under the law*. He argued that "equality" in taxation meant *equality in sacrifice*.

The ability-to-pay approach was also popular with other classical economists and political writers of that period. One reason was their focus on revenue rather than expenditure. As pointed out in Chapter 1, the classical economists explored the various possible functions of government spending, but their usual prescription was to keep expenditures at a minimum. They considered the question of how to apportion taxes with the least sacrifice, but they did not extend the ability-to-pay notion to the logical conclusion that the government should redistribute income in order to maximize welfare. To the exponents of laissez faire, government intervention on this scale would have been undesirable.

Adam Smith, as quoted earlier, defined "equality" of taxation in terms of ability to pay:

The subjects of every state ought to contribute toward the support of the government, as nearly as possible, in proportion to their respective abilities;

that is, in proportion to the revenue which they respectively enjoy under the protection of the state.

The index of ability here is the revenue or income of the individuals. In previous periods "wealth" might have been designated the appropriate index; however, as industrialization continued and more transactions were carried on in terms of money, the appropriate base became income.[11]

Many factors complicate the consideration of the proper base for taxation. Should leisure be included in income? What about income not spent on consumption? If the latter is saved and invested, should the resultant income be taxed again? Would not this "double taxation" make for greater sacrifice? Similar questions arise in the attempt to determine the tax *rate* which imposes equal sacrifice. There is also the question of what precisely is meant by "equal" sacrifice.

CONCEPTS OF EQUAL SACRIFICE

The classical economists were not specific about "equality" of sacrifice. Three concepts of equal sacrifice may be distinguished: equal absolute, equal proportional, and equal marginal (or "least aggregate").[12] Taxes which impose "equal absolute" sacrifices are those which cause the same loss of total utility to each taxpayer. "Equal proportional" sacrifices are imposed when the ratio of lost utility relative to total utility is the same for every taxpayer. Taxes imposing "equal marginal" sacrifices reduce each taxpayer's income to the point where the marginal utility of income of each is the same.

Figure 2.2 is helpful in illustrating these concepts. We must assume that preference patterns are known and identical; therefore, the total utility curve OGC is representative for any taxpayer. As income is added, total utility increases but at a decreasing rate. In other words, the marginal utility of income diminishes; the income recipient gets less enjoyment out of each additional dollar. Let us compare two taxpayers, A and B. A's income is OA and B's is OB. Before taxes A's total utility is AC and B's is BG.

---

[10] See Mill, *Principles of Political Economy*, ed. W. J. Ashley (London: Longmans, Green, 1921).

[11] Smith, however, would exempt all income below the subsistence level from taxation.

[12] These were outlined by A. G. Cohen-Stuart and F. Y. Edgeworth. See Cohen-Stuart, *Bijdrage tot de Theorie der progressieve Inkomstenbelasting* (The Hague, Netherlands: Martinus Nijhoff, 1889), and Edgeworth, *Papers Relating to Political Economy* (London: Macmillan, 1925). A good outline of the "equal sacrifice" concepts is given in Musgrave, *The Theory of Public Finance*, pp. 95–102.

Assume further that the total tax bill is AT. If we tax so as to impose *equal absolute sacrifice*, we must reduce the total utility of A and B by the same amount. The dotted lines in Figure 2.2 depict this case. Note that $CD = GJ$; thus, equal amounts of total utility have been taken from each taxpayer. Measuring the amount of the tax on the horizontal axis, we find the tax to A is PA while the tax to B is KB. Imposing equal absolute sacrifice means a larger tax bill for the high-income individual, A, because of the diminishing marginal utility of income. The sum of both taxes is equal to the total tax bill ($PA + KB = TA$).

If we tax so as to impose *equal proportional sacrifice* (dashed lines), we equate the ratio of the utility lost to the total utility of each taxpayer. Thus we equate GI/GB to CE/CA. By taxing so as to equate these ratios, we make the tax burdens equal with respect to their relative impact on total utility. The amount taken from B, BL, and the amount taken from A, AN, sum to fulfill the tax bill requirement. Again A's tax bill is larger, owing to the diminishing marginal utility of income.

Taxes imposing *equal marginal* sacrifice would be the most progressive of the three. In fact both A's and B's income would be reduced to the same amount, OM. As the solid line in Figure 2.2 shows, the equal-marginal-sacrifice tax takes AM from A and BM from B. Marginal utility is simply the rate at which total utility increases as income increases; in other words, it is the slope of the total utility function. If we assume identical utility patterns, a reduction of both incomes to OM has the result of leaving both A and B at the same point on the total utility curve (F) and thus with the same marginal utility of income. This tax is said to cause the least aggregate sacrifice because the aggregate amount of utility lost is less than in the other cases. Since the marginal utility of income diminishes as income increases, taxes which hit the higher income groups hardest are the least costly in terms of total utility. The logical conclusion of this approach is that, in order to maximize welfare, incomes should be equalized. In cases where the amount of the tax bill is less than the difference between incomes, A must pay the whole tax bill plus a *transfer* to B so that their incomes may be equal.

Let us pause to consider the implications of these various concepts. In the first place, the assumptions we accept initially in order to make these comparisons are somewhat unrealistic. Although research continues, very little has been accomplished in the effort to analyze and compare individuals' preference patterns. Indeed, the new welfare economics declares that interpersonal comparisons of this nature cannot be made. The assumption of identical preference patterns, although useful in presenting the concepts above, is untenable. Finally, it is again appropriate to ask what "value judgments" are involved. A choice between equal absolute, equal proportional, or equal marginal sacrifice must be derived from some notion of what is "just" or "equitable."[13]

QUESTIONS INVOLVING DIMINISHING MARGINAL UTILITY OF INCOME

The two crucial difficulties involved in imposing "equal-sacrifice" taxes have been shown to be (1) the value judgment as to what "equality" means and (2) the fact that utility or preference patterns are unknown. But since the equal-sacrifice concept is important, let us proceed a short way further, temporarily assuming these difficulties resolved. We find that the method of taxing to impose equal sacrifice is still not immediately obvious.

Assume that all preference patterns are known and identical to that depicted in Figure 2.2. The special features of this function are that it starts from the origin and that its slope is such that the percentage change in utility is the same as the percentage change in income. This means that the change in marginal utility is just equal to the change in income.[14] Consequently, the function makes a good *starting point* for asking what sort of taxes are required under the three concepts of equal sacrifice. Now, if we wish to impose equal absolute sacrifice, the tax rate structure will be proportional.[15]

---

[13] Musgrave outlines the positions of some writers: Adam Smith and J. S. Mill both failed to specify the character of the "equal sacrifice" they advocated. "Cohen-Stuart argued that there was a clear preference for equal proportional sacrifice because this would leave unchanged relative positions in terms of total utility. Sidgwick and Marshall favored equal absolute sacrifice, while others such as Carver interpreted equality in terms of equal marginal sacrifice. Edgeworth, and later Pigou, held that there was no logical or intuitive choice between the equity principles of equal absolute and equal proportional sacrifice. Arguing on welfare grounds, they considered equal marginal sacrifice the only proper rule, not as a matter of equity, but because it met the welfare objective of least aggregate sacrifice." (The latter objective also requires a value judgment.) Musgrave, *Theory of Public Finance*, p. 98, which includes references to the arguments cited.

[14] Hence the marginal utility function derived from this total function would be a rectangular hyperbola.

[15] But if the utility schedule is steeper, as in Figure 2.3, *progressive* rates will be required to obtain equal absolute sacrifice. And if it is *flatter*, as in Figure 2.4, *regressive* rates will be required. The point is that even if we decide to assume utility functions identical, we still must know the *rate* at which utility changes with income before we can decide on the tax rate structure.

FIGURE 2-3

Total utility case #1

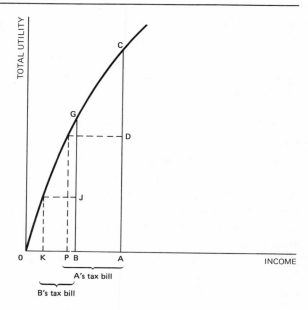

FIGURE 2-4

Total utility case #2

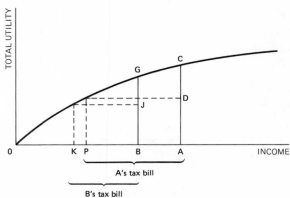

If we choose to impose equal proportional sacrifice for persons with utility patterns like that in Figure 2.2, our rate structure must be progressive.[16] As income increases, the horizontal portions of the dotted lines will draw closer together; hence, upper income groups can pay progressively more and yet make equal (proportional) sacrifice.

To impose equal marginal sacrifice upon utility patterns similar to Figure 2.2 maximum progression is required. This remains true for any utility function for which marginal utility declines as income rises. Only this rather extreme choice can allow us to make the rate structure decision without precise knowledge of the rate at which utility changes with income (that is, the slope of the utility function).

Now let us again consider the basic assumptions of the ability-to-pay approach. The proposition that individual preference patterns can be quantified and in turn compared has already been examined and questioned. It has been noted that many economists rule out *any* analytical inquiry involving interpersonal comparisons. If this is the case, then the whole ability-to-pay approach is useless. But let us continue in order to see whether, if the assumption of diminishing marginal utility of income holds, at least something can be said about the effect of taxes on the welfare of individuals.

Several questions remain concerning the assumption of diminishing marginal utility of income. It is usually assumed that income within the so-called subsistence level has an infinitely high utility. Of course this level differs according to what the individual considers the basic " essentials " of life. Moreover, what is considered "subsistence" may change through time. It is generally accepted that as income rises above this "level," the marginal utility of additional increments of income declines. But there is disagreement as to how much marginal utility of income diminishes at higher income levels. It should be remembered that the marginal utility of income is something quite different from the marginal utility derived from obtaining greater quantitites of a particular commodity. It is easy enough to believe the proposition that as one obtains more and more sport coats, the satisfaction derived from each addition is lower. But additions of income allow the recipient to purchase from among the entire range of commodities. Moreover, additions to income might have the effect of changing tastes (although theoretically one's "tastes " include all possible income and expenditure alternatives). A change in income may engender new aspirations. The individual discovers that he can just about afford a cabin in the mountains. He suddenly becomes highly desirous of the marginal income that will allow him to purchase it. In other words, his utility pattern has changed.

---

[16] This is because as income increases, marginal utility diminishes faster than average utility (the ratio of total utility to income). If the function were such that marginal utility declined at the same rate as average utility, proportional taxes would be called for. If marginal utility declined less rapidly than average utility, only regressive taxes would impose equal proportional sacrifice.

FIGURE 2–5

Least aggregate sacrifice
with unknown preference
patterns

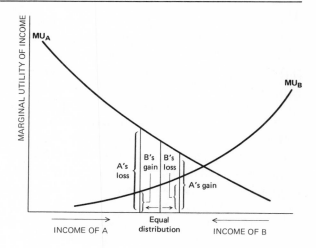

Additional possibilities of changing tastes appear when it is recognized that persons base their notions of well-being on their neighbor's condition as well as their own. If a promotion involves a move to a wealthier neighborhood, one is quick to adjust his "standard" of living upwards. Moreover, if one's neighbors begin to exhibit a higher standard of living, it is natural to emulate them. This is known as "keeping up with the Joneses." Similarly, if acquaintances of a lower income group begin to spend on a level closer to one's own, it is natural to attempt to "keep ahead of the Smiths." In either case the effect is to raise one's marginal utility for additional income.

Finally, we should note that time can be an important factor. Tastes tend to harden into habits. Luxuries become necessities. The utility lost by an individual who has to give up a Rolls Royce he has come to think of as a "necessity" may be much greater than that lost by a *nouveau riche* whose taxes cause him to lose his Rolls Royce. And of course over time new styles, new modes of transportation, new products—in short, whole new sets of living conditions—evolve. These factors are in part a response to changing tastes but at the same time tend to alter tastes themselves.

These observations lead us to conclude that the preference patterns of individuals within the economy are neither identical nor stable through time. It follows that there is no one way in which marginal utility diminishes with income. Indeed, on occasions the marginal utility of income may in fact shift upwards.

LEAST AGGREGATE SACRIFICE WITH UNKNOWN PREFERENCE PATTERNS

If we acknowledge that preference patterns are neither identical nor stable, it is difficult to make a case for any of the "equal"-sacrifice tax rate structures. For even if we could decide which principle of equal sacrifice was most appropriate, we would need exact knowledge of all preference patterns to implement it. Professor Abba P. Lerner of Michigan State University has considered the more realistic situation where preference functions are neither known nor identical but exhibit declining marginal utility of income.[17] His argument is illustrated in Figure 2.5. The economy is composed of two individuals, A and B, whose marginal utility of income diminishes. However, the exact slope and position of the curves are not known by those making decisions about taxes. In Figure 2.5 we assume that both A and B have equal incomes (as shown by the center middle vertical line). A's income is measured from the lefthand side and B's from the right. Hence, A's MU of income slopes downward to the right and B's slopes downward to the left.

If the decision makers knew the precise shape of A's and B's curves and desired to promote maximum aggregate welfare, they would tax and transfer so as to equalize the marginal utilities of A and B.[18] But in the absence of this knowledge a move away from equal distribution of income may be in the wrong direction. Suppose the decision is made to tax A and transfer that amount to B, as illustrated by the lefthand vertical line. We see that A's loss is the entire area beneath MU_A, whereas B's gain is the area beneath MU_B. The difference between these is the net loss in total utility.

Now suppose that the decision makers decide to tax B and give to A as depicted by the vertical line on the right. In this case there is a net gain in total utility, since A's gain is greater than B's loss. The net gain of this latter alternative, however, is less than the net loss incurred under the first. If we assume that either alternative has an equal chance of being decided upon, it is best always to move toward an equal distribution of income.

Proceeding from the utilitarian goal of maximizing aggregate welfare, Lerner concludes that in the absence of known preference patterns, least aggregate sacrifice is most likely attained by a program of maximum progression in taxes.

---

[17] Abba P. Lerner, *The Economics of Control* (New York: Macmillan, 1944).
[18] Thus Lerner is assuming the decision makers have chosen to impose equal marginal sacrifice.

FIGURE 2–6

Marginal utility and
disutility in budget
action

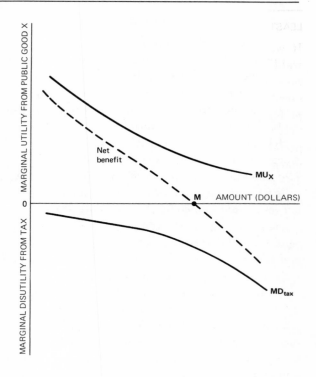

THE CONTRIBUTION OF A. C. PIGOU

Professor A. C. Pigou's work has done much to reconcile the benefit
and ability-to-pay approaches. Formerly, those using the ability-to-pay
approach had been absorbed only in questions involving the revenue side
of the ledger. Discussions centered around the question of how taxes
might be implemented so as to cause the least amount of sacrifice. But let
us, following Pigou, consider the welfare of the individual taxpayer in
terms of not only the sacrifice imposed by public financing, but also the
benefit.

The benefits accruing to an individual are in the form of his consumption of public goods. The costs imposed are in the form of income which
taxes take away. The "sacrifice" imposed by taxes occurs because the
income could have been used to purchase goods on the private market.
The benefits or utility from the consumption of these private goods may
be seen as opportunity costs incurred in the production of the public
goods. Pigou expressed these relationships in terms of the marginal utility

and marginal disutility created by devoting additional amounts of income to certain goods.[19] If the marginal utility for the production of each good is equal to the marginal disutility caused by paying for it—either in the marketplace or via taxes—then the optimum allocation of resources has been achieved. This optimum allocation refers to choices between different public goods as well as between goods in the public and private sectors. Figure 2.6 illustrates the "correct" case. The production of public good X has been carried to point M, where the marginal utility derived from X is just equal to the marginal disutility imposed by the taxes necessary to pay for its production. As long as there is a positive net benefit from devoting more and more income to the production of good X, expenditures and taxes should be increased.

Pigou's analysis is useful because the ability-to-pay approach is extended to the expenditure as well as the revenue side of the budget. The problems inherent in aggregating from individual preferences to social preferences are not solved. The marginal utility in Figure 2.6 supposedly can represent that of society; however, in order to arrive at what "society" wants, one must first know the shape of all individual preference patterns and then make a value judgment as to whose utility is to be maximized. If the output mix forthcoming from the decision-making process of the free enterprise economy (or a "model" of it) is to be considered appropriate, value judgments must be made as to the initial distribution of economic and political power within the system and the processes by which this power is exercised. The marginal disutility resulting from taxes involves the same questions: Again the social disutility must be derived by aggregating individual disutilities. Moreover, the final disutility for any amount of tax depends on how the tax is to be distributed among individuals. Pigou would impose taxes so as to cause the "least total sacrifice"; that is, he would impose "equal marginal" sacrifice by means of completely progressive taxes. This choice of tax programs is in itself a "value judgment."

The point is that if we are to speak of the optimum allocation and distribution of goods, it is necessary to make certain assumptions about

---

[19] It is necessary, of course, to speak in terms of marginal rather than total values if we are to arrive at an optimum "balance." The appropriate question does not concern the *total* utility an individual receives from expenditures on education versus those on highways but, rather, whether the individual would prefer a little more spending on education and a little less on highways.

individual preference patterns and to resolve certain value judgments.[20] In following the benefit approach to relating individual welfare to public financing it will be useful to keep these insights in mind.

THE BENEFIT APPROACH

THE EARLY DEVELOPMENT OF THE BENEFIT APPROACH

In the seventeenth century, political theory usually explained government activity in terms of the "contract theory of the state." According to this theory, the state provided the service of protecting the individual in return for taxes. If the terms of this contract were seriously misconstrued by the state, the ruler risked the danger of being overthrown. Initially this explanation was put forward by political theorists to whom the arrangement seemed part of the "natural law." But it appealed also to theorists who saw the "contract" relationship simply as an outgrowth of human behavior.

The benefit approach was upheld by the classical economists of the eighteenth and nineteenth centuries, who used it effectively in their arguments for liberal legislation. But while Smith, Ricardo, J. S. Mill, and others eschewed the attempt to use utility as a measurement of value, Jeremy Bentham (1748–1832) developed a complete system of social ethics based on the assumption of the measurability of pleasure and pain. By equating pleasure with goodness and pain with evil, one could simultaneously judge the efficiency and morality of particular economic and political activities. If all individuals were assumed to have *identical* pleasure-pain reactions, this "felicific calculus" could be extended to include public as well as private activity. Thus, the benefits of public fiscal policies could be evaluated in terms of the happiness contributed to society.

In the course of applying the benefit approach to specific situations, the classical political economists become aware of certain of the necessary assumptions outlined in the previous sections. First, as in Bentham's case, some assumptions must be made as to how individuals' preference patterns are related; otherwise no measurement can be made of the pleasure and pain involved in an activity. The legitimacy and efficacy of attempting to compare individual preference or welfare positions are and have been seriously questioned. Temporarily we, like Bentham, will again assume that individuals possess identical preference patterns—an assumption that will receive more attention as our study proceeds.

The benefit approach did not necessarily lead early political economists to advocate that individuals contribute equal amounts to the public till. Reasoning from the observation that the main function of government was protection, it was most often argued that individuals should pay according to the amount of wealth government helped them protect. Hence, most of the earlier writers favored a tax proportional to income.[21]

That the argument inherently assumed *protection* as the state's primary legitimate function seems odd today. However, it must be remembered that most writers in the eighteenth and early nineteenth centuries, Adam Smith included, felt that government functions should be held to a minimum.[22] Their observations had been that most government expenditures were wasteful. Consequently, less attention was given to the question of "balancing" benefits and costs and more to the question of minimizing the sacrifice inherent in paying taxes.

THE BEGINNINGS OF THE VOLUNTARY EXCHANGE APPROACH

In the latter part of the nineteenth century a new perspective developed which renewed emphasis on the benefit approach. Taxes came to be considered as *voluntary payments* to the government for services rendered. The perspective changed from explaining taxes as "just" in light of benefits received to explaining expenditures and taxes as part of welfare maximization.[23] We have noted that a question crucial to the benefit

---

[20] More will be said on this subject in a later section of this chapter.

[21] For example, Montesquieu, McCulloch, and Senior favored the proportional tax. Others, however, favored progressive taxes. Rousseau and Sismondi favored progressive taxes, since they felt that the wealthy benefited relatively more from protection. Bentham and Adam Smith favored proportional taxes for income over and above a minimum subsistence (in essence this is a progressive system). John Stuart Mill, reasoning that the poor were protected by government from the economic power of the wealthy, rejected the benefit approach because it seemed to argue for a regressive tax system.

[22] In *Wealth of Nations* Smith argued that only three governmental functions were required for the economic system to function. The first two, "protecting the society from the violence and invasion of other independent societies," and "establishing an exact administration of justice," fall within the argument above. The third duty, "erecting and maintaining certain public institutions and public works," while not considered as important, also lends itself to Smith's argument for taxing in proportion to income. Obviously, many public institutions and public works enhance the ability of individuals to earn income; thus payment of taxes according to income is justified.

[23] Among the earlier contributors to this new perspective were Antonio de Viti de Marco, M. Pantaleoni, U. Mazzola, and Emil Sax. English translations of some of their works and others can be found in Musgrave and Peacock, *Classics in the Theory of Public Finance.*

FIGURE 2–7

The Lindahl model of expenditure and tax shares

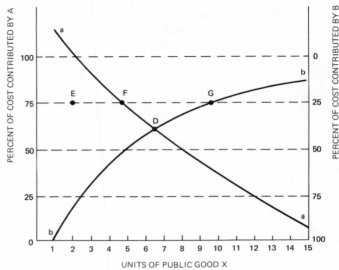

approach is whether the government will respond to voters in such a way as to maximize welfare. These early writers recognized that optimum allocation of society's resources required that the government increase expenditures to the point where the taxes paid were just equal to the marginal benefits received. At this optimum allocation marginal benefits would equal marginal costs for each individual in the society (as depicted in Figure 2.1).

The exchange relationship between the individual and the government was thought of as being like market exchange except that taxes were the prices of public services. It was recognized, though, that public goods and services, not being subject to the exclusion principle, must be *consumed in equal amounts by all*. Thus it would seem impossible to find the right combination of taxes and expenditures for each citizen. One contributor, de Viti de Marco, reconciled these difficulties by assuming that the *demand* for public services was proportionate to an individual's income. This would indicate that a proportional income tax would best maximize welfare—provided, of course, that the voters could effectively dictate the quantity provided of each public service.

De Viti de Marco, however, did not endorse proportionate taxation. Instead, on entirely different grounds, he opted for *progressive* taxation. He argued that the marginal dollar meant less to the wealthy. While additional dollars add to total utility, the amount of happiness added by each marginal dollar diminishes. Consequently, if the cost to the wealthy is to be equated to the benefit received, they must be taxed progressively. Yet, while de Viti de Marco and others demonstrated how welfare might be maximized through the provision of services and voluntary payment, the rationale still rests on the tenuous assumption that the government will provide the correct amount of each public service.

The Swedish economist Knut Wicksell (1896) extended the dimensions of the benefit approach by examining the political requirements for achieving the appropriate amount of public financing to maximize welfare. He saw the democratic form of government as a necessary part of the process of reconciling individuals' wants.[24] Wicksell had a high respect for the will of the individual, yet he realized that it was not reasonable to expect any decision-making system to achieve *complete unanimity*. An appropriate goal, therefore, was "approximate unanimity." One method of achieving a high degree of agreement would be to present combinations of expenditures and taxes to the public for their approval or disapproval. Different combinations would be presented, until one passed by the margin designated as "approximate unanimity."[25] Wicksell noted, however, as had others before him, that even in this system a "proper" distribution of income is a prerequisite if welfare is to be maximized.

THE CONTRIBUTION OF ERIK LINDAHL

The writings of Erik Lindahl further illuminated the political aspects of realizing individual wants through public fiscal activity.[26] Lindahl recognized that the two major variables to be decided were (1) the quantity of output of the public good, and (2) the percentage of the cost to be borne by each individual.

Let us follow Lindahl's argument by considering Figure 2.7. The model is composed of two individuals: A and B. *Their demand for social*

---

[24] Knut Wicksell, "A New Principle of Just Taxation" in Musgrave and Peacock, *Classics in the Theory of Public Finance.*

[25] The process of referendums on tax changes often used in localities in the United States is not too different from Wicksell's scheme, since the tax proposals are usually tied to a specific expenditure proposal. However, Wicksell's definition of "approximate unanimity" is more stringent.

[26] For a more thorough presentation of Lindahl's contributions see Musgrave, *The Theory of Public Finance*, pp. 72–78. Also see Musgrave and Peacock, *Classics in the Theory of Public Finance*, for excerpts of Lindahl's writings.

good X is represented by the percent of the cost each is willing to share at various levels of output. For example, individual A, shown by the function *aa*, would be willing to contribute over 100 percent of the cost in order to produce 1 unit. As the output of good X increased, however, his marginal utility from it would decrease. He would be willing to finance only 75 percent of the cost of producing $4\frac{1}{2}$ units and only 25 percent of the cost of producing 13 units. B's desire that good X be produced is represented by *bb* (note that the right vertical axis registers B's willingness to contribute and that the scale starts from the top). Whereas B would contribute only 13 percent if 15 units were produced, he would, if necessary, contribute 100 percent in order that 1 unit be produced. Obviously there is a unique solution at point *D*; 6 units of output are produced, with A contributing 65 and B 35 percent of the cost. According to Lindahl, at any amount less than 6 units both A and B are willing to contribute more than is necessary to finance output—hence both A and B desire to increase output. He therefore concludes that the equilibrium at *D* will be reached. Lindahl's conclusions thus tend to reinforce Wicksell's: If voters under a democratic system are offered a means of voluntarily choosing between alternative expenditure and tax plans, they will settle upon a welfare-maximizing plan.

Musgrave points out a serious shortcoming of the Lindahl argument: The voters will not reveal their preferences regardless of the voting system used.[27] This problem is inherent in the nature of public goods. Since the exclusion principle does not operate, all individuals benefit from production of the good regardless of their share of the cost. The fallacy may be illustrated in terms of Lindahl's model (Figure 2.7). Suppose the current production of public good X is at point *E*. Two units are being produced, with A bearing 75 percent of the cost and B 25 percent. We assume that each individual votes to expand output at the current distribution of costs. A will vote for output *F* (5 units) and B will vote for output *G* (9 units). But A will not voluntarily contribute to the *G* level of output. Instead, if the 75-25 percent cost share is to be maintained, point *F* is the solution. There is no assurance that B will be willing to move from point *F* to point *D*. His gains (having more of good X) might be more than offset by his losses (sharing a higher percent of the cost). The final solution depends on the relative gains and losses incurred by A and B and the possible bargaining into which they might enter. Musgrave contends, moreover, that neither will wish to reveal his preferences. With large numbers of voters similar results supposedly occur. Since each voter can have little effect on output by changing his contribution, he will be reluctant to do so. In fact, if one's share of the cost is in any way dependent on his revealed preferences, he will find it profitable to understate them.

Our analysis leads us to ask two questions: First, how can preferences best be revealed through voting? and, second, how may the institutional structure facilitate this process? We will explore these questions at length in the next two chapters. Before that we must cope with the difficult concept of a "unique" welfare maximum. It turns out that even if preferences are revealed there is no unique solution unless other assumptions and value judgments (as indicated in previous arguments) are made.

THE "UNIQUE" SOLUTION QUESTIONED: THE NEW WELFARE ECONOMICS

The notion of a one "best" allocation of resources in the economy has always been intriguing. In Chapter 1 we went to some lengths to outline the conditions under which competition would work towards such a unique welfare-maximizing allocation of resources. At the same time we described ways in which the public sector would have to augment the competitive market system. We noted, however, that the tools of analysis of the "new" welfare economics were insufficient to prescribe the best public sector response to various types of market imperfections. As we might suspect, it is impossible to construct a model leading to a unique welfare-maximizing solution if we must abide by the rigorous constraints under which Pareto placed the "new" welfare economics.

Nevertheless, it is useful to consider the notion of the "unique" solution and to do so using the analytical approach of Pareto. The basic difficulty Pareto sought to overcome was the fact that utility can neither be measured nor compared among individuals. Although we shall have to go beyond Pareto's criteria to derive a "unique" solution, it is informative to know just how far we can go within his constraints.

Our model will utilize indifference curves.[28] The beauty of indifference curves is that they allow us to describe an individual's preference pattern without establishing a unique standard by which utilities can be measured and compared.

---

[27] See Musgrave, *The Theory of Public Finance*, pp. 79–80.

[28] If a more thorough review of indifference curves is required, the student may consult any microeconomic theory text.

FIGURE 2–8

Indifference patterns

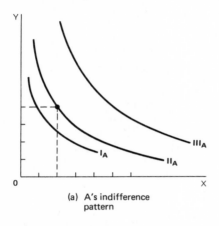

(a) A's indifference
pattern

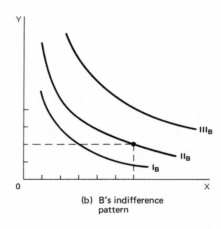

(b) B's indifference
pattern

FIGURE 2–9

The Edgeworth-Bowley box
showing gains from trade

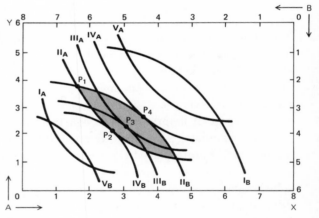

Let us begin by visualizing an imaginary economy with only two individuals: A and B. Each has an initial holding of the commodities X and Y as shown in Figure 2.8; individual A owns four units of Y and two of X. The indifference curve II_A shows the various combinations of Y and X which in A's opinion would give him the same amount of satisfaction—that is, he is indifferent as to which of the combinations represented by II_A he holds. He would, of course, prefer more of both X and Y to the alternatives on II_A. All positions to the upper right of II_A show higher levels of satisfaction. The indifference curve III_A shows another group of combinations to which A is indifferent, yet all of these combinations are preferred to any of those on II_A.

The slope of the indifference curve shows the rate at which the individual can substitute one of the goods for another and still have the same amount of satisfaction. The convexity of each curve demonstrates the assumption that as the mix of goods becomes heavily loaded with, say, Y, it takes increasingly more Y to make up for a small loss of X and still maintain the same level of satisfaction. B's preference pattern has a similar but not identical shape. B's initial holding is two Y's and six X's. If A and B have different rates (marginal rates of substitution) at which they are willing to trade X for Y, there are gains to be had from trading. This proposition may be demonstrated by use of the "Edgeworth-Bowley" box diagram (see Figure 2.9).

This box is constructed by rotating B's preference map 180 degrees so that its X and Y axes are parallel to those of A's preference map. The dimensions of the box are determined by the initial amounts of goods held. Thus we see that there are six Y's (with A holding four and B two) and eight X's (with A holding two and B six). B can now increase satisfaction by moving to indifference curves to the lower left of II_B, while A continues to wish to move upward and to the right of II_A. Consequently, a movement to any point in the shaded area will leave both individuals better off than before while on the boundary one is better off and the other is no worse off. The greatest gain possible for A (if B is to be left as well off as before) is to the point P_4, where II_B is tangent to IV_A. Likewise, the greatest gain possible for B is to the point P_2, where IV_B is tangent to II_A. From the little we know of the preferences and bargaining talents of A and B it is impossible to predict the final equilibrium point. We can observe this only after the fact. Let us assume that equilibrium is reached at point P_3. The two indifference curves III_A and III_B are tangent. Trading has ceased, because the marginal rates at which each is willing to substitute one good for another are now equal. A has traded one Y to B for one X, and both individuals are better off. During the process of trading, a common rate at which Y will be exchanged for X and vice versa has been arrived at. We see that this exchange rate, the marginal rate of substitution, is also the price ratio between Y and X:

$$MRS_{X \text{ for } Y} = \frac{P_X}{P_Y}$$

FIGURE 2–10

The Edgeworth-Bowley box showing a Pareto equilibrium

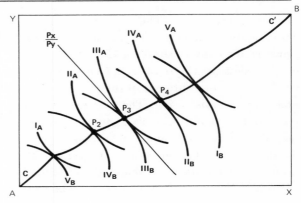

FIGURE 2–11

The allocation between private and public goods

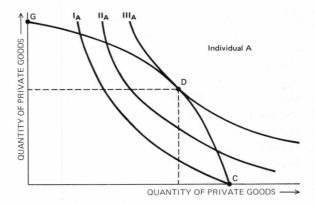

FIGURE 2–12

The allocation between private and public goods

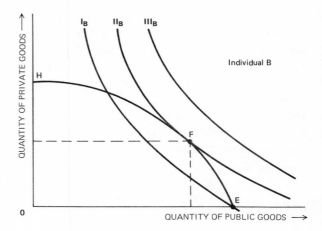

We recall that equilibrium is reached when the marginal rates of substitution are equal. This is shown in Figure 2.10 as the points along the line CC', defined as the "contract curve." We also recall that a "Pareto optimum" is defined as an equilibrium such that any further gain by an individual could only come at the expense of another. Once the contract curve is reached, no other trading is possible under the Pareto optimum criterion unless the dimensions of the box are changed. In the real world economy, of course, the dimensions of the box are constantly changing in response to changes in technology and quantities of goods.

We are now in a position to make two important observations about distribution of goods and welfare within our model.

Observation 1. The Pareto optimum criterion makes no distinction as to the welfare of A or B along the contract curve CC'; however, the initial distribution of goods affects this outcome. Hence the initial distribution must be assumed to be "acceptable" if the model is to be used.

Observation 2. Changes in the welfare of A and B take place during trading in the initial movement to the contract curve and in response to changes in the dimensions of the Edgeworth-Bowley box. In order to go beyond the Pareto optimum criterion and speak of welfare maximizing in a dynamic setting, we must also assume that the *process* by which these tradeoffs are made is "acceptable."

These propositions bear directly on the question of deriving a social welfare function and finding a unique welfare-maximizing combination of private and public goods. Let us proceed to the private-public good case, still using the Pareto criterion.[29]

Consider whether it is possible to reconcile A's and B's preferences with respect to public as well as private goods (see Figures 2.11 and 2.12). Initially A has the amount of private goods shown by point C and B has the amount shown by E. It is possible to devote resources to the production of public goods, though this will reduce the amount of private goods by drawing resources away from their production. Our indifference curves and production possibilities are drawn so that higher satisfaction can be attained by shifting to some combination of public and private goods. Let us assume first that A is directing the economy and may choose the

[29] See Paul Samuelson, "The Pure Theory of Public Expenditures," *Review of Economics and Statistics*, vol. 36, no. 4 (November 1954), pp. 387–389, and "Diagrammatic Exposition of a Theory of Public Expenditures," *Review of Economics and Statistics*, vol. 37 (November 1955), pp. 350–356. Also see Musgrave's interpretation in *The Theory of Public Finance*, pp. 80–84.

combination of private and public goods. His only restriction is that he must leave B at least as well off as he was before. This condition is satisfied if B is kept at some combination located on his indifference curve I. A is left to explore different combinations of resource uses. The production possibility curve CDG is derived so as to show the different combinations of private and public goods which are available to A *while still fulfilling the requirement to keep B as well off as he was at point E.* Individual A will obviously choose combination D, which allows him to reach the level of satisfaction represented by III_A.

If individual B were directing the economy, he would choose another combination of private and public goods. Assume that EFH represents the production possibilities open to B if his only restraint is to keep A as well off as he was originally at point C. Individual B will desire combination F, since that combination allows him the greatest possible level of satisfaction: II_B.

Now suppose that neither individual A nor individual B has complete control of the economy. The outcome is again indeterminate. There is no unique solution. Almost certainly A and B will agree to move from their original positions to some combination between D and F. If they are free to trade, they will bargain on the amount of public goods produced (which must be consumed equally by both A and B) along with the amounts each has left to devote to private goods. Within our simple two-person model a Pareto optimum equilibrium will in fact be attained. However, the final solution depends in part on the bargaining prowess of the individuals, and, just as in the Edgeworth-Bowley box illustration, instead of a "unique" solution there are a number that would fulfill the Pareto conditions.

Observation 3. While it can be demonstrated that welfare-maximizing behavior *may* lead to an equilibrium solution for all private and public good production, the Pareto criterion allows for a number of such optima. Hence no "unique" solution (in the Benthamian sense of the greatest total welfare) can be discovered via the approach of the "new" welfare economics.

The student should not despair that we are devoting so much effort to finding out the *limitations* of economic analysis. A major responsibility of economists is to reveal the value judgments necessary to analysis—and value judgments abound in decisions of public finance. Our observations thus far lead us to conclude that judgments must be made concerning the initial distribution of economic and political power as well as the economic and political processes themselves. Even then we find that the concept of a "unique" welfare maximum has little meaning.

It follows that economic analysis cannot be used to demonstrate that there exists some "ideal" system of free competition and voting which, if we could adopt it, would provide maximum efficiency and welfare. And we have dealt with only the difficulties which appear at the level of rather abstract theory; "real world" implementation of some "ideal" system would involve many more. On the one hand our analysis has laid bare inconsistencies in the various attempts to formulate *policy norms* based on an ideal such as the unique social optimum. We have also demonstrated that analysis of public sector activities which relies too heavily on such norms can easily be misleading. On the other hand our examination has been useful in *revealing* some of the *necessary value judgments* inherent in public choice decisions such as the tax rate structure. Thus we have provided a background for the next phase of our study: a look at the mechanics of making public choices.

Let us not lose sight of our initial purpose: to provide perspectives for analyzing the efficiency of the economic and political system in providing private and public goods and services. We will, of course, proceed to analyze the "real world" economic situations involving public sector finances, even though we have found *no definitive norm* by which to evaluate each situation. Our "real world" system does provide means for resolving the questions of income distribution, public goods production, and macroeconomic policy. We do, in fact, have elected administrators, congressmen, lobbyists, and so on who do bargain with each other and settle upon mutually advantageous agreements as to expenditures and taxes. In the process of arriving at these decisions, individuals operate within the context of our democratic system and express their preferences through voting. In the next chapter we will continue to ask how individual preferences might be translated into public sector resource allocation. Since we are to focus on public sector budgeting, we must consider the part played by the voting process.

3
PUBLIC CHOICES
AND VOTING

ARROW'S CRITERIA FOR A RATIONAL VOTING SYSTEM

Considerable analysis has been focused recently on the question of relating individual choice to the budget through voting.[1] Much of the discussion has asked whether such an ordering of social preferences can be expressed. Let us first consider whether majority voting can lead to an unambiguous result. Professor Kenneth Arrow has presented the problem succinctly in the form of a "paradox of voting."[2] Suppose there are three voters, A, B, C, and three budget alternatives, high, H, medium, M, and low, L. The voters rank their preferences 1, 2, and 3; their orderings are shown in Figure 3.1. We observe that individual A prefers L to M to H (an thus L to H). Individual C prefers H to L to M (and thus H to M). Suppose we proceed by pairing alternatives, deciding the winner by majority vote, and successively pairing the winner with another alternative. If we start by pairing H to M, we find that M wins, since A and B rank it higher than H. We now compare M to L and find that L wins. If the community were "rational," we would expect an ordering of L to M to H. But if we take a ballot comparing H to L, we find that H is preferred. It turns out that the winner depends on the sequence in which the votes are taken. The results are *ambiguous*.

Arrow claims that voting results can be considered a rational representation of the social preference function only under the following conditions:[3]

1. The voting must give rise to a *unique* social ordering. The results must be consistent regardless of the order in which the vote is taken.
2. The social ordering must respond positively to alterations in individual values, or at least not negatively. Thus if one alternative, say M, rises in the estimation of individuals and all other orderings stay the same, we expect that it rises, or at least stays the same, in the social ordering.
3. The elimination of one alternative, say M, should not affect the relative rankings of the remaining alternatives.
4. The social preference function is not to be imposed. The ordering must result from free choice among *all* possible alternatives.
5. The social preference function is not to be dictatorial.

While some of these conditions are met by the "paradox-of-voting" example, clearly the first one is not met, since the result is ambiguous. No unique social ordering can be found; the result depends on the order in which the vote is taken. In such a situation it would be impossible to derive a community preference ordering using majority voting. Obvi-

58

ously, we must be able to say something more about the character of preference orderings if unambiguous results are to be assured. Let us begin by examining a case where the outcome is determinable. Consider Figure 3.2. Individual C has changed his preference orderings to H to M to L. The outcome is now determinate. If we start by pairing H to M, M wins. We then pair M to L, and M wins again. Regardless of the voting sequence, M will win a majority.

SINGLE-PEAKEDNESS IN PREFERENCE ORDERINGS

What characteristic of the individuals' preference patterns led to the unique solution? The difference between the two cases can be seen best by plotting the alternatives as in Figures 3.3 and 3.4.[4] In Figure 3.4 (the determinate case) all orderings are single-peaked, so that in going from H to L *one does not go down and then up.* In the situation posed we obtain a determinate result when votes are taken by successive pairs

---

[1] See, for example, Kenneth Arrow, *Social Choice and Individual Values* (New York: Wiley, 1951); Duncan Black, "On the Rationale of Group Decision-making," *Journal of Political Economy*, vol. 56, no. 1 (February 1948), pp. 23–24, and "The Decisions of a Committee Using a Special Majority," *Econometrica*, vol. 16, no. 3 (July 1948), pp. 245–261, and "Wicksell's Principle in the Distribution of Taxation," in J. K. Eastman, ed., *Economic Essays in Commemoration of the Dundee School of Economics* (London: Culross, 1955); Howard R. Bowen, *Toward Social Economy* (New York: Holt, Rinehart & Winston, 1948), James M. Buchanan, *Public Finance in Democratic Process* (Chapel Hill: University of North Carolina Press, 1956), *The Demand and Supply of Public Goods* (Skokie, Ill.: Rand McNally, 1968), with Robert D. Tollison, eds., *Theory of Public Choice* (Ann Arbor: University of Michigan Press, 1972); Anthony Downs, *An Economic Theory of Democracy* (New York: Harper & Row, 1957); Clifford Hildreth, "Alternative Conditions of Social Ordering," *Econometrica*, vol. 21. no. 1 (January 1953), pp. 81–94; A. K. Sen, *Collective Choice and Social Welfare* (San Francisco: Holden-Day 1970); and Gordon Tullock, "The General Irrelevance of the General Impossibility Theorem," *Quaterly Journal of Economics*, May 1956, pp. 256–270, *Toward a Mathematics of Politics* (Ann Arbor: University of Michigan Press, 1967).

[2] Arrow, *Social Choice and Individual Values*, p. 3. Arrow states that the paradox of voting seems to have been first pointed out by E. J. Nanson [*Transactions and Proceedings of the Royal Society of Victoria*, vol. 19 (1882), pp. 197–240].

[3] Arrow, *ibid.*, chap. 3. Alternative criteria for evaluating voting systems are suggested by James S. Coleman, "The Possibility of a Social Welfare Function," *American Economic Review*, December 1966, pp. 1105–1122; Clifford Hildreth, "Alternative Conditions for Social Orderings," *Econometrica*, vol. 21 (January 1953), pp. 81–94.

[4] The diagrammatic representation of preference orderings is similar to that used by R. A. Musgrave in *The Theory of Public Finance* (New York: McGraw-Hill, 1959), p. 120.

FIGURE 3–1

Preference ratings, the voting paradox I

	INDIVIDUALS		
ALTERNATIVES	A	B	C
H	3	2	1
M	2	1	3
L	1	3	2

FIGURE 3–2

Preference ratings, determinate outcome I

	INDIVIDUALS		
ALTERNATIVES	A	B	C
H	3	2	1
M	2	1	2
L	1	3	3

FIGURE 3–3

Preference ratings, the voting paradox II

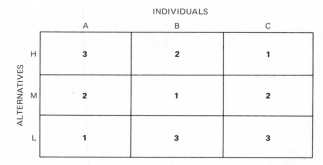

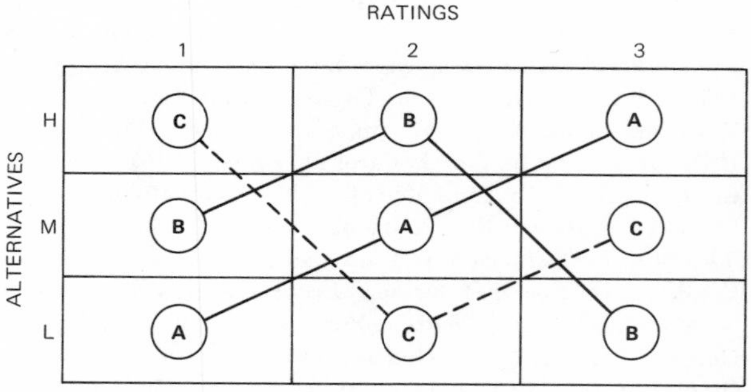

FIGURE 3–4

Preference ratings, determinate outcome II

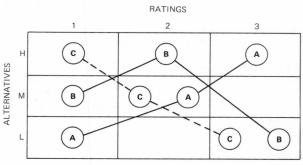

(regardless of the order). In the situation depicted in Figure 3.3 we see that the ordering of individual C starts at H, then goes down to L and back up to M.

Actually, although the figures depict the *nature* of single-peakedness, more specification is in order. What the concept of single-peakedness implies is that the voters have consensus as to the system of relating alternatives to each other. In the examples above the voters had to agree on the relationship high to medium to low. The system of relating alternatives may go from hot to moderate to cold or from dark to medium to light or from conservative to moderate to liberal. What is necessary is not that each individual regard the same alternative as his first choice, but that he honor the consensus relationship between alternatives when picking his second, third, fourth, and subsequent choices. Assume, for example, that the order 100, 90, 80, 70, 60 in Table 3.1 is the consensus ordering and that the alternatives represent public sector budgets. The choices of a liberal are shown in part (a) of the table and those of a moderate in part (b). It is permissible for the moderate to choose 80 first and then higher and lower budgets away from this optimum. But the ranking of the eccentric individual shown in part (c) violates the " single-peakedness " characteristic, since his skips over 70 and ranks 60 third, even though 70 is closer to 80.

From this it follows that the " oddball " in the voting paradox (Figure 3.3) is individual 3, who ranks budgets H, L, M, thus creating ambiguity. Had he abided by the " ground rules " of the accepted high to medium to low relationship between alternatives, the voting results would have been determinate.

Professor Duncan Black has proposed that it is appropriate to assume that the choices of voters in many voting situations do in fact follow the single-peak rule—that is, that there is general consensus on how the alternatives relate to each other.[5] Our examples provide a good case for his argument. The general budget alternatives that citizens vote on involve higher or lower levels of spending rather than a myriad of different ways of accomplishing some goal.

We are now in a position to hypothesize that the more homogeneous a society is and the more numerous the individuals within it are who accept the same criteria for ordering preferences, the more likely it is that rational voting results occur. As we shall see, however, the question

---

[5] See Black, " On the Rationale of Group Decision-Making " and " The Decisions of a Committee Using a Special Majority."

TABLE 3–1

Single-peakedness in
preference orderings

	(a) Liberal		(b) Moderate		(c) Eccentric	
Alternative	Rank	Alternative	Rank	Alternative	Rank	
100	1	100	4	100	4
90	2	90	2	90	2
80	3	80	1	80	1
70	4	70	3	70	5
60	5	60	5	60	3

becomes more complex when a larger number of alternatives are to be
voted upon simultaneously.

A DIGRESSION ON THE CONCEPT OF CONSENSUS

Let us reflect for a moment on some of the broader implications of our
examination of voting techniques and welfare. We have observed that
if determinate results are to follow, it is crucial that for a given voting
situation the pattern of an individual's choices be single-peaked. This
observation leads us to reconsider the nature of individual preferences,
especially as they incorporate social as well as private wants.

Professor Kenneth Arrow has made some interesting comparisons of
the assumptions inherent in welfare economics and those inherent in
political philosophy as to the nature of individual preference functions.[6]
In our analysis we started from the assumption that individuals order
both private and public wants on the basis of the satisfaction they receive
from each additional unit of the good or service in question. Very little
distinction was made between the moral character of public as opposed
to private goods.[7] According to the idealist school of political philosophy
there is a *general will* common to all members of society, which may
or may not be revealed and implemented depending on the society's
institutional structure. Central to the argument of the several members
of this school (which includes Rousseau, Kant, T. H. Green, and others[8])
is the existence of a general conception of what should be society's goals.
This latter ordering of wants may seem to be in conflict with the individual's more immediate preferences. According to Kant the ordering
of preferences by the individual follows from three imperatives: the
pragmatic, the technical, and the moral. The pragmatic imperative is the
individual's impetus to seek his happiness. The technical imperative is

the necessity to know the means required to carry out given ends. These two imperatives lack the *ultimate* necessity characterizing moral obligation; they are contingent in nature, while the moral imperative is categorical. Moreover, *the moral imperative has complete interpersonal validity.*

In Arrow's opinion:

The moral imperative corresponds to our concept of social ordering, in a sense, but it is also an individual ordering for every individual; it is the will which every individual would have if he were fully rational. . . .

The idealist doctrine then may be summed up by saying that each individual has two orderings, one which governs him in his everyday actions and one which would be relevant under some ideal conditions and which is in some sense truer than the first ordering. It is the latter which is considered relevant to social choice, and it is assumed that there is complete unanimity with regard to the truer individual ordering.[9]

We are left with an interesting parallel between the question posed by the idealist school, whether the pragmatic imperative can be brought into coincidence with the moral (true) imperative, and our present question, whether voting techniques can be used to reveal some best (welfare-maximizing) social ordering.[10] As social scientists we must ignore the question of whether some preferences are more "moral" (categorically speaking) than others. Indeed, we have difficulty even conceptualizing a unique welfare-maximizing allocation of resources; hence it would be folly to assume we could derive voting techniques to reveal individuals'

---

[6] Arrow, *Social Choice and Individual Values*, pp. 81 ff.

[7] We did note that satisfaction can derive from altruistic as well as selfish motives, and we designated goods whose production created externalities of the altruistic type as "merit" goods. We noted, however, that often an activity (such as education) produces effects which are desirable from both selfish and altruistic perspectives, so it is hard to designate which of the two motives is more influential. In any event it is obvious that "publicness" can derive from motives other than the altruistic one.

[8] See J. J. Rousseau, *The Social Contract*, English translation, 2nd ed. (New York: Putnam, 1906); I. Kant, "Fundamental Principles of the Metaphysic of Morals," in Kant's *Critique of Practical Reason and Other Works on the Theory of Ethics*, trans. T. K. Abbott, 5th ed. (New York: Longmans, Green, 1898), and T. H. Green, *Lectures on the Principles of Political Obligation* (New York: Longmans, Green, 1895).

[9] Arrow, *Social Choice and Individual Values*, pp. 81–82.

[10] It is precisely from this perspective that Rousseau comments: "The principle of majority rule must be taken ethically as a means of ascertaining a real 'general will,' not as a mechanism by which one set of interests is made subservient to another set. Political discussion must be assumed to represent a quest for an objectively ideal or 'best' policy, not a contest between interests." Rousseau, *The Social Contract*, pp. 165–166, as quoted in Arrow, *ibid.*, p. 85.

FIGURE 3–5

An individual's function
for two public goods

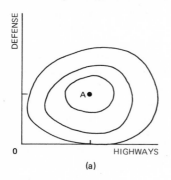

(a)

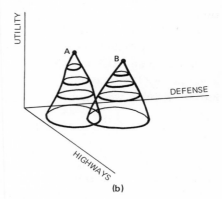

(b)

FIGURE 3–6

Utility functions for two
persons for two public
goods

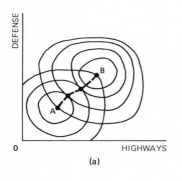

(a)

(b)

"true" preferences in line with some "best" allocation of private and
public activity. Yet our task is to analyze the decision-making processes
governing public sector economic activities, and we would find it difficult
if not impossible to proceed without some criteria for evaluating the
different processes. One intriguing analogy to the pragmatic versus moral
imperative is the emphasis on the problem of individuals' *expressing*
their preferences. We will use this as a point of departure as we analyze
voting techniques, budget procedures, and other political institutions in
subsequent chapters.

CONCURRENCE AND THE NUMBER OF ISSUES AND VOTERS

As Gordon Tullock has demonstrated, the acceptability of the results of votes depends importantly on the ratio of the number of issues to voters.[11] It turns out that many difficulties associated with small-number situations (including the voting paradox difficulty) lose importance in large-number situations.

Let us proceed by utilizing a special variation of the individual's utility function. This function, pictured in Figures 3.5(a) and (b), shows the utility received by the individual when various amounts of two public goods are produced. The utility function is not the type we have formerly worked with; *it does not purport to show total utility* but only the individual's preferred output of defense and highways *given his tax share and preferences for and holdings of other goods*. Figure 3.5(b) shows the utility function in three dimensions. There is one combination of defense and highways that gives the individual the highest level of utility. That combination is point A. Figure 3.5(a) is an aerial view of 3.5(b). The indifference curves represent lower levels of utility for combinations further away from point A.

Now suppose there are only two individuals in the economy and they are to decide on the best public good output. Their preference patterns are shown in Figures 3.6(a) and (b). Our experience with regular utility functions leads us to conclude that the two will decide on a combination somewhere along the contract line AB. The contract line represents tangencies of A's and B's indifference curves. Any point on this line is Pareto optimal in that, once attained, no movement can occur without one of the parties being worse off.[12] Of course, we have no way of judging among the positions on the contract line without making interpersonal utility comparisons.

The set of Pareto optimal combinations increases if we add another voter (assuming that he is not located on the contract line AB). The new situation is depicted in Figure 3.7. Actually *any point within the area bordered by the ABC contract lines fits the Pareto optimum criterion*. At this point it is appropriate to register some disappointment with the Pareto criterion, since its usefulness seems highly questionable in the

---

[11] *Toward a Mathematics of Politics.* The discussion that follows draws heavily on Tullock's second chapter.

[12] Since our utility functions are not total functions, however, there is still the possibility of tradeoffs using private goods, tax shares, and other variables we have excluded from the model.

FIGURE 3–7

Utility functions for
three persons for two
public goods

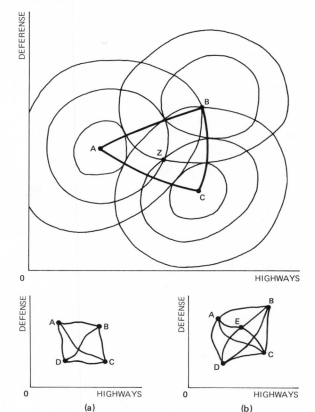

FIGURE 3–8

Utility functions for
four and five persons for
two public goods

situations we have depicted. It seems desirable to be more specific about preferred positions. We will argue that positions more to the center of the bordered area are in general preferable to those near or on the border. We will define *voter concurrence as the tendency to move to the center of the Pareto optimal area*. In Figure 3.7 voter concurrence would be more enhanced by point Z (or a point near Z) than points A, B and C or a point on the contract line *ABC*. Our preference for more central positions involves a value judgment which is inherent in some of the welfare norms we have already associated with the perfectly competitive model. An important attribute of the model is that each individual has complete control over the combinations of goods he wishes to purchase. Where joint consumption of public goods is necessary, the individual must give up the prerogative to specify the exact amounts he consumes. Yet inherent in the Pareto criterion and the Wicksellian unanimity rule is the judg-

---

ment that each individual should have a significant part in the decision. Thus a voting system which takes no account of some individual preferences would violate these norms. Suppose, for example, individual A in Figure 3.7 were given power to dictate the amounts of defense and highways to be produced. He would choose point A. Suppose instead that the decision was left to majority vote and B and C colluded to pick a point on the line BC. In both examples the decision left out the preferences of one or more of the affected parties. Only with a voting system accounting for all parties would a solution near the center result. Thus we have linked the concept of voter concurrence with the norm that all affected individuals should participate in the decision.

Let us seek a general rule for the way the Pareto optimal set behaves as more voters and issues are added. First observe Figures 3.8(a) and (b). We observe that as more persons are added, more of the contract lines cut through the Pareto optimal set. As demonstrated previously, individuals have incentive to move towards agreement on a contract line; hence, agreement towards the center (as opposed to the boundaries) of the Pareto optimal set is enhanced if contract lines cut through the center.

On the other hand, let us add another public good, education, by using the third dimension of Figure 3.9. With three issues and four people the expected Pareto set will be a tetrahedron. Here, again, we find no contract lines crossing the center; hence we are less sure that a given voting procedure will lead to what we have tentatively judged to be better concurrence. It turns out that it is just those situations where *the number of issues is one less than the number of voters* which are least likely to have contract lines cutting through the center of the Pareto optimal set.

Now let us evaluate these results. We will find that voter concurrence is greatly enhanced as the number of voters increases relative to the number of issues. Once again consider Figure 3.8(a). The tendency to move towards the outside edge of the Pareto set (lines *AB*, *BC*, *CD*, and *DA*) is somewhat offset by possible agreement between *A* and *C* or *B* and *D*. Obviously restrictive voting procedures of some sort are preferable to a situation encouraging perpetual tradeoffs along the outside of the Pareto set. And it would seem most likely that new rules, if adopted, would suffice to move the final solution towards the center of the Pareto set. Voter concurrence is enhanced even more in Figure 3.8(b), where agreements between A and E, A and C, B and E, and B and D are all likely to produce movement towards the center.

But, as anticipated, the most difficult situations arise where the number

FIGURE 3–9

Utility functions for
four persons and three
public goods

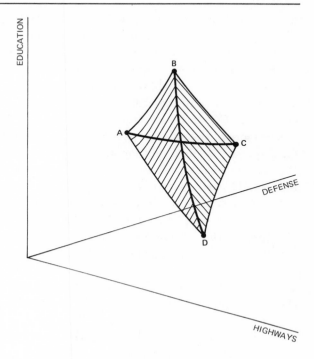

FIGURE 3–10

The voting paradox with
three persons and two
public goods

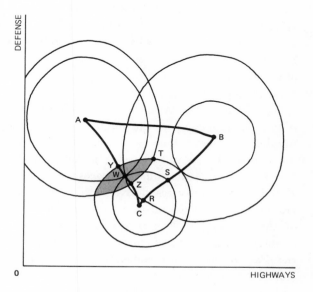

of issues is one less than the number of voters (Figures 3.6, 3.7, and 3.9). Let us emphasize this point by considering the use of majority voting in the three-person, two-public-good model.[13] Consider Figure 3.10. No combination towards the center such as T can be attained; in fact, the voting paradox may occur. Start by assuming that A and C collude. They can both gain by switching from T to a point in the shaded area. The contract line would suggest a point between Y and Z, possibly W, since both A and C would move to higher indifference curves. But if point W is reached, B now has incentive to retaliate by (1) colluding with C and moving to a point on the line BC (where C can be even better off than he is at W) *or* (2) colluding with A to move to a point on the line BA (where A can be even better off than he is at W). For example, if B chooses to collude with C, he can offer him a position between S and R, and both B and C will be better off (closer to their optima at points B and C, respectively) than they were at W. Within the context of the model the possibility of endless cycling is quite real. The situation makes great demands on any voting rule which may be used. It would have to cope with the voting cycle problem and at the same time make allowance for minority interests (as, for example, B's if A and C were to collude and choose point W).

Fortunately, most "real world" voting situations involve large numbers of voters relative to issues and, as demonstrated, the results here are much more acceptable than Arrow's criteria would seem to imply.[14]

---

[13] We recall that in our initial small-number voting models (as shown in Figure 3.2) the voter holding the median position, M, always prevailed (when a determinate result existed). This is because M was the second choice of the liberal (who preferred H to M to L) and also the second choice of the conservative (who preferred L to M to H). If the issues above were voted on *separately*, the median voter would prevail in each case.

[14] Tullock concludes: " . . . majority voting will, indeed, always be subject to the paradox of voting, but . . . this is of very little importance. . . . Any choice process involving large numbers of people will surely be subject to innumerable minor defects, with the result that the outcome, if considered in sufficient detail, will always deviate from Arrow's conditions. The deviation may, however, be so small that it makes no practical difference." *Toward a Mathematics of Politics*, p. 38.

Tullock uses additional diagrams to demonstrate that in large-number cases majority voting leads (in ways similar to the models described above) toward what we have defined as voter concurrence. Cycling would occur only as the center was approached, at which time proposals further from the center might win. But in most cases, Tullock argues, the area of disagreement will be so small that "most voters will feel that new proposals are splitting hairs, and the motion to adjourn will carry." *Ibid.*, p. 41. In Tullock's opinion the results at this point will be acceptable even though they do not completely fulfill Arrow's criteria of a rational system.

FIGURE 3–11

Voter concurrence with
changing tax shares

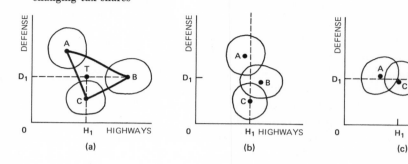

(a) (b) (c)

CONCURRENCE AND TAX SHARES

Now let us consider the relationship between tax shares and voter concurrence. It is rather easy to demonstrate that tax shares can be manipulated so as to increase voter concurrence. Indeed, this was implicit in our discussion of welfare-maximizing resource allocation, the benefit principle, and so on. The possibility of varying tax shares somewhat mitigates the discord arising from the indivisibility and nonassignability of public good benefits.

Consider again the simple three-person, two-public-good model as shown in Figure 3.11(a). We recall that if output decisions are voted on separately, using majority vote, the median voter will prevail each time. Thus point T will be reached. If both issues are considered at once, a voting paradox may well occur. It is important to remember, however, what sort of special utility functions we are dealing with. *They are not the usual total utility functions but merely the utility derived from the two public goods in question.* Hence the quantities and prices of all other utility-producing goods are taken as *given*. Moreover, the individual's income and *tax share* are also taken as given. It follows that a change in the individual's tax share will *shift* the utility functions shown in Figure 3.11(a). Assume that the government is going to produce amount H_1 and wishes to manipulate tax shares to achieve greater voter concurrence. In Figure 3.11(b) tax shares of individuals A and B have been manipulated so as to shift their optimum closer to the output level H_1. In Figure 3.11(c) tax share manipulation shifts the optima of A and C towards output level D_1. Theoretically a tax plan could be devised that would move the optima of all three to the same point on the diagram.

The next logical question is: How do we find the tax share plan which allows us to make the moves described above? No easy answer is possible, since in the real world the differences in individual preference functions are not neatly uniform and predictable. Even so, considerable work has been done on how particular taxes affect the individual, and frequent resort is made to these studies when tax decisions are made. We will mention here only two general observations, postponing a more thorough examination until Part III.

In the first place we know that most publicly produced goods are not purely public, having *all* benefits completely indivisible and unassignable. It seems likely that voter concurrence would be enhanced by a tax share plan which differentiated among taxpayers on the basis of these direct benefits. The funding of highways is a good example. While most of us benefit indirectly from our system of highways, those who receive the most benefits are the frequent users. It follows that a tax share plan which varied with usage would be more likely to improve voter concurrence. Reconsider Figure 3.11(a). We would expect B to be the frequent user of highways and A the infrequent user. If we imposed taxes according to use, the preference patterns might well be shifted as shown in Figure 3.11(b). The present policy of paying for highways from gasoline taxes essentially performs this operation. Infrequent highway users are much more content with present highway expenditures than they would be if they shared a greater percent of the cost; while the frequent users are less inclined to push for greater expenditures that will be accompanied by higher gasoline prices.

Another general observation we can make concerns the relationship of a person's income to his preferences for public goods. For many public goods we expect a *positive income effect*. As his income increases, he desires more of all kinds of goods and services including those produced by the public sector. Let us illustrate, using a simple model where only two goods are produced: a private good, food, and a public good, defense.[15] If both the price of food, P_f, and the tax rate, T_d, remain

---

[15] The utility function for this model (see Figure 3.12) is shown by standard indifference curves. Since we are assuming only two goods in the economy, these curves depict *total* utility rather than the partial functions used just previously. Within the relevant range the individual's utility increases with more of both goods.

FIGURE 3–12

Individual preferences for
public and private goods

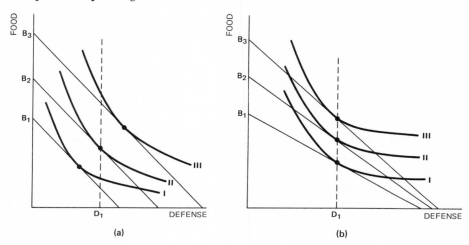

(a)　　　　　　　　　　(b)

stable as the individual's income increases, the budget constraint shifts out from the origin in a parallel fashion.[16] As depicted, the utility-maximizing combinations of food and defense include more of both goods as income increases. But, of course, the individual is not free to determine the benefits he receives from defense, since only one quantity can be produced for the whole economy. If that quantity were D_1, he would be "satisfied" only if his income were B_2. If his income were B_1, he would think "too much" was being spent; but if it were B_3, he would think "too little" was being spent.

As Figure 3.12(b) shows, *progessive* income tax rates could be used to improve concurrence over the *proportional* rates inherent in Figure 3.12(a).[17] We can extend these results to our three-person model as shown in Figure 3.11. If the differences in A's, B's, and C's preferences on defense spending are due primarily to income differentials, a progressive tax can be used to shift their (partial) utility functions in the manner shown in Figure 3.11(c).

VOTING ON TAX SHARES

In actual practice many difficulties arise in the use of differential taxes to improve voter concurrence. Since voters (like consumers in the private market) can better maximize utility if the marginal costs (of taxes) are equal to the marginal benefits (of public goods), there would seem to be a natural tendency in a democracy for an efficient tax system to evolve. But can we expect any voting procedure to produce mutual agreement on tax shares? Within any political system, interest groups are working to use the fiscal machinery to further their own interests. Moreover, the tax share question is fundamentally different from that of determining the level of public activity. If we take the revenue requirement as given, the tax share question becomes a zero-sum game,[18] where the gains (lower taxes) of one group must be just equal to the losses (higher taxes) of another. The benefits here are not indivisible (as in the case of public good production) but are in the form of dollars, whose benefits are completely divisible and assignable. It is naive to expect an individual or group not to try continually to lower their share of the tax burden—since, after all, the benefits of public goods are enjoyed regardless of the individual's tax payment.

In the most ideal sense the tax payment is a voluntary exchange of taxes in return for government services. This analogy to the free exchange of the private market was explored in Chapter 2. But note that the difficulty in the tax share question is that *benefits and costs cannot be linked*. To prove this point, let us indulge ourselves by considering a model which purports to show how tax shares and public good output *can* be simultaneously decided upon in a voluntary manner.

We recall that Erik Lindahl attempted to develop a two-person model within which an equilibrium solution could be attained between two variables: (1) the quantity of output of a public good and (2) the percentage of the cost to be borne by each individual. We reproduce the model in Figure 3.13. There are two individuals, A and B, whose demands (*aa* and *bb*, respectively) for the one public good are represented in terms

---

[16] The budget constraints for all individuals in an economy cannot, of course, be legitimately represented as straight lines. In the first place, the rate at which food and defense can be substituted for each other for the whole economy depends on the quantities of inputs and technology—that is, the production function. Second, it is not within the individual's prerogative to substitute one for the other at the P_f/T_d ratio. What we are assuming is that the individual perceives the P_f/T_d ratio as the rate at which he can vote to trade off public for private goods in the immediate area of the equilibrium point.

[17] The parallel budget lines in Figure 3.12(a) imply that the same tax rate applies as income increases. Thus the rate structure is proportional. In Figure 3.12(b) the tax rate becomes steeper as income increases.

[18] Game strategy in public choice is examined in the next section. The use of the concept of zero-sum game here is self-explanatory, the sum of gains and losses from a change in tax shares being equal to zero.

FIGURE 3–13

The Lindahl model of expenditure and tax shares

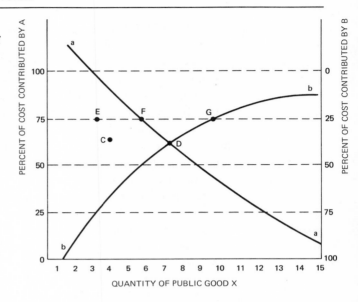

of the percent of the cost of production each is willing to pay. For each person higher levels of output of the public good are acceptable only if he pays a smaller percent of the cost. A cursory glance at Figure 3.13 would indicate that bargaining between the two individuals would lead them to equilibrium D—6 units produced, with A's tax share 65 percent and B's share 35 percent. It may be argued, for example, that if we start from position C both A and B will be willing to expand output to position D. Presumably we can extrapolate from this model to argue (as did Wicksell) that voters can operate under a democratic system and arrive at a welfare-maximizing combination of tax share and expenditure. This presumption necessarily includes the question of just how institutions provide for the emergence of such choices in a large-number setting —and thus it is exactly the question we now wish to pursue. But first let us recall Musgrave's criticism of the Lindahl model: *that the equilibrium at point D is not guaranteed*! If you *start* from a position such as E in Figure 3.13, individual A will wish to move to position F, while individual B will desire position G. It is by no means certain that B will be willing to pay a larger percentage of the cost to move from E or F to D. Moreover, Musgrave argues that strategy will becloud the bargaining, in that neither will be willing to reveal his preferences. If one's tax share is dependent on his revealed preferences, he will find it profitable to understate them.

It seems that the spectre of "revealed preferences," "strategy," and the like has raised its head much too often and destroyed our neat little models. We now ask: Just how crucial is strategy in real world situations in which large numbers of voters have imperfect knowledge and very complex fiscal choices to make? Just how often does the voter (and/or his representative) resort to the strategy of not revealing preferences? In most "real world" voting situations there is little or no connection between the preferences revealed for public goods expenditures and the tax share of the individual voter. We recognize, of course, that part of the reason tax shares are not usually linked with expenditure proposals may be precisely the "revealed-preferences" problem. As we examine real world fiscal institutions it will be pertinent to ask: What if any effect does the "revealed-preferences" problem have on the institutional structures?

We observe that many types of institutions have arisen to cope with the complexities of fiscal decision making. Many of our public choices, it turns out, are worked out by representatives, in committees, where resort to strategy, logrolling and tradeoffs may well occur. We will find the insights from our small-number models directly applicable. In other situations, popular vote by large numbers is decisive and other models may be employed. But let us not evade our initial question: Can voter concurrence be enhanced by voting for the *tax share* question along with public good output levels? The answer is *no*; considering the two questions simultaneously greatly reduces the degree of concurrence.

It might seem that limitations in the *tax share* choice might affect our ability to decide on the budget level and hence the level of public good output. A simple model will suffice to show that *once tax shares are fixed* the size of the budget can then be decided upon. Consider the simple two-person model shown in Figure 3.14.[19] Since the good in question is a pure public good, it will be *jointly* consumed at the one level of output to be agreed upon. The tax shares have already been decided. Each of the two individuals (A and B) knows the price he will have to pay at various levels of output; therefore, demand curves can easily be derived for each person. As output is expanded, the "price" each has to pay depends on the aforementioned tax share. His quantity demanded is dependent on the price and the relative marginal utility derived from increasing output.

---

[19] Although the context differs, this model relies on one developed by Buchanan in *The Demand and Supply of Public Goods*, chap. 3.

FIGURE 3–14

Two-person agreement on
budget level and public
good output

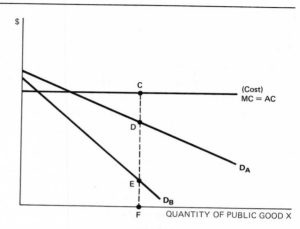

Assume also that "constant costs" prevail at different levels of output. With no "economies" or "diseconomies" of scale, marginal and average costs of increasing output are the same.

The final equilibrium is shown as point F in Figure 3.14. Since their demand curves represent utility (maximized via the equi-marginal rule), both A and B will wish to move as far to the right as possible. They will vote to expand output to point F, where their joint tax share (EF and DF) just covers the cost of production, CF (note that $EF = CD$).

What this model implies is that, with tax shares fixed, voters can agree on public good output level. In practice the tax share decision is in fact divorced from expenditure decisions by budgeting rules and conventions in Congress and other institutions in the fiscal decision-making process. The procedure of divorcing the tax share decision from the public good output level decision does not at first seem appropriate, owing to our predilection for equating marginal costs and benefits. But, because of the nature of the benefits and costs of the revenue decision (being direct and assignable benefits and costs), it can be argued that it is more efficient to have the two decisions divorced. Indeed, an argument to be presented in Chapter 4 would make the revenue share decision a Constitutional issue, so as to further divorce it from frequent consideration.

VOTING TECHNIQUES OTHER THAN THE MAJORITY RULE

The majority rule has been shown to be rather cumbersome in many of the voting models we have used. In small-number situations cyclical majorities often occurred. More important, there is no assurance that the rule is the most efficient to maximize satisfaction. While most voters prefer the majority result to no action at all, the preference of the median voters always holds sway. In the simple models we have employed the majority rule offers no way to account for differences in the intensity of feelings between voters. In other words the voting procedures we have used make no allowance for the individual's *level* of utility. Can we hope for better results from the use of other voting rules? Let us consider several possibilities, subjecting them to the critical test of voting on tax shares and expenditures simultaneously.

WICKSELL'S "RELATIVE UNANIMITY"

The Swedish economist Knut Wicksell had great empathy for the interests of minorities, so much so that he would have preferred that *complete unanimity* be required before any addition to the public budget be adopted. Wicksell's technique for obtaining complete (or if necessary only "relative") unanimity has been outlined in Chapter 2. It is now appropriate to evaluate this method further.

Each expenditure plan was to be accompanied by a tax plan and the combination matched against the option of no change. Successive proposals were to be made, each with a slightly different expenditure and tax plan, until one received approval of the required unanimity or until a reasonable number of combinations were defeated, in which case no budget change would be made.

Reductions in the budget were to be handled in a similar fashion. Certain expenditures were to be linked with certain taxes, and votes were to be taken on whether to discontinue this specific part of the budget. But Wicksell would require only a small percentage of the voters for the effecting of discontinuance. Use of this technique, like the other, would enhance the minority's wishes ability to influence the outcome. Thus voter concurrence may improve. But it would also increase the possibility of having less than optimum expenditure on public goods.

VOTING UNDER THE PLURALITY RULE

Use of the plurality rule is also more responsive to the desires of the minority, yet it does not assure this responsiveness by putting undue restrictions on possible solutions. In addition, the plurality rule allows for consideration of several alternatives simultaneously, so that the arbitrariness of the sequence of voting is reduced.

TABLE 3–2

Voting for budget size with
alternate tax plans—case I

	A (High income)		B (Medium income)		C (Low income)	
Budget	Progressive tax	Regressive tax	Progressive tax	Regressive tax	Progressive tax	Regressive tax
Small	3	4	6	5	4	3
Medium	2	5	3	4	5	2
Large	1	6	1	2	6	1

TABLE 3–3

Voting for budget size with
alternate tax plans—case II

	A (High income)		B (Medium income)		C (Low income)	
Budget	Progressive tax	Regressive tax	Progressive tax	Regressive tax	Progressive tax	Regressive tax
Small	1	2	6	5	4	3
Medium	3	4	3	4	5	2
Large	5	6	1	2	6	1

Voters rank all alternatives, giving the highest points to first choice, and so on. If there are six choices, the first gets 6 points; the second, 5 points; the third, 4 points, and so on, as demonstrated in Tables 3.2 and 3.3. The models presented in Tables 3.2 and 3.3 are useful for demonstrating a difference of major consequence between the majority and the plurality rule. The three voters A, B, and C are choosing among three budget sizes (small, medium, and large) with either a progressive or a regressive tax plan. Of the six options individual A prefers regressive tax, large budget and thus awards it 6 points; he awards regressive tax, medium budget 5 points, and so on. Now aggregate the points given to each plan in Tables 3.2 and Tables 3.3. In Table 3.2 the progressive tax, small budget is favored. If we had used the majority rule to vote on alternative pairings, we would have obtained the same winner. But in Table 3.3 we find that, while use of the majority rule is ambiguous, use of the plurality rule shows the progressive tax, large budget to be the winner with 12 points.[20]

It behooves us to ask whether one can legitimately assume that the progressive tax, large budget is the best choice rather than the several others that could have won under the majority rule. We admit that the allotment of points carries the tenuous assumption that intensity of satisfaction or dissatisfaction varies evenly between choices ranked first, second, third, and so on. Although this assumption is unrealistic for most comparisons, the plurality rule certainly offers greater accuracy in recording intensity of desire than does the simple majority technique.

Arrow, we may note here, argues rightly that the plurality rule (as well as point voting) runs counter to his third condition for consistency: that the elimination of one alternative should not affect the relative rankings of the remaining alternatives.

Let us illustrate using Tables 3.4 and 3.5. Suppose we have a situation similar to that posited above. We are voting on budget size with alternate tax plans. The priorities are set as in Table 3.4, and under either the majority or the plurality rule the regressive-tax small-budget plan is chosen (with 14 points). Suppose, however, that the regressive-tax medium-budget plan is found to be infeasible and is dropped as an alternative. The new rankings are shown in Table 3.5. Now the regressive-tax large-budget choice wins the plurality vote with 12 points. Under the majority rule the regressive-tax small-budget plan would still win. Arrow concludes that this demonstrates a weakness of the plurality and point vote system. Just how crucial this consideration is depends on one's judgment as to the "irrelevancy" of the regressive-tax medium-budget plan. It may be argued that the shift from regressive tax, small budget to regressive tax, large budget is not inconsistent but in fact better reflects intensity of desire, given the new set of alternatives and the fact that each voter in assigning points is not certain which will win.

Another method of revealing preferences, "point voting," allows even more sophistication in revealing the intensity of satisfaction or dissatisfaction for various public budget plans.

POINT VOTING

When a point voting system is used, each voter is allotted a certain number of points and allowed to distribute them among the choices as he pleases. Ideally he can distribute points in approximation of his relative preference among the alternatives. He may give all of his points to one

---

[20] We must note, however, that these results are not general; there still remain situations in which the plurality rule offers no unambiguous solution.

TABLE 3–4

Voting for budget size with
alternate tax plans—case III

	A (High income)		B (Medium income)		C (Low income)	
Budget	Progressive tax	Regressive tax	Progressive tax	Regressive tax	Progressive tax	Regressive tax
Small	1	6	1	6	3	2
Medium	2	5	2	5	4	1
Large	3	4	3	4	6	5

TABLE 3–5

Voting for budget size with
alternate tax plans—case IV

	A (High income)		B (Medium income)		C (Low income)	
Budget	Progressive tax	Regressive tax	Progressive tax	Regressive tax	Progressive tax	Regressive tax
Small	1	5	1	5	2	1
Medium	2	0	2	0	3	0
Large	3	4	3	4	5	4

TABLE 3–6

Voting for budget size with
alternate tax plans—case V

	A (High Income)		B (Medium Income)		C (Low Income)	
Budget	Progressive tax	Regressive tax	Progressive tax	Regressive tax	Progressive tax	Regressive tax
Small	0	0	15	15	10	5
Medium	0	0	10	10	15	5
Large	20	40	5	5	20	5

Total points for each plan

Plan	Points	Plan	Points
Regressive tax, large budget	50	Progressive tax, small budget	25
Progressive tax, large budget	45	Regressive tax, small budget	20
Progressive tax, medium budget	25	Regressive tax, medium budget	15

---

alternative and none to the rest. Obviously such a system will often yield different results from those of the majority or plurality rules.

Suppose that in the situation shown in Table 3.3 we now use " point voting." Sixty points are given to the voters to divide among the six alternatives in accordance with their preferences. We see from Table 3.6 that A assigns all sixty points to the large-expenditure plans. Perhaps he is alarmed at the communist threat and feels greater defense spending is needed. However, of the two tax plans he favors the regressive one, which now wins with a total of 50 points.

Again we must consider the various value judgments inherent in a system. How do we arrive at the total points to be awarded each voter? Obviously, without a common utility measure there is no satisfactory answer; the assigned point spread might not be appropriate. Moreover, awarding the same number of points to each voter will not allow for differing intensities among individuals. Once again we face the dilemma of dealing with interpersonal utility comparisons.

Even in the " point voting " system it is possible to have situations with indeterminate results. But obviously the technique allows for finding a winner much more frequently than the majority or plurality rules.

A further aspect of this survey no doubt has been bothering the student —and quite obtrusively in the example above. It was quite obvious in the point voting problem of Case V that A determined the result by placing most of his points on the regressive-tax large-budget plan. Why did not B and C anticipate this and assign their own points in large blocks as well? The answer, of course, is that we have implicitly assumed that the voters choose honestly, without regard to strategy. As we shall see below, if strategy enters the voting process the results become even more ambiguous. In passing we note that point voting, while it allows for more flexibility in expressing intensity of desire, also allows the use of more strategy; consequently, it may actually be less satisfactory than the other systems.

STRATEGY AND GAME THEORY IN BUDGET VOTING

Strategy does in fact play a major role in the voting processes by which the public budget is formulated. The problem of unrevealed preferences, we recall, is basically the problem of voters' wishing to conceal their preferences for strategic reasons; namely, they wish others to pay for the public goods consumed by all.

TABLE 3–7

Payoff matrix for a
two-person, constant-sum
game (strictly determined)

A's Strategies

B's Strategies

	a'	b'
a	6	5
b	7	4

The voting techniques discussed offer different possibilities for strategy. For example, in the " point voting " system let us suppose that all three voters have some idea of the others' preferences. It seems obvious that B and C will collude to produce some result other than regressive tax, low budget. Given that C prefers progressive taxes while B prefers small budgets, the result will probably be either progressive tax, small budget or progressive tax, medium budget. If A foresees their collusion and is more concerned about communism than about his tax bill, he may try to influence the outcome towards progressive tax, medium budget; or, better yet, he may attempt to collude with C and produce the outcome progressive tax, large budget. The point is that when the voting procedure involves strategy, an understanding of the relation of the budget to individual wants requires analytical tools we have not yet discussed.

Since von Neumann and Morgenstern's *Theory of Games and Economic Behavior*[21] appeared in 1944, considerable attention has been given to strategy as a part of economic behavior. So far the most enlightening applications of game theory have been to various oligopolistic market situations. Our immediate interest is to see how the perspectives of game theory might help in analyzing public sector decision making. Since these perspectives emphasize the effects various strategies have on the outcome of interdependent activities, they are quite appropriate for our present purposes. Let us examine some that may be useful.

The purpose of game theory is to determine and explain standards of "rational behavior" for the participants in situations where their actions are interdependent. Such a situation is called a "game," and it is usually assumed that all possible courses of action (or "strategies") open to the "players" are known. Moreover, each player must know the full set of alternatives open to him and his opponents. Thus, when the game involves chance each player knows the probabilities assigned to all alternatives.

Let us first consider the class known as "strictly adversary" games in which the preferences of the opponents are diametrically opposed (as, for example, those of voters A and C in the situation depicted by Table 3.2). Within this class, "constant-sum" games are those with a fixed sum of goods to be distributed among the participants. Within this latter category, "zero-sum" games are those in which the winnings of one player must be exactly matched by the losses of another. In such a game it follows that the players are strict adversaries. While this simple case is a good starting point, it obviously has little relevance to most of the voting "games" of interest in this study. In the voting among budget alternatives the choices include many where gains are not offset by losses.

Using the case of a constant-sum, strictly adversary, "strictly determined" game, let us consider an assumption about behavior known as the Neumann-Morgenstern "minimax" principle. Assume there are two players A and B who can choose between two alternatives. The game's "payoff" matrix is shown in Table 3.7. Assume the game is worth 10 points. *The "payoff" is shown in terms of what A will receive, with B getting the residual.* Player A gets to determine the row (a or b) and B the column (a' or b'). Obviously, A wishes to maximize his winnings, but he is aware that B will choose the column so as to minimize his (A's) winnings. Player A would benefit most if he chose b and B chose a'. However, in the event that A chose b, B would surely choose b' in order to minimize A's winnings at 4. Consequently, A selects the strategy which maximizes the minimum he will get. Thus strategy a is his minimax. The strictly determined result of the game is the solution ab'.

In many "games" no unique solution can be determined. On the other hand, a "mixed strategy" solution does exist for every constant-sum game.[22] To illustrate, let us assume that the voting strategies of two individuals A and B are interrelated as shown by the payoff matrix in Table 3.8. The game has a constant sum but, if each voter uses minimax strategy, the result is not strictly determined. If A chooses row b (his "minimax"), B will choose column b'. However, as play progresses, A sees that B always chooses b' and realizes that his best strategy is to choose a and receive 5 instead of 4. Eventually B will begin to anticipate A's choosing a and will himself choose a' to lower A's winnings to 1.

[21] John von Neumann and Oskar Morgenstern, *Theory of Games and Economic Behavior* (Princeton, N.J.: Princeton University Press, 1944).
[22] This has been demonstrated by von Neumann and Morgenstern, *ibid.*

TABLE 3–8				B's Strategies	
				a'	b'
Payoff matrix for a two-person, constant-sum game (nonstrictly determined)		A's Strategies	a	1	5
			b	6	4

This change of strategy will continue until each player arrives at the best way to alternate strategies so as to get the greatest value from the game.[23]

EVALUATION OF THE GAME THEORY APPROACH

Our meager introduction has barely suggested the imaginative work being done under the broad heading of "game theory"—yet we have gone far enough to recognize some of the difficulties.

One difficulty is the choice of a behavioral assumption upon which to predict the choices of the participants. The minimax principle requires one player to assume that his rival will always take the least desirable strategy from the former's point of view. This assumption, while valid in "zero-sum" games, is hardly applicable in the voting which determines public finances. Here often the alternatives involve many different expenditure and tax plans, not all of which match one party's benefits against another's losses. The analytical tools needed to examine these more complex alternatives have yet to be developed.

Another difficulty is acquiring the knowledge we have assumed as to the values of different strategies to the participants. The values we have used presumably represent the "utility" of each player. Moreover, it has been inherently assumed that each player's utility may be assessed in terms of a *unique* index. The difficulty of assigning different values to different players for each element in the matrix can be overcome (although the game becomes more complicated); but the crucial problem is that we cannot derive values for payoff matrices in terms of *utility* unless we know the utility functions of the individuals involved. Unfortunately, the situations involving voting for public goods are not conducive to providing information for interpersonal utility comparisons and even less so when strategy enters the picture. It would seem, then, that once again we are confronted with the difficulties of measuring utility, making interpersonal comparisons, and so on.

Unfortunately, it can be readily demonstrated that *if strategy is present,* the welfare-optimizing alternative is not likely to be reached under the plurality or point voting procedures. Consider the nonzero-sum game payoff matrix shown in Table 3.9. We assume tenuously that the values shown are of the same order as the utility received. The different choices represent different budget plans and the scores represent the marginal benefits (net of opportunity costs) which will accrue to the various participants from a change to either of the alternative budget plans. Player A's winnings are shown in the lower left portion of each block and B's in the upper right. Under either point voting or plurality voting

---

[23] We begin by assuming that A chooses a one-fifth of the time and b four-fifths. On the other hand, B chooses a' one-fourth of the time and b' three-fourths. The expected value of the game from A's standpoint is

$$V_A = \left(\tfrac{1}{5}\right) \cdot \left(\tfrac{1}{4}\right) \cdot (1) + \left(\tfrac{4}{5}\right) \cdot \left(\tfrac{1}{4}\right) \cdot (6) + \left(\tfrac{1}{5}\right) \cdot \left(\tfrac{3}{4}\right) \cdot (5) + \left(\tfrac{4}{5}\right) \cdot \left(\tfrac{3}{4}\right) \cdot (4)$$

$$V_A = \begin{pmatrix} \text{A's probability} \\ \text{of choosing} \\ a \end{pmatrix} \cdot \begin{pmatrix} \text{B's probability} \\ \text{of choosing} \\ a' \end{pmatrix} \cdot \begin{pmatrix} \text{value} \\ \text{of} \\ aa' \end{pmatrix}$$

$$+ \begin{pmatrix} \text{A's probability} \\ \text{of choosing} \\ b \end{pmatrix} \cdot \begin{pmatrix} \text{B's probability} \\ \text{of choosing} \\ a' \end{pmatrix} \cdot \begin{pmatrix} \text{value} \\ \text{of} \\ ba' \end{pmatrix}$$

$$+ \begin{pmatrix} \text{A's probability} \\ \text{of choosing} \\ a \end{pmatrix} \cdot \begin{pmatrix} \text{B's probability} \\ \text{of choosing} \\ b' \end{pmatrix} \cdot \begin{pmatrix} \text{value} \\ \text{of} \\ ab' \end{pmatrix}$$

$$+ \begin{pmatrix} \text{A's probability} \\ \text{of choosing} \\ b \end{pmatrix} \cdot \begin{pmatrix} \text{B's probability} \\ \text{of choosing} \\ b' \end{pmatrix} \cdot \begin{pmatrix} \text{value} \\ \text{of} \\ bb' \end{pmatrix}$$

$$V_A = .05 + 1.20 + .75 + 2.40 = 4.40$$

Thus the value of the game is 4.40 to A. However, we recall that A's and B's strategy ratios were picked arbitrarily. We expect each player to keep adjusting this strategy so as to make the value of the game higher if possible. *It turns out* that B can reduce A's winnings by choosing b' more often. Player A will respond by choosing a more often, and the final ratios will be

for A: $a \ldots \tfrac{2}{6}$ for B: $a' \ldots \tfrac{1}{6}$

$b \ldots \tfrac{4}{6}$ $b' \ldots \tfrac{5}{6}$

and the value of the game for A is:

$$V_A = \left(\tfrac{2}{6}\right) \cdot \left(\tfrac{1}{6}\right) \cdot (1) + \left(\tfrac{4}{6}\right) \cdot \left(\tfrac{1}{6}\right) \cdot (6) + \left(\tfrac{2}{6}\right) \cdot \left(\tfrac{5}{6}\right) \cdot (5) + \left(\tfrac{4}{6}\right) \cdot \left(\tfrac{5}{6}\right) \cdot (4)$$
$$= 4.33$$

Thus, if both participants follow the behavioral assumption of minimaxing, a unique "mixed strategy" solution exists for the game.

TABLE 3–9

Payoff matrix for a
two-player nonzero-sum
game

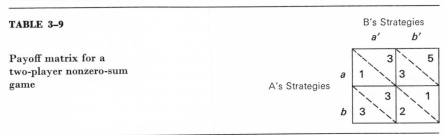

combination ab', with a value of 3 to A and 5 to B, would win. If strategy
enters, however, B in attempting to maximize his minimum might pick
a' while A might pick b. Thus the values received would be 3 for B and
3 for A—a solution clearly less than "optimum." We will not attempt a
rigorous specification of the conditions necessary for the outcome $a'b$.
Obviously, the results depend on the characteristics of the decision-
making process and on whether logrolling, tradeoffs, and other strategies
may enter. We have demonstrated that in some situations where strategy
enters, social welfare may be reduced. On the other hand, we have also
demonstrated that voting systems which are more responsive to intensity
of voters' feelings allow a greater scope for strategy (recall the example
of use of strategy in the point voting example). We must conclude that
in evaluating voting systems there will often be a tradeoff between the
responsiveness of a system to intensity of voter feeling and the various
harmful effects which the use of strategy may produce. Evaluation of
any particular voting process would necessarily include analysis not only
of the mechanics of the voting rules but also of the relationship between
the issues and the voting behavior of the participants.

In order to predict voter behavior we must know something of the
incentives (the cost-benefit pattern) inherent in the various choices. The
game theory perspective gives insight as to how these incentives might
be translated into strategic behavior by voters, committeemen, and others
in the budgeting process. For greater insight let us further explore some
of the incentives that are at work in determining voter behavior.

SOME MODELS OF WELFARE-MAXIMIZING VOTING BEHAVIOR

An individual may play one or more of many roles in the process of deciding the economic activities of the public sector. His participation in the
election of representatives may range from nonvoter, to voter, to party

worker, to campaign manager, and even to candidate as well. On a particular tax or spending issue he may participate as a voter, a letter writer, an agency head, a budget official, a congressman or senator, or in any number of other roles. In examining the budgetary process in Chapter 5 we will analyze the interaction among individuals and groups in budgeting. Our focus now will be primarily on the individual as voter.

What are the costs and benefits of going to the polls and casting your vote? Let us first consider only the *direct* costs and benefits. On the cost side we should compute the expense of time and transportation in the trip to the polls. We may also include the expense of inquiring as to the possible benefits and costs of the choices to be made. These costs seem trivial, but what is important is the comparison of costs and benefits, and *the direct benefits acquired through voting are usually minuscule.*

On the benefit side we include the rewards forthcoming if your party, representative, or issue wins. These are *net* benefits—over and above those expected if the other side wins. In order to translate these benefits into the actual rewards from *voting*, however, we must reduce them by the probability factor of *our vote's* influencing the outcome. We should also reduce them by the probability factor of our being correct in our assessment of the benefits.

For many years model builders yielded to the temptation of assuming that all individuals voted; but, as Downs has demonstrated, it is quite rational for most individuals *not to vote*, especially if only direct economic benefits and costs are calculated.[24] There are, of course, additional considerations which work to increase voter participation. For example, many voters get utility from the act of voting itself, because it is their patriotic duty. Similarly, the cost of acquiring information may be negative. For many people, being "well informed" is part of their job, a hobby, perhaps necessary to their participation in cocktail party conversation, and so on. The assessment of benefits, on the other hand, might include not only the direct benefits to the individual but all benefits flowing to friends and relatives, the whole city, state, or nation. Indeed, an individual voting for a candidate promising a new foreign policy might feel that he is benefiting the whole human race for generations to come.

Finally, the effectiveness of a particular vote does not always hinge on

[24] Anthony Downs, *An Economic Theory of Democracy* (New York: Harper & Row, 1957).

whether the issue wins or loses. Note is taken of dissenting votes even in a national election. A few liberals voted for Goldwater in order to reduce the "mandate" which Johnson seemed certain to receive. Moreover, certain interest groups, such as farmers, blacks, and labor, may expect to receive benefits from voting regularly as a group.

MOTIVES BEHIND INDIVIDUAL FISCAL CHOICES

Can the benefits from fiscal choices be measured so that subhypotheses can be formulated and tested? When political campaigns are waged many issues are expressed in measurable terms. It is at least assumed by politicians that economic self-interest plays a large part in voter choices. It is not difficult for an individual to be able to determine which policies will give him a greater real return. A survey conducted by the Survey Research Center of the University of Michigan in 1960 and 1961 indicated that economic self-interest was a significant (though not necessarily dominant) variable in determining the fiscal choices of respondents.[25] Low-income individuals generally favored public programs such as transfers to the poor, aged, and unemployed; hospital and medical care; and education; while high-income groups generally favored aid to small businesses and highway expenditures. However, the high-income groups also favored expenditures on education and aid to the aged, two programs which tend to redistribute real income from the wealthy to the poor. Other empirical studies also support the observation that both lower and higher income groups often support the extension of certain types of public activities.[26]

Another interesting finding was that higher income groups were relatively more favorable to expansion of public programs of all kinds. This result does not necessarily refute the basic hypothesis that individuals vote to maximize their self-interest, even under a progressive tax system. As income increases, individuals wish to obtain more goods from the public as well as the private sector. As more and more direct benefits are obtained from private goods, the indirect benefits to be obtained from additional public expenditure become relatively more attractive. If the relative attractiveness of public goods increases faster than the costs associated with progressive taxes, it follows that the higher income groups would be more favorable to increased public spending. These observations suggest caution in the use of models basing voter behavior primarily on income maximization.

Additional reservations appear to be warranted by other surveys.

James Q. Wilson and Edward C. Banfield of Harvard make observations of voting behavior by income group in municipal referenda.[27] Here there is often a close link between the particular benefits and proposed taxes. Testing the hypothesis that voters act to maximize net family income, they found as expected that the poor favored programs where they received direct benefits; the middle income classes opposed such redistributive programs. However, again the upper income groups often favored spending programs where they did not seem to benefit directly in relation to the cost.[28]

As one surveys the studies attempting to formulate and test hypotheses about voting behavior, three general problems appear. The first problem is to build a model of the individual's voting behavior as he makes fiscal choices. Human beings are complex and have complex motives for behaving as they do. We have seen that we must be cautious in assuming that they behave so as to maximize monetary income.

The second problem is that of finding pertinent data which lend themselves to quantification. The benefits and costs to individuals are not always quantifiable. Where altruistic motives are a significant factor, the problem is difficult indeed. But even when selfish self-interest can be assumed paramount, one is still faced with the previously discussed difficulties of revealing preferences for public goods. The more indirect the nature of the goods and services, the less likely quantifiable data are to be found. This leads to our third general problem: the difficulty the individual himself has in determining the value of benefits he secures from publicly provided goods and services. It has been traditionally

---

[25] The results were reported by Eva Mueller, " Public Attitudes toward Fiscal Programs," *Quarterly Journal of Economics*, vol. 77 (May 1963), pp. 210–235.

[26] See James Q. Wilson and Edward C. Banfield, "Public Regardingness as a Value Premise in Voting Behavior," *American Political Science Review*, vol. 58 (December 1964), and W. C. Birdsall, "A Study of the Demand for Public Goods," in R. A. Musgrave, ed., *Essays in Fiscal Federalism* (Washington, D.C.: Brookings, 1965), pp. 235–294.

[27] James Q. Wilson and Edward C. Banfield, "Voting Behavior on Municipal Public Expenditures," in *The Public Economy of Urban Communities*, ed. J. Margolis (Baltimore, Md.: Johns Hopkins Press, 1965), pp. 74–91.

[28] We note again that high-income groups tend to favor more spending because as they spend more on private goods the public goods become relatively more attractive. Moreover, the tax pattern proposed in local referenda is often fairly regressive and almost never as progressive as the federal personal income tax. Hence, it is not surprising that upper income groups usually endorse the proposition that public goods should be produced at the lowest possible level of government.

assumed that the individual possesses perfect knowledge of the benefits and costs of fiscal choices. But, as noted, the assumption is tenuous even when we apply it to analysis of the private sector. Information problems are even more crucial when we analyze the individual's behavior in making fiscal choices.

These three problems indicate the difficulties of building and testing models of individual voting behavior. The motives behind any voter's choices are complex, and it is difficult to express them so as to obtain quantifiable data to test. Even so, substantial work is going on in this area, and these studies promise to fill in our knowledge of how voters behave in response to variations in the costs and benefits inherent in public choices.

RECURRENT CHOICE SITUATIONS

An important factor in evaluating the *costs* of choice participation is the frequency with which the choice is to be made.

In the usual theoretical models, choices are assumed to be one-time costless phenomena. Consequently the models—particularly in microeconomics—are very often misleading if taken as a description of consumer or firm behavior. Actually, the manager of a firm may find that his costs and revenues shift frequently over time. It is often difficult for him to make precise calculations of marginal revenue and cost at a point in time, and he cannot make such calculations as demand and cost curves shift through time. Instead, he finds it *more efficient* to anticipate and "average out" expected shifts. The result is the widely observed practice of "cost-plus" pricing—which, although seemingly inefficient at a point in time, may well be the most efficient pricing procedure through time. Consumers also face the problems of inadequate knowledge about products and of costs in acquiring knowledge. Instead of spending all of their energy and time researching the merits of various products, they develop rules of thumb—such as loyalty to certain brands. In a grocery store the shopper has an overwhelming variety of options to choose from, so that minute analysis of the benefits derived from each possible combination would be costly if not impossible. Lacking information on quality differentials, the shopper will often choose by seemingly "irrational" rules—such as packaging, sales gimmicks, or some extraneous information recalled from an advertisement. The more rational approach would be to develop rules of thumb—such as loyalty to certain brands.

Public choice situations are often analogous. Where information is difficult to obtain, the cost may be too high to warrant voting in a one-time referendum. This is why most complex nonrecurrent decisions are left to elected representatives and administrative officials.

Where choices are recurrent, it becomes worthwhile for the voter to do some research. It also pays him to develop "rules" or "conventions" to follow. Hence, for the individual voter, knowledge of how a particular individual or party stands on particular issues would seem to be more important if (1) the individual or party is to be considered in more than one election and (2) the "issues" require recurrent decision making.

In order to link "issues" and party, voters must put some effort into informing themselves of the actual benefits and costs of the programs in question. We might ask: How "aware" are voters of costs and benefits?

VOTER "AWARENESS" OF COSTS AND BENEFITS

Several studies have been made to determine the individual's "awareness" of the costs and benefits of public programs. In separate surveys it was found that only slightly over one-half of the respondents could estimate their liability under the personal income tax to within plus or minus 10 percent.[29] Surveys by the Institute of Economic Affairs in Britain indicate that individuals also err in estimating the costs of governmental spending programs even when these programs involve primarily direct benefits.[30] Respondents were found to substantially underestimate costs of the National Health Service. Although only one-fifth of the costs are met through individual contributions to that fund, 36 percent of the respondents thought such contributions covered the full cost. Similarly, 35 percent of the respondents thought the full costs of public pensions were paid by the pensioners, whereas only 10 percent is actually paid. Interestingly enough, the costs of public education—

[29] Norbert L. Euick, "A Pilot Study of Income Tax Consciousness," *National Tax Journal*, vol. 16 (June 1963), pp. 169–177, and "A Further Study of Income Tax Consciousness," *National Tax Journal*, vol. 17 (September 1964), pp. 319–321, and J. V. Wagstaff, "Income Tax Consciousness under Withholding," *Southern Economic Journal*, vol. 32 (July 1965), pp. 73–80. The results are also borne out by Bruce L. Gensemer, Jane A. Lean, and William B. Neenan, "Awareness of Marginal Income Tax Rates among High-Income Taxpayers," *National Tax Journal*, vol. 17 (September 1965), pp. 258–267.

[30] *Choice in Welfare*, Institute of Economic Affairs (London, July 1963 and July 1965). The results of the 1963 study were evaluated by Ralph Harris and Arthur Seldon, "Welfare and Choice," *The New Society*, no. 43 (July 1963), pp. 14–16.

a good with fairly direct benefits but financed with less direct costs (general taxes)—were substantially overestimated.

Such studies show very little individual ability to identify the benefits of public activities with their costs. They also imply that the institutional structure may play a part in the individual's consciousness of costs and benefits, and they lead to some interesting speculation as to the influence of "directness" or "indirectness" in public financing.

VOTER AWARENESS AND THE "DIRECTNESS" OF BENEFITS AND COSTS

It is reasonable to assume that the more *direct* are costs and benefits of specific programs, the more aware is the individual. Even though "publicness" implies substantial indirectness in the consumption of public goods and services, the institutional means of providing such goods may differ in terms of directness. There is limited room for varying such "pure" public goods as national defense in such a way as to increase or decrease their "directness" to the individual. But where certain of the benefits are divisible, more alternatives are available. Some of these alternatives have been noted in other connections. Friedman's voucher plan for financing education would doubtlessly make parents and children more aware of the costs of education. A similar plan could be used for veterans' medical benefits. Presumably the cost figures posted along new interstate highways also aid individuals in assessing costs and benefits.

Although it seems plausible that "directness" in taxing and spending increases individual "awareness," very little research has been directed toward this question. Rational fiscal choices require such "awareness," so it is important to know the fiscal institutional arrangements under which it is enhanced. Since localities often provide similar services under different fiscal arrangements, it may be fruitful to compare the "awareness" of individuals under the different systems.

When tax structures feature indirect rather than direct taxes, we would expect individuals to be less informed as to the amount they are paying. Studies by Gunter Schmolders of the University of Cologne, Germany, show that taxpayers are often unaware of which items are taxed and which are not.[31] They generally know what types of goods are taxed but have little idea of the rates imposed.

One method of increasing awareness would be to submit all budget proposals to referenda of the Wicksellian type. The complexity of modern budgets precludes this practice; moreover, the expenses of presenting fiscal alternatives to the public in referendum form would no doubt offset the possible benefits.

It would seem that awareness would be increased when certain taxes were used and "earmarked" for certain public activities. In this way both voters and their representatives would find it easier to compare costs and benefits from these activities, especially if the taxes were in some way related to the activity.[32] Gasoline taxes are often earmarked for highway expenditures. Perhaps taxes on liquor should be earmarked for rehabilitation of alcoholics and those on cigarettes should be earmarked for cancer and heart disease research. The appropriateness of earmarking depends on the characteristics of the tax and the public activity. In short, the tax should be such that the yield will correspond to the amount needed for the activity. Second, it should be such that the voter can recognize the connection between the tax and the activity and can gauge the cost relative to the benefit.

CHOICES UNDER DIFFERENT TAX PLANS

How might different budgeting procedures influence the amount spent on various public activities? We will see that when more than one budget item is voted on at the same time, the combination of items included can be of strategic importance in determining the outcome. For example, the director of a city's recreation program may or may not wish to have his budget requests considered along with the school budget. Organizations which depend on contributions, such as the Heart Fund or a local rescue squad, may or may not choose to join the United Fund, depending on which method of fund raising they think is more effective for them. James Buchanan has outlined the relationship between revenue sources and the *demand* for the public activity.[33]

---

[31] Gunter Schmolders, "Unmerkliche Steuern," *Finanzarchiv*, vol. 20 (1959), pp. 23–34.

[32] While our present focus is on the individual as a voter in the budget process, the "earmarking" method reminds us that an important aspect of translating individual wants into public policy is the part played by representatives, administrators, and budget officials in the budgetary process. This aspect of public financing will be examined in some detail in the chapters that follow. We note in passing that earmarking reduces the flexibility of administrative officials. This can become crucial as needs change during long budget periods. If the earmarked tax system requires constitutional changes, the legislature loses additional flexibility.

[33] Buchanan, *Public Finance in Democratic Process*, pp. 72 ff.

TABLE 3–10		Proposal X	Proposal Y
Minority coalitions to increase spending proposals	Individual A	Strongly favor	Mildly oppose
	Individual B	Mildly oppose	Strongly favor
	Individual C	Mildly oppose	Mildly oppose

We are familiar with the concept of relatively *inelastic demand*. It can refer either to an area on the demand function or the shape of one function relative to others. In either case the more inelastic the demand curve *the less effect changes in price have on changes in quantity*. This means that the monopolist, if faced with rising marginal costs, could raise his price and know that consumers would not reduce their purchases proportionately. In terms of the budgeting process, relatively inelastic demand means that voters will be reluctant to reduce the quantity of the public good or service even if greater expenditure is required.

It follows that the supporters of a particular activity will benefit if they can "tie in" with an activity producing another good or service whose demand is relatively inelastic. If the two are considered simultaneously, the combined expenditure will be larger than otherwise.

Another important "tie in" consideration is how demand may shift. Over time, changes in population, incomes, tastes, and so on will shift the demand for public activities. Consequently, it is beneficial to "tie in" your activity with one whose demand not only is relatively inelastic but expands through time.

On the other hand, supporters of a particular activity will resist unfavorable "tie ins" with activities whose demand is less inelastic and less likely to expand.

The nature of the revenue plan also plays a part in the effectiveness of "tie ins." The activity with relatively inelastic and expanding demand will benefit from a separate budgeting, to include perhaps an earmarked revenue source. Conversely, other activities will want to "tie in" to more general revenue sources. Buchanan concludes that since tying-in can result in greater overall support for spending and since bureaucrats inevitably favor increases in spending, they will support switching to general rather than earmarked financing.[34] This in turn will encourage greater than optimum budgets and misallocation of resources among activities. Presumably the separation of budget items allows each to be considered independently and enhances the possibility that each will be carried to the point where marginal benefits are equal to marginal costs.

The argument above suggests that, in general, "tie-ins" are to be discouraged in the budget processes. Some interesting exceptions may occur, however, when it seems desirable to allow minorities to express the intensity of their wants. Vote trading is less likely to occur under earmarked taxes and other institutions which discourage "tie ins." Consider Table 3.10. The majority of individuals mildly oppose both proposals. If tradeoffs are discouraged (say through earmarked taxes or other methods), both proposals will fail. If tradeoffs occur, however, individuals A and B may collude to approve both proposals.

If the present model seems to reinforce the argument that "tie ins" increase public spending, the result is accidental. The model could have been constructed with two minority groups who each *strongly oppose* a proposal and collude to defeat both. Thus, instead of a general conclusion we are left with two observations: (1) the outcome of budget voting depends on the way in which activities with different demand characteristics are linked together and (2) the choice between different methods which encourage or discourage tie ins, tradeoffs, and so on may well involve a value judgment among the interests of different groups of voters.

TAX STRUCTURES AND VOTING BEHAVIOR

Let us briefly consider how particular tax structures affect voting behavior. We will not attempt an exhaustive investigation now, since this question is inherent in much of what follows in Parts II and III. We would expect individuals to favor those tax structures under which they expect their relative burden to be smaller. In a study made by Elizabeth Jane Likert David, high-income groups were found to prefer sales taxes (which are regressive) over income taxes, whereas low-income groups preferred the opposite. And predictably, property owners were less inclined to favor property taxes than were renters.[35]

Similarly, we would expect the structure of the political jurisdiction to influence the nature of fiscal choice making. We would expect that where the tax structure allowed local voters to shift the burden to others, more expenditure would be forthcoming. If, for example, a large portion of the taxable property in a locality belonged either to persons outside

---

[34] Buchanan, *ibid.*
[35] David, "Public Preferences and the Tax Structure: An Examination of Factors Related to State and Local Tax Preferences" (University of Michigan Microfilm, 1961).

FIGURE 3–15

Partial utility function, voters with identical preference functions

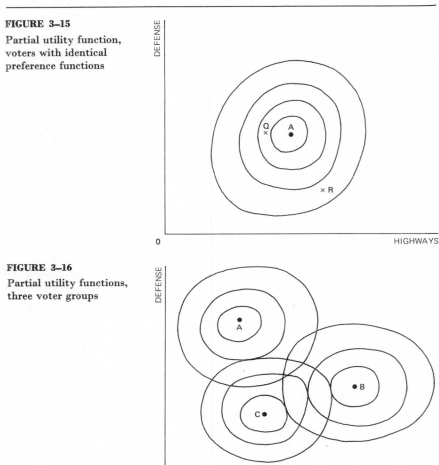

FIGURE 3–16

Partial utility functions, three voter groups

the jurisdiction or to a small proportion of the local voters, one would predict relatively larger public budgets than would otherwise be the case.[36] The observations concerning direct versus indirect tax and spending arrangements (mentioned above in connection with earmarked versus general funding) also apply to the different possible forms of political jurisdictions. Thus, when political jurisdictions make for more directness in voter estimation of costs and benefits, more or less of the activity will be desired depending on the elasticity of its demand. Empirical evidence gathered by Julius Margolis shows that communities which finance public schools from general funds tend to spend more on education than when they are divided into smaller districts and taxed accordingly.[37]

VOTER CONCURRENCE AND POLITICAL PARTIES

How well do political parties respond to the preferences of the voters they represent? An ideal model could be described as follows: The goal of the party is to maximize votes. In order to accomplish this goal the party seeks to calculate voter preferences and build a platform consistent with them. If a party does a poor job of calculating preferences, it will be supplanted by a party which does a better job.

Consider the model shown in Figure 3.15. A " partial " utility function similar to the ones used previously is shown, except it now represents the wishes of all voters instead of an individual. All voters are assumed to have identical functions, with the optimum at A. Now suppose there are two parties, each attempting to win voter support by adopting a platform which reflects voter preferences. If Q and R are the combinations of Defense and Highways the parties promise to deliver, the one promising Q will win. The same results would hold if voters' utility functions were evenly distributed around point A; the party with the platform closest to A would receive the majority vote. This model explains why the national parties tend toward the center of every issue and why it is often difficult to distinguish between the positions of Presidential candidates.[38]

But suppose there are distinct interest groups of voters instead of an even distribution around one point. Consider Figure 3.16 and assume A, B, and C are the optima of three separate groups made up of individuals with identical preference functions. The situation looks disturbingly similar to the voting models used earlier, and in fact the results are analogous. Political parties will position themselves with regard to issues so as to achieve a majority coalition. And, as with the voting models,

---

[36] Studies by Otto A. Davis and others lend support to these hypotheses. See Davis, "Empirical Evidence of Political Influences upon the Expenditure Policies of Public Schools," in Margolis, *The Public Economy of Urban Communities*, pp. 92–111.

[37] Margolis, "Metropolitan Finance Problems: Territories, Functions, and Growth," in *Public Finances: Needs, Sources and Utilization*, (New York: National Bureau of Economic Research, 1961).

[38] The argument above, attributable to Harold Hotelling and Anthony Downs, has been somewhat bastardized for the making of subsequent points below. For a better appreciation read Downs, *An Economic Theory of Democracy*.

FIGURE 3–17

Partial utility functions, "voter concurrence"

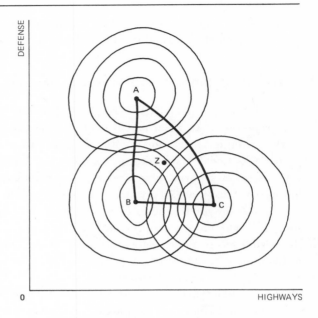

situations may occur where the number of national issues and the number of parties encourage cyclical majority coalitions. Although unstable coalitions of several political parties are the pattern in several other countries, in the United States we typically choose between two parties with remarkably similar platforms. The latter phenomenon, which was explored by Hotelling, occurs when there is high degree of "voter concurrence." In many other voting situations, however, distinct interest groups are attached to widely separated issue-positions, and the resultant tendencies are centrifugal. In many local elections for city council, for example, each candidate clearly attempts to represent a particular interest group. Similarly, the structures of political parties which have evolved in several European countries contain a number of interest-group oriented parties, none of which can gain a majority without forming a coalition with one or more of the others.

THE MINIMUM COALITION

If we drop the assumption that parties attempt only to maximize votes, we open the possibility of further centrifugal tendencies. A party itself is typically a coalition, and any analysis of its goals is complex. However, it is fairly safe to assume that those who have substantial control of a party at any one time will have preferences which differ from those of any particular interest group to which they may appeal. These party leaders will wish to move the party to a position which maximizes their own position and still win. Instead of maximizing votes, they will try to form the minimum winning coalition consistent with their own goals.[39] This may on occasion involve alienating one or more interest groups in order to secure another. It follows that a party may often benefit from emphasizing certain issues in order to form a minimum coalition from the divisions which result.[40]

VOTING COSTS AND VOTER CONCURRENCE

Reconsideration of cost factors in large-number voting reveals yet another possible centrifugal tendency. With positive costs for voting, an individual is not likely to vote unless the alternatives presented approximate his preferences. Consider Figure 3.17 and assume that each group is composed of an equal number of voters with identical preference functions. Under certain voting procedures it would be possible to reach " voter concurrence " at a point somewhere near the center of the Pareto set of optima (say point Z).

But suppose there are positive costs for voting such that if the alternative is further than three utility levels from the optimum the individual will not vote, since expected benefits have fallen below costs. The possibility of finding voting procedures leading to Z is reduced. It is more likely that the final result will somehow be determined by groups B and C and lie somewhere on the contract locus between. On the other hand, lower voting costs might allow a three-party system to evolve. An institutional structure wherein the political parties themselves negotiated compromises among the three positions could substantially reduce the costs to the voter of researching all of the alternatives, and so on. This reduction in costs might be adequate to make participation worthwhile for the voters in group A.

The models indicate that the final arrangement of parties and the possible coalitions and compromises depends importantly on the costs of voter participation.

---

[39] See William Riker, *The Theory of Political Coalitions* (New Haven, Conn: Yale University Press, 1962).

[40] An excellent example of this tactic is the campaign conducted by the Republicans in the 1970 elections. Much of the rhetoric of Vice-President Agnew was aimed at polarizing various groups of voters.

VOTING COSTS AND PUBLIC CHOICE INSTITUTIONS

Our examination of the relationship between economic welfare and voting has produced some ambiguous results. On the one hand, powerful forces are at work to bring about "acceptable" results in the *large-number* voting situations which are most common. These acceptable results would occur almost regardless of the voting procedure used. On the other hand, there remain many public choice situations where "acceptable" results can be attained only if a favorable institutional structure can be found.

Our task in the next two chapters will be to examine the nature of public choice institutions. In completing this task we will deal with some of the questions we are now leaving unanswered. In our examination of budgeting procedures, for example, we will observe how various institutions nave arisen in response to the several kinds of costs involved in the individual's participation in the public choice process. In anticipation of this discussion, let us summarize some of the kinds of costs would-be voters encounter.

THE CHOICE PARTICIPATION PROBLEM

The "choice participation" problem occurs when the costs of participating in a public choice are so high that a significant number of affected individuals do not participate in the decision-making process. We have already observed that in many situations, if only direct benefits are considered, the "rational" voter will not bother to vote. But voting is only one of the methods of public decision making which may be too costly to warrant participation by the average citizen. There are a number of ways in which the average citizen might influence, say, our trade relations with Chile. But the marginal benefits to the individual are extremely low relative to the costs involved in finding out just what our policy is, keeping up with trade legislation, writing congressmen, and so on. But we would hardly wish to leave the decision up to a "general" referendum in which only those with more immediate interests (such as the officials of the major competitors to Chilean imports) turned out to be the only voters. A more reasonable institutional structure is to have our representatives make the decision—hopefully with the interests of the voters at heart.

However, it takes only minimal familiarity with our nations' tariff and import quota system to realize that the choice participation problem has not been fully resolved. Although all of us as consumers are affected by our nation's system of tariffs and import quotas, the interests of consumers are rarely considered. Much more influential are the lobbying efforts of those industries which may be directly affected by changes in the system. Other flagrant examples of the choice participation problem are given by the behavior of many of the regulatory commissions at the federal and state levels. Consumer interests are rarely represented in an adequate manner at the commission hearings. In contrast, the regulatory commissioners become quite intimate with the interests and problems of the regulated industries and eventually come to feel that their major responsibility is to insure that the industries make a "fair" return. Consumers are directly affected by the actions of the commissions, but the benefits to any one individual are not sufficient to offset the costs of his actively seeking to influence commission rulings.

Theoretically, new forms of organization could appear which would allow the individual to participate at a cost low enough to be commensurate with the expected benefits. Several consumer groups have appeared in recent years which solicit contributions for the purpose of lobbying for consumer interests. A remarkable feature of the "Ralph Nader phenomenon" and other such groups, however, is that only a minute fraction of the individuals for whom these efforts are being made actually contribute in any way. The choice participation problem is still operative.

THE FREE-RIDER AND REVEALED-PREFERENCES PROBLEMS

The "free-rider" and "revealed-preferences" problems are similar to the "choice participation" problem in that in both cases the individual's action will not greatly affect the benefits received. Yet instead of the *costs* of participation being the problem, the free rider receives benefits *in spite of not participating*. Thus there is an actual benefit from not participating. In cases where there are a large number of voters and tax-payers, essentially the same amount of public goods will be produced even if the individual escapes payment. Moreover, since the benefits are indivisible, the individual can partake equally. The free-rider problem is, of course, basic to our initial "lighthouse" definition of public goods and explains why coercion of the taxpayer by the public sector is necessary.

An aspect of the free-rider problem of importance to our discussion of voting models is the "revealed-preferences problem."[41] The ideal model

---

[41] We will use the term "revealed-preferences problem" to refer to the "free-rider problem" as it pertains to the difficulty of getting voters to reveal their preferences when tax shares are to be decided along with expenditures.

would feature voting on expenditures and taxes simultaneously, so that marginal benefits and costs could be compared directly. This would require that each voter reveal his preferences and pay taxes in accordance with his benefits. However, since essentially the same amount will be produced anyway, it becomes good strategy for the voter *not to reveal his preferences*. Consequently, the revealed-preferences problem is a major difficulty in developing theoretical voting models which link expenditures with taxes.

Wicksell, in his work with voting models, recognized the problem and attempted to overcome it by requiring *unanimity* for an approval of referenda including both expenditures and tax shares. If unanimity is required, the vote of every individual becomes crucial. He cannot use the strategy of concealing his willingness to pay taxes.

In reality it would be difficult to convince every voter that a particular referendum was in fact a "take-it-or-leave-it" proposal and that the public officials would not eventually find some other method of providing the benefits in the event that all proposals sent to the voters failed.

The free-rider problem is apparent in the dismal record of local referenda. It is very often fatal for a locality or state to offer a proposal which requires an increase in taxes. Even if higher taxes are inevitable in the long run, many voters will vote "no" in hopes that their immediate tax burden will not be increased.

If tax and spending decisions are too widely divorced, we may encounter the free-rider problem in reverse. This aspect of the problem, known as the "diffusion effect," is felt to be of significance in budget situations such as "pork barrel" bills, where expenditures have direct benefits for certain groups of individuals. The individual may reason that, since the tax input is *given*, he must push for expenditures which give him and/or his constituents special benefits. But if all groups engage in this activity, the budget will be inefficiently large and will include items best handled in the private sector.

THE EXPERTISE AND MINUTIAE PROBLEMS

Finally, let us specify two aspects of public decision making which often add to the costs of individual participation. Many public choices which must be made are quite complex. The more expertise required and the more minutiae which must be assimilated, the less likely it is that the average voter will be willing or able to participate directly in the decision. The average voter cannot be expected to decide on the value of a particular component of an ABM system. Nor can he be expected to cope with the billions of small and large public expenditure decisions which must be made during the budget process. The sheer bulk of decisions necessitates delegation of much responsibility to appointed and elected bureaucracy. The problem becomes how to handle complex and multitudinous choices efficiently and yet also in the interests of the voters.

In this chapter we have examined various voting models in which individual preferences are related to voting behavior in various public choice situations or models. In the process of this examination we have observed that the institutional framework within which the choices are made is crucial. The question to which we now proceed is: How can public choice institutions work to provide public sector economic activity consistent with the preferences of voters?

II

PUBLIC ACTIVITY AND PUBLIC CHOICE INSTITUTIONS

4.
TECHNIQUES FOR
MAKING PUBLIC CHOICES

In attempting to link individual preferences to public activity we have repeatedly questioned the part played by the institutional setting within which public choices are formulated and then implemented. Already we have had occasion to resort to simple models which necessarily presume various voting procedures, taxing and spending institutions, and so on. Analysis of the processes of implementing fiscal choices becomes increasingly difficult as the economic model is expanded to contain more units and more complex interrelationships. Part of the difficulty arises because the character and scope of the functions of the public sector itself become more complex. A large part of the analytical task is that of discovering the role and influence of the various institutional structures through which these priorities are implemented. In Part II we will seek to further describe this institutional structure—to include the different tax instruments, administrative and legislative organizational arrangements, budgeting procedures, and expenditure programs—in order to analyze its impact on the process of translating individual preferences into public financing.

We begin by describing the fiscal functions of the public sector in general terms. We note that a specific program may affect several of our public wants simultaneously. Consider the public housing program. The building of federal housing directly affects the allocation of our resources between the public and private sector. By making use of public financing, we funnel into housing more resources than would have been committed if the private market had been left to determine their allocation. At the same time the rent payments are so low as to represent a subsidy to the occupants; hence, income distribution is affected as well as the resource allocation. Finally, we note that the timing and nature of the spending and taxation involved will have an effect on aggregate demand and supply and hence on unemployment and/or inflation. Thus we see that a particular program may affect our economic goals in various ways.

Owing to the rapidly changing nature of our economic environment and the flexibility of our democracy to adapt to changing dispositions of its citizenry, neither our fiscal choices nor the particular functions of government required for their implementation are well defined at any one moment in time. The task of examining and evaluating government activity would be much more precise if the appropriate norms (that is, public wants) were more specifically defined. We must, however, be content with designating as legitimate several broad functions of government.

The economic functions of our government, as initially conceived by the Constitutional Convention, allowed for a limited scope of public activity. The list of functions was similar to that proposed by the classical economists and consisted primarily of providing for those goods and services which we have termed " public." Moreover, the range of public goods and services was more narrowly conceived than at present. It is important to reflect that governments before that period had shown a propensity to thwart rather than to promote the individual and collective economic goals of the majority of citizens. The record of governments seemed to be one of hindering rather than promoting such social goals as equitable distribution of income and economic stability and growth. Through time, the public sector has assumed more responsibility in accomplishing these goals. Later in this study we shall examine more comprehensively the reasons for the growth of the public sector. The immediate task at hand is to formulate analysis of budget policy as it relates to implementing our fiscal priorities.

Without attempting to describe the fiscal functions of government in detail, let us place them in three broad categories: (1) the allocation of resources between private and public *goods and services*, (2) the *distribution of income* among individuals within the society, and (3) *macroeconomic policy* to include provision for full employment, a stable price level, and economic growth.[1] These objectives are quite distinct; yet, specific legislative proposals often affect more than one of them. More importantly, the interrelationships of the activities of the private sector and the public sector must be considered simultaneously when budgetary decisions are made.

THE MUSGRAVIAN MODEL OF BUDGET IMPLEMENTATION

Professor Richard A. Musgrave uses an interesting model for analyzing these interrelationships.[2] He imagines a Fiscal Department whose responsibilities include the three categories listed above. To carry out these functions the Fiscal Department is assumed to be organized in three branches. We shall call these the Public Goods, the Income Distribution, and the Macroeconomic Policy branches.

THE PUBLIC GOODS BRANCH

The task of the manager of the Public Goods Branch is to provide for the correct allocation of resources between private and public goods. For the moment we assume that social priorities concerning macroeconomic policy and income distribution are being accomplished by the other branches. Moreover, we assume that the voting mechanism somehow reconciles individual preferences and presents to the Public Goods Branch a set of priorities to be implemented. Our initial concern is to see how these priorities can be implemented in the simplest way. We anticipate by stating that the problem is to draw resources from the private sector and to produce public goods without upsetting the income distribution or macroeconomic policy goals.

The "publicness" of economic activities, we recall, results from externalities with which the private market cannot cope. If all of the conditions necessary for perfect competition[3] were met, no such externalities would be created, and there would be no need for the Public Goods Branch. The price mechanism would translate individual preferences into prices, and firms, motivated by profits, would allocate resources efficiently. We have seen, however, that public activity may be required if one or more of the necessary conditions are not met.

Initially assume that only one condition is missing: the requirement that all benefits and costs created by an activity be divisible and assignable. This would be true if some of the goods to be produced were public goods such as defense. In the absence of the exclusion principle the private market will not allocate a sufficient amount of resources to these activities. The task of the Public Goods Branch is to reallocate resources so as to devote the appropriate amount to the production of public goods.

Presumably the Public Goods Branch manager possesses the information necessary to produce the appropriate quantity of each public good. Ideally, the problem of distributing resources among public goods is solved by equating marginal social benefits with marginal social costs. The quantity of a particular public good should be increased as long as the marginal benefits (in terms of "utility") are greater than the benefits *which would be derived* from using the resources to produce more of some

---

[1] The following analysis of budget policy based on these three functions depends heavily on the theoretical model elaborated by Richard Musgrave in "Principles of Budget Determination," *Federal Expenditure Policy for Economic Growth and Stability by Panelists before the Subcommittee on Fiscal Policy* (Washington, D.C.: U.S. Government Printing Office, 1957), pp. 108–115, and in *The Theory of Public Finance* (New York: McGraw-Hill, 1959).

[2] Musgrave, *The Theory of Public Finance*.

[3] As outlined in Chapter 1, p. 12 ff.

FIGURE 4–1

The "correct" quantity of public good X

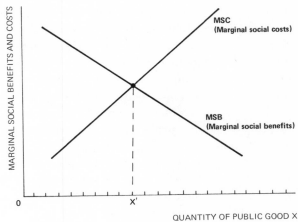

other good. These "would be" benefits may be termed the marginal social costs or the "opportunity costs" of producing the particular public good in question. Adding to our interstate highway system requires the use of labor; of grading, hauling, paving, and other machinery; and of gravel, concrete, and other resources which would have been devoted to the production of other goods. While it may be difficult to estimate marginal social costs in terms of the value of the "other goods," a rough estimate may be obtained from the market prices placed on the resources used—because input prices already reflect the value of their marginal product in alternative uses.

Figure 4.1 illustrates the concept of equating marginal social benefits and costs for a particular public good, X. The "correct" quantity is seen to be OX'. At smaller quantities it is still possible to add to social welfare by increasing X, since the costs of doing so are less than the benefits.[4]

It is further recognized that the MSB function shares all the difficulties associated with deriving a social welfare function (as outlined in Chapter 2).

In practice, of course, it is apparent that public officials do not always make decisions about public good production in the manner ascribed to the manager of the Public Goods Branch. Some of the reasons are (1) lack of knowledge on the part of public officials as to the equi-marginal principle, (2) lack of information as to the preference patterns of voters and marginal social costs and (3) lack of adequate incentives to promote the interests of constituents when these differ from the more immediate interests of the public official.

These difficulties are not always as serious as they sound. The process of compiling budget estimates necessarily involves matching costs with the proposed quantities. Moreover, the judgments budget officials make during the process of formulating the budget usually are not whether to start or discontinue entire programs but whether or not to slightly increase or decrease the various existing programs. Thus in a sense many of their judgments *are* made at the margin. And while these expenditure estimates usually include only the more obvious costs (which may differ from the full opportunity costs), they do at least furnish a rough guide to the relative value of resources being used in the production of the different public goods. Moreover, as we shall see later, there is increasing awareness of the spillover effects attendant upon public programs, and attempts are being made to quantify these benefits or costs where possible.

THE ALLOCATION OF RESOURCES THROUGH TIME

If our Public Goods Branch manager were confronted with the question of how best to apportion consumption of resources between the private and public sector *during only one time period,* his responsibilities would be greatly simplified. Upon learning the preferences of the citizenry, he would tax away the amount of funds necessary to withdraw the appropriate quantities of resources from the private sector and then he would use them to provide the desired collective goods. The only fiscal tools required would be taxation and public spending. Since the goods and services would be consumed in either the private or the public sector in one time period, there should be no reason for the Public Goods Branch to have an unbalanced budget. Assuming no effect on the price level, when resources are transferred from the private sector to the public sector a corresponding amount of spending power should be transferred by taxation.

It does not follow, however, that all publicly financed goods will be consumption goods. Indeed, resources may be used in either investment or consumption in the public sector just as in the private sector. Allocating resources to investment involves transferring benefits from one

---

[4] Since goods are interdependent in their ability to create utility, the marginal social benefit function will not be as stable as depicted in Figure 4.1. For example, if public good X were highways, the marginal benefits derived would depend on the number of automobiles in use and vice versa. If more highways were built, more cars would be built, and in turn the total and marginal benefits derived from different quantities of highways would change; that is, the MSB function would *shift*.

TABLE 4–1	Private sector		Public sector

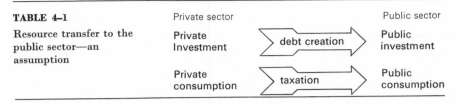

Resource transfer to the public sector—an assumption

	Private Investment	debt creation	Public investment
	Private consumption	taxation	Public consumption

time period to another and if we are to analyze such transfers our model needs additional assumptions. Let us assume a full employment economy such that all resources will be employed regardless of the amount used in either sector. Let us further add the rather heroic assumption that additional taxes cause people to reduce consumption (rather than investment) while public debt creation causes people to reduce private investment (rather than consumption). This assumed relationship is illustrated in Table 4.1. As will be noted later, under certain market conditions taxes may reduce private investment as well as private consumption. Likewise, public debt creation may not be matched exactly by a reduction in private investment. In either case aggregate demand may be affected so as to produce unemployment or inflation. For the present let us assume that the Public Goods Branch manager can and does implement his portion of the budget so that private consumption is appropriately reduced by taxation when public consumption is provided, and private investment is appropriately reduced by public debt creation when public investment is called for. By using this budget rule, the manager can allocate resources to public goods and services so that their marginal benefits equal marginal costs through time. With regard to the present, taxpayers give up private consumption for public consumption, equating the marginal benefits and marginal costs involved in each private or public expenditure. And in both the private and public sectors, individuals can compare the benefits of discounted future returns from investment to their costs. *Theoretically, public investment is financed through debt, so that in each period the present period's marginal benefits from previous investments coincide with the present period's marginal costs involved in paying off and servicing the debt incurred in financing the particular project.*

The Public Goods Branch manager formulates his portion of the budget in accordance with the desires of the citizenry and the costs associated with producing various goods. Assuming that a "proper" income distribution has been accomplished by the Income Distribution Branch, "proper" welfare-maximizing expenditure decisions can now be made on each private and public good. This optimal budget will be where the expenditure on each good or service is such that marginal benefits from its production equal the marginal opportunity costs of drawing the required resources away from the production of other goods or services (as explained in connection with Figure 4.1).

If we momentarily assume away the nonmarket externalities making for quasi-public goods and natural and man-made monopolies, our Public Goods Branch manager can simply use the fiscal tools of taxation and public expenditure to allocate resources in accordance with desired public consumption. And he can use public debt creation and expenditure on public investment to allocate resources according to expected benefits and costs in future time periods. Taxes, debt, and expenditure are managed so that they have no effect on income distribution or aggregate demand and supply.

THE INCOME DISTRIBUTION BRANCH

The imaginary division between the Public Goods and the Income Distribution branches is useful in illustrating the fundamental difference between these two functions of the public sector. The provision of public and quasi-public goods is a problem of allocating resources so as to maximize welfare. In considering this question, we normally assume that a " proper " distribution of income exists and then proceed to examine the process by which each individual uses his economic power to influence the allocation of resources. The distribution question is only indirectly related to the question of allocating resources. The redistribution of income can be limited to taxes and transfers of money. Any effects on resource allocation are a secondary result of the different tastes of those taxed and those who have received additional income.

Within the context of our model the duties of the Income Distribution Branch manager are quite simple. He receives directions from the citizenry as to what constitutes a " proper " income distribution.[5] Then he uses

[5] Here again heroic assumptions are necessary in order for *all* individual preferences to be expressed, reconciled, and implemented in a plan for redistributing income. Our examination of the tools of welfare economics demonstrated that formulating such a plan within the context of the " unique welfare-maximizing resource allocation " is dubious at best and would certainly be impossible under the constraints of the " new " welfare economics. However, our political system does in fact produce legislation designed to redistribute incomes. It behooves us to develop some criteria for analyzing redistributive programs. Our approach here is to build a simple model and to ask what assumptions, value judgments, and so on are in fact necessary.

taxation to reduce the income of some persons while using transfer payments to increase the income of others. Since the manager of the Public Goods Branch is assumed to be accomplishing his task, it is unnecessary for the Income Distribution Branch manager to make public expenditures which involve the public sector in decisions as to how resources are to be allocated. Francis Bator makes the distinction between government expenditures which exhaust resources—"exhaustive expenditures"—and those which do not—"nonexhaustive expenditures."[6] The expenditures of the Income Distribution Branch involve only the latter. No resources are "used up" by the Distribution Branch. Instead, purchasing power changes hands within the private sector.

Several disquieting considerations arise when we anticipate whether or not our political processes yield an "ideal" redistribution program. Since the majority vote is basic to our system and since the "rich" are a small minority, it would seem probable that the majority would exploit the rich via the public sector redistribution function. One rather obvious factor is that redistribution legislation is formulated through political processes which feature representative government, separation of powers, budgetary traditions, conventions, and the like rather than by a simple majority vote. The system was in fact designed to lessen the possibility of a minority's being exploited. At the same time rich individuals are able to use their wealth to attain political power in ours as in most political systems. Moreover, experience shows that changes in tax laws are usually incremental in nature, even when thorough overhaul is needed. It does not appear that public redistribution programs are vulnerable to rapid revision by newly formed coalitions of interest groups.

Yet another factor working against majority "exploitation" of the redistribution function is the fact that social and economic mobility within our system is high. Middle-income individuals will be unlikely to "soak the rich" if they perceive the possibility of becoming rich themselves, especially if they think the redistribution institutions may well still be in effect.

In the final analysis it is perhaps naive to anticipate any sort of "legitimate" consensus about redistribution to be revealed through our political system. Certainly interest groups are at work seeking to use the redistributive process to increase their wealth at the expense of others. And even if we assume that individuals possess "objective" judgments as to what constitutes "proper" redistribution, the judgments are probably "washed out" in most voting situations by more immediate motives. The difficulty here is akin to the philosophical problem posed in Chapter 3: does the " pragmatic imperative " conflict with the realization of " moral " choices? Our question is whether decision-making institutions can be utilized which will somehow sublimate the individual's prospects for immediate gain via redistribution and instead reveal his " true " preferences as to the " proper " redistribution policy. This in turn leads us back to the more general question: What impact do various fiscal institutions and techniques have on the revelation and implementation of public choices? Later, when we examine the institutions of the budget process in more detail, we can add more substance to our speculation that certain institutions tend to mitigate the possibility of the redistribution function's being misused by majority coalitions seeking immediate gains.

SEPARATING PUBLIC GOODS AND INCOME DISTRIBUTION DECISION MAKING

Separating redistribution from the public goods decision making is analogous to the problem of isolating it from the more immediate interest motives. Here again we shall see that within the budgetary process, institutions have evolved which help to separate these two decisions. For example, tax and expenditure bills originate in different committees in Congress. It is obvious that decision making is facilitated if these issues can be separated. Analysis of the marginal costs and benefits of public goods production is difficult enough without redistribution considerations being added. We recall the added complexity (and difficulty of resolution) when the simple voting models in Chapter 3 were expanded to include both alternate tax rates as well as spending plans.

James Buchanan has suggested that separation of the redistribution question be further isolated from other public decision making.[7] The *tax rate pattern* could be made a *constitutional* question, with extraordinary voting procedures required for the making of changes. One possibility might be to allow each citizen *one* opportunity (say at age 30) during his lifetime to express his preferences on the proper rate schedule. The rate schedule would change only as the summation of all votes dictated. This

---

[6] Francis M. Bator, *The Question of Government Spending* (New York: Harper & Row, 1960).

[7] James M. Buchanan, *Public Finance in Democratic Process* (Chapel Hill: University of North Carolina Press, 1967).

FIGURE 4–2

The interaction of
aggregate supply and
demand

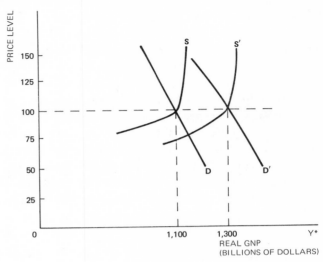

scheme would require the individual to use the long-run view when expressing his preferences and would allow public goods decision making to be divorced from redistribution decisions.

While the theoretical division between public goods and income distribution decisions makes for neatness in our theoretical model, implementation of budget policy in this way is not always feasible. Many public goods and services include aspects both of income redistribution and of resource allocation between the private and public sectors. Consider, for example, public housing. The provision of low-cost housing to certain families is certainly a form of income redistribution. At the same time, to the extent that more of our economy's resources are devoted to housing than would have been, this program affects the allocation of resources. Similarly, many expenditures on welfare, medical care, foreign aid, veteran benefits, and so on affect income distribution but also change the composition of goods produced in the economy. Yet, while such programs complicate an evaluation of the impact of our budget, their benefits seem to outweigh their costs.

In our model, however, the Income Distribution Branch manager uses only the fiscal tools of tax and transfer, and the problem of financing public goods is divorced from the income distribution problem. Consequently, income distribution decisions are made so as not to affect the allocation of resources, and the Public Goods Branch manager can carry out his function without worrying about income distribution. Finally, we note that the budget of the Income Distribution Branch is balanced so as not to affect aggregate demand and supply.

THE MACROECONOMIC POLICY BRANCH

There is little disagreement that our government can and should take actions to promote full employment, price stability, and economic growth. Since the Great Depression of the 1930s the government has used both monetary and fiscal tools with increasing proficiency. Part IV of this book deals at length with these macroeconomic aspects of budget policy; however, a brief introduction will be given here.

The interaction of aggregate supply and demand. First, it is necessary to recognize that fiscal and monetary policy must be coordinated if macroeconomic goals are to be realized. Very simply, in order to achieve stable economic growth, aggregate demand must increase as fast as but not faster than aggregate supply. As Figure 4.2 illustrates, a stable price level can be maintained only if shifts to the right in potential supply are compensated by shifts in aggregate demand. Over time, changes in technology and the availability of resources make for greater productive capacity. Such changes are illustrated in Figure 4.2 as a shift to the right in the aggregate supply curve S'. If aggregate demand shifts accordingly, greater output can be attained with no change in the price level.

Inherent in the shape of the aggregate supply curve are certain economic relationships mentioned previously. At the output range we may call " capacity," there is a limit to what more can be added to real output during the time period in question. Consequently, the aggregate supply curve rises sharply. If aggregate demand were increased too rapidly, the price level would rise as shown in Figure 4.3(a).

Unfortunately, prices will not as easily adjust downward. If aggregate demand does not keep pace, the demand curve will not cross supply at the capacity output, but instead real output will fall to point B—a situation where considerable unemployment exists. Under the assumptions of the *classical economists*, such a situation could not occur, since prices would adjust downward. But in the less-than-perfect competition of American capitalism, prices of commodities and inputs do not always adjust downward at the full employment level of GNP. Consequently, insufficient aggregate demand will result in unemployment rather than a lower price level. This situation is illustrated in Figure 4.3(b). The line D' illustrates a short-run decrease in demand. And, as is inherent in

FIGURE 4–3

Aggregate demand and
supply showing inflation and
unemployment

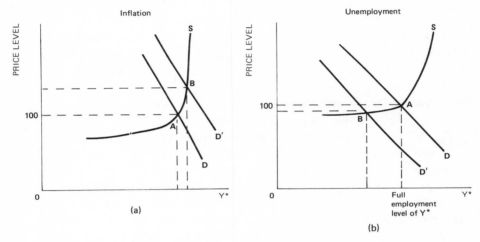

(a)

(b)

the elastic portion of the aggregate supply curve, prices do not adjust
downward so as to maintain GNP at the highest attainable level; hence,
some resources are either unemployed or underemployed.

The composition of aggregate demand. The basic logic of monetary and
fiscal policy is to manipulate aggregate demand so as to compensate for
shifts in aggregate supply and keep the price level stable. In order to
accomplish this task, one must predict how much spending will result at
different levels of income. The basic Keynesian model (we recall from
introductory economics) breaks down aggregate spending into the following components: consumption, C; investment, I; and government spending, G. National income, Y, is simply the total of these three:

$$Y = C + I + G$$

The simple model includes only one variable, consumption, which is made
a function of income:

$$C = a + bY$$

In the familiar function above, a is the intercept while b is the rate at
which consumption changes with changes in income (the marginal

propensity to consume). The crucial point made by the simple model is that, as income expands, consumption will not expand at the same rate. Any attempt to adjust aggregate spending to aggregate supply must account for the behavior of consumption in response to income. At the same time, attention must be given to the expected spending flows of investment and government spending. Investment spending is perhaps the most volatile of the three components and the most difficult to predict.

Macroeconomic policy, of course, requires not only predictions of potential spending patterns but positive action to manipulate aggregate demand. The monetary and fiscal tools available allow the public sector to adjust any of the three components: consumption, investment, or government spending. Monetary authorities work through open market security operations, rediscount rates, or reserve requirements to change the money supply, the rate of interest, private investment, and thus, finally, aggregate spending. Alternatively, fiscal tools such as tax incentives, income tax increases (or cuts), transfer payment increases (or cuts), or for that matter changes in " exhaustive " expenditures may all be used to expand or contract aggregate demand.

For the moment let us simply state three working rules for our imaginary Macroeconomic Policy Branch. When aggregate demand is insufficient to maintain full employment, we should increase transfer payments or cut taxes so as to provide more spending power. When aggregate demand is too great, so that inflation results, we should decrease spending power by increasing taxes or decreasing transfer payments. These fiscal tools must be used in conjunction with coordinated monetary policy. Finally, fiscal and monetary policy should enhance stable economic growth by adjusting tax rates and the money supply to provide the appropriate amount of aggregate demand commensurate with the economy's growing productive capacity—the latter being illustrated by a shift to the right of the aggregate supply curve (see Figure 4.2).

It is, of course, the responsibility of the Macroeconomic Policy Branch manager to order his activities so as not to interfere with those of the other branch managers, who, presumably, are accomplishing their respective goals. Accordingly, he adjusts aggregate demand with taxes or transfers which are proportional with respect to the income distribution goal of the Income Distribution Branch. And, theoretically, he should accomplish his task using only one fiscal tool: either *taxes or transfers* (but not both). Consequently, his budget *should not be balanced*!

If governmental "exhaustive" expenditures are used for macroeconomic policy, their use must agree with the goals of the Public Goods Branch.

Predictably, real world implementation of macroeconomic goals cannot be so neatly separated from the goals of the Public Goods and the Income Distribution branches. As we shall see, "exhaustive" government expenditures are effective and perhaps necessary stabilization tools in certain situations. Likewise, it may prove a difficult task to arrange tax or transfer adjustments so as to avoid affecting income distribution. Indeed, if inflation or recession has already begun, income distribution has already been adversely affected, since, in either case, the impact is disproportionate.

A SIMPLIFIED MODEL OF THE FISCAL DEPARTMENT

Before considering more of the questions posed by our model, let us briefly summarize the basic interrelationships by utilizing a simple version of our theoretical model.[8] As outlined above, the budget is planned with three goals in mind: (1) proper distribution of income, (2) appropriate allocation of resources between private and public goods, and (3) provision for stable prices, full employment, and economic growth. Let us assume that we have an economy composed of only two individuals, Mark and Victor. These two jointly produce an annual gross national product valued at $100. Mark receives $70 in wages for his part in production, while Victor receives $30.

The Income Distribution Branch. Mark and Victor jointly decide that a " proper " distribution of wealth should not exceed a 60 percent to 40 percent range from the average income. Distribution is adjusted accordingly by taxing Mark $10 and transferring it to Victor. Now Mark has $60 and Victor $40.

The Public Goods Branch. Putting on their hats as managers of the Public Goods Branch, Mark and Victor now formulate that part of the budget. It is agreed that each individual will spend 50 percent of his income on public goods. Since Mark now has $60 and Victor has $40, they are taxed $30 and $20, respectively. The revenue from these taxes, $50, is then spent to produce the desired public goods.

The budget of the Public Goods Branch is balanced; hence, it has no effect on the macroeconomic goal. We also note that the income distribution goal has not been disturbed, since the relative distribution remains the same.

The Macroeconomic Policy Branch. Mark and Victor (acting as a two-man Council of Economic Advisers) analyze productivity trends and foresee that, owing to changes in technology, aggregate supply in current prices will increase to $120 in the coming year. Realizing that prices will not readily adjust downward, they decide that aggregate spending must be increased. In this rather peculiar economy there is no investment spending, so the increase must be in the form of consumption or government spending. Since government spending is already set at $50, $70 more in aggregate spending is required. But care must be taken not to upset the other goals.

Since it has been decided that 50 percent of spending will be on public goods, they now allocate $10 more for that purpose. It follows that they now must manipulate consumption so that $60 will be spent. They find, however, that the marginal propensity to consume is only .6. Consequently, in order for Mark and Victor to spend $60, their combined incomes must be $100. Therefore, a transfer is made, $30 to Mark and $20 to Victor. This final income distribution is in keeping with the original goal.

Table 4.2 summarizes the activities of the Fiscal Department. We see that each branch has a balanced budget except for the Macroeconomic Policy Branch, which posts a deficit of $60. We also observe that the budget of the Income Distribution Branch includes no "exhaustive" expenditure; that is, no resources are withdrawn from the private sector and exhausted in the production of public goods. Instead, the income distribution goal is accomplished by transferring funds from one individual to another. In contrast, the Public Goods Branch uses taxes to withdraw spending power from the private sector for the purpose of producing public goods. The Macroeconomic Policy Branch, however, necessarily must adjust both public and private spending if the desired balance between sectors is to be retained.

Our simple model has been quite useful in illustrating several important aspects of how these three basic goals are accomplished by the public sector. At the same time it has demonstrated the fundamental interrelationships inherent in the application of fiscal tools to simultaneously accomplish all three goals. Even in our simple model it was not easy to account for these interrelationships; we shall see it is much more difficult in "real world" budgeting.

---

[8] This model is quite similar to that used by Musgrave in "Principles of Budget Determination."

TABLE 4–2

The fiscal department's
budget

The income distribution adjustment

Private sector		Income distribution branch	
Mark	$70 income		
	—10 tax	Taxes	+ $10
	⎯⎯		
	60 disposable income		
Victor	$30 income		
	+10 transfer	Transfer	— $10
	⎯⎯		
	40 disposable income	Balance	0

The public goods adjustment

Private sector		Public goods branch	
Mark	$60		
	—30 tax	Taxes	+ $30
	⎯⎯		
	$30 disposable income		
Victor	$40	Taxes	+ $20
	—20 tax	Government spending	
		on public goods	— $50
	⎯⎯		
	$20 disposable income	Balance	0

The macroeconomic policy adjustment

Private sector		Macroeconomic policy branch	
		Government spending	
Mark	$30	on public goods	— $10
	+30 transfer	Transfer	— $30
	⎯⎯		
	$60 disposable income		
Victor	$20		
	+20 transfer	Transfer	— $20
	⎯⎯		
	$40 disposable income	Balance	— $60

IMPLEMENTATION CONSIDERATIONS ARISING FROM THE MODEL

INTERGOAL FISCAL NEUTRALITY

A major reason for presenting Musgrave's model was to illustrate how
several fiscal functions may be integrated into one budget. The difficulty
comes in finding techniques which allow for fulfilling a particular function
while remaining "neutral" to others. With respect to the three functions

---

outlined for the model we found that: (1) the Income Distribution Branch could tax and transfer so as to effect income distribution while remaining neutral to the Public Goods and Macroeconomic functions; (2) the Public Goods Branch, using a balanced budget of proportional taxes and, of course, "exhaustive" expenditures, could accomplish its task of producing public goods while being "neutral" to the other functions; and (3) although the Macroeconomic Policy Branch would often operate with an unbalanced budget, the nature of its macroeconomic tools is such that they would not need to affect income distribution or resource allocation. Obviously, interfunctional fiscal neutrality is desirable, because it makes for more precise appraisals of the separate functions. But, as we noted in developing the model, other considerations often offset the advantages of intergoal neutrality. We will only briefly summarize these considerations before examining others.

THE PROVISION OF QUASI-PUBLIC GOODS

In our discussion of externalities we noted that they may be categorized as relating either to production or consumption. When the public sector provides quasi-public goods which exhibit *externalities of consumption*, it necessarily affects *income distribution* as well as public good production. We have previously mentioned some governmental activities which fall into this class: federal housing, medicare, veterans' benefits, the food stamp program, education. The key factor is that it is only when these goods are consumed by the recipient that external benefits accrue to others.

When such goods are produced, it is necessary to calculate their effect in terms not only of public good production but of income distribution as well. Theoretically, such goods as housing and education, whose consumption creates externalities, could be provided simply by income redistribution. The problem is that the income recipients would not necessarily spend their income on the goods they were supposed to. The provision of quasi-public goods with consumption externalities must include assurance that the recipient of the benefits does indeed consume the good. Hence children are required to go to school, and the monetary advantage offered by federal housing is available only to its tenants. The choice of financing techniques differs according to the nature of internal and external benefits provided.

INTERSECTOR NEUTRALITY IN PUBLIC FINANCING

"Neutrality" in fiscal activity is defined as the ability to be effective without disturbing the established *price ratios* within the private sector.

FIGURE 4-4

Welfare maximization
as depicted with a total
production possibility
function, social
indifference curves and a
price ratio

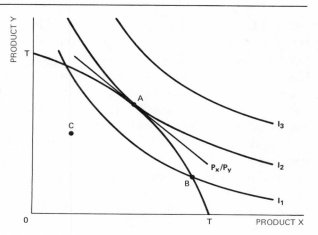

FIGURE 4-5

The effect of an excise
tax on welfare maximi-
zation

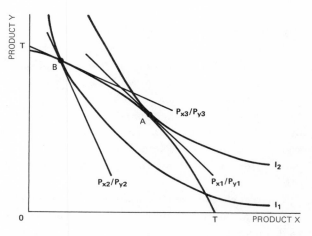

Inherent in the definition is the assumption that there is something good
about the established price ratios. We have developed the notion of how
an optimum welfare-maximizing allocation of resources occurs in a perfectly competitive economic system. All price ratios set within this model
reflect all benefits and costs associated with the commodities and the
factors used in production. In such a never-never world, fiscal activity
which needlessly upset these price ratios would certainly be undesirable.
Let us demonstrate this by temporarily assuming that all conditions of a
welfare maximum exist. In Figure 4.4 the welfare-maximizing equilibrium
is shown at point A. The production possibility function, TT, shows the
possible combinations of society's two products, X and Y. Perfectly com-

---

petitive markets react so as to equate the consumers' preferences as to the relative attractiveness of goods (marginal rate of substitution) to producers' abilities to adjust output composition (the marginal rate of transformation). In other words,

$$MRS_{xy} = \frac{P_x}{P_y} = MRT_{xy}$$

The attainment of this equilibrium depends on the success of the price mechanism in communicating consumer desires, relative scarcities, the productivity of inputs, and so on within the system. Only with the correct price ratios can consumers communicate their desires correctly to producers. Under these conditions the welfare-maximizing position at A would be attained.

More realistically, the allocation of resources and corresponding price ratios will be consistent with some position which meets neither the condition of optimality (point A) nor the condition of "efficiency" (somewhere on TT). Output levels will be somewhere inside of TT, say point C.

We are now in a position to reconsider the possible ramifications of "nonneutral" fiscal activity on the private sector. If current prices correspond to the allocation "C," it is possible that a change in prices may move the economy to a more favorable position. We designate such a result as "positive nonneutrality." If fiscal activity results in price changes which move the economy further from the optimum, such an effect is termed "negative nonneutrality."

Part III will present a more complete analysis of the behavior of firms in response to taxes and other fiscal activity. For the moment let us simply state that firms in certain market situations are able to shift the burden of certain types of taxes forward to consumers or backward to the suppliers of inputs. In either case, tax shifting involves a change in prices. Taxes which are shifted involve some form of nonneutrality.

While we have defined nonneutrality quite rigorously, caution should be observed when this criterion is used to evaluate nonneutrality in terms of welfare optimization. In our model in Figure 4.5 point A is a good reference point from which to evaluate other output and price combinations. Unfortunately, in real-world situations we cannot define "optimum" allocation with the same precision. Consequently, we cannot always be certain whether a particular "nonneutral" change is "positive" (moving towards better resource allocation) or "negative" (moving towards worse resource allocation).

NEUTRALITY IN TAXATION

Taxes necessarily impose a burden on the taxpayer. The difference between the burden it is necessary to impose and that which is actually
imposed may be defined as "excess burden."[9] Intersector neutrality
would require that no excess burden be imposed by unnecessary interference with the market mechanism. It is pertinent to compare the excess
burdens which result from different methods of taxation. We will again
use the perfectly competitive model as developed in Chapter 2.

We wish to compare the "neutrality" of a specific excise tax with that
of a tax which is independent of output of a specific good (such as a head
tax, a lump-sum tax, a general income tax, or a general sales tax).
Assume that we are comparing an excise tax on X with an income tax.
Both taxes are imposed so as to withdraw a certain quantity of resources
from the private sector. We assume that TT in Figure 4.5 shows the
possibilities *after* the resources have been withdrawn. The income tax
enables the public sector to withdraw resources so that the production
possibility curve TT is established. Producers, maximizing profit, respond
to the desires of consumers. The rate at which producers find it profitable
to produce X relative to Y (the marginal rate of transformation) depends
on the price ratio, P_{x_1}/P_{y_1}, which in turn depends on the rate at which
individuals are willing to substitute X for Y (the marginal rate of substitution). This equilibrium is attained at point A in Figure 4.5.

No such equilibrium is possible with a specific excise tax. The tax on X
drives a wedge between the new price and that which would attain in
free exchange. The consumer again adjusts his marginal rate of substitution to the price ratio, P_{x_2}/P_{y_2}. However, the producer adjusts to the
price ratio without the tax (P_{x_3}/P_{y_3}). The new equilibrium, B, is at a
lower level of satisfaction. We see that the imposition of a specific excise
tax creates both the burden of withdrawing the necessary resources and,
by interfering with the price mechanism, an "excess burden." From the
standpoint of neutrality the specific excise tax is undesirable. We note,
however, that the assumptions made in order to designate point A as
optimal are not met in the real world; therefore, the nonneutrality of the
specific excise tax *may* turn out to be "positive" rather than "negative."

The preceding analysis offers an opportunity to comment on some possible nonneutral effects of the general income and sales taxes. The implicit
assumption that work effort is fixed does not necessarily hold when income
taxes are introduced. The benefits accruing from work income are now
more costly than those associated with leisure, and so, presumably, more

leisure will be taken. On the other hand, we note that if the individual's tastes are such that he is reluctant to give up the standard of living supported by his former income, he may have incentive to work harder than before. At present little evidence has been given to clarify the net effect of these two influences.

The general sales tax may also have nonneutral effects. Although we have implicitly assumed that the consumption and saving habits of consumers would remain unchanged, a sales tax will make consumption relatively more expensive than saving. Here again, however, we cannot be sure that the imposition of a general sales tax will cause consumers to save more than before. Indeed, if the consumer wishes to continue his old purchasing habits, he will *reduce* rather than increase his savings. The net effect of the nonneutrality of the sales tax, like that of the income tax, has not been satisfactorily determined.

In Part III we will examine in detail the effect of different taxes on the behavior of the firm and individual. Our brief description here has demonstrated that the choice of fiscal tools may have important effects on resource allocation.

THE PROVISION OF PUBLIC AND QUASI-PUBLIC GOODS

THE DEGREE OF GOVERNMENTAL DECISION MAKING

The benefits of pure public goods are primarily indivisible and are generally provided with no user charge. Purely private goods require no public activity, since the market provides them at appropriate prices. It is with quasi-public goods and situations involving monopoly or monopsony that fiscal techniques become a matter of controversy. One useful way of categorizing these techniques is with respect to division of decision-

---

9 The concept of excess burden has received much attention in economics. We will be interested in it when we consider the microeconomic analysis of specific taxes in Part III. Analysis of excess burden has been approached from the traditional welfare perspective where interpersonal comparisons are allowed: see Alfred Marshall, *Principles of Economics*, 8th ed,(London: Macmillan, 1930) chap, 13, and A. C. Pigou, *A Study in Public Finance*, 3rd ed. (London: Macmillan, 1951); in terms of the newer welfare criteria: M. F. W. Joseph, "The Excess Burden of Indirect Taxation," *Review of Economic Studies*, vol. 6, no. 3 (June 1939), pp. 226–231; and from the general equilibrium perspective: Earl R. Rolph and George F. Break, "The Welfare Aspects of Excise Taxes," *Journal of Political Economy*, vol. 57 (July 1949), pp. 46–54, and Milton Friedman, "The Welfare Effects of an Income and an Excise Tax," *Journal of Political Economy*, vol. 60, no. 1 (February, 1952), pp. 1–24.

making power between private and public sectors. Without restating the case for the efficiency of the competitive market, we offer the following proposition:

Proposition: When competitive markets may be utilized, it is better to leave the maximum amount of decision making within the private sector.

There are often several methods by which quasi-public goods may be provided. Consider the provision of hospital care for veterans. This service is currently provided to veterans in hospitals owned and operated by the federal government. Several other alternatives are possible. One alternative would be for the government to contract with particular private hospitals to care for all veterans within a geographical area. Another would be for the government to allow veterans to go to any hospital of their choice and to reimburse their charges. The latter two alternatives obviously allow much more of the necessary decision making to be accomplished within the private sector.

The following fiscal techniques involve greater-to-smaller degrees of public sector decision making:

1. *Public sector produces the final good and all intermediate goods.* There are few if any examples of this type of public activity in the United States. However, practically all goods produced in the Soviet Union fit this category.
2. *Public sector agency makes a decision at one or more stages of production.* This may be the final stage or some intermediate stage. Decisions as to the final use of helicopters by the U.S. Army are made entirely by the public sector, while many production decisions such as plant location, input sources, and so on are left to the private sector. On the other hand, decisions as to the final use of our annual crop of corn are made primarily within the private sector, while substantial decision making in the area of acreage allotments and the like is performed by the government.
3. *Regulation and/or subsidies at one or more stages of production.* The transportation and communication industries often feature substantial regulation and subsidization. For example, not only are the airlines regulated as to which air routes they can fly, but they are given mail contracts and other subsidies as well.
4. *Licensing and taxation.* Government licensing sets standards and limits entry into certain fields. Taxation may also be used to affect resource allocation. Specific taxes change relative price ratios between taxed and non-taxed goods. Taxes on cigarettes have at least some effect (although a surprisingly small one) on the quantity demanded. Often, licensing and taxing may be used together to restrict entry and prescribe behavior in certain markets.

5. *Indirect macroeconomic tools.* The government uses monetary and fiscal policy to affect aggregate demand. The fiscal tools of general taxes and expenditures may be used for this purpose. Theoretically, changes in taxes and expenditures can be made in such a way as to not upset the desired balance between public and private sector resource allocation.

6. *Moral suasion and advertising.* Moral suasion and advertising may also be used by the public sector to influence decision making. Presidential wage-price guidelines or specific comments about steel prices may be partially effective.

Similarly, government advertising has been employed to a limited extent in such areas as public health and education. If such advertising is effective, individuals' preferences are influenced, and in turn they may support increased expenditure on certain public goods and services. John Kenneth Galbraith and several other commentators argue that public goods and services suffer a considerable disadvantage vis-à-vis private sector goods owing to the overabundance of advertising for private goods and the relative paucity of advertising for public goods.

The choice of the technique depends, as we have noted, on the nature of the good and the market within which it is produced.

THE CHOICE OF FINANCING TECHNIQUES FOR QUASI-PUBLIC GOODS

Quasi-public goods (in contrast to purely public goods) offer some benefits which are divisible by quantity and quality. According to the nature of benefits derived, it may or may not be feasible to differentiate among users in dispensing the benefits. There are a number of ways in which the nature of benefits suggests different fiscal rules for public activity. We mention only a few.

Quality differentials in quasi-public goods. First consider the case where the "impurity" rests in possible quality variations afforded consumers of the public activity. Police and fire protection are essentially public goods, but there is certainly opportunity to vary the quality of service among taxpayers. Police may, for example, patrol the Providence Hill and business areas more frequently than the ghetto areas. Fire stations may be located closer to one section of town than the other. Where such variation is possible, political pressure will often be used to secure benefits. But the point is that the possibility of varying quality of service allows for correlation between services and charges. For example, if certain businesses or areas of town want police protection, street cleaning, or some other service extended beyond the quality deemed adequate, it may be efficient to furnish them with quality differentials at higher charges.

User charges for divisible benefits. A related procedure may be used when purely divisible benefits are attendant to the public activity. A frequent example is the operation of public forests and parks. Such scenic areas may produce indivisible benefits for conservationists, clean-air enthusiasts, aesthetes, and so on, and at the same time provide specific benefits to individuals who utilize camping, boating, swimming, and fishing facilities. Hence, direct user charges are appropriate for the latter services.

It is often difficult to determine the appropriate private method of financing, the appropriate quantity benefits, and who should pay. In such situations political controversy is inevitable. And this is as it should be— for several alternatives may present themselves and usually more than one interest group will be involved. Ideally, there will be a method available so that the private benefits may be charged for on a user charge basis, while the collective benefits may be paid for from general taxes. This is roughly the way lunches at public schools are financed. Direct charges to students are used to finance a substantial part of the cost; but, in addition, federal and state funds are added to increase the quality of these lunches. This is because the external benefits are greater than those financed simply by user prices. Taxes are also used to finance lunches for those students whose parents are hard pressed to pay for them. It is felt that every child " merits " at least one good meal a day.

Another example of user charges is the method used for highway construction and maintenance. The primary source of revenue, gasoline taxes, is in effect a user charge. Generally speaking, the more gas you buy the more you drive and, consequently, the more wear and tear you create on the highways. Additional funds come from license fees and tolls, which vary usually according to the type of highway user involved. There are also marginal benefits in excess of those to which the exclusion principle applies; consequently, general taxes provide additional funds. Mixed financing is also employed in the provision of some parks, museums, monuments, recreational facilities, and health programs. Generally, the appropriate mix of direct user charges and general taxes should be determined by the relative importance of the private and collective benefits involved.

Unfortunately, it is not always possible to find the right combination of user charges, general taxes, or other revenue tools to account for the private and collective benefits produced by a particular good. Moreover, we should note again that, even though external benefits exist, the divisible benefits will often provide enough incentive so that the appropriate amount of the good or service is produced in the private sector without public financing.

The choice of techniques when there are nonmarket externalities may include alternatives other than taxes and user charges. Laws may be framed to internalize such externalities as air and water pollution, unkept property, the razing of historical sites, and so on. The factory whose smoke ruins the widow's laundry may be required by *law* to install a filter or pay damages.

In other situations as well, the nature of the benefits may make user charges undesirable. The most important quasi-public good, education, certainly creates direct benefits to the children in school, but since "consumption" by children of all family income levels is desired, no charges are made. Public swimming pools offer another example where public sector activity may be warranted to provide for widespread "consumption." But in this latter case a small user charge is usually employed.

The question of consensus again. As illustrated by the quasi-public goods education and swimming pools, "publicness" depends not only on the supply characteristics of a good but on community attitudes as well. To take the public swimming pool example again, there may be general consensus in some communities that swimming for children helps the community in several ways, such as reducing juvenile delinquency, building healthy bodies, and providing psychic benefits to those who enjoy knowing children have a place to swim. Other communities may be less cohesive. Many persons in a town's Providence Hill area may feel no affinity with the ghetto children. They may feel, for example, that "we have already gone too far in helping the blacks, especially since we are already paying dues at the country club where our own children swim."

Consensus is also important in determining the revenue-producing institutions which may be utilized. In some communities a door-to-door campaign of voluntary contributions may be successful in providing funds for public activities. In others the "free-rider" problem may quash this possibility. During World War II patriotism was effectively called upon to make rationing work, but it is doubtful that such a system could work during peacetime. Similarly, while the effectiveness of our tax institutions depends primarily on public coercive power, it is greatly enhanced by a general respect for our government. Most of our taxes depend importantly on compliance by the individual or firm being taxed.

In this section we have outlined several different methods which can be used to provide for public and quasi-public goods. We have observed that different methods involve varying degrees of governmental decision making. Similarly, different revenue methods can be used to apportion the costs of quasi-public goods between the collective benefits and the individuals who receive direct benefits. Finally, we have observed that the choice of techniques depends in part on the nature of attitudes held by the community itself.

THE TAX-OR-SUBSIDY PRESCRIPTION

Most of the public and quasi-public goods we have been considering exhibit externalities which accrue when the good is used or " consumed." Another type of externality is more closely associated with the production of a particular good or service. A firm or individual pursuing some activity in the private sector may create external benefits or costs which in turn affect others. Here, again, the appropriate policy depends on the nature of the externality in question. The solutions range from public sector production to less direct methods, such as moral suasion.

Let us first examine the possibility of using taxes or subsidies to encourage behavior which accounts for the externalities. In situations where *external costs* are created during the production process a *tax* may be used either to encourage a shift to different production methods or to reimburse the injured parties. One of our initial examples of an externality, the factory smoke and the widow washerwoman, could well lend itself to this sort of solution. Depending on the other alternatives available (such as smoke filters, shutting down the factory, and so on), the best solution might be to tax the factory owner and reimburse the widow.

Where external benefits are created in the production process, it may be appropriate to encourage this activity through subsidies. The subsidies can be paid for by taxes on individuals or from general revenue, according to who benefits from the externalities. When the production of a particular product requires research which in turn may be useful for many other purposes, it is appropriate that it be financed in part by government subsidies.

In general, the major problems in finding the optimum tax or subsidy prescription stem from the fundamental difficulty of relating " welfare " to economic activity. We often suffer from a serious lack of knowledge—especially if we attempt to evaluate benefits and costs with no market prices available. Our discussion of " positive " and "negative " nonneutrality also gives us pause for thought. Presumably, whenever there is a question of public intervention, one or more of the conditions for optimum resource allocation by the private sector are missing. Any compensating public activity will be " nonneutral "; but can we be sure it will be " positive "? The so-called "theory of the second-best" warns that when several conditions are missing, public action leading to what seems to be the second-best solution may in fact have *negative nonneutral effects.* For example, firms are given special tax treatment for new investment spending, since such spending has salutary external benefits for the economy as a whole. However, if these tax benefits help larger firms squeeze out smaller firms, the competitive nature of those markets may be reduced. A nonneutral fiscal action that seemed to be " positive " may in fact be " negative."

An important observation made by Coase[10] and by Buchanan and Stubblebine[11] is that in tax-subsidy situations not only the initial action but the *alternatives* open to the persons acted upon must be considered. It would seem, for example, that an airport authority should reimburse nearby homeowners who are disturbed by the noise of jet airplanes. But what should be the policy relative to homes built *after* the airport has been established? Admittedly the airport authority has control over the activity making the noise, but the building of new homes is under the control of others. One solution would be to hold the airport responsible to the property owners at the time the nature of the externality became apparent. Thus the airport would be responsible for paying damages according to the initial effect the externality had on the then present value of the property. Presumably this initial effect would reflect all of not only the current costs but the costs expected in the future. After all, future buyers would purchase the property at a price discounted because of the noise nuisance. The point is that tax-subsidy prescriptions must be designed to account *for all alternatives open to all parties* affected by the externality.

[10] Ronald Coase, "The Problem of Social Cost," *Journal of Law and Economics*, vol. 3 (October 1960), pp. 1–44.

[11] James M. Buchanan and W. C. Stubblebine, "Externality," *Economica* (November 1962), pp. 371–384.

FIGURE 4-6

The natural monopoly case: price regulation with subsidy

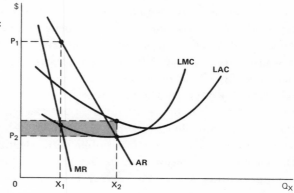

There are numerous examples of government intervention in which the secondary externalities seem not to have been anticipated. For example, the federal government has attempted to improve the cotton grower's terms of trade by acreage allotments, price supports, and other measures designed to keep prices up. Subsequently, however, textile firms, faced with foreign competition which can buy cheaper cotton, have successfully argued for direct subsidies and import quotas. Situations where the externalities are interrelated offer even more complex problems for public sector activity. Consider, for example, the government's "proper" role in the transportation industry. Federal grants and subsides of different sorts have been given the railroads and the airlines. Federal, state, and local levels of government help finance the highways and roads for trucks and automobiles. Any program to "save the railroads" will, of course, have an impact on the profitability of the airlines, trucking, bus lines, and other competing forms of transportation. All three levels of government affect the several different forms of transportation in different ways: laws, regulatory agencies, and direct and indirect subsidies and taxes. A change in any one policy will have ramifications that affect related firms and may require compensatory policy changes.[12]

NATURAL MONOPOLY: REGULATION AND SUBSIDY

The tax-subsidy prescription for the natural monopoly depends on the revenue and cost functions the firm is facing. In some situations very little governmental decision making may be required; others may require so much that the choice between private and government management may be made simply on the grounds of expediency. In Part III we will consider the impact of public finances on microeconomic behavior. Let us anticipate by briefly considering the regulation, taxation, and/or subsidization of the natural monopoly.

The resource misallocation attendant upon natural monopoly situations was described in Chapter 1. Since the optimum size firm is large relative to market demand, there is not room for other firms to enter and compete. Figure 4.6 illustrates such a case. In the absence of regulation the firm, equating MR and LMC, would produce quantity X_1 and charge price P_1. This solution meets neither the test of efficiency nor that of welfare maximization. In terms of efficiency we note that a long-run average cost could be reduced considerably by increasing output. In terms of welfare maximization we note that the price does not reflect marginal costs and thus consumers are misinformed when dictating society's allocation of resources. The price-quantity combination which apparently would bring society closer to optimum allocation is P_2 and X_2, the point at which price reflects long-run marginal costs. Consequently, the correct policy would be to regulate the firm's price at P_2. Obviously the firm will lose money at this price, since price is below long-run average costs. A subsidy equal to the shaded area must be paid to the firm if it is to make a normal profit.

A number of goods and services seem to exhibit characteristics similar to those depicted in Figure 4.6. Many are found in the transportation and

---

[12] Some of the theoretical and analytical difficulties of following what seem to be obvious tax-subsidy prescriptions are illuminated by James M. Buchanan and M. Z. Kafoglis, "A Note on Public Goods Supply," *American Economic Review*, vol. 53 (June, 1963). Baumol and others have commented that difficulties may arise if attention is focused on the marginal externalities while the second-order conditions are not met. Stated in mathematical terms, the attainment of a maximum (say of welfare or profit) requires that the marginal values (first derivatives) be set to zero. In addition, certain second-order conditions must hold to assure that you are not at a saddle point, a minimum, or some other point which is not the actual maximum. The problem is analogous to finding the top of a mountain when there are several small peaks and plateaus. The second-order conditions help describe the area around the point where the first-order conditions are met. In terms of the familiar factory-vs.-washerwoman example, the marginal (first-order) conditions will tell us whether the two parties can reach an agreement (*given* the presence of smoke); whereas the second-order conditions will tell us something about the context within which the agreement is reached: is it really a maximum?

Baumol demonstrates that when externalities are present, the attainment of the first-order conditions is often insufficient, since the very presence of externalities can work towards a breakdown of the second-order conditions. See William J. Baumol, "External Economies and Second Order Optimality Conditions," *American Economic Review*, vol. 54 (June 1964).

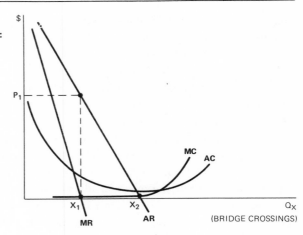

FIGURE 4–7

The natural monopoly case: marginal costs zero

communications industries. Possible examples are postal services, telephone, toll roads, transit authorities, railroads, airlines, and city bus lines. Many of these are often in the position of requiring subsidies even though the services they produce feature benefits which are primarily divisible, so that direct user charges may be used to defray the majority of the costs. Our analysis would indicate that a net loss in such ventures may in fact be closer to the optimum situation than is often supposed.

The extreme "decreasing cost" case exhibits marginal costs which are zero. Consider the classic example of a bridge with operating expenses which do not vary with the number of bridge crossings within the relevant demand (see Figure 4.7). The demand curve, AR, shows the crossings that will be made if various prices are charged. The implication, however, is that since marginal costs are zero, no charge at all should be made unless overcrowding happens to result. Any charge above zero would arbitrarily reduce bridge crossings to below the optimum amount—thus resources would be misallocated.

Observe that there are two different types of situations where the consumption of additional units creates zero marginal costs. In introducing the concept of public goods we used the illustration of the lighthouse, whose beams were available to all with no extra cost. Similarly, a radio broadcast retains its quality no matter how many persons are listening. And within certain limits the number of persons crossing a bridge may vary with little change in costs.

An important feature of the "publicness" of the lighthouse case, however, was that the benefits of the beams were not divisible and assignable to specific persons. Since no one could be excluded, there was no incentive for a private market entrepreneur to build the lighthouse and attempt to sell the beams to customers; consequently, public sector action was required. The "publicness" of the natural monopoly case, however, does not derive from the indivisibility and nonassignability of the benefits, but from the fact that profit maximization will lead to a misallocation of resources. In the bridge example the profit-maximizing output level, X_1, would be where MR is equal to MC. Welfare maximization, however, would require X_2 crossings.

Analysis of the zero-marginal-costs case is useful for short-run considerations; but its validity for long-run planning is limited. In the long run all costs are variable. Hence one would be hard pressed to imagine a case where long-run marginal costs are zero. In the bridge example a "long-run" period would include ample time to consider various sizes of bridges and various methods of paying for them. The number of crossings would depend on the size of the bridge to be built—allowing for more crossings would require positive marginal costs.

NATURAL MONOPOLY: PUBLIC VERSUS PRIVATE PRODUCTION

Where public control is required because of a natural or man-made monopoly situation, there are many alternative methods of production. Let us consider the provision of postal service, where the benefits are divisible but public intervention is required. User charges can be used to pay for at least a large part of the cost of providing the service. Conceivably, postal service could be provided by a private firm. Although some aspects of the operation would have to be regulated, most decisions —such as recruitment of personnel, utilization of transportation, the design of post offices, and the colors of mailboxes—could be left within the private sector. Recently the Postal Service has been reorganized to increase its independence and allow it to operate more like a private corporation.

Where natural monopoly situations exist, it is often debatable whether the second-best solution is reliance on detailed decision making by governmentally operated agencies or reliance on private market decisions augmented by government regulation. For the most part, Americans have made the latter choice. Public utilities, such as electric power and telephone and telegraph systems as well as railroads and other transportation facilities, are operated in most European countries by the government. But in the United States it is usually thought preferable to take advantage of the incentives of the private market whenever possible. Of course, the final judgment as to how much decision making we can leave within the private sector depends importantly on the nature of the good and the degree of competition in the particular resource markets.

Predictably, economists are divided in their opinions as to which goods and services government should produce. Most agree, however, that government agencies should be relied upon only when they are more efficient than private enterprises would be.

Milton Friedman has proposed (perhaps seriously) a plan for publicly financed but privately operated school systems.[13] Under this plan students would be given grants to attend any school their parents preferred. The schools would be privately operated—subject to certain specifications, of course. Presumably, the schools which offered the highest quality education would be the more successful in attracting students. There would be incentive for educators to innovate and to emulate successful methods of others. In this way, it is argued, the incentives of the private market economy could be useful in promoting a more efficient educational system.

There are, of course, many objections to such a plan. It may be argued, for instance, that the present system benefits from economies of scale which would be lost if it were broken up into smaller educational plants. It is questionable that a system of private schools would be able to communicate and share new teaching methods as efficiently as the present systems do. A more obvious objection is the wide diversity in educational opportunity which would probably develop between children of different income groups.

But the point here is that the question of public financing does not necessarily entail public operation; and certainly, one of the necessary criteria for deciding in favor of public operation is *efficiency*. Finally, we must note that one's judgment in such matters often depends on one's opinion of the relative efficiency of the private sector and the public sector. Obviously, it takes great faith in private enterprise to assume that it would be more efficient than the present public school system. We would prefer, whenever possible, to take advantage of the competitive forces of the private sector in the production of quasi-public goods. Unfortunately, however, many market situations do not exhibit sufficient competition to warrant such a policy.

PUBLIC FINANCING AND GOVERNMENTAL BOUNDARIES

If the benefits from a particular public project—say, a port facility—accrue primarily to a certain *geographical area*, it would seem appropriate to tax the citizens of that area to build the harbor. When quasi-public goods are involved, often the social benefits may be financed out of general funds while special taxes may be placed on a certain locality which enjoys more direct benefits. But since most public good benefits are indivisible, it is often difficult to ascertain the geographical boundaries within which they are enjoyed.

The question is often quite complex. The geographical area to which benefits accrue depends on the nature of the public good. The benefits from police and fire protection accrue primarily to the locality they serve. The benefits from recreational facilities accrue primarily to those in one locality or region, depending on the facility in question. On the other hand, the benefits from a consistent judicial system, an educational system, or a national defense system cover wider areas. Basically, two problems are involved in deciding how taxes should be allocated geographically. First, what groups benefit (and how much does each group benefit)? Second, what level of government should finance the activity? It may be difficult to decide which budget functions should be carried out at which level. We observe that each individual's assessment of the presence and extent of an externality is dependent on his own utility function and may be quite different from others. Where some individuals perceive extensive externalities others see none.

Theoretically votes could be taken to determine the geographical importance of a specific externality. These votes would indicate the most efficient governmental unit for this function. Tiebout and Houston point out that economies of scale in public production are not as important as they may seem since many goods and services do not have to be produced by the local government units themselves but can be contracted for with other governmental units or private industry.[14] A more basic difficulty is that the boundaries of governmental units are not flexible. Since present boundaries and tax structures set parameters for tax incidence there will

[13] See Friedman, *Capitalism and Freedom* (Chicago: University of Chicago Press, 1962), chap. 6.
[14] C. M. Tiebout and D. M. Houston, "Metropolitan Finance Reconsidered: Budget Functions and Multi-level Governments," *Review of Economics and Statistics*, vol. 44 (November 1962).

be groups which oppose any change which may make them bear a heavier part of the burden. Similarly these groups will resist an intergovernmental shift in functions which may make them worse off.

Even if voting procedures could be found to reveal the most efficient government unit for a particular function it may not have the most efficient taxing instruments for matching benefits and costs.

With these reservations in mind we formulate the following:

Proposition: Public functions should be carried out at the lowest level of government at which they can be efficiently accomplished.

This proposition expresses a bias for federalism, affirming that the level of government more immediate to the individual should be able to respond to his preferences and is thus better able to match costs and benefits. On the other hand the term " efficiently " is somewhat ambiguous here, and we can reformulate the proposition so as to mitigate any undue bias towards decentralization:

Proposition: Where taxing capacities differ among regions, the appropriate government level to carry out a function depends on consensus as to the geographical scope of the benefits and costs created.

This proposition emphasizes the idea that citizens' consensus as to the geographical scope of the benefits and costs indicates the proper level of government. By way of illustration, let us examine our own notions about the proper government level to carry out the *public education* function. Where do the benefits accrue? One spillover effect is the satisfaction we get from knowing educated young people have greater economic opportunity. Do we limit our concern to children in our family? in our community? in our state? in our nation?

Another consideration is the direct economic benefits afforded to individuals and firms by a better-educated work force. For example, a firm which draws workers from a nearby city will benefit from greater educational effort by that city. It follows that if the makeup of externalities is such that all cities within a state have mutual benefits from educational expenditures, but at the same time their taxing capacities differ, the state is the appropriate level; otherwise the budget decisions made by the different cities will not reflect all of the social benefits and costs associated with the public education function.

A SUGGESTION

As our study proceeds, the student on occasion will benefit by stopping, taking stock of the concepts thus far presented, and *applying* them in a thoughtful evaluation of the current federal, state, and local budgets. This is one such occasion.[15]

Several perspectives may be used for applying many of the concepts thus far developed. Consider the following possibilities: (1) analyzing the data *by function* by employing the arguments in Chapters 1 and 4 used to *justify* public sector activity: (2) evaluating government expenditures and taxes in terms of the *marginal benefits* and *costs*; (3) breaking down expenditures and taxes by *level of government* and pondering whether the present distribution of functions is most appropriate, and (4) considering present and *alternative methods* of accomplishing these functions with different divisions between private and public sector decision making.

In using the first perspective, we might well attempt to categorize public activities as to their impact on the distribution of income and on the production of public and quasi-public goods, or their macroeconomic effect on full employment, stable prices, and economic growth. Questions which might arise are: Which activities may be classified as pure public goods and which as quasi-public goods? Which activities are primarily transfer payments and thus involve no "exhaustive expenditures"? On the other hand, which items affect more than one goal—say both intersector resource allocation and income redistribution?

In using the second perspective, we might well employ the concepts of the benefit and ability-to-pay approaches. From the "voluntary exchange" point of view, which taxes may be considered as payments for specific expenditures? Or more generally: "Who benefits" and "who pays"? And how do the major taxes stand up under the equal sacrifice criteria?

[15] There are several convenient sources for current budget data with which the student should become familiar. Federal expenditures are presented annually in *The Budget of the United States Government* (Washington, D.C.: U.S. Government Printing Office), a volume which includes the Budget Message of the President, information by function, and summary tables and statistical information. Current compilations of state and local budget data are much more difficult to come by; however, one of the best sources is the *Statistical Abstract of the United States* (Washington, D.C.: U.S. Government Printing Office), which is also published annually. It contains a guide to the most current state statistical abstracts and other sources of statistics. Another convenient source is the series *Facts and Figures on Government Finance* published by the Tax Foundation, Inc.

In using the third perspective, we might analyze the nature of the benefits produced by the activities carried out at the various levels of government. Do the benefits and costs accrue primarily to those within the geographical area in question? Does the governmental body have responsive decision-making institutions and adequate taxing power?

Finally, in using the fourth perspective, we might speculate as to what alternative fiscal techniques might be used. For example, what are the alternatives to the publicly managed old age, unemployment, and medical insurance programs? What would be the results of relying on the private sector for a greater portion of the necessary decision making?

Undoubtedly, one result of this preliminary examination of budget figures will be to open up a Pandora's box of additional questions: What are the mechanics of the macroeconomic policy of changes in taxes and expenditures? Who in fact bears the incidence of the taxes we use? How do taxes affect the economic behavior of individuals and firms? And (the question to which we now turn) how do different budget institutions affect the realization of public choices?

5

CHOICES AND BUDGETING AT FEDERAL, STATE, AND LOCAL LEVELS

Now let us apply the insights gained in the last few chapters to an examination and evaluation of "real world" budgeting. We begin by focusing on the budget process itself. As we move along, we will employ the perspectives gained previously—to include fiscal goals, principles, rules, and so on—at the same time, of course, developing new perspectives appropriate for analysis of the budget situation in question. We will provide the basis for the next chapter's suggestions on how our budgeting processes may be improved. These arguments will be made in terms of "cost-benefit analysis" or "program budgeting," a frame of reference whose widespread adoption in recent years is having significant impact on fiscal reform.

THE BUDGET PROCESS

The primary function of the budget process is to provide efficiency in decision making on public expenditures and revenues. Theoretically, the budget could be compiled by staging a series of Wicksellian-type referenda. Given the acceptance of certain value judgments (with which we are familiar) and the assumption that every voter possesses *perfect knowledge*, we might even make a case for the Wicksellian technique providing for an *optimum* budget. By optimum budget we mean that combination of public expenditures and revenues which corresponds with welfare-maximizing resource allocation. In the real world, of course, several conditions preclude the Wicksellian approach. Of utmost importance are the difficulties stemming from the size and complexity of the budget and the expertise required to judge many of the public programs. These conditions necessitate our leaving budget formulation to representatives. Yet even with this added dimension we may still analyze budgeting in the context of welfare-maximizing resource allocation. Now, however, the principal question becomes that of how *efficient* the institutional framework is in realizing public wants via representative government.

A basic difficulty stemming from the size and complexity of the budget, is, of course, the *costs* in time and energy required to make decisions. Thus, we expect budget institutions to be arranged so as to reduce these costs. We may also expect that, in choosing between budget processes, there is often a tradeoff between efficiency and wider representation.

The executive and legislative branches have developed procedures which allow for systematic presentation and review of expenditure proposals by the many agencies of the public sector. The basic function of the executive branch is to execute the budget. In addition, it has the responsibility of compiling the initial proposals. The legislative branch, whose primary function is to enact the budget, also participates in its formulation and oversees its execution. Both branches have a vast array of agencies (some of whom are semi-independent) which participate in the budget process. Although Congress has its own experts on various facets of the budget, it must rely heavily on the executive branch for raw data and statistics. Our major interest is in the interaction of these agencies during the budget process. An outline of the budget cycle will serve as a preview of types of decisions which must be made. The budget cycle includes the functions of formulation, enactment, execution, and control. We first consider the federal budget cycle.

FORMULATION

The preparation of the federal budget begins at the "ground floor" level some eighteen months before the fiscal year is to begin. These lower levels of the organization pyramid have a myriad of titles: agency, division, department, office, and so on; but for simplicity let us term the lower levels (such as the local Soil Conservation Service Office) "Agencies" and the higher levels (such as the Department of Agriculture) "Departments." In the initial phase preliminary estimates at the "agency" level and at the Office of Management and Budget (OMB) are made more or less *independently*. Moreover, the Cabinet, the Council of Economic Advisers, and other Presidential advisors—and of course the President himself—are considering the possible shape of the final budget.

Estimates are generally *incremental* in nature; that is, they are made in terms of adjustments to the current expenditure levels. Assessment is made of how much is being spent presently, and costs are usually projected under the assumption that the present functions will be continued —or perhaps increased at the present rate of expansion. While the agency may have ambitions of taking on new functions or drastically changing its present activities, it probably has neither the authorization nor the cost figures it needs in order to include such alternatives as part of its preliminary estimates. Within most governmental agencies, in fact, a formal and lengthy procedure is followed when lower-level units wish to expand their operations. The procedures typically involve the submission of standardized forms to higher-level agencies which demonstrate the need for expanded services; a formal investigation by the higher-level

---

agency; and then recommendations and perhaps tentative approval based on future budgetary allotments. It follows that the lower agency units are not likely to use the preliminary budget estimate as an occasion for broaching requests for significant changes in their expenditures.

Soon after initial efforts are made to project the incremental spending of existing programs, the Office of Management and the Budget in cooperation with the Council of Economic Advisers, the Treasury, and other Presidential budget advisors attempts to formulate tentative budget guidelines and to discuss them with the President.

After the initial guidelines are formulated, they are disseminated to the departments and agencies along with requests for preliminary budget estimates. During this phase of the budget process there is considerable interaction among agencies, intermediate organizational units, and the departments, as different groups present their cases for more favorable treatment. If the agency is requesting an increase which substantially overshoots its guideline, it must naturally employ an aggressive selling program.

The results of this preliminary bargaining are compiled by the OMB and presented to the President in late June. He may at that time attempt to establish priorities in line with the broad goals he, his Cabinet, and his advisors have formulated. The OMB in turn formulates more rigorous guidelines and ceilings and requests the departments and agencies to make formal specified requests.

During the summer months (July-September) of the year prior to the start of the budget, the departments and their agencies work up the formal requests based on the OMB's ceilings and guidelines. While the possibilities of change are somewhat reduced at this point, aggressive agencies may still attempt to argue their case with the higher-level organizational units or even the President.

Early in the fall OMB personnel begin compiling the final figures for the budget. The director and other staff members coordinate the compilation of the final figures, which are in turn reviewed by the President. Statements justifying the final expenditure figures are composed with the help of the agencies and departments. The entire budget is then drawn together in December for presentation to Congress by the President in the annual Budget Message.

ENACTMENT

The budget is never considered in toto by Congress but is broken down into appropriations and revenue bills, each of which is studied by a special committee and then presented to the House or Senate. Appropriations bills originate in the House. The House Appropriations Committee farms out the President's budget recommendations to twelve subcommittees, where intensive study and hearings take place. The subcommittee recommendations are compiled in the form of an appropriations bill, which is submitted to the Appropriations Committee and in turn to the floor of the House. These appropriations bills then are forwarded to the Senate, where once again they are considered by a subcommittee before being reported to the floor. Differences between the House and Senate versions of the bills are ironed out by a Joint Committee and the compromise versions resubmitted to both Houses for their approval. Throughout the enactment process the President's option to veto serves as a constraint on Congress. Since a two-thirds majority in both houses is required to override the veto, a certain amount of consensus is required when items are included that are likely to provoke a veto.

The enactment phase takes the better part of the first half of the year and often runs over July 1, requiring an extension of current expenditure patterns and some guessing on the part of agencies.

EXECUTION

The actual allocation of the funds to agencies is the responsibility of the Office of Management and the Budget (a situation which allows the OMB some flexibility in determining actual expenditures). Department and agency directors also have some flexibility in the use of funds according to the specificity of the allocation.

CONTROL

There are several overlapping systems of control and audit in the execution phase. The OMB, the departments, and the agencies have well-defined reporting procedures which serve the dual purpose of an accounting by the organizational unit of its own activities and of control by higher echelons. In addition, the departments and intermediate organizational units systematically audit the "books" and activities of lower echelons. Congress also keeps tabs on the use of funds through its own auditing agency, the General Accounting Office.

THE GAMES BUDGETERS PLAY—I: FEDERAL BUDGETING

EVOLUTION OF THE RULES OF THE GAME: CHECKS AND BALANCES, SEPARATION OF POWERS, AND PARALLEL REVIEW

One of the focal questions running through our discourse has been how individual interests can be combined and resolved in the process of deciding upon resource allocation. One aspect of the private sector model was the Pareto criterion that free trade would not be entered into unless at least one individual was better off while *none were worse off*. We asked whether such free exchange would lead to an allocation of resources that could be considered " optimal," and we concluded that there are serious difficulties in visualizing a social optimum under such assumptions. It is even more difficult to make judgments about how individual wants are translated into resource allocation through the public sector. Decision making through majority voting certainly cannot be said to conform to the Pareto criterion that no one is allowed to be made worse off. However, the checks and balances which have evolved within our budgetary systems help mitigate the possible abuses to the minority that would occur if straight majority voting were used to determine the budget.

Over the years, the principles of separation of power and checks and balances applied by James Madison and his cohorts have remained effective, even though the institutions making up the budget system have changed markedly. The founding fathers built into our government system a separation of powers among the three branches of the federal government, among the states and the federal government, and between the House and the Senate. They did not foresee the demands that would be placed on the decision-making process as the budget grew larger and more complex. However, as the budget process has evolved through the years, checks and balances have been extended into the interplay of executive agencies, House appropriations committees, Senate appropriations committees, the House Ways and Means Committee, and numerous other agencies and committees which hold strategic positions in the process. In the executive branch, for example, one observes the checks and balances of competing agencies within the ever-present constraint of the OMB. The Council of Economic Advisers, the Treasury, the Federal Reserve, and other agencies also play influential roles in the budgetary process.

We will not attempt a thorough examination of the implications of the " separation of power " and " checks and balances " concepts in terms of political theory. Instead, let us outline the limited way in which we will use them. We take " separation of powers " to mean the delegation of authority to perform certain governmental functions to certain branches or levels of government. The idea is to disperse power among different bodies by dispersing the different governmental *functions*. We take " checks and balances " to mean giving more than one governmental body *influence over the same function*, thus requiring cooperation if the function is to be accomplished. Thus, to a certain extent, the two ideas work in opposite directions.

In practice we have no clear-cut separation of powers; instead, the different branches of government have "clusters" of decision-making powers, all of which overlap to some degree with the "clusters" of other branches. To the extent that these powers and functions overlap, checks and balances inevitably come into play.

The existence of checks and balances requires that the different branches resolve their differences in order to change the "status quo." In terms of the budget process, each of the several units participating holds a certain amount of veto power. The units in question use their veto power to extract concessions from the other participants. Since agreement must be extracted from all participants, a system of checks and balances, although it allows for a wider representation of interests, is obviously inefficient in terms of "getting things done."

In our study of the budget process a third concept will also be useful. "Parallel review" of budget proposals is necessary if the separate participants within the budget process are intelligently playing their roles of checks and balances. By "parallel review" we mean that the separate congressional committees, OMB agencies and other participants in the budget process cannot exercise their roles by a cursory glance at budget proposals. Since proposals are often lengthy and complex, thorough review by separate bodies is expensive and time consuming. Each body is required to organize itself so that it can come to agreement within itself. And each separate body is required to develop sufficient expertise to intelligently review the proposals.

THE QUESTION OF EFFICIENCY AND CONFLICT RESOLUTION

Our previous discussion has revealed that the dispersion of budgetary powers usually allows for interests other than the majority to play a part in the decision-making process.[1] Yet "parallel review" by separate bodies makes certain organizational demands. A major factor of the complexity of budgetary decision making stems from the expertise required to evaluate the costs and benefits of a particular program. The administrative agencies themselves are populated by experts in the activity in question, but the voter and his representative have no such training. In order to exercise its decision-making responsibility, Congress has found it necessary for some of its members to specialize and to develop expertise in certain areas of the budget. The appropriations committees of the House and Senate are specialized, in that their members devote considerable time and study to the part of public activity that their committee oversees. In addition, the congressmen develop their own staff of experts and solicit the advice of other experts in their review of agency requests.

The objective of wider representation is at odds with efficiency when separate consideration of complex proposals requires large and expensive staffs for each organization. When the judgments to be made require considerable expertise, the decision-making group must *defer* some of its power to a smaller, more expert, and more efficient group. Thus, although Congress has many members, representing a wide range of interests, only a few congressmen can thoroughly and intelligently review any one section of the budget.

Two other phenomena also encourage either formal or informal relinquishment of decision-making power. Both considerations stem from our earlier analysis. First, we must ask whether certain many-faceted budget issues could be resolved at all if left to some sort of majority vote system. Our analyses of various voting situations suggests that when the number of issues is large (relative to the number of participants), there exists ample incentive for reaching agreement. As the number of issues is increased, the percentage of the total issue space accounted for by the Pareto optimal area shrinks rapidly.[2] Nevertheless, procedures for accomplishing the necessary tradeoffs must be found, and when issues are numerous the time factor becomes an important limitation.

A second and related question is whether many of the decisions to be made constitute an irreconcilable dilemma for congressmen. A congressman represents many interest groups. A voting system which relies on floor votes on each separate issue might well alienate enough of his constituents to make reelection impossible regardless of his voting behavior. Instead of allowing for the direct *confrontation* of all interests at one point in the budget process, conflict resolution takes place in committees, subcommittees, agencies, and so on, and diverse interests are given opportunity to be effective at various points along the path of budget proposals.

---

[1] In some situations the legally constituted institutions may require too much dispersion. Then there may arise more inclusive organizations, such as political machines, which are more " efficient " but may severely limit the range of interests which participate.
[2] See Chapter 3 and Gordon Tullock, *Toward a Mathematics of Politics* (Ann Arbor: University of Michigan Press, 1962), pp. 24 ff.

CONFLICT-REDUCING CONVENTIONS IN CONGRESS

Congress reduces conflict and allows for specialization by breaking up the budget into parts and allowing specialized committees considerable decision-making power. The members of these committees seem willing to focus their attention on the technical relationships and the testimony of " experts " rather than on the value judgments involved. That is, they attempt to couch decisions in terms of " efficiency " rather than the " welfare " of their constituents. It follows that considerable power is conferred on the committee chairman, who exercises control over the content and timing of the legislation to be considered. Congressmen further delegate decision-making power to committees and their chairmen by restricting debate when budget legislation reaches the floor. *In the House only alternatives offered by the committee itself can be considered.* The Senate floor debate offers a little more freedom to amend; however, the convention of deferring to the " expertise " of the committee is so strong in both Houses that there is little chance of altering a bill on the floor.

If the preferences of committee chairmen reflected the interests of the majority of congressmen, little would be lost by yielding power to them. But by yet another convention, committee chairmen are chosen by seniority, and the resultant appointments can at times seem quite irrational. Thus we find committee chairmanships heavily populated by southern and western congressmen typically more conservative than most of their colleagues. The seniority convention is another aspect of the deference to " expertise " at the expense of a system more responsive to majority preferences. Indeed, states where more turnover of representatives occurs would seem to be better barometers of changing public tastes than those where there is little turnover.

Further examination of the committees reveals additional ways in which direct conflict is bypassed. The House Appropriations Committee is typically divided into twelve subcommittees, each of which considers one broad program area of the budget. For example, one subcommittee studies the requests of the Department of Defense; another, the requests of the Department of Agriculture and related agencies; another, Health, Education and Welfare, and so on. As noted, the subcommitteemen develop considerable expertise in working with these departments, and to a certain extent they identify with these agencies and their programs. Moreover, the individual congressmen get to know the specialists in the agencies under their jurisdiction and form an opinion of their capability. An effort is made to appoint subcommittee members who will not rock the boat. This may mean appointing men whose constituency is not directly affected by the programs to be considered. It certainly means appointing men who are willing to make tradeoffs rather than insist on costly confrontations. Even within a committee a certain amount of specialization occurs as particular members devote themselves to studying particular agencies. And here, as elsewhere in the budget process, the " expert's " judgment is respected, and reciprocal respect can be counted upon when one's own expertise is on the line. Consequently, the success of a particular agency in getting funds may depend on its ability to " cultivate " one or two congressmen on the appropriate subcommittee.

But even within a subcommittee many judgments require tradeoffs; and there are conventions governing these decisions. Such tradeoffs are facilitated by the nature of appropriations bills. One starts with the assumption that the old level is " sacred " and the amount of the increment is in question. Since the medium is " money," almost any ratio of exchange can be established. Usually some parts of a program can be cut or spread through time in such a way as to accommodate opposing positions.

There are, of course, limits to what any one congressman can do on behalf of an agency. One constraint is the power of the committee chairman; and certainly there are limits to how much one committeeman will defer to the " expertise " of another. A broad parameter is that defensible criteria must accompany each request as it is presented on the floor of the House. If pushed too far, the " silent majority " may balk and call the committee's recommendation into question.

The Senate appropriations committees roughly parallel those of the House. Separate committees consider the appropriations bills originating in the House, and a high degree of deference is shown to the expertise of the committee. Differences in degree, however, are worth examining. In the Senate more emphasis is put on the *program* rather than the minutiae of each bill. Two factors may help to explain this: First, the House has already considered the bill in detail and some deference is given its work. Second, a senator represents a wider constituency and therefore is concerned more with the big picture than how a specific item in the budget affects a particular city or county.

Whereas in the House the effort is made to staff committees with members who can be objective—this may mean that the department or agency has no major operation in the congressman's district—no such effort is made in the Senate. Several of the committee members may have a direct interest—perhaps opposing interests, so that the resulting bargaining often involves more bottlenecks and less deference to the opinion of others.

ROLE PLAYING IN THE BUDGET PROCESS

An interesting phenomenon is that the Senate usually increases budget requests where the House has reduced them. [3] In attempting to interpret these and related phenomena it is helpful to consider the "roles" which the various actors within the budgetary process feel obligated to play. In an interesting and provocative study Aaron Wildavsky has ascribed certain roles to budget officials and congressmen. [4] Agency and department officials are expected to be *advocates of increased appropriations*. Agency personnel are more aware of the contributions of their own program than of the programs of other agencies. Moreover, they naturally tend to feel that their endeavors are "significant" in terms of social welfare. Besides, the larger their program in terms of personnel, budget, and so on, the greater power, prestige and salary of the agency official.

We have already noted some of the techniques used by agencies to gain increased appropriations in the bargaining within the department and vis-à-vis Congress. First, they tend to pad their bid, both because other agencies do the same and so that higher levels within the process (the higher agencies, departments, the OMB, and Congress) can make cuts and get credit for economizing. Alternatively, they can seek broad public support for their activity. The National Aeronautics and Space Administration has been especially adept at gaining public support through publicity. Other strategies include effecting a tie-in with the activities of another popular agency or servicing some popular "need." Hence, one should not be surprised when agencies in the Department of Agriculture or the Department of Transportation justify one of their programs as necessary to our national defense. One variation of this technique is for an agency to cultivate a relationship with a particular interest group which is organized and can be expected to give political support when called upon. Such a group may also help to cultivate and reelect particular congressmen—especially those on the appropriate budget committee.

The dominant role of the Office of Management and Budget, according to Wildavsky, is to help the President carry out his purposes. [5] The OMB attempts to create proposals which implement the priorities of the President (and his advisors) as to resource allocation among the various departments and agencies with due consideration for the macroeconomic policy goals, income redistribution, and (importantly) the attitude of the public towards taxes. Since the agencies typically fulfill their role as *advocates*, the OMB rarely has to push for the programs the President wishes to expand. But the OMB's responsibility to *curtail* proposals which expand expenditures and *taxes* beyond politically acceptable levels must be exercised frequently.

The prevailing role played by the House Appropriations Committee is *guardian of the taxpayer's money*. This role is conditioned by the advocate role of the agencies. Committee members see themselves as faithful guardians standing off masses of avaricious, irresponsible bureaucrats. A review of the record does in fact reveal that House Appropriations subcommittees almost invariably cut the budget proposals they consider.

The Senate Appropriations Committee, on the other hand, must play the role of a *court of appeal*—in part because the House has played its role so well.[6] Another reason may be that the constituency of the senator is broader than that of the congressman. Several factors encourage the member of a House Appropriations subcommittee to be more frugal than his counterpart in the Senate: First, his constituency is smaller and he is less likely to have groups which *directly* benefit from the appropriations in question. Second, we have observed that in the House, as opposed to the Senate, an effort is made to appoint members who have little direct stake in the appropriations to be considered. Finally, we have noted that floor debate—where the broader issues might be given more play—is more limited in the House. In the final analysis it seems natural that the House subcommittee member is more attuned to his constituents as taxpayers—since they are directly affected by taxes—rather than as recipients of the social benefits of the proposed expenditures.

---

[3] See Richard F. Fenno, Jr., *The Power of the Purse: Appropriations Policies in Congress* (Boston: Little, Brown, 1966), and Aaron Wildavsky, *The Politics of the Budgetary Process* (Boston: Little, Brown, 1964). Fenno traced the path of a large number of reductions made by the House. The Senate appropriations committees voted to increase the House figure in 63 percent of the cases.

[4] *Ibid.*

[5] *Ibid.*, pp. 35–47.

[6] Professor Fenno quotes one senator as follows: " We on the Appropriations Committee are placed in an embarrassing position. We believe in economy. We are trying to bring about economy. Yet we are receiving bills from the House with exceedingly large cuts. The argument is made, ' Do not worry about that. The Senate will take care of it.' " *The Power of the Purse*, p. 538.

In general these same factors encourage the Senate to restore some of the cuts made by the House. As mentioned, the Senate's role is at least in part forced upon it by its position vis-à-vis the House. We have also suggested that the broader scope of the senators—in terms of both constituency and decision-making procedure—allows for better appreciation of the social benefits (as opposed to direct private benefits).[7]

CONFLICT RESOLUTION AND TAXES

The revenue side of the budget offers even more opportunity for irreconcilable conflict than does the expenditure side. Indeed, when we consider the nature of the conflict, it seems incredible that agreement can ever be reached. In our examination of welfare voting models we toyed with the notion that linking taxes with expenditures would encourage better resource allocation. More sophisticated models, however, revealed difficulties in that approach. The " free-rider problem " in particular greatly reduced the possibility of deciding the best combination of public activities and the tax share question as well.

The tax share question, after all, is distinctly different from the public goods decision, since the benefit from reduced taxes, namely *money*, is almost infinitely divisible. We are no longer deciding between the most preferred combination of, say, defense and highways; instead, we are deciding how much money an individual pays in taxes and how much he has left to exchange for any of the many available private goods. Naturally, each person wants to reduce his tax load as much as possible, and so the Chapter 3 models featuring multiple issues and voters do not apply.

Several " public " considerations do apply, such as: the psychic benefits the altruists find in income redistribution, the political dangers inherent in overconcentration of wealth, and generally held ideas about fairness and equity in taxes. But it is safe to assume that these considerations would be secondary in most situations where one's tax share was put to the vote. If the judgment is made that the tax share decisions should include the broader, " objective " considerations, it follows that the decision should not be made using voting procedures which allow for free debate, vote trading, coalitions, unlimited amendments, and so on.

Thus, tax legislation, instead of being formulated on the floor of the House and Senate, is relegated to committees where several conflict-reducing conventions are honored.

THE HOUSE WAYS AND MEANS COMMITTEE

The House Ways and Means Committee, like the House Appropriations Committee (and its subcommittees), operates under the conventions of *deference to expertise* and *restrained partisanship*. Members are chosen who will be likely to address their tasks in a pragmatic rather than a reformist manner. Chairman Wilbur Mills emphasizes technical competence and professionalism rather than party affiliation. Members of the opposition party are allowed to participate in the discussion on equal terms and even to associate their names with those parts of legislation on which they work.

The conventions of budgeting by increments (focusing on current and past budget figures and making small adjustments to them) and deference to expertise are adhered to in legislating taxes as in legislating appropriations, but in slightly different ways. Now and then reform seems to be in the air. The President or perhaps the Ways and Means Committee on its own initiative will begin to " ponder " wholesale changes in tax law. Such activity soon has the desired effect of reminding the favored interest groups of their indebtedness to Congressman Mills, Senator Long, and others. There is always the outside chance that the ritual will bear fruit. What is more likely is that changes in tax legislation will be small and incremental in nature. Few tax shelters will be eliminated, and those that are changed will be modified only slightly. When the tax bill reaches the floor, it will be subject to the closed rule: Only the bill and amendments cleared by the committee will be considered. Instead of allowing wholesale debate, House members prefer to defer to the committee.

THE SENATE FINANCE COMMITTEE

The differences between House and Senate with regard to tax policy are similar to those with regard to expenditure budgeting. The Senate Finance Committee exhibits less homogeneity than does the Ways and

---

[7] It is intriguing to ponder whether the Senate's view does indeed offer better insight into the social benefits of public goods production. What seems to be implied is that the relative liberality of the Senate is connected with the greater breadth in each senator's constituency. Supposedly, the congressman's view is narrower because it is more concerned with individual interest groups—as opposed to the public welfare. This line of discussion might in turn lead us back to the philosophical inquiry introduced in our discussion of voting. For example, can we say that the person representing the broader view can better identify public wants and interpret the appropriate " social ordering " which the exigencies of more immediate bargaining tend to confuse? Our previous development of such questions has revealed that " answers " are not readily at hand, at least not to the economist as such.

Means Committee, and its members show less deference to each other's expertise. Moreover, the closed rule is not followed when tax legislation reaches the Senate floor; amendments are offered and sometimes adopted. Senate amendments usually have the unfortunate effect of reducing rather than enhancing the generality, neutrality, and horizontal equity of tax legislation. This result is not surprising in light of our previous discussion. In our survey of public goods voting models, wider representation was considered beneficial; but in deciding who will bear the tax burden, wider representation often provides excessive opportunity for potential free riders.

After passage by the Senate, differences in the two versions of the tax bill are ironed out in the Joint Committee on Internal Revenue Taxation. Here again it would seem that straightforward majority voting could easily end in irreconcilable conflict, especially since the compromise must pass both Houses before being signed—or vetoed—by the President. But the makeup of the Joint Committee is conducive to the bargaining which must take place. Members are drawn from the House Ways and Means Committee and the Senate Finance Committee. Moreover the specialists, consultants, and so on who have worked with the bill help again in this stage, thus providing substantial continuity in information and perspectives as well as personnel.

The final result is conditioned by the role played by the President and by the OMB and other Presidential advisors, who exercise considerable influence throughout the legislative process. In the first place, the President has the option of initiating tax legislation. Even when it is initiated in the House Ways and Means Committee, ample opportunity is given for the Budget Director and his staff to offer counterproposals. And, of course, the President may use his considerable leverage with party members at various stages of the enactment. To the extent that macroeconomic considerations are relevant, the President's Council of Economic Advisors will offer their testimony. Throughout the process the threat of Presidential veto is ominous, especially to tax legislation not initiated by the President, since, unlike appropriations bills, tax legislation can often be put off till another year.

THE EXECUTION AND CONTROL STAGES OF FEDERAL BUDGETING

The President and his administration play the most important role in the execution phase of the budgetary process, for in the end it is the administrative agencies which must implement the programs. Congress and various levels within the organizational structure are limited in how much authority they can wield through specifying the procedures to be used by those below them. Hence the President, in exercising his responsibility to execute the budget, may to a certain degree circumvent the intentions of Congress. The President has a particular advantage with respect to programs he does not support in that he may be able to reduce, delay, or even abolish programs funded by Congress. Congress, however, is often aware when the President does not support certain programs and consequently will specify exactly when and how expenditures are to be made. Moreover, Congress is aware that it must play the role of watchdog to see that its wishes are carried out. Hence, while the administration attempts to enhance its control through the accounting procedures it requires of the agencies, the General Accounting Office, headed by the Comptroller General, audits the budget on behalf of Congress. In addition, Congressional committees continually investigate, hold hearings, and so on to keep Congress informed of the status of the legislation it has passed.

THE VOTING MODELS RECONSIDERED

Let us further consider the voting models presented in Chapter 3 and indicate their use in evaluating the federal budget process.

The models with small numbers of issues and voters were used to demonstrate that voter concurrence is most difficult in situations where the numbers are about equal. It is also true, however, that voter concurrence is difficult when there are large numbers of both issues and voters. The models suggested that voter concurrence is enhanced when either issues substantially outnumber voters or voters substantially outnumber issues.

Yet when participation costs are considered, the possibilities are substantially altered. Suppose, for example, that the issues are very complex. A high cost of analyzing the issues will reduce the net benefits from participating, even when the numbers of voters are small. On the other hand, even relatively small voting costs will reduce participation as the number of voters increases. This is because the individual's degree of influence over the final decision diminishes as the number of voters increases.

It is appropriate, then, that the federal budget, which features a large number of issues pertaining to a large number of persons, be formulated through representative government. The ideal system would allow for efficiency and at the same time reduce the costs of participation so that the preferences of all individuals might be considered. There are, of course, several layers to the decision-making process. There are usually a few "big issues" which concern the whole populace and lend themselves to mass participation. These issues can be decided by a general referendum. In a sense the national Presidential and Congressional elections serve this purpose, since the candidates and parties do in fact run on the "big" issues. Even so, and despite the admittedly high costs, the limited use of national referenda for voting on specific issues is disappointing.

The minutiae and expertise problems arising from the millions of complex decisions inherent in public sector activity necessitate many of the formal budget procedures. Many decisions are left to the administrators who carry out the public sector activities on a day-to-day basis. Also, as outlined, many of the minutiae are filtered out as recommendations travel upward through agency channels. Yet the budget, when it reaches Congress, still features so many unresolved issues that numerous conflict-reducing rules, procedures, conventions, and the like are required. We noted also that the procedures feature parallel levels of expertise to cope with the complexity of the issues while at the same time retaining the division of powers so necessary for the expression of minority interests. By the same token the procedures allow for tradeoffs to be accomplished within committees and between the two Houses and the Executive. As portions of the budget pass through various committees and subcommittees, opportunity is offered minority groups to interdict their progress and effect desired tradeoffs.

The free-rider problem is essentially avoided by the separation of expenditure and revenue decisions. Since taxes are divorced from expenditures, however, the diffusion effect (wherein each representative pushes for special benefits for his constituents) is encountered. Moreover, the frequent passage of "pork barrel" legislation demonstrates that the problem has not been completely eradicated. Even so, the practice of granting substantial power to committees and the practice of choosing "objective" committee members certainly reduces the diffusion effect. Since floor debate offers little opportunity for the individual House representative to "tack on" special-interest expenditures, he must resign himself to essentially a "take-it-or-leave-it" choice.

THE GAMES BUDGETERS PLAY—II: STATE AND LOCAL FINANCE

The institutional setting of state and local finance differs from the federal situation in several important ways. And as we shall see, these differences

---

cause the state and local participants to adopt roles which differ from those of their federal counterparts. The conventions, traditions, and other rules of the game also reflect the different institutional setting.

States differ according to economic conditions, ranging from heavily industrial to agrarian. These differences are reflected not only in the economic functions required of the public sector but also in the political organizations and, in turn, the budgeting institutions. The major determinant of variations in per capita expenditures turns out to be differences in per capita personal income among states. It follows that in those states with higher personal income more is spent on promoting efficiency in the budget process itself.

Often within one state there are wide differences in the economies of different geographical sections. These differences are carried over into political organizations and influence the budgetary processes.

In most states and localities, public representatives and budget officials receive low pay and work with small, inadequate staffs. These conditions usually do not allow " parallel review " to play as important a role as it does in the federal budget process. The separate branches of state and local governments are unable to include in their staffs the specialists so necessary to make judgments on complex budget proposals.

The constitutional parameters within which state and local budgets are formulated also create budgetary processes different from those on the federal level.

LIMITATIONS ON BORROWING

State and local governmental units are subject to many debt limitations imposed by voters through the years in response to unfortunate borrowing experiences. These limitations include constitutional restrictions on certain types of taxes, specification of tax rates, prohibitions against certain taxes, and debt ceilings. Most states require either constitutional change or a statewide referendum to finance increased expenditure by borrowing. Many other types of restrictions on indebtedness are also imposed. For example, nine states will not underwrite the debt issued by their own agencies. If these agencies borrow, the absence of state backing usually means higher interest payments.

States have not only imposed debt limitations upon themselves but upon localities and other subordinate governmental bodies as well. These limitations may simply impose a ceiling based on some formula; more frequently a referendum is required for the debt to be expanded.

It is difficult to tell the extent to which these restrictions have limited state and local borrowing. In every state there have appeared financial innovations and new governmental units which can circumvent the old restrictions. In fact, a study by Mitchell shows that on a statewide basis, governmental units with relatively strict debt limitations have found means to borrow as much debt as less restricted units.[8] He did, however, find that the restrictions encourage substitution of nonguaranteed for general obligation debt.[9] Circumventing the restrictions requires other types of adjustments, such as shifting expenditure decision making away from one unit to another, which may have "nonneutral" effects on resource allocation. Other studies indicate that debt restrictions do, in fact, limit debt levels, primarily by *inhibiting spending* rather than by causing local governmental units to substitute tax finance for debt finance.[10] It follows that the net effect is to restrict the flow of resources from the private to the public sector.

EARMARKING TAXES

Another self-imposed restraint frequently used in state and local budgeting is *earmarking*. Certain taxes are to be used only for certain purposes. Often the user-charge rationale is evident: Funds from gasoline taxes, driving licenses, and vehicle registrations are designated to be spent on highways and roads; hunting and fishing license fees go to wildlife and park programs. The revenue devices which are earmarked, however, are not always user charges. Revenues may be earmarked for purposes unrelated to the revenue sources. For example, revenue from alcohol taxes is often earmarked for schools. In many states the funds allocated in this manner account for a large proportion of the budget. Agencies naturally favor having a dependable source of revenue to insure against the fickleness of the legislature and governor, and often they take advantage of their strong position in budget decision making to push for earmarking. Earmarking does allow user charges to be designated to the service in question, and this, perhaps, facilitates marginal benefit—marginal cost comparisons (although this is only relevant if the tax rate is adjusted accordingly). But earmarking also reduces the flexibility of budget decision makers, especially when the supply of good revenue-producing taxes is limited.

LIMITATIONS ON TAXING AND THEIR EFFECTS

Constraints on taxing are also important limitations on budgeting at the state and local levels. In many cases constitutional changes or referenda are required for changes in tax rates. Limitations on taxing powers, like those on debt financing, have in fact exerted great influence on the evolution of the governmental structure itself.

In order to circumvent constitutional taxing and/or debt limitations states will spin off semi-independent "authorities." This is often done when the new authority's service can be financed at least in part by user charges, as for bridges, turnpikes, port services, housing, and so on. These authorities can sell their own debt to be paid primarily from charges for the service. School districts, regional water and sewage authorities, and the like have also evolved because of the tax and debt limitations imposed on localities by the states. In some situations the resultant configuration may better wed decision-making power, technical constraints, and voter preferences; in other cases the opposite occurs. The semi-independent authorities and agencies naturally become less responsive to the governor and the legislature (or the mayor and city council). Instead, authority directors are more inclined to follow their own goals, which may include: (1) maximizing the quantity and quality of the service provided, (2) maximizing the profit made by the authority, or (3) maximizing the power and prestige of the director while "satisficing" one or more of the other goals. Resource allocation under either of the last two goals is unlikely to be optimal. And even if the first goal is pursued, the separation of various activities from the normal budgeting process curtails overall assessment and control of the budget by the elected participants of the budget process. For example, the New York Port Authority seems to behave as a profit seeker, and thus its behavior is adequately controlled to the extent that its projects create assignable costs or benefits. But projects involving transportation and communication often involve externalities—otherwise public sector activity would not be required. Indeed, as we demonstrated in the bridge-crossings

[8] William E. Mitchell "State and Local Government Borrowing," in Murray E. Polokoff, ed., *Financial Institutions and Markets* (Boston: Houghton Mifflin, 1970) and "The Effect of Debt Limit on State and Local Government Borrowing," *The Bulletin*, New York University, Institute of Finance, no. 45 (October 1967).

[9] General obligation bonds pledge the "full faith and credit" of the governmental unit to include resources from all forms of taxation. Nonguaranteed or revenue bonds are to be paid only from a specified source and have no claim to the other revenue sources.

[10] See Thomas F. Pogue "The Effect of Debt Limits: Some New Evidence" *National Tax Journal*, vol. 23 (March, 1970); Advisory Commission on Intergovernmental Relations, *State Constitutional and Statutory Restrictions on Local Government Debt*, Report A-10 (Washington, D.C.: U.S. Government Printing Office, 1961) and B. U. Ratchford, "State and Local Debt Limitations," *National Tax Association*, Proceedings (October 1958).

model in Chapter 4, in certain public sector activities, operating *losses* are more appropriate than profits.

VARIATIONS IN POWER AND BUDGETARY ROLES AMONG STATES

From state to state there are wide variations in the distribution of power among party, agency, executive, and legislature. In most states the balance of power shifts between the two major party divisions. The major campaign issues, of course, concern state public finances, and in fact the positions of the state party on national goals may differ widely from those of the national party. In some states considerable power is concentrated in the hands of a few, but even within a so-called " one-party " state the party organization must provide for the interests of groups representing various geographical regions and differing economic and political philosophies.

The interplay of different interest groups in any one state depends both on party organization and on the formal institutional structure within which budget determination takes place. Where the governor is weak and the legislature lacks expertise, the agencies have greater discretion. Where the governor is strong, (1) he will exert control over the agencies in formulating the budget, (2) his recommendations will hold great weight with the legislature, and (3) he will be able to control the execution of the budget with some degree of flexibility. In most states the legislature is relatively weaker than its counterpart at the federal level; however, in those states where it is strong, its committees develop the capability of critical review in the formulation and enactment stage as well as substantial control during the execution phase.

The governor may exert pressure on the budget in several ways. Through his political party, for example, he may have substantial influence which extends over the boundaries between governor and agency director or legislator. One factor affecting the governor's power is his control over appointments to agencies which spend much of the state's money. In many states heads of important agencies (education, highway, and so on) gain office through popular election. Moreover, many agency heads are semi-independent from both governor and legislature. Another factor that varies among states is the nature of the governor's review over agency requests and his veto power over the appropriations made by the legislature.

It is enlightening to observe what types of figures are included in the format of the budget document as received by the legislature. In about *half* of the states expenditure figures for the current and past year are listed along with not only the governor's recommendation but that of the agency as well. The use of this format obviously encourages an incremental approach. At the same time, it dilutes the force of the governor's recommendation by directly comparing it with that of the agency. In the other states the budget document does not include the agency's recommendation, although here again several strategies (from "cultivating" particular legislators to simply appearing before the appropriations committees) are open to the agency.

A major source of the governor's influence is his power to veto.[11] In forty states the governor may veto certain items of an appropriations bill while accepting others.

In many states the governor is restricted in his budget review and the manner in which budget recommendations are made. In thirteen states the budget director is not appointed by the governor but is either elected or appointed by the legislature or a Civil Service Commission. In several other states (Florida, West Virginia, Mississippi, North Dakota, and South Carolina) the governor merely chairs a budgetary board of elected administrative heads and representatives appointed by the legislature. In Indiana the budget is formulated by a legislature-appointed board to which the governor appoints but a single member.[12] A major factor to keep in mind when assessing the formulation of the budget by boards composed of legislators and agency heads is that many of the agency heads are *not* appointed by the governor but either are elected directly or are semi-independent.

CONTAINED SPECIALIZATION IN BUDGET CONSIDERATION

We recall that many features of the federal process evolved because of the expertise in budget review and the necessity of reducing conflict where it proved too costly. " Contained specialization " is a term coined by Professor Ira Sharkansky to describe the institutions which have evolved to make budget decisions by providing expertise and insulation from

---

[11] Except in North Carolina.

[12] For a more thorough examination of restrictions on governors' power in budget formulation see Joseph A. Schlesinger, " The Politics of the Executive," in Herbert Jacob and Kenneth N. Vines, *Politics in the American States* (Boston: Little, Brown, 1965).

costly conflicts. A committee formed to cope with such decisions exhibits the following characteristics: "elite status, intensive specialization among participants, and ability to manage partisanship and other sources of conflict within decision-making bodies, and the acceptance of specialists' recommendations by other officials in government."[13]

At the state level contained specialization in budget review has not evolved as it has at the federal level. As a result, in many states the separate budgeting groups of the different branches of government do not have adequate resort to expert analysis, and their roles as "checks and balances" are weakened. Factors restraining this development include the typically high turnover in state legislatures (and hence in the committees themselves), limited use of the seniority rule, and no acknowledged obligation to annually reinstate committee chairmen or members. A study by Theodore Mitan revealed that in many states the vast majority of committee chairmen had legislative experience of one year or less.[14]

Financial restraints work against contained specialization in two ways. Meager pay to legislators seriously curtails the time one can afford to devote to this public service and thus contributes to high turnover and lack of legislative experience. Moreover, funds for specialized assistance to committee members are practically nonexistent.

The "rules of play" which have evolved in the state budget process feature even more reliance on incremental decision making than at the federal level. While the distribution of power differs among states, we have noted several general features:

1. There is neither time nor money for thorough review by specialists within the legislative branch (and in some cases within the governor's office as well).
2. The decentralization of agencies results in piecemeal budget formulation which, owing to restraints on the governor's budget power, carries through to the enactment phase. No opportunity arises in any stage to evaluate alternative ways to accomplish tasks traditionally assigned to a particular agency.
3. Budget documents usually are expressed in such a way as to encourage budgeting by increments. Current and past figures are outlined by the agency along with the present request. Crude program criteria, such as number of children in school, number of roads paved, number of personnel employed, often become mechanistic formulas which substitute for a review of costs and benefits.

STATE AGENCIES AND PUBLIC CHOICES

We noted the advantageous positions given to many state agency heads by such factors as restrictions on the governor's part in budget formulation, reliance of the legislature on mechanistic formulas in the absence of parallel specialization, and so on. Many agencies' positions are further enhanced by their semi-independence from both governor and legislature. But what are the goals of the agency likely to be? And how might they differ from the public choices that might be expressed by the citizenry under other decision-making processes?

An important goal for most agency heads, no doubt, is to increase the quality and quantity of the service they provide. Agency heads, like most of us, are convinced that their own contribution is highly beneficial and should be expanded. Moreover, they probably want to keep up with or surpass their counterparts in agencies in other states. Finally, it is probably the case that the prestige and salary of the agency head grow with the size of the agency in terms of persons employed and services rendered.

The "nonneutrality" we would expect from having certain agencies "too powerful" would tend to involve the devotion of "too many" resources to the service in question. *This is not to say, however, that the nonneutrality is necessarily negative.* If in the past too few resources have been devoted to this activity, the nonneutrality is positive in direction. On the other hand, we may easily list many possible goals of the agency head which would lead toward negative nonneutrality. He might, for example, indulge his preferences for redheaded secretaries and plush office furniture at the expense of more efficient resource allocation.

Where user charges are employed to finance various public services, an agency head will often emphasize the "profit goal." While such a goal is expected of firms in private enterprise, when employed for public enterprise it often makes for misallocation of resources. Public activity almost by definition involves externalities which cannot be accounted for by the private market mechanism. Hence, when a public agency follows the "profit goal," these externalities are necessarily ignored.

---

[13] Ira Sharkansky, *The Politics of Taxing & Spending* (New York: Bobbs-Merrill, 1969), p. 38.

[14] Theodore Mitan, *State and Local Government; Politics and Processes* (New York: Scribners, 1966).

Two other aspects of the execution of state budgets deserve mention. First, we note that regulatory boards and agencies appointed by the governor and/or the legislature, like their counterparts at the federal level, often take on a complexion more favorable to the regulated industry than to the consumer. The basic reason for such a development is that the consumer-voter lacks knowledge and shows little interest while industry officials demonstrate intense interest by making political contributions and so on. Another reason is the lack of expertise on the part of the governor and the average legislator, so that a regulatory board often turns out to be made up of "experts" from the industry itself and/or legislators from law firms representing the industry.

A final comment concerns the diversity among states in the control state agencies exercise over local agencies. Centralization of financing is usually accompanied by centralization of decision making. One may observe, for example, wide diversity in centralization of decision making in public education. In some states the state Board of Education sets strict standards for every phase of education, including course offerings and course content. In other states more decision making is done at the local level by school boards, city councils, superintendents, principals, and teachers. This leads us again to one of our central questions: How do we determine the most efficient level of decision making for a particular public activity? Before delving further into this question, however, we will more closely examine budgeting at the local level.

BUDGETING RULES AND PUBLIC CHOICE INSTITUTIONS OF LOCALITIES

DIVERSITY IN LOCAL BUDGET INSTITUTIONS

Localities exhibit an even greater variety of budgeting procedures than do states. Certain basic similarities necessarily prevail: The executive and agencies work together to *formulate* the budget, which is then subjected to the scrutiny of an elected legislature (the city council) empowered to *enact* the budget; agencies then must *execute* the budget, a process over which both administrators and legislators attempt to exercise some *control* through various reporting and auditing procedures. But many budget decisions are made in ways which preempt, bypass, or circumvent this general procedure. Frequently the clear-cut separation of powers among governmental branches seen at the federal and state levels is not found at the local level. The budget of a municipality reflects a complex conglomeration of decisions made by several types of governmental bodies. School districts, water and sewage authorities, regional planning districts, and so on often overlap with local government boundaries. Membership on these agencies, authorities, boards, and the like may be appointive, elective, or some combination of the two. The many legislative-type decisions made by these hybrid bodies are difficult to analyze in terms of voter preferences, since their position with respect to the voter is often ambiguous.

THE QUESTION OF LOCAL AUTONOMY

In the two areas accounting for most local expenditures—education and welfare—local decision making is significantly circumscribed by state and federal prerogatives.

The federal government has largely left spending decisions on education to the states and localities. There is considerable diversity among states as to the extent of local autonomy. Typically, where states accept responsibility for raising a large portion of the revenue for education they are more likely to specify how the money is to be spent: teacher salaries, teacher accreditation, curricula, textbooks, and so on. Moreover, where state governments provide a large portion of education funds, they assign them on the basis of some formula related to need (number of school-age children, average daily attendance, and the like), thus accomplishing considerable redistribution between rich and poor localities.

The position of the school board vis-à-vis the city council and mayor is another crucial factor in the local budgeting process. The school board may be appointed or elected. In either case it offers some insulation for the city council and mayor from dissatisfied parents, and, more important, it allows for specialization and (in appointive positions especially) accumulation of expertise. The school board may display one or more of the aforementioned budgetary "roles" according to its position in the institutional structure. Often, when defending its recommendations to the city council for inclusion in the budget, it will play the role of *advocate*. If this role is overplayed, however, the city council will feel obligated to act as "defender of the taxpayer." A favorite ploy of the city council in such situations is to pick a somewhat arbitrary figure for educational expenditures within which the school board, superintendents, and principals must make adjustments. In utilizing this ploy the city council can still claim to be giving due consideration to taxpayers, the balance between educational and other local needs, and the expertise of the school board and education officials; yet at the same time the council avoids associating itself with the approval or disapproval of controversial programs.

In contrast to the small part it plays in deciding educational expenditures, the federal government is quite specific as to how states and localities are to dispense welfare payments. The federal provisions detail the administrative organization, the criteria to be used in designating recipients, the nature of the benefits, and other requirements that must be met if federal matching funds are to be made available. Only those few states who grant benefits greater than those allowed by the federal program may exercise some freedom in deciding how the additional funds will be spent. Similarly, localities have little discretion unless they choose to go farther than the states.

THE MAKEUP AND ROLE OF THE BUDGET COMMITTEE

The parts played by mayor, city manager, city council, and the agencies in budget *formulation* differ from locality to locality. In some cities the city manager and his staff work on behalf of the mayor and city council to *coordinate* agency participation in budget formulation. In some cities a budget committee of the city council may play an active role in the formulation phase. Another alternative is review and formulation by a joint committee made up of personnel from both the council and the administrative officers (to include the city manager, the treasurer, other officers, and perhaps even the mayor himself).

Usually the mayor has the prerogative to appoint several or all of the budget committee. This prerogative understandably gives him considerable power in budget formulation. Agency recommendations normally go directly to this committee, where they are reviewed along with testimony by agency heads and others. After review, the budget requests are usually sent back to the agency with recommended changes (or perhaps a " ceiling "), to be resubmitted for compilation and presentation to the full council. Consequently, an agency may find it difficult to appeal to either the full city council or the general public at open hearings, since by that stage its original proposals may have already been substantially modified.

RULES AND CONVENTIONS IN BUDGET COMMITTEES

Lack of expertise and the desire to avoid costly conflict lead the budget committee and the full council to employ budgeting rules and conventions similar to those used at the state level. Full evaluation of programs is avoided by relying on incremental comparisons. The structure of budget review favors small, if any, percentage changes in the major categories in the budget.

Several studies indicate that the elected officials like to avoid favoring one agency over another; hence, they attempt to give "equal" treatment. John P. Crecine, in a study of budget rules employed in municipalities of the Cleveland, Detroit, and Pittsburgh areas, reports that precedent is important in deciding how much each agency will be awarded.[15] When aggressive agencies are able to apply pressure for more money, they often may be more successful than the less aggressive agencies. On the other hand, the less aggressive agencies are seldom cut unless a general percentage cut is ordered. Where several aggressive agencies are competing for more funds, a typical solution is to give each an equal percentage increase.

In analyzing the decision-making strategy of the municipal budget committee, it would be unfair to imply that the substitution of incremental rules for programmatic values stems entirely from "politics" (that is, the desire to avoid conflicts which may reduce the politician's support among his constituency, and the like). Another dilemma of the decision maker is his frequent lack of the knowledge or expertise to choose between good and bad programs either on a short- or a long-run basis. Moreover, the costs of using procedures affording "perfect knowledge" would usually be preclusive. Even *if the only goal of the decision makers were to follow voters' preferences, their best strategy with imperfect knowledge would include occasional resort to an incremental convention.* When one does not know which departments are spending "too much" and which are spending "too little," the best strategy may be to order equal percentage cuts or increases.

One ploy often used to avoid making specific budget decisions is to approve a total figure for an agency rather than approve specific programs. Thus the responsibility to cut back on certain programs is left to the agency. A benefit of this procedure is that it leaves the agency free to adjust expenditures to its most crucial needs. Unfortunately, the goals of agency personnel do not entirely coincide with those of the community.

When agencies are left with the burden of cutting budget requests, studies indicate that expenditures on maintenance and long-life

[15] John P. Crecine, *Governmental Problem Solving: A Computer Simulation of Municipal Budgeting* (Skokie, Ill.: Rand McNally, 1969).

equipment are cut first, while nonadministrative and administrative salaries are cut last. Although it is difficult to demonstrate conclusively, it seems obvious that the practice of placing the responsibility of budget cuts back onto the agencies encourages them to favor salaries over capital equipment and long-range program planning.

INTEREST GROUPS AND FORMS OF LOCAL GOVERNMENT

Forms of local government differ widely, but one of two general alternatives is taken with respect to (1) the decision-making power of the professional manager vis-à-vis that of the mayor, and (2) the method of selecting council members. Cities where considerable power rests with the mayor generally select council members from districts, whereas those with a city-manager orientation generally select them from " at large " constituencies. The cities of the mayor-and-council-districts orientation tend to spend more (and tax more) than their counterparts of the other orientation.[16] Some of the decision-making models outlined previously help us assign reasons for this. It may be that the mayor-and-council-districts orientation provides more opportunity for specific interest groups to voice their demands for particular public services. Perhaps these demands, once voiced at the council level, have a good chance of passage, since the conservatively biased budget conventions mentioned above have been bypassed.

On the other hand, special interest groups apparently are less successful in effecting their demands through professional city managers and councils elected in at-large contests. It is probable that the " diffusion effect " is more powerful in the mayor-and-council-districts setting. The fact that councilmen are more likely to represent special interest groups lends support to this hypothesis. There may, in fact, be a prisoner's dilemma: Each group must push its own demands for spending, knowing that others will be achieving theirs as well and that the net result will be greater taxes for all, with the final budget pushed beyond the point where marginal benefits equal marginal costs for the goods and services produced.

SOME ECONOMIC FACTORS AFFECTING LOCAL SPENDING

Many studies have attempted to relate differences in local spending to various economic factors.[17]

1. *Local wealth.* The factor having by far the highest correlation with state and local per capita spending is *wealth*. This means that the legisla-

tive body in the relatively poor community does not really have the option to emulate its counterpart in the wealthy community. Since wealth explains most of the differences in spending among localities, relatively small scope remains for the other factors. The per pupil expenditure on education in cities in New York state compared to that in, say, cities in Maine or Virginia is not so much a social choice as a reflection of the high income level of New Yorkers.

Differences in wealth appear to impose more stringent constraints on localities than on states, in part because of the revenue instruments to which localities are limited. The state can tax more types of wealth, and more progressively; consequently, states may spread the tax burden in different ways so as to overcome differences in wealth. Many local taxes (such as sales taxes) are not difficult to escape; even property taxes can be avoided by moving one's residence and/or business establishment. Moreover, many communities are afraid to tax property too heavily lest local businesses move and new industry prove more difficult to attract.

2. *Population density.* There is a negative relationship between population density and per capita spending by city governments on streets, highways, and related transportation facilities. Although several factors are no doubt at work here, the most plausible explanation stems from the supply side: that there are *economies of scale* in the provision of transportation facilities in urban areas.

Conversely, there is a positive relationship between population density and spending on crime prevention, traffic control, law enforcement, sanitation, and public health. Here again the supply side offers explanations: some concerning technical diseconomies of scale, others concerning breakdowns in aspects of the social system vulnerable to overcrowding, loss of identity, and the like.

---

[16] See Robert L. Lineberry and Edmund P. Fowler, "Reformism and Public Policies in American Cities," *American Political Science Review*, Vol. 61 (September 1967), pp. 701–716.

[17] See, for examples: Robert C. Wood, *1400 Governments* (Garden City, N.Y.: Anchor Books, 1962); Harvey E. Brazer, *City Expenditures in the United States* (New York: National Bureau of Economic Research, 1959), Woo Sik Kee, "Central City Expenditures and Metropolitan Areas," *National Tax Journal*, vol. 18 (December 1965), pp. 337–355; Howard G. Schaller, ed. *Public Expenditure Decisions in the Urban Community* (Washington, D.C.: Resources for the Future, 1963), Bernard H. Booms, "City Governmental Form and Public Expenditure Levels," *National Tax Journal*, vol. 19 (June 1966), pp. 187–199; and Jesse Burkhead, *Public School Finance* (Syracuse, N.Y.: Syracuse University Press, 1964).

3. *Proportion of owner-occupied dwellings.* A negative relationship also exists between the proportion of owner-occupied dwellings and local expenditure per capita. This time the more plausible explanations seem to stem from the demand side. Home owners feel the impact of property taxes directly, and where they have political clout they are more likely to exercise conservative bias against new spending. Although usually most of the property tax on rental property is passed on to the renter, he is less likely to see the connection between new public services and higher rents. Even so, the tendency of the home owners to demand relatively less in the way of public services is somewhat surprising, since this implies that the positive income effect (in which the wealthier home owner demands more public services) is offset.

4. *Proportion of residents in suburbs.* A positive relationship exists between the proportion of metropolitan suburb dwellers and the expenditure of central cities. Of the many factors involved, the differences in economic and social organizational requirements are no doubt important. Greater demands are placed upon the central city for parking areas, traffic control, and public utilities and services for the employment, shopping, and recreational facilities enjoyed by the commuters. Moreover, the flight of population to the suburbs gives additional impetus to the phenomenon known as "urban blight" (to be considered later).

We make two observations in passing. First, even though more is spent by central cities with high suburb-dweller ratios, it is obvious that the problems of the central cities are not being solved. Second, it is not simply a matter of suburbanities escaping the tax burden for problems they create. Those who commute to work, to shop, and to enjoy recreation do in fact pay general sales taxes, excise taxes, other indirect taxes, and in some instances even local income taxes—yet they utilize only partially the public expenditures on education, welfare, sanitation, and so on. As we shall see in later chapters, most urban fiscal problems stem from mismatches among public choice institutions, economic incentives and private and public needs; these in turn foster dislocations in economic activity, land use, transportation facilities, and the like, and create impossible fiscal demands upon local governments.

LONG-RANGE PLANNING AT THE LOCAL LEVEL

We have examined a number of barriers to long-range fiscal planning at the local level. In the first place, we noted several types of legal and other restrictions that limit the capability of the locality to finance long-term projects thorough taxation and debt creation. This often means that the costs of school buildings, sewage treatment plants, waterworks, and other long-term projects cannot be spread over the periods in which the benefits are received.

Second, we have noted that the localities themselves have inhibited long-range planning by adopting various budgetary rules and conventions. The rules and conventions which encourage incremental budget adjustments and "equal" treatment for all agencies are particularly inimical to long-range planning.

Third, we note the planning difficulties created by geographical overlapping of districts, municipalities, regional authorities, and so on. Moreover, many local planning prerogatives have been preempted by other levels of government. This latter phenomenon may on occasion work towards better planning if it enables localities to overcome the difficulties imposed by the abovementioned laws, rules, and conventions. Two fiscal devices that on occasion have worked for the introduction of better long-range budget planning are special districts and federal and state aid programs. As noted above, special-purpose authorities can often be set up under debt and taxing regulations which are much more liberal than those imposed on municipalities. Moreover, the new decision-making procedures within the new body usually afford more opportunity for taking advantage of specialization and expertise. More important, the conservatively biased conventions of the existing local bodies are avoided (although restrictive conventions will eventually evolve in the new bodies as well). Often federal or state aid programs will *require* that a long-range plan (to include consultation with outside experts, and so on) be effected as a part of the new program.

There is a large body of literature which explores the possibility of employing new budget procedures to overcome some of the difficulties we have noted in our survey of federal, state, and local budgeting. We are now in a position to examine some of these proposals. Our survey of budget procedures has revealed that present procedures, rules, and conventions were not forged with only our efficiency criteria in mind. We have also gained some appreciation for the requirements new budgetary procedures must meet if they are to be economically and politically feasible.

6
PRESCRIPTIONS FOR IMPROVING BUDGETARY PROCEDURES

Our examination of public sector budget processes has tended to further erode our confidence in our governmental institutions as efficient vehicles for translating individual preferences into resource allocation. The evolution of institutional structures necessary to cope with difficulties such as the " free-rider " problem, the " diffusion effect," the " voting paradox," and the expertise and minutiae problems may proceed in directions which are not appropriately responsive to voter preferences. The danger is enhanced when the goals of the direct participants in the budget process, say congressmen, differ from the goals of the voters. For example, congressmen *must* find ways of reducing conflict and arriving eventually at decisions, and they prefer to do so in such a way as to enhance their chances of reelection. The preferences of voters would bear more weight if issues were settled openly; but, instead, important issues are settled in committees where only a narrow range of voter interests are represented.

But let us trudge onward in the face of adversity and offer prescriptions for improving budgetary procedures. We will have the audacity to proceed by employing our original approach, the comparison of marginal benefits and costs. We recognize, however, not only the difficulties of estimating benefits and costs but also the fact that any prescriptions must account for the goals and expected behavior of the public officials themselves.

COST-BENEFIT ANALYSES

The general term for the prescriptive rules we are about to examine is cost-benefit analyses. We will use the term in its broad sense to cover all the various models and techniques economists have used which stem from the basic cost-benefit perspective. We proceed with caution, aware that social scientists at times become so enamored of elegant analytical tools that they forget their limitations.

Cost-benefit analyses are attempts to consider *all* costs and benefits of economic and political actions. Inherent in these attempts are two somewhat conflicting goals: (1) to include *all* costs and benefits even where they defy precise measurement (as is usually the case where " externalities " exist) and (2) to quantify these marginal costs and benefits where possible. A major aspect of the approach is the inclusion of all reasonable *alternatives*, even when these include programs by agencies other than those traditionally thought to have hegemony in the area in question. To follow this approach is no small task. It is difficult enough in the private sector for, say, the manager of a firm to find quantified

174

data relevant to all the alternatives of a policy he is considering; but decision making in the public sector involves public goods with benefits and costs which have not (and perhaps cannot) be reduced to quantifiable terms.

Budget information usually is available only in terms of *costs* along departmental lines by types of inputs (such as salaries, typewriters, bulldozers, gasoline, paper clips). Since so many additional data estimates and value judgments are required if all costs and benefits are to be included, how can we proceed? As economists, we cannot—not unless we are willing to make various assumptions, approximations, and guesses and to frame our analyses within given sets of value judgments. Of great value here is the economist's penchant for organizing information in ways that allow marginal benefits and costs to be compared, at the same time pointing out the necessary value judgments. Essentially this means that economists have a knack for asking the right questions and framing them in meaningful ways.

Actually the cost-benefit approach envisions the combining of data and analyses from various disciplines. Consider the decision on supplying water to an urban area. Engineers, chemists, and ecologists as well as sociologists, political scientists, and economists may offer important insights. Engineers and chemists could suggest the technology of alternative water systems. Ecologists could attempt to predict their impact on the ecosystem—how changes in water, air, availability of food, will affect the balance of plant and animal life. Sociologists, political scientists, and economists could suggest how each of the alternatives would affect individual and group behavior and the life of the community. The role of the economists in particular would be to sum up and attempt to quantify the costs and benefits of using alternative water systems. The final choices, of course, would have to be made by voters, their representatives, and appointed public officials.

CONVENTIONAL AND COST-BENEFIT METHODOLOGY COMPARED

To further explain the cost-benefit approach let us compare it with conventional methodology. We do so by recalling some of the behavior of budget decision makers.

First, we recall that existing budget procedures encourage empire building on the part of officials at various levels. The traditional emphasis on costs means that an official's "importance" is judged not so much by the benefits produced but rather by the size and costs of organizations under his responsibility; consequently, he finds it rewarding to push for expansion of his organization well beyond the point where marginal benefits equal marginal costs. Under the cost-benefit approach an attempt is made to compare output and cost data for programs through time. A frequently used cost-benefit technique attempts to change the *budget format* (and perhaps even the organizational structure) so that the *criteria* by which budget officials evaluate agencies is stated in terms of *programs* and their *goals*. If such changes are successfully implemented, they not only encourage better decision making in budget formulation but reorient the goals and behavior of agency officials at all levels. There are, of course, costs in changing budget formats, and too frequent use of this technique would negate its benefits.

Second, the traditional emphasis on costs creates different types of influences on officials at different levels. The lower-level department head, we have noted, finds it rewarding to expand his operations. He realizes that he will be operating under some cost constraint; however, his immediate goals are an expanded and more "efficient" program with more personnel, better working space and equipment, and so on. His behavior is influenced by something akin to the "diffusion" effect. He focuses on requirements rather than costs. Higher-level agency officials rely heavily, of course, on observations and reports of their staffs in evaluating the performance of agencies under their responsibility, yet they must also rely importantly on budget reports made up primarily of cost data. And administrative and legislative officials at subsequent stages in the budget process find it even more difficult to make choices in terms of benefits as well as costs when no performance criteria are included. Several of the methods of employing performance criteria will be examined below.

Third, the treatment of time in the budget format differs in cost-benefit and conventional approaches. The conventional approach usually covers only one year, comparing current figures with those proposed for the year ahead. Under the cost-benefit approach the attempt is made to consider an entire program from beginning to end, possibly embracing a number of years. At any one time some programs are being started while others are being completed, so that focusing on annual cost figures alone can be quite misleading. Moreover, once a program is begun, the costs of discontinuance may be quite large—a situation that, unfortunately, encourages officials to use subterfuge in expanding their operations. They may employ foot-in-the-door techniques to start programs which higher officials will be obliged to continue in subsequent budget periods. A related technique is the purposeful shading of cost figures, which can be raised later. The Pentagon, in collusion with private contractors and their " friends " in key positions in Congress, are masters at using these methods of subterfuge. At the present writing cost " over-runs " on current military programs alone are exceeding $34 billion.

COST-BENEFIT TECHNIQUES: PROGRAM BUDGETING

Several of the techniques we have included under our broad term *cost-benefit analyses* have been implemented in the past few years under the more specific term *program budgeting*. These techniques, at first termed " performance budgeting," were introduced in certain municipal planning and Defense Department programs in the 1950s. Under Robert McNamara a concentrated effort was made to introduce program budgeting in the Defense Department in 1961. The initial success of these techniques led to President Johnson's decision in 1965 to introduce them to the entire federal budget. The results so far have been mixed: some obvious improvements in efficiency in some departments, some obvious failures, and some promising modifications. It will be still some time before the overall picture can be assessed.

Program budgeting differs from the conventional process in three ways. First, an effort is made to express the budget in terms of goals. More specifically, *performance criteria* are formulated, and the budget is reorganized along program lines instead of by input costs. Second, an effort is made to fill out the program outline with *intermediate missions*, so that program elements may be utilized at all possible levels. One advantage of the use of performance criteria *over time* is that it allows evaluators to compare present and past performances by the organization in question. Third, there is an effort to outline the outputs produced and inputs required over the entire program period rather than one or two years. This requires that past as well as future expenditures and output be included. If successful, this approach allows evaluators to consider both the short- and long-run effects of the program.

Certain difficulties are presented when the more specific program budgeting techniques are used to try to implement the broader cost-benefit goals. In organizing data for budgetary review there is necessarily a tradeoff between emphasizing quantifiable missions (persons educated,

pilots trained, road miles paved, and so on) and emphasizing contributions made to the broader goals. Generally speaking, the former emphasis
allows for more definite performance criteria for judging intermediate
organizational units but does not include perspectives useful for making
judgments in terms of the entire program.

There are, then, several important and difficult steps in program
budgeting. The initial difficulty is in developing appropriate " missions "
or " performance criteria." These must lend themselves to quantification,
yet take account of the major benefits and costs associated with the
unit's activities; otherwise, they may reward behavior which is not
compatible with the program's real goals.

A second and related difficulty occurs when a single agency is simultaneously active in several different programs. Since economies of scale
(in administrative and support costs and so on) are usually present, the
assignment of portions of the agency's costs to various programs is
necessarily arbitrary. In practice it turns out that the missions of *most*
agencies affect more than one program goal; but specifying the relationship of an agency's activities to one goal necessarily muddles the evaluation of its relationship to other goals. For example, suppose you are
evaluating the performance of the agency responsible for coordinating
educational grants to veterans. These grants affect educational institutions, income distribution, employment opportunities, social patterns,
and many other factors relating to a multitude of broad and specific
" goals." Thus it is difficult to set up performance criteria for this agency.
If you set up accounting procedures and performance criteria along the
lines of the effects on the educational levels attained by veterans, it may
become more difficult to judge the effects on the employment opportunities open to the recipients. The point is that when several goals are
important, the accounting procedures and performance criteria used
must be flexible enough to allow for judgments in terms of each of the
goals.

It follows that a third difficulty arises once the program budget format
is decided. Namely, decision makers will find it difficult to analyze the
interdependencies among programs. How does a highway program affect
alternative urban renewal plans? Questions of this sort remain, and may
be made even more difficult, under a program budget format which
features specific performance criteria.

A fourth difficulty is the *assessment of costs and benefits* once performance criteria have been chosen. The usual practice, as noted, is to calcu-

late some cost per performance unit—tanks built, Job Corps trainees graduated, or whatever. This format, however, encourages focusing on the *average* instead of the marginal benefits and costs. The appropriate question when maximizing efficiency is not: " What is the average cost per unit? " but " What are the costs and benefits in expanding or contracting the activity? " Will administrative overhead, cost of facilities, and so on expand proportionately? Have useful techniques been forged which will lower future costs? Or, on the other hand, are costs rising because of shortages of land, talented administrators, and other scarce resources?

When public activities and institutions are already organized along appropriate program and goal lines, the implementation of program budgeting is greatly enhanced. But when agencies of two different organizations play a part in accomplishing the same goal, their activities may not complement each other. One organization may not have incentive to design the accounting procedures and performance criteria of its own agencies to complement the work of other agencies in accomplishing the same goal. Furthermore, competition among departments working on a goal may be quite harmful. It becomes clear that program budgeting is not universally applicable and that the rule for implementation is again in terms of benefits and costs. It seems to follow that program budgeting is advisable where specific, independent missions may be identified and where the organizational structure can accommodate these independent missions. Changing the budget format will make for little improvement unless the cost-reward incentives for the budget officials are also efficiently linked to the missions. If the change allows the same bargaining relationships, vested interests, and so on to remain intact (or even perhaps creates more detrimental relationships), the results will be negative.

In each case *all* of the costs and benefits of implementing changes in the budgetary process need to be considered. Experience has shown that program budgeting methods are often inadequate and should be supplemented with other perspectives and techniques.

COST-BENEFIT TECHNIQUES: ADDITIONAL PERSPECTIVES

Besides program budgeting, the rubric " cost-benefit analysis " includes several other approaches. Certain methods and techniques used in examining the complexities of interrelated programs and missions are

TABLE 6–1

Hypothetical programs for
a city's recreation planning

	Participants			
	Young children	Teens	Young married	Older persons
1. Playground equipment	×			
2. Organized play for children	×			
3. Craft centers and directors	×	×	×	×
4. Tennis courts		×	×	
5. Swimming and wading pools	×	×	×	×
6. Additional organized sports		×	×	
7. Teenage social and recreation centers		×		
8. Public golf course		×	×	×

termed "systems analysis." Others, used in making comparisons between alternative operations designed to accomplish a specified goal,
are termed "operations research."

Under either approach the basic cost-benefit question is asked: How
can resources best be allocated ("economized") to fulfill certain goals?
The perspectives are familiar. Where costs are given, the effort is to
minimize costs; and where both outputs and inputs are to be adjusted,
maximization follows the equi-marginal rule. We are not, of course,
confined to the familiar consumer-oriented models of maximization
under perfect competition. Indeed, we cannot easily isolate the economic
aspects from the political, sociological, engineering, and other aspects of
the real world problems we confront. Instead, a multitude of disciplines
must be employed—the situation may call for the skills of the engineer,
the lawyer, the military strategist, the biologist, the ecologist, the
urban planner, and others. This is necessary because cost-benefit
analyses consist of choice making within complex *systems*, with the
choice to be made among all feasible alternatives.

Some of the systems with which cost-benefit analyses have been used
most effectively are water use and power production (which must involve, among other things, analyses from the ecological perspective),
transportation systems (which necessarily involve analyses of the input
and output market systems in question), and urban planning (which
necessarily involves analyses of the area's economic, sociological, and
political patterns).

These analyses are carried out with a constant interplay of analytical techniques against goals, principles, and criteria. The goals may be stated in broad or specific terms. Within the context of these goals, we have seen that it may be desirable to derive principles and rules by which to modify and stabilize decision making in situations of uncertainty and of recurrent choice. It is crucial to cost-benefit analysis that goals be defined in such a way as to allow the deletion of obviously inferior alternatives. It is important, too, that uncertainty be given due consideration, and that adaptability and flexibility receive proper weight in the evaluation of alternatives.

Several familiar rules of economic analysis are fundamental to the cost-benefit approach. A basic technique is the building of models—that is, making assumptions about priorities and behavior, simplifying the interrelationships among entities within the system, and making predictions on the basis of the expected responses to possible changes in the variables. Another familiar technique is the calculation of the " opportunity costs " involved in choosing one alternative over the others. And, finally, information may be organized to allow comparisons and choices in terms of the equi-marginal rule.

AN EXAMPLE: RECREATION PLANNING

A hypothetical example will illustrate the use of these techniques in public sector decision making. Suppose we are involved in planning for the recreational needs of a city of 200,000. Specifically, we are the Recreation Committee of the City Council and we are considering various proposals our recreation officials have prepared with the help of outside recreation experts and local contractors and architects. For many years our city has recognized the need to expand its recreational program, and now it has raised its yearly appropriation to $400,000. The city has six well-distributed parks but each has little equipment. The only administered recreational activity involves summer baseball and softball leagues in white middle-class sections. Table 6.1 lists the possible programs and the groups which would participate in each.

Our committee's primary goal is to maximize the benefits created by the program. Each committee member, besides feeling responsible to the community as a whole, is influenced also by his own preferences and those of his family, neighbors, and business associates as well as those of

TABLE 6–2		4 lanes	6 lanes
Swimming pool alternatives	Cost (in thousands of dollars)	70	90
	Benefits (in swimmers accommodated per day)	308	360
	Ratio of benefits to cost	44/10	40/10

TABLE 6–3		A	B	C	D
Cost-benefit comparisons through time	Cost	$100	$100	$200	$200
	Benefit after one year	$105	$150	$210	$280
	Benefit-cost ratio	1.05	1.50	1.05	1.40

the particular groups of voters who helped elect him. While the immediate question is now to allocate funds for the coming year, the city's long-run recreational needs must also be considered. In choosing among the alternatives, two of the principles we will attempt to follow are (1) coordination of current and long-run recreation plans and (2) maintenance of flexibility to provide for known and unknown recreational needs of the future.

Knowing the various prices associated with each program, we on the Recreation Committee must formulate a recreation plan in terms of an optimum program mix. When we choose a program, we must be aware of the opportunity costs of giving up other programs—not only the recreational benefits foregone but other costs as well. If, for example, many of the young blacks of the community are unemployed and restless and there has been racial tension, the failure to implement programs to occupy their energies might be costly in terms of burned buildings, hospital bills, and so on. Another cost to each councilman is the political support of particular groups pushing for specific programs: tennis players, or golfers, or persons living near proposed playground areas.

The student may wish to further specify the model. Certainly the cost-benefit approach requires more specification and not just in terms of costs. Benefits such as the number of people involved in each program, the effect on community morale and cohesiveness, and the added attractiveness of the community to new industry should be considered. Again, both long-run and short-run planning are required: What, for example, is the cost pattern *through time* of a particular mix of programs? How do the programs interrelate to accomplish the broader goals? What economies in administration, maintenance, and so on may be realized with various combinations of programs?

Answering these questions is the essence of cost-benefit analysis. After attempting to evaluate *all* benefits and costs, we make the final choice in terms of the equi-marginal rule. That is, we find the proper mix by carrying each program to the point where marginal benefits are equal to marginal costs (to include opportunity costs).

SOME POSSIBLE ERRORS IN ASSESSING BENEFIT-COST RATIOS

The difficulty of quantifying benefits and costs may lead to some errors of interpretation. Recall, for example, the swimming pool program discussed earlier, and consider Table 6.2.

These benefit-cost ratios, while interesting, should not be taken as "the" criteria. In fact, they are not very useful in making an "equi-marginal" judgment and may be quite misleading. The marginal evaluation is not reflected in the ratios—the pertinent question is: Are we willing to pay $20,000 to accommodate 52 more swimmers per day? The marginal benefit-cost ratio is 26/10. It is important that additional criteria be used to evaluate these benefits: How many potential swimmers are there in the area's population? And, on the assumption of diminishing marginal benefits from additional expenditures on swimming pools, how do these benefits fit in with the broader recreation goals? What benefits may be created by spending the $20,000 on another program or by leaving it with the taxpayer? Thus we note two errors which may result from the attempt to reduce benefits and costs to quantifiable terms: (1) the criteria may tend to draw attention away from other pertinent information and the primary goals themselves, and (2) the criteria may encourage judgments to be made on *average* (44/10) rather than marginal adjustments.

Other errors are easily made in comparing benefits and costs over time. Let us use a rather straightforward example, as shown in Table 6.3, where costs and benefits have been reduced to monetary terms. Perusal of the benefit-cost ratios indicates choice B which returns $150 for the $100 cost. Again, however, the choice may not be simply a question of maximizing the average benefit-cost ratio. We must know whether the alternatives are mutually exclusive. Suppose the rate of return is 8 percent in other alternatives and we have no cost constraint; then we naturally choose *both* B and D. On the other hand, with a budget constraint of $100, we must of course choose B.

TABLE 6–4

Resource transfer to the
public sector

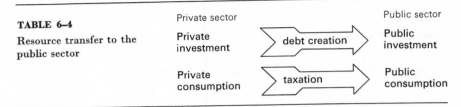

Now suppose the alternatives are mutually exclusive. Is alternative B (which carries the highest benefit-cost ratio) the best choice? Not necessarily!—because in order to initiate project B we must forego project D, which yields a net gain of $80 of benefits. Consideration of all other public and private investment opportunities would probably demonstrate that the benefits from project D should not be given up. In deciding among alternatives with different yields through time, the ideal method would be to compare the benefit-cost ratio of each alternative to a general rate of discount. Such a discount rate would reflect the rate at which society is generally willing to put off present for future consumption (given their preferences and the productivity of investment through time). The current interest rate structure can be taken as a rough approximation of the social discount rate. In using this or any other concept, however, it has been amply demonstrated that public choices based on benefit-cost ratios must be made with care.

THE SOCIAL RATE OF DISCOUNT

The choice of a rate of return by which to evaluate public activities has several interesting facets.[1] Assessing the time streams of benefits and costs of a particular alternative is only part of the problem. The decision also rests on the rate of return for other public investments and the multitude of rates found in the private sector. When marginal adjustments are to be made, it is important to ascertain the rates of projects being curtailed as well as those being expanded.

Let us begin by recalling the basic public sector, private sector model discussed in Chapter 4, where public consumption goods are financed by taxation (which appropriately reduces private consumption) and public investment projects are financed by public debt creation (which appropriately reduces private investment).[2] Suppose that the market for capital is perfectly competitive and that there is a single rate of return on private investment which in turn is equal to the single private rate of discount, r_p. Assume also that we have decided upon the rate of discount applicable to public investment, the social rate of discount, r_s, and that it in turn is equal to the rate at which the public sector can borrow (which is, of course, the private rate). Thus

$$r_s = r_p.$$

With resort to this rate each public investment expenditure can be carried to the point where the rate of return (including all benefits) is equal to the cost of obtaining funds (including *all* opportunity costs).

Now let us consider situations in which $r_s \neq r_p$. Unless careful consideration is given to all factors affecting the demand and supply of private investment funds, the correct policy prescription may not be found.[3] We will proceed by using the two-sector model and outline the various possible forms of imbalance which may occur between the four categories of resource use: private and public investment, private and public consumption. As Table 6.4 illustrates, we assume that public debt creation will be used to transfer funds (and resources) from private to public investment and taxation will be used to transfer funds (and resources) from private to public consumption. (The transfers illustrated are simplifications; actually debt creation includes readjustments in both private investment *and consumption*, just as taxation may reduce private investment as well as private consumption.)

We start with the assumption of an optimum balance among the four categories. Now consider some of the factors which may shift the demand for private investment funds. First we note that the demand for such

[1] A few of the recent articles and books exploring the question are: Stephen A. Marglin, "The Social Rate of Discount and Optimal Rate of Investment," and "The Opportunity Costs of Public Investment," *Quarterly Journal of Economics*, vol. 77 (February and May 1963), pp. 95–111 and 274–289; and *Public Investment Criteria* (Cambridge, Mass.: MIT Press, 1965); Martin S. Feldstein, "Net Social Benefit Calculation and the Public Investment Decision," *Oxford Economic Papers*, vol. 16, N.S. (March, 1964), pp. 114–131, and "The Social Time Preference Discount Rate in Cost-Benefit Analysis," *Economic Journal*, vol. 74, no. 2 (1964), pp. 360–379; Arnold C. Harberger, "On the Opportunity Cost of Public Borrowing," in *Economic Analysis of Public Investment Decisions: Interest Rate Policy and Discounting Analysis*, Hearings before the Joint Economic Committee, 90th Congress, 2nd Session (Washington, D.C.: U.S. Government Printing Office, 1968).
[2] This outline of the investment decision follows that of Richard A. Musgrave, "Cost-Benefit Analysis and the Theory of Public Finance," *Journal of Economic Literature*, vol. 7, no. 3 (September 1969), pp. 797–806.
[3] Owing to their neglect of simple demand and supply models, many of the cost-benefit studies lead to confusing results. The articles in the preceding footnotes may be read and compared as examples of studies with confusing results.

FIGURE 6–1

Figurative shifts in demand
between the two sectors

Private sector

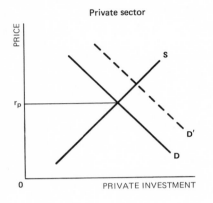

Public sector

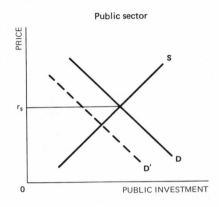

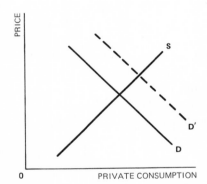

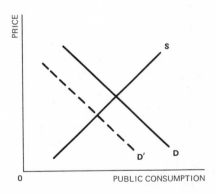

funds is derived from the demand for private consumption. Ideally, the discount rate reflects the choices that consumers with perfect knowledge make between present and future consumption, given the production possibilities. Some interesting arguments follow, however, if the assumption of perfect knowledge is dropped. It is often argued, for example, that individuals are inordinately aware of their immediate needs and not sufficiently aware of social needs—especially those of future generations. This argument has several aspects. One is that the rapid pace of our society does not allow adequate reflection of public needs. If it did, presumably more resources would be made available for public investment. A corollary is that our institutions inordinately favor private consumption choices over all investment (both private or public). It is contended, for example, that advertising "warps" the individual's preference ordering towards private sector consumption, while there are no offsetting advertisements for public goods. At the same time the decision-making process—given the free-rider problem, and so on— understates individual tastes for public goods. For these and other reasons, it is argued, demand for private consumption is higher than it should be. Consequently, the demand for funds for private investment— a "derived" demand, since the investment is undertaken to produce future consumption goods—is also higher relative to the demands for public consumption and investment goods.

The results of these demand shifts are depicted in Figure 6.1.[4] The solid lines represent the ideal equilibrium, where $r_s = r_p$. The dotted lines indicate the shifts that take place under the condition where, say, advertising and the institutional structure inhibit individuals from voicing their true preferences for public goods. The demand for private investment is shown to be shifting to the right as a complementary response to the increased demand for private consumption goods. To the extent, however, that the increase in private sector consumption substitutes for private sector investment, this shift will be reduced.

Consumers, firms, voters, and legislators all tend to overestimate the value of private relative to public production. At first glance it might seem that increased demand for private sector consumption might replace demand for private sector investment; but recall that the demand for investment funds comes from firms, not consumers, and firms respond to increased sales by expanding capacity. The shift in private sector demand for investment funds will, of course, increase private sector investment and raise the rate of interest. The shift away from public investment will dampen the increase in r_p, since there is some competition between private and public securities for the same funds. There may also be pressure on the supply of private investment, since the shift in consumer preferences towards present consumption should cause them to reduce planned saving. We recall, however, that the supply of

---

[4] The reader may well object to the rather simplistic depiction of demand and supply relationships in the two sectors. In order to specify the model properly, one would need to give considerable time and effort to the outlining of the assumptions about the institutional framework and so on. Moreover, actual measurement of the values portrayed is impossible. The depiction, therefore, is highly figurative.

private investment funds is more dependent on firms' retained earnings and government monetary policy than on individual savings plans. The final outcome, as depicted in Figure 6.1, depends on two effects: (1) overestimation of the value of private investment and upward pressure on r_p and (2) underestimation of r_s. Both effects tend to reduce public investment to a less than optimum level.

Our model can also be used to depict disequilibria between r_s and r_p when the disequilibrating forces work towards "too much" public spending. Logrolling, tie-ins, the diffusion effect, and other factors in the budget process can tend to shift effective demand for public sector consumption and investment. In this case the shift in demand for public investment would be to the right. The apparent social rate of discount would be higher than the ideal rate. A secondary effect of the increased demand for investment funds by the public sector would be to drive up the rate of interest, thus reducing private investment below its optimum level. Consequently, arguments can be made that too many resources are being devoted to public good production and that the actual social rate of discount on public investment is too high, even though it may *appear* to be lower.

There are other factors which are said to create shifts in the *supply* of investment funds. An important one is that no account is taken of the social costs and benefits created when externalities are created by private sector production; consequently, the prices of some resources used in private sector consumption and investment do not reflect the real opportunity costs. It follows that the supply curves for private investment and consumption may be to the left or the right of the "ideal" depiction in Figure 6.1 according to whether the spillover effects result in net social losses or gains.

Another factor making for disequilibrium between r_s and r_p is the treatment of risks in the private and public sectors. It is argued that the treatment is uneven because, while owners of firms may suffer irretrievable loss for unwise investment, government (presumably because of its ability to spread risks and its impressive power to raise revenue) faces lower risks when investing.

Making judgments about the supply of investment funds raises complex questions about the nature of competition in banking and public sector macroeconomic policy. Loaning practices of banks are subject to the oligopolistic nature of the markets within which they operate. Moreover, the interest rate is manipulated by the public sector (either directly through Federal Reserve operations or indirectly through government spending or tax measures) to achieve balance between aggregate demand and supply. It is logical, of course, that public policy encourage the appropriate balance between investment (private and public) and consumption (private and public) at the same time it is promoting full employment without inflation. Our question, however, is: How can we determine r_s? How is it related to r_p? And we observe that, if the interest rate itself is a by-product of macroeconomic policies, it cannot also be taken as an approximation of r_s. If the interest rate (r_p) is being manipulated to cure a short-run economic fluctuation, it is not likely to reflect the choices that would be made by the community under ideal conditions between present and future consumption. Moreover, since the long-run trend in r_p reflects short-run macroeconomic policies, even it cannot be taken as an exact approximation, although it would seem to be more reliable than the current r_p at any given point in time.

In summary, we see that the problem of estimating r_s (with respect to either specific economic activities or the entire economy) requires analysis of the behavior of r_p in response to macroeconomic fluctuations and policies and imperfections in the monetary and credit institutions of the private market.

An underlying problem, if we are to apply r_s to choices among alternative public sector programs, is that of estimating individual preferences for the benefits from the program in question.

COST-BENEFIT ADJUSTMENTS WHEN $r_s \neq r_p$

Now suppose we have "solved" the problem of estimating r_s and have found that $r_s \neq r_p$. The next problem is to find the best policy for either curing the cause of the maladjustment or compensating for it. As we might anticipate, the cure depends on the nature of the illness.

Let us first suppose that the maladjustment arises from factors affecting *demand*; insufficient effective demand for private investment causes "too little" investment, and $r_p < r_s$. The most obvious prescription is to correct the cause. Suppose, for example, that the case involves a quasi-public good being produced in the private sector. Since part of the benefits are indivisible, they will not be marketable, and the investment in that industry will be less than optimal. Depending on the nature of the benefits, several options are open. Perhaps the law or other market institutions could be changed to allow the producer to charge for the benefits produced. Alternatively, the government may give tax incentives, subsidies, or provide investment funds at reduced rates. As a last resort the government may be required to usurp substantially all of the production decisions: investment, hiring, firing, production techniques, and so on, as it did when it entered into the production of electricity as the Tennessee Valley Authority.

The latter method essentially calls for public production of goods with primarily divisible benefits. Although private investment may be partially displaced by public investment, the result may be in fact the "second best" solution. Musgrave observes that many cost-benefit analysts often become engrossed in the criteria for replacing private with public investment and do not adequately explore the possibilities of encouraging private investment. He notes, however, that "... public investment as a policy instrument can neither raise the level of private investment to include projects which would be profitable if r_p were reduced to r_s, nor can it lengthen the structure of private investment to that which would hold at r_s."[5] Many factors affect the determination of whether an economic activity is more efficiently provided by private or public organizations. While the investment criterion is important, it obviously should not always be the controlling factor, since it may not account for all opportunity costs.

Fortunately, our simple two-sector model offers us some help in assessing opportunity costs of public investment. To demonstrate, let us again start with a model with full employment, perfect capital markets, and the equilibrium of r_s and r_p. When government withdraws resources, they are taken from either private investment or consumption or both. Assuming such shifts are in response to shifts in demand, there is no net burden in the process. Private investors, we recall, carry investment expenditure to the point where marginal returns equal marginal costs. When funds are shifted from private to public investment, the least profitable (and presumably the least welfare-producing) projects will be displaced. Similarly, if funds are withdrawn from private consumption, consumers will forego their least satisfying purchases.

Generally speaking, when a shift from private to public investment is called for, debt creation should be used; whereas taxes should be used for withdrawing resources from private consumption. This basic model and prescription offer a good starting point; but when the particular tax and/or debt instrument used produces nonneutral effects on the relationship between investment and consumption, compensating adjustments must be made. The specification of these adjustments depends on the particular effects produced.[6]

Now suppose that we have "too much" private investment, resulting from maladjustment in the *supply* of investment funds. The supply function has shifted to the right, forcing down r_p. Again, if feasible, the most appropriate policy is to remedy the *cause*. If this is a general phenomenon encompassing the whole private sector, the appropriate response would be to use monetary and/or tax policy to increase r_p and encourage reallocation of resources towards the proper balance between private and public investment. If the inequality pertains to a specific industry, more specific tools must be used to reduce the amount of resources invested in that industry. The possibilities, as outlined previously, include such things as special taxes, regulatory agencies, or nationalization of the industry.

Now let us consider adjustments where $r_p > r_s$ (again r_s is assumed to be known and is the "welfare-maximizing" discount rate). Suppose first that the factors are on the supply side—say, an imperfection in the capital markets which causes the cost of capital to be arbitrarily high and private investment curtailed to a less than optimum level. In this situation we have "too little" private investment and presumably "too much" private consumption. To the extent that budget officials curtail public investment in response to the higher rates, public investment also falls below the optimum level. The most appropriate adjustments would be directed at allowing the real costs of capital to be reflected; in this example, some reorganization or regulation of the capital markets may be appropriate. Alternatively, other governmental encouragements to private investment may be required.

If the factors causing $r_p > r_s$ are from the *demand side*, the picture is quite different. Suppose that private investment (and consumption) are *above* optimum levels because various social spillover effects are not being adequately accounted for in the private markets. A current example is the widespread pollution of streams and rivers by private companies. The result is that prices are often lower to consumers and the returns to these companies higher than if all externalities had to be reflected in costs.[7] Now, the movement to more efficiency requires *less* investment and consumption in these industries. Various alternatives are open for public sector activity. The most appropriate would be legislation or other governmental activity to cause these costs to be

---

[5] Musgrave, "Cost-Benefit Analysis, and the Theory of Public Finance," p. 801.

[6] The effects of various tax instruments on economic behavior will be examined in detail in Part III.

[7] In terms of demand and supply curves, this means that the *supply* (costs) of the private consumption goods are lower (to the right) than appropriate. This in turn causes the firms' *demand* for private investment goods to be greater (to the right) than appropriate.

internalized. Another prescription—certainly not always the most desirable—would be to use taxes to discourage investment and consumption in these industries, reducing market rate of return to the neighborhood of r_s. The funds would be reallocated to other activities in the public and private sectors.

In summary, three important points have been made about the use of a social discount rate. First, the cost-benefit approach offers no definitive procedures for finding a unique social rate of discount. While considerable insight can be gained from considering the demand and supply factors which may cause disequilibria between r_p and r_s, eventually an attempt must be made to account for the "preferences" of the affected individuals. Choices involving time preference add another dimension of complexity.

Second, analyses must include consideration of *all* opportunity costs. Couching the discussion in the two-sector model enhances one's ability to consider the costs created in one sector when resources are withdrawn for use elsewhere. The demand and supply models aid in the analysis and prescription for cases where $r_s \neq r_p$. However, the prescription should include an attempt to correct the factors making for the imbalance between private investment and consumption. Displacement or augmentation of private with public investment or vice versa necessarily creates further nonneutralities and requires even more complex assessments of opportunity costs.

Third, our examination has demonstrated that public investment alternatives cannot be considered in isolation. Our two-sector model, breaking down resource allocation into four categories (public and private investment and public and private consumption), demonstrated some of the interdependencies which must be considered. It was observed that the simple demand and supply models are useful in prescribing remedies when $r_s \neq r_p$.

The outline of public sector techniques presented in Chapter 4 suggests some of the alternatives. Implementation requires further knowledge of just how taxes affect economic behavior of firms and individuals as well as the macroeconomic consequences. These subjects will be examined in Parts III and IV, respectively.

THE MEASURABILITY OF COST-BENEFIT CRITERIA

A basic dilemma arises for cost-benefit analysts when they attempt to include *all* benefits and costs, since some of these strenuously resist quantification. The lack of "data" is not the real problem. One may compile tons of data—prices, quantities, and so on—without improving and perhaps even diminishing one's ability to choose among alternatives. On the other hand, we can often find surprisingly pertinent "data" about rather esoteric activities such as the "value" of a concert, a beautiful tree, or a babbling brook. Our central question is whether existing decision-making procedures adequately reflect the important costs and benefits. For many economic activities private markets provide prices which do account for all costs and benefits. Where actual prices are missing, they can often be augmented by other physical measures which aid in the estimation of real costs and benefits. McKean categorizes the types of data in terms of measurability:

1. gains and costs that can be measured in monetary units (for example, the use of items like typewriters that have market prices which presumably reflect the marginal evaluation of all users);
2. other commensurable effects (impacts of higher teacher salaries, on the one hand, and of teaching machines, on the other hand, on students' test scores);
3. incommensurable effects that can be quantified but not in terms of a common denominator (capability of improving science test scores using a new teaching technique and its capability of reducing the incidence of ulcers among students); and
4. nonquantifiable effects.[8]

We note that the "publicness" characteristic of public goods belies any expectation that any public sector cost-benefit analyses will contain only data of the first category. Similarly, no public activity will include only effects of the last category. Instead, analyses are more likely to include elements of each category. The major difficulty, then, is the combination of the different types of data and value judgments.

The essence of the problem is (1) to search out the pertinent data that are available, (2) to combine and organize the data in an appropriate format, and (3) to pinpoint the value judgments, assumptions, and the like inherent in the various choices. Where value judgments abound, cost-benefit analysis cannot, of course, furnish definitive answers. For example, cost-benefit analysis is helpful in predicting the ramifications of

---

[8] Roland N. McKean, *Public Spending* (New York: McGraw-Hill, 1968), p. 141.

present population trends, but ethical judgments are necessary in questions such as the "sanctity of life," the "quality of life," and euthanasia.[9] If, however, the values in question are generally accepted, cost-benefit analysis can then proceed to provide and organize information so that it can be *systematically* examined and evaluated.

Now let us consider the measurability problem as it evidences itself in various situations:

Where the activity's benefits and costs are divisible and assignable. Measurement here presents little difficulty. The cost-benefit decision is to choose among various techniques of compensating for the market failure. We have previously examined cases where, although goods exhibit divisible benefits, the situation may warrant public activity. In a natural monopoly situation, for example, the options range among public ownership, public regulation, no regulation with antitrust activity and so on. Value judgments must be made in choosing among the alternatives, but there is little difficulty in measuring the costs and benefits associated with the good itself. The price mechanism of the private sector can be utilized.

Where none of the activity's benefits and costs are divisible and assignable. Our classic example here is the "lighthouse" model. Measurement of benefits becomes difficult because they are indivisible and unassignable. The market price will not reflect marginal evaluations. We may, of course, resort to criteria such as the market value of boats to be saved each year, the number of lives saved each year and so on. Such data may be helpful, but their use in the form of benefit-cost ratios must be undertaken with caution, since each involves value judgments.

Where the activity exhibits nondivisible and nonassignable benefits and costs but is an intermediate rather than a final good. Consider the cost-benefit information provided in the following situations: a new canal reduces costs of transporting goods by boat; a job training program increases earning potential of trainees; improved public health care reduces hospital costs of recipients. While the intermediate activity may exhibit public good characteristics and require public sector production, certain of the benefits associated with the final good may lend themselves to measurement via the price mechanism. In these cases cost-benefit analysis has been most helpful; indeed, cost-benefit analysts owe much of their success to their ability to demonstrate the intermediate nature of public activities and find measurable data pertaining to the final goods.

CHOICES AND THE BUDGET: SUMMARY COMMENTS

Our examination of the budget sequence reveals a complex organizational structure populated by officials and other personnel whose own priorities encourage certain types of behavior. These individual priority patterns may often yield behavior at odds with what voters would prefer. Our survey shows that when cost-benefit analyses are made, a detailed examination of the effect of institutional structures on decision making is essential.

Our introduction to cost-benefit analysis has only suggested some basic perspectives and techniques which may be used to cope with some of the difficulties inherent in public decision making. We can but suggest in a general way when and where these methods can be successfully instituted. Our discussion above reveals that measurable information is more readily available in some situations than in others. It naturally follows that the *cost* of finding information must be an important factor in determining the structure of the proposed budget institutions.

The costs of changing the budget process (say, the costs of acquiring additional information, expert opinions, and so on) must be weighed against the benefits expected from better resource allocation. Some important possible costs are incurred when decision-making authority is readjusted among budgetary agencies. Let us consider some of the benefits and costs involved when budget decision-making authority becomes more concentrated in one agency. One possible benefit is that decision-making power is given to those who have the broader view and will compare more alternatives. Second, there may be economies of scale in the budgetary process itself; that is, similar decisions for similar activities can be handled more efficiently by a central agency. Centralization may also tend to offset some of the inefficient practices of budgetary officials (such as empire building and "foot-in-the-door" ploys) which result from the cost-reward incentives in less centralized budget structures.

But the centralizing of decision making increases "efficiency" at the expense of allowing a wider group of interests to play a part. As our voting models demonstrated, the more flexible systems (allowing for tradeoffs and so on) are more likely to account for differences in preferences, even though they may sometimes be unwieldy. In this regard we note that concentration may increase the danger of "big" mistakes.

---

[9] The act of painlessly putting to death persons suffering incurable and painful illness.

Concentration often means the loss of inventive diversification, especially when there was formerly a rivalry between public agencies. The loss of diversification and competition may change the nature of conflict among budgetary officials so as to make it more costly. Instead of diversified, competing units, you have factions within the unit itself fighting for control. The result may be shifting coalitions, rapid personnel turnover, frustration, and similar problems.

Flexibility and innovation may be further reduced, because concentration of decision making requires more formal processes with set procedures. The central decision maker must now make most of the decisions formerly made by his subordinates; consequently, he must set precedents, screen out many decisions, and set patterns for recurrent decisions. Unusual situations are handled badly—if at all. Lower officials often find that a bureaucrat's "hands are tied." Each unexpected situation must be referred to a higher authority or ignored. The flexibility of the higher official may be also curtailed. Once precedents are set and positions taken, lower-level officials may presume that the "standard operating procedure" will always be followed. The higher-level officials must, in effect, make promises which cannot easily be broken. They must allow certain vested interests to become stabilized and institutionalized. The setting of procedures, so necessary to centralized decision making, reduces flexibility at all levels.

As this discussion indicates, changes in the structure of budgeting involve both benefits and costs. Even the decision on how to structure the decision-making process should itself be exposed to cost-benefit analyses with due regard to the marginal costs and benefits.

In the next chapter we will attempt a general survey of the development of American public finance institutions. In the process we will also attempt to apply many of the concepts, models, and insights we have just acquired.

7
ECONOMIC GROWTH AND THE PUBLIC SECTOR

THE BASIC MODEL OF PUBLIC SECTOR GROWTH

Little expertise is required to recognize that public sector activity has been increasing over time. This trend is a popular topic of discussion among laymen as well as economists. Three questions are familiar: Why does the government spend so much? Why has the government been taking a greater share of national income? Why doesn't the government spend on things we want? These questions run in various forms throughout this investigation. We now ask them in the context of the history of U.S. public sector growth. Several models, including some already developed, will be useful.

The familiar model featuring an aggregate production possibility function and a social preference function offers a good starting point. Again we assume only two possible alternatives, private good Y or public good X, as shown in Figure 7.1. Given the social preference functions I_1, I_2, I_3 and the production possibility curve PP, the welfare-maximizing combination of output will be at A. Now assume that growth occurs as technology changes and supplies of resources increase. The new production possibilities are shown by $P'P'$ and the new equilibrium by B.

Without reviving the argument of whether the social optimum at A or B can be identified and/or reached, let us simply use the model to frame some rather fundamental statements. First, we observe that as the economy grows through time, *more* of both private and public goods will be demanded.[1]

While it is theoretically possible that the actual amount of public or private activity be *reduced* through time, the more relevant question is the *relative* amounts of private and public activity. This question is more interesting because of the observed tendency in the Western economies for output in *both* sectors to increase but for public sector activity to increase its relative share of resources. Our model is useful for demonstrating two different types of influence in this direction. Either *demand* or *supply* (or both) factors may provide the impetus toward public

---

[1] It would, of course, be possible to draw a model where point B would be above and to the *left* of point A, even within the context of our assumptions of diminishing marginal utility (making the I functions convex to the origin) and diminishing marginal productivity (making the P function concave to the origin). Our purpose here, though, is not to make a proof but simply to illustrate the expected relationships.

FIGURE 7–1

Basic model of public
sector growth, example 1

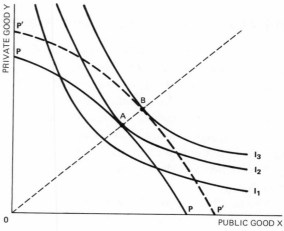

FIGURE 7–2

Basic model of public
sector growth,
example 2

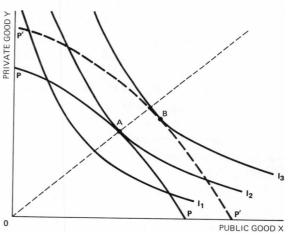

FIGURE 7–3

Basic model of public
sector growth, example 3

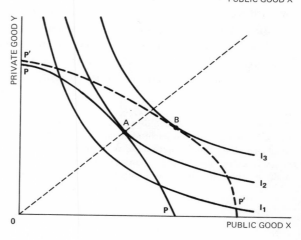

activity. Note that in Figure 7.1 P' P' and I_2 are situated such that A and B are on a ray from the origin. Thus no relative shift has occurred in the percentage of production (in real terms) devoted to either sector. In Figure 7.2, however, the social preference pattern (I_1, I_2, and I_3) is situated so that a relatively greater proportion of output is accounted for by the public sector (B is to the right of a ray from the origin). The shift has been influenced by demand factors. Anticipating our examination of actual events, we may hypothesize that as the economy has grown more wealthy, public goods such as defense, education, and highways have become *relatively more attractive* (at the margin) than additional clothing, food, housing, vehicles, and the like.

Figure 7.3 shows another type of influence which may cause a relative shift towards public good production. This time, factors on the supply side are responsible. As growth occurs, new technology and previously existing economies of scale favor public good production. Again anticipating our more thorough examination, we may hypothesize that with growth, *economies of scale* and *changes in technology* are experienced in the production of defense, education, highways, and so on, so that they become relatively less expensive than private goods. Hence, we have another explanation for the relative shift to public sector activity.

WAGNER'S LAW OF INCREASING RELATIVE IMPORTANCE OF THE PUBLIC SECTOR

The work of German economist Adolph Wagner (1835–1917) adds new dimensions to our investigation. Whereas our preliminary remarks utilized a simplified model, Wagner was much more thorough and ambitious. Wagner hypothesized a functional relationship between industrialization and the relative importance of public sector activity. He then set out to test his hypothesis by examining the industrialization process in various countries—Britain, the United States, Germany, Japan, and France. To Wagner the statistical evidence seemed to reveal a "law" that social progress caused increasing public sector activity: "The law is the result of empirical observation in progressive countries, at least in Western European civilization; its explanation, justification and cause is the *pressure of social progress* and the resulting changes in the relative spheres of private and public economy. . ."[2] Wagner saw these required functions taking three forms.

1. law and order—especially those forms necessary for market operation;
2. public production of material goods—especially in industries with economies of scale and large capital requirements; and
3. other economic and social activities such as education, banking, and postal services.

Wagner examined factors on both the demand and supply side of public sector activity and explained how they *interact*. Changing production and marketing arrangements affect and are affected by social organization in two ways: (1) organizations within the economic system change to accommodate new *production* and *marketing* arrangements, and (2) social and political organizations change to accommodate the new *social* relationships among persons. One requirement of the first category of changes is that the public sector takes on certain functions which facilitate implementation of new production and marketing techniques. As mentioned, these functions may include regulation or public production of certain material goods. Industries such as basic fuels and metals, communications and transportation, and banking exhibit these characteristics and create important external economies.[3]

In the second category, organizational and expenditure requirements arise from new social patterns, including urbanization, specialization of labor, and centralization of administration in both private and public activities. According to Wagner the net effect of these growing interdependences is a higher relative resource allocation to the public sector. These changes in the infrastructure of social organization in turn have feedback effects on economic organizational requirements, thus enabling even higher rates of economic change.

In examining the evolution of public and private activities Wagner foresaw increasing *centralization* in lower and higher levels of government and in the private as well as public sectors. His predictions followed his view of the inevitable role of the "state." On the one hand, increasing interdependence naturally made centralized administration in public activities more efficient. On the other hand, large-scale production processes became more feasible, and efficiency called for public rather than private production. The latter trend would be accentuated by what Wagner saw as weaknesses in large private firms: the joint stock companies. He thought that they were inefficient, wasteful, and unstable and that the mistakes they made were procyclical. Consequently, the citizenry would eventually require the public sector to assume all those functions which featured natural monopoly, high uncertainty, and large fixed capital requirements.

Obviously, the functional relationships Wagner sought to trace are complex. The growth patterns of the countries he chose to examine did indeed exhibit an overall tendency towards a relative increase in public sector activity. Understandably, however, he was not very successful in reducing the complex factors involved in changing social and economic relationships into simple functional relationships. In the process of industrialization many important variables are changing simultaneously in manufacturing, marketing, and communications. Among countries with differences in culture and natural resources we would expect variations in the pattern of economic growth, manifesting themselves in different requirements for public sector activity. Hence, it would be difficult to predict that one category of resource use will increase faster than another without examining the pattern of growth for the country in question. The Wagner hypothesis, however, is an interesting one to test with regard to the U.S. experience, and it offers us a valuable model to use in viewing the interrelated growth of the private and public sectors.

THE MARXIAN PROCESS OF SELF-DESTRUCTIVE CAPITALISM

To Marx, of course, the impetus for social and political change stemmed *entirely* from the changes in economic well-being and class conflict brought about by changing technology.[4] Marx saw that the capitalistic system bore within itself the seeds of its own destruction. In fact, he presented three distinct theories of how it would destroy itself: (1) through capital accumulation and a falling rate of profit, (2) through overproduction in certain industries, and (3) through underconsumption.

Under the first theory, firms would seem to be in a sort of *prisoner's dilemma* which required each of them to accumulate more capital in

[2] Adolph Wagner, *Finanzwissenschaft*, 3rd ed. (Leipzig, 1890), part I, p. 16. Italics added.
[3] We observed earlier that these activities have been accomplished differently in different countries. Whereas in the Western European countries most are public industries, in the United States they are more or less regulated. If these industries had become public, the relative importance of the U.S. public sector would, of course, be significantly greater.
[4] Karl Marx and F. Engels, *Capital* (New York: Modern Library, Random House, 1932).

order to compete. As the capital stock increases, however, the ratio of fixed to variable capital (the "organic" composition of capital) will also increase. This process, according to Marx, leads to unemployment as capital is substituted for labor. A growing "reserve army" of unemployed tends to drive down wages to the subsistence level.

Periodically, capital accumulation would lead to short-run profits and higher wages in certain industries. However, the increase in wages would subsequently lead to reduced profits, a decrease in investment, and finally to a crisis and recession. During each such cycle the situation would become worse as more capital was accumulated and the reserve army grew.

The second theory featured another sort of *prisoner's dilemma*, this time a result of the capitalist's imperfect knowledge of his competitor's plans. Each capitalist adjusts his own production to market demand, but, as many firms act simultaneously, overproduction occurs. This is turn leads to falling profits, reduced investment, and an economic crisis. The army of the unemployed grows during these periodic crises.

The third theory focuses on the lack of aggregate demand relative to increasing capacity. With a growing reserve army of unemployed and with wages at the subsistence level, the necessary increase in demand cannot come from the working classes. Yet the capitalist cannot furnish the required purchasing power, since he himself is forced by competition to reinvest. It follows that overproduction will occur periodically, leading inevitable to a fall in profits, reduced investments, and so on.

As the system proceeds toward destruction, the ownership of capital becomes more concentrated. Small businesses that neglect to accumulate more capital are destroyed, and the remaining firms seek protection by combining in trusts.

The role of the public sector is determined by the capitalist. In Engels' words: "It is as a rule the state of the most powerful economic class that by force of its economic supremacy becomes also the ruling political class and thus acquires new means of subduing and exploiting the oppressed masses."[5] The search for new investment opportunities leads capitalists to seek them in other countries. The role of the state thus becomes imperialistic as new colonies are secured for investment. On the domestic scene, big business uses the public sector to limit competition and to keep the exploited working force in check. In the end, however, the reserve army of the unemployed, its ranks swelled by recurrent crises, will revolt and create a new economic system.

THE SOCIAL OVERHEAD CAPITAL HYPOTHESIS

A hypothesis closely akin to Wagner's observes that a nation's industrial development requires certain types of public "investment." Increasing returns from capital formation are possible from both sectors; but in order for the gains from specialization, external and internal economies of scale, and so on to be fully exploited in the private sector, *social overhead capital* in the form of education, highways, railroads, communications, stable banking, law and order, and the like must be subsidized or directly provided by the public sector.

Social overhead capital, then, refers to public sector investment activity which *enables* rapid industrialization. As formulated by Professor Paul Rosenstein-Rhodan of MIT, the terms in the concept have the following meanings:

1. "social" refers to the implicit externalities;
2. "overhead" implies a necessary fixed cost or precondition for private sector development; and
3. "capital" implies that the nature of the activity is investment.

Building a highway in an underdeveloped country usually requires that resources be diverted from present consumption to investment. But once this fixed cost has been committed, *externalities* appear in the forms of reduced input costs for firms and reduced marketing costs for consumer goods. The combined effect of these characteristics requires the public sector to take a major role in the provision of social overhead capital. It is not sufficient that the system generate surplus income available for reinvestment. Conditions must be such that a large proportion be invested in social overhead capital.

The social overhead capital hypothesis can be expressed in any of three ways, depending on the direction of causation inferred. It may be argued that the technological requirements of inevitable industrial change *require* public sector activities accommodating such change. Alternatively, emphasis may be placed on those innovators who perceive new ways of utilizing public sector activity to encourage industrialization and economic growth. Finally, the hypothesis may treat causation as an *interaction* among changing social, political, and economic needs and the changing organizational patterns. Obviously, either of the first two perspectives is

[5] F. Engels, *The Origin of the Family, Private Property and the State* (Chicago: Charles Kerr, 1902), p. 208.

preferable to the last if one wishes to develop a model where simple functional relationships may be specified. But since the third case best approximates reality, the first two can be used only sparingly.

W. W. Rostow uses a form of the social overhead capital hypothesis in his ambitious attempt to designate the stages of economic growth.[6] He identifies four stages:

During the *transitional period* social overhead capital is being developed, usually with the aid of foreign capital. Generally the necessary transition in the political and social structure of the traditional society takes place in response to outside influences, such as a military threat from a foreign nation or the observation of economic progress.

During the *takeoff period* one or more major industries in the economy develop rapidly, "yielding profits a large proportion of which are reinvested in new plant; and these new industries, in turn, stimulate, through their rapidly expanding requirement for factory workers, the services to support them, and for other manufactured goods, a further expansion in urban areas and in other modern industries plants. The whole process of expansion in the modern sector yields an increase of income in the hands of those who not only save at high rates but place their savings at the disposal of those engaged in modern sector activities."[7]

During the *drive to maturity* self-sustained growth occurs (for around 60 years), as a high rate of reinvestment allows for a rounding out of the supporting industries and a shift in the composition of output where it has comparative advantage in world trade. These changes, which often require more sophisticated processes, will test the adequacy of the social overhead capital.

An *age of high mass consumption* may occur if the social and political situations allow for a shift towards industries producing consumer goods —especially consumer durables and services. According to Rostow the automobile was the decisive element in ushering in this stage in the United States, beginning with Henry Ford's assembly line in 1913–1914 and maturing in the 1920s and in the postwar decade 1946–1956.

The social overhead capital concept implies that a large proportion of resources must be funneled through the public sector. We would expect public sector activity to increase relative to private sector activity during Rostow's transition and takeoff stages. Although social overhead capital continues to be built up during the latter stages of takeoff and the drive toward maturity, Rostow's argument would seem to indicate a leveling off or even decline in the relative importance of public sector activity.

Presumably the fixation upon consumer durables in the age of high mass consumption would encourage lower relative public sector activity. We will entertain this possibility in Chapter 8.

INNOVATIONS AND INVESTMENT

Innovations were central to the growth theory of Joseph A. Schumpeter, who was an economist and finance minister in Austria before coming to Harvard.[8] In the works cited, he presented two concepts important to the analysis of economic development: (1) the notion that *innovation* in the hands of the *entrepreneur* is often the spark to economic growth and (2) the notion that development often takes place *in cycles*. The two concepts were combined in Schumpeter's explanation of the development process: Entrepreneurs use new innovations to make profits and spark expansion. New investment creates simultaneously more output and more spending power. Moreover, a multiplier effect on investment occurs because of the *externalities* created by interdependent sectors.

In subsequent periods, however, overexpansion occurs. Output at first cannot keep up with demand and, because of the lag in supply, profits remain high. The imitators of the original innovators are not quite as astute and tend to overestimate the possibilities. Unfortunately, the banking system obliges imitators and speculators with an overexpansion of credit. Meanwhile, diminishing returns are accruing in the use of the factors of production.

Eventually the bubble bursts, credit contracts sharply, and business failures and unemployment increase. A long period of readjustment must then precede the opportunity for a new wave of innovations.

THE DISPLACEMENT EFFECT

It seems appropriate once again to acknowledge that the perspectives we are developing will not give birth to a *definitive theory* of public sector growth. Instead, they will be used merely as *frames of reference*. Peacock

---

[6] W. W. Rostow, *The Stages of Economic Growth: A Non-Communist Manifesto* (New York: Cambridge University Press, 1960).

[7] *Ibid.*, p. 8.

[8] See Schumpeter, *The Theory of Economic Development* (Cambridge, Mass.: Harvard University Press, 1934; published in Germany in 1911), and *Business cycles* (New York: McGraw-Hill, 1939), 2 vols.

FIGURE 7-4

Total government
expenditure and gross
national product in
the United Kingdom
at current prices,
1890–1955

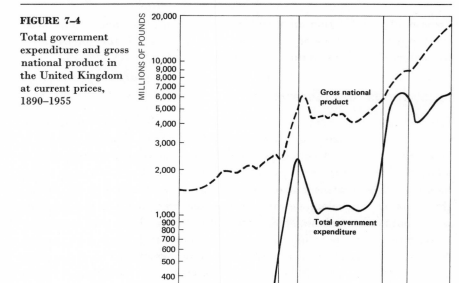

and Wiseman's study of public sector growth in Britain from 1890 to 1955 partakes of this spirit of investigation.[9] They concluded that *exogenous* factors were of great importance in explaining the evolution of public expenditure. Whereas the Wagner analysis featured a self-contained model of interaction between public and private sectors, to Peacock and Wiseman the data seemed to reveal that outside forces (such as war or a major world monetary crises) brought about responses changing the relative balance between public and private sector. And whereas Wagner's "law" seemed to require that public sector expenditure expand in proportion to GNP, it seemed obvious to Peacock and Wiseman that the growth in public expenditure was less regular and quite different from the pattern of GNP growth. Instead, the pattern of public sector growth in the United Kingdom seemed to be subject to a *displacement effect*. Major social disturbances such as war, of course, changed resource use dramatically. Figure 7.4. illustrates that "the plateaus of expenditure establish themselves at successively higher levels, and the share of government expenditure in national product remains much greater after the wars than it was immediately before them."[10]

The revenue side of the budget seemed to be the key. Wagner had foreseen the possibility of lulls in the growth of public sector activity due to the lack of revenue, but Peacock and Wiseman made this the center of their hypothesis. We have observed that both the institutional structure of the budget process and the nature of public goods encourage a cleavage between ideas about public expenditure levels and ideas as to a reasonable burden of taxation. Economic change may very well bring about new ideas concerning public expenditure, but "when societies are not being subjected to unusually violent pressures or disturbances, people's ideas about the 'tolerable' burden of government taxation tend to be fairly stable."[11] In periods of peace the types and levels of taxation available to government officials are limited by political considerations. Thus, according to Peacock and Wiseman, government activity may rise in such periods "but if so it will do so at a steady and relatively unspectacular rate, curbed by such economic factors as the disincentive effects of high marginal rates of tax and also by popular notions of tolerable tax burdens and by the degree of political control exercised by the citizens over their government, but encouraged by a rising output per head."[12]

As we turn to examine data of American public sector growth, let us remind ourselves that several of the insights gained in our outline of budgeting procedure and behavior will be useful. We recall, for example, that the presence of *costs in decision making* leads to various formal and informal institutional arrangements which attempt with mixed success to increase decision-making efficiency. We examined various problems which bear on our present inquiry into the absolute and relative growth of public sector activity. The *choice participation problem* occurs when the individual's marginal cost of entering into the decision making are greater than expected benefits. When changes in the institutional structure do not account for this problem, the forthcoming composition of expenditures is likely to be unpopular, especially if many individuals

---

[9] Alan T. Peacock and Jack Wiseman, *The Growth of Public Expenditure in the United Kingdom* (Princeton, N.J.: Princeton University Press, 1961).
[10] *Ibid*, p. 26.
[11] *Ibid.*, p. 26.
[12] *Ibid.*, p. 27.

feel that they have been somehow disenfranchised by the political process. In the process of economic development the dimensions of the choice participation problem change according to the responsiveness of the institutional structure. If we assume that bureaucrats continually desire to expand their respective areas of responsibility, the diminution of voter control occasioned by the choice participation problem will lead to overexpansion of the public sector. Again, the importance of the *free-rider problem* and the *diffusion effect* depends on the institutions of budgeting and how they change through time in response to political, social, and economic development.

Public sector growth is further illuminated when we recall some of the "*games*" *budgeters play*. We should keep in mind the costs and benefits affecting the behavior of elected and appointed public officials. We recall, for example, their frequent resort to *conflict-reducing conventions* which change the process of budgeting and in turn affect the size and composition of the budget.

A CURSORY VIEW OF PUBLIC SECTOR GROWTH IN THE UNITED STATES, COLONIAL TIMES THROUGH 1900[13]

Three striking phenomena are evident from a cursory review of U.S. public spending. First, we observe the drastic changes in spending during *wars*. The postwar trends seem to display the *displacement effect* predicted by Peacock and Wiseman but not to the extent of Britain's experience. Second, public sector activity (especially that of states and localities) seems to be significantly affected by *the business cycle* (and vice versa). Third, there seem to be discernible *stages* in our economic development which have called forth a changing and growing role for the public sector. Now let us describe this process with occasional references to the hypotheses and models already presented.

COLONIAL TIMES THROUGH 1860

COLONIAL TIMES THROUGH 1800

Although many Americans later embraced the laissez faire formula for public-private relationships, the prevailing economic philosophy during colonial times and the early years of nationhood was mercantilism.[14] A popular notion is that the brave souls who first settled the land were seeking religious and political freedom. No doubt some of them were, but profit was the primary motive for most settlers and those who furnished funds for their transportation. And the public sectors of Europe and their American extensions attempted to provide the legal and fiscal framework (through land grants, legal monopolies, and various types of tariffs and taxes) necessary for profitable economic ventures.

The often noted coincidence of the Declaration of Independence and Adam Smith's *Wealth of Nations* in 1776 reflected, among other things, a change in economic philosophy away from mercantilism and towards a laissez faire role for the public sector. However, mercantilism was an important element of the political philosophy of the Federalists— especially as articulated by Alexander Hamilton. As Secretary of the Treasury he advocated encouraging growth in trade through subsidies, tariffs, treaties, navigation laws, and establishment of a central bank. Federal government spending increased from a $4.3 million average in 1789–1791 to $10.8 million in 1800. The war had left the government with what most people felt was a huge debt, but Hamilton showed no particular interest in paying it off. In fact he used it as a macroeconomic tool, increasing payments when money was tight and postponing them when money was easy. Instead of being reduced, the debt increased from $77.2 million in 1789–1791 to $83.0 million in 1800.

Even so, expenditures on internal improvements were miniscule. The federal budget then, as now, was oriented towards defense—45 percent went to interest on the debt and another 40 percent went to current defense spending. Localities made allocations for internal improvements, but they seem appallingly low by almost any standards. There were few

[13] Excellent sources for more information are: Charles H. Hession and Hyman Sardy, *Ascent to Affluence* (Boston: Allyn & Bacon, 1969); Paul Studenski and Herman E. Krooss, *Financial History of the United States* (New York: McGraw-Hill, 1952); D. C. North, *The Economic Growth of the United States, 1790–1860* (Englewood Cliffs, N.J.: Prentice-Hall, 1961); Frank W. Tuttle and Joseph M. Perry, *An Economic History of the United States* (Cincinnati: South-Western, 1970); Joseph M. Peterson and Ralph Gray, *Economic Development of the United States* (Homewood, Ill.: Irwin, 1969); Shepard B. Clough and Theodore F. Morburg, *The Economic Basis of American Civilization*, (New York: Crowell, 1968); Herman E. Krooss, *American Economic Development*, 2nd ed. (Englewood Cliffs, N.J.: Prentice-Hall, 1966). For historical statistics and sources see Department of Commerce, *Historical Statistics of the United States: Colonial Times to 1957*, and National Bureau of Economic Research, *Trends in the American Economy in the Nineteenth Century* (Princeton N.J.: Princeton University Press, 1960).

[14] The term mercantilism refers to a broad group of sixteenth-, seventeenth-, and eighteenth-century ideas and practices that prescribed various types of government aid to the burgeoning merchant class. The government was to take an active part on behalf of certain merchants and industries by granting monopolies, setting up tariffs, and so on.

roads and no municipal water and sewage systems. Local expenditures ranged from zero in many frontier towns to $1.80 per capita in New York City.

JEFFERSONIANISM, 1800–1809

The contrasts between Jefferson's and Hamilton's brands of Federalism are well known. Hamilton's economic philosophy was a strange mixture of mercantilism and Adam Smith. He was impressed with Smith's vision of the growth of national wealth through economic development. He also shared Smith's insights into the interdependence of the different sectors of the economy. However, his vision of intersector growth was national rather than international, and he felt government intervention necessary to promote trade and industrialization in the Northeast.

Jefferson also appreciated the concept of an interdependent economy, but his version was more attuned to the French physiocrats' than to Smith's. He saw land as the source of true wealth and landowning farmers as the ideal base of democracy. Jefferson had no desire to promote rapid development in trade, industrialization, and population concentration. The political and social virtues fostered by the secure independence of the farmer were superior to those engendered by the necessary interdependence of the factory, the market, and the city. The role of federal government should be confined to maintaining law and order, enforcing contracts, and national defense. Above all, the government should work to *reduce* rather than increase interdependence and possible conflict among individuals, regions, and nations.

A major goal of Albert Gallatin, Jefferson's Secretary of the Treasury, was to dismantle the Federalists' fiscal system. Another somewhat conflicting goal, reducing the federal debt, necessitated retention of a system of tariffs; but the Federalists' internal taxes were repealed. As it turned out, success of the administration in reducing the debt (to $57 million in 1808) depended on greatly increased foreign trade (and increased customs revenue) rather than the reductions in expenditures for which Gallatin had hoped.

Unfortunately, this increase in trade, a result of the Napoleonic wars, was short-lived, since it jeopardized American neutrality at a time when meager defense spending had left us unprepared for war. Both the French and British forbade our trading with the other and seized our ships that disobeyed. Jefferson's response (aimed primarily at the British—since the French navy had been destroyed) was to threaten and later enact a counterembargo. The Embargo Act of 1807 prohibited American vessels from visiting foreign ports, forbade foreign vessels from carrying American goods, and put restrictions on imports. The embargo, a rather noble attempt at substituting nonviolent coercion for war, failed. The British, owing to the revolution in Spain, were able to shift their trade to South America. Moreover, the little damage inflicted on Britain affected mainly the working class, who at that time had little power in Parliament. But the embargo had disastrous effects at home. Exports fell from $108 million in 1807 to $22.4 million in 1808. Several hundred thousand workers were unemployed, and many firms connected with foreign trade went bankrupt. The effect on federal revenues was devastating; they fell from $17.1 million in 1808 to $7.8 million in 1809. This situation was relieved only partially by the passage of the Non-intercourse Act, which prohibited only trade with Britain and France. Yet, as war became increasingly imminent, Gallatin clung to his goals of debt reduction, sole reliance on import duties for revenue, and minimal defense expenditures. He did, however, work out an ill-fated theory of war finance.

THE WAR OF 1812

Gallatin's plan for financing war with Britain was to use existing taxes to meet the regular governmental expenses while *borrowing* to meet the extraordinary costs of war. Supposedly this would minimize the disruptive effects on the economy. But after one successful loan the government's credit rating dropped precariously, and further offerings returned only a fraction of the loan's face values. The federal debt soared from a previous low of $45.2 million in 1811 to $127.3 million in 1815. The only other revenue source available was import duties—hardly to be relied upon during a war with the world's greatest sea power. Customs averaged only $8.8 million during the period 1812–1815. In 1813 Congress finally enacted some internal taxes (on slaves, buildings, distilled spirits, financial instruments, and several other licenses and excises), but these produced little revenue and failed to ease the fiscal crisis. These difficulties were augmented by a breakdown of the nation's financial system, which, after the closing of the Bank of the United States in 1811, had become dependent on the often depreciated notes of state banks. The role of the federal level of the public sector in encouraging growth left something to be desired.

THE PRECONDITIONS FOR "TAKEOFF"

During Jefferson's two terms and the War of 1812, in spite of the difficulties mentioned above, the economy had grown in its ability to produce an agricultural surplus. After the war this trend was accentuated. Moreover, while the philosophy of limited intervention prevailed for the federal finances, state and local governments greatly increased expenditures on the social overhead capital so necessary for increased trade, specialization, and subsequent industrial growth.

The buildup of private and social capital in the period between the wars was erratic and at times misdirected. The liberal land sales policies of the federal government had the salutory effect of rapidly expanding the frontier; at the same time, however, they had the effect of reallocating capital and labor to regions where transportation facilities were not yet established and the economies of interdependent markets could not be exploited.[15]

The leading sectors of the economy during this period were the staple crops—cotton in the South and grains in the Midwest. This dependence on agricultural exports led, in the now familiar pattern of developing nations, to wide income fluctuations in response to price changes in the international market. Immediately after the war, growing industrialization and poor harvests in Europe led to a great European demand for our staples. This produced a land boom in the South and West—which, fed by speculation and easy credit, turned into a " bust " when increased supplies here and in Europe forced prices down. The ensuing depression lasted from 1818 to 1823. After slow growth in the 1820s, profits from the export of staples inaugurated another boom in 1836–1837. This boom also featured increased land speculation, a rapidly expanding money supply, and investment from abroad. It was followed by a severe depression, which lasted from 1839 to 1843. A similar depression occurred in 1858–1859, again triggered by a crisis in international credit! In the latter case, however, the boom and downturn were augmented by events in the domestic industrial sector, especially the railroad industry.

The Schumpeter analysis offers considerable insight into the time paths of these fluctuations. Their initial impetuses, although not strictly " innovations," were responses to situations *outside* the system, and they led from true innovation to overexpansion by imitators and thence to depression. The long lag between the shift in demand for the staple and the increase in supply, as new land was finally brought into production, provided ample opportunity for the turning of profits, for continued land speculation and eventual overproduction. Liberal credit expansion also contributed to the three upswings. In the 1815–1817 boom, credit was provided primarily by the state banks; however, British exporters also provided credit on the rising quantities of finished goods shipped to America. Inflationary pressure was further fueled by the Second Bank of the United States, chartered in 1816. It expanded credit excessively in 1818 and 1819 and then, when the crash came, tightened credit precariously.

REGIONAL DIFFERENCES AND PUBLIC SECTOR RESPONSE

Now let us consider the character of development in the South, Midwest, and Northeast and examine the part played by the public sector in each case. The economy of the South depended increasingly on the staple crop, cotton. The mode of production was the plantation system based on slavery. Cotton production was highly labor-intensive, so that most of the "capital formation" took the form of investment in slaves. Substantial economies of scale encouraged an increase in the average size of farms to 800–1000 acres. The nature of economic development gave little impetus to public activity. Urbanization was relatively slow; the economic system did not demand free public education; and while some expenditures were made on improving transportation, nature had already provided navigable rivers and ports. The uneven distribution of wealth, lack of urbanization, and the nature of the transportation system provided insufficient aggregate demand to allow for substantial development of marketing and manufacturing industries.

Development in the Midwest was quite different from that in the South. Initially farms were small and dispersed. As transportation facilities were developed, subsidiary industries grew up in small towns to process farm surpluses. Small manufacturers of retail goods also appeared in response to increased consumer demand. Southern agricultural development

[15] According to some economists this reallocation and others actually retarded growth and caused a decline in per capita income in the 1820s. See Robert F. Martin, *National Income in the United States, 1799–1938* (New York: National Industrial Conference Board, 1939). For an opposing argument and several other views see Simon Kuznets, "National Income Estimates for the United States prior to 1870," *Journal of Economic History* (Spring 1952), and W. N. Parker and F. Whaternby, "The Growth of Output before 1840," *Trends in the American Economy in the Nineteenth Century* (Princeton, N.J.: Princeton University Press, 1960).

enjoyed economies of scale and increased specialization in a single crop; development in the Midwest gained from the *externalities* involved in interdependent growth of several sectors. *Consequently, the Midwest development encouraged relatively more public sector involvement in transportation and education.* Innovations in transportation were rapid; the steamboat greatly enhanced industrial development in the Mississippi Valley from 1815 to 1860; the opening of the Erie Canal in 1825 dramatically reduced transportation costs between midwestern and northeastern urban areas and ports; and still later the railroad facilitated this route of trade.

Economic development in the Northeast immediately after the war was mixed. The region continued to develop important lines of trade and communication. Efficient transport of merchandise to America and of cotton and other staples to Europe required that the same vessels be used for both. The northeastern ports, especially New York, had acquired an early lead in transport facilities, banking, and other institutional arrangements which helped them become the center of trade. Innovations, such as an effective auction system, the transatlantic packet service, and later the Erie Canal, greatly facilitated trade and insured New York's dominance.

Manufacturing in these states was subject to both favorable and unfavorable influences. During the embargo and the war, manufacturing had benefited tremendously from growing markets protected from foreign competition. After the war, however, these industries were subjected to severe foreign competition, and only the fittest survived. One of these, the cotton textile industry of New England, developed an innovative factory system that was quite successful. This industry, in true Schumpeterian fashion, also spawned the textile machinery industry. Together, these two industries trained the technicians and entrepreneurial talent which would, in the 1830s, introduce the factory system to many other industries—woolen manufactures, men's clothing, boots and shoes, and so on. In the 1840s and 1850s the metalworking skills and techniques developed for textile machinery were put to use in the locomotive and machine tool industries.

THE PUBLIC SECTOR, SOCIAL CAPITAL, AND TAKEOFF

It is a popular notion that America's industrialization in the eighteenth century occurred in the context of a laissez faire economic system and that very little public sector activity took place or was required. This view is understandable if one focuses on the Jeffersonian and Jacksonian philosophies of government which held sway at the federal level during much of this period. However, the part played by state and local governments—especially in providing social capital for the expansion of markets—was quite significant.

The construction of the Erie Canal has been singled out by Schumpeter and others as a major innovative spark in igniting spending on *social overhead capital*. The canal, financed by state bonds, was begun in 1817 and completed in 1825. Governor Clinton of New York was a key figure in this dramatic act of public sector entrepreneurship. When completed, the canal revolutionized trade between East and West. The average freight charge for shipments between Buffalo and New York dropped from 19.12 cents per ton-mile (via wagon and the Hudson River) to 1.68 cents per ton-mile. This changed the economic structure of both regions. The western states were now able to dispose of their agricultural surpluses at higher eastern prices. At the same time they were able to shift from subsistence farming toward production of staple crops for which they had a comparative advantage. The improvement in the West's terms of trade provided surplus real income and a larger consumer market for Eastern manufactures. As trade increased, economies of scale were realized both in eastern manufacturing and western farming. Profits to manufacturing induced new investment both in finished goods industries and in construction and manufacturing equipment industries as plants were expanded. During the 1830s and 1840s trade along this route continually expanded, reaching $10 million in the mid-thirties and $94 million in 1853.

The impact of the Erie canal and other successful *public-private social capital ventures* was dramatic. Between 1820 and 1837 state governments borrowed approximately $175 million. In fact, Schumpeter suggests that the public and private imitators of the Erie canal offer an excellent example of how an innovation can lead to expansion, induced investment, *overexpansion* (particularly of credit), and finally to financial panic and recession. One important aspect of the shift in resources was that labor was taken from agriculture and other short-run production and employed in long-run capital production. Thus, while consumer income and demand were increasing, the supply of consumer goods was temporarily curtailed. Meanwhile, the money supply was expanded precariously by state banks and the Second National Bank under the directorship of Nicholas Biddle. The money supply fluctuated dramatically upon anticipation of the withdrawal of the National Bank's federal deposits after Andrew Jackson's overwhelming victory in 1832. However, Jackson subsequently distributed federal funds to the state banks and added further inflationary pressure by distributing funds from public lands sales to the state governments.

The financial activities of the public sector aggravated the severe depression of 1837–1843. The default and repudiation of many state obligations accentuated the financial crisis in the private sector. Between 1841 and 1842 eight states defaulted on interest payments on bonds issued during the social capital craze. An important result was loss of confidence by British lenders, who added to the credit crunch by withdrawing their funds.

As a result of the depression, several *fiscal constraints* were placed upon the role of state legislatures in public and private finance. Many state constitutions were changed so that referenda were required when state-backed obligations were incurred. In addition, the chartering and regulation of state banks was made much more stringent.

Let us briefly summarize some factors that influenced economic development and public sector activity during this transitional period. The economy was still essentially agricultural, with staple crops providing a surplus (over subsistence) for export. Growing dependence on the international market made the economy subject to its fluctuations in prices, made all the more volatile by time lags in the sequence of higher prices, land clearance, and finally overabundance of crops. Besides land settlement, surplus capital secured during these expansionary periods was devoted to building social overhead capital in the form of education and better transportation facilities.

Different levels of the public sector played quite different roles. Federal government activity, except for very active land acquisition and subsequent sale to the public, was relegated to a passive role in the philosophy of Jeffersonian and Jacksonian democracy. In the 1820s and 1830s state governments aggressively mobilized private and public funding of social overhead capital.

Even so, the importance of the public sector in providing services and in generating income was still not large relative to total income. R. F. Martin has estimated that in 1819 all governments generated only 1.9 percent of total income, and in 1839 the figure was 2.4 percent.[16] The relative unimportance of the public sector as a factor *directly* affecting aggregate demand is perhaps fortunate, since, as we have seen, federal and state governments both followed policies that were usually procyclical. At the same time, however, we have seen that public sector policy, especially at the state level, encouraged the buildup of social capital during this period.

THE TAKEOFF PERIOD, 1843–1860

Let us continue to use the Rostovian schema in our examination of private and public sector activity in the period 1843–1860.[17] Rostow's model is useful to us primarily for pedagogical reasons. It would be difficult to make the case that the period 1843–1860 can be termed "take-off" in any precise way. In the first place, the data on industrial production and the like are scanty. Second, the economic relationships in Rostow's model are not specified well enough for us to be able to easily differentiate between stages.[18] With reference to the takeoff stage itself, most studies indicate that periods in the 1820s and 1830s as well as the period after the Civil War also may qualify. For example, Rostow claims that takeoff occurs with a change in the rate of productive investment from less than 5 percent of national income to over 10 per cent; but R. E. Gallman concludes that this rate ran between 9 and 14 percent in the periods before and after Rostow's "takeoff."

Nevertheless, several studies of American economic growth do in fact support the view that an upward jump or shift took place in national income in the late 1830s and early 1840s.[19] The paucity of good data precludes any final conclusions, but estimates of gross national product

---

[16] Martin, *National Income in the United States, 1799–1938*, p. 87.

[17] Rostow designated the period 1843–1860 as the American "Takeoff." He sees it as involving two different periods of expansion: " . . . the first, that of the 1840s, marked by railway and manufacturing development, mainly confined to the East—this occurred while the West and South digested the extensive agricultural expansion of the previous decade; the second the great railway push into the Middle West during the 1850's marked by a heavy inflow of foreign capital. By the opening of the Civil War the American economy of North and West, with real momentum in its heavy-industry sector, is judged to have taken off." *The Stages of Economic Growth*, p. 38.

[18] Some pertinent critiques are: S. Kuznets, " Notes on the Take-Off," in *The Economics of Take-Off into Sustained Growth*, ed. W. W. Rostow (New York: St. Martin's, 1963), and reviews of Rostow's *The Stages of Economic Growth* by W. N. Parker in *American Economic Review*, December 1960, p. 550; A. K. Caincross, *The Economic History Review*, April 1961, p. 450; and D. C. North, "A Note on Professor Rostow's 'Take-Off' into Self-Sustained Growth," *The Manchester School*, January 1958.

[19] See Goldsmith, "Long Period Growth in Income and Product, 1839–1960," in *New Views on American Economic Development* (Cambridge, Mass.: Schenkman, 1965), pp. 337–361; R. L. Andereano, "Trends and Variations in Economic Welfare in the United States before the Civil War," *ibid.*, pp. 131–167; R. E. Gallman, "Estimates of American National Product Made before the Civil War," *ibid.*, pp. 168–186; R. E. Gallman, "Gross National Product in the United States, 1834–1909," in *Output, Employment and Productivity in the United States after 1800*, National Bureau of Economic Research Studies in Income and Wealth, vol. 30 (New York: Columbia University Press, 1966); Martin, *National Income in the United States, 1799–1938*.

TABLE 7–1		1820	1830	1840	1850	1860
Population growth in the United States, 1820–1860	Population in millions	9.6	12.8	17.0	23.1	31.2

show a five-year jump from $2.32 billion in 1849 to $3.53 billion in 1854, an increase of over 50 percent.

The two leading sectors were agriculture and railroads. The export of staple crops remained highly dependent on world prices. Even more specialization was accomplished as transportation facilities were improved, opening the way for further benefits from comparative advantage. At the same time many innovations were introduced—crop rotation, fertilization, new livestock breeds, new plows, the reaper, the thresher, and other types of machinery.

The basic innovation was the railroad, and its growth spawned innovations not only in trade and marketing but in machine manufacturing and the iron and steel industries as well. Moreover, it further encouraged the agricultural revolution in the Midwest—a phenomenon begun in the canal era.

As trade increased between the Midwest and the Northeast, significant *economies of scale* and *externalities* were experienced in the iron industry. This resulted from its vertical integration not only with railroads but with other industries as well. The economies of scale and changes in technology here created downward shifts in firms' cost curves in other industries, leading to new innovations in related industries which used iron as an input (stoves, farm machinery, etc.) and those which produced inputs for iron production (the mining of coal and iron ore). Later in the 1850s simple light-metal products were manufactured which featured standardized interchangeable parts. Power was put to use to run specialized machines. Specialized machine tools replaced many of the skills of the craftsman. These firms turned out such products as firearms, timepieces, and tools.

INVESTMENT AND THE PUBLIC SECTOR

In a country just developing its industrial sector, the crucial question is whether or not conditions are favorable for a sustained flow of investment funds. What part did the public sector play in encouraging investment?

As in the 1820s and 1830s, different levels of the public sector took different directions. The federal level did little to provide credit, leaving to states the responsibility of regulating banking. The so-called Independent Treasury system was reinstituted, which required that Treasury funds be kept out of private banks. Thus in the early 1850s, when the federal budget was running substantial surpluses, this policy acted to drain the nation's money supply. States encouraged the growth of state banks; the system expanded from 696 banks in 1844 with loans of $265 million and notes in circulation of $75 million to 1562 banks in 1860 with loans of $692 million and notes in circulation of $207 million. Moreover, states and localities often joined with private individuals in quasi-public financial ventures. In outlining the growth of such mixed operations, Hartz points out that the public-private joint firm originated in the late eighteenth century in banking and began to have considerable impact in transportation ventures in the 1820s.[20]

SOCIAL AND POLITICAL CHANGE AND PUBLIC SECTOR ACTIVITY

Demographic changes from 1820 to 1860 profoundly changed the social structure of the United States and the prevailing attitudes as to the proper role of the public sector. Rostow has noted that the United States and a small company of other European-settled countries escaped many of the constraints on growth present in traditional, stabilized societies, where vested interests resist change. Social organization in the United States was in a continual state of flux. Table 7.1 offers a major part of the explanation; population more than tripled in the 40 years from 1820 to 1860. Immigration continually undermined the social tendencies to hold certain groups in their " stations." Thus considerable mobility was offered to the the the laborer and entrepreneur.[21]

---

[20] L. Hartz, *Economic Policy and Democratic Thought: Pennsylvania, 1776–1860* (Cambridge, Mass.: Harvard University Press, 1948).

[21] The extent of mobility and its effect on wage rates have often been overemphasized. The historian Frederick Jackson Turner [*The Frontier in American History* (New York: Holt, Rinehart & Winston, 1921), pp. 259, 275] presented the theory that the West offered a " safety valve " to the labor market in the Northeast, thus draining off surplus labor and keeping wages high. Later historians and economists elaborated the idea. Actually, wages in the Northeast were not high enough to finance travel to and acquisition of land in the West. See, for example, C. H. Dankof, " Economic Validity of the Safety-Valve Doctrine," *The Journal of Economic History*, vol. 1 (1941), pp. 96–106.

TABLE 7–2

Percentage distribution of
U.S. population by region,
1800–1860

Year	Continental United States	North-east	South	North Central	West
1800	100.0	50.0	50.0	—	—
1820	100.0	45.4	45.4	9.2	—
1840	100.0	39.6	40.7	19.8	—
1860	100.0	33.8	35.4	29.0	1.9

Source: Hession and Sardy, *Ascent to Affluence*, p. 321, as adapted from P. B. Kenen, "A Statistical Survey of Basic Trends," in Seymour E. Harris, ed., *American Economic History* (New York: McGraw-Hill, 1961), p. 68.

The impetus of immigration, together with the freedom from traditional constraints, necessitated continual reallocation of resources. These conditions plus the prevailing Jeffersonian political philosophy ruled out the use of the public sector to resist economic change. Indeed, we have observed that state governments, far from resisting change, acted instead as Schumpeterian entrepreneurs in building the social overhead capital so necessary for industrialization.

Although the public sector participated directly in the financing of social overhead capital, the actual income it generated remained small relative to national income between 1820 and 1860. The situation in which public sector activity increases as a percent of national income—as prescribed by Wagner's law—did not develop. But during this phase the state and local governments were taking on new functions—in the true Wagnerian sense—in *response* to the changing technology of economic development. As we have observed, the public sector was active in financing canals and then railroads. But roads, water supply, sewage, bridges, and other business-oriented facilities were also built. Expenditures on education and fire and police protection also increased. However, localities in general were slow to respond to the social needs created by the growth of industrial cities. Since rapid immigration kept wages low, the political power of the new immigrants also tended to be low. The diversity of immigrant nationalities made social and political consensus difficult to achieve. Clubs, lodges, and other social organizations developed along ethnic lines rather than in terms of the entire community. When the political potential of the immigrants was eventually organized, it followed these neighborhood lines; consequently, no comprehensive political structure developed. Coalitions of interest groups would obtain power and seek to further the interests of their groups. Municipal government was often corrupt, the rewards going to a favored few. This political and social balkanization provided no broad planning and was unresponsive to the social needs being created.

On the national level political lines tended to polarize in the 1840s and 1850s. There were two parties, the Whigs and the Democrats, and although both parties had a rather limited view of the possibilities of federal action, their platforms favored the philosophy that the public sector should encourage economic development. There was substantial disagreement on just how the federal government should proceed; the prescription of each party followed in general the interests of the sections and income groups from which the party drew support. The Democrats were more conservative and generally represented the agrarian interests. They expressed fear of the potential financial monopolies of Philadelphia and New York; instead, they favored competition in banking and no central bank. Tariffs and land sales were favored as revenue sources; however, both revenues and expenditures should be kept low.

The Whigs desired more active public sector support of industry. They insisted that high tariffs, by protecting domestic industry, would help the whole country. A national bank and more federal influence over banking were also favored. The Whigs also proposed federal support of internal improvements designed to facilitate commerce. These goals, however, were consistently thwarted by the Democrats, who held power for most of this period.

Successful political accommodation between agriculture and industry had been achieved in the Northeast, but the conflict between the Northeast and the South could not be resolved peacefully. The two regions, as noted, were developing in different directions, the southern economy becoming more and more dependent on cotton and tobacco. The southern manufacturing, transportation, and marketing industries were outstripped by those of the Northeast, the latter experiencing economies of scale and other externalities of growth. The concentration of trade, manufacturing, and banking in the Northeast was a growing concern of the southern planters, who felt that they were being exploited. The panic of 1857, although weathered better by the South than by the North, accentuated southern frustration over dependence upon northern financial institutions.

In 1800 a rough political "equilibrium" obtained between North and South. Table 7.2 illustrates the shifts in regional population which ultimately shifted the political power of the regions. The South's portion of the population had fallen to 40.7 percent in 1840 and to only 35.4 percent in 1860. As northern interests became more influential, the role of the state changed. Higher protective tariffs were allowed. The northern manufacturers were free to trade with the South, but the South could not import from Europe. The terms of trade disadvantaged the South relative to other suppliers of staples to Europe because high tariffs prevented the purchase of European finished goods and thus created a dollar shortage in Europe. The political balance between the Whigs and Democrats was disrupted by the demise of the Whigs, the birth of the Republican Party, and finally the dissolution of the Democratic Party in 1859.

THE ROLE OF THE PUBLIC SECTOR DURING THE CIVIL WAR

The public sector's role during the Civil War was a significant departure from its role in previous wars. There had been wars in the past that touched every individual in the countries involved, but never before had the public sector been required to play such an important role in allocating society's resources towards the war effort.

Neither the Union nor the Confederacy had the fiscal know-how to finance and organize the massive reallocation of resources required, and both managed badly. As it turned out, victory for the North depended heavily on its reallocating its resources without experiencing the almost complete disruption of the economy which occurred in the South.

CONFEDERATE PUBLIC FINANCING

The wartime public finances of both North and South were chaotic. The South began with no fiscal system at all, while the Union relied for revenue primarily on tariffs which would have been inadequate even had foreign trade continued at its prewar level. It is understandable that, as the end drew near, the borrowing power and currency of the Confederacy disintegrated. What many students of the period find more significant is that the breakdown of the South's fiscal apparatus was a major factor in the outcome of the war.[22] They contend that, long before the armies of the Confederacy were threatened with defeat, fiscal maladjustment was wreaking havoc not only on the process of directing resources to the war effort but on every market within the economy.

Memminger, Treasury Secretary for the Confederacy, proposed a tax program much too conservative for the impending war effort. The few trifling taxes and the small bond issue put all of the pressure on currency issue. The Produce Loan Act of 1861 provided that government 8 percent bonds could be purchased on pledges to pay in agricultural commodities. Only about two-thirds of the $34 million of these pledges was collected, and, owing to the Union blockade, the Confederate government was able to ship only a small amount to Europe for trade.

As the war intensified, Memminger was forced to rely on currency issue. Over $311 million in bonds and currency were issued during 1861. In later years the amounts increased: 1862—$268 million; 1863—$517 million; 1864—$456 million; the total exceeded $1.5 billion during the life of the Confederacy. It was not until 1863 that Memminger was able to extract realistic tax legislation from the Confederate Congress. The law included sales, excise, property, and income taxes as well as a 10 percent tax *in kind* on agricultural products. Even so, the revenue raised from taxes represented only 1 percent of the total.

Drastic fiscal action would have been required to hold the economy of the South together during the war years. Basic to the problem was the Union blockade. Thwarting it would have required both a concerted military effort and government organization of marketing. Even without military victory at sea, however, some semblance of economic order could have been achieved by government use of subsidies, credits, and the like to direct the flow of resources and keep businesses intact. The demise of the planter economy and the increasing inflation caused by excessive currency issue engendered the collapse of the market system. The government lacked the expertise to organize and regulate the production, transportation, and distribution processes required for the war effort.

UNION PUBLIC FINANCE

On the Union side, Congress was quick to react when it became obvious that expenditures would greatly exceed original estimates. In August of 1861 Congress instituted a property tax and an income tax and raised customs duties. Congress also authorized abolition of the Independent Treasury system, so that the Treasury's fiscal actions could be tied in directly not only with the specie available in its own subtreasuries (where all federal funds were kept in the form of specie) but with that available in the private banking system as well.

[22] C. Eaton, *A History of the Southern Confederacy* (New York: Macmillan, 1959) and C. W. Ramsdell, *Behind the Lines in the Southern Confederacy* (Baton Rouge: Louisiana State University Press, 1944).

TABLE 7–3

Expenditures, revenues and
debt of the Union,
1861–1865 (in millions of
dollars)

Year	Expenditures	Revenues	Surplus or deficit	Total gross debt
1861	$ 66.5	$ 41.5	$ — 25.0	$ 90.6
1862	474.8	52.0	—422.8	524.2
1863	714.7	112.7	—602.0	1119.8
1864	865.3	264.6	—600.7	1815.8
1865	1297.6	333.7	—963.8	2677.9

Secretary Chase, however, attempted to retain the Independent Treasury system in the face of a still woefully inadequate revenue system, increased military requirements, and a worsening trade situation, by borrowing $150 million from the private banks to be paid in specie. Since private banks held only $63 million in specie and its turnover had been reduced by hoarding, a crisis was precipitated, and in December of 1861 private banks and the federal government suspended payment in specie. Congress took the initiative to provide for the issue of Treasury notes to be used as legal tender. Representative E. G. Spaulding, a member of the House Ways and Means Committee, argued that the revenues (to include the government bond sales) would be exhausted within thirty days. Secretary Chase reluctantly endorsed this view. In February of 1862 the Legal Tender Act passed, authorizing the issue of $150 million in the Treasury notes which soon became known as " greenbacks."

Even though these notes were made legal tender for almost all debts and were convertible into federal bonds, their value was discounted, falling by 25 percent the same year and reaching a low of only 35 cents to the dollar in mid-1864. These further depreciations came as a result of additional issues of greenbacks which brought the total to $450 million. Looked at another way, the depreciation of the greenback was simply a sympton of the perverse fiscal policy of relying primarily on credit to finance the war. Our brief introduction to macroeconomic policy was enough to demonstrate that diversion of resources from private to public use requires a corresponding *exchange* of spending power. But without an adequate overhaul of the revenue structure the public sector depended on increasing its own spending power relative to that of the private sector. It would, of course, have been much less inflationary to obtain purchasing power by selling bonds instead of by issuing notes which were themselves legal tender; however, the first option, as noted, was not open in 1862.

The issue of greenbacks was only one factor leading to inflation. The public sector continued to borrow as much as possible from commercial banks. During the war the latter source accounted for 40 percent of revenue, whereas the issue of paper money accounted for only 13 percent. The private banks were far from stable, and all currencies fluctuated according to war news and foreign relations, both of which were usually unfavorable until the late stages of the war.

As the war continued, mobilization occurred at a rate previously unimaginable. Table 7.3 shows the aggregate figures of public sector activity on the Union side. Expenditures soared from $66.5 million to $1297.6 million. Revenues (excluding borrowing), while not keeping pace with expenditures, increased more than eightfold. Increased borrowing was unavoidable, and the debt rose from $90.6 million to $2677.9 million.

The requirements of the war economy led to substantial overhaul of both public and private financial institutions. The Revenue Act of 1862 was very inclusive. In addition to higher customs, new taxes on general sales, excise, inheritances, and licenses were imposed as well as a tax on income that became quite important by the end of the war. The revenues produced by this system increased from $41.5 million in 1861 to $558.0 million in 1866.

War finance has often been singled out by historians as a helpful stimulant to economic development. Union expenditures in the Civil War have been so interpreted, some writers even claiming that the war ushered in the "industrial revolution." The North was in fact suffering from mild unemployment in 1860 and the war industries quickly put these people to work. More important, the war brought tremendous profits to certain industries—providing investment capital for later periods. Actually, however, the net effect of the war was to impede economic development in the Northeast—while the effect on the South was devastating.[23]

It is, of course, impossible to specify how the war altered what might have been. As outlined earlier, significant shifts were taking place in the economic development of both the Midwest and the Northeast. During the war, trade between these two sections continued to expand. The

---

[23] See, for example, T. C. Cochran, "Did the Civil War Retard Industrialization?" *Mississippi Valley Historical Review*, September 1961.

agricultural output of the Northwest increased rapidly. Traffic over the Erie and Pennsylvania railroads increased by 100 percent. United States export of foodstuffs (crude and manufactured) increased from $51 million in 1860 to $126 million in 1862. The tremendous surge in population of the previous periods insured growing aggregate demand, a trend facilitated by the issue of greenbacks and the wartime deficit financing.

The prewar growth in manufacturing in the Northeast continued; however, the war finance was selective: the former leading sectors—cotton textiles and railroad building—now lagged while war industries prospered. In general, technological change slowed down, although mass production and standardization occurred in the industries mentioned. The purchasing policies of the Armed Forces naturally favored the large, dependable firm; consequently, business concentration was encouraged along with economies of scale and standardization.

In the South a desperate attempt was made to industrialize, ultimately failing as a result of financial collapse as well as military defeat. The Jeffersonian tradition of laissez faire constrained the public sector in its necessary function of organizing resource allocation in the southern economy. Workers with industrial skills were scarce, and many were drafted. When machinery broke down, often its parts could not be replaced. Consequently, in the latter stages of the war, recruits were required to furnish their own uniforms and weapons and often had to acquire their own food. In the end the southern economy was almost completely decimated—the railroads destroyed, homes and factories burned, one-third of the livestock eliminated, farm machinery wrecked, and the assets of banks reduced from $51 million in 1860 to $15 million in 1865.

PUBLIC SECTOR GROWTH IN THE DRIVE TO MATURITY, 1866–1900

Let us again, for reasons of pedagogy, resort to the Rostovian schema. During the "drive to maturity" stage economic growth takes on a self-sustained character (some 10–20 percent of national income being steadily invested) and the initial leading sectors are replaced by new ones. We have already questioned Rostow's separation of this stage from others, intimating that this period was in many respects simply a continuation of processes begun earlier. Our primary interest here, however, revolves around the question of intersector technological change and the demands placed upon the public sector. For in a very real sense this ability of public and private institutions to accommodate technological change is crucial to economic development. Both the Marxian and Rostovian models are interesting because they posit various demands on the public sector in the various phases of growth. Obviously it is not necessary for us to accept either their assumptions or predictions in order to use the models as vehicles of exposition.

First consider the economic growth aggregates presented in Tables 7.4 and 7.5. From the period 1869–1873 to the period 1889–1893 real GNP (measured in 1929 prices) almost trebled. And per capita income, even in the face of massive immigration, rose from $223 to $405. As in the prewar period both the agricultural and manufacturing sectors led the economic growth. By 1894 the United States was the world's leading manufacturing nation. Some insight is offered by Robert Gallman's estimates in Table 7.5 of the relative contributions of different sectors of economic growth. Value added is the value of output less the value of commodities used up in production.[24] Since both agriculture and manufacturing contributed greatly to increased production, the shift in relative importance of value added is more gradual than usually supposed. Using 1879 prices, we see that the relative value added in the takeoff period shifted from agriculture's $.99 billion and manufacturing's $.49 billion in 1849 to agriculture's $1.49 billion and manufacturing's $.86 billion in 1859. During thirty years after 1869, agriculture's value added grew from $1.72 billion to $3.92 billion but was surpassed by the value added in manufacturing: $1.08 billion to $6.26 billion.

Additions to the factors of production were an important element of the continued growth. Immigration was high throughout the period. During the 1866–1873 boom it increased from 359,957 (1866) to 459,803 (1873). It slacked off during the ensuing depression to 138,469 in 1877, later fluctuating to an all-time high of 788,992 in 1882 and back down to 334,203 in 1886. Between 1887 and 1893 immigration remained high— between 400,000 and 600,000—but averaged below 300,000 for the remainder of the century. Total population over the years 1869 to 1899 increased from 40 million to 75 million. The nation's stock of capital was also growing dramatically, as shown by Table 7.6. In fact it grew so rapidly that the stock per member of the labor force rose from $3520 in 1869 to

---

[24] Viewed from the income side, it is the net income generated for the factors of production within a particular sector. Since the emphasis is on production of real goods, the total value-added figure differs from GNP in that it excludes all "services" (such as medical care and education) and the costs of transportation and distribution of the final goods.

TABLE 7-4

Gross national product, total and per capita income, in current and 1929 price, 1869-1893

Year	Current prices		1929 prices	
	Total (in billions of dollars)	Per capita (in dollars)	Total (in billions of dollars)	Per capita (in dollars)
1869–1873	6.71	165	9.11	223
1872–1876	7.53	171	11.2	254
1877–1881	9.18	186	16.1	327
1882–1886	11.3	204	20.7	374
1887–1891	12.3	199	24.0	388
1889–1893	13.1	204	26.1	405

Source: *Historical Statistics of the United States*, p. 139 ; see p. 132 for commentary on sources.

TABLE 7-5

Value added by selected industries and value of output of fixed capital, in current and 1879 prices, 1839–1899 (in billions of dollars)

Year	Total	Agriculture	Manufacturing	Mining	Construction	Value of output of fixed capital
			Current prices			
1839	1.04	0.71	0.24	0.01	0.08	0.20
1844	1.09	.69	.31	.01	.08	· · ·
1849	1.40	.83	.45	.02	.11	.31
1854	2.39	1.46	.66	.03	.23	· · ·
1959	2.57	1.50	.82	.03	.23	.62
1869	4.83	2.54	1.63	.13	.54	1.51
1874	5.40	2.53	2.07	.15	.65	· · ·
1879	5.30	2.60	1.96	.15	.59	1.64
1884	7.09	2.84	3.05	.20	1.01	· · ·
1889	7.87	2.77	3.73	.28	1.10	2.82
1894	7.83	2.64	3.60	.29	1.30	· · ·
1899	10.20	3.40	5.04	0.47	1.29	3.47
			1879 prices			
1839	1.09	0.79	0.19	0.01	.11	.25
1844	1.37	.94	.29	.01	.13	· · ·
1849	1.66	.99	.49	.02	.16	.39
1854	2.32	1.32	.68	.03	.30	· · ·
1859	2.69	1.49	.86	.03	.30	.73
1869	3.27	1.72	1.08	.07	.40	1.09
1874	4.30	1.98	1.69	.11	.52	· · ·
1879	5.30	2.60	1.96	.15	.59	1.64
1884	7.30	3.00	3.22	.23	.86	· · ·
1889	8.66	3.24	4.16	.35	.92	2.72
1894	10.26	3.27	5.48	.39	1.12	· · ·
1899	11.75	3.92	6.26	.55	1.02	3.35

TABLE 7–6	Year	Gross capital stock (in billions of dollars)	Gross capital stock per member of the labor force
Growth in capital stock and capital stock per laborer, 1869–1899 (in 1929 prices)	1869	$ 45	$3,520
	1879	71	4,160
	1889	116	5,220
	1899	190	6,660

Source: Simon Kuznets, *Capital in the American Economy* (New York: National Bureau of Economic Research, 1961), Table 3, p. 64. Copyright 1961 by Princeton University Press for the National Bureau of Economic Research.

$6660 in 1899. These additions of capital, which embodied new technology, resulted in a tremendous increase in productivity for the growing work force.

THE CHAOTIC PATH OF MATURITY AND PUBLIC SECTOR ACTIVITY

The growth outlined above was chaotic, and the fluctuations have many of the characteristics of the Marxian, Schumpeterian, and Rostovian models. The fluctuations were keyed by irregular waves of investment and accompanied by monetary difficulties, the public sector playing an important part in creating both problems.

The leading sector after the Civil War continued to be the railroads. In his brief analysis Schumpeter explained the period's growth fluctuations in terms of the pattern of investment in railways and related industries. The rapid rise in railroad mileage continued in *spurts* into the 1870s and then subsided; one last spurt in railroad investment occurred in the middle eighties before a sudden decline in the nineties. As Table 7.7 indicates, the cyclical growth of the period followed the pace of railroad investment. The most severe contraction occurred in October 1873 and lasted for 65 months.

TREASURY POLICY AND FLUCTUATIONS IN INVESTMENT

Public sector policy accentuated the fluctuations in growth in two important ways: by fostering monetary instability and by direct but uneven incentives to railroad investment. The development of the national

Source: Robert E. Gallman, "Commodity Output in the United States, 1839–1899," Conference on Research in Income and Wealth, *Studies in Income and Wealth*, vol. 24 (New York: National Bureau of Economic Research, 1960). Copyright 1960 by Princeton University Press for the National Bureau of Economic Research. Also presented in *Historical Statistics of the United States*, p. 139; see p. 133 for additional commentary on sources.

TABLE 7–7

Business cycles and their
duration, 1867–1897

Business cycle			Duration in months		
Trough	Peak	Trough	Expansion	Contraction	Full cycle
Dec. 1867	June 1869	Dec. 1870	18	18	36
Dec. 1870	Oct. 1873	Mar. 1879	34	65	99
Mar. 1879	Mar. 1882	May 1885	36	38	74
May 1885	Mar. 1887	April 1888	22	13	35
April 1888	July 1890	May 1891	27	10	37
May 1891	Jan. 1893	June 1894	20	17	37
June 1894	Dec. 1895	June 1897	18	18	36

Source : Arthur F. Burns and Wesley C. Mitchell, *Measuring Business Cycles* (New York : National Bureau of Economic Research, 1946), p. 78. Copyright 1946 by the National Bureau of Economic Research.

banking system gave the federal government great potential for controlling the money supply to promote orderly, stable growth. The 1866 legislation had encouraged state banks to join by levying a prohibitory tax of 10 percent on their notes; within four years 90 percent had joined the federal system. This potential, however, was not used wisely. Obsessed with the goal of attaining the prewar parity with the British pound, the Treasury followed a policy of *contracting* the money supply so as to lower domestic prices and raise the value of dollars in terms of pounds. Unfortunately, prices in Britain were also falling, and so, despite stringent and painful monetary restraint, it was not until 1879 that the Treasury achieved its goal. Fortunately, money expansion via checking accounts helped to partially offset the dwindling supply of banknotes. Forced to rely on their own devices for expanding credit, the private banking system developed some questionable practices. Bank deposits grew from $758 million in 1866 to $5,486 million in 1896 as banks pyramided reserves through correspondent banks (which usually were New York banks). Consequently, the failure of any large firm whose stock was held by one of the large New York banks would generate panic throughout all interrelated banks. Commercial banks' tendency to concentrate in short-term rather than long-term investment made these fluctuations even more volatile.

From 1867 to 1879 prices declined 3.5 percent per year, with the most severe declines occurring during the 1873–1879 depression.[25] Finally, in

1879, the price level had been reduced sufficiently to resume specie payments at the pre-Civil War parity between the pound and the dollar. After that time the money supply grew sporadically; the growth rate from 1879 to 1881 was over 19 percent, but from 1892 to 1897 it was zero.

A short-run monetary crisis was brought on in the early 1890s by a combination of factors: an unfavorable balance of trade, a financial crisis in Britain requiring repatriation of investment funds, and suspicion attendant on our use of silver to back dollars.

The movement to use silver backing had had a long history among populist groups and, of course, the silver industry. Farmers and small businessmen, ever suspicious of the powerful eastern banks, were made even more dependent on them by the Treasury's program of decreasing the money supply. The Sherman Silver Purchase Act, a result of these political pressures, required the Treasury to purchase silver and issue Treasury notes. The stipulation that Treasury notes could be redeemed in gold led, along with the other factors mentioned above, to a severe "gold drain."

President Cleveland began desperate efforts to replenish the gold supply: the Silver Act was repealed, four separate bond issues were sold, and finally J. P. Morgan and August Belmont agreed to attempt to "peg" the price of gold by purchasing it for the U.S. Treasury. After all these efforts had failed, Treasury Secretary Carlisle finally succeeded with yet another bond issue. Achieving a more stable monetary situation, however, was not sufficient; and not until the presidency of McKinley did high agricultural yields, new investment in the marketing and retailing industries, the defeat of the silverites, and increased productivity bring full economic recovery.

During this period the nature of public sector aid to the railroads accentuated the fluctuations in economic growth. There is little question that the extension of the railroads created innumerable externalities, so

---

[25] For the 1867–1879 period the money supply [including all gold, state and national banknotes, U.S. notes (greenbacks) and bank deposits] rose only 1.1 percent per year. Moreover, according to Friedman and Schwartz, the rate at which money circulates, its "velocity," declined by 1 percent. As these figures indicate, a healthy 3.6 rise in output occurred in spite of monetary instability and erratic investment. Milton Friedman and A. J. Schwartz, *A Monetary History of the United States, 1867–1960* (Princeton, N.J.: Princeton University Press, 1963), p. 34.

that public sector support was appropriate. But the story of the railroads demonstrates the need for careful consideration for the structure of the industry and the macroeconomic consequences when public sector aid is given.

Huge land grants were given railroad companies to allow them to expand into new areas which were not immediately profitable. Investment in railroads fluctuated as major projects were undertaken with public support and later proved to provide low profit margins.

The long 1873–1879 depression was triggered by the collapse of an attempt to finance the Northern Pacific Railroad. A panic followed as the banks closely connected with the venture failed and sent vibrations through the system.

The process followed the Schumpeterian schema. Since railroads had overextended in the past (in response to governmental stimuli), their returns were low and there was little incentive for new investment.

The 1879 boom was again accompanied by investment overexpansion in the railroad, steel, and related industries, which culminated in panic, banking failures, and a depression in the years 1883–1885. Practically the same order of events recurred in the upswing which lasted until 1893; a downturn followed low returns in railroads, steel, and the like and international financial fluctuations. Again several railroad companies and many banks collapsed.

What peculiar characteristics of the railroad industry made investment so volatile? Our knowledge of externalities provides some interesting insights and explains why the public sector policies were inappropriate. Two types of externalities were present. In the first place, the obvious spillover effects inherent in improved transportation warranted support through the public sector. But, as we have seen, the subsidies given were inappropriate. The gifts of lands acted as a one-shot bonanza which encouraged speculative investment. What was required was stable, long-range support and planning that took account of the related growth of other industries.

A second and related peculiarity of the railroad industry is its large preponderance of fixed to variable capital. This characteristic creates technical externalities which preclude reliance on the free market to ensure efficient, welfare-maximizing competition. Railroads have a high proportion of their capital tied up in engines, cars, and tracks, and their operating costs are relatively low. On routes where there was no competition, monopoly profits were frequently available, but where routes were competitive, pricing often became "cutthroat." When fixed costs are high, short-run marginal costs tend to be less than average costs, making for situations when profit maximization may call for prices which do not cover costs. There were, in fact, rate wars in the 1870s and 1880s. At the same time railroads exploited their monopoly positions on routes where no competition was present. These developments made some sort of regulation by the public sector inevitable.

INDUSTRIAL CONCENTRATION AND NEW DEMAND FOR PUBLIC SECTOR ACTIVITY

The growing necessity of new forms of public sector intervention was not restricted to the railroad industry. A rapid increase in concentration of industry was taking place in several sectors of the economy as gains from better transportation and new technology were consolidated. The firms, seeking to gain monopoly profits and avoid cutthroat competition, turned to holding companies, interlocking directorships, and trusts. The passage of the Sherman Antitrust Act in 1890 did little to dampen the trend, since the courts chose not to enforce it.

The process of industrial concentration and public sector support in certain sectors of the economy resembled uncomfortably the Marxian scenario of development.

THE MARXIAN PREDICTION AND PUBLIC SECTOR ACTIVITY

The developments lead us to reconsider the Marxian prediction that under capitalism the powerful industrialists would manipulate public sector activity to their own ends. Instead of complete domination of the public sector by a few industrialists, we find numerous interest groups at work attempting to use the political sphere to their advantage. The industrialists achieved considerable success by working through the Republican party. The Senate in the 1880s and 1890s became known as the "Millionaires' Club."

The Republicans, however, were not without opposition. White Southerners began to regain control of their region as Republicans relied less on Negro votes. Farmers in all areas were becoming politically active in response to their increased dependence on the finished products of the Northeast. They argued that while their products were being sold under pure competition they were being exploited by the railroads and were buying goods produced under monopoly conditions. Local and state political parties were formed around contacts made in Grange organizations. These groups successfully agitated for state regulation of railroads and warehouses. At first the Supreme Court upheld these state laws.[26] In 1886, however, the court reversed its position[27] and in essence circumvented the states' authority in this area. This ruling, however, necessitated regulation at the federal level, and in 1887 the Interstate Commerce Act was passed.

Federal tariff legislation was an area of public sector activity where these interest groups conflicted. Farmers and small businessmen opposed the high tariffs set by the Republican administrations; however, because the laws contained *direct benefits* for many different interest groups, general antitariff laws continually failed to pass Congress.[28] President Harrison's victory in 1888 was taken as a mandate for even higher tariffs. The McKinley Act of 1890 raised tariffs on wool, iron, and steel. Later, however, voters connected the higher tariffs with subsequent inflation, and the Republicans lost ground, but attempts to reduce tariffs during Cleveland's second term as President met with repeated failure. The few reductions contained in the Wilson-Gorman Act of 1894 were ineffective, yet subsequent deepening of the recession led many voters to believe that lower tariffs were the cause. McKinley's victory over Bryan was again interpreted by the Republicans as a mandate for higher tariffs, and the Dingley Act of 1897 brought the highest duties in our history.

The impact of the high tariffs on income distribution favored the protected industries at the expense of consumers, farmers, and small businessmen. The federal surpluses resulting from tariff revenues further reduced spending power within the economy. Eventually these surpluses became embarrassing to Congress, and they expanded spending on such items as battleships and higher pensions for Civil War veterans.

Although blunders were certainly made in macroeconomic policy, tariff policy, regulation of industry and so on, the most glaring deficiency in federal economic policy was what was left undone. The federal sector seemed oblivious to crying needs in health, education, welfare, and roads as well as the opportunities for use of fiscal policies to influence employment and spending power. One reason for federal inaction was the decentralization of power bases within the political structure. Power within the political parties did not allow for the formulation of national goals but rested in state and local organizations. Local bosses and interest groups sought to use state and local government to promote their particular interests. Their efforts were usually kept in check by the resistance of opposing groups.

A prevailing attitude of laissez faire inhibited public sector activity in the areas of regulation and fiscal policy. Adam Smith's argument had been powerfully reinforced by the British philosopher Herbert Spencer, who linked it with the Darwinian theory of survival of the fittest. This argument held that the slings and arrows of the business cycle destroyed only the weakest (that is, the inefficient) firms; hence, the government should not interfere with this natural and beneficial cleansing of private enterprise. In a similar spirit, public works to provide employment and spending power were eschewed.

Thus the general picture of economic growth and public sector activity was uncomfortably close to the Marxian schema. Business cycles seemed to be increasing in frequency and severity. There seemed also to be long periods with excess capacity in certain industries and too few investment opportunities. Moreover, little inclination was shown to use the public sector to restrain the tendencies toward concentration of income and economic power. The Spanish-American War and the growing American " presence " in the Far East seemed to indicate growing imperialism. There were, of course, some mitigating circumstances: Lower transportation costs and better communication encouraged competition and efficiency. New technology, capital formation, and expanding markets belied Marx's prediction of the increasing misery of the proletariat. Moreover, although the Populist movement had had only limited success in gaining its immediate goals, it argued forcefully for an expanded economic role for the public sector. Even so, there remained the question of whether the process would lead inevitably to its own destruction, and the answer depended on whether or not Americans had the will and the means to regulate and redirect certain forces within their economic system.

[26] In *Munn* v. *Illinois* (1877) the court ruled that a state could regulate business practices which affected the public interest.

[27] *Wabash, St. Louis and Pacific Railroad* v. *Illinois* (1886).

[28] We have here another application of the prisoner's dilemma concept. It is possible that most parties would have been better off with lower tariffs; however, the tendency of each representative to focus on the benefits and costs of his specific interest groups prevented any general reduction. There were, of course, other reasons for the failure of the antitariff legislation. For example, those who stood to benefit most from high tariffs were industrialists, whose economic power could be translated into political power via campaign contributions and the like. On the other hand, the damage done by a tariff to a particular consumer was not large enough to warrant political activity on his part.

8
PUBLIC CHOICES IN THE MASS CONSUMPTION ECONOMY

What part is played by the public sector in the mass consumption economy? In this chapter we examine the changing requirements and possibilities for public sector activity in an economy that has reached "maturity." Many of the theoretical models used in the last chapter will help provide perspectives and hypotheses for our investigation. Several new ones also will prove helpful.

HYPOTHESES ON POSTINDUSTRIAL PUBLIC ACTIVITY

According to Rostow's outline, the society reaching industrial maturity would evolve towards one of three alternatives:

1. *Pursuit of external power and influence.* This choice has proven especially attractive to countries where nationalism runs high. It occurs where the citizens share a belief in the nation's destiny to rule and where the nation has ample opportunity to expand. In the 1930s Germany and Japan, and in the late 1940s Russia, succumbed to this alternative.
2. *Welfare state.* This direction beckons as real incomes increase and the inability of private markets to provide for public wants becomes evident. The public sector is called upon to accomplish such goals as redistribution, increase of leisure, public health, public education, and old age insurance.
3. *Mass consumption.* This social choice is most likely to prevail if the society is democratic, is not seriously threatened from outside, and can allow consumer sovereignty to dictate economic development.

As we have observed, the basic question at this stage becomes not how to generate *more production* but how to generate the *right amount of demand.* The relative importance of the public and private sectors obviously depends on the social choices meted out by the society. If the nation's primary pursuit is external power through military means, the public sector will no doubt command a much greater proportion of the resources. Likewise a shift towards the welfare state would entail a larger role for the public sector, especially if accompanied by a significant shift towards public production of private goods. On the other hand, Rostow's mass consumption alternative would seem to lean toward decreasing the relative importance of public sector activity. As we shall see, our present system combines the three alternatives, yet even its "mass consumption" aspects create considerable demand for public sector activity.

236

THORSTEIN VEBLEN

Thorstein Veblen, like Marx, attempted to analyze the *interaction* between economic development and the institutional framework within which it occurred.[1] But while Marx based his theories on the British economy, Veblen based his on the American economy as it reached industrial maturity.

Veblen began by analyzing man's fundamental instincts, which he defined as: parenthood, workmanship, acquisitiveness, and curiosity. The *institutions* that evolved in any economy were shaped by the exercise of these instincts, given the constraints of technology and scarce resources.

Veblen's theory of the development of American capitalism features the interaction of two instincts: the acquisitive accumulation of wealth and the pleasures derived from producing serviceable, well-engineered products. Veblen, like Marx, emphasized the importance of economies of scale and capital formation in encouraging concentration in market power. Moreover, the acquisitive instinct encouraged collusion to drive out competitors. But it seemed to Veblen that concentration was necessary and in fact beneficial, since it allowed for economies of scale and the reduction of cutthroat competition.

One unfortunate result of the collectivization of the economy was the replacement of the "captains of industry" (who were not only entrepreneurs but engineers who derived satisfaction from producing useful products) by the "captains of finance," who were more interested in building financial empires than in producing functional goods.

Veblen, like Marx, saw the capitalistic system squeezed by continually depressed profit rates as a result of capital accumulation and competition. But Veblen was more optimistic about the alternatives. One remedy was growing demand for wasteful consumption. This demand could come from either the public sector, as in the form of expenditure on war, or from the private sector, in the form of "conspicuous consumption." Veblen foresaw manufacturers *creating demand* through aggressive advertising. But he was not sympathetic with the "conspicuous consumption" alternative, since it undercut the more noble instincts and created a feeling of inferiority among the low-income groups.

A more palatable and lasting remedy for depressed profits and cutthroat competition, according to Veblen, was increased consolidation in

---

[1] See Veblen, *The Theory of Business Enterprise* (New York: Scribners, 1904) and *The Vested Interests and the State of the Industrial Arts* (New York: Viking, 1933).

business. Although incipient competition would always threaten, real progress and growth would occur in these industries which could temporarily free themselves from it.

KEYNES AND THE STAGNATIONISTS

Since the theories of John Maynard Keynes are central to currently accepted macroeconomic theory and will be outlined in Part IV, we will not dwell on them here. We note, however, that the "Keynesian Revolution" has slowly but surely changed the generally held ideas of government responsibility towards employment, inflation, and economic growth.

The nature of Keynesian "intervention" in the economy is essentially *indirect*. The models feature such terms as aggregate demand and supply, consumption, investment, and government spending. The rather optimistic premise is that the government can produce economic growth with full employment and stable prices without direct controls on private enterprise. The Keynesian analysis is primarily aimed at the problems inherent in what we, following Rostow, have labeled the mass consumption economy. The central question becomes how to provide the right amount of aggregate demand as the capacity of the economy grows.

Within the broad umbrella of "Keynesian economies" there are many different schools of thought as to just what is required of the public sector if aggregate demand is to be manipulated successfully. One interesting offshoot of the Keynesian analysis prescribes ever-increasing public sector spending to stave off a seemingly inevitable stagnation of the economy. The *Stagnationists* (as the economists who espoused this argument in the 1930s were known) started with the belief that *consumption spending* was a stable function of income that would not increase fast enough to absorb the economy's expanding output potential.[2] One possible solution would be an increase in private investment spending that would compensate for the savings consumers were withdrawing from the spending stream. But the Stagnationists held little hope that private investment spending would keep pace with the increase in savings. In the thirties and early forties the innovations taking place did not seem adequate to stimulate the vast new consumer markets that would be required. Consequently, as the capital stock increased, businessmen would face alternatives of lower profitability. The Stagnationists' prescription for offsetting underconsumption was massive doses of government spending. Taxes, of course, could not be raised correspondingly, since this would further reduce needed consumer spending. The long-run fiscal outlook was increased public spending and continuous deficit financing.

Though many aspects of the Stagnationists' argument have been refuted,[3] it still appears in various forms. For example, it is currently fashionable to argue that private consumption spending would not be adequate if we were to reduce defense spending significantly.

The more generally accepted version of the Keynesian analysis holds that both consumption and private investment (not just government spending) can be manipulated so as to provide the correct amount of spending; consequently, fiscal policy involves a *choice* between the aggregate components. For example, in the early 1960s when the Kennedy administration was pledged to "get the economy moving again," it faced the choice of encouraging private investment, encouraging consumption, or increasing government spending.

GALBRAITH AND SOCIAL BALANCE

Some of John Kenneth Galbraith's observations on public sector growth make interesting hypotheses as to the nature of public sector growth in the mass consumption stage. Running through two of his books, *The Affluent Society*[4] and *The New Industrial State*,[5] are several theses on how our economic development has led to misallocation of resources. One important hypothesis (virtually impossible to test with economic analysis) is that individual preferences (and thus social preferences) are manipulated by advertising towards private sector consumption. In terms of our basic model this "social imbalance" appears in Figure 8.1, the dotted lines representing the new preference pattern. This effect would, of course, accentuate the Rostovian trend towards less public sector activity in the mass consumption stage.

The composition of consumption, according to Galbraith, is determined by the management of large firms who are free from stockholder control. Funds for investment are generated from within the firm and are not

---

[2] The stable consumption function, $C = a + bY$, where $C =$ consumption, $Y =$ income, and a and b are constants (b being the marginal propensity to consume), is, of course, basic to the simple Keynesian model and will provide the starting point for our analysis in Part IV.

[3] See Chapter 17.

[4] (Boston: Houghton Mifflin, 1959).

[5] (Boston: Houghton Mifflin, 1967).

FIGURE 8–1

Social balance with a shift
in preference functions

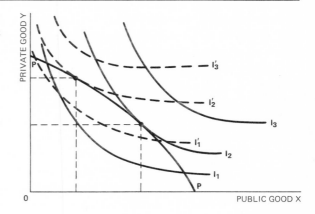

subject to the vicissitudes of capital markets. Management seeks to minimize the risk and uncertainty of the marketplace by developing products for which *want creation* is most efficient. There are exceptions to the trend toward the oversupply of private sector goods, but these exceptions also derive from management's desire to minimize risks. Management has found that government can be of great use in reducing risks—by government "regulation" of a particular industry, or by producing public goods for which riskless contracts are awarded, or by means of government guarantees (such as price supports and rent supplements) on essentially private sector goods. The results of these and other influences are an imbalance in the *composition* of goods in both the private and public sectors and a net overall excess of private relative to public expenditure.

Although the Galbraithian argument is open to criticism on several grounds, we will not now subject it to rigorous scrutiny; instead, we will use it and the other *hypotheses* as vehicles for our examination of the growth of public sector activity.

WHY MASS CONSUMPTION?

Historians and economists alike have seen the 1890s and early 1900s as a turning point in the development of the American economy. Rostow, with the benefit of hindsight, has designated this as the transition period between the drive to maturity and high-level mass consumption. We have noted Rostow's outline of three routes various nations have taken as they reached maturity. According to him a nation has three choices: (1) *imperialism*: "national pursuit of external power and influence; that is, the allocation of increased resources to military and foreign policy "; (2) *the welfare state*: "the use of powers of the State, including the power to redistribute income through progressive taxation, to achieve human and social objectives (including increased leisure) which the free-market process, in its less adulterated form, did not achieve "; or (3) *the mass consumption society*, which features "the expansion of consumption levels beyond basic food, shelter, and clothing, not only to better food, shelter, and clothing but into the range of mass consumption of durable consumers' goods and services."[6] Each nation reaching this stage develops in a direction which combines these possibilities in a unique way. The direction depends on many variables: technology, the nation's relations with other nations, its resources, and its internal political, social, and economic relationships. It is not very illuminating to think of a "nation" making a public choice. It is more useful to examine individual preferences and behavior in the context of a changing institutional structure. We ask (1) what part specific economic and political institutions played in the formulation of public choices; (2) whether these institutions *efficiently* realized the changing preferences of individuals and groups, and (3) how the public choice institutions themselves underwent change.

The direction of change in American political and economic institutions was difficult to predict during these years.

Pressures toward the welfare state were not strong. The group nearest to a broadly based movement eliciting government aid were the Populists, but they did not ask for social welfare programs. On the other hand, potential pressure in that direction was growing along with increased inequality of wealth, frequent business fluctuations, and economic stagnation caused by insufficient aggregate demand.

Pressures toward imperialism were much stronger. The expansion of markets was now slowing as the frontiers were reached and the rate of immigration slowed. America's experiences in the Spanish-American War and the Philippines as well as its trade relationships with many countries were evidence of imperialistic tendencies. The object lesson offered by World War I, however, somewhat dampened the American voter's appetite for this direction of development.

The temporary inappropriateness of other alternatives was, however, only a necessary, not a sufficient condition for the shift to a mass

---

[6] W. W. Rostow, *The Stages of Economic Growth: A Non-Communist Manifesto* (New York: Cambridge University Press, 1960), pp. 73–74.

consumption economy. The shift required several basic changes in private and public sector institutions.

First, it required a change in the structure of business organizations. The trend towards management specialization continued and was augmented by what Frederic W. Taylor popularized as "scientific management," the use of set procedures and incentive pay. A related development, which served to increase the flexibility so necessary in the shift towards mass consumption, was the birth of modern research and development methods in World War I.

Second, the shift required the rise of a whole new set of institutions and techniques adapted to discovering consumer wants, creating effective demand, and providing credit for the purchase of consumer durables.

Third, it required a stable financial climate both for creditor and debtor. One necessary condition was a more stable banking system; a more general requirement was the taming of the business cycle.

Fourth, new legislation and public regulation were required to mitigate against the worst excesses that past laissez faire, pro-big-business policies had created. As industrial concentration increased, some protection was demanded by consumers, investors, and the general public.

THE CHANGING ECONOMIC SYSTEM

Just how great were the changes in market structure and business organization? Many economists refer to the massive reorganizations that occurred from 1889 to 1903 as the first merger movement.[7] The period featured rising prices and a retardation in the rate of development of new markets. Partly in response to these factors, a new breed of innovator appeared, the professional promoter of business combinations. His success depended on recognition of the growing promise of new types of consolidation as means of adapting to changes in transportation, new market orientations (with new economies of scale in production and marketing), and the growth of the stock exchange.

The initial result of lower transportation and marketing costs was to create a situation with "too many" small, inefficient firms selling slightly differentiated products. This type of monopolistic competition, however, was not stable, and it tended towards oligopoly as new economies of scale were realized and brand names associated with quality and dependability were developed. Subsequently, consolidation and direct collusion or price leadership became possible. The steel industry provides an example of unusually effective price leadership. Under the leadership of Judge Gary of the United States Steel Corporation, the price of steel rails stayed at $28 per ton from May 1901 until April 1916, and later at $43 per ton from October 1922 until October 1932. As the trend towards large-scale firms and concentration in industry continued, countervailing powers appeared in the form of labor, farming, and professional organizations. Individuals were seeing opportunities to use various organizational forms to promote their interests. This trend of substituting collective for individual decision making has been described by Kenneth Boulding as the Organizational Revolution.[8] According to Veblen, "captains of industry" were being replaced by "captains of finance" as business enterprise evolved towards collective action.[9] Veblen saw this move as inevitable, not only because of economies of scale but also because of the coercion it allowed one group to exercise upon current and potential competitors.

Veblen also saw a fundamental change taking place in the business cycle. Prior to 1873 the cycles followed a familiar pattern: a boom led eventually to a financial collapse of capitalized values, which later acted as a spur for another increase in investment spending. But after 1873 the cycles seemed to lack this purgative effect. In recessions, devaluations of capital assets were matched by declining costs of new capital goods; consequently, depressions became more persistent. We have observed that to Veblen only curtailed competition through massive concentration offered a reprieve from persistent depression. Mass consumption did not seem a possible alternative, given the trend towards greater rather than less income inequality. Conspicuous consumption among the wealthy could only tend to mitigate the problem of advancing efficiency. Expenditure by the public sector would provide mixed blessings. To the extent that public sector aid to railroads, highways, and so on increased manufacturing efficiency, it would only accentuate the problem. War was a distinct cure, since it not only was wasteful but provided a palliative to the sense of "relative" poverty of the laboring

---

[7] For more detailed description see, for example, J. S. Bain, *Industrial Organization* (Homewood, Ill.: Irwin, 1959), Kenneth E. Boulding, *The Organizational Revolution* (New York: Harper & Row, 1953), and R. L. Nelson, *Merger Movements in American Industry, 1895–1956* (Princeton, N.J.: Princeton University Press, 1959).

[8] Boulding, *The Organizational Revolution*.

[9] Veblen attempted to analyze the organizational revolution in his *Theory of Business Enterprise*.

TABLE 8-1

Percentage shares of value
of finished commodities,
1899–1929 (in producers'
1913 prices)

Commodity class	1899–1908	1909–1918	1919–1929
Consumer perishable	58.7	55.1	47.7
Consumer semidurable	19.5	19.2	18.9
Consumer durable	10.0	12.9	20.2
Producer durable	11.9	12.8	13.2

Source: W. H. Shaw, *Value of Commodity Output since 1869*
(New York: National Bureau of Economic Research, 1947),
p. 17. Copyright 1947 by the National Bureau of Economic
Research.

TABLE 8-2

Net capital formation
among sectors, 1900–1912
(in millions of dollars)

	Net capital formation
Agriculture	$ 4,677
Mining	1,855
Manufacturing	8,133
Nonfarm residential construction	14,995
Government construction	6,045
Transportation and other public utilities	12,005
Steam railroads	5,212
Electric railroads	1,995

Source: S. Kuznets, *Capital in the American Economy* (New
York, National Bureau of Economic Research, 1961), Table
R-35, pp. 610–611. Copyright 1961 by Princeton University
Press for the National Bureau of Economic Research.

masses. The fundamental change, however, must come in the form of
an organizational revolution.

The story of the automobile industry demonstrates quite well some
of the strengths and weaknesses of Veblen's argument. The automobile
did in fact have initial success as a "plaything for the idle rich" and has
continued to be a beautiful example of the American yen for status
symbols, with frequent style changes and advertising often appealing to
one's baser instincts. Yet the automobile has become a mass consumption
product and has in true Schumpeterian fashion engendered tremendous
investment opportunities. Its rank in terms of value of output relative
to other industries rose from 150th in 1899, to 77th in 1904, to 21st in
1909, 7th in 1914, and first after 1925.

The automobile exemplifies Veblen's failure to recognize the possibilities of mass consumption. Necessary conditions for such development
include both lower production costs of consumer goods and a distribution
of income sufficient to allow adequate demand. But Veblen and Marx
failed to anticipate that changes in technology could raise labor productivity and wages. Many of the new techniques raised the value of labor's

marginal product relative to that of capital. The use of electric power in manufacturing increased significantly. From 1902 to 1917 the production of electric power increased from 2507 million to 25,438 million kilowatt-hours. The introduction of overhead wire for electric trolleys changed patterns of living and working in many communities.

Favorable terms of trade enjoyed by farmers in the early 1900s also eased the income distribution problem. Increased demand for farm products came from the growing urban population and European markets. Later, although the supply of farm products was increasing rapidly, the increase in demand associated with World War I and its aftermath kept farm prices high until the late 1920s.

The growing importance of consumer durables in the economy is illustrated in Table 8.1. The big shift came in the 1920s. Producer durables also showed steady gains in spite of the Veblenian prediction that investment values would suffer in both absolute and relative terms.

Table 8.2 shows the sectors in which new capital formation was taking place. The trend towards urbanization required almost $15 billion in new nonfarm housing plus substantial expenditures on highways, streets, trolleys, water systems, and other public utilities.

PUBLIC SECTOR RESPONSE TO CHANGING ECONOMIC INSTITUTIONS

The changing structure of private sector institutions created new demands for public sector activity by a variety of political and economic organizations. The trend of consolidation in industry (outlined in the last chapter) continued. Investment bank trusts and increased use of the stock market created new methods of mobilizing and controlling investment funds. John Moody's data on trusts indicate that, of the 318 listed, only 98 (with over $1 billion total capital) were born before 1898 while 234 (with over $6 billion total capital) were born between 1898 and 1904.[10]

Increased consolidation of industry was accompanied by increased use of the public sector by "big business" to further its own interests. The factors allowing this development spotlight the difficulties of too much separation and diffusion of power in the decision-making process. At the state and local levels of government the dispersal of power between governor and legislature, between mayor and council, and among many independent and semi-independent boards and commissions created a

[10] John Moody, *The Truth About the Trusts* (New York: Moody, 1904).

need for centralization of power outside the formal structure. This need was filled by political machines. These machines consolidated their power with patronage systems and the provision of services to certain voter groups (particularly immigrant groups). The staying power of local machines was augmented by connections with powerful statewide machines. Big businesses in turn could provide payoffs and campaign funds for favorable treatment. All but a few states in the early 1900s were controlled by alliances between big businesses and political machines.

A factor hindering reform was the generally held "deterministic" attitude towards economic development, which left little room for positive action by the public sector. Gradually this attitude lost ground. The Populist Movement had popularized the idea that social change could be influenced by government, and now more pragmatic views of man's possibilities appeared in the movement termed "Progressivism." Philosophers William James and John Dewey and economists Richard Ely, Simon Patten, and Henry Adams attacked the determinist positions. The Progressive movement, however, was primarily a middle class, "grass roots" reaction to exploitation by big business and political machines and to the spectre of class conflict.

The Progressive movement started as a number of separate movements to reform local and state politics and to attempt to use government to control banking and big business as well as big government. Although most of the leaders were fairly well-to-do farmers, small businessmen, and professionals, they were discontent with their lot as consumers in this age of rapidly rising expectations. The results came at first in the form of scattered victories over local party machines. Such machines were particularly difficult to dislodge, owing to their patronage systems and their connections with the state machines; consequently, it was not until the defeat of a statewide machine in Wisconsin by Robert La Follette in 1900 that a thorough-going reform movement was begun. Wisconsin enacted legislation to control railroads, banks, and public utilities and to mitigate some of the hardships visited upon workers, especially women and children. The lead was followed by several other states, and innovations were added, the first minimum wage law being passed by Massachusetts in 1912 and the first effective workmen's compensation law by New York in 1910.

At the federal level the movement found its initial leadership in Theodore Roosevelt. The response of his adminstration to the economic consequences of growth and the organizational revolution was to accept consolidation as inevitable and to attempt to direct it more in accord with social welfare. Roosevelt proved adept at using the powers of his office and his control over his party to pursue his programs. Early successes included settlement of the anthracite coal strike and prosecution of the Northern Securities Company, a railroad holding company. Later he supported legislation to control railroads and to strengthen the role of the Interstate Commerce Commission by giving them the power to fix rates. Subsequent regulatory efforts by Roosevelt and then Taft proved more difficult to get through Congress; however, both presidents aggressively prosecuted the more flagrant business combinations through the courts. The Standard Oil and American Tobacco cases were started during Roosevelt's administration and won during Taft's.

Roosevelt's bolt from the Republican party allowed Democrat Woodrow Wilson, running on a modified Progressive platform, to win the Presidency and control of Congress. Under Wilson major victories were won in changing the tax structure: lowering tariffs and adopting income taxes.

In 1913 the Sixteenth Amendment to the Constitution cleared the way for the federal income tax on corporations and individuals. Attempts had been made in the 1880s and 1890s to reduce tariffs and introduce income taxes, but the Constitution held that direct taxes could be imposed only in such a way as to be apportioned among states according to their population. The Civil War income tax had been challenged, but the Supreme Court found it not to be a direct tax in the meaning of the Constitution.[11] The Court later reversed itself when ruling against the personal income tax legislation of 1894.[12] The Sixteenth Amendment gave Congress the power to impose income taxes without regard to apportionment among the states. The Tariff Act of 1913 contained an individual and a corporation income tax.

The Federal Reserve System was created in 1913 to cope with the instability of the banking industry that resulted from the consolidation of financial resources among banks. The Fed's organizational structure reflected compromises with conflicting interest groups. Farmers and small businessmen desired that the federal government take a greater part in insuring the availability of credit. Conservatives, however, pushed for decentralized control. The resulting legislation provided for a system

---

[11] *Springer* v. *United States.* 102 U.S. 586 (1880).
[12] *Pollock* v. *Farmers' Loan and Trust Co.*, 157 U.S. 429; 158 U.S. 601 (1895).

TABLE 8–3

Federal government
finances, 1915–1925 (in
thousands of dollars)

Year	Expenditures	Receipts	Surplus or deficit	Total gross debt
1915	760,587	697,911	−62,676	1,191,264
1916	734,056	782,535	48,478	1,225,146
1917	1,977,682	1,124,325	−853,357	2,975,619
1918	12,696,702	3,664,583	−9,032,120	12,455,225
1919	18,514,880	5,152,257	−13,362,623	25,484,506
1920	6,403,344	6,694,565	291,222	24,299,321
1921	5,115,928	5,624,933	509,005	23,977,451
1922	3,372,608	4,109,104	736,496	22,963,382
1923	3,294,628	4,007,135	712,508	22,349,707
1924	3,048,678	4,012,045	963,367	21,250,813
1925	3,063,105	3,780,149	717,043	20,516,194

TABLE 8–4

Wholesale price index,
1914–1918

July 1914	100
December 1915	106
December 1916	147
December 1917	183
November 1918	206

of twelve regional banks, controlled in part by the region's private banks. It is interesting to note that, as the Fed has accepted a more important role in national macroeconomic policy, the same organizational structure has been used, although decision making has become more centralized.

The Democrats' antitrust and regulatory legislation showed a slight change in voter attitudes toward the consolidation movement. Instead of simply *punishing* firms for violations of the Sherman Act, provisions were made under the Clayton Act and the Federal Trade Commission to *prevent* the occurrence of situations encouraging monopoly practices. The Wilson administration also supported extension of federal financing in several areas: highway construction, vocational education, and federal employee workmen's compensation.

Continuing fluctuations in economic activity led to increasing voter awareness of the need for a public sector role in this area. The Federal Reserve Act was only a partial solution. Excessive speculation brought on the " rich man's " panic in 1903, which featured a panic on the stock market and a contraction in investment. The 1907 recession started as another rich man's panic but went much deeper, owing in part to perverse monetary and fiscal policy. The prevailing debt management policy was to reduce the debt whenever possible; consequently, the recovery stage of the recession was undercut by the policy of reducing the debt and in turn the money supply. The 1913 recession also deepened into depression, being reinforced by reduction in European trade and investment owing to the Balkan War. It was not until the war prosperity of 1915 that the economy was able to break out of its chronic malady of instability.

FINANCING WORLD WAR I

World War I was financed under the familiar theme "borrow now and tax later." These methods had repercussions in the postwar period. Actually the initial intention of the Wilson administration was to cover at least half of the war expenditures with new taxes. A glance at Table 8.3, however, is sufficient to reveal why tax legislation did not keep up with expenditures. Before World War I the highest wartime government expenditure was $1.3 billion in 1865; and the highest peacetime expenditure was $.8 billion in 1916. But expenditures skyrocketed to $18.5 billion by 1919. The increase in revenues from $783 million in 1916 to $6695 million in 1920 was also unprecedented but far short of what was required. The large deficits were met primarily by the sale of Liberty bonds, saving certificates, and stamps. Unfortunately, a substantial part of the debt was acquired by banks, which could use the debt in turn to fulfill their reserve requirements; consequently, the sale of bonds to banks did not withdraw sufficient spending power from the private sector and, when coupled with increased federal spending, caused inflationary pressures. In March 1918 the government securities owned by private bank members of the Federal Reserve reached over $3 billion.

Table 8.4 demonstrates the war's inflationary effect on prices. At first, government price controls on essentials and exhortations not to buy luxuries restrained aggregate demand. But pressure mounted with increased defense expenditures, until inflation finally became so rampant that in mid-1918 even the price controls collapsed. The 1918 wholesale price index rose to 206 percent of the 1914 base.

The economic integration accompanying industrial development made for new wartime relationships among public and private sector institutions. Now practically every sector of the economy could be included in the war effort. The War Industries Board was established under the chairmanship of Bernard Baruch. Direct controls were placed on the

TABLE 8-5

National income growth
during the 1920s

Year	National income (in billions of dollars)	Real income per capita in 1929 prices
1921	$59.4	$522
1922	60.7	553
1923	71.6	634
1924	72.1	633
1925	76.0	644
1926	81.6	678
1927	80.1	674
1928	81.7	676
1929	87.2	716

Source: Simon Kuznets, *National Income and Its Composition, 1919–1938* (New York: National Bureau of Economic Research, 1941). Copyright 1941 by the National Bureau of Economic Research.

transportation and fuel industries, and these, along with other indirect controls, were used to insure that governmental priorities were adhered to. Further consolidation and standardization were encouraged. The War Industries Board found it more expeditious to deal with trade associations and the like rather than with individual businesses. An important insight we gain here is that consolidation of decision making in private sector institutions facilitates direct participation in those decisions by the public sector.

THE GOLDEN TWENTIES

Economic conditions in the 1920s were particularly favorable for the flowering of the mass consumption economy. This period of prosperity witnessed continued growth in some areas of public sector activity, particularly in providing social overhead capital. Yet at the same time it allowed the postponement of public sector assumption of responsibility in several other important areas.

The United States' position in international trade and finance had changed dramatically during the war. It emerged from the war a creditor nation with a favorable balance of trade. Foreign demand for its products plus a policy of monetary "ease" by the Fed created a postwar boom which facilitated a rapid reconversion to peacetime production. Moreover, the government continued to make loans to the Europeans, which further encouraged exports. Furthermore, the inflationary fiscal policy used during the war provided substantial spending power for consumers

---

with pent-up demands for housing, automobiles, and other consumer durables.

In fact, spending increased much more rapidly than the supply afforded by the reconversion process, and predictably it resulted in inflation, speculation, overexpansion of credit, and a short panic and recession in 1920 and 1921. The monetary policies of the Fed during this period did not inspire confidence. In the inflationary period the Fed felt obligated to provide easy money as an aid to the Treasury in marketing its final Victory Loan. During the decline and on into 1921, however, the Fed's policy was deflationary.

The changes in national income from 1921 to 1929 are presented in Table 8.5. National income increased from $59.4 billion to $87.2 billion, and per capita income in 1929 prices increased from $522 to $716. The leading sectors were the construction, automobile, and other industries producing consumer durables. The use of electricity was expanded in manufacturing and in consumer goods such as radios and kitchen appliances. The automobile industry exemplified Schumpeter's description of how one innovative industry can accelerate economic growth. New techniques were applied to mass production and mass distribution. Other innovations were spawned in related industries: steel, rubber, and plate glass.

The organizational revolution begun earlier in the century moved into its second phase in the twenties. A second great wave of mergers occurred. Trends toward concentration developed in many sectors: the automobile and related industries (including oil) and the public utilities. Many consumer goods industries were reorganized, as advertising and improved distribution methods increased market potential.

FACTORS CONTRIBUTING TO THE GREAT DEPRESSION

The initial impetus of the Great Depression was the 1929 stock market crash. This was followed by a general financial collapse, which saw over 4000 banks fail in the year 1933 and demand deposits contract from $22.6 billion in 1929 to $14.4 billion in 1933. Table 8.6 gives the basic outline of the depression in terms of the aggregate figures. Gross national product fell from $103.1 billion in 1929 to $55.6 billion in 1933, while unemployment rose from 1.6 percent to 12.8 percent. We postpone examination of the macroeconomic dynamics at work until Part IV. The question we ask now is: What was the nature of economic change

TABLE 8-6

National income and
employment, selected years,
1929–1945 (in billions
of dollars)

| Year | Gross national product | Federal | | Surplus or deficit | Unemployment (percent) | Money supply |
		Expenditures	Receipts			
1929	$103.1	$ 3.1	$ 3.9	$ .7	1.6	$26.5
1931	75.8	3.6	3.1	— .5	8.0	23.6
1933	55.6	4.6	2.0	— 2.6	12.8	19.5
1935	72.2	6.5	3.7	— 2.8	10.6	25.6
1937	90.4	7.7	5.0	— 2.8	7.7	30.3
1939	90.5	8.8	5.0	— 3.8	9.5	33.6
1941	124.5	14.0	9.2	— 4.8	5.6	45.4
1943	191.6	78.9	25.1	—53.8	1.1	72.3
1945	211.9	95.2	50.2	—45.0	1.0	99.2

which allowed for the depression and what basic demands did it make for public sector activity? The figures in Table 8.6 demonstrate that the depression was not simply the familiar cycle of overexpansion and speculation followed by panic, recession, and the inevitable upswing. Instead, some weaknesses in the system were revealed which indicated the need for a fundamental change in the role of the public sector. It was not simply a question of how to employ the surplus of a growing economy, as intimated in the Rostovian model; instead, a fundamental change in political and economic institutions was required, more on the magnitude of the Marxian scheme.

One basic weakness the collapse revealed was the continuing fragility of the financial system and the inadequacy—if not perversity—of the Fed's monetary policies. More important, the economic system itself had undergone basic change. The proportion of fixed to variable capital had continued to grow as the economy had advanced. This, along with the commitment to producing for mass consumption, particularly consumer durables, created a critical dependence on sustained aggregate demand.

In the later 1920s the rapid rate of investment spending in certain industries had created capacity that was threatening to saturate their markets. Residential and commercial construction had in fact peaked in 1925. Moreover, questionable lending practices of banks and inflated capital values gradually laid the groundwork for a drastic shift in the expectations of consumers and businessmen. The postponable nature of consumer durables allowed consumers to cut purchases of new output drastically. For example, car registrations (and presumably car use) declined only slightly from 1929 to 1932 while new car sales shrank to one-fourth their 1929 level.

The financial crisis and reduced consumer spending caused business-men to shift their expectations downward and cut back investment. In our later examination of macroeconomic theory we shall see that a reduction in investment may have two effects: one via a "multiplier" effect, as spending is cut not only for a particular investment project but for all the subsequent businesses and consumers through whose hands the spending power would have passed; and one via an "acceler-ator" effect, since when a producer cuts investment and output, there is a much greater percentage reduction in the production of *capital goods* used to produce that output. Both effects seem to have interacted to contract spending during the Great Depression.

Not only was the depression severe, it was long. After a partial recovery in the mid 1930s yet another downswing occurred in 1937. Unemploy-ment rose back up to 10.4 percent for 1938 and, as Table 8.6 indicates, it was not until World War II that full employment was reached. The basic problem was a long-term shortage of aggregate spending. It seemed to many economists that we had entered a period of chronic spending shortage for which the economic system contained no self-corrective mechanism. The simple Keynesian model offers an explana-tion of why consumption expenditure could not be expected to provide the needed stimulus. Consumers spend only a *part* of additional incre-ments of income, and, if higher equilibrium levels of aggregate spending are to be reached, either additional investment or government spending must compensate for the increase in consumers' savings. The Stagna-tionists' interpretation of the situation, as outlined earlier, was that little private investment could be expected, since previous capital forma-tion had oversaturated most markets and no new innovations seemed to be forthcoming. The only cure, it seemed, was massive doses of govern-ment spending.

There is some disagreement as to whether the Keynesian prescriptions were in fact attempted during the Great Depression. Government spending did increase and deficits occurred in the federal budget in every year. The 1936 federal expenditures, $8.4 billion, were over twice federal revenues, $4.0 billion. In most years, however, deficits occurred because of the automatic reduction in governmental revenues as incomes and spending declined. President Roosevelt took office promising to "balance the budget," and he endorsed deficit spending only when it became obviously a necessary by-product of some of the New Deal programs. Moreover, after the semi-recovery in 1935 and 1936 tax rates were raised and contributed to a second slump. Only the massive doses of federal expenditure on the war finally created sufficient aggregate demand.

Our present task, however, is not to evaluate macroeconomic policy but to consider the changes in the individual's concept of the proper role of the public sector in response to this crisis. Needless to say, the public's mood shifted drastically. Business leaders, once positive they were self-made men and secure in the knowledge of their own innate superiority, took to jumping out of buildings. Arguments extolling the virtues of the laissez faire, free enterprise system were temporarily sidetracked. The Roosevelt administration, although it did not know precisely what needed to be done, was committed to do whatever was necessary to restore the economic system. Programs designed to furnish direct relief and work were instituted. Direct relief grants began under the Federal Emergency Relief Administration (FERA). A program of national public works to employ the able-bodied was begun under the Public Works Administration (PWA) in 1933; however, it proved difficult to implement rapidly and was supplemented by the Works Progress Administration (WPA), whose program involved direct relief and "make-work" projects.

The New Deal also showed a new attitude towards government intervention in certain "sick" industries: construction, agriculture, and the merchant marine. The agricultural program included loans, subsidies, and acreage allotments and other "emergency" measures that are still with us.

The federal sector also started significant welfare programs, an area heretofore the responsibility of states and localities. The Social Security Act of August 1935, which provided old-age insurance and aid to the handicapped, is the basis for our present public insurance programs. In addition, the federal government began extending its grants to the states in a wide range of social welfare programs.

The Revenue Law of 1935 expanded the use of the personal and corporation income taxes and made the rate structure much more progressive. Increased taxes were hardly in order, as the economic relapse of 1936 demonstrated; however, the 1935 act laid the groundwork for heavy reliance on the income tax in World War II.

FINANCING WORLD WAR II

In one respect the high rate of unemployment now turned out to be a boon, since the new war industries were able to bid for workers in a depressed market. But the job market quickly changed, owing to the requirements of the armed forces and industry. And while the individual's spending power was increasing, the composition of output was shifting away from consumer goods.

The government again turned to debt creation to reduce spending power in the private sector. A series of Victory Bond drives were used. The federal debt rose from $45 billion in 1940 to $278 billion in 1945. A large portion of the debt was sold to commercial banks which had the immediate effect of reducing their reserves and curtailing credit. However, the Federal Reserve subsequently bought these bonds thereby reinstating the bank's reserve position. Moreover, the Fed's purchases were paid for by printing money. This monetizing of the debt by increasing the money supply provided inflationary pressures which had to be stemmed by stringent rationing.

Although increased tax revenue did not keep pace with expenditures, it increased over ten times its 1939 level, and the change in composition was significant. The trend towards more reliance on the personal and corporation income taxes was accelerated. By 1944 personal exemptions had been reduced to $500 and rates ranged from 23 to 94 percent. An important aspect of the change was that direct taxation of the low- and middle-income groups now became the backbone of the federal tax system. The total income tax liability for incomes under $10,000 increased from $174 million in 1933 to $10,763 million by 1944, while the liability of the $10,000-to-$50,000 group increased only from $305 million to $3432 million.

The scope of public sector intervention in the private economy was to become even more pervasive during World War II. In passing, however, we make an important distinction between the Keynesian "new economics" and the nature of intervention during the New Deal. The Keynesian focus is on aggregates such as Investment, Consumption, and Government Spending. Its prescriptions call for manipulating these aggregates and consequently can be administered in ways which are essentially neutral to goals of income distribution and resource allocation. The basic thrust of the New Deal (although Roosevelt espoused Keynesian ideas in the late 1930s) was to mitigate economic inequality, to break down concentration of economic power, to create economic

TABLE 8–7	Year	Gross national product (in billions of dollars)	Unemployment (percent)
Postwar economic growth	1945	$211.9	1.9
	1946	208.5	3.9
	1947	231.3	3.9
	1948	257.6	3.8
	1949	256.5	5.9
	1950	284.8	5.3
	1951	328.4	3.3
	1952	345.5	3.0
	1953	364.6	2.9
	1954	364.8	5.5
	1955	398.0	4.4
	1956	419.2	4.1
	1957	441.1	4.3
	1958	447.3	6.8
	1959	483.7	5.5
	1960	503.7	5.5
	1961	520.1	6.7
	1962	560.3	5.5
	1963	590.5	5.7
	1964	632.4	5.2
	1965	684.9	4.5
	1966	749.9	3.8
	1967	793.9	3.8
	1968	865.0	3.6
	1969	931.4	3.5
	1970	976.8	4.9
	1971	1,046.8	5.9
	1972 (prem)	1,153.0	5.5

opportunity for the underprivileged, and to intervene directly in certain industries where the nature of competition brought unacceptable results.

The Keynesian question of just how much government expenditure was required to stimulate the economy was never answered, since federal war expenditures quickly reached and overshot that figure. War expenditures rose from $1.4 billion in 1940 to $81.2 billion in 1945. The fiscal problem immediately became one of controlling inflation.

CHANGES IN THE STRUCTURE OF THE ECONOMY AFTER WORLD WAR II

Many economists feared that reconversion to peace would be accompanied by a return to the mass unemployment of the 1930s. Instead, there was a period of rather steady growth until 1954. The 1954–1961 period was one of slow growth with recurrent recessions, some of which featured both high unemployment and inflation. Agressive fiscal policy during the mid-sixties fostered renewed growth and lower unemployment. The precarious balance of the full-employment economy in the late sixties was upset by a very rapid expansion of expenditures on the war in Vietnam, which was not matched by increased taxes until much later. Inflationary pressures born in the Johnson-Humphrey administration matured rapidly under the Nixon-Agnew administration's policy of "gradualism," which relied primarily on tight money. This policy produced a lengthy recession-with-inflation similar to that experienced in the Eisenhower-Nixon years. Wage and price controls, initiated in August, 1971, were only partially effective due to their lack of generality. Unfortunately the wage and price controls were not accompanied with measures designed to adequately increase demand (and output) in those sectors with high unemployment. Consequently, the return to growth without inflation was sluggish.

Table 8.7 shows the growth of GNP from 1945 to 1972. Five recessions have interrupted economic growth in the postwar period—1948–1949, 1953–1954, 1957–1958, 1960–1961, and 1969–1971. The annual percentage increase in GNP over the period 1948–1956 was 4.7 percent. The period began with a high level of pent-up demand and a more than adequate supply of credit. During the war years consumers had "used up" their consumer durables—especially automobiles and housing. At the same time new technology, developed during the war effort, became available to produce new consumer goods. These factors accounted for a *shift* in individual consumption behavior. The annual increase in expenditures on consumer durables was 6.8 percent in the period 1948–1956. After an initial cutback in the immediate postwar years, defense expenditures furnished a strong stimulus which accelerated during the Korean war and has remained high in subsequent years. The annual increase during the 1948–1956 period was 22.4 percent.

By contrast the annual increase in GNP in the 1957–1963 period was only 3.0 percent, while unemployment averaged 5.5 percent per year. The extraordinary rate of increased expenditure on consumer durables fell to 3.4 percent annually as some markets became saturated; and, although defense expenditures remained high, the annual percentage increase fell below 3 percent.

As the economy languished in the late 1950s under the conservative economic policies of the Eisenhower-Nixon administration, the feeling grew that the economy had matured to the point where slow growth, high unemployment, and recessions were inevitable. It became popular to argue that in an economy with highly specialized employment, high levels of "structural" unemployment occurred as certain industries declined and its workers experienced difficulty in adapting to other occupations. The economy's potential growth became a central debate topic in the 1960 presidential campaign and was a significant factor in Kennedy's narrow win. Kennedy's promise to "get the economy moving again" was not honored immediately; but, as his term progressed, more aggressive fiscal policies were pursued. In 1962 efforts were made to stimulate private investment by accelerating depreciation rates and offering a 7 percent tax credit on new investment. A more drastic step was taken in 1964 when a cut in personal income taxed injected $10 billion into the economy. The economy responded vigorously to these stimulants, with GNP rising from $520.1 billion to $793.9 billion between 1961 and 1967 while unemployment dropped from 6.7 to 3.8 percent.

The mechanics of these macroeconomic policies will be examined in Part IV. What is significant for our present examination is that during this period the public sector was *successful in stimulating private sector demand*. In other words, it is not necessary to rely on the Stagnationists' formula for fiscal policy, which relies entirely on doses of government spending; instead, a social choice is available. Macroeconomic policy can in fact be carried out with due regard for the resource allocation goal (between the private and public sectors), as portrayed in our idealistic Fiscal Department model in Chapter 4.

It will not be known for some time whether or not economic growth can in fact be maintained with unemployment at the 4 percent target of the economic advisors to Kennedy and Johnson. When rising defense expenditures threatened to overheat the economy in early 1966, several steps were taken—including a speedup in collection of corporate income taxes, the reversal of certain scheduled excise tax reductions, an already scheduled increase in social security tax rates, and a new graduated withholding system on individual income taxes. In addition, a tight money policy was followed which quickly produced a sharp contraction in homebuilding. However, further measures, including the suspension of the investment tax credit, were required before business investment was slowed.

The respite these policies brought from inflationary pressures was to be short-lived. War expenditures, which had risen from $49.6 billion in 1965 to $56.8 billion in 1966, now soared to $70.1 billion in 1967 and

$80.2 billion in 1968. The load was too much for monetary policy to bear alone, especially since housing construction was already depressed. As economists became aware of the enormity of the war expenditures, efforts were renewed to impose an income surtax, suggested in 1966 as an alternative to monetary policy. The tax, however, was not enacted by Congress until mid-1968, long after the seeds of inflation had been planted.

Most economists underestimated the inflationary pressures at work in the economy in 1968 and 1969. The Nixon-Agnew administration chose to use a tight monetary policy; however, their initial efforts resulted in higher interest rates but little reduction in spending and inflation. Even tighter monetary restraints finally brought rising unemployment along with inflation.

As inflation and unemployment continued, the administration continued to rely on monetary restraints and to make periodic statements that the economy was responding according to predictions. But an inflationary "psychology" persisted even in the face of rising unemployment. The large unions and corporations continued to post dramatic wage and price increases. The situation encouraged firms both large and small to use any monopoly power they had to raise prices. The "prisoner's dilemma" concept is useful for describing the effect of inflationary "psychology." Each wage earner and firm was well aware that if all wages and prices were increased, inflation would persist. Yet if the individual union or firm could raise its wages or prices, it could gain at the expense of the others. Moreover, if the individual union or firm showed restraint, it would suffer, since the other unions and firms would push up wages and prices anyway. Consequently, each union and firm, in attempting to maximize its own position, behaves in a way which is mutually harmful.

Another disturbing aspect of the inflation-recession showed up in the behavior of firms as the expansion of market demand finally slowed. Firms continued to raise prices, while at the same time they cut back on new investment and in some cases laid off workers. Thus, even as aggregate demand slowed, prices continued upward in response to a general curtailment of aggregate supply.

Eventually, broad public support grew for government-imposed controls over wages and prices. And in August of 1970 Congress passed a bill giving the President the power to stabilize wages and prices. The President had not asked for this power, and he refused to use it until another full year of high inflation and unemployment had passed. In the meantime the U.S. balance of payments had steadily deteriorated, partly in response to the continuing strength of the postwar economic recovery of Japan and the European countries and partly in response to domestic inflation.

On Sunday night, August 15, 1971, President Nixon utilized "prime time" to announce a dramatic shift to aggressive macroeconomic policy. He outlined a number of steps, some taking effect immediately and others requiring Congressional approval. A wage, price, and rent freeze was imposed to start immediately and last for 90 days. The freeze covered essentially all wages and prices—even those which had been contracted for, as long as they were not in effect as of August 15.

Two other significant steps were the "floating" of the dollar and a 10 percent surcharge on the value of imports. "Floating" the dollar was accomplished by ending the U.S. policy of buying gold at $35 an ounce. The immediate aim was to allow the dollar to be "devalued" relative to other currencies. Both steps were aimed at making American goods relatively cheaper than foreign goods, thus discouraging imports and "creating jobs" at home.

The program also included some rather significant steps favoring business investment and profits. The investment tax credit was to be restored at 10 percent, and the automobile excise tax of 7 percent was to be dropped. Consumer spending was to be stimulated in 1972 by an advance of the effective date of increased (by $100) exemptions on the personal income tax.

In keeping with the fight against inflation (but at odds with the aim of stimulating spending) the President promised to reduce the federal budget. "Savings" were to be accomplished by postponing the proposed welfare reform and general revenue sharing.

The intended effect of the program was expansionary, especially since Congress was not likely to reduce the budget by the amount indicated by the President. In general, then, the aim was to stimulate spending and output with the hope that the increase in aggregate supply would be sufficient to compensate for inflationary pressures, once the wage-price freeze was lifted. This is not to say, however, that only the "net effect" was important. Policy aimed at several goals should appropriately include several different tools. And although these goals (reducing inflation, increasing employment, and improving the balance of trade) are somewhat conflicting, it is still possible, at least theoretically, to find a combination of tools which aids in the attainment of all three simultaneously. We will postpone an evaluation of the Nixon program until Part IV, when we have an opportunity to examine the mechanics of the fiscal tools in more detail. Our present task is to reflect briefly on the changes in our economic system which made these choices necessary.

Our outline of the growth of the private and public sectors has suggested why readjustments were required in the part played by the public sector to combat inflation and to restructure America's international monetary policy. At the end of World War II United States dollars emerged as the basic currency used for liquidity in international trade and as a reserve to bolster confidence in the currency of the countries holding them. The use of the dollars for these purposes was enhanced by the U.S. pledge to sell gold for dollars at $35 an ounce. However, as Western Europe and Japan prospered, the value of their currencies relative to the dollar increased. The currencies of West Germany and Japan tended to be "undervalued" in terms of the dollar. Moreover, the reluctance of these countries to revalue their currencies enhanced the attractiveness of their exports and aggravated the U.S. balance of payments problems. The immediate aim of the decision to stop buying gold at $35 an ounce and to impose a 10 percent surcharge on imports was to encourage other countries to value their currencies upward. The long-run implications were that international monetary relationships would have to be reorganized with more flexible exchange rates and a new basis for furnishing reserves for countries requiring backing for their currencies.

Our historical outline also suggests economic developments which permit inflation-recession to persist and which necessitate direct intervention by the public sector. One factor is the continued concentration of economic power, coupled with the postwar trend towards "countervailing power." The trend towards national markets where a few oligopolists compete has continued. An important feature of oligopolistic competition has been the increasing dependence on nonprice competition; the firm depends more on advertising and related marketing techniques to retain its market position.

Since the 1930s labor unions have grown and become powerful in the oligopolistic industries. In many situations the growth of labor unions has tended to overcome a monopsony situation and raise wages without negative effects on resource allocation or efficiency. In other situations, however, harmful effects have been created. For example, in some oligopoly situations labor unions can obtain raises in wages that can readily be passed on to consumers in the form of higher prices. When all of the oligopolists are included and the market demand is relatively inelastic, there is little decline in quantity sold when prices are raised. Increases in wages and other costs are taken as a signal for all firms in the industry to raise prices. Firms continue to rely on nonprice competition, even when their sales begin to diminish as a result of general inflation and government monetary and fiscal restraint.

The attempt by individual firms to keep profits up by raising prices in response to higher costs creates the *prisoner's dilemma* mentioned above. This effect is so strong that it persists even in the face of diminishing sales and rising unemployment.

Many economists argue that direct government intervention in the form of wage and price controls is required to deal with an inflation-recession of the type described above. It is argued that once the inflationary psychology is broken, the economic incentives of labor unions and firms are changed so that their behavior is no longer mutually harmful.

During the 90-day wage-price freeze of August-November 1971, a Phase II program of guidelines and supervision was worked out. It featured limits on wage (5.5 percent) and price (2.5 percent) increases, a Pay Board and a Price Board to oversee and adjudicate the controls. The Phase II controls worked remarkably well during their 14 months of operation. The annual rate of inflation for the month of December 1972, had slowed to 2.4 percent. By that time the economy was responding to deficit budgets and monetary "ease" of the previous two years. In fact, the rate of investment was accelerating at a pace which suggested renewed restraint. However, residual "cost-push" factors were still evident especially in those sectors (such as food costs) not covered by controls. Although the economy was expanding, unemployment was still high and inflationary psychology was still prevalent.

Under these circumstances President Nixon's announcement of the Phase III reduction of controls was premature. Rent control was given up completely. The Pay Board and the Price Commission were abolished. Voluntary compliance to guidelines was urged. The resultant price jump in February, a result of both "demand-pull" and "cost-push" factors, reached a 9.6 percent seasonally adjusted annual rate, the sharpest one-month climb in 22 years. The surge included a food-price rise at a 26.4 percent adjusted rate. In response to public outrage over rising food costs, President Nixon placed ceilings on the prices processors', wholesalers', and retailers' charge for meats. Another immediate result of the Phase III controls was a second international monetary crisis which destroyed existing exchange rates and forced the "floating" of all major currencies. The "silver lining" of these events was that the dollar was devalued to rates favorable for increased exports and the basis was laid for progress toward a more flexible and workable system of exchange rates. It remains to be seen whether the optimum combination of controls and incentives can be found to deal with the inflation-recession phenomenon. Equally important is our recognition that basic structural changes in our market system are required if the self-regulatory competitive forces are to be revived. *As we turn to a closer examination of our current public " needs " we will find that the constraints placed on our public choices by the macro-economic environment are crucial.* A significant factor constraining these choices in the last several years has been the chronic "cost-push" inflationary pressure inherent in our economic system.

It is important to note that wage and price controls are associated neither with the traditional Monetarist nor the Keynesian policy prescriptions. One Monetarist position is that the money supply should be expanded at a stable rate with no monetary or fiscal manipulation to upset the self-regulating mechanics of the competitive system. The other Monetarist position is essentially the same, except that more faith is placed in aggressive monetary countercyclical policy. The traditional Keynesian position also eschews direct controls, but favors manipulating aggregate demand with emphasis on fiscal policy. Tax increases or cuts, investment tax credits, or changes in government spending are used to influence the components of aggregate demand: consumption, investment, and government spending. Relevant questions to be answered during the 1970s are what types of direct controls are needed and in what economic situations. Can we utilize a wage-price freeze to halt an inflationary spiral and then resort to the more indirect methods in "normal" times? Or does the public demand that the public sector be represented when labor and business bargain over wages and prices? Finally, a related question is: Given the trends away from private competition in our economic system, what role can the public sector play in changing those trends, enhancing competition, and reducing the necessity for direct public sector intervention?

POLITICS AND PUBLIC CHOICES IN POSTWAR BUDGETS

Now, instead of focusing on public sector economics as a *response* to changing economic relationships, let us again view the public sector, and especially the budget process, as a means through which individual

TABLE 8-8	Year	Total	Defense	All others
Federal expenditures, 1946–1952 (in billions of dollars)	1946	$60.4	$55.5	$4.9
	1947	39.0	33.3	5.7
	1948	33.1	28.3	4.8
	1949	39.5	31.1	8.4
	1950	39.6	30.1	9.5
	1951	44.1	37.3	6.8
	1952	65.4	57.6	7.8

and collective preferences are implemented. Let us consider some of the political and social developments which affected the composition of postwar budgets.

THE TRUMAN ADMINISTRATION

The postwar period began under the administration of Harry S. Truman, who became President upon Roosevelt's death. Truman soon initiated efforts to extend the New Deal programs and introduce new social legislation for national health insurance, increased minimum wages, federal housing, and regional development projects. His efforts met strong opposition. Reaction against the new public sector activities grew stronger with postwar prosperity. Businessmen decided they were, after all, "self-made men," and the campaign coffers of conservative politicians began to fill. Republicans in 1946 won control of both Houses of Congress for the first time since the 1920s. Most of the legislative battles during the next few years were won by the Republicans. Not only were the administration's programs defeated, but tax reductions and the Taft-Hartley bill were pushed through in spite of Presidential vetoes.

By some strange quirk of the electorate Truman was returned to the Presidency again in 1948 in a surprising political upset. His "new" program, which he labeled the Fair Deal, contained most of the programs he had championed in previous years. Most of these were soundly defeated during the next four years. His major domestic successes were the Housing Act of 1949, the raising of the minimum wage from 40 to 75 cents per hour, and the extending of the number of persons covered by social security.

As Table 8.8 illustrates, defense-oriented expenditures continued to dominate and determine the trend in federal expenditures. The Red scare immediately after the war was heightened by the communist takeover of China, several sensational spy trials, and Senator McCarthy's use of the Senate as a kangaroo court for alleged communists. The outbreak of the Korean war and the subsequent Cold War firmly entrenched the so-called military-industrial complex as a major factor in determining the composition of public spending.

In the 1952 campaign the Republicans were again heavy favorites, aided on this occasion by a frustrating war, the Soviet threat, and incidents involving corruption in several areas of government. In this campaign and the next Adlai Stevenson outlined a new brand of liberalism, which eschewed many of the old spending prescriptions and concentrated on programs for improving economic *opportunity* for the minority groups and the *quality* of American life. However, the war, the Red scare, and a well-financed campaign featuring the personal appeal of General Eisenhower guaranteed Republican victory.

THE EISENHOWER ADMINISTRATION

One beauty of being a conservative President is that it is much easier to curtail new spending programs than it is to inaugurate them. In general, the Republican administrations from 1952 through 1960 attempted to "hold the line" in the face of changing social needs.

We have outlined the basic changes in the economy and the effects of the pre-Keynesian macroeconomic theories that were used on the economy. Paradoxically enough, attempts in the late 1950s to "balance the budget" in the face of reduced demand for consumer durables always seemed to backfire. Any veteran of a college economics course could have explained that by further reducing aggregate demand the government would only produce more unemployment and lower rates of profit. Consequently, the automatic reduction in tax revenue and increase in welfare and unemployment compensation would lead to even less "balance" in the budget.

Table 8.9 reflects the Republicans' attempts to hold the line on federal expenditures. After the Korean war, expenditures were reduced to $64.6 billion. Defense expenditures, however, started another upward trend in 1956. The hoped-for reductions in the "welfare state" did not occur; instead, the social security program and the federal government's part in welfare were enlarged. Meanwhile, the structure of the economy had been changing. Urbanization and suburbanization were placing overwhelming demands on states and localities for schools, public utilities, hospitals, roads, and welfare. The prime source of revenue for localities, the property tax, had been overextended both in terms of equity, it

TABLE 8-9

Federal budget expenditures
by function, 1952–1960 (in
billions of dollars)

	1952	1953	1954	1955	1956	1957	1958	1959	1960
Defense[a]	51.6	56.9	52.9	47.3	47.2	50.0	54.3	55.4	52.5
Interest	5.9	6.6	6.5	6.4	6.8	7.3	7.7	7.7	9.3
Health, labor, welfare and education	2.2	2.4	2.5	2.6	2.8	3.0	3.4	4.4	4.4
Agriculture	1.0	2.9	2.6	4.4	4.9	4.6	4.4	6.5	4.8
National resources	1.3	1.4	1.2	1.1	1.0	1.3	1.5	1.7	1.7
Commerce, transportation and housing	2.7	2.6	.9	1.6	2.2	1.5	2.1	3.4	2.8
General government	1.5	1.5	1.2	1.2	1.6	1.8	1.4	1.6	1.7
Total	65.4	74.3	67.8	64.6	66.5	69.4	71.9	80.7	77.2

[a] Includes international affairs and finance, veterans' services and benefits.

TABLE 8-10

State and local expenditures
by function, 1946–1960 (in
billions of dollars)

Year	Total	Education	Highways	Public welfare	Health and hospitals	Police and Fire	Financial administration	Insurance trust	Utility and liquor stores	Other
1946	$14.1	$ 3.4	$1.7	$1.4	$ .8	$ .8	$ .7	$1.3	$1.7	$ 2.3
1948	21.3	5.4	3.0	2.1	1.2	1.1	.9	1.2	2.4	4.0
1950	27.9	7.2	3.8	2.9	1.7	1.3	1.0	2.4	2.7	4.8
1952	30.9	8.3	4.7	2.8	2.2	1.5	1.2	1.7	3.1	5.4
1954	36.6	10.6	5.5	3.1	2.4	1.8	1.4	2.4	3.5	6.0
1956	43.2	13.2	7.0	3.1	2.8	2.1	1.6	2.4	4.1	7.0
1958	53.7	15.9	8.6	3.8	3.5	2.4	1.8	4.2	4.7	8.8
1960	61.0	18.7	9.4	4.4	3.8	2.9	2.1	4.0	5.1	10.6

being a highly regressive tax, and feasibility, since tax law usually required referenda to extend local taxes and these often failed.

Table 8.10 outlines the changes in state and local spending from 1946 through the Eisenhower years. The increase in educational expenditures reflects not simply rising quality but the onslaught of the World War II "baby boom," which caught almost every community unprepared in spite of ample forewarning. A basic difficulty for the localities was that they depended on the state government for power to tax. Yet even where the income tax and general sales tax were available to the locality, the collection expense and tax avoidance were more severe problems at the local level. A basic constraint at the state level was that representation in the state legislatures did not reflect changes in population shifts. Rural interests dominated the state legislatures and resisted efforts to redistrict and to expand taxes and expenditures to meet the needs of the growing cities.

Instead of being able to shift responsibility back to the states and localities, the federal government felt pressed to help meet some of their growing needs. The interstate highway system was begun, to be financed in large part by a federal trust fund supported by a federal gasoline tax. Federal aid for public welfare and the building of hospitals was increased; however, proposals to increase federal aid to education were blocked by southern congressmen, who rightly feared that the federal government would use such financial support as a lever to speed up racial integration in the public schools.

In summary, changes in the public sector budgets reflected the changing voter priorities of a mature and urban mass consumption economy. The public wants of many groups were not realized, and several excesses of the mass consumption economy became increasingly evident. The rise to affluence was creating wide disparities between the newly affluent middle- and high-income groups and certain pockets of poverty in the inner cities, Appalachia, and other areas. At the same time the media explosion helped certain industries to literally inundate the reader, listener, and viewer with advertising designed to create demand for their products. Moreover, many of these industries, as well as municipal governments, were exploiting natural resources in ways that were becoming real threats to the environment. Finally, in his Farewell Address in 1961, President Eisenhower issued an ominous warning:

Until the latest of our world conflicts, the United States had no armaments industry. American makers of plowshares could, with time and as required, make swords as well. But now we can no longer risk emergency improvisation of national defense; we have been compelled to create a permanent armaments industry of vast proportions. Added to this, $3\frac{1}{2}$ million men and women are directly engaged in the Defense Establishment. We annually spend on military security more than the net income of all United States corporations.

This conjunction of an immense Military Establishment and a large arms industry is new in the American experience. The total influence—economic, political, even spiritual—is felt in every city, every statehouse, every office of the Federal Government. We recognize the imperative need for this development. Yet we must not fail to comprehend its grave implications. Our toil, resources, and livelihood are all involved; so is the very structure of our society.

In the councils of government we must guard against the acquisition of unwarranted influence whether sought or unsought, by the military-industrial complex. The potential for the disastrous rise of misplaced power exists and will persist.

We must never let the weight of this combination endanger our liberties or democratic processes. We should take nothing for granted. Only an alert and knowledgeable citizenry can compel the proper meshing of the huge industrial and military machinery of defense with our peaceful methods and goals so that security and liberty may prosper together.

THE "NEW LIBERALISM" OF JOHN F. KENNEDY

The fiscal arguments used by John F. Kennedy in the 1960 election were compelling. Recessions in the late 1950s had disenchanted many people as to Republican macroeconomic policy; and the problems of economic imbalance mentioned above were becoming more pressing. These advantages plus a pleasing television charisma allowed him to post a very narrow victory over Richard Nixon.

Kennedy's brand of new liberalism contained many of the arguments outlined in the Stevenson campaigns of 1952 and 1956. The traditional liberal approaches had featured *more money* to solve problems of particular groups while using legislation and *regulatory agencies* to shore up cracks in the competitive system. These policies usually had the secondary aim of insuring voter support from a majority coalition. What Kennedy attempted to do was to emphasize broad social goals and translate these into specific public policies.

Kennedy's legislative accomplishments were much less impressive than his success in lifting individual and social aspirations. Although the Democrats had a slim majority in Congress, Republicans found it easy to defeat Kennedy's proposals with the support of southern Democrats. Administration-backed tax reforms, medicare, aid to education, civil rights, and urban programs all went down to defeat. On the other hand, certain of the Roosevelt and Truman programs—social security, public housing, and the minimum wage—were expanded.

THE MILITARY-INDUSTRIAL COMPLEX

Table 8.11 details federal budget expenditures by function in recent years and reveals the growth of the military-industrial complex. From 1960 to the height of the Vietnam war in 1968 defense expenditures grew from $54.4 billion to $96.7 billion.

During this growth process the predictions of President Eisenhower came true with a vengeance.[13]

It is almost a law of nature that large sustained expenditures on a particular function will encourage the growth of a large network of formal and informal alliances which enter into the expenditure decision-making process. It is not surprising, then, that the Defense Department has extended its influence not only into the armaments industry but into related industries as well. Congressmen whose districts stand to prosper are also Pentagon advocates. Moreover, through direct grants and agencies, such as the National Science Foundation, the Defense Department has substantially altered the pattern of education and research. Vested interests related to defense contracts have developed among labor and in those favored geographical regions.

These changes have had some disturbing effects on the decision-making process. Most important, of course, is the encouragement such a reinforced system of support gives to the allocation of a greater than optimum amount of resources to the military-industrial complex. Also disturbing are the inroads the Department of Defense has made in assuming the major decision-making prerogatives in the *legislative* as well as the *executive* branch. American foreign policy is strongly influenced by military concepts of "power," "spheres of influence," the "domino theory," and the like. Another disturbing feature of defense spending decision making is that the usual constraints of the market are missing. Not only is there no way to adequately estimate the worth of most of the expensive new armaments, but also costs are usually a secondary consideration.

Several of the less appealing of the budget conventions and procedures outlined in previous chapters come into play in determining defense allocations. The complexity of the defense programs and the expertise necessary for their evaluation require that a few persons in key agencies and committees have considerable power in determining the alternatives to be considered. A few congressmen and senators have gained considerable notoriety by directing the flow of defense contracts to their districts to enhance their industrial and commercial growth.

---

[13] A considerable amount of literature is appearing which treats this subject. Two works which outline the development are Seymour Melman, *Pentagon Capitalism* (New York: McGraw-Hill, 1970), and William Proxmire, *Report from Wastelands* (New York: Praeger, 1970).

TABLE 8–11

Federal budget expenditures
by function, 1960–1974[a] (in
billions of dollars)

	1960	1964	1966	1968	1970	1972	1974
Total	$92.2	$118.1	$130.7	$178.8	$196.6	$231.9	$268.7
Defense[b]	54.4	67.6	72.7	96.7	96.3	96.1	99.7
Interest	8.3	10.8	11.3	13.7	18.3	20.6	24.7
Agriculture	3.3	5.5	2.8	5.9	6.2	7.1	5.6
Natural resources	1.0	2.6	2.2	1.7	2.5	3.8	3.7
Commerce and transportation	4.8	3.0	6.8	8.0	9.3	11.2	11.6
Community development and housing	1.0	.0	.4	4.1	3.0	4.3	4.9
Education	1.3	1.3	2.5	7.0	7.3	9.8	10 .1
Health and income security	18.8	25.9	33.2	43.5	56.8	82.0	103.7
General government	1.3	2.3	2.3	2.6	3.3	4.9	6.0

[a] Data for 1974 are estimated from the budget.
[b] Includes international affairs and finance, space research and technology, and veterans' benefits and services.

One ploy used by the military in collusion with industry and occasionally with congressional committees has been the cost overrun. Often projects have been started with budget estimates well below what the actual costs are known to be. These foot-in-the-door techniques have been successful in adding over $10 billion a year to the defense budget for a number of years.

The shift towards defense industries has, of course, had a substantial impact on the composition of industry and employment in the United States. Seven favored states account for over half of all defense industry. The ordnance, aircraft, and electrical industries are heavily dependent on defense contracts. Moreover, owing to the concentration of these industries and the specialization required, any slowdown in defense spending would necessitate significant planning and aid to relocate these resources.

A number of attempts have been made in recent years to curb the more flagrant excesses of the military-industrial complex. Implementation of some of the budgeting techniques outlined in Chapter 6 has already helped illuminate the actual costs of programs. In addition, some defense contracts now include severe penalties for cost overruns and delays. It has also been suggested that the Defense Department's foreign policy role be curtailed, perhaps through reorganization of the Cabinet. Another proposal would create an independent civilian agency to exercise final authority over all procurement and contracts for the armed forces. These proposals, if accompanied by increased public awareness of the social choices involved, could lead to a significant shift in resources to urgent domestic needs.

POVERTY AND THE JOHNSON ADMINISTRATION

The legislative record of the Johnson administration contrasts sharply with that of the Kennedy administration. In the 1964 campaign the tragic assassination of President Kennedy and the Republican nomination of conservative Barry Goldwater helped Johnson to a landslide victory and a comfortable majority in both Houses of Congress. In short order he was able to enact many of the measures Kennedy had originated. Enacted, besides the 1964 income tax cut, were the Medicare program, a major aid-to-education act, and the Civil Rights Law of 1965.

The new trends in spending of the Johnson "War on Poverty" are outlined in Table 8.11. Expenditures on Health and Income Security increased from $25.9 billion in 1964 to $43.5 billion in 1968. Over the same period federal expenditures on education increased from $1.3 billion to $7.0 billion. Many pilot programs were also started to search for ways to eliminate the *causes* of poverty rather than just the symptoms. Most of these attempts have revealed that cures are not easy to come by, since the cycle of poverty usually derives from a family's entire social and economic environment—including educational and vocational opportunities and aspirations, nutrition, health, and so on. Obviously, programs designed to cure these ills will be more expensive in the short run than the traditional giveaway techniques.

The welfare programs have always been criticized for destroying the incentives of the poor. In the face of rising tax bills to meet defense expenditures and the growing array of other public needs at the federal, state, and local levels, the "taxpayer revolt" in the late 1960s and early 1970s has focused special criticism on the aid to families with dependent children (AFDC). Figure 8.2 shows the rapid increase of welfare payments of this type, which now account for more than two-thirds of those persons on welfare. The AFDC program has the effect of discouraging marriage and encouraging desertion so as to make the mother and children eligible for payments. These and other aspects of the welfare program, including

FIGURE 8–2

Number of persons
receiving welfare

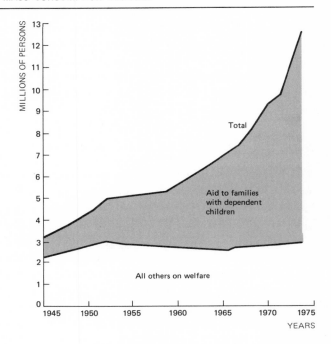

disincentive effects and inefficient administration, led the Nixon administration to back the "negative income tax plan" as a substitute for
existing programs. This plan, explained in more detail in Part III, makes
welfare payments a part of the personal income tax program except that
those families below a certain base receive a payment instead of paying
taxes. As a family moves towards higher income levels it receives smaller
amounts until it reaches a breakeven point. Nixon's plan, termed the
Family Assistance System, also features expanded vocational training
and aid to child day-care centers.

The negative income tax appeals to conservatives and liberals alike
on the basis of its promised efficiency. However, the attack on the basic
causes of poverty has been slowed by the Indochina war. Johnson's idea
of a "Great Society" with job opportunity for all never really got off
the ground. In fact, his efforts to increase both domestic and war expenditures without appropriate tax measures were a major cause of the
inflationary spiral. The Nixon adminstration, its hands full with the
unpopular Indochina war and a policy committed to stop inflation,
found itself limited in its capacity to restructure the welfare system.

PUBLIC CHOICES OF THE SEVENTIES:
THE DILEMMA OF URBAN FINANCES

THE NATURE OF URBAN BLIGHT

The trends in economic development mentioned earlier have placed great pressures on the fiscal capacities of America's urban communities. In the absence of adequate aid from the federal and state levels many are at the point of virtual collapse. While the population migration towards the cities has continued, the flight of industry and the middle and higher income groups from the central city has eroded the tax base, increased the crime rate, and caused growing areas of urban blight.

In the wake of the exodus, land and capital—buildings, plants, roads, and so on—have been left behind. However, capital in these forms does not particularly enhance the productivity or well-being of the remaining low-income groups; instead, the buildings deteriorate and property values fall. A *prisoner's dilemma* speeds the process. If all property owners would cooperate to keep their property in repair, the process would be stemmed. But if urban blight appears imminent, it doesn't pay the individual to refurbish; instead, it pays to get out as soon as possible— preferably before the surrounding properties have become run down. Often this process spreads urban blight into areas which otherwise would furnish suitable housing. One method of avoiding urban blight is for the property owners in a neighborhood to organize in recognition of their mutual dependence. More often the prisoner's dilemma prevails and urban blight, once begun, is accelerated.

Urban governments have been obliged to increase their outlays for public services: police and fire protection, sanitation, health education, transportation, and welfare. The welfare costs of cities have skyrocketed as a result of the continued influx of southern Negroes and immigrants with few skills but high fertility. Needs are expanding in geometric proportion while the tax base is eroding. The exodus from the city increases the tax burden on those who remain; and if the city attempts to raise taxes in order to pay for the growing needs, it simply speeds the exodus. On the other hand, political support for increases in government salaries and welfare payments grows as government workers and welfare recipients become a significant proportion of the electorate. These and subsequent observations will lead us to conclude that programs to ease the urban crises must take account of the cost-reward incentive patterns of the workers, consumers, firms, and politicians involved.

GOVERNMENTAL BOUNDARIES AND COSTS AND BENEFITS

The problem of externalities spilling over governmental boundaries is aggravated because of the wholesale balkanization of our metropolitan areas into numerous municipalities, counties, townships, and special districts. Often these boundaries are a matter of historical accident, and those of a particular governmental unit do not coincide with its functions. The degree of difficulty involved in reorganizing these governmental units depends on the nature of the vested interests and the political power wielded by the particular unit. The state government has ultimate authority to determine the composition of most government units within its boundaries, hence it is at this level that most reorganization battles take place.

Julius Margolis has analyzed the fiscal problems of urban communities in terms of the *spatial organization* of the economic activities which take place there.[14] Margolis starts from the proposition that every activity must occupy a unique site within the city. The market can dictate the right *amount* of heavy industry, light industry, business goods and services, personal goods and services, and so on; but an important role of government is not only to organize the public goods and services but to organize spatially all economic activities within the city.

Margolis observes that over time locational sites within the cities are highly substitutable. We have observed, for example, how mobile residential housing is in response to such stimuli as taxes and racial integration. This mobility can be beneficial in allowing firms to respond to the benefits of locating near complementary activities. At the same time, however, it allows firms, homeowners, and workers to escape paying for some of the services they receive and costs they create. The problem is aggravated when a metropolitan area is balkanized in many separate governing units with little flexibility. Since each of the governmental units has *veto* power over its own jurisdiction, it will not cooperate with other units if the *costs* to its inhabitants are greater than the *benefits*. Often the governmental units are caught in a *prisoner's dilemma*. If all units would cooperate—say in coordinating property tax rates or zoning ordinances—then all would be better off; but as long as one could be better off by not cooperating, it is probable that none will. The incentive patterns of the governmental decision makers may be unconducive to intergovernmental coordination. On the one hand, they are not inclined to give up responsibilities for which they receive pay and other rewards; and on the other hand, they will refrain from changes whose costs to their constituents are obvious even though greater but less obvious benefits will accrue to the community.

AN EXAMPLE: URBAN TRANSPORTATION

Urban transportation exemplifies the several types of interrelationships which may exist in an urban public activity. Planning for urban transportation obviously requires *area planning* by all of the relevant governmental units within the metropolitan area. To be efficient, highways, streets, railroads, subways, and bus routes must often cross governmental boundaries. Not only must the planning be coordinated, but, if all benefits and costs to the different areas are to be accounted for, some method of *joint funding* will have to be implemented. This in turn opens up the opportunity for some of the governmental divisions within the metropolitan area to "free ride," by declining to assume their fair share of the cost of the transportation network.

Other externalities are inherent in the close relationships among the different forms of urban transportation. The benefits and costs deriving from subway service depend on the highway system, buses, taxis, and so on. Trucks, taxis, buses, and private autos are jointly dependent on the road system. Consequently, when one mode of transportation is subsidized, the others are affected in one or more ways. Moreover, there are often social costs involved; for example, when the automobile is used in the central city, it creates air pollution and traffic congestion and requires parking area.

The more governmental units involved in transportation, the more difficult coordination becomes, especially since it is less likely that costs for an areawide plan will coincide with benefits for each unit. In practice, various agencies at different levels of government necessarily make decisions in piecemeal fashion. The federal and state governments subsidize private automobiles and trucking by building highways. At the same time, regulatory agencies are using other criteria to adjust the routes and rate structures of the railroads and airlines. The methods used often are not adequate for including all benefits and costs. For

---

[14] Julius Margolis, "Municipal Fiscal Structure in a Metropolitan Region, "*Journal of Political Economy*, June 1957, pp. 225–236 and "Metropolitan Finance Problems: Territories, Functions, and Growth," National Bureau of Economic Research, in *Public Finances: Needs, Sources, and Utilization* (Princeton, N.J.: Princeton University Press, 1961), pp. 229–293.

example, the federal and state governments subsidize automobile transportation through gasoline taxes, which act as user charges. But in the central cities automobiles cause air pollution, traffic congestion, and other problems, which are not matched with higher charges. And, as we have mentioned, the balkanization of metropolitan governmental units inhibits *areawide* coordination of more efficient transportation systems. Consequently, transportation problems become more acute and—along with urban blight, pollution, crime, growing welfare rolls, and high taxes—add impetus to the flight of persons and firms away from the central city.

POLITICAL REORGANIZATION, REVENUE SHARING, AND USER CHARGES

Several perspectives suggested in earlier chapters are helpful in analyzing urban fiscal problems and prescribing solutions. The most obvious fiscal maladjustment is that the geographical boundaries of the governing units do not coincide with the fiscal problems. The commuters from Suburbia do not pay for many of the services they receive from the city. Moreover, there are a number of externalities created by and imposed on the cities that we are just beginning to recognize. The cities have always attracted the rural poor from our country and abroad and they continue to bear this burden. However, national standards of education and welfare have been rising as the cities' tax base has been eroding. Moreover, the talented central city dwellers who take advantage of the educational expenditures, vocational training, and so on also join the exodus.

REORGANIZING METROPOLITAN GOVERNMENTS

Several approaches have been suggested for solving the problems of the cities. Let us begin by examining methods of accounting for the spillover effects mentioned above. The ideal solution is to create a metropolitan government which has adequate revenue sources and can provide services and planning for the whole metropolitan area. Within the context of this broad governing unit, responsibility could be delegated (with consent of the state government) to more narrowly based agencies for services best provided at that level. But can we expect the present institutional structure to develop in these directions? The prospects are rather gloomy. There are too many vested interests fixed within the present arrangement of balkanized governmental boundaries, various overlapping agencies, and the like. In the process of reorganization some of these interests would be impinged upon; thus, to the extent that they can impede reorganization, they will do so. Some of the more prominent reorganizational struggles involve the consolidation of adjoining cities and towns as a metropolitan area grows. In the course of the decision making over a consolidation proposal, arguments are put forth which on the one side outline the interdependence of the units and the benefits from consolidation and on the other side outline the special interests of each party. As long as one of the parties has veto power and feels that the proposal is not sufficiently beneficial, it will defeat it.

There are, of course, ways in which consolidation and reorganization reduce the capability of the governmental units to reflect the wishes of citizens. The existence of various governmental units within a metropolitan area offers the advantage of directly representing the preferences of those people. A necessary proviso is that these smaller units do in fact represent the interests of people within them. Three questions are involved: (1) whether preferences differ between the different areas, (2) whether the governmental units actually voice these preferences, and (3) whether the nature of the public goods involved allows production of different amounts for the different groups. If preferences do in fact differ, the arguments for having separate units participate in the decision-making process may parallel those for the separation of powers and for checks and balances within the state and federal systems. The gains realized when groups can maximize their welfare by making tradeoffs, and the attendant protection against "too much" concentration of power, may outweigh the advantages of an efficient centralized metropolitan government.[15]

Moreover, if there are obvious mutual benefits, governmental units can cooperate to realize them. They can, for example, cooperate to organize broadly based agencies and authorities which have taxing authority and planning capabilities. Where the benefits of the service are divisible, *user charges* can be employed. Cities already rely on user charges to meet some of the costs of water treatment, public transportation, and other services, but resource allocation would be further enhanced if more of the direct benefits of public services were financed in this way.

---

[15] For further examination of effects of centralization on budgeting see Charles M. Tiebout and David B. Houston, "Metropolitan Finance Reconsidered: Budget Functions and Multi-level Governments," *The Review of Economics and Statistics*, vol. 44 (November 1962).

TABLE 8–12	Year	Total	Education	Highways	Public welfare
State and local expenditures	1950	$ 27.9	$ 7.2	$ 3.8	$ 2.9
by function, selected years	1955	40.4	11.9	6.5	3.2
1950–1976 (in billions of	1960	61.0	18.7	9.4	4.4
dollars)	1965	86.7	28.6	12.2	6.3
	1970	148.1	52.7	16.4	14.7
	1976[b]	261.1	96.2	19.6	34.5

Year	Health and hospi- tals	Police and fire	Financial Adminis- tration and general control	Other general[a]	Insur- ance trust	Utility and liquor stores	Basic urban services[c]	Admin- istra- tion[d]	Other[e]
1950	$ 1.7	$1.2	$1.0	$ 2.7	$2.4	$2.7			
1955	2.5	1.9	1.4	3.7	2.8	3.9			
1960	3.8	2.9	2.1	10.6	4.0	5.1			
1965	5.4	3.9	2.8	15.5	5.0	7.1			
1970	9.7	6.5	4.7	20.5	7.3	9.5			
1976[b]	18.5						24.7	35.5	32.1

[a] Includes police and fire, sanitation and sewerage, recreation, housing and urban renewal, and other general expenditures.
[b] Estimate by Schultze et al., *Setting National Priorities: The 1972 Budget* (Washington, D.C.: Brookings, 1971) p. 142.
[c] Includes police and fire, sewerage, recreation, housing and urban renewal, and transportation and terminals
[d] Includes administration and general control, general public buildings, interest on general debt, employment services, and miscellaneous functions.
[e] Includes utility deficit, debt retirement and contributions to retirement systems.
Source: 1950–1970, Department of Commerce, Bureau of the Census.

Yet, while certain situations lend themselves to intergovernmental cooperation, we have outlined several ways in which the haphazard balkanization of governmental units over the years has led to serious maladjustments in the planning and budgeting processes of localities. An important point is that *the state government must bear ultimate responsibility for reorganizing metropolitan governments.* This is because the states *create* the local governments and have authority over the laws under which they may be reorganized. The states, for example, control the conditions under which localities may vote to consolidate. They also control the revenue and debt regulations under which different types of local government may cooperate. Indeed, an important proportion of local funds pass through state hands. Thus the state can use significant financial incentives to encourage or enforce reorganization. We see, then, that the fiscal crises of the cities are directly tied to those of the states. In fact, the budgets of localities, states, and the federal government must be considered together.

GENERAL REVENUE SHARING AND RISING DEMANDS FOR STATE AND LOCAL SPENDING

Table 8.12 illustrates the tremendous growth of state and local expenditures since 1950. The changes in our economic system creating these needs have been outlined above. Total expenditures increased from $27.9 billion in 1950 to $148.1 billion in 1970 and consisted of increases in all major state and local functions: education, highways, and public welfare. Increases in school-age population, higher standards for teachers and facilities, and the extension of college-level education to a much greater proportion of the population are all important factors in the growth of educational expenditures from $18.7 billion in 1960 to $52.7 billion in 1970. And although the rate of growth in population is slowing, demands for better services, more vocational training, and rising costs promise continued increases during the 1970s. The population boom and the needs created by urbanization during the 1960s are reflected in the increases on highways ($9.4 billion to $16.4 billion), on public welfare ($4.4 billion to $14.7 billion), on health and hospitals ($3.8 billion to $9.7 billion), and on police and fire protection ($2.9 billion to $6.5 billion).

Table 8.13 illustrates sources of revenue on which states and localities have drawn to finance increased expenditures. State and local revenue increased from $60.3 billion in 1960 to $150.1 billion in 1970. The major contributors were the property tax ($16.4 billion to $34.1 billion), the sales taxes ($11.8 billion to $30.3 billion), the individual income tax ($2.5 billion to $10.8 billion), and the corporation income tax ($1.2 billion to $3.7 billion). Although impressive, the increase in state and local revenues has been insufficient to meet the growing needs of states and localities. In the late 1960s and early 1970s a "fiscal crisis" of major proportions developed in a few of our states and most of our large cities. Four factors contributed:

First, a combination of rapid inflation and recession increased the costs of public services while dampening the increase in revenues.

Second, taxpayers virtually revolted against further increases in taxes. This last factor is especially crucial for localities, since local tax changes more often require local referenda. Moreover, the move to urban areas does not seem to have been accompanied by increased taxpayer awareness that in urban areas more public services are needed and their cost is greater.

TABLE 8–13

State and local revenues by
source, selected years
1950–1976 (in billions
of dollars)

Year	Total	Property	Sales	Individual income	Corporation income	Federal grants	Other
1950	$ 25.6	$ 7.3	$ 5.2	$ 0.8	$0.6	$ 2.5	$ 9.2
1955	37.6	10.7	7.6	1.2	0.7	3.1	14.3
1960	60.3	16.4	11.8	2.5	1.2	7.0	21.4
1965	87.8	22.6	17.1	4.1	1.9	11.0	31.1
1970	150.1	34.1	30.3	10.8	3.7	21.9	49.3
1976[a]	251.7	50.2	43.5	22.0	6.2	45.4	84.3

[a] Estimate by Schultze *et al.*, *Setting National Priorities: The 1972 Budget* (Washington, D.C.: Brookings, 1971) p. 142.
Source: 1950–1970, Department of Commerce, Bureau of the Budget.

Third, there is the difficulty, given the present institutional structure, of matching revenue resources with needs. The states have recourse to an impressive array of revenue sources, including the personal income tax, but the current distribution of political power often inhibits the use of these resources to meet the pressing needs of the cities. At the same time, states differ widely in needs and taxing capability.

Fourth, state and local public *needs* have been expanding faster than GNP. As outlined previously, increases in population, rising per capita income, and urbanization have created demands for public sector services. Population growth has created needs for more schools, hospitals, and other public services. Urbanization has created more traffic, trash, air and water pollution, crime, and urban "blight." Many public goods and services are complementary to the private goods purchased as incomes rise; for example, as the number of cars per family increases, greater demands are created for highways and traffic control.

In their examination of national priorities and the budget, Schultze, Fried, Rivlin, and Teeters have attempted to estimate roughly what roles inflation, increased workload, and increased quality of services have played in the expansion of state and local spending.[16] All three factors have been important. Rising prices have accounted for the largest proportion (43.8 percent) of the growth in spending, while increased scope and quality of services also have played an important part (30.0 percent). Increases in workload accounted for another 26.2 percent.

Estimates of future needs and revenue sources project a continued disparity between the two. Schultze et al., for example, project state and local revenues at existing tax rates (and with current federal grant programs expanded to account for price and workload increases) to reach $251.7 billion by 1976. And if expenditures increase at the same rate as they did during 1965–1969, they will reach about $261.1 billion by 1976. The annual gap between revenues and expenditures will be about $10 billion. This gap would seem less formidable were it not for the taxpayer revolt and the fact that the cities and states with the greater needs are those with limited capabilities.

There are several approaches the federal government might take to relieve the fiscal crises of the states and cities. The most promising, *general revenue sharing*, was inaugurated in a limited program in late 1972. This is the practice of *earmarking* a portion of federal revenues for distribution to the states and/or cities according to some formula. The shift towards this method encourages greater reliance on the federal income tax and more decision making at the state and local levels. A suggested alternative would be for the federal government to give a *tax credit* for taxes paid to states. While this would increase state and local revenue capacity in theory, in reality positive action (which has been inadequate in the past) would still be required of the states. Moreover, a federal tax credit would not solve the problem of distributing funds to the states and cities with the greatest needs.

Another alternative would be for the federal government to increase its *special grants* to states and localities. As Table 8.13 shows, the federal special grant programs have increased considerably in recent years. Often the joint administration of these programs turns out poorly because of its complexity and the uncertainty of depending on rather fickle and often tardy congressional appropriations committees. A related and more rational alternative would be for the federal government to take over one of the major state and local *functions* rather than increase its participation in the form of special grants. We have considered the question of federal implementation of the negative income tax and related programs which would relieve the states and localities of a rather large portion of their expenditures on public welfare. We have also noted the argument that the geographical spillover effects of public welfare programs make it an appropriate federal function. Some observers, however, contend that greater general revenue sharing is needed even if the federal government does take over the major burden of public welfare.

Let us outline the pros and cons of expanded general revenue sharing.

[16] Charles L. Schultze, Edward R. Fried, Alice M. Rivlin, and Nancy H. Teeters, *Setting National Priorities: the 1972 Budget* (Washington, D.C.: Brookings, 1971), pp. 134–157.

First, in describing the nature of the fiscal crises facing the cities and states we have noted that there are wide disparities between resource capabilities and needs. Neither the tax credit alternative nor the federal takeover of welfare would accomplish the neccessary distribution of funds to the states, cities, and agencies in accord with the needs that have been described. Many advocates of "no strings attached" revenue sharing argue that the lower levels of government are more responsive to the needs of their constituency and are better equipped to mold programs to meet those needs. They go on to argue that the different governmental bodies should be left free to innovate and thus provide a variety of approaches. The skeptics of general revenue sharing argue that state and local governments are often *less* responsive to public needs. They point out that fewer people vote in state and local elections, political power is often too diffused (thus making room for political machines to take over), the pay for state and local representatives is too low, and the budget processes have many weaknesses. Moreover, states and localities have not shown the initiative for reform so necessary if their problems are to be dealt with. For example, the state legislatures, often controlled by agrarian and suburban interests, have often been insensitive to the needs of the cities.

As general revenue sharing is expanded, two key issues will spark controversy: the formula for distributing funds to states and/or localities and the fiscal controls (including institutional reform) to be required. Many different formulas have been suggested. Most agree that distribution should be according to need—but what need? Education? Welfare? Urban blight? Transportation? Even after we decide which need or needs to focus on, what data can be gathered to estimate differences in need among cities and states?

Another suggestion is that the formula include distribution by *effort*, say, with respect to a state's current tax burdens relative to per capita income. This would encourage states to increase their own revenue production.

Another suggestion is to make revenue sharing contingent on reform of budgetary and administrative institutions by state and local governments. This proposal runs counter to the "no strings attached" argument; however, a major cause of the present dilemma is that the existing institutional structure has not responded even where the revenue capacity has been present. A related question is whether funds should be "passed through" the states to the local governing bodies. Presumably this could be accomplished on the basis of differences in need among localities. Implementing the "pass-through" of funds to the local bodies may present major difficulties and could necessitate substantial changes in governmental structure because of major differences in governmental structure within and among states. For example, if the goal of the revenue sharing is to distribute funds for education, we find different degrees of centralization of decision making among states. In some states the local school board is quite powerful and even has revenue-raising authority; in others the state government makes most decisions and distributes the major portion of educational funds.

BUDGET CONTROL VIA ANNUAL CEILINGS

The budget battles waged between Congress and President Nixon in the mid-1970s elicited many criticisms of the budget process that we have examined in earlier chapters. For example, in seeking public support for his budget cuts, Nixon used several arguments: (1) that Congress was subject to the pressures of interest groups who, through key persons on key committees, could exercise undue influence; (2) that since expenditure and revenue decisions were divorced and expenditure decisions were divided among several appropriations committees, Congress tended to spend irresponsibly. Nixon claimed that the executive has a better perspective from which to view the budget as a whole. With respect to the overall size of the budget there are of course two facets: (1) the relative size of public versus private spending, and (2) the impact of the budget on inflation and employment.

In 1972 Nixon used these arguments to justify his vetoing and impounding of funds. Actually several public choice alternatives were involved. Within the budget Nixon chose to maintain defense spending at its wartime level while curtailing programs aimed at creating jobs, education, income maintenance, urban redevelopment, and cleaning up the environment. Presumably the Democratically-controlled Congress would have chosen other ways to cut expenditures. Alternatively, the macroeconomic requirements for lower aggregate spending could have been met by raising taxes if Congress had been satisfied that its spending decisions reflected public preferences as to the best allocation of resources.

The budget battles of 1973 and 1974 were particularly fierce. Nixon insisted that Congress keep itself within a $250 billion ceiling for fiscal year 1973. When Congress failed to do this, Nixon used the pocket veto and impounding to enforce the $250 billion ceiling. Although the courts found several of Nixon's cutbacks illegal, they were for the most part effective; and Congress failed to override his vetoes.

All of this brought considerable pressure on Congress to "get its own house in order." And it established a joint committee to work out means of establishing and implementing annual budget ceilings and revenue goals. At this writing Congress favors such a plan; however, its implementation will be extraordinarily difficult. For even if Congress can agree on a ceiling each year, its implementation will involve setting limits for each of the appropriations sub-committees. Obviously setting the overall limit and more specific limits will require yet another decision-making layer complete with conflict-reducing devices, deference to expertise and so on. The study committees recommended the following plan:

(1) Budget committees would be established in the House and Senate. The House committee would have twenty-one members; seven from the Appropriations Committee, seven from the Ways and Means Committee, and seven from other committees. The Senate Committee, (fifteen members) would have five from the Appropriations Committee, five from the Finance Committee, and five from other committees.

(2) The budget committees would present resolutions each year setting the overall spending ceilings to include the *ceilings for the various subcommittees of the appropriations committees.*

(3) Any amendment offered when an appropriations bill reached the floor would have to include a proposed compensatory cut elsewhere or a tax or debt adjustment.

(4) In September and December readjustments in ceilings could be made by the budget committees to reflect new economic developments (to include new revenue estimates). If required to meet the new debt limit, the December bill could include a tax surcharge.

It is by no means certain that the proposed plan will be acceptable to Congress. It will be interesting to see what new budget institutions evolve within Congress in its attempts at self-regulation via budget ceilings.

A FINAL COMMENT

In the preceding chapters we have examined the interaction among economic growth, private and public wants, and changing private and public choice institutions.

A basic technique we have used is to utilize rather simple but abstract models and concepts to analyze ever-changing "real world" public choice problems.

The ideal laissez faire model which features perfect competition in every market has provided a norm for evaluating "real world" governmental functions. The growth models of Wagner, Marx, Veblen, and Rostow, while not yielding definitive results, have provided frames of references for examining the public sector response to changing economic conditions—industrialization, urbanization, and the many types of externalities created by increasing interdependence. Our development of voting models and concepts has provided insight into the political and economic forces at work within the budgetary institutions of the public sector. Our analysis of such factors as conflict-reducing conventions and the veto power inherent in our system of checks and balances, has offered insight into the various ways our budget rules and institutions may lead to misallocations of resources. Our analysis of the indivisible nature of public good benefits versus the direct benefits of private goods, the effect of advertising and the like, has demonstrated the possibility of social imbalance between the private and public sectors.

Our introduction to public choice problems and their analysis has been very general. The student is encouraged to use the models, concepts and perspectives for more intensive examination of the specific public choice issues. New questions are constantly presenting themselves: What are the public choice considerations of new arms control agreements, changing trade relations with the Common Market, Congress' shift away from strict seniority rules for appointing committee chairmen, the Nixon Administration's practice of cutting programs specifically funded by Congress, the introduction of the negative income tax, and changes in wage and price controls?

In the process of using the concepts developed above to analyze "real world" issues many questions are raised which require better understanding of the effects of taxes and expenditures on individual economic behavior, income distribution, and on the macroeconomic variables. In Parts III and IV we will attempt to provide a framework for answering these questions.

III
MICROECONOMICS AND
THE PUBLIC SECTOR

9
MICROECONOMIC EFFECTS ON THE INDIVIDUAL: SOME BEHAVIORAL MODELS

What sorts of economic behavior can we expect from individuals and firms in response to various public spending and taxing policies? Can the burden of some taxes be shifted more easily than others? Who actually pays? These questions have been raised on several occasions in previous chapters and bear importantly on some of the conclusions we have reached. It is now time to go behind the assumptions concerning economic behavior and the incidence of taxes and expenditures and to look at the multitude of individual decisions making up their aggregate effects.

We begin by examining some behavioral models of the individual as consumer and input owner. (In later chapters we will consider the behavior of the firm.) We again work from the assumption that an individual seeks to maximize welfare; consequently, we will be building on some of the basic models introduced previously. Before examining the particulars of expenditures and taxes, let us further develop these basic models with respect to, first, a consumer in response to nonneutrality among private goods; second, a consumer in response to nonneutrality among private and public goods; third, an input owner in response to nonneutrality among consumption and investment; fourth, an input owner in response to nonneutrality among investment alternatives; and, finally, an input owner in response to nonneutrality among employment opportunities.

NONNEUTRALITY AMONG PRIVATE GOODS

The question, "How do consumers respond to nonneutral taxes and transfers?" has come up on several occasions, and we have employed the basic model of welfare-maximizing behavior. In Parts I and II we used the model to develop criteria by which to evaluate taxes and transfers. *Neutral* taxes and transfers were defined as those which did not affect the price ratios established in private sector markets. Such taxes and transfers do not change the relative desirability of commodities but do, of course, change the individual's purchasing power. Conversely, *nonneutral* taxes and transfers do change price ratios and encourage the consumer to substitute one good for another.

Consider the familiar indifference curve model shown in Figure 9.1.[1] Given the budget constraint, the individual adjusts purchases so as to

---

[1] Note that these indifference curves depict the usual utility model in which food and clothing are assumed to be the only two goods available. We recall that the special "partial" utility functions used in Chapter 3 featured a utility peak at the most desired combination of two public goods, and it was inherently assumed that *other* private or public goods could be acquired with the funds not used on the two in question.

FIGURE 9–1

Consumer response to
neutral transfers and taxes:
the normal good case

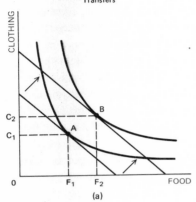

Transfers

(a)

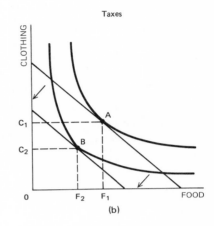

Taxes

(b)

FIGURE 9–2

Consumer response to neutral
transfers and taxes: the
inferior good case

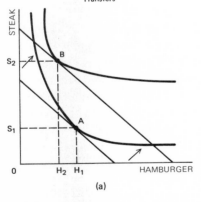

Transfers

(a)

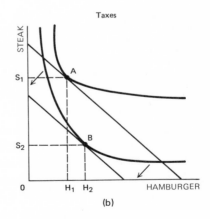

Taxes

(b)

reach the highest level of utility attainable. This equilibrium occurs at
point A, where the slope of the indifference curve (the marginal rate of
substitution) is equal to the slope of the budget constraint (the ratio of
commodity prices):

$$MRS_{FC} = \frac{P_F}{P_C}$$

What happens if we introduce a transfer or a tax which changes income but has no effect on the price ratio? The budget constraint shifts in a parallel fashion. A neutral transfer [Figure 9.1(a)] shifts the budget constraint *out* from the origin, and the new equilibrium, *B*, features an increase in the purchases of both food and clothing. A neutral tax [Figure 9.1(b)] shifts the budget constraint towards the origin, where at the new equilibrium less of each good is purchased.

A somewhat obvious but important fact has become clear: the effect of a *neutral* tax or transfer is exactly the same as a change in *income*. Figure 9.1 is not to be interpreted as showing the two commodities being purchased at the same ratio as income changes. In fact, maintaining the same ratio would require that equilibrium points follow a ray drawn from the origin, and this does not necessarily hold even for normal goods. The proportion of the budget spent on a commodity at different income levels depends on the shape of the indifference curve. Purchases of some goods, known as inferior goods, may in fact be *reduced* as income increases. Such a phenomenon is depicted in Figure 9.2(a). As the income of the individual is increased (say by means of a transfer of money), he reduces his purchases of hamburger from H_1 to H_2. The converse may also occur. As shown in Figure 9.2(b), the individual increases his purchases of the inferior good as his income is reduced by a neutral tax.

Now let us consider the effects of nonneutral taxes and transfers. Assume that the individual is awarded a transfer in the form of food stamps, which in effect reduces the price he pays for food [Figure 9.3(a)]. The price of clothing, on the other hand, remains the same, so that the shift in the budget constraint *rotates* outward. Consequently, the new equilibrium at *E* is the result of both an *income* and a *substitution effect*. Using our knowledge of the income effect, we may now isolate that part of the total adjustment which results from *substitution* at the new price ratios. First we draw an imaginary budget constraint tangent to the original indifference curve but parallel to the new budget constraint (thus it features the new price ratio). The shift from *B* to *E* obviously is due to the income effect.[2] It follows that the movement along the indifference curve from *A* to *B*, the substitution effect, is due solely to the change in the price ratio.

The effect of a nonneutral tax, depicted in Figure 9.3(b), is analogous. Assume an excise tax is placed on food while no tax is placed on clothing.

---

[2] Note that the dotted line and the new budget constraint are parallel, just as in Figure 9.1 the budget constraints are parallel.

FIGURE 9–3

Consumer responses to nonneutral taxes and transfers

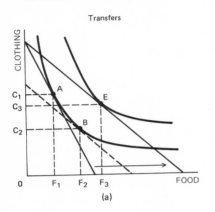

(a)

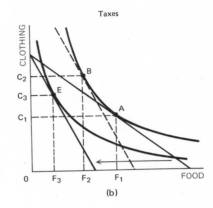

(b)

The budget constraint rotates in towards the origin, and the shift from A to E includes both a substitution (A to B) and an income (B to E) effect.

The substitution effect of a nonneutral tax or transfer will also influence the individual to buy more of the good whose price becomes relatively smaller. We have seen, however, that the income effect may work either in the same direction or against the relative price change (substitution effect). The income effect of a normal good works in the same direction as the relative price change; that is, an increase (or decrease) in income makes for an increase (or decrease) in quantity purchased [as depicted in Figures 9.3(a) and (b)]. As we have seen, however, the income effect of an inferior good may work against the substitution effect; that is, an increase (or decrease) in income may result in a decrease (or increase) in quantity purchased.

We have now made several observations that will furnish the basic building blocks for our forthcoming examination of taxes and public expenditures:

1. A change in taxes or transfers may affect consumer choices in two distinct ways: by changing the relative prices of commodities and/or by changing the individual's income.

2. A change in the composition of purchases caused by a *neutral* tax or transfer depends only on the income effect. The normal case exhibits a positive rela-

tionship between income and quantity purchased; but in certain cases, termed inferior goods, quantity purchased will change in the opposite direction.

3. A change in the composition of purchases caused by a *nonneutral* tax or transfer involves both an income and a substitution effect. The substitution effect will always influence the individual to purchase more of the good whose price is lowered relative to other prices. The income effect may augment the substitution effect (in the case of normal goods) or may tend to partially offset it.[3]

We may now make a further observation:

4. The repercussions of the substitution effect on purchases of other goods depend on their relationship with the taxed good. The demand for a close substitute or a complement for the taxed good will shift. For example, an excise tax on beer may cause the individual to shift to a substitute, say liquor. At the same time his demand for pretzels, a complement to beer, will fall. It follows to predict the economic effects of a nonneutral tax or transfer we must estimate the "cross-elasticity relationships"[4] among all goods which may be affected.

An important part of our subsequent analysis will concern the different degrees in neutrality found in taxes and transfers. The federal tax on personal income obviously is more neutral than several of the excise taxes; yet, as we shall see, even income taxes create some substitution effects, and since excise taxes are usually imposed on goods with inelastic demand, they may occasion little substitution.

PUBLIC GOODS AS SUBSTITUTES OR COMPLEMENTS FOR PRIVATE GOODS

Having considered the relationship among taxes, transfers, and the choice among private goods, we next ask: How does public good production

---

[3] The student familiar with price theory will recall that in a very special case the income effect may be stronger than the substitution effect, thus defying the law of demand (a negative relationship between price and quantity). This possibility, known as Giffen's paradox, is discussed in most microeconomic theory texts.

[4] Cross-elasticity of demand is a measure of the responsiveness of demand to changes in the price of other goods. More specifically, it is

$$n_{zy} = \frac{\text{percentage change in quantity demanded of good X}}{\text{percentage change in price of good Y}}$$

The closer the goods are related (as substitutes or complements), the larger the quantity reaction to a price change, and thus the greater the numerical value (positive or negative) of the cross-elasticity.

FIGURE 9–4

A shift in preferences in
response to production of a
complementary public good

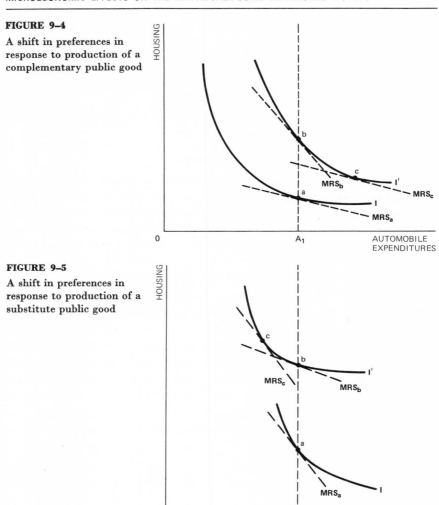

FIGURE 9–5

A shift in preferences in
response to production of a
substitute public good

affect choices among private goods? Fortunately, answers are quickly
forthcoming if we simply extend the results of the models just presented.

Public good production may effect the choice among private goods in
one of three ways: (1) by leaving their relative attractiveness unchanged,
(2) by complementing one of the private goods, or (3) by substituting for
one of the private goods.

The first possibility needs little explanation. What is required is that the production of the public good does not change the rate at which individuals are willing to trade one good for another. In terms of our indifference curve model this means that the marginal rate of substitution (the slope of the indifference curve) remains unchanged. It is unlikely, for example, that an increase in defense expenditures will have much effect on an individual's choice between apples and oranges.

Public production of a complement to a private good will, however, change the rate at which individuals are willing to trade. The complemented good will become relatively more attractive. For example, the benefits from expenditures on automobiles are increased by greater public expenditures on highways. A rigorous diagrammatic presentation of complementarity would require three dimensions, since three goods are involved; however, the two-dimensional drawing in Figure 9.4 will illustrate the points we wish to make.

In order to retain a basis for comparison we arbitrarily hold automobile expenditure constant at A_1. An increase in highway expenditure shifts the indifference curve (and the whole pattern of indifference curves) from I to I'. In the process the slope of the indifference curve (the marginal rate of substitution, MRS) becomes *steeper* as shown by the slopes of the dashed lines at a and b. Thus, automobile expenditures are relatively more attractive, and at any given price ratio the individual would substitute automobile for housing expenditures. For example, if the original price ratio between housing and automobile expenditures (the dashed line at a) still obtained, the individual would wish to move from b to c (note the dashed line at c is parallel to that at a); in other words, he has incentive to increase automobile expenditure.

The third possibility involves public good production which substitutes for a private good. Obviously, the private good would become less attractive relative to other private goods. Figure 9.5 depicts such a case. Suppose expenditures are increased on a public activity, public education, which substitutes for private education. The indifference curve pattern would shift in the manner shown by I and I'. The slope, MRS, at output level E_1, would *decrease*. Thus, private education would become less attractive, and there would be a tendency to substitute expenditures on private housing for those on private education.

We pause here for an important observation. Any evaluation of the costs and benefits of a public good expenditure must take into account the good's substitute and/or complementary relationship with other goods

FIGURE 9–6

The income effect of a
proportional tax rate,
public and private goods

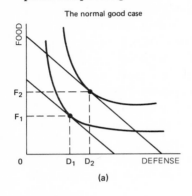

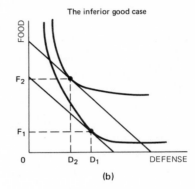

(a)

(b)

FIGURE 9–7

Individual preferences and
the indivisibility of public
good supply

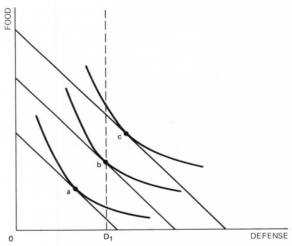

and the individual's welfare-maximizing behavior in response to its
production.

NONNEUTRALITY BETWEEN PRIVATE AND PUBLIC GOODS

In Chapter 3 we considered how taxes might enhance agreement among
individuals as to the best level of public good production. At that time

we were interested in how the economic impact of various taxes on individual welfare might affect his voting behavior. Since the choice involves both private and public goods, let us briefly reconsider the model.

We recall that we cannot legitimately speak of "neutrality" with respect to the *price ratios* between private and public sector goods, since the latter are not priced in the private sector. Even so, it is useful to assume that the price/tax ratio approximates the rate at which the individual thinks he can trade off public for private goods. We assume also that only two goods, food and defense, are produced in the economy and that the tax is a *proportional income tax.*

Consider Figure 9.6(a). Since the tax rate is proportional, the price/tax ratio does not change as income increases. Consequently, any desire to move towards additional food or defense depends entirely on the income effect. As income increases, the individual, if he could determine the amount of defense to be produced, would desire both more food and more defense. Thus, by definition, both are normal goods (that is, they exhibit a positive income effect).

Can some public goods be considered *inferior goods*? Figure 9.6(b) depicts the case of an individual who desires that less be spent (and less taxes be levied) for defense as his income increases. This is not the typical case, but several more realistic possibilities immediately come to mind. Increases in an individual's income level to where he can afford to own and operate his own automobile may well result in a desire to *reduce* public spending on (and taxes for) public transportation. Demand for public recreation facilities may also decrease as incomes increase. Higher income individuals find they prefer private recreation—say, the country club swimming pool rather than a public pool; consequently, they desire to reduce expenditure on (and taxes for) public recreation.

Unfortunately, the wishes of the individual as to the level of public good production are likely to be frustrated. Since public good supply is indivisible, the amount produced cannot be that which maximizes individual satisfaction in the usual sense. Briefly consider Figure 9.7 and the conclusions reached in Chapter 3. Assume that majority vote is used to determine output and that preference functions of individuals within the economy are similar. The middle income voters will determine the level of defense to be produced, D_1. Lower income groups will desire less defense (and less taxes), and upper income groups will desire more defense (and more taxes, again assuming that the proportional tax share plan is fixed). If, however, the public activity in question is an *inferior*

FIGURE 9–8

A progressive tax which offsets a positive income effect

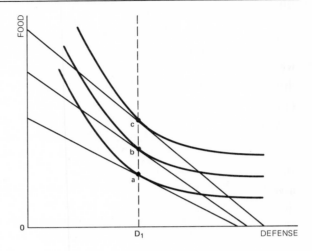

FIGURE 9–9

Present versus future consumption; income tax

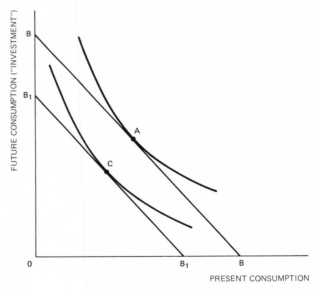

public good, the situations of individuals with different incomes are re-versed. The median income groups still determine the output level, but the lower income groups now desire greater output (and taxes) while the higher income groups want less output (and taxes).

Another dimension is added if we relax the requirement that taxes be proportional. With progressive taxation it is possible to set rates so that all individuals are "satisfied" with the amounts of a normal public good produced (see Figure 9.8). The tax rate increases with income and exactly offsets the income effect. If the rates were less progressive, we would still have dissatisfaction in the same direction (lower income groups desiring less defense and higher income groups desiring more) but to a lesser degree. On the other hand, too much progressivity will lead the higher income groups to advocate less spending on defense and the lower income groups to advocate more.

We have observed several different ways the tax structure can affect the welfare-maximizing choices made by individuals of different income groups. Without knowledge of individual preference patterns we cannot predict the response of a particular individual, but our observations do allow us to form testable hypotheses. For example, we would expect that under proportional or regressive income tax rates higher income groups would favor increased output of normal public goods while lower income groups would favor less. Similar reasoning can be used to formulate hypotheses concerning progressive tax rates and inferior public goods.

NONNEUTRALITY BETWEEN CONSUMPTION AND INVESTMENT

Let us suppose now that one may dispose of one's income only by spending on a single "consumption" good or else by investing. "Investment" here is used in the financial sense and does not necessarily involve the decision by a firm to employ additional real capital.

The individual's response to a tax depends on his initial motivation for saving and investing. The usual motivation is to postpone consumption. With a positive rate of return there is the additional incentive of being able to consume more in the future than is possible in the present. Another reason for saving is simply to accumulate wealth and its attendant advantages—economic and political power, security, prestige, and so on.

We first consider only the alternatives of present consumption and future consumption. (Figure 9.9). Income is fixed at BB. The slope of BB incorporates the rate of return on financial investment. There is only one possible investment alternative and we assume it involves no risk or uncertainty. The shape of the indifference curves depends on the individual's predilection between present and future consumption. We assume that both are subject to the law of diminishing marginal utility of income.

FIGURE 9–10

Present versus future consumption; tax on present consumption

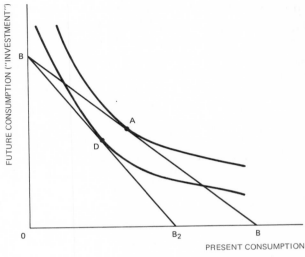

FIGURE 9–11

Present versus future consumption; tax on future consumption

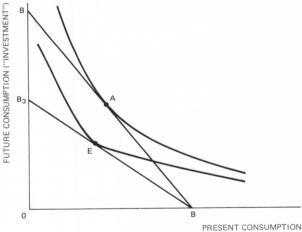

Hence, as one is substituted for the other, it loses its relative attractiveness. The initial equilibrium is at point A. We will consider three basic ways a tax may be imposed: on income (excluding interest), on future consumption, or on present consumption.

A TAX ON INCOME

A tax imposed on income which excludes interest has no substitution effect. Line BB is shifted parallel towards the origin: $B_1 B_1$. The new equilibrium at C reflects only the income effect.

A general sales tax (on present and future consumption) would have the same effect as a proportional income tax in our simple model since all income must be spent on either present or future consumption. A general sales tax gives no incentive to substitute, since it has no influence on the relative prices (both present and future consumption are taxed at the same per cent).

A TAX ON PRESENT CONSUMPTION

A different result occurs when the tax is imposed only on present consumption. Such a tax causes a shift in the budget constraint similar to that shown by BB_2 in Figure 9.10. Both an income and a substitution effect are included in the adjustment from equilibrium A to D. While the income effect is toward reduction of both present and future consumption, the substitution effect encourages future over present consumption. If it is the purpose of the fiscal authorities to reduce consumption temporarily —say, during a period of inflation—the tax on present consumption is more appropriate than a tax on both present and future consumption, because both the income and substitution effects encourage reduction of present consumption. Thus the tax's duration—or rather the duration expected by the individual—is crucial in determining response to the tax.

A TAX ON FUTURE CONSUMPTION

A tax on future consumption is shown in Figure 9.11. The budget constraint shifts from BB to BB_3. In the process of moving from equilibrium A to E the individual experiences both an income and a substitution effect—the latter an encouragement to substitute present for future consumption.

Without precise knowledge of individual preference patterns we cannot predict the effect of such a tax on present consumption. The income effect and the substitution effects are operating in different directions. In Figure 9.11 the income effect outweighs the substitution effect, so that present consumption is slightly reduced. It is quite possible that the substitution effect could be stronger than the one pictured; in fact, it could outweigh the income effect so as to keep consumption at the pretax level or even increase it. The result again depends on the individual's reasons for saving and investing. To the extent that he has a consumption *goal* for the future period the income effect will encourage even greater saving; but to the extent that he is merely maximizing welfare through either present or future consumption the change in prices will influence him towards present consumption. All taxes on saving, financial investment, or return to financial investment have the effect of increasing the relative attractiveness of present over future consumption as described above.

ADDITIONAL OBSERVATIONS

In practice, several factors complicate the responses indicated by our simple model. These will be explored in succeeding chapters; but we can make several important observations here by simply considering our models and assumptions.

We have, for example, assumed that consumers are rational and that their expectations about prices and future government activity are stable. Moreover, our limited knowledge of the shape of individual preference patterns may lead to erroneous predictions. For example, it may be important to know the determination with which individuals pursue certain savings or consumption " goals." If an individual has a target amount of savings and future consumption—such as sending his son to college—he will vigorously resist income and substitution effects even though they discriminate against future consumption. If, on the other hand, the individual is determined to maintain his present level of consumption—say, because he must " keep up with the Joneses "—even significant changes in the price ratio may not reduce his current consumption.

By requiring that income be spent on consumption in either the present or the future we have implicitly excluded the possibility of accumulating wealth for its own sake—that is, for prestige, economic or political power, and so on. The inclusion of this additional variable to our model complicates it considerably, but the direction of the influence of various taxes is not difficult to ascertain. A tax on income (excluding interest) still has no substitution effect. A tax on wealth, of course, discriminates in favor of present and future consumption over wealth.

If there is incentive to accumulate wealth, a general sales tax (on future and present consumption) will give more encouragement to saving than would an income tax. It follows also that a tax on returns from investment discriminates against both wealth accumulation and future consumption. Correspondingly, a tax on present consumption favors both wealth accumulation and future consumption, while a tax on future consumption favors both wealth accumulation and present consumption.

Another important omission is the consideration of a tax structure with multiple rates. Assume again that only present and future consumption are possible. If progression is added to the tax rate structure, no change is needed in the model depicted in Figure 9.9. Again there is no substitution effect, since the *marginal* rate at which present and future income is taxed does not change. On the other hand, if a tax on present consumption were made progressive, it would *accentuate* the substitution effect which favors future consumption. Similarly, if a tax on future consumption were made progressive, it would accentuate the substitution effect favoring present consumption.

Let us compare our federal personal income tax with a general sales tax (on both present and future consumption). Since the income tax covers both present and future income (including income from past investment), it obviously gives less encouragement to wealth accumulation than would a general sales tax. As we shall see in the next chapter, however, our personal income tax structure gives some encouragement to wealth accumulation and future consumption through preferential treatment for some forms of income from investment (that is, the favorable treatment given capital gains).

Finally, we observe once again the limitations of our partial equilibrium models. For example, while the budget constraints used may illustrate the rates at which an *individual* can substitute present for future consumption, these rates cannot hold for massive changes at the aggregate level. We are just looking at how the individual will respond to different tax rates. For the economy as a whole, however, resource supply, technology, and all factors making up the economy's *production possibility function* determine the rate at which present and future consumption can be substituted.

NONNEUTRALITY BETWEEN FINANCIAL INVESTMENT ALTERNATIVES

In the previous section we examined possible individual responses to taxes as they affect a choice between present and future consumption. We assumed there was only one financial investment opportunity[5] and one rate of return. We now ask: In what ways may taxes affect the choice among financial investment alternatives?

[5] Again we differentiate between financial investment and real investment. The former may involve only bidding up the price of existing stocks and bonds, while the latter implies utilization of real capital goods.

FIGURE 9–12

Choice of optimum
risk-yield combination

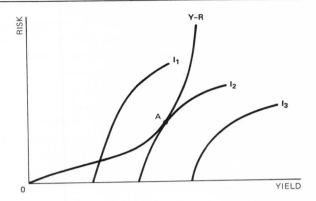

FIGURE 9–13

Choice of optimum
risk-yield combination:
proportional income tax
with no loss offset

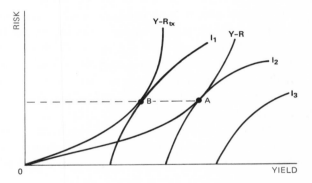

Individuals as input owners and as managers of firms employ available funds in investment ventures which may or may not involve the use of real capital. Typically there are alternatives of various degrees of risk and yield. The relevant ones range from low risk and low yield to high risk and high yield; alternatives which offer lower yields for the same risk are not relevant. Such a spectrum of relevant alternatives may be described as in Figure 9.12. The risks and yields of *various asset combinations* are shown, the risk (in percentages) is measured on the vertical axis and the yield (in percentages) is measured on the horizontal axis. If we assume that prices are stable, holding cash involves no risk. Thus the function representing the optimum risk-yield combinations, *Y-R*, starts from the origin. The lower-yield, lower-risk alternatives may include savings accounts and bonds, perhaps mixed with certain holdings of cash. Changing the portfolio to include higher-yield and higher-risk ventures causes the curve to become steeper—convex from below.[6]

The individual's preference pattern is shown by the indifference curves: I_1, I_2, and I_3. The individual receives greater satisfaction with greater yields. Each curve starts from the yield axis at a higher level of riskless yield, and each exhibits the individual's increasing disutility for risk.[7] Along each curve the individual is shown to be indifferent among certain combinations of low yield and risk and those featuring higher yield and risk. Owing to the increasing disutility of risk, the curve flattens out at higher risk-yield combinations. Hence, an equilibrium occurs at A, which represents the most satisfactory portfolio. At this point the individual's portfolio includes several types of investment featuring varying amounts of risk and yield. The overall combination of risk and yield is that which best matches his preferences.

Taxes affect the yield-risk function in various ways. An important consideration is whether losses can be offset against gains in income when taxes are computed.

A proportional income tax that does not permit loss offsets will shift Y-R upward and to the left proportionately as shown in Figure 9.13. The movement to the new equilibrium, B, includes both income and substitution effects. The income effect relative to risk is inverse: More risk is taken to offset the tax's impact on income. The substitution effect works in the opposite direction: The tax has made Y-R steeper, thus risks are now more expensive relative to yield, and there is incentive to substitute towards lower risk. Without precise knowledge of the individual's preference pattern we cannot know if the net effect will result in the amount of risk taking depicted in Figure 9.13. The result depends on the relative strengths of the income and substitution effects.

If, on the other hand, losses are fully offset, the tax will create no substitution effect.[8] If both losses and yields are reduced by the same percentage, the imposition of the tax does not change the relative attractiveness of the different combinations. The effect on high-risk, high-yield portfolios is proportional to the effect on low-risk, low-yield portfolios. Thus

---

[6] See R. A. Musgrave, *The Theory of Public Finance* (New York: McGraw-Hill, 1959), pp. 312–345, for a more thorough derivation of this function.

[7] The pattern of the "risk taker," a person who enjoys a certain amount of risk, might start upward and to the *left* before bending back to the right.

[8] This situation amounts to the government's sharing equally in the losses as well as the gains incurred. As we shall see in subsequent chapters, the U.S. income tax regulations provide loss offsets in many cases.

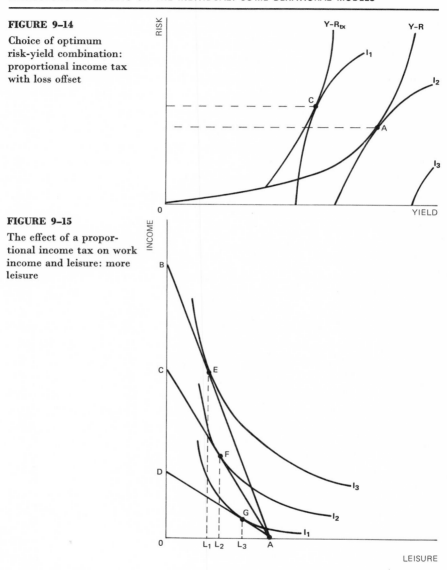

FIGURE 9–14

Choice of optimum risk-yield combination: proportional income tax with loss offset

FIGURE 9–15

The effect of a proportional income tax on work income and leisure: more leisure

no incentive is given to *substitute* towards low-risk alternatives. Indeed, if the income effect is in the direction posited above, we must predict an increase in the willingness to take risks. This prediction (depicted in Figure 9.14) is reinforced by the observation that the addition of a tax with loss offset increases the government's share in risk taking. This latter effect, added to the individual's private risk taking, should increase total risk taking in the economy.

The commonly held notion is that our present income tax structure *reduces* risk taking. Our model implies that income taxes with loss offsets encourage *greater risk taking*. We withhold final comment, however, until we have examined the specific provisions of our tax laws.

NONNEUTRALITY BETWEEN TYPES OF EMPLOYMENT AND BETWEEN WORK AND LEISURE

We may employ the basic model of individual preferences once again to answer the question: What kind of effects may taxes and transfers have on the choice among types of employment? Theoretically at least we can simply assume that the individual can choose the optimum combination of employments in the same way he chooses the optimum combination of private goods. The basic difference is that most individuals can hold only one job at a time and thus are not free to make marginal adjustments among hours spent at various types of employment.

Given these limitations, however, we observe that taxes or transfers on certain types of employment create incentives to substitute. For example, a license fee to operate a taxi may force some individuals to change to another occupation. On the other hand, the housework done by a housewife and the vegetable garden grown for personal use by a farmer yield real income that escapes the income tax (and the sales tax as well). Such tax exemption is a factor (although perhaps a small one) encouraging individuals to choose those occupations. A truly general income tax would, of course, have no such substitution effects, since the income from all types of employment would be taxed equally.

A substitution effect possible even under a general income tax (or transfer) is the choice between leisure and work. It is often argued that the income tax, by changing the price ratio between income and leisure, makes leisure relatively more attractive, so that leisure is substituted for work income. As we shall see, this result depends on the individual's preference patterns. The usual argument—that income tax reduces work effort—is depicted in Figure 9.15. The individual's preference pattern between income and leisure is represented by the indifference curves I_1, I_2, and I_3. The individual is endowed with a certain amount of time—say 24 hours a day—which he can devote to leisure or income. If he devotes all

FIGURE 9–16

The effect of a proportional income tax on work effort and leisure: more work

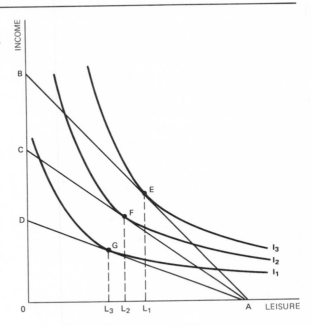

his time to work, he can earn the amount OB. In the absence of an income tax, the line AB represents the wage rate at which he can work. Maximizing satisfaction, he adjusts income and leisure to point E. The number of hours devoted to leisure is OL_1. The remaining hours, L_1A, are devoted to work.

Now introduce a proportional income tax by shifting the price ratio between income and leisure to AC. It can be seen that as one substitutes work for leisure by moving from A to O, proportionately less income can be earned. The individual now substitutes leisure for work, moving to point F. He now spends OL_2 hours in leisure. Similarly, if the tax is increased to AD, leisure becomes even more attractive and OL_3 hours are taken.

While the preference pattern depicted in Figure 9.15 might represent an individual's preference between two commodities, there is some question as to whether it accurately depicts the relationship between income and leisure. The main difference between the usual two-good preference pattern and the income-leisure relationship is that in the latter the individual will resist changes in income which may move him to what he considers an undesirable level of income. That is, the *individual's desire to exchange leisure for income at the new price ratio may be offset by his desire to maintain his old standard of living.* This "income effect" of the tax may be so powerful that the individual will actually work *more* after the tax. These considerations are built into the preference pattern depicted in Figure 9.16. The indifference curves, I_1, I_2, and I_3, are drawn so that as the tax becomes greater, income becomes more desirable relative to labor. Without the tax, the individual chooses OL_1 hours of leisure and L_1A hours of work. With the tax AC, he chooses OL_2 hours of leisure and L_2A hours of work. The greater the tax, the more he substitutes leisure for work.

The actual response on the part of most individuals is probably somewhere between those pictured in Figures 9.15 and 9.16. It is likely that the desire to remain at the present standard of living partially offsets the tendency to substitute leisure for income at the new price ratio. It is a simple matter to translate the results of these models into observations about the effects of income transfers. Under a tax system which includes negative income taxes both are relevant, since some individuals will be receiving transfers while others are paying taxes. Obviously, the net effect of such a tax system on employment is not easily predicted, and we will reserve further evaluation until we have examined more closely the provisions of particular tax plans.

We have developed models for examining several modes of individual response to public sector expenditures and taxes, and we have seen that expenditures and taxes affect the behavior of individuals in their roles as consumers, savers, investors, and workers. In the next several chapters we will use these models to gain further insight into the microeconomic effects of our taxes and expenditures.

10
PERSONAL INCOME TAXES
AND SUPPLEMENTS

Taxes and supplements to personal income are central to the study of public financing for several important reasons. In the first place, the personal income tax provides more revenue than any other source. In the budgets of the last several years it has provided approximately 60 percent of federal and 13 percent of state tax revenue. Second, personal income taxes and supplements are important tools for macroeconomic fiscal policy. The reasons are their relative *size*—changes in income taxes and supplements can generate large shifts in aggregate spending; and their *generality*—they directly affect all income earners, carrying the impact of fiscal actions to all parts of the economy. Finally, they score well in the various efficiency criteria we have developed. For these reasons economists have traditionally advocated use of personal income taxes and supplements in preference to other alternatives.

Our major tasks in this chapter are to analyze the effects of income taxes and supplements on the welfare and economic behavior of the individual. Analysis of their significance as a tool for macroeconomic policy will be deferred to Part IV.

We begin by outlining some of the major provisions of the federal income tax.

AN OUTLINE OF FEDERAL PERSONAL INCOME TAX PROVISIONS

In theory the steps for determining personal income tax liability are simple: you add up all income, subtract certain deductions and exemptions, and apply the tax rate to the remaining "taxable income." The procedure in practice is quite complicated and furnishes employment for hundreds of thousands of tax accountants and lawyers.

As we might anticipate from our earlier discussion of ability-to-pay theories, the notion of "equal sacrifice" is used in the normative analysis of personal income taxation. It is important not only in evaluating the rate structure but in the rather basic task of *defining* the concept of income itself. If equal sacrifice is to be attained, it must first be decided who the "equals" are. Moreover, a necessary corollary of horizontal equity (equal treatment for equals) is "unequal" treatment for "unequals." In other words, even if two individuals receive the same amount of monetary income, they may be "unequal" in important ways that we want to take into account. Hence two concepts of income necessarily emerge as important: *adjusted gross income*, which approximates an individual's accretion of wealth, and *taxable income*, which supposedly accounts for most of the important inequalities among individuals.

310

ADJUSTED GROSS INCOME

The base for the federal income tax is quite simply all income accruing to an individual taxpayer within a calendar year. All wages, salaries, dividends, rents, royalties, and other monetary payments are included.

Difficulties arise immediately, however, in deciding just what is and is not income. Among the major sources of income-in-kind not taxed are the real income to the family in the form of services produced by the housewife, the rent value of owner-occupied houses, the food grown and consumed on farms, and many of the "expenses" of salesmen and executives. When income-in-kind is obviously a part of wages or salary, it is taxable. However, most income-in-kind, although not explicitly excluded by tax regulations, has not been considered taxable income by the Internal Revenue Service.

Capital gains are not taxed until the year they are realized. If capital gains are not realized during the lifetime of the individual, they are not taxed at all. Under the present system "short-term" capital gains, defined as those assets held less than six months, are taxed as regular income. Gains from assets held for longer periods qualify for preferential treatment. Only 50 percent of such realized gains are included in the tax base. Capital losses, however, are not accorded equal treatment. Unless a capital loss is offset by capital gains plus $1,000, it may not be deducted from the tax base. The primary reason for excluding yearly capital gains and certain types of income-in-kind is that they do not involve price transactions, so it is difficult to estimate their monetary value.

In addition, a few income payments that do involve price transactions are excluded for "meritorious" or other reasons. This category includes social security benefits, unemployment compensation, certain veterans' payments, certain types of payments to members of the armed forces (such as subsistence and quarters allowances and hazardous duty pay), and fellowship and scholarship grants. Interest from state and local government securities is also exempted, but primarily for reasons of precedent.

DEDUCTIONS AND TAXABLE INCOME

One may take two types of deductions from adjusted gross income to find taxable income: The first type covers various personal expenditures which may be unduly "unequal" between individuals; the second type covers personal exemptions accounting for different family situations. There is a shortcut available for many individuals (around 30 million returns), who

TABLE 10-1

Federal individual income
marginal tax rates, 1973 (percent)

Taxable income (dollars)	Married couples (separate returns)	Single persons	Heads of households	Married couples (joint returns)
0 – 500	14	14	14	14
500 – 1,000	15	15	14	14
1,000 – 1,500	16	16	16	15
1,500 – 2,000	17	17	16	15
2,000 – 3,000	19	19	18	16
3,000 – 4,000	19	19	18	17
4,000 – 6,000	22	21	19	19
6,000 – 8,000	25	24	22	19
8,000 – 10,000	28	25	23	22
10,000 – 12,000	32	27	25	22
12,000 – 14,000	36	29	27	25
14,000 – 16,000	39	31	28	25
16,000 – 18,000	42	34	31	28
18,000 – 20,000	45	36	32	28
20,000 – 22,000	48	38	35	32
22,000 – 24,000	50	40	36	32
24,000 – 26,000	50	40	38	36
26,000 – 28,000	53	45	41	36
28,000 – 32,000	53	45	42	39
32,000 – 36,000	55	50	45	42
36,000 – 38,000	55	50	48	45
38,000 – 40,000	58	55	51	45
40,000 – 44,000	58	55	52	48
44,000 – 50,000	60	60	55	50
50,000 – 52,000	62	62	56	50
52,000 – 60,000	62	62	58	53
60,000 – 64,000	64	64	58	53
64,000 – 70,000	64	64	59	55
70,000 – 76,000	66	66	61	55
76,000 – 80,000	66	66	62	58
80,000 – 88,000	68	68	63	58
88,000 – 90,000	68	68	64	60
90,000 – 100,000	69	69	64	60
100,000 – 120,000	70	70	66	62
120,000 – 140,000	70	70	67	64
140,000 – 160,000	70	70	68	66
160,000 – 180,000	70	70	69	68
180,000 – 200,000	70	70	70	69
Over 200,000	70	70	70	70

may apply adjusted gross income directly to a simplified tax rate schedule
which automatically accounts for family size and the other usual deductions.

Personal expenditures in the first type of deduction include: interest
payments, medical and dental expenses (exceeding 3 percent of adjusted
gross income), charitable contributions, casualty and theft losses (ex-

ceeding $100 for each loss), and taxes paid on income, general sales, property, and gasoline to state and local governments.

The taxpayer has two options for computing his deductions. Those whose expenditures in these categories are not extraordinary may take a *standard deduction* instead of itemizing the deductible expenditures.

The standard deduction has been an important provision since its inception in 1944. Its importance, however, declined over the years as conditions changed but tax law exhibited its well-known rigidity. In 1944 the standard deduction was taken on 80 percent of all returns, but as incomes rose and deductions were expanded the percentage declined to 56.5 in 1968. The 1969 tax law increased the 1944 allowance of 10 percent of adjusted gross income (maximum $1000) to 15 percent (maximum $2000) in 1973 and thereafter. The floor to the standard deduction was $200 (plus $100 for each exemption claimed) but was replaced in the 1969 law by a "low-income allowance" of $1000 from 1972 on.

The other major type of deduction, personal exemptions, also remained rigid for many years before the 1969 law. At that time the allowance was graduated upward from the former $600 level to $750 in 1973 and thereafter.

Obviously these different types of deductions could be varied in a number of ways to vary the impact of the tax among individuals. In the next section we will examine the rationale behind the deductions and their effect on income distribution.

THE RATE SCHEDULES

Additional discrimination among individuals according to family situation is accomplished when the tax rate is applied to taxable income. There are four separate rate schedules for the categories: married couples (separate returns), single persons, heads of households, and married couples (joint returns). As outlined in Table 10.1, the rates range from 14 percent on the first $500 of taxable income to 70 percent for a single person's income over $100,000 and a married couple's joint income over $200,000.

The advantage given to married couples filing jointly is obvious when we compare the rate structure in column four with the others. The usual argument for such preferential treatment is approximately the same as that given for exemptions for dependents, with the additional idea that the "family" may be thought of as a single, joint, economic venture. In actuality the joint return is a historical happenstance stemming from community property laws in a few states. Because the Supreme Court allowed married couples within those states to split their income and file separately (thus taking advantage of the lower rates), other states enacted similar laws to give their citizens similar benefits. Finally in 1948 Congress was forced to provide the splitting option on a national scale.

A related justification for income splitting is the recognition that the personal exemptions do not adequately account for the responsibilities towards children (educational expenses and so on), especially among medium and upper income groups. It would appear, however, that some other provision could best fit this need, since the splitting provision applies equally to families with no children.

The preferential treatment given married couples is, of course, resented by single individuals, especially those who have dependents they support. We recall that the real income produced by the housewife is not subject to the tax. In addition, the rates set by the 1969 tax law limit the single individual's liability to 120 percent of any comparable bracket of the joint return.

Yet another rate structure provides relief for persons who although unmarried must play the role of breadwinner for dependents and are thus declared " head of household."

It may pay a married couple whose incomes differ widely to file separately so that one of them can take advantage of the lower tax bracket (with progressively lower rates) into which they will fall. At the same time the higher income partner may claim most of the deductions. However, the rate structure is obviously designed to reduce the attractiveness of this option, since it favors the joint return.

Although the rate structures include rates for taxable incomes over $100,000 and $200,000, very few individuals fall into these brackets. In 1968 only 7000 of the 73,700,000 returns filed fell into the $100,000-and-over bracket. In fact, 97 percent of the returns filed and 80 percent of the tax revenue came from the $10,000-and-below brackets.

From 1913 until today tax payment has been " voluntary "—meaning that the individual is not only required to pay the tax but must bear the responsibility and expense of figuring his liability and seeing that the goverment receives the right amount. From 1913 to 1942 taxes were paid quarterly in the *following* year. This system worked hardship on those with fluctuating incomes, since people tend to spend income when it is received. During the expansion of the federal revenue structure during World War II a new principle emerged: that the income tax is due when the income is earned. Since that time an approximation of the tax has been *withheld* from the paycheck of most wage earners. The withholding system now accounts for approximately 80 percent of federal personal income tax revenue.

The top withholding rate is 27 percent (from 1973 on). Thus higher income individuals must either make a declaration of estimated tax (and pay extra amounts in installments due April 15, June 15, September 15, and January 15) or voluntarily increase their withholding payments.

THE RATE STRUCTURE AND THE ABILITY-TO-PAY AND BENEFIT PRINCIPLES

What connections can we make between the theoretical arguments in Chapter 2 attempting to relate individual welfare and public sector activity and the rate structure of the personal income tax? No direct parallel can be drawn between theoretical abstractions and "real world" institutions, but we can still make some interesting observations.

We recall that the "ability-to-pay" approach focuses on the "sacrifice" imposed on various individuals by a given tax rate structure. If *equal sacrifice* is desired, it follows that individuals must somehow be taxed according to their welfare. In order to accomplish this with the personal income tax, we must assume that income is a good index of welfare and that we know the rate at which welfare increases with income.

The assumption of diminishing marginal utility of income, we recall, has been used to justify progressive rates. This argument has been undermined considerably by the admonition of Paretian welfare economics against interpersonal utility comparisons. If preference functions are not identical, which certainly they are not, it cannot be said that progressive taxation minimizes sacrifice. Upon reflection, however, we realize that *no* form of taxation can be justified under the strictures of the Paretian criterion unless both sides of the budget are considered and some sort of Wicksellian voting scheme can be found which avoids consumption externalities, free-riders and similar problems. With regard to taxes alone perhaps the most appealing—though hardly rigorous—argument is that of Abba Lerner: With declining marginal utility of income (and preference patterns unknown) the tax system *most likely* to minimize total sacrifice is one which tends to equalize income.[1] But even the assumption

[1] See Chapter 2, p. 43.

of declining marginal utility of income may not always hold. Hence the ability-to-pay argument for progression is tenuous.

Can we apply the benefit principle to an evaluation of the income tax? Since expenditures are separated from taxes in the budget process, the link between the costs and benefits of a particular tax is severed. As we have outlined, individuals acting as voters, politicians, bureaucrats, and so on make benefit-cost judgments in the public choice activity, but only in the broadest sense do taxpayers make judgments about the benefits and costs associated with their income tax payments. We have noted previously that the *voluntary exchange* argument of Di Viti di Marco has been used to correlate the "benefits" from defense spending (the major exhaustive federal expenditure) with the "costs" imposed by the personal income tax (the largest revenue source). The argument is that individuals who possess greater wealth derive greater benefit from having it defended. Thus they should pay higher taxes. Yet higher taxes do not necessarily mean a progressive rate structure. In order to justify progressiveness additional assumptions (such as diminishing marginal utility of income) are required. However, the myriad of other ways in which expenditures and taxes affect individuals certainly beclouds the cost-benefit evaluation of the income tax as such.

In the final analysis the rate structure and deductions are a result of our representatives' ideas about equity, the need for revenue, and the pressure of various interest groups. Inherent in our discussion of the negative income tax concept was the recognition that the rates derive directly from our "distribution goal." And to the extent that we can talk about a general "distribution goal," it derives from many ideas including benefit and ability-to-pay norms and equalitarian concern. Especially important is the recognition that even though our economy offers considerable mobility, the income-earning potential of many individuals is limited.

Can we say that the tax structure reflects the "distribution goal" of citizens? In our idealized model of the Fiscal Department we assumed that the citizenry revealed its preferences to the Income Distribution Branch manager who then implemented them. Our later discussion of voting models led to questions as to whether a voting procedure could be found which would reveal these preferences. Moreover we noted later that if tax rates are subject to frequent change, the short-run, "zero-sum-game" considerations of competition among interest groups may take precedence over the longer-run, social "norms" such as "equal sacrifice" and "equitable" distribution. We hypothesized that a more indirect decision-

---

making procedure featuring checks and balances and separation of powers may better reveal social "norms." Under the present system the decision is made jointly by Congress (where it is regulated by committees which give deference to expertise and specialization) and the Administration and is *not subject to frequent change.* While the present system is cumbersome it may better reflect accepted "norms" than a more responsive system subject to shifting coalitions seeking their more immediate interests.

THE NEGATIVE INCOME TAX

It is a simple step from considering the redistributive effects of the income tax to the idea of a negative income tax—a tax schedule which involves transfers to those who earn less than some designated minimum level.

It is obvious that an income tax *as such* can do nothing to alleviate the need of families below the exemption levels and can do very little for those in the lower tax brackets. The present method of transferring income to these groups involves a myriad of programs for aid to dependent children, medical and retirement insurance programs, and aid to the blind, deaf, and otherwise disabled. Coverage differs widely from locality to locality; moreover, a large percentage of those low-income individuals who can work but are disadvantaged because of lack of training, talents, or opportunity get no relief at all. It follows that a negative income tax program could be used to supplement existing welfare programs so as to provide more general coverage. Alternatively, the exemptions and deductions of the negative income tax could be modified in such a way as to *replace* many of the existing welfare transfers. The negative income tax, of course, cannot be expected to provide the retraining and incentive necessary for many of the disadvantaged to realize their productive potential. Consequently the negative income tax would have to be augmented by such programs.

THE BASIC MECHANICS

Computation of the individual's taxes (or transfers) would remain essentially the same as under the present system: one adds up gross income, figures exemptions and deductions, and pays taxes according to the rate schedule. But the individual whose exemptions and deductions are greater than income would receive a transfer instead of paying tax. In practice, those receiving transfer payments would get them on a regular basis throughout

FIGURE 10-1

A negative income
tax plan with $3000
minimum income
and $5000 break-even
income

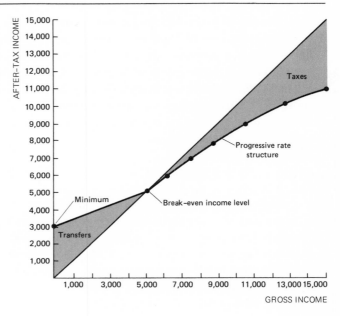

the year, just as most of those paying taxes now have them withheld. The transfers would be based on estimated income for the year. It would hardly be logical to pay "subsistence" transfers in a lump sum at the end of the year.

Two basic variables must be decided when implementing the negative income tax: the *minimum* (or "guaranteed") income level and the *break-even* income level. The minimum income level is the amount the family unit will receive even if it has no income. The break-even point separates the lower income levels where income is supplemented and the higher income levels on which taxes are imposed. In addition, of course, tax rates below and above the break-even point must be set. Below the break-even point the tax rate may be thought of alternatively as a transfer reduction rate.

Now let us demonstrate the basic mechanics of the tax. The most logical approach is to relate exemptions directly to the minimum income level.[2] Suppose we decide on a minimum income allowance of $4000 for a family of four. We allow only personal exemptions and set them at $1000 for each member.[3] Consequently, a family of four with no income would have $4000 in exemptions and would receive a $4000 transfer payment from the government. With the first of our three variables decided, we find that the choice of one of the remaining two variables automatically determines the third. That is, if we choose both a minimum income allowance and a break-even income level, the rate at which supplements are reduced automatically follows. For example, if we decide to set $5000 as the break-even point and tax proportionately, we *must* use an 80 percent rate. The family making $5000 would get to keep only $1000 over and above their $4000 guaranteed income. Alternatively, if we set the rate at 50 percent, the break-even level would not be reached until the $8000 income level.

These calculations indicate the dilemma we face in setting these variables. On the one hand we want the minimum income to cover basic "poverty level" income needs for those who cannot work; and yet we cannot afford to set the break-even point so high that it destroys the usefulness of the tax as a producer of revenues. At the same time, if these two levels are relatively close, the high marginal tax rate required would seriously dampen the individual's incentive to earn additional income. A tradeoff between the goals is necessary.

Figure 10.1 presents a hypothetical negative income tax plan. The minimum income level (for the family of four) is set at $3000 and the break-even level is $5000. If proportional tax rates are used, a rate of 60 percent is required. The transfer reduction could be made progressive, say starting with only 20 percent for the first $1000, but this necessitates higher marginal rates approaching the break-even level. For incomes above the break-even level a progressive rate structure is shown with exemptions included.

Many different variations of the negative income tax plan have been presented in recent years. One interesting aspect of the concept is that it is supported by both liberal and conservative economists. The plans have been termed "guaranteed income," "family assistance," and "minimum income" as well as "negative income tax" plan. Some of the plans incorporate different sorts of exemptions and work incentives, but

---

[2] Otherwise the two rate schedules will overlap. This phenomenon is not too critical, since presumably the individual would be given the option of the most favorable treatment and there need be no abrupt shift in the marginal tax rate. It is important in such cases to specify when you are referring to the gross or taxable "minimum" income level.

[3] It would be a simple matter to further differentiate exemptions according to family situation. For example, we could allow $900 for each parent and $600 for each child. The logic behind such a policy derives from the fact that there are economies of scale in family provision of the subsistence level of income.

the basic approach is the same. Our subsequent investigation will reveal that the present system bears revision, and revision in the direction of the negative income tax plan is certainly an attractive option.

INCOME DEFINITIONS AND EROSION OF THE TAX BASE

"DEFINING INCOME"

In order to better evaluate the efficiency of current tax provisions, let us consider two questions: (1) Just how can we best measure "income"? (2) Does the definition of income used for tax purposes coincide with ours?

There are institutional as well as theoretical problems involved in defining income for tax purposes. The following three perspectives are helpful: (1) the *flow* of purchasing power into the hands of the invididual, (2) the *accretion* of wealth or economic power available to the individual, and (3) the use of income by the individual to provide *utility* (primarily via consumption).

The flow concept sees income as the goods and services received by the individual for the part he plays in the economic system. During any one period, certain goods and services become available to him. He is able to purchase them only when he has immediate access to the necessary purchasing power. Following this concept, it would seem appropriate to tax purchasing power at the time when it *flows into* the hands of the individual. The income tax base then would be a compilation of the monetary income actually realized in market transactions by an individual during a given period.

A related alternative developed by Robert M. Haig and Henry Simons is to view income as the accretion of wealth or economic power.[4] Following the latter concept, it would seem appropriate to tax all economic power when it *accrues* to the individual, whether or not he chooses to actually exercise it via some market transaction.

The difference in these two approaches shows up in the treatment of capital gains. Suppose the value of a stock held (but not sold) by an individual increases in value during a particular tax period. Does the increase in value constitute taxable income? It *does not* under the flow concept, since gain has not been realized and made immediately available as purchasing power to the individual. It *does* under the accretion concept, since the gain whether realized or not represents economic power *potentially* available to the individual.

The third perspective, advocated by Irving Fisher, focuses on the utility derived from income—the goods and services the individual withdraws from the system and consumes.[5] In practice this tax would be essentially a general sales tax, since "income" would be considered realized only when used to purchase goods and services. It would still be possible to "individualize" such a tax by requiring each individual to keep account of all his purchases. Consequently, exemptions and deductions could be applied to this tax base and a graduated rate structure used.

Capital gains would not be taxed under the procedure described above. Moreover, in the Fisher view, any system under which income is taxed when first received (such as the flow or accretion alternatives) should not tax returns on investment, since this would amount to *double taxation*. This follows from the view that income is realized only when used to consume goods and services. Money going towards savings and investment should not have been taxed in the first place; however, such taxation certainly should not be imposed on investment returns in subsequent periods.

If we accept the definition of income as the act of consuming, Fisher's argument is cogent; however, from either the flow or the accretion perspective no double taxation is involved.

The choice among these three approaches involves a value judgment and lends itself to some rather sophisticated philosophical inquiry. The Sixteenth Amendment simply gave Congress authority to tax income "from whatever source" derived, with no specific definition of income. What has evolved is a tax on what we might term Net Flow Income. Our outline of tax provisions reveals that capital gains are not taxed until they are realized and that several exemptions and deductions are allowed before the tax rates are applied.

TREATMENT OF CAPITAL GAINS

Capital gains accrue with increase in market value of an asset which is not part of the seller's stock in trade. Their proper treatment for tax purposes has been an enigma. Under the accretion approach capital gains would be taxed as income when they occurred. Unless capital gains are realized—that is, unless they involve a price transaction—they do not fall within the flow concept. Taxation under the accretion approach

---

[4] See Robert M. Haig, *The Federal Income Tax* (New York: Columbia University Press, 1921), and Henry C. Simons, *Personal Income Taxation* (Chicago: University of Chicago Press, 1938).

[5] Irving Fisher, *The Nature of Capital and Income* (New York: Macmillan, 1906). A more recent argument for this type of tax has been put forth by Nicholas Kalder, *An Expenditure Tax* (London: Allen & Unwin, 1955).

would be difficult. Not only would unrealized capital gains be hard to estimate for tax purposes, but imposition of the tax would probably require untimely shifts in resource ownership.

Treatment of capital gains under federal tax law has varied. From 1913 to 1921 realized capital gains were treated as ordinary income. In 1929 a distinction was made between ordinary income and income from capital gains (income for capital gains was taxed at a maximum rate of 12.5 percent). It was held that only property held for over two years for personal use was subject to special treatment. Property held as inventory, such as land held by a real estate developer, would not qualify. This definition was made more specific in the Revenue Acts of 1934, 1936, and 1942.

The present treatment of capital gains has changed very little from the rates established in 1942. Capital gains, if realized within six months, are treated as ordinary income. For assets held longer than six months only 50 percent of the realized gain (net of any short-term capital loss) is subject to tax. This figure is then added to the taxpayer's adjusted gross income and taxed at the appropriate rate. The *maximum* rate at which capital gains are to be taxed was set at 25 percent for many years but graduated upward by the 1969 law to 35 percent (in 1972 and after).

Two important aspects of capital gains treatment derive from use of the flow rather than the accretion concept. In the first place, since capital gains may accrue over a number of years, the tax liability incurred in the year of realization shifts the taxpayer into an inordinately high tax bracket. The consequences would be more severe, of course, if realized capital gains income were counted as regular income. Second, the present tax treatment allows one to escape income from capital gains merely by dying. The recipients of the estate are, of course, subject to inheritance tax, but the capital assets are valued at current value and there is no income tax liability on the capital gain.

Several aspects of the treatment of capital gains, then, have important effects on income distribution. First there is the question of whether they should be taxed at all. If one were to accept the Fisher argument over the flow or accretion concepts and exempt capital gains from taxation, this would undoubtedly lead to greater income disparity, since the higher income groups receive a relatively greater proportion of their income from this source.

Another aspect concerns the time period in which gains are taxed. Since the flow concept of income is used, capital gains are taxed only when realized. One reason often given for preferential treatment is that capital gains may accrue over a number of years and if treated as ordinary income would place the individual in an inordinately high tax bracket when realized. This argument in itself seems insufficient to warrant the favoritism now displayed. An alternative would be to treat capital gains as ordinary income and to provide the option to average them in the same way other irregular receipts may be averaged. Yet another argument is that the corporation income tax falls primarily on capital and, consequently, to treat capital gains as ordinary income would be another sort of double taxation. We will attempt to examine the overall effects of the entire tax structure in Chapter 14. We note in passing that the capital gains treatment afforded by federal income tax allows substantial relief for upper-income individuals.

PERSONAL EXEMPTIONS

The fundamental argument for the personal exemption is that low-income families with children must provide for *subsistence* and cannot be expected to pay taxes. The more dependents the low-income family has, the higher the subsistence level, although the increase is not proportional. At higher income levels the exemption provides for only small differences in the tax bills of families with different numbers of children.

The real value of personal exemptions has decreased drastically since 1913, partly as a result of reductions legislated during the two world wars and partly as a result of inflation. By 1969 the exemption was worth approximately one-fifteenth its 1913 value. The 1939 exemption of $600 was reduced by inflation to one-third that amount (in 1939 prices) in 1969.

The 1969 legislation took into account the impact of inflation on the exemption, the realization that the primary function of the exemption was to account for the family situation at low income levels, and recent research aimed at defining "poverty" levels of income. The legislation not only raised the personal exemptions but provided for a *low-income allowance* ($1000) which was aimed directly at the problem of lowering the tax burden for the lower-income family while avoiding the high revenue loss of increased exemptions at all income levels.

DEDUCTIONS

Of the deductions which may be claimed under the income tax law, few seem justified on ability-to-pay principles.

The largest deductions at all levels—for interest payments and for state and local taxes—certainly cannot be justified on the ability-to-pay principle. The deduction for payments on interest is a quite important source of tax relief to the medium-income families (in the $5000 to $20,000 levels) who are purchasing new homes. There may be some grounds for the interest deduction if we treat homeowners as " merit " individuals, but this reasoning seems rather tenuous, since more direct methods could be used. The deduction also holds, of course, for those making payments (which include interest) on other durable consumer goods.[6]

The deduction of state and local taxes has little foundation except historical precedent. It cannot be justified on the ability-to-pay approach. And it would also be difficult to argue that the " separation of powers " principle somehow justifies such treatment. A remaining possibility is to argue that the deduction offers partial redress for the " inefficiencies " of particular state and local taxes, but this offers little promise. On the contrary, to the extent that state and local taxes have beneficial effects on, say, resource allocation, their deduction for federal income tax purposes partially offsets these effects. For example, one of the important deductions is for state and local gasoline taxes, and their commendable role as " user charges " is partially offset. As a " user charge " the gasoline tax falls more on individuals who are heavy users of the roads and highways. The taxes in turn are used to finance the building and maintenance of roads and highways. The tax relief afforded the heavy road user by the tax deduction reduces his overall tax burden relative to those individuals who use roads less. Finally it would seem that income tax deductions for state and local taxes help redress the regressivity of the state and local taxes. But the lower income groups receive little help from this provision since their incomes are so low that they either owe no taxes at all or utilize the standard deduction.

The deduction for charitable contributions is obviously in direct contradiction to the ability-to-pay principle; its only rationale is that it provides incentive for " meritorious " behavior. Given the lack of public sector support for the arts, medical and other research, higher education, and the like, such encouragement of gifts to nongovernmental agencies performing these functions may be justified by the " public " nature of the externalities involved.

Deductions for medical expenses certainly qualify on the basis of the ability-to-pay principle. Indeed, extraordinary medical expenses are often so large that the tax relief given by the present deduction to low-income families is insufficient to allow them to stay solvent. It seems ironic that our present system allows the lower-income taxpayer to be "wiped out" while the chronically poor are able to receive free medical care.

The standard deduction is justified only by the existence of the other deductions. Since all taxpaying units qualify for some deductions and since their computation is burdensome, a 15 percent standard deduction is allowed in lieu of itemizing. But suppose we were able to eliminate all deductions except those which were clearly justified on the basis of the ability-to-pay principle. It would then be possible to reduce or abolish the standard deduction as well. This would not necessarily mean that federal income tax revenues would be higher. Such a change could be accompanied by changes in the *rate structure*. The resulting tax legislation would offer improved *neutrality*, greater *horizontal equity*, and a rate structure better reflecting the proportion of actual income that is going to the public sector.

Reducing deductions is difficult for Congress, owing to opposition from the groups most benefited. In the 1969 legislation Congress *raised* the standard deduction, thus in an inverse way reducing some of the inequity caused by the special deductions by making the standard deduction relatively more attractive.

EROSION OF THE INCOME TAX BASE

The net effect of the exemptions and deductions is considerable erosion of the tax base. Figure 10.2 shows the influence of various provisions on *effective rates* of the federal income tax. These estimates, based on calculations by Pechman, demonstrate the importance of various provisions at different income levels.[7] The actual maximum effective rate is about 35 percent. The personal exemptions are important at the low income levels, while deductions and capital gains are most important at the higher levels. Income splitting becomes an important source of tax avoidance at around $15,000 and remains important until very high levels.

---

[6] There is considerably greater justification for interest deductions in cases where the purchase relates directly to a person's business and thus should be considered a cost against income.

[7] Joseph A. Pechman, *Federal Tax Policy*, rev. ed. (New York: Norton, 1971), Figure 4.2 and Table C.11.

FIGURE 10–2

Influence of various
provisions on effective rates
of the federal individual
income tax

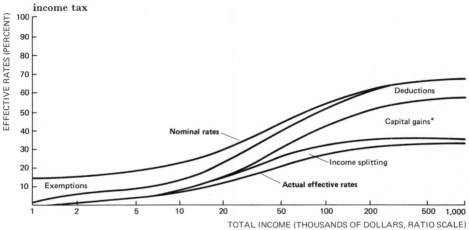

Source : Special tabulation based on a file of about 87,000 federal individual income tax returns for 1966. Calculations based on rates exemptions, and other provisions of the Tax Reform Act of 1969 scheduled to apply to calendar year 1973 incomes. Joseph A. Pechman, *Federal Tax Policy*, rev. ed. (New York : Norton, 1971), Figure 4.2 and Table C.11.
* Includes the effects of preference items and the maximum tax on earned income.

FIGURE 10–3

The income tax and the
excise tax compared in
terms of neutrality: the
individual's preference
pattern

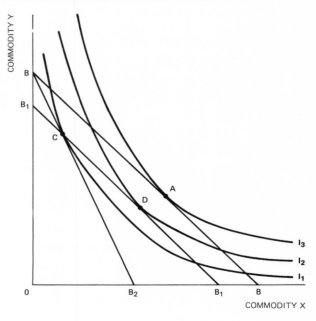

In addition to differences in the abilities of different individuals to avoid taxes, the special provisions, exemptions, and deductions have nonneutral effects on individual economic behavior.

EFFECTS ON ECONOMIC BEHAVIOR OF THE INDIVIDUAL

NEUTRALITY BETWEEN PRIVATE SECTOR GOODS

Our basic indifference curve model would indicate that, better than any other of the taxes in our system, the personal income tax fulfills the criterion of neutrality between private sector goods. Certain provisions interfere with the price mechanism and these will be examined subsequently. First, however, let us review the argument that a *general* income tax falls on all types of income and consequently *cannot be shifted*. This argument has been presented with reference to individual choice between commodities and types of employment. Since the income tax does not change relative price ratios, no incentive is provided for consumers to substitute one commodity for another. Thus the tax does nothing to impair the allocation by competitive forces of resources to the production of commodities offering the greatest marginal benefits relative to costs. Similarly, since the tax cannot be avoided by changing one's occupation or investment portfolio, the tax does nothing to impair resource allocation via its effect on input price ratios.

We have inferred that the income tax by virtue of its neutrality (which features an *income* but no *substitution* effect) will allow the individual to achieve a higher level of satisfaction than will a nonneutral tax. Let us demonstrate this with more precision by directly comparing the two in terms of indifference curves. The model in Figure 10.3 features the preference pattern (I_1, I_2, and I_3) of one individual. We start with the budget constraint BB, no tax, and an initial equilibrium at A.

Suppose that an excise tax on good X is imposed. The price of good X is raised, so that the greatest quantity that can be bought by the individual is now OB_2. The new budget constraint BB_2 gives the combinations now available at the new price ratio. The excise tax is nonneutral *by definition*, since the price ratios set by the market have been disturbed. Moreover, the individual's satisfaction has been lowered from I_3 to I_1. The new equilibrium point is at C. An income tax can be used which provides the same amount of revenue but allows the individual to adjust purchases so as to attain a greater level of satisfaction.

FIGURE 10–4

The income tax and the
excise tax compared in
terms of neutrality: social
indifference curves

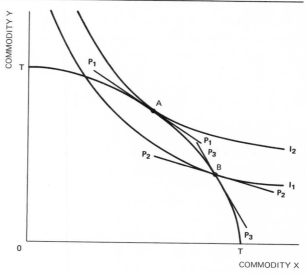

Line $B_1 B_1$ is drawn at the same distance from the original budget line
as point C. Regardless of the combination of output chosen under the
price ratio $B_1 B_1$, the income of the individual will be reduced by the
same amount as with the excise tax. *Thus the revenue provided the public
sector is the same in either case.* Since the slope of the budget line $B_1 B_1$ is
the same as that of line BB, it is obvious that the income tax is neutral
in its effect on the original price ratio. Yet the individual moves to combination D, thus enjoying a higher level of satisfaction, I_2.

We may gain further insight by making the excise vs. personal income
tax comparison in terms of production possibility curves and social indifference curves. Consider Figure 10.4. The production possibility curve is
represented by TT. The economy can produce only goods Y and X,
and the society's preferences are represented by I_1 and I_2, the necessary
value judgments being somehow resolved. If perfect competition prevails,
the price mechanism will direct the economy towards an equilibrium at
point A. Welfare will be maximized. Now suppose an income tax is
imposed but the proceeds are not spent—that is, the public sector requires
no *resources* from the private sector. At first glance, it would seem that the
production possibilities must be reduced.[8] But recall that no resources are
withdrawn from the private sector and we are assuming a competitive
model. Consequently, there is no reason to doubt that prices will adjust
so that the equilibrium at point A will once more be attained.

If an excise tax is imposed, there is still no reason within our model to suppose that firms will not be efficient and will not attain an output somewhere on TT. But the excise tax, say on good Y, will drive a wedge between the price the consumer pays and the price at which the firm is remunerated. Hence, instead of P_1P_1, two different price ratios obtain. Now the consumer looks at P_2P_2 and adjusts consumption accordingly. Meanwhile, the producers are adjusting to P_3P_3. At the new equilibrium point B the level of satisfaction is lower.

The arguments above lend support to the contention that the personal income tax scores well in terms of neutrality, especially when compared to the excise tax. It is necessary to remember, however, that nonneutrality does not always lead to a reduction in welfare. Such a conclusion holds only under necessary value judgments concerning distribution and so on and the assumption of a perfectly competitive model. It may be, for example, that certain prices are already distorted by monopoly elements. An excise tax may in fact lead to a price ratio and resource allocation which is more "optimum." In other words, noneutrality may well be more appropriate than neutrality.

It is important to observe, as we postulate differences in individual behavior under present proportional and progressive income taxes, that a switch to progressive rates involves both an income and a substitution effect. Consider the model illustrated by Figure 10.5. The economy is composed of only two people; and only two goods—one public and one private—are produced. The production of the public good is fixed at $\bar{S}$. Again assuming that each individual presumes tradeoffs between private and public goods would be made at the present tax-price ratio, we see that at the given level of public good output the low-income individual prefers less; he would prefer to move from position a to position b. The high-income individual prefers more; he would prefer to move from position e to position f.

Assume a progressive tax is introduced. The new tax-price line is $A'A'$. The income effect raises the low-income individual to I_3. Moreover, since

---

[8] Here we have inadvertently stumbled into an argument which requires assumptions about macroeconomic variables. If we assume that prices (to include factor prices) are completely flexible, our argument holds. If, however, prices have downward inflexibility, a reduction in spending power (as a result of the tax) may cause unemployment and an equilibrium somewhere *inside TT*. Alternatively, we may assume that the tax was imposed because of an anticipated excess of aggregate demand, so that the reduction in spending power does not require a general reduction in prices.

FIGURE 10–5

Substitution of a progressive
for a proportional income tax

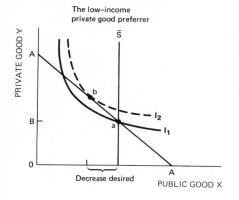

The low–income
private good preferrer

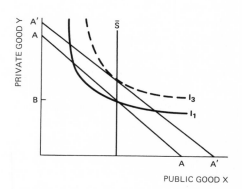

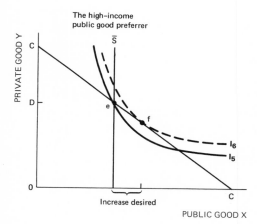

The high–income
public good preferrer

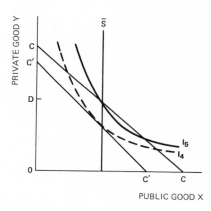

the slope of the tax-price ratio has changed, there is a substitution effect. Providently, the combined effect on the individual is to make him satisfied with the existing private good-public good production. For the high-income individual the new tax-price function is $C'C'$. His income is reduced, and both the income and substitution effects combine to move him to the position where he no longer desires an increase in the production of public good Y.

The above does not purport to be another argument for progressive taxation. The reduction in the welfare of the high-income individual precludes such an argument, unless knowledge of preference patterns and necessary value judgments concerning interpersonal utility comparisons are given. Instead, our intent is to show the direction of income and substitution effects of replacing proportional with progressive income tax. For the low-income individual a more progressive income tax would cause more of the private good to be purchased, and there would be less incentive for him to work for a reduction of public expenditures. For the high-income individual private spending would necessarily be reduced, and there would be less incentive for him to work for an increase in public expenditures.

Little empirical work has been done to test these specific hypotheses. However, some of the studies on voting behavior referred to in Chapter 3 lend them support. It was noted that higher income groups often vote for public expenditure and tax referenda which seem to benefit other income groups disproportionately. This would imply that the *income effect* causes high-income taxpayers to vote for public goods and services even when the more direct benefits of those services go primarily to the lower income groups. Another factor working in the same direction is that most state and local taxes are regressive; thus the tax burden of the high-income individual increases at a slower rate than his income.

VISIBILITY

The individual's behavior in response to changes in income depends, as pointed out, on what tradeoffs he *thinks* might be made. There is no assurance that the individual is aware of the marginal tax rate applicable to his income. Studies by Norbert Enrick and Joseph Wagstaff indicate that rate consciousness is often limited.[9] Both found that over half of those sampled erred in estimating their income tax by plus or minus 10 percent. Moreover, as Table 10.2 shows, more than a fourth of the total erred by over plus or minus 20 percent. The above hypotheses are, as stated, not dependent on exact knowledge of tax rates by the individual.

---

[9] Norbert L. Enrick, "A Pilot Study of Income Tax Consciousness," *National Tax Journal*, vol. 16 (June 1963), pp. 169–173, and "A Further Study of Income Tax Consciousness," *National Tax Journal*, vol. 17 (September 1964), pp. 319–321; and J. V. Wagstaff, "Income Tax Consciousness Under Withholding," *Southern Economic Journal*, vol. 32 (July 1965), pp. 73–80.

		Percent of sample population	
TABLE 10–2			
Income tax consciousness— Enrick and Wagstaff studies	Range of percentage tax error	Enrick studies	Wagstaff study
	± 0 to 10%	53	52
	± 10 to 20%	21	17
	Over ±20%	26	31
		——	——
		100	100

Sources: Enrick, "A Pilot Study of Income Tax Consciousness" and "A Further Study of Income Tax Consciousness"; Wagstaff, "Income Tax Consciousness under Withholding."

The apparent lack of tax consciousness on the part of individuals makes their choices very rough indeed.

Interestingly enough, it was revealed that lower income groups tend to overestimate their tax burden and higher income groups tend to underestimate theirs. If this is true, lack of awareness of actual rates may tend to accentuate the frustration by different income groups over a given supply of a public good. Assuming a public good with a positive income effect, the lower income groups think their taxes are higher than they actually are and are thus given double impetus to work for lower public good production; the higher income groups think their taxes are lower than they actually are and thus work for greater public good production.[10]

A surprising result in the Wagstaff study is that withholding of taxes does not seem to promote tax awareness.[11] In situations where the weekly check is attached to a slip itemizing withholding and other deductions, visibility would seem to be enhanced. But in general, withholding by deducting tax before income actually becomes "visible" tends to decrease tax awareness.

NONNEUTRALITY BETWEEN CONSUMPTION AND INVESTMENT

In the preceding chapter the argument was presented that an income tax which excludes interest is *neutral* with respect to present and future consumption.

Assuming that the interest rate is set, the individual will adjust to an equilibrium where he is satisfied with the amount he consumes in the present period and the amount he saves and invests to provide for future consumption. (Our simple model does not include the possibility of saving for its own sake.) Hence a tax which affects both present and future consumption proportionately (and does not affect the rate at which they can be substituted for each other) will not produce a *substitution* effect.

If interest is taxed, however, the relative attractiveness of present over future consumption is increased.

Using this model, we can argue that our present income tax provisions, which include income in the form of interest, favor present over future consumption. Similarly, we can say that the inclusion of stock dividends and capital gains as income also favors present over future consumption. This, of course, is not the same question asked earlier concerning the appropriate definition of income and whether or not returns on investment " should " be taxed. We are asking what effect present treatment has on individual behavior. The answer, obviously, is that if the returns from investment were no longer taxed, the change would have a substitution effect in favor of present saving (and investing) for future consumption. We also note that the present favorable treatment given capital gains (relative to interest and stock dividends) creates a substitution effect, encouraging those types of investment in which returns accrue in the form of capital gains.

It is difficult to predict the net effect that an increase (or decrease) in the present tax would have on aggregate saving and investment. Where the substitution effect may be in the direction of present consumption, the income effect may partially offset its influence. Studies which seek to reveal individual motivation behind investment decisions attest to a strong "income effect" which maintains savings goals in the face of reductions in income. Young married couples tend to base savings on future educational needs for their children, middle-aged couples save to meet retirement goals, and older persons save in order to make bequests to their heirs. In such cases of *target saving*, increases in taxes would be met by increases in saving effort.

Another factor which seems to reduce the impact of taxes on saving is the aforementioned lack of awareness of marginal tax rates by individuals.[12] Reduced tax consciousness affects the choice between consumption and saving in two ways—both favoring saving. In the first place,

---

[10] The arguments do not hold, of course, for "inferior" public goods or for a progressive rate structure which offsets the positive income effect.
[11] Wagstaff, "Income Tax Consciousness Under Withholding," pp. 79–80.
[12] Enrick, "A Pilot Study" and "A Further Study," and Wagstaff, "Income Tax Consciousness."

lack of awareness of the aggregate tax burden tends not to detract the saver from his original goals. Second, lack of awareness of the *marginal rates* tends to dampen the *substitution effect* (the latter being in the direction of reduced saving). Studies of the investment behavior of upper income individuals indicate that marginal income tax rates have little influence in the investment decision-making process.[13]

Yet another observation serves to mitigate the prediction that the income tax "discriminates" against saving. In the partial equilibrium model used to illustrate the choice between present and future consumption, the rate of return on investment was assumed as "given." In the real world this rate for the economy depends on sales and costs; for the economy as a whole, it depends on aggregate demand and supply, technology, and so on. The federal government (or Macroeconomic Policy Branch, to allude once more to our imaginary Fiscal Department) has taken upon itself the responsibility of providing for appropriate amounts of aggregate spending on consumption and investment. The personal income tax is only one of several tools which may be employed. Monetary authorities affect the rate of interest by manipulating the supply of money. Similarly, real investment may be encouraged by use of the investment tax credit in the corporate income tax. Thus, while our microeconomic analysis reveals certain aspects of individual investment behavior under the personal income tax, conclusions about their aggregate effects will be postponed until Part IV.

NONNEUTRALITY BETWEEN FINANCIAL INVESTMENT ALTERNATIVES

The theoretical perspective for evaluating tax effects on the choice between financial investment alternatives was drawn in the last chapter. In the model presented, the owner of investment funds was seen to have alternatives ranging from low yield with low risks to high yield with high risks. Correspondingly, there are risk-yield combinations among which the individual is indifferent. In equilibrium the individual will have chosen that risk-yield combination which promises to give him the highest attainable level of satisfaction. Personal income taxation without loss offsets was shown to produce both income and substitution effects. The loss of income induces the individual to increase his risk and yield in order to regain the former income level. Since, however, risks are now relatively more costly, the influences of the substitution effect is in the direction of less risk taking. The net effect of these opposing incentives cannot be predicted without knowledge of individual preference patterns.

Prediction is more easily made under the income tax with full loss offsets, since no substitution effect occurs. The surprising prediction is that risk taking will increase. Since the government is now a partner and shares both gains and losses, it also bears a part of the risks. And individuals, desiring to regain lost income, will choose to bear additional risks. The loss-offset model essentially shows choices to be made by the large diversified investor under present federal personal income tax provisions. Before the tax base is established, all losses are deducted from gains. Thus, in all cases where losses do not exceed gains, the government shares revenue loss. Since small investors generally cannot afford to diversify their portfolios, loss offsets for them often are not full —certainly not for those who go bankrupt.[14] In order to fully offset losses the Treasury would have to refund losses at the same rate at which gains would have been taxed.

For gains subject to progressive rates the yield-risk function becomes progressively steeper, owing to progressively greater tax on high-risk, high-yield alternatives. In response to an increase in an already progressive tax the individual will move to an equilibrium which reflects both an income and a substitution effect. Unlike the proportional tax with loss offset, the substitution effect of the progressive tax may result in less risk-taking, as depicted in Figure 10.6. For a shift from another tax to a progressive income tax of equal yield, the effect on individuals would differ according to size of income, amount of tax formerly paid, and the progressivity of the new rates.

EMPIRICAL STUDIES OF INVESTMENT BEHAVIOR

Since the income tax creates somewhat offsetting income and substitution effects in the choice between risk and yield portfolios, it is not surprising that empirical tests have given mixed results. Studies based on the interview technique reveal that tax considerations are not a major influence

[13] See R. Barlow, H. E. Brazer, and J. N. Morgan, *Economic Behavior of the Affluent* (Washington, D.C.: Brookings, 1966), and an earlier study by J. K. Butters, L. E. Thompson, and L. L. Bollinger, *Effects of Taxation: Investment by Individuals* (Boston: Graduate School of Business Administration, Harvard University, 1953).

[14] There is no provision for carrying over losses of personal income to past or future tax years; however, capital gains, we recall, are not taxed until the year they are realized. Thus the investor has some flexibility in matching losses with gains. Business operating losses may be carried back three years and (if this does not use them up) forward for five years.

FIGURE 10–6

Choice of optimum risk-
yield combination:
progressive income tax with
loss offset

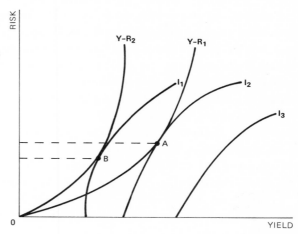

one way or the other in investment decision making.[15] Where positive responses to income tax changes are found, the results are mixed: some individuals shift to portfolios of *more risk* and some to portfolios of *less risk*.[16]

More significant influences on investment behavior stem from the specific provisions. The capital gains feature is the most important. It increases the willingness of individuals to take risks. Moreover, growth stocks, which often involve greater risk and greater potential yield, are given preference over more stable dividend-producing stocks and bonds.

In order to convert stocks into gifts or to put them in trusts, the giver must realize the capital gains and pay income tax on them. But since the income tax on capital gains can be permanently escaped by dying before they are realized, there is incentive to pass them via inheritance instead of gifts. With respect to this decision, however, the death and gift taxes are complementary, and we will analyze the net effect in Chapter 14. We conclude in passing, however, that the ability to escape income taxes on capital gains at death tends to encourage retention of funds in " growth " stocks.

Finally, certain provisions influence the timing of financial investing. The six-months criterion for capital gains treatment encourages the investor to hold stock at least that long. Another "lock-in" effect occurs after gains have been made, simply because tax payment can be deferred until the gain is actually realized. On the other hand, individuals with high income in one particular tax period are encouraged to sell those

assets that have declined in value in order to obtain a loss for tax purposes. Yet another "lock-in" effect derives from the escaping of gains
taxation at death. The elderly individual, attempting to maximize the
value of his estate at death, is encouraged not to sell currently held
assets even if more profitable alternatives present themselves unless the
foreseen profit *more* than compensates for the necessary tax on capital
gains.

FINANCIAL INVESTMENT BY FIRMS

Gains may also be subject to business rather than personal income taxes.
While the analysis of management behavior will be examined in the next
chapter, it is appropriate to anticipate that examination with respect to
financial investment decisions. First we recall that the asset, say a
security, is treated as an investment subject to capital gains treatment
if held by an individual; or if held by an investments dealer, it is treated
as stock in trade. If the asset is held by a *firm*, not only are taxes on
investment yield different, but the goals and behavior of management
may be quite different from those of private individual investors.

Several models of management decision-making behavior will be developed; we mention now only a few aspects which may affect risk taking.
For firms where management and ownership are closely interrelated, any
additional taxation on gains has a rather direct income effect. As demonstrated above, the expected response when returns from investment are
taxed will be *increased* risk taking. For firms where management and
ownership are separated, management may have a certain target volume
of profits which they and the stockholders regard as acceptable. A tax
which reduces yield below this target may lead to increased risk taking
on the part of management. If the reduction does not affect the profit
target, no change in the risk-yield portfolio may occur—unless, of course,
other goals important to management have been thwarted. The criteria
the firm uses in promoting its officers will be influential in deciding the
way an officer adjusts the firm's portfolio. It may be that moderate
success with no "blunders" is the best strategy for promotion. If so, the
executive is *less likely* to divert funds to high-risk, high-yield portfolios
in response to increased taxes.

[15] Barlow, Brazer, and Morgan, *Economic Behavior of the Affluent*; Butters, Thompson
and Bollinger, *Effects of Taxation*.
[16] See Butters, Thompson, and Bollinger, *Effects of Taxation*.

Finally, we observe that for firms (as well as for high-income individuals) the larger the portfolio, the more likely it is that any forthcoming loss can be completely offset against gains for tax purposes.

NONNEUTRALITY BETWEEN TYPES OF EMPLOYMENT AND BETWEEN WORK AND LEISURE

The generality of the personal income tax limits its nonneutral influence between types of employment. Thus, here again, it scores well relative to other taxes on the *neutrality criterion*. There are, however, limitations to its generality, and these produce nonneutral effects. More specifically, the effects derive from not including leisure and many types of income-in-kind in the income tax base, and from various tax exemptions, loopholes, and so on which may induce the individual to change his occupation.

The exclusion of services produced by a housewife no doubt induces many women to choose that occupation rather than one with a taxable income. Similarly, the omission of goods and services produced and consumed on the farm gives added incentive to those considering a farming career. More generally, the omission of do-it-yourself projects may induce persons to choose occupations with spare time for such nontaxed work. The tax obviously places a premium on occupations which offer nonmonetary rewards. Such rewards may come in the form of the intellectual stimulation found in academia, the pleasant surroundings of the office worker or the forest ranger, or the prestige of the medical profession.

Employers as well as employees are aware that fringe benefits such as contributions to pension plans, income in kind (such as a good, inexpensive cafeteria, attractive and comfortable working quarters, and so on), are strong incentives in occupational choice, especially since they are not taxable. Hence, more of the economy's resources are devoted to these types of real income than would be the case if real income were included in the tax base.

Choice among safe versus risky or uncertain occupations may also be influenced by the tax structure. The analysis here is similar to that of the choice among investment portfolios. For any increase in the income tax the *income effect* is likely to influence the individual towards a more risky occupation in order to attain his target income level, if any. With progressive rates, however, the substitution effect is likely to be quite persuasive. Since the high yields, which may be associated with high risks, are taxed progressively, the attractiveness of the low-risk profession is increased. A related influence may be the discrimination against occupations where income is irregular relative to the tax period. The tax's limited averaging provisions coupled with progressive rates make occupations with more regular income relatively more attractive.

Most studies[17] have found little empirical evidence that the considerations mentioned above have substantial impact on occupational choice. Consequently, only the arguments and the *direction* of the effects have been presented, and no attempt has been made to establish their possible significance. Since occupational choice often involves many factors over which the individual may have little control, the part played by taxes is difficult to ascertain. One study found evidence that the tax has the effect of reducing the willingness of *executives* to transfer to other jobs with higher salaries.[18] Here again many factors enter into decisions to change jobs, but high marginal tax rates obviously diminish the effectiveness of a higher income compensation for harder work, moving, and so on and may on occasion be decisive.

THE CHOICE BETWEEN WORK EFFORT AND LEISURE

The basic model for analyzing the choice between work and leisure was presented in Chapter 9. A proportional income tax was shown to produce *both* an income and a substitution effect. The nonneutrality derives from the fact that the real income created by leisure is not included in the base of the personal income tax; hence, the tax on income makes leisure relatively more attractive. As was shown, however, the income effect of a tax increase may be towards more work in order to maintain a desired income level and may offset the substitution effect.

If tax rates are progressive, as in the personal income tax, the substitution effect is heightened, and there is more likelihood that leisure will be substituted for work. Consider Figure 10.7. The entire amount of time available to the individual is OA. Initially the wage rate—the rate at which income can be substituted for leisure—is given by the slope of BA. The initial equilibrium is at E, where OL_1 hours are devoted to leisure and L_1A to work.

---

[17] See, for example, Herbert G. Grubel and David R. Edwards, "Personal Income Taxation and the Choice of Professions," *Quarterly Journal of Economics*, February 1964), pp. 158–163.

[18] T. H. Sanders, *Effects of Taxation on Executives* (Boston: Graduate School of Business Administration, Harvard University, 1951).

FIGURE 10-7

The effects of a proportional and a progressive income tax on work effort and leisure

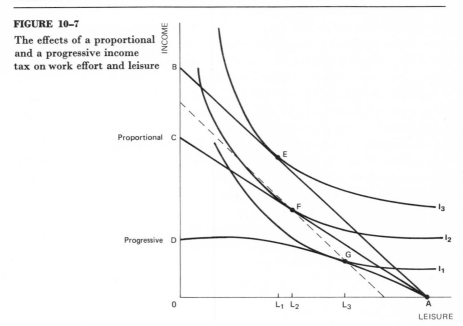

A proportional tax is represented by the reduction of possible income to AC. In the case depicted, the inducement to exchange leisure for work (the substitution effect) more than offsets the inducement to maintain the original *level of income* (the income effect). The new equilibrium at F features more leisure, OL_2. Now introduce a progressive rate structure, AGD. The amount taxed is shown to be equal for both taxes by the dotted line passing through the two equilibria F and G (since it is parallel to the income constraint BA). But the substitution effect is greater under the progressive tax, and more leisure, OL_3, is taken.

Even though the analysis demonstrates that the substitution effect is reinforced by progressive rates, there is little empirical evidence that the effect is sufficient to reduce work effort. Most individuals responding to interview studies reply that taxes have little net effect on work effort. Apparently, then, the income effect of taxes offsets the substitution effect. That the income effect works against the substitution effect is supported by interviews conducted with 2997 families, which revealed an inverse relationship between wage rate and hours worked.[19] Two British studies indicate that, in general, income effects offset substitution effects even for workers and professionals who have considerable discretion over hours worked.[20]

Such results agree with more general interview studies of higher-income individuals in the United States.[21] Tax rates have little effect on work effort even for executives in higher tax brackets. In general, other factors, such as a sense of accomplishment, power, prestige, and working conditions, are more important in the individual's attitude. But to the extent that tax rates do influence work effort, some individuals are motivated to work harder while others are motivated to work less.

In summary, the simple model of welfare-maximizing behavior has been useful in outlining the various factors influencing the individual's response to taxes. We have seen that some of the more frequently held ideas are not true. For example, we demonstrated that income taxes do not invariably reduce work effort, as generally assumed, but may in fact increase work effort according to the individual's goals. The use of these basic models along with further empirical studies will continue to provide insights into the effects of current and proposed tax provisions.

WORK EFFORT UNDER THE NEGATIVE INCOME TAX

A major concern in the decision to adopt the negative income tax is its effect on the supply of work effort. A frequent argument against the tax-transfer is that it would severely curtail the work incentives of the poor. In part this judgment depends on a judgment as to why the poor are poor. Are they "lazy," or are they "disadvantaged." The "lazier" they are, the more willing they will be to trade off work effort for leisure. On the other hand if they are ambitious but disadvantaged with respect to work opportunity, they will be less willing to trade off work effort (and more money) for leisure. Considerable analysis is currently being undertaken to predict responses to the negative income tax. These studies range in approach from the traditional behavioral models to questionnaire surveys and pilot demonstration programs.

---

[19] J. N. Morgan, M. H. David, W. J. Cohen, and H. E. Brazer, *Income and Wealth in the United States* (New York: McGraw-Hill, 1962).

[20] A sample of 1429 workers carried out for the Royal Commission on the Taxation of Profits and Income produced vehement declarations of the disincentive influences of taxes. Yet only a small number of those interviewed actually reduced work effort. See *Royal Commission on the Taxation of Profits and Income: Second Report* (London, 1954). A 1956 study of 306 London solicitors and accountants by George Break also met with much talk but little action. But even when a liberal interpretation is given, it is found that while 20 percent experience or anticipate impairment of incentives, over 30 percent experience the opposite effect. See Break, "Income Taxes and Incentives to Work: an Empirical Study," *American Economic Review*, vol. 47 (September 1957), pp. 529–549.

[21] See for example, Barlow, Brazer, and Morgan, *Economic Behavior of the Affluent*, and Sanders, *Effects of Taxation on Executives*.

FIGURE 10–8

Negative income tax, work
income, and leisure

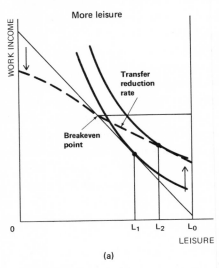

(a)

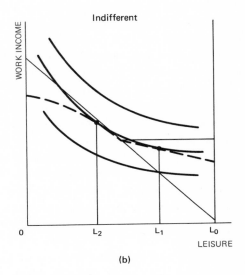

(b)

FIGURE 10–9

Work opportunity and the
negative income tax

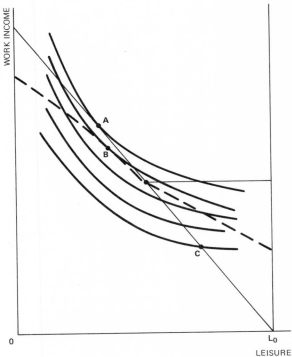

While there is some doubt as to whether the *traditional analysis* favors more or less work in response to a positive income tax, there is no doubt with regard to the negative income tax. For in the latter case *both* the income and substitution effects work in the direction of taking *more leisure*. Figure 10.8(a) demonstrates the effect of a negative income effect on the person receiving low work income. The substitution effect, obvious in the new slope of the dotted line, creates a more attractive rate at which leisure can be substituted for work income. And under the assumption that leisure is a "normal good," we expect one to "consume" more leisure as his income increases.

We could, of course, draw a preference pattern so that less leisure would be taken in response to the negative income tax. We can even draw a case where the individual is *indifferent* between two work-leisure combinations as in Figure. 10.8(b). But the basic conclusion of the traditional preference function model is to support the argument that the negative income tax will encourage the poor to substitute leisure for work effort.

It would seem, then, that a favorable argument for the negative income tax's effect on work effort must rest on the hypothesis that the poor have not been given *opportunity* to work as much as they would like. Our model is useful in illustrating these assumptions. Suppose instead of the individual being able to adjust the amount of leisure he takes (point *A* in Figure 10.9), he is obliged by lack of opportunity to take more (point *C*). It follows that under a negative income tax program he still may wish to reduce rather than increase his leisure. As Figure 10.9 shows, the individual would prefer position *B* to *C* even though the new tax program requires him to reduce his leisure and pay taxes on his work income.

Several conclusions follow: On the one hand, the negative income tax encourages less work effort for low income individuals if the assumptions of our basic model are met. On the other hand, if the assumption that individuals have the opportunity to work all they want to is not met, they may still desire more work after a change to the negative tax. We observe, finally, that the response to the negative income tax would involve a number of related variables such as whether work opportunities are increased and whether the disincentives of other parts of welfare program are removed.

INCOME TAXES AND MACROECONOMIC POLICY

Since an examination of macroeconomic policy will be presented in Part IV, we offer here only a few comments about the impact of the personal income tax on the goals of price stability, full employment, and economic growth. Of primary note is the fact that the personal income tax is one of the most powerful weapons in the arsenal of the fiscal authorities. The 1964 tax cut and the 1968 surtax attest to the importance of the income tax in macroeconomic policy.

The generality of the tax is again the feature which makes for its high rank under the macroeconomic policy criteria. Admittedly the effectiveness of the tax often depends somewhat precariously on the whim of particular congressmen.[22] However, once enacted, a change in the tax, say an increase, can become immediately effective via greater withholding deductions from a large percentage of wage earners, and higher payments are soon forthcoming from those self-employed persons who are required to make periodic tax payments.

As continued use is made of the income tax as a macroeconomic tool, the public and their congressional representatives will become more inclined to approve of rapid employment of the tax when needed. However, it is natural to expect that tax increases will be harder to enact than tax cuts. Moreover, once an inflationary mood of expectations has set in, as in the late sixties, the effectiveness of additional taxes is reduced by dissaving and rising costs, especially if the money supply and credit are allowed to expand.

When only slight countercyclical fiscal action is required, the present tax structure *automatically* obliges. This is because during inflation spending power increases are dampened as individuals advance to *progressively higher* tax brackets. The opposite occurs in recession, thus leaving progressively more spending power in the private sector.

The income tax treatment of capital gains is said to have a nonneutral effect on the prices of stocks which supposedly makes for instability in the stock market. The tax encourages the retention of stocks that have increased in value, since taxes do not have to be paid until the stocks are sold; consequently, supply becomes more inelastic during a bull market, and this accentuates the boom. Supposedly, then, the "lock-in" effect is procyclical. However, the effect, if it occurs, cannot be very strong, since empirical studies have failed to reveal evidence of such an effect.

Attaining a satisfactory growth rate requires not only attention to full employment and stable prices but a proper balance between consumption and investment through time. For example, aggregate supply in this period depends not only on full employment during this period but investment in preceding periods. Similarly, aggregate demand depends on consumption and the profitability of investment in past, present, and future periods. The income tax is an important tool in controlling consumption so that this proper balance can be attained.

Returning to our imaginary fiscal model, we note that the income tax recommends itself because of its neutrality towards other goals such as resource allocation and income distribution. Theoretically, at least, the income tax can be used to regulate aggregate demand without upsetting price ratios in the private sector or the relative distribution of income. In order for the latter goal to be accomplished the tax bill of all individuals would have to be increased (or decreased) proportionately. If in fact the rate structure of the tax already reflected the desired distribution goal, the 1968 income surtax would have approximated this requirement. Yet, as we have observed, the ability of certain groups to avoid the tax makes it highly unlikely that such a goal, however defined, is met precisely. Indeed, the imposition of the surtax enhanced the relative position of those who successfully avoid the tax.

Finally, we note that to the extent the tax is nonneutral—and we have examined several ways in which it seems to be—its employment as a macroeconomic tool disturbs price ratios and thus may misallocate resources. Of course, in order to be certain that such nonneutrality has a negative impact on social welfare we must ascertain whether existing price ratios and resource allocation were optimal. Nonetheless, in spite of the nonneutral effects and other deficiencies of specific provisions, the many attributes of the personal income tax are sufficient for us to favor its use as the basis of our tax system.

SOME ALTERNATIVES CONSIDERED

INCREASING TAX VISIBILITY

As we shall discover, the other taxes in our system do not fare as well as the present income tax under our efficiency criteria. Its attributes for implementing our basic fiscal goals have been noted: (1) income redistribution is facilitated, since the base of the tax is income and progressive rates can be uniformly applied, (2) stability and growth goals are enhanced by the generality of the tax, which can quickly effect a change in aggregate consumption; and (3) generality of the tax also allows for neutrality (with respect to private sector price ratios) when purchasing

---

[22] For example, Wilbur Mills, Chairman of the House Ways and Means Committee, held up the 1968 surtax legislation interminably while inflationary pressures steadily built up.

power is withdrawn. In terms of the Fiscal Department model used in Chapter 4 we demonstrated that use of the personal income tax should, in theory, be helpful to voters in ascertaining just what the public sector is doing with respect to their major national priorities. In terms of the real world, of course, it is difficult to assess the impact of the tax as part of the overall picture, owing to the complex ways in which the budgets of federal, state, and local governments affect our goals. Nevertheless, use of the personal income tax as an important source of revenue adds to the voter's ability to assess public sector activity.

Several exemptions under the present tax law, such as veterans' benefits and combat pay stem from "merit" considerations. Orderly decision making would require that these considerations be met by transfer payments rather than by provisions which tend to muddle the overall assessment of the distribution goal. It is difficult, for example, to evaluate the impact of our progressive structure of tax rates, since the tax base is significantly eroded by the tax provisions.

Net progressivity is tied to exemptions and deductions as well as to the rate structure. The basic personal exemption of $750 is justified by its exemption of "subsistence-level" income. This aim could be accomplished in a more straightforward manner by integrating exemptions with the rate structure so as to clarify the effect on income distribution. The exemptions and rate structure would, of course, take account of differences in the number of dependents in the family taxpaying unit. In addition, the "subsistence-level" exemption will have to be changed periodically to reflect the changing value of the dollar and, more importantly, people's notions of "subsistence-level" income.

Our emphasis on visibility leads us to advocate replacement of the present system of welfare payments and the personal income tax with the *negative income tax*. As outlined previously, the *negative income tax* plan would supplement those family units whose income was below the "subsistence level." The income supplements would be reduced as income rose to a "break-even" level, after which taxes would be paid at higher levels of income. Visibility to the average citizen would be enhanced not only because of the integration of the rate structure with "subsistence-level" exemptions, but because the existing complex system of income supplements for the most part would be made part of the negative income tax system. The impact of these integrated taxes and supplements on our income redistribution goals would then become much more visible.

CAPITAL GAINS RECONSIDERED

The favorable treatment given capital gains under current provisions depends on the use of the flow as opposed to the accretion concept of income. The time-period question is resolved by taxing income only when "realized" and then at a reduced rate. The use of the accretion concept would involve considerable difficulty in annually assessing the value of many types of capital and appears to be impractical for that reason. However, the inequity generated by progressive rates and irregular realization of capital gains can be remedied by a more liberal averaging provision. It would be too lenient to propose strict averaging and still maintain the present option not to average; however, more liberal rates could be applied to the present framework. With full taxation of capital gains the present rate structure might well be amended. With more liberal averaging and full capital gains taxation (which thus could not be escaped by death), a more rational application of rates would be possible and the "lock-in" effects (if any) would be reduced.

THE EXEMPTIONS RECONSIDERED

The exemption of various other types of income creates distortion of distribution and resource allocation goals. One of the more flagrant loopholes for those in higher tax brackets is the exclusion of returns on state and local securities. Admittedly their inclusion in the personal income tax base would require states and localities to pay higher interest; however, there are better ways than this for the federal government to aid state and local financing.

Life insurance proceeds also are exempt from income taxation, although they include not only "pure" insurance but returns on investment and returns on reinvested earnings. Under the flow concept there again may be argument for present treatment, since the returns on investment are not actually in hand. However, under the accretion concept such returns should be taxed.

Nonmonetary income of various types also lends itself to taxation. Housework and many do-it-yourself projects would be difficult to evaluate monetarily; however, the evaluation of owner-occupied housing and many types of fringe benefits from employers presents fewer difficulties. The difficulties are of two types. The major difficulty is, of course, that of finding figures upon which to base taxes. Often, but not always, assessment data of owner-occupied housing is readily available and firms have records of expenditures on their employees. In the latter connection, however, a second difficulty occurs: the question of separating out what is consumption for the employee and what are legitimate business costs. This problem leads us to the much broader question discussed below.

COSTS VERSUS CONSUMPTION

Many activities considered consumption under present tax provisions are necessary to the production of income. For example, food, shelter, and clothing are necessary to the health of the laborer, yet they cannot be counted as a deduction against income earned. On the other hand, filet mignon is hardly an appropriate deduction in this respect. In fact, most expenditures on food, clothing, and shelter have a dual nature as both consumption and cost. One alternative might be to treat a minimum level of expenditure on these items as a "subsistence" level necessary for earning income. The present $750 personal exemption may be justified in this way; however, the amount allowed is not in line with that needed.

Educational expenditures also have elements of consumption and investment. The liberal arts college certainly offers more than training to enhance one's monetary income. On the other hand, graduate school is a prerequisite investment for the card-carrying professor of economics. Here again, while exact differentiation between costs and consumption is not possible, it would seem appropriate that some portion (perhaps an arbitrary percentage) of educational costs be deductible.

Many business expenses which have strong elements of consumption are deductible. In some occupations travel, entertainment, elegant meals, and so on are written off as necessary business costs. Trips by the owner to an orange grove in Florida, or rental housing in Stowe, Vermont, may allow vacation expenses to be deducted as costs. Similarly, the expense of building a fishing pond for the pleasure of a farmer and his friends will often be deducted.

Several of the questions posed here with regard to personal income tax will be reconsidered in Chapter 14 in an assessment of the tax system as a whole. What seems to be negative nonneutrality when we consider only one tax may be, in fact, positive in light of other taxes and expenditures. Our final evaluation must await this more general perspective.

11
MICROECONOMIC EFFECTS ON THE FIRM: THE SHIFTING AND INCIDENCE OF TAXATION

Suppose an excise tax is imposed on a commodity. One is tempted to say that the retail price of the commodity will be raised and the consumer will bear the tax burden; but this answer depends on the nature of the market. Suppose consumers can easily switch to other products. It may not be profitable for the firm to raise prices in an attempt to recoup losses.

Suppose instead that the producing firm does not purchase *inputs* in a competitive market but is a monopsonist (the sole buyer from many sellers). It may be profitable to shift the burden of the tax backward to the suppliers of inputs. It is not always immediately obvious who pays certain taxes.

In this chapter we will examine the conditions under which tax shifting may take place. *Shifting* simply means passing the burden of a tax from one person to another—the question being: Who pays?

Two more concepts will also be useful: the *impact* and the *incidence* of taxes. The "impact" of a tax is its initial effect on the firm or person who must make payment to the governing body. For example, the retail excise tax is initially imposed by the government on *retail stores*. The impact of the tax is on them, although they are expected to shift the tax to consumers. The "incidence" of a tax is the final resting place of the burden of the tax. To pursue the example of the excise tax, we may observe that the incidence is typically thought to be shifted to the consumer in the form of a price increase. Actually, others may also bear the incidence of the tax. If the tax reduces retail profits, the owners and employees of the firm supplying the goods may also bear some of the burden.

Since the shifting and incidence of taxes may be complex, we find "models" useful in analyzing their effects. In using models, we assume certain things are "constant," so that we may focus on what seem to be the most important relationships.

We will usually begin our examination of a tax using "partial equilibrium analysis"; that is, analyzing the equilibrium tendencies of firms (or other economic units) in a particular market. There are of course important methodological differences between partial and general equilibrium analysis. What seems to hold true for a particular firm or market may not hold true when the entire economy (and the general equilibrium to which it tends) is considered. We will find it necessary to shift to the general equilibrium perspective in order to check the validity of our "partial" models. We begin by examining tax shifting and incidence in terms of the partial equilibrium models of the firm.

FIGURE 11-1

Market demand and supply
in the immediate period

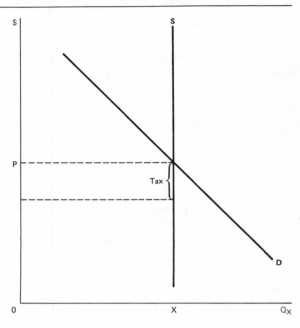

TAXES, DEMAND, AND SUPPLY

Taxes on output do not affect the demand for that output but rather its
supply (or cost); yet the demand relationship is quite important in determining incidence. We recall that market demand refers to the summation
(horizontal) of all consumer demand in a particular market.[1] Similarly,
market supply is the summation of quantities firms will supply at various
prices.

The time period involved is crucial. While certain things such as technology and the prices of inputs are "held constant" regardless of the time
period, other factors are acknowledged to vary with time. Consequently,
it is useful to distinguish between the following three time periods: the
immediate period, the short run, and the long run.

THE IMMEDIATE PERIOD

In the immediate period very little affecting the supply can be changed.
Consider, for example, the farmer whose crop of tomatoes has been har-
vested. Regardless of the price he can do little to change the quantity
supplied. Similarly, the market supply, which is the summation of all

farmers' supplies in the market area, is also unresponsive to changes in price (see Figure 11.1). It is drawn as a straight line parallel to the vertical axis—it is completely inelastic.[2] If a tax is imposed, there is no chance of shifting the tax "forward" to the buyers. Since there is no way to change the quantity supplied, price must remain at P. Hence, the incidence of tax goes "backward" to the supplier.

SHORT-RUN AND LONG-RUN COSTS

Unless otherwise specified, the factors affecting demand are assumed to remain constant in all three time periods. Actually we differentiate among the time periods according to the firm's flexibility in using inputs. In the

---

[1] More rigorously, it is a schedule of the quantitites of a particular good which will be bought at different prices during a specific period of time. We initially assume that everything affecting the quantity bought, except price, is held constant. This includes the number of consumers, consumer tastes and incomes, and the prices of related goods. If the price of good X changes, we move along the demand curve to another quantity demanded; but if one of the factors we have "held constant" (such as consumer income) changes, the whole demand curve shifts.

[2] The concept of elasticity is quite useful in measuring the effects of taxes. The student should recall that price elasticity of demand refers to the relative responsiveness of changes in quantity to changes in price. The elasticity coefficient can be expressed by the following formula:

$$E_d = \frac{\text{percentage change in quantity demanded}}{\text{percentage change in price}}$$

In terms of discrete changes the average coefficient may be arrived at by the formula:

$$E_d = \frac{\dfrac{\text{change in quantity}}{\text{sum of quantitites}/2}}{\dfrac{\text{change in prices}}{\text{sum of prices}/2}}$$

Suppose price changes from \$5 to \$4 while the quantity demanded changes from 2000 to 4000. The formula becomes

$$E_d = \frac{\dfrac{2{,}000}{6{,}000/2}}{\dfrac{1}{9/2}} = 3.00$$

When the relative change in quantity is greater than the relative change in price, the curve is said to be relatively elastic ($E_d > 1$). When the relative change in quantity is less than the relative change in price, the curve is said to be relatively inelastic ($E_d < 1$). When the relative changes are the same, E_d is said to be unity ($E_d = 1$).

FIGURE 11-2

Total, average, and marginal
costs

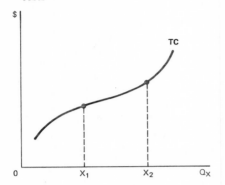
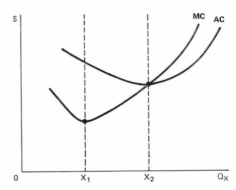

FIGURE 11-3

Long-run average and
marginal costs

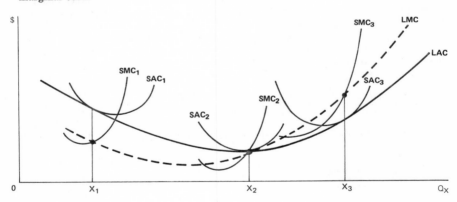

immediate period we assumed no flexibility—the firm's supply was fixed.
In the short run some inputs are fixed but others are variable. Thus, the
firm may increase or decrease output by increasing or decreasing the use
of the variable inputs. In the usual " model" of firm behavior featuring
only two inputs, one input (" labor ") is assumed to be variable in the
short run while the other (" plant ") is assumed to be fixed. Since there
are fixed and variable inputs, changes in the quantity of output involve
increasing and diminishing returns.[3]

The long-run assumptions concerning supply—or costs—are the same as those of the short run with but one exception: all inputs are now considered variable. Looking over the long-run alternatives, the executive can choose any plant and labor combination consistent with the available technology. There is one optimum plant size and there is one optimum combination of inputs (say, labor and plant).[4]

The elasticity concept is also used to describe the supply relationship. We can see that in Figure 11.1 the supply curve is completely inelastic; a large change in price will produce no measurable change in quantity.

An important aspect of the shifting and incidence of taxes is the effect of taxes on costs. Consider the effect of an output tax on short-run costs shown in Figure 11.4. The tax on output is an additional variable cost. Suppose the tax is on cigarettes. For each pack the firm produces and sells, it must pay more tax; hence, both the marginal and the average costs are raised. Consider now the effect of a tax which is independent of output. Suppose a retail store is required to purchase a license in order to operate. The tax has no connection with output; it must be paid regardless of the amount of business done by the retail store—it is a fixed cost of doing business. In Figure 11.5 this shows up as a shift

---

[3] It is important to remember that output can be increased only by adding units of the variable input. Look at Figure 11.2. As output is increased to point X_1, decreasing marginal costs are experienced. But at that point, diminishing returns to the variable input begin to be experienced, and marginal costs start rising. Finally, at point X_2, average costs also rise. This is the most "efficient" output for this plant, since average costs per unit of output are minimized. Here fixed and variable inputs are being used in the most efficient combination.

[4] Long-run average and marginal costs can be stated in terms of the short-run curves. Since short-run cost curves correspond with a particular fixed plant size, we may view the long-run alternatives as a series of short-run cost curves consistent with the different plant sizes. In Figure 11.3 each short-run curve represents a different plant size. The long-run average cost curve is not simply a summation of the lowest points of particular short-run average curves, but rather it is an envelope of the short-run curves (see Figure 11.3). At only one output, X_2, does the lowest point on a short-run average cost curve coincide with the lowest long-run average cost per unit of output. It is at this output, X_2, that long-run average costs are minimized, reflecting the fact that the optimum plant size is being used along with the most efficient combination of labor and plant.

The long-run marginal cost is the short-run marginal cost associated with the lowest short-run average cost for a particular output (as shown for outputs X_1, X_2, and X_3). Note that at a less-than-optimum size plant and output the appropriate short-run marginal cost is below the short-run average cost, while at a greater than optimum plant size the appropriate short-run marginal cost is above the short-run average cost.

FIGURE 11–4

The effect of a tax on
output on TC, AC, and MC

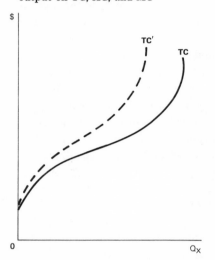

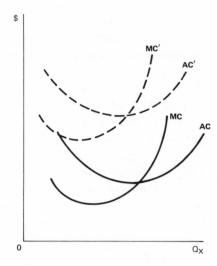

FIGURE 11–5

The effect of a tax independent of output on TC, AC,
and MC

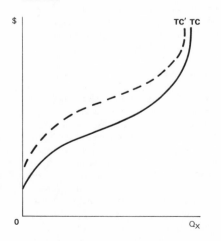

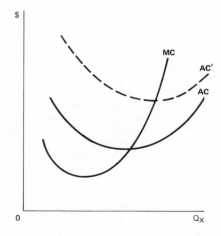

---

upward of the total cost curve. At any given output the old and new total cost curves have the same slope. The vertical distance between the old and new total cost curves would represent the amount of the tax. Since this new cost is independent of output, marginal costs do not change. Average costs, which are simply TC/X, do shift upward.

We are now in a position to examine the firm's reaction to changes in taxes as they affect the firm's cost curves. The firm's reaction will depend on the demand curve it faces, which in turn, depends on the type of market within which the firm operates. We will investigate these market situations and examine the response of firms within them to various taxes. Market types are usually classified as follows: pure competition, pure monopoly, oligopoly, and monopolistic competition. The basic difference is in the number of firms operating in the market. This, in turn, affects the demand curve the firm faces. For example, in pure monopoly only one firm is in the market; consequently, it faces the entire market demand curve. In pure competition, however, so many firms are in the market that the individual firm has no control over price; consequently, the highest price at which the firm can sell is *the* market price, and so this becomes the firm's demand curve.

PURE COMPETITION

How do taxes affect the firms in perfectly competitive markets? The firm takes the market price as given. Since it can sell all it wishes without affecting price, its demand curve is horizontal at the market price. Average revenue,

$$\frac{total\ revenue}{x}$$

and marginal revenue,

$$\frac{change\ in\ total\ revenue}{change\ in\ x}$$

are both equal to market price. The firm, maximizing profit, produces at that quantity of output where marginal cost (MC) is equal to marginal revenue (MR).

FIGURE 11–6

Taxes in a model of pure
competition

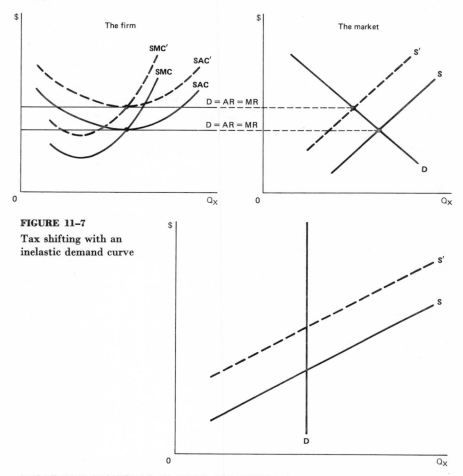

FIGURE 11–7

Tax shifting with an
inelastic demand curve

SHORT-RUN INCIDENCE IN PURE COMPETITION

If costs to the firm change, the market supply curve shifts.[5] In Figure 11.6 we see the effects of a *tax on the output*, X. As the firm's
average and marginal costs shift up, the market's supply also shifts up.
The market, and the firms within it, tend to a new equilibrium where
$S' = D$ and where $MC = MR$ (and $AR = AC$).

What can be said of incidence in the short run in a purely competitive
model? The illustration (Figure 11.6) is somewhat arbitrary, since it starts

and ends in the equilibrium position. In actual market situations, some firms will usually be experiencing abnormal profits while others experience losses. With the addition of the tax to marginal and average costs, the market price will start rising. Some firms may find that their variable costs are now greater than revenue—in which case they may cease to operate or else plan to leave the industry when the opportunity arises. In the meantime, however, before the number of firms adjusts, all firms will experience smaller profits or even losses until the market price adjusts upward. The resultant market price and quantity depend on the relative elasticities of the demand and supply curves of the industry in question.

If the market supply curve is completely inelastic—as in the case of the immediate period—the entire cost will be borne by the firms and input owners (as depicted in Figure 11.1 above) and the price will remain the same. If the market demand curve is completely inelastic—as in Figure 11.7—all of the tax will be completely shifted forward. The same quantity of output will be produced, but the market price will be raised by the exact amount of the tax. The entire incidence of the tax will be on the consumer. *The percentage of the tax which shows up as a price increase may be taken as a rough index of how much the incidence is shifted forward.*[6]

Figure 11.8 illustrates how the impact of a tax depends on the relative elasticity of the market supply curve. The curves are drawn so that we start from the same equilibrium where $S = D$. The added tax is depicted as a vertical shift of the same amount for each supply curve. S_e, the relatively elastic supply curve, shifts to $S_e{}'$, and the new equilibrium is at P_e and X_e. S_i, the relatively inelastic supply curve, shifts to $S_i{}'$, and the new equilibrium is at P_i and X_i. The more elastic supply schedule makes for a greater change in price and quantity. This indicates that a larger percentage of the incidence has been passed forward. This result

---

[5] Remember that the market supply curve is simply the summation of the quantities all firms would supply at various prices. In perfect competition the supply of each firm is its marginal cost curve. Thus market supply is simply the summation of all firms' marginal cost curves. To illustrate this, recall how each firm determines output by equating MR with MC. If market price rises, the firm again equates the higher price (which is the firm's AR and MR) to its MC to determine output. From this perspective it is easy to see that the firm's MC curve is actually its supply curve. And the market supply curve is the summation of the MC curves of the firms. Consequently, if the MC for each firm changes, the market supply curve shifts.

[6] This index cannot be considered as a measurement of welfare lost, however. The latter depends upon the alternatives open to the consumers in question, the effect of the tax on their incomes, and the shape of their particular *preference patterns*.

FIGURE 11–8

Tax shifting with different elasticities of supply

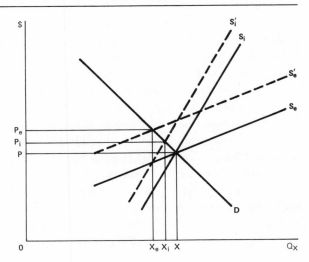

FIGURE 11–9

Long-run equilibrium for the firm in perfect competition

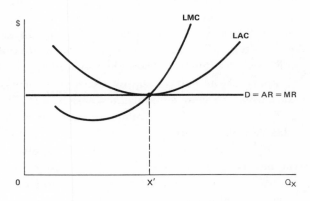

FIGURE 11–10(A)

The increasing-cost industry and tax shifting

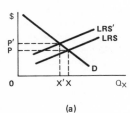

(a)

FIGURE 11–10 (B)

The constant-cost industry and tax shifting

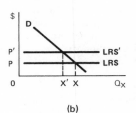

(b)

FIGURE 11–10 (C)

The decreasing-cost industry and tax shifting

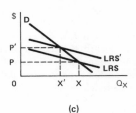

(c)

is expected because of the relatively greater elasticity of S_e. What the greater elasticity means is that the input owners are flexible and thus can respond readily to changes in prices by moving to other occupations; thus, the tax cannot be shifted to them.

LONG-RUN TAX INCIDENCE IN PURELY COMPETITIVE MARKETS

Next consider how taxes affect costs in the long run. We start from the firm's long-run equilibrium position.[7]

It is often the case that as demand increases over time, some input costs will change. The *long-run supply curve* (*LRS*) is upward sloping, horizontal, or downward sloping according to whether the costs of inputs increase, remain constant, or decrease. The slope of the long-run supply curve is crucial in determining the long-run incidence of a tax in a particular market. Figure 11.10(a) depicts an industry which experiences increasing input costs as it expands. The addition of a tax shifts the long-run supply curve upward. Part of the tax is shifted forward and part backward according to the relative elasticity of demand and supply. The more elastic the supply curve, the more of the tax is shifted forward. The increasing-cost industry is considered to be the most frequent case. However, it is appropriate to note that (owing to the greater flexibility of resources over time) the long-run supply curve is more elastic than the short-run curve. Accordingly, there is less chance a tax will be shifted backward to the resource owners for the long run. In the so-called "constant-cost" industry, the long-run supply curve is completely elastic; hence, all of the tax is shifted forward [see Figure 11.10(b)].

The last possibility, the "decreasing-cost" industry, also deserves mention. Since we are not examining the question of possible changes in technology, there are few markets which will fit the decreasing-cost description. What is required is that costs of inputs decrease as the industry expands. This situation may occur if the input industries experience economies of scale as they expand to supply more inputs. In such a case the long-run supply curve is downward sloping, as in Figure 11.10(c), and the increase in market price is greater than the tax (or rather greater than the vertical shift in the long-run supply curve brought about by the tax).

---

[7] Since there is free entry, firms will enter the market as long as abnormal profits are available. Market price will be driven down so that each firm's revenue just covers costs. Firms will produce that output at which costs are lowest—that is, where $AR = LAC = MR = LMC$ (Figure 11.9).

FIGURE 11–11

Pure monopoly and
a tax on output

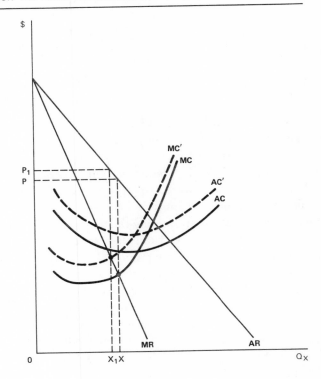

PURE MONOPOLY

Tax incidence at the other extreme of the spectrum of market types, pure monopoly, can more readily fall on the owners of the firm, since they may be experiencing abnormal profits. Tax shifting again depends on the nature of change in costs and the slope of the demand curve. We recall that in the pure monopoly model only one firm faces the market demand curve, which is negatively sloped. Sales can be increased only by lowering market price; hence, marginal revenue falls faster than the price itself.

SHORT-RUN TAX INCIDENCE IN PURE MONOPOLY CASES

Let us again start from a profit-maximizing equilibrium and observe the firm's response to the imposition of a tax on output. In Figure 11.11 the original profit-maximizing equilibrium is at output X and price P (the average abnormal profit being the difference between AR and AC at that output).

Now recall the discussion of taxes and costs. A tax related to output shifts both marginal and average costs as depicted in Figure 11.11. Since marginal costs have shifted up to MC', the new equilibrium of MR and MC' will result in a higher price, P_1, and a lower quantity, X_1.[8] The tax

---

[8] The monopolist's response to an excise tax can easily be portrayed with simple calculus. Assume he has the following demand and total cost functions:

$P = \alpha - \beta X$
$TC = aX^2 + bX + c$

where α, β, a, b, and c are all positive. It follows that his total revenue function is:

$TR = \alpha X - \beta X^2$

The monopolist maximizes profit by equating marginal revenue with marginal cost.

$$MR = \frac{d(TR)}{dX} = \alpha - 2\beta X$$

$$MC = \frac{d(TC)}{dX} = 2aX + b$$

$2aX + b = \alpha - 2\beta X$
$2aX + 2\beta X = \alpha - b$
$2X(a + \beta) = \alpha - b$

$$X = \frac{\alpha - b}{2(a + \beta)}$$

This, the profit-maximizing output level, can be substituted into the demand function to find the profit-maximizing price:

$P = \alpha - \beta \left[\dfrac{\alpha - b}{2(a + \beta)} \right]$

$P = \alpha - \dfrac{\beta(\alpha - b)}{2(a + \beta)}$

$P = \dfrac{2\alpha(a + \beta) + \beta(b - \alpha)}{2(a + \beta)}$

If the government places a tax on output the monopolist will add it to his cost function. Since the tax varies directly with output, X, his total cost function becomes :

$TC = aX^2 + (b + t)X + c$

and his marginal cost function becomes:

$MC = 2aX + b + t$

His new profit-maximizing output level can be attained by equalizing MR and the new MC.

$2aX + b + t = \alpha - 2\beta X$
$2aX + 2\beta X = \alpha - b - t$
$2X(a + \beta) = \alpha - b - t$

$$X = \frac{\alpha - b - t}{2(a + \beta)}$$

FIGURE 11–12

Pure monopoly, a tax on output with different elasticities of marginal costs

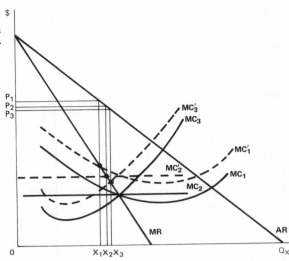

has been partially shifted forward. *The percentage shifted forward depends on the relative slopes of the marginal revenue and marginal costs curves.* The more inelastic the demand and marginal revenue curves, the *greater* the portion of tax shifted forward. The marginal cost curve may be downward sloping, constant, or upward sloping, as depicted in Figure 11.12. In the diagram the vertical distance by which costs are increased by the tax is the same for each case. The resultant price increase is greatest when marginal costs are downward sloping.[9] In the case of constant marginal costs, MC_2, the price change will be less than in the decreasing-cost case but greater than the more typical case of increasing marginal costs. While it is possible that MC may be downward sloping and result in a price increase greater than the tax, in most cases only a part of the tax will be shifted forward. Part of the incidence to the firm will be a reduction in its abnormal profits.[10]

Thus the after-tax quantity will be less than the before-tax quantity.

$$\frac{\alpha - b - t}{2(a + \beta)} < \frac{\alpha - b}{2(a + \beta)}$$

The new profit-maximizing price becomes

$$P = \alpha - \beta \left[\frac{\alpha - b - t}{2(a + \beta)} \right]$$

$$P = \alpha - \frac{\beta(\alpha - b - t)}{2(a + \beta)}$$

$$P = \frac{2\alpha(a + \beta) + \beta(b - \alpha + t)}{2(a + \beta)}$$

which if compared to the before-tax price shows that the after-tax price will be higher:

$$\frac{2\alpha(a+\beta)+\beta(b-\alpha+t)}{2(a+\beta)} > \frac{2\alpha(a+\beta)+\beta(b-\alpha)}{2(a+\beta)}$$

As we expected, the tax on output, through its direct effect on costs, causes the profit-maximizing monopolist to raise price and restrict quantity.

Finally, let us examine the differences between the prices and quantitites:

$$\Delta X = \frac{\alpha-b-t}{2(a+\beta)} - \frac{\alpha-b}{2(a+\beta)} = \frac{-t}{2(a+\beta)}$$

$$\Delta t = \frac{2\alpha(a+\beta)+\beta(b-\alpha+t)}{2(a+\beta)} - \frac{2\alpha(a+\beta)+\beta(b-\alpha)}{2(a+\beta)} = \frac{\beta t}{2(a+\beta)}$$

The changes depend directly on the slopes of the revenue and cost functions. The decrease in quantity will be less than one half the tax rate and the increase in price will be less than one half the tax rate.

[9] It is theoretically possible for the downward slope of the MC curve to be greater than that of MR. In this case the result of a tax would be a lower price, and the incidence shifted backward would be greater than the amount of the tax.

[10] Since the primary purpose of an excise tax might be to raise revenue, let us consider the problem of maximizing tax revenue. The problem lends itself to simple calculus. Assume the monopolist has the following total revenue and total cost functions:

$$P = \alpha - \beta X$$
$$TC = aX^2 + bX + c$$

where α, β, a, b, and c are positive.

Previously we found the monopolist's profit-maximizing quantity to be

$$X = \frac{\alpha-b-t}{2(a+\beta)}$$

the tax rate, t, directly influencing the monopolist's behavior.

Thus the tax revenue function becomes

$$T = tX = \frac{t\alpha - tb - t^2}{2(a+\beta)}$$

To maximize tax revenue we take the derivative, set it equal to zero, and solve for t.

$$\frac{dT}{dt} = \frac{\alpha-b-2t}{2(a+\beta)} = 0$$

$$\alpha - b - 2t = 0$$

$$\alpha - b = 2t$$

$$t = \tfrac{1}{2}(\alpha - b)$$

This tax rate will provide the maximum possible revenue assuming the second-order condition holds:

$$\frac{d^2 T}{dt^2} = \frac{-2}{2(a+\beta)} = \frac{-1}{a+\beta} < 0 \text{ (recall } a, \beta > 0)$$

FIGURE 11–13

Pure monopoly with a tax
independent of output

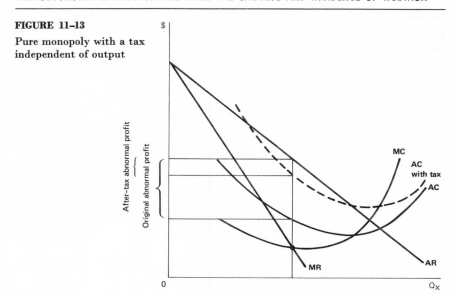

If the tax is independent of output, such as a tax on abnormal profits,
the incidence will not be shifted forward but will be borne by the monopolist. Abnormal (or "economic") profits are defined here as those returns
to the owners of capital that are *over and above* the normal returns in that
industry. These normal returns are necessary if the appropriate amount
of capital is to be attracted to the industry. Since they are rightly considered a cost they have already been accounted for in the cost functions.
Abnormal profits are shown in Figure 11.13 as the amount by which
average revenues exceed average costs. The argument that the monopolist
must bear the incidence is simple: The profit-maximizing price and output
have already been chosen. Now if a tax is imposed that does not affect
marginal costs, *MC*, the profit-maximizing price and output will not
change either. The tax reduces the monopolist's abnormal profit. Raising
the price would only reduce the monopolist's profits further. Similarly,
the monopolist cannot offset the tax by increasing output (and, necessarily lowering price), since at greater outputs marginal costs are greater than
marginal revenue; that is, total costs are being increased faster that total
revenue.

It is often difficult for the student to believe that it is not in the interests of the pure monopolist to raise his prices when taxed. The student
may benefit by thinking through the present example several times in

order to assure himself that, indeed, the profits of the monopolist will be smaller if he changes from the original profit-maximizing price and output combination.

Even so, a few words of caution are in order. In the first place, the pure monopolist model is an abstraction. While some firms find themselves with significant control over the price in a well-defined market, few, if any, monopoly situations are " pure " in the sense that they face no competition whatsoever. More important, in most real market situations the firm will not be operating precisely at the profit-maximizing price-quantity combination—possibly because of the monopolist's imperfect knowledge or his fear of antitrust actions. If the firm was not actually maximizing profits before the tax, it may be able to raise prices after the tax and suffer no loss in profits. This is especially true in industries where the possibility of antitrust action has kept prices below the profit-maximizing level.

LONG-RUN TAX INCIDENCE IN THE PURE MONOPOLY CASES

The long-run pure monopoly case differs from the purely competitive case. Where there is some barrier to entry by other firms, no inherent force points the way to an equilibrium where price is equal to average cost at the low point on the long-run average cost curve.[11]

Taxation and regulation of monopoly may take either of two approaches: the " socially optimum " or the " fair return " approach. The " fair return " approach is the one generally used by regulating authorities. The authorities attempt to set prices so that the firm can cover costs to include a fair or " normal " return to capital. Since we have already included " normal profit " as a cost in deriving the LAC curve, the fair return price would be set where $AR = LAC$. At that point there would be no abnormal profit. The effects of price regulation on a pure monopoly

---

[11] The profit-maximizing output (where $MR = LMC$) may be at a less than optimum size plant [Figure 11.14(a)], an optimum size plant (b), or a greater than optimum size plant (c), depending on the cost condition of the firm relative to market demand. Case (a) is the most likely, since it represents the case where the market is small relative to the optimum size plant; it thus represents all cases where the barriers to entry are " natural," such as the public utilities, transportation, and communications. Diagram (c) is somewhat misleading if it is taken to imply that costs increase simply because there is one " best " plant size and any larger plant size necessitates greater average costs. If demand is sufficient, the monopolist can simply build more plants of the optimum size. It is more appropriate to attribute increasing LAC [as in diagram (c)] to " inefficiencies " in large organizations rather than simply a greater than optimum plant size.

FIGURE 11-14

Profit maximization in pure
monopoly with different
demand-cost relationships

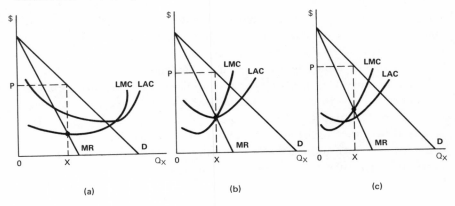

(a)   (b)   (c)

FIGURE 11-15

Pure monopoly and the fair
return price

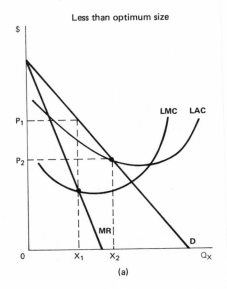

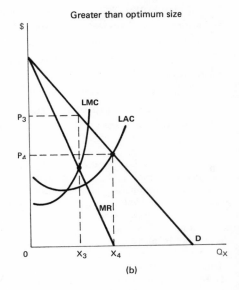

of less-than-optimum size are shown in Figure 11.15(a). Without regulation the monopolist sets price at P_1 and quantity at X_1. If the regulators take the fair return approach and estimate costs and demand correctly, they will set price at P_2. If the firm is at less-than-optimum size, as is the usual case, it must produce at X_2 in order to cover cost and earn a normal profit. If it happens, however, that the firm is at a greater-than-optimum size, the fair return price would not insure that it would produce the quantity demanded, X_4. The regulated price presents what amounts to a horizontal demand curve to the firm. Since the firm can sell only at P_4, that price becomes marginal revenue as well as average revenue. The firm will desire to produce where P_4 equals LMC. At that output there will again be an abnormal profit, and the regulating authorities may again lower the "fair return" price. If this procedure is continued, the price and quantity will gravitate towards $P = LMC = LAC$ (the optimum size); however, the quantity produced will be less than that demanded.

The basis of the socially optimum approach is to achieve a welfare-maximizing resource allocation. As outlined in Chapter 2, if the prices to which consumers adjust purchases reflect the marginal costs incurred in producing the good, the allocation of resources in response to these choices will be that which maximizes welfare within the economy. Hence, if the socially optimum price is to be set, it is fixed where $LMC = D$.

Consider Figure 11.16. Prices P_1 and P_3 in diagrams (a) and (b) would occur if the firms set price in order to maximize profit. Prices P_2 and P_4 would be set if the regulating authority implemented the socially optimum approach.

Where there is insufficient demand relative to the optimum size firm [where LAC is lowest—diagram (a)], the firm requires a *subsidy* in order to break even. This is because the price set, P_2, is less than LAC at the appropriate output level, X_2.

Where demand is excessive relative to the optimum size firm, a *tax* is required to prevent the firm from making abnormal profits. This is because the socially optimum price P_4 is greater than LAC at X_4, thus allowing the firm to make abnormal profits unless taxed.

OLIGOPOLY

Pure competition and pure monopoly are abstract extremes of the spectrum of market types within our economy. Actual market situations lie somewhere between. In examining some of these cases, we will start near the monopoly extreme and continue towards pure competition.

FIGURE 11–16

Pure monopoly and the
socially optimum price,
tax and subsidy

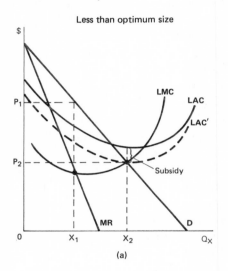

Less than optimum size

(a)

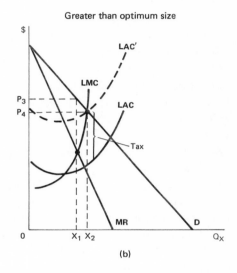

Greater than optimum size

(b)

"Oligopoly" is the market situation where sellers are "few." There are innumerable types of interrelationships among firms in market structures thus classified. In each case the activity of one firm has repercussions on the others. Since the products of all firms are quite similar, one firm can cut price or advertise and take customers away from its rivals. Such actions, however, would probably bring about retaliation of some kind. As a result, various types of formal or informal arrangements may arise among firms. Unless oligopolistic firms can communicate and reach agreement on mutually advantageous behavior, they are likely to find themselves in a "prisoner's dilemma." If each firm tries to gain a larger part of the market by undercutting its rivals' prices, the group as a whole will suffer as a price war lowers revenues for all. What seems to be profit-maximizing behavior for the individual will reduce profits for the group as a whole. In most oligopoly situations it is to the advantage of the rival firms to organize and collude.

Professor Fritz Machlup of Princeton has suggested classifying oligopolistic market situations according to the degree of collusion and organization present among firms. His three categories are: organized-collusive, unorganized-collusive, and unorganized-noncollusive.

THE ORGANIZED-COLLUSIVE OLIGOPOLY

It is possible for an organized-collusive oligopoly—a cartel—to operate exactly as a monopoly, in which case it would react in the same way to tax increases. But problems regarding the market shares and conflicting interests of the cartel members often can be resolved only by a bargaining process; thus the maximized abnormal profits are usually not realized. An analysis of how a cartel sets prices and quantities and how it would react to a certain tax would necessarily involve knowledge of the political arrangements within the particular cartel.

THE UNORGANIZED-COLLUSIVE OLIGOPOLY

It is illegal in the United States for firms to formally organize and collude on prices. This is one reason for including the unorganized-collusive category. Under this classification we find markets in which firms establish informal agreements as to prices and market shares while attempting to avoid antitrust prosecution. The method of collusion may range from clandestine meetings of executives in hotel rooms to tacit agreements on price leadership. One disconcerting feature of many market situations within this category is that even when firms informally agree not to compete in terms of price, they often will resort to what seems to be cutthroat competition in the form of costly advertising and so-called " quality" changes. One unfortunate outcome is that consumers are bombarded with competing advertisements which often tend to offset each other. Another unfortunate outcome is that increases in advertising costs increase the cost of entering the industry, further reducing the possibility of price competition among firms.

No attempt will be made here to explore all of the complexities of the diverse cases within this category. One observation is appropriate. Where firms are not formally organized and yet seek to collude, the imposition of a tax will probably be taken as a signal for all firms within the market to shift the tax foward by raising prices. This is especially true where the collusive firms have been hesitant to raise prices under the threat of antitrust action. Consequently, the nature of the tax—whether on output or independent of output—does not matter in such situations. In either case the firms may be able to shift most of the incidence of the tax forward.

THE UNORGANIZED-NONCOLLUSIVE OLIGOPOLY

In situations where there is no organization and little or no collusion, much depends on what one firm *expects* others to do in the way of retalia-

FIGURE 11–17

The Sweezy solution
with an output tax

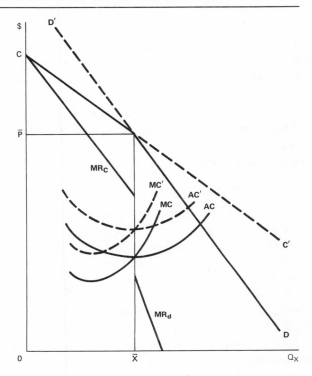

tion. If an entrepreneur has no idea of the response of others, he does not know what sort of demand curve he himself is facing. Using the duopoly cases, economists have shown that the *assumptions as to the expected retaliation* are crucial to the resulting market price and quantity.[12]

Paul Sweezy has presented a model which is useful in depicting the probable results of tax changes in a stable, noncollusive, unorganized oligopoly situation where retaliation is expected to take the form of price cuts.[13] Consider the demand curve in Figure 11.17. We must assume that somehow a market price has already been established at $\bar{P}$. The product the firm sells is a good substitute for those of the other firms in the market. Thus, in the absence of retaliation, the demand curve would be CC'. We assume that if the firm wishes to raise its prices above those of the market, its competitors will acquiesce, since some of its customers will turn to their products. If, however, it desires to lower prices, it can expect retaliation. In the case depicted, let us say that the firm expects rivals to match its price cuts and thus lower its demand to $D'D$. At higher prices the relevant demand curve is CC' and at lower prices $D'D$; thus, the relevant marginal revenue curves are MR_C and MR_D. The interesting feature of the Sweezy solution is the discontinuity of the marginal revenue curve at output $\bar{X}$. The profit-maximizing rule for all types of markets is to produce where $MR = MC$. Thus, for any cost configuration which results in MC's crossing the discontinuous part of the MR curve, it is practical for the firm to produce output $\bar{X}$ and to continue to honor the market price, $\bar{P}$.

For example, suppose a tax on output raises average and marginal costs from AC and MC to AC' and MC'. Since $MC' = MR$ in the discontinuous area, the firm will retain price $\bar{P}$ and quantity $\bar{X}$, although its abnormal profits have been reduced. In such a situation firms are likely to be unresponsive to changes in taxes either on output or independent of output.

It is clear that there are varying responses to taxes among oligopoly situations. In situations where firms collude and act as a monopolist, we would expect a response similar to a monopolist's: A large part of the tax on output would be shifted forward but none of a tax independent of output would be shifted. Yet in situations where there are unrealized abnormal profits, a tax (either dependent on or independent of output) may act as a signal for the market price to be raised. Finally, in some situations (as in the Sweezy solution) no change in market price may occur, even though the tax may change marginal costs.

---

[12] In the initial presentation of the duopoly case Augustine Cournot assumed that each firm expects his rival never to change his output. In the zero-marginal-cost model used by Cournot, the monopoly solution is to produce one-half the perfectly competitive result. If we use his assumption as to the reaction of firms, the result of a duopoly solution is that two-thirds of the competitive level of output is produced. As more firms are added, the output level and price approach the perfectly competitive solution. See Augustine Cournot, *Recherches sur les principles mathématiques de la théorie des richesses* (Paris, 1938) [English translation (by Nathaniel T. Bacon): *Researches into the Mathematical Principles of the Theory of Wealth* (New York: Macmillan, 1897)]. Another model suggested by Joseph Bertrand and developed by F. Y. Edgeworth embodies the assumption that firms believe their rivals will maintain a constant price—though of course they will not. Under this assumption there is no stable solution; price fluctuates up and down. See Joseph Bertrand, "Théorie mathématique de la richesse sociale," *Journal des Savants* (Paris, 1883), pp. 499–508; and F. Y. Edgeworth, *Papers Relating to Political Economy* (London: Macmillan, 1925), vol. I, pp. 111–142. Edward Chamberlain has presented yet another model in which the duopolists recognize their mutual interdependence; both then realize their advantage in setting price at the monopoly price and equally sharing the market. See Chamberlain, *The Theory of Monopolistic Competition* (Cambridge, Mass.: Harvard University Press, 1933), pp. 46–51.

[13] Paul Sweezy, "Demand under Conditions of Oligopoly," *Journal of Political Economy*, vol. 47 (1930), pp. 568–573.

FIGURE 11–18

The long-run effect of an
output tax in monopolistic
competition

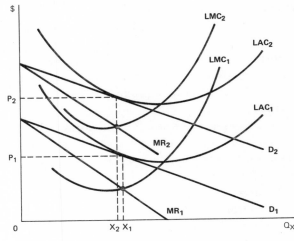

TABLE 11–1

Market types and the firm's
demand for inputs

	Firm's relationship to input market	Firm's relationship to output market
Situation 1	perfect competition (no influence over input price)	perfect competition (no influence over output price)
Situation 2	perfect competition (no influence over input price)	monopoly (control over output price)
Situation 3	monopsony (control over input price)	perfect competition (no influence over output price)
Situation 4	monopsony (control over input price)	monopoly (control over output price)

MONOPOLISTIC COMPETITION

Another market classification—monopolistic competition—is used to describe a large diversity of market situations. Monopolistic competition
lies closer to pure competition than to pure monopoly. There are many
sellers of slightly differentiated products. Since there are many sellers,
price adjustments by one firm have little effect on other firms. No retaliation is in order. Since entry is free, firms will continue to enter as long as
abnormal profits occur. Competitive forces will tend towards prices and
output where $P = LAC$.

The short- and long-run results of a change in taxes are similar to those
in the purely competitive model. Although no market supply or demand

---

curve can be drawn—since the products are slightly differentiated— reference to the purely competitive case is informative. A tax increase shifts each firm's costs upward, and aggregate supply shifts to the left. In the short run, firms will suffer losses and will attempt to cut back production. Some will eventually leave the market. As market price rises, firms will again cover costs (to include a normal profit).

In the long run there will be sufficient time for inputs, including capital, to leave the industry. Since entry is free, the long-run equilibrium occurs at a price and output where there are no abnormal profits. At that point, $P_1 = LAC_1$ and $LMC_1 = MR_1$ as in Figure 11.18. The monopolistically competitive firm is just covering costs (to include a normal profit).

Suppose a tax on output raises each firm's cost to LAC_2 and LMC_2. At first, firms suffer losses and attempt to cut back production. The aggregate supply curve shifts to the left. Firms begin to leave the industry and continue to do so until a normal profit can be earned. This exodus will raise the demand curve of the remaining firms to the point where once again price equals average costs. Price will have risen to P_2.

TAXES ON INPUTS

There are innumerable models one could construct to depict the behavior of firms in the input market. Most of our remarks, however, will be in the context of the situations listed in Table 11.1.

PERFECTLY COMPETITIVE INPUT MARKET—PERFECTLY COMPETITIVE OUTPUT MARKET

The perfectly competitive model has been introduced earlier in the text. The firm's demand for an input, termed the value of the marginal product (VMP), is simply the marginal product of the input times the price of the commodity produced. If we let the input be represented by I and the output by X, the firm's demand for I is

$$VMP_I = MP_I \cdot P_X$$

It is downward sloping, since MP_I decreases as more I is employed. In a competitive output market P_X is not affected by one firm's activity, since the firm is small relative to the market. Similarly, the supply (average input cost curve) the firm faces is horizontal, since in a perfectly competitive input market the amount employed by any one firm is insignificant.

FIGURE 11-19

Input tax in perfectly competitive input and output markets

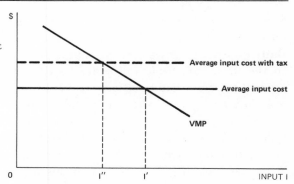

FIGURE 11-20

Equilibrium combination of inputs (isoquant perspective)

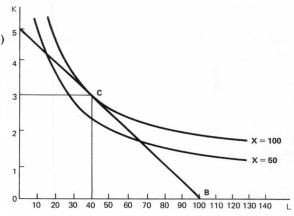

When a tax is imposed on the firm's use of an input, the *short-run effect* is to raise average (and marginal) cost of employing that input.

The new equilibrium, depicted in Figure 11.19, will be at a lower employment level I''. The corresponding output market is depicted in Figure 11.6. Since the tax is related to short-run production costs, both AC and MC shift. Assuming the tax to be on all firms, the market price will eventually rise. In the interim most firms will experience decreased profits or increased losses. In the long run some firms will necessarily leave the market, since at a higher price less of the commodity will be purchased. The equilibrium for the remaining firms will be at the low point of the new long-run average cost curve (which includes the input tax).

The new cost curve reflects the input adjustments made by the firm in response to the new input price ratio. This adjustment is best depicted by reference to the firm's production function.[14] Suppose a tax is imposed on labor as depicted in Figure 11.21. The budget constraint is reduced to AB' and the amount of L employed is L''. Figure 11.21 is drawn so that no change in K is required for equilibrium, but in many cases an adjustment in K would be called for. If K is " fixed " in the short run, however, a new equilibrium featuring a change in K cannot be attained until time is allowed for such adjustment.

The long-run equilibrium for firms remaining in the industry will be at the low point on the long-run average cost curve; however, whether

---

[14] Here again the student unfamiliar with production function theory may wish to refer to a text in microeconomic theory, since only a summary introduction is offered here.

The isoquant perspective of the production function shows the different combinations of inputs which may be employed to produce a *particular level of output*. Look at Figure 11.20. Assume that the isoquant $X = 100$ shows the combination of two inputs, L and K, required to produce 100 units of the commodity X. We note that the slope of the isoquant shows the rate at which K can be substituted for L (or vice versa) while still maintaining the same output level. This rate, the Marginal Rate of Technical Substitution, simply shows the productive contribution (marginal product) of one input relative to another at different points on the isoquant. Thus,

$$MRTS_{LK} = \frac{MP_L}{MP_K}$$

The firm's budget constraint shows the different amounts of K and L which can be purchased with a particular budget, say $5000. If units of K cost $1000 each, expenditure of the entire budget on K would employ 5 units. If units of L cost $50 each, the entire budget would employ 100 units. It can be easily shown that the slope of AB, the *rate* at which L can be substituted for K, is P_L/P_K.

The firm adjusts to point C, the highest output that can be reached given the budget constraint. At that point the slope of the isoquant is the same as that of the budget constraint:

$$MRTS_{LK} = \frac{MP_L}{MP_K} = \frac{P_L}{P_K}$$

This is, of course, the same equilibrium as that shown earlier by the equi-marginal rule:

$$\frac{MP_L}{P_L} = \frac{MP_K}{P_K}$$

Our reason for analyzing how the firm adjusts inputs with respect to prices and productivity will become clear in the text. Taxes may change the relative prices of inputs, and we are interested in how firms respond to taxes. In short, the firm responds to a change in the price of an input by adjusting the use of that input with respect to the use of other inputs. The new equilibrium combination of inputs to which this adjustment process leads depends on the *relative productivity* of the inputs.

FIGURE 11–21

Short-run adjustment to a
tax on one input (isoquant
perspective)

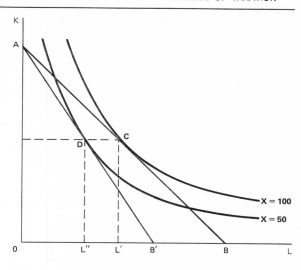

FIGURE 11–22

Long-run adjustment to a
tax on one input (isoquant
perspective)

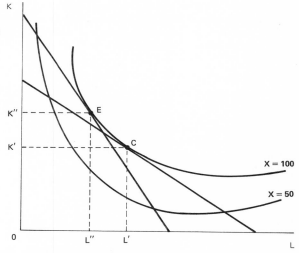

each firm is producing more or less than before depends on how the new
input price ratio affects the firm's choice among given production techniques. In Figure 11.22 we assume the original output level, 100 units, is
retained. The assumed change in the price ratio causes the firm to substitute K for L. A larger budget is required to reach the new equilibrium
E. Here again the equilibrium conditions hold:

$$MRTS_{LK} = \frac{MP_L}{MP_K} = \frac{P_L}{P_K}$$

Two long-run adjustments tend to cushion the tax's incidence on the price paid the input. First, we have shown that in the long run the firm is free to adjust the combinations of inputs it uses. The shift will involve using more of the inputs *complementary* to the taxed input. This means that the productivity of the remaining units of the taxed input will increase. In terms of Figure 11.18 this means that VMP shifts to the right (recall that MP_I is a component of VMP).

Second, if the inputs of the other competitors are similarly taxed, *the market price of the commodity will eventually rise.* Since P_X is also a component of VMP, the latter will shift to the right. The time required for this adjustment depends on the flexibility the firms may exercise in varying the use of the input. If the taxed input is "fixed" in the short run, it follows that a long-run adjustment will be required before the full effect on market price will be completed.

In summary, the firm's flexibility to use complementary inputs and the eventual rise in market price (of the commodity) will cushion the tax's incidence on the input's price.

PERFECTLY COMPETITIVE INPUT MARKET—PURE MONOPOLY OUTPUT MARKET

The pure monopolist's evaluation of additional inputs reflects the fact that output price must be lowered if sales are to be increased. Hence his demand for an input, marginal revenue product, diminishes both because of the input's diminishing marginal product and the diminishing marginal revenue associated with the increase in output:

$$MRP_I = MP_I \cdot MR_X$$

The firm's response to an input tax, shown in Figure 11.23 is similar to that of the perfect competitor except that MRP_I is lower than VMP_I and less of the input is hired than would be if the market were competitive.[15] The imposition of the tax causes the average input cost to be raised by the amount of the tax. In adjusting to the tax, the monopolist will substitute other inputs for the taxed input. The rapidity of this adjustment depends on the flexibility of the inputs in question. The long-run adjustment will be similar to that described above and depicted in Figure 11.22,

---

[15] Recall that $VMP_I = MP_I \cdot P_X$ whereas $MRP_I = MP_I \cdot MR_X$. In a perfectly competitive output market $P_X = MR_X$. But in a monopoly market $MR_X < P_X$. We should note that the VMP_I depicted in Figure 11.23 is derived from the different prices of the monopolist's demand curve and thus is not directly comparable to a VMP_I derived from a single market price established in a competitive market.

FIGURE 11–23

Input tax in perfectly
competitive input market
and a pure monopoly output
market

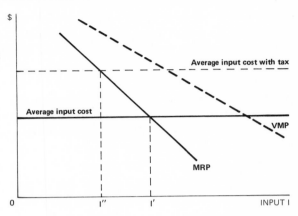

FIGURE 11–24

Input tax on the monopsonist
operating in a perfectly
competitive output market

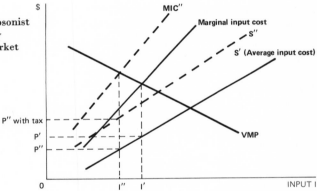

FIGURE 11–25

Input tax on the monopsonist
operating in a pure monopoly
output market

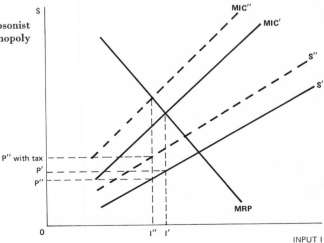

except that the long-run equilibrium for the monopolist is not likely to be at the most efficient ("least cost") level of output.

It is appropriate to recall our earlier analysis of the monopolist's response to taxes on variable versus fixed costs (Figures 11.11 and 11.13). A tax on an input which is variable in the short run (and thus affects short-run marginal costs) will cause the monopolist to immediately raise output price. A tax on a "fixed" input does not raise short-run marginal cost; consequently, the burden will be borne by the monopolist until he can adjust his input mix.

MONOPSONY INPUT MARKET—PERFECTLY COMPETITIVE OUTPUT MARKET

As the only buyer in the input market, the monopsonist faces an upward-sloping input supply curve. As noted in Chapter 1 (see Figure 1.8), marginal input costs, MIC, rise faster than average input costs, since all inputs must be paid the higher price necessary to employ additional units. Hence the monopsonist (the market's sole buyer) equates MIC and VMP and pays price P' (see Figure 11.24). A tax on a variable input will cause average and marginal costs to be higher. Equating MIC' with VMP, the monopsonist reduces employment to I'' and pays the input P''.

Our earlier observations about possible short- and long-run adjustments to VMP are still valid, since we are again facing a perfectly competitive output market. The input's VMP will shift to cushion the tax's incidence on the input price as the firm adjusts its input combinations (with inputs complementary to the taxed input) and as market price rises. The rapidity with which these adjustments take place depends on the firm's flexibility in adjusting the combination of inputs.

MONOPSONY INPUT MARKET—MONOPOLY OUTPUT MARKET

Little imagination is needed to continue the analysis to the monopsony-monopoly case. As illustrated in Figure 11.25, the firm will equate MIC and MRP, hire quantity I' of input I, and pay P'. The imposition of a tax will shift S' and MIC' to S'' and MIC'', as shown in Figure 11.25. The new equilibrium will be at I'' employment and P'' input price.

As time and input flexibility permit, the firm will adjust its input mix so as to include a greater proportion of the nontaxed inputs. Hence MRP_I will shift and cushion the initial impact of the tax on the price of the input.

The student may wish to ponder the possibility that MR_x (and thus MRP_I) will be affected by an input tax.

OLIGOPSONY AND IMPERFECT KNOWLEDGE

The models posed above provide a basis for postulating hypotheses as to the shifting and incidence of taxes on inputs. It has been evident that as additional variables are introduced, the partial equilibrium models become increasingly complex. The models we have considered are the polar extremes on the continuum of market types—ranging from one buyer or seller to an infinite number of buyers or sellers. In between, one or more of the assumptions associated with these models may be missing, and the behavior of firms may differ accordingly. We have noted, for example, that in an oligopoly situation the firm's response to a change in cost—perhaps an input tax—may or may not include raising the price of the commodity. The response depends on the nature of the interrelationship among firms. The firm may or may not know what to expect of the others.

Similarly, if there are only a few buyers in the input market (an oligopsony situation), the response to a tax on inputs again depends on the way firms are interrelated. Firms may have decided not to compete against each other by offering a higher price for a certain type of input. Their response to a tax on that input is uncertain, but it is possible that they would collude to impose most of the burden on the input owners. Alternatively, a new tax may precipitate a price war by upsetting a stable market arrangement.

SOME ALTERNATIVE HYPOTHESES OF FIRM BEHAVIOR AND THEIR IMPLICATIONS FOR TAX SHIFTING

We have made certain assumptions concerning the behavior of firms that deserve further attention. We have, for example, abstracted from reality in assuming that a firm has precise information as to the shape of its cost and revenue functions. In addition, we have assumed that the firm has but one goal, maximizing profit. Finally, we have assumed that the decision makers within the firm are of one mind with no conflicting interests. Obviously, these assumptions do not square with reality; but this objection by itself is not sufficient. After all, any "model" is an abstraction from reality, and the models presented above are a description of the equilibrium to which profit-maximizing behavior is tending rather than a theory of the process of decision making within the firm.

What is important to us is whether these assumptions lead us to make erroneous predictions about the firm's behavior—especially its response to changes in fiscal policy.

THE IMPACT OF UNCERTAINTY ON FIRM BEHAVIOR

One hypothesis about firm behavior under uncertainty makes for predictions markedly different from the usual marginalist models. In many situations, it is held, the manager has little information as to the elasticity of demand. His procedure for setting price is simply to determine the firm's "full" costs (to include both fixed and variable costs) and to add to this a conventional markup. After setting price at this figure, he adjusts the firm's output so that he can fill all orders. Of course, the adjustment to greater quantities of output affects his costs (and hence his price), but the equilibrium to which he is adjusting is where demand is equal to average total cost ("full costs" plus the conventional markup).[16]

If this hypothesis is correct, businessmen pay much more attention to costs than to demand in establishing price. Significantly, the firm will attempt to shift taxes even if they affect only average (and not marginal) costs. Such a convention obviously makes for behavior different from that previously predicted. The pure monopolist, for example, would attempt to shift not only those taxes directly related to output but all other taxes as well. Consider Figure 11.26. The profit-maximizing price-quantity combination would be $P_1 X_1$, where $MR = MC$. But presumably the monopolist figures average costs, sets his price, P_2, by adding his conventional markup, and adjusts output so as to fill the quantity demanded at that price. Since costs change with output and demand is unknown, the firm will not immediately arrive at $P_2 X_2$; however, it will adjust to that equilibrium. If it happens that the monopolist's idea of a "proper" markup approximates the actual opportunity costs of using capital in this industry, the average costs plus markup will be approximately the same as the average costs depicted in previous models. Consequently, the price-quantity chosen by the monopolist may include no "abnormal" profit. More likely the monopolist will realize his favorable position and opt for a healthier return on his investment—higher than that depicted in

---

[16] Some of the earlier empirical work was done by R. L. Hall and C. J. Hitch, "Price Theory and Business Behavior," *Oxford Economic Papers*, vol. 2 (May 1939), pp. 12–45. Also see R. F. Harrod, "Price and Cost in Entrepreneurs' Policy," *Oxford Economic Papers*, vol. 2 (May 1939), pp. 1–11. For more current evidence and observations see D. C. Hague, "Economic Theory and Business Behavior," *Review of Economic Studies*, vol. 16, no. 3 (1949), pp. 144–157; and A. C. Cook, N. F. Dufty, and E. H. Jones, "Full Cost Pricing in the Multiproduct Firm," *Economic Record*, vol. 32 (May 1956), pp. 142–147; and I. F. Pearce, "A Study in Price Policy," *Economica* vol. 23, N.S. (May 1956), pp. 114–127.

FIGURE 11–26

The pure monopolist
practicing markup pricing

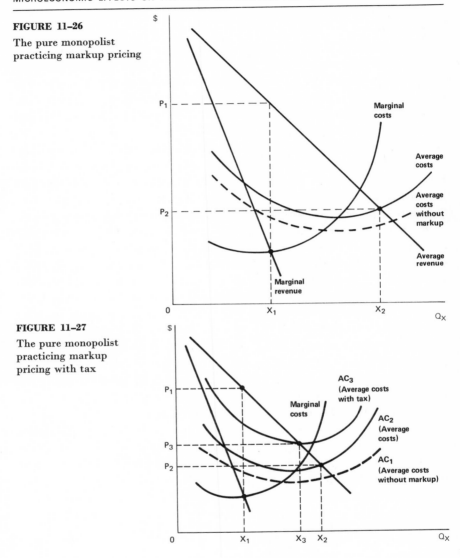

FIGURE 11–27

The pure monopolist
practicing markup
pricing with tax

Figure 11.26; and the price-quantity combination would be closer to that
which maximizes profits, P_1X_1.

In either case, an increase in taxes can be passed on if the firm is willing
to sell a smaller quantity. The firm may increase price and fully recoup its
tax payments, since an increase in price moves it in the direction of the
profit-maximizing price and quantity. Figure 11.27 depicts such a case.

A tax is imposed which is independent of output; it affects only average costs. The new average costs, plus markup, are labeled AC_3. The price that will be set is P_3, and, at that price, quantity X_3 can be produced and sold. Such a solution does not require the monopolist to reduce his markup.

If the firm is determined to maintain a particular level of total profits, it may be able to do so—assuming, of course, that its pretax price-quantity combination did not maximize profits.[17] In any case a higher price will require less output. If total profits are to be maintained, it will be necessary to raise price by an amount great enough to compensate for the tax *and* the loss in sales; hence, price must be raised by more than the original markup ratio.

In market situations where uncertainty about demand prevails and markup pricing is practiced, the usual response is to attempt to shift taxes to the consumer. Where the conventional markup leaves substantial unrealized profits, successful tax shifting is possible regardless of the nature of the tax. If, on the other hand, the firm is already realizing all possible profits, the attempt to pass on taxes which are unrelated to output will result in a reduction in possible profits (or an increase in losses).

An important question is whether the presence of markup pricing in markets infers that profits are not being maximized. Considerable research is being focused on the decision-making processes through which markup conventions evolve and are changed. An important observation is that markups tend to be higher where abnormal profits are more readily attained. When demand is increasing, markups are raised; and when demand is declining, they are lowered. What this evidence suggests is that while day-to-day uncertainties require the use of markup conventions, the longer-run determination of the markup reflects profit-maximizing behavior as predicted by the marginal models.

OTHER FACTORS IN THE FIRM'S DECISION-MAKING PROCESS

The assumption that the one goal of the firm is profit maximization is somewhat dubious. The persons and groups within the decision-making process of the large corporation, for example, have a myriad of interests, some of which may be in conflict with the firm's attaining maximum profit.

---

[17] Here the term "profits" refers to the return forthcoming from the markup. Loosely defined, it is a return on investment. This may or may not be the same as a normal return to investment in that industry. Economists consider the normal return to capital to be a part of costs and include it in the average cost function.

TABLE 11-2

The 200 largest nonfinancial
corporations classified by
type of ultimate control,
1929 and 1963

	1929			1963		
	Number	Assets (in millions of dollars)	Percent of assets	Number	Assets (in millions of dollars)	Percent of assets
Private ownership	12	$ 3,367	4	None	$ 0	0
Majority ownership	10	1,542	2	5	3,307	1
Minority control	46.5	11,223	14	18	28,248	11
Legal device	41	17,565	22	8	8,765	3
Management control	88.5	47,108	58	169	224,377	85
In receivership	2	269	0	None	0	0
	200	$81,073	100	200	$264,697	100

Source: Berle and Means, *The Modern Corporation*, Table VI, p. 358. The 1929 figures are from the study by Berle and Means for their first edition. The 1963 figures are from a similar study by Robert J. Larner, "Ownership and Control of the 200 Largest Non-financial Corporations, 1929 and 1963," *The American Economic Review*, vol. 56, no. 4, part I (September 1966), pp. 777 ff.

Where decisions emanating from the process differ from those prescribed by simpler models, it is necessary to inquire into the interaction of the interest groups within the organization. In some firms, even large corporations, control rests with one person or family. In others, decision-making power may be diffused among various groups, with labor, management, and stockholders (not to mention government) exercising different amounts of influence.

Often a small group of stockholders can exercise substantial control. Where thousands of individuals own a few shares each, those owning 20 or even 10 percent may have effective control. The pyramiding of control through holding companies, interlocking directorates, and the like allows a small minority effectively to increase their influence.

Do the goals of the controlling minority differ from those of the disorganized majority? The basic interest of both groups is that the company prosper, thus increasing dividends and the value of the stock. But one way in which the interests of the smaller and the larger stockholder might diverge is in the choice between dividends and company growth (and hence growth of the value of stock). We might suppose that the larger stockholders are wealthier and more likely to prefer an increase in stock value to dividends. This is due to the favorable tax treatment given to capital gains—a benefit more advantageous to the wealthy than to the middle and lower income groups. A reasonable hypothesis is that a wealthy minority may effectively influence the policy of the company towards long-run growth as opposed to declaring greater dividends. Presumably this hypothesis is testable. In companies controlled by a wealthy minority we would expect to see growth emphasized at the expense of dividends. Owing to its greater interest in long-term growth in sales, the controlling group is less willing to pass on the incidence of a tax on output. A related hypothesis is that the wealthy minority is more responsive to incentives to investment such as investment tax credit. These hypotheses have not yet been adequately tested, and until empirical evidence warrants their acceptance they must remain hypotheses.

There are limits to minority stockholder control. A basic reason for the small stockholder's lethargy is his feeling that the decisions made by the controlling group will accord with his own interests. When serious discord is present, proxy fights often develop, and the small stockholder is given an opportunity to vote for a group more closely aligned with his interests.

A more important aspect in the trend away from majority ownership control is the increased decision-making power of management. The fact of substantial management control is easily observable in many of our larger corporations. Studies over the last forty years by Adolf Berle, Gardiner Means, and others show that management control has increased substantially.[18]

Table 11.2 illustrates the direction and extent of this change. The 1929 figure reflects substantial management control. Of the 200 largest firms, 88.5 were estimated to be controlled by management with little outside interference. But 1963 shows a significant increase in management control; by that time 169 of the largest 200 were management controlled, and these figures accounted for 85 percent of the assets.

The importance of these firms is significant and increasing. In 1950 the 200 largest manufacturing firms held 46.7 percent of all assets in manufacturing. By 1965 the share had increased to 55.4 percent. If, in fact, the goals of the persons controlling most of these corporations are significantly

[18] See A. A. Berle and G. C. Means, *The Modern Corporation and Private Property* (New York: Macmillan, 1932); J. Burnham, *The Managerial Revolution* (New York: John Day, 1941); R. A. Gordon, *Business Leadership in the Large Corporation* (Washington, D.C.: Brookings, 1945); and O. Knauth. *Managerial Enterprise* (New York: Norton, 1948).

FIGURE 11–28

The pure monopoly
management with the dual
goals of a satisficing profit
and maximum sales

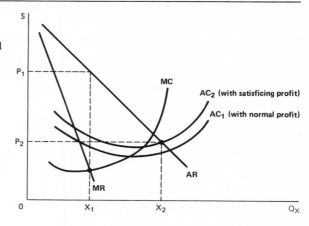

different from the profit-maximization assumption of the traditional models, further consideration is warranted. Indeed, considerable economic inquiry into the implications of the separation of ownership and control has been and will continue to be made. We must ask whether management has different goals, how these goals make for different economic behavior, and whether this behavior makes for a different response to government fiscal activity.

One of the most frequently stated hypotheses concerning management-controlled firms is that profit "targets" act as a sort of threshold for other goals. Management will work hard to achieve an acceptable level of profit; however, once this goal is reached, other goals become more important—perhaps having a company plane, redheaded secretaries, or whatever. This behavior is called *satisficing*. Management is said to seek to satisfy one or more targets which are thought to be important to the owners, such as a certain yearly profit total or a percent of the market sales. After these goals are met, others can be pursued, such as management salary, community prestige, political and economic power, and so on.

Professor William Baumol argues that management's primary goal after satisficing some minimum profit target is to increase sales. An increase in sales is accompanied by an increase in the size of the corporation and hence in the responsibility held by management. A related assumption is that increased responsibility acts as a better justification for greater management salaries than does increased profits. In addition, an increase in sales and firm size increases the power and prestige of management. In its simplest form a model with these assumptions can be graphed in much the same way as the markup model. Here, however, average costs include not a " markup " but a profit target which will satisfy the stockholders. In Figure 11.28 the profit-maximizing combination of price and output is P_1X_1. AC_1 depicts average costs with a normal profit. Owing to the firm's monopoly position, stockholders expect a greater return, as depicted by AC_2. Once this target is met, however, management sets price so as to maximize sales. The price-output combination P_2X_2 accomplishes both goals.

It is difficult to tell what response management will make to an increase in taxes in this situation. Management may, of course, be able to raise price, compensate for the tax, and retain the original profit target regardless of whether the tax is on output or profit. However, the additional tax may be used as an argument to induce stockholders to accept a lower return; consequently, management may be able to maintain sales at close to the former level. In this latter respect the " satisficing " model differs from the " markup " model. In the " markup " model the firm increased price in order to recoup the old level of profits; in the " satisficing " model management may desire that part of the tax burden be absorbed by the owners so as to minimize sales reduction.

When we extend our examination to consider priorities other than profits and/or sales, our models become more complex. Additional complexities arise if an attempt is made to consider the process by which conflicting interest groups influence the firm's decision-making process. The nature of the organization and the process of decision making affect the substance of the firm's decision and, more specifically, the firm's reaction to fiscal policy. We have briefly considered possible conflicts between owners and management. In addition, conflict may arise between groups within management, between management and labor, and between groups within labor. The nature of conflict resolution between these groups may be an important determinant of the firm's response to governmental fiscal activity. We outline a few possibilities:

Within labor the conflicting groups may be the younger members and the older members with seniority—the latter group will be the last to be laid off. Let us assume that the younger group is aware that raising the price of the final output necessarily involves a reduction in sales, production and the labor force. However, since the senior union members will be last to be laid off, they will be willing to trade off employment for higher wages. If the senior members are in control, the union's influence will be used to maintain or raise wages. If a tax is imposed on the firm (whether on output or profit), the union will encourage management to pass it on to consumers in the form of higher commodity prices.

This last point reveals another possible conflict between interest groups within the firm. Suppose the management in question is prone to maximize sales (after satisfying its profit target.) Suppose the union in question is prone to maximize the wages of its senior members. The union's attitude to an additional tax on the firm is to pass it on to the consumer in the form of higher prices. Management, on the other hand, will attempt to induce labor and the stockholders to bear some of the burden—thus maintaining sales. The net effect depends on the relative power and bargaining skill of the opposing groups.

Many other conflicts of goals may arise within the structure of the firm's decision-making process. In many cases the response to fiscal activity may differ from that predicted by the traditional models of microeconomic theory. This is not to say that the traditional models must be completely discarded in favor of different, more recent models. Instead, it is better to view the traditional models as helpful in abstracting from the complexity of reality and in formulating general hypotheses; but where the traditional models lead to erroneous predictions, they must be restructured to include all of the important variables.

While empirical tests indicate merit in the more recent analyses, their validity is often limited to certain market situations. Until more concrete results are attained, it seems best to use the traditional models for deriving general hypotheses about tax shifting and incidence and to employ additional variables and perspectives where appropriate.

In chapters that follow we will examine more closely the taxes used by the public sector. We will have the opportunity to employ both traditional models and more recent approaches to the analysis of incidence and shifting of particular taxes.

12
THE CORPORATION INCOME TAX

The corporation income tax, like the personal income tax, has important implications both as a major source of revenue and as an influence on economic behavior. In fiscal year 1974, for example, the expected revenue was approximately $37.0 billion, over 14 percent of federal revenues. This ratio has declined in recent years as shown by Table 12.1. The main reason for the low level of receipts in the early seventies was of course the recession. The corporation income tax is highly responsive to the business climate.

The corporation income tax shares many of the favorable features of the personal income tax with regard to its generality and neutrality. The tax's incidence, however, is hard to trace, and its burden is not clearly visible to the individual taxpayer. Consequently, the individual's ability to make benefit-cost judgments concerning private versus public goods is reduced. As we shall see, the answers to several important questions depend on tracing the tax's incidence. These questions, along with some other interesting aspects of tax shifting, will be analyzed with resort to the perspectives developed in the previous chapter.

The early use of the tax stemmed not from any esoteric tax theory but from the need for revenue during the Civil War. We recall, from our outline of public sector growth, that until passage of the Sixteenth Amendment both the personal and the corporation tax were considered unconstitutional, since they were not apportioned among the states according to population. Consequently, the 1909 tax was passed under the guise of an excise tax. The actual justification used, however, was that corporations owed their legal existence to the state and were recipients of important privileges such as limited liability for shareholders, the availability of capital through the stock market and retained earnings, and the possibility of perpetual life.

Over the years the rates have tended to be proportional, starting with a 1 percent rate in the 1909 tax. During both world wars the rates were raised substantially, up to 12 percent in 1918 and up to 15–24 percent on base income in 1943 with a surtax on other income ranging from 10–16 percent. The proportional rate structure was returned in 1950, and for the period 1951–1963 the rate structure was 30 percent on the first $25,000 with an additional surtax on income over that amount. The present rate of 22 percent on the first $25,000 with a surtax of 26 percent has been in effect since 1965. The result, of course, is semi-progressive, since the rate on the first $25,000 is 22 percent and the combined rate on the remainder is 48 percent. However, the basic effect is proportional

	Year	Total tax collections	Corporation income and profits	Percent total
TABLE 12–1	1929	$ 3,541	$ 1,096	31
Federal corporation income	1938	5,550	1,029	19
tax returns selected fiscal	1949	40,934	11,554	28
years 1929–1973 (in millions	1959	80,856	18,092	22
of dollars)	1962	107,662	20,523	19
	1965	120,332	21,579	18
	1968	153,676	28,665	19
	1969	187,792	36,678	19
	1970	193,844	32,829	17
	1971	188,392	26,785	14
	1972	208,649	32,166	15
	1973a	224,984	33,500	15
	1974a	255,982	37,000	14

a Estimate.

since approximately 95 percent of all corporate income is subject to the 48 percent rate.

The rates of state corporation income taxes are also generally proportional and range from 1.0 and 12.0 percent among the 43 states which impose them. After many attempts the first successful state tax on corporate income was developed by Wisconsin in 1911. By 1929 sixteen others had followed its lead. The depression years 1931–1937 encouraged another rash of new enlistees bringing the total to 30. In 1971 43 states imposed the tax, and it accounted for a little over 5 percent of revenue from state sources. Most of the states are adapting their provisions to accord with those used by the federal government so that the tax bases will be similar.

A number of cities in Kentucky, Michigan, Missouri, and Ohio have low-rate corporation taxes on net profits. Typically the taxes are supplementary to taxes on personal income and on unincorporated businesses.

Since state and local provisions are similar to federal provisions and since the federal tax is the most important quantitatively, our discussion and analysis will center on the federal tax.

THE CONCEPT OF CORPORATE INCOME

Little can be gained by trying to draw an analogy between income as received by individuals and "income" upon which corporations pay taxes. Whereas practically all income received by the individual is the base for the personal income tax, the corporate "income" tax base is the residual after "costs" are deducted from receipts.

It would at first seem more appropriate to call the corporation income tax the " corporation profits tax." We recall that profits—or rather more precisely *abnormal profits*—can be defined as the difference between total revenue and costs (costs being defined by the economist as the return to *all* factors of production including a normal return to the owners of the capital used). However, a second incongruity appears if the corporation income tax is considered a tax on " profits," since present provisions do not allow the firm to deduct a normal return to the stockholders' capital as a cost of operation. The incongruity is increased in that payments to capital borrowed from sources other than stock issues *are* counted as a cost for tax purposes. We are left with the conclusion that the corporation " income " tax is a tax on abnormal profits and the normal return of capital supplied by stockholders (but not on the normal return of capital from other sources).

The procedure by which a firm arrives at its tax base is as follows: Gross receipts are calculated by summing all revenue received during the tax period (exclusive of income from investments). From this figure Costs of Goods Sold is subtracted. To arrive at the Costs of Goods Sold figure the firm typically starts with the value of inventory at the beginning of the year, adds all costs of material and supplies, wages and salaries, and other production and marketing costs, and subtracts from this total the year-end inventory.[1]

The difference between Gross Receipts and Costs of Goods Sold is Gross Profit. Other forms of income, primarily income from the firm's investment such as royalties, dividends, rents, and capital gains, are now added to Gross Profit to obtain Total Income.

Finally, Net Profit or Loss, the tax base to which the rate will be applied, is obtained by subtracting certain expenses and deductions from Total

---

[1] The estimation of the cost of materials used and the value of inventory is not as straightforward as it seems. In the first place the pricing of goods-in-process can become complicated, since goods may be in various stages of production. Hence, formulas for estimating the worth of goods (based on the proximity of the good to completion and the costs of inputs thus far committed) must be devised. Another question in connection with the valuation of materials used arises when, during the year, their prices have changed. Should it be assumed that the inputs used first are always those which were purchased at the earliest time (and at the lowest price, assuming that prices have risen)? This method of accounting for material costs, termed first-in, first-out or *fifo*, was traditionally the only acceptable one. Since World War II, however, a more liberal method, last-in, first-out or *lifo*, has been allowed. The latter method, allowing a higher figure for cost deductions if prices are rising, is naturally preferred by most firms.

Income. Among the more important of the expenses allowed are depreciation and depletion. In addition, the firm is allowed to deduct 85 percent
of all dividends received from its own investments. Both depreciation and
depletion allowances can be legitimately considered *costs*, since both represent the "using up" of assets in the process of production. Depreciation is the loss in value which occurs as such items as equipment, machinery, and buildings are used in the process of production. Depletion occurs
where natural resources such as minerals, ore, gas, oil, clay, sand, and
rock are extracted from one's property. In both cases there is controversy
as to the method and degree of the allowance made. These arguments will
be presented below.

DEPRECIATION

The value of machinery, equipment, plant buildings, and so on depreciates
as they are used. It is appropriate that this loss in value be counted as a
cost. In practice, depreciation is one of the expenses subtracted from Total
Income to find Final Net Profit. Only the original cost of the machine
may be depreciated over time. No account is taken of the fact that rising
prices may make replacement costs higher.

We must be careful to distinguish between actual (physical) depreciation and the *Internal Revenue Service's definition of depreciation for tax
computation purposes*. Several methods are available to the firm for calculating depreciation for tax purposes. Since counting the depreciation
deduction as a cost against income reduces tax liability, the business, in
the majority of cases, is better off to take advantage of depreciation
methods which allow for as quick a write-off as possible regardless of
whether it coincides with actual (physical) depreciation. The sooner depreciation is taken, the longer the firm can have the use of the funds it
would otherwise have paid as tax. Of course, only the full amount of the
cost can be deducted, and if the business uses a large part of the cost of
the machine as depreciation in the early years of a machine's life, less will
be available to deduct later. In subsequent periods, then, taxes will be
higher; but the firm will have had the use of these funds during the
meantime.

The Treasury traditionally provided *conservative* formulas by which to
compute the depreciation deduction—with respect to both the expected
life of equipment and the distribution of the write-off over the life period.
The "straight-line" rate is the traditional method of dividing depreciation over the estimated life of equipment. By this method, the total cost

is divided by the number of years and the average amount of deduction is applied to each year. In 1954, the Treasury provided two more liberal alternatives: the "double-declining-balance" and the "sum-of-the-digits" methods. The double-declining-balance method "doubles" the average of the remaining deduction each year. This method allows deductions of two-thirds of the original cost during the first half of the equipment's estimated life. The sum-of-the-digits method apportions the deductible cost by multiplying it by a fraction whose numerator is the number of years remaining in the equipment's expected life and whose denominator is the sum of the years of useful life.

Suppose, for example, that a machine is purchased for $500 with an expected life of 5 years. The denominator of the fraction is $5 + 4 + 3 + 2 + 1 = 15$. The numerator for the first year is 5. Consequently the allowable deduction is

$$\frac{5}{15} \times \$500 = \$166.67$$

For the next year the denominator remains the same but the numerator is 4, and so on. This method allows the company to deduct almost three-fourths of the cost during the first half of the life of the equipment.

The length-of-life guidelines have also been reduced in recent years. In 1942 the Internal Revenue Service set guidelines for over 5000 categories of capital goods based on their average lives. These guidelines have been reduced twice in recent years and on both occasions the primary justification has been to stimulate new investment. In 1962 the guideline life categories were reduced and simplified. The overall reduction in guideline lives was about 15 percent resulting in a significant savings for corporations. Another substantial reduction in the length-of-life guidelines was approved in the Revenue Act of 1971. Guidelines were reduced by 20 percent. This speed-up in tax reduction supposedly frees investment funds for the firms and in turn stimulates new employment and so on. However, its introduction in periods when overcapacity is high (as in 1962 and 1971) no doubt reduces its effectiveness. The macroeconomic policy considerations will be discussed in later sections and in Part IV.

DEPLETION ALLOWANCES

The logic behind the depletion allowance is similar to that which counts depreciation as a cost—but in this case the asset being "used up" is a natural resource. When minerals, oil, or gravel are removed from a person's or firm's possession, they cannot be restored; thus their removal is counted as a legitimate cost in the process of determining net profit and tax liability.

There is little disagreement about the legitimacy of depletion deductions, but there is much controversy about the nature and degree of present provisions. The controversy occurs because depletion allowances have been used for purposes other than just compensating the resource owner for the value of the natural resource extracted from his land.

The argument for making depletion allowances greater than the real cost of depletion is that some allowance should be made for risks and expenses incurred in exploration and development in the extractive industries.[2] Opponents of this position argue that the depletion allowances do little to compensate those small companies whose "risks" do not pay off. Only those companies large enough to spread their risks are rewarded. Moreover, the firms which take the risks in exploration may not be the firms which produce from a particular oil field, mine, or quarry. Finally, even if it is accepted that raising depletion allowances is an appropriate way to compensate for exploration costs, it remains that present allowances exceed any reasonable estimate of costs associated with these risks. Since the value of the resource when discovered is difficult to estimate, firms are allowed to deduct a percentage-of-sales revenue as a depletion allowance regardless of the original investment. For forty years, 1929–1969, the allowance for oil and gas stood at 27.5 percent in spite of repeated attempts to reduce it. A new rate, 12 percent, was established in the surprisingly inclusive 1969 tax legislation. Other allowances range from 22 percent for uranium and sulfur to 5 percent for gravel and oyster shells.[3]

If we accept the argument that depletion allowances are still too liberal, what are the repercussions on resource allocation? More resources are attracted to the extractive industries than would be the case if the tax were neutral. The advantage inherent in the depletion allowances will be "capitalized" to an extent, in that capital will continue to flow into the extractive industries until the rate of return on that capital drops to the normal rate of return. The real rate of return (without the special allowance) will be lower than normal, since relatively too many resources are being devoted to these industries. These industries' output prices will be lower than they would be without this form of favoritism. The oil industry, however, has found that the demand for oil products is fairly inelastic and has been able to obtain governmental aid in the form of restrictions on output and import quotas. Consequently, they have been able to maintain the price of oil at roughly twice that of the world market.

While it is not argued that depletion is not a legitimate business cost which should be used to reduce the firm's tax liability, we have seen that much doubt surrounds the notion that additional uses, such as bonuses for exploration expenses, should be made of the depletion allowance. The argument is not that depletion allowances as such are not warranted but that the present ones are too liberal. The implication is that they have a nonneutral affect on price ratios and hence disturb the forces working toward welfare-maximizing resource allocation.

TAX CRITERIA APPLIED TO A CORPORATION "PROFITS" TAX

Now let us lay the foundation for applying the tax criteria and the analytical tools developed in Chapter 11 to current provisions.

The tax base of the corporation income tax is abnormal profits plus the return to stockholder capital. First consider the consequences of the tax if it were only on abnormal profits. We will see that there is no shifting and that the tax is neutral.

Assume initially, then, that all costs including a normal return to stockholders can be deducted when figuring tax liability. Thus, only abnormal profits are taxed. Normal profits, the incentive necessary to attract the appropriate amount of capital to the industry, are not taxed.

Next consider the short-run equilibrium of the firm in perfect competition. The firm is enjoying abnormal profits and is producing at X', as shown in diagrams (a) and (b) of Figure 12.1. A 50 percent tax on abnormal profits is imposed. Demand, of course, is unaffected. Within the area where abnormal profits may be experienced, costs are raised by the amount of the tax. The *total* amount of the tax is shown by the shaded area in (a), while the *average* amount is shown in (b). The firm would gain nothing by changing output in an attempt to avoid the tax; such a change would

---

[2] A corollary to this argument urges special encouragement for the domestic extraction industries in order that supplies will be available in case of war. This argument is questioned in that the incentive is tied to depletion rather than exploration. Thus the bonus given in the form of liberal depletion allowances encourages reduction rather than preservation of our natural resources.

[3] The maximum total allowance for all cases is 50 percent of net income from the property.

FIGURE 12–1

The tax on abnormal profits
on a firm in perfect
competition (short run)

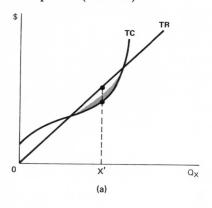

(a)

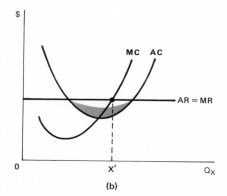

(b)

FIGURE 12–2

The tax on abnormal profits
on a firm in perfect
competition (long run)

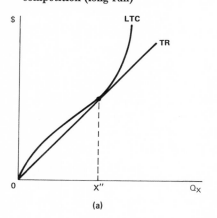

(a)

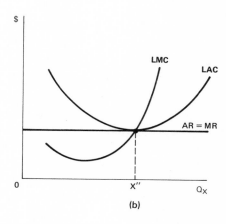

(b)

only reduce abnormal profit. Depiction of the long-run equilibrium is even
simpler. Free entry has forced market price to the low point on the long-
run average cost curve. As shown in Figure 12.2, there are no abnormal
profits, so no tax would be levied. We conclude that in perfect competition
no incentive exists for shifting the tax in either the short or the long run.

The effect of the tax on the pure monopoly is similar. No shifting is possible in either the short or the long run. In the long-run case depicted in Figure 12.3, a 50 percent tax is shown in the shaded area. The equilibrium between MR and LMC (long-run marginal cost) continues to be at the original output (X').

In situations of monopolistic competition and oligopoly similar results are found. Where the long-run monopolistic competition equilibrium is devoid of abnormal profits, there will be no profits to tax. In oligopoly situations where collusion takes place and monopoly profits are realized, the result is like that in pure monopoly. Only in certain oligopoly situations may firms increase prices and escape some of the tax's impact on abnormal profits. Where there is uncertainty, difficulty in colluding, or danger of antitrust action, it may well be that oligopolists have been *unable to maximize profits*. If the tax is taken as a signal by all to raise prices, the profits from which the tax is taken may be expanded and part of the incidence successfully passed on. However, in all cases where profit was already being maximized, no shifting could occur.

Although this tax differs markedly from our present corporation tax, let us briefly observe how it fares under the tax criteria. Our observations will be useful in subsequent analysis. Does the tax enhance welfare maximization through optimum resource allocation, income distribution, and a stable and growing economy?

The abnormal profits tax scores its highest mark in terms of the neutrality standard. As demonstrated in Figures 12.2 and 12.3, there is little shifting in response to the tax; consequently, prices established in the private market remain the same. Unless perfect competition reigns in every market, of course, there is the possibility that nonneutrality would improve resource allocation. Yet unless misallocation is evident, neutrality is to be preferred.

By reducing monopoly profits, the tax has several additional effects, some on resource allocation and others on income distribution. The first effect results from transfer of purchasing power from monopoly firms to public sector. Whether or not this transfer brings us closer to optimum resource allocation depends on how the monopoly originally used these funds. If, on the one hand, the monopolist had invested these funds to increase the production of a good where social benefits exceed costs—which is often the case for a monopolized good—the tax may do more harm than good. If, on the other hand, the funds generated by the

FIGURE 12–3

The tax on abnormal profits
on a pure monopoly

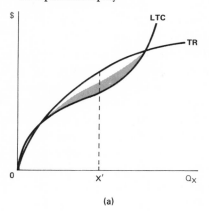

(a)

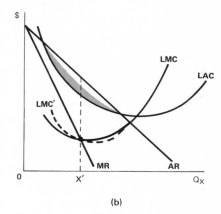

(b)

monopoly position are used extravagantly and wasted, the reallocation would be favorable.

It would seem that diminution of monopoly profits would enhance the accomplishment of the distribution goal—part of which, we recall, requires that input owners receive payment according to the value of their marginal products. By reducing the difference between VMP and the return to some inputs in monopoly, the abnormal profits tax reduces the redistribution necessary by other means.[4]

The tax's macroeconomic effect depends primarily on its impact on investment spending. If we *assume* that the firms would spend these funds on real investment, and if the latter is needed in order to attain the proper level of aggregate demand and the proper rate of growth, then the tax could do more harm than good. The opposite may also be true. In any event, it is clear that a tax on abnormal profits may have macroeconomic effects.

Now that we have explored the characteristics of our " model " corporation tax, it is appropriate to examine the economic effects of the actual corporation tax. The model will serve as a basis for comparison.

IS THE CORPORATION INCOME TAX SHIFTED?

Unlike the tax described above, the corporation income tax is imposed on a base that *includes* the normal return to capital supplied by stockholders. To the extent that the tax is on a factor of production, marginal costs are affected, and the firm's response will be to change quantity and price. Let us consider the question from the following three perspectives: short- and long-run partial equilibria for the single firm and general equilibrium of the whole economy.

The short-run equilibrium model supports the contention that no shifting takes place. Although the tax is on an input, it is on a "fixed" input, capital. Short-run output costs are not affected, since the tax is independent of output in the short run.[5] Consequently the pre-tax quantity-price combination remains the one most profitable to the firm.

In the long run, however, *all inputs are variable*, and a tax which affects any input will change long-run marginal costs. In long-range planning the firm whether monopolist or perfect competitor will adjust output accordingly. The rise in market price will depend on relative elasticities of market demand and supply (or of marginal revenue and costs for the monopoly). Since prices and quantities are affected, it follows that some tax shifting occurs.

A more general view, however, somewhat undermines the argument that the incidence may be shifted in the long run. This view requires that we anticipate the government's policy with regard to stability and growth. First assume that the government is passive and does not offset the tax's reduction of the money supply available in the private sector. Assume further that the government does *not* increase its expenditures by the amount of the tax. Now reconsider the firm's attempt to pass along the incidence of the corporation income tax in the form of higher output prices and lower input prices. Without an increase in spending power, consumers cannot spend enough money to buy the goods at the higher prices. One possibility is that *output prices* and *input prices* will fall simultaneously, as input owners realize they must accept lower remuneration and firms conclude that output prices should be lowered. This is possible because although demand (and marginal revenue) is lower, costs are also lower. In the process of this backward shifting, a wedge has been placed between the return stockholders get from their capital and its costs to firms; hence, the owners of other factors of production will benefit relatively. A more likely possibility is that prices will not readjust downward quickly enough and the macroeconomic consequences would be a reduction in employment and real GNP.

---

[4] Here again we observe that the implication that monopoly profits result in a "bad" distribution is derived from the acceptance of the perfectly competitive model as a norm.
[5] As shown in Figure 11.5, p. 354.

Now assume that the government follows an aggressive fiscal policy aimed at providing adequate spending power. Hence, more spending power will be furnished to compensate for an increase in the corporation income tax. Thus, forward shifting may be accomplished—the wedge between capital costs and the firm's return would be compensated for by increased output prices. It follows that the relative returns to stockholder's capital and to owners of other inputs could remain unchanged with forward shifting. However, several related effects remain to be considered.

Since World War II the usual trend in prices has been inflationary. Within this context it is difficult to designate and measure shifting, if any, attributable solely to corporation income tax. In 1968, the income surtax was applied to the corporation as an anti-inflationary measure. If indeed the tax is shifted forward, the wisdom of such a fiscal policy is doubtful. The continued rise in prices did nothing to discredit the argument that the tax is shifted forward.

Other complications in measuring the tax's incidence derive from the different degrees of competition we find in different markets. From the models considered above we have concluded that short-run shifting is unlikely but partial long-run shifting may occur, the probability increasing if aggregate purchasing power is being expanded. Yet if we extend our analysis to oligopoly and monopolistic competition and to situations involving price leadership, imperfect collusion, markup conventions, and so on, we recognize that no one answer to our question will suffice. We temporarily conclude that in situations where profits are not being maximized prior to the tax there is more likelihood of forward shifting. Such situations may occur, for example, when management is merely " satisficing " a profit goal, when a " markup " convention is being used, or when collusive oligopolists have restrained themselves for fear of antitrust action.

SOME EMPIRICAL ANALYSES OF INCIDENCE

Empirical analyses by economists demonstrate the difficulty of measuring the incidence of the tax. Several major studies yield conflicting results.

STUDIES INDICATING SUBSTANTIAL SHIFTING

The theoretical models presented above have been severely challenged in recent years by several major empirical studies, which purport to show that corporations have managed substantial forward shifting of the corporation income tax. The methodology used has differed widely.

Eugene M. Lerner and Eldon S. Hendrikson examined the rates of return on investment for all manufacturing firms during the 25-year period 1927 to 1952 and concluded:

Even though the effective tax rates have fluctuated from about 9 to 63 percent, and even though there is no evidence that the corporate income tax is passed on completely in the short run, the rate of return on investment after taxes has fluctuated around an almost level line over this quarter century.[6]

Since the rate of return has not been affected by tax increases, they conclude that complete forward shifting has been accomplished. During this period aggregate demand increased rapidly—especially at the time when taxes were increased. The authors recognize this but nevertheless argue that corporations can and do respond to the tax in their long-range plans.[7]

Other statistical studies by John Clendenin and Sidney Houston revealed that corporations had managed to maintain their intended rate of return.[8] Each therefore concluded that the tax had been shifted forward. But here again no satisfactory method is given for isolating such factors as increasing aggregate demand, technological advances, and so on from what is purported to be the firm's " response " to increased taxes. Nevertheless, in interpreting the results of these studies, Don Soule has suggested that the burden has been passed on to the consumer in two ways.[9] First, the corporation tax, by reducing retained earnings, is particularly harmful to those firms which primarily depend on financing from that source. Those firms with better access to outside financing—recall that borrowed funds are not taxed but counted as costs—are better able to adjust to changing market conditions. In other words, the tax may make unprofitable a firm which otherwise might have provided services at lower costs than the firms which survive and expand. A second part of the tax burden has been shifted in the form of higher prices—or in some cases by failure to pass cost reductions on to the consumer.

[6] E. M. Lerner and E. S. Hendrikson, "Federal Taxes on Corporate Income and the Rate of Return in Manufacturing, 1927 to 1952," *National Tax Journal*, vol. 9 (September 1956), pp. 193–202.

[7] " . . . the corporate tax has become a part of the long run horizon of profit-making firms." *Ibid.*, p. 202.

[8] J. C. Clendenin, "Effects of Corporate Income Taxes on Corporate Earnings," *Taxes*, June 1956; G. Sidney Houston, "Taxation and Corporate Enterprise," *Annals of the American Academy of Political and Social Science*, November 1949.

[9] Don M. Soule, "Shifting of the Corporate Income Tax: A Dynamic Analysis," *Journal of Finance*, vol. 14, no. 3 (September 1959), pp. 390–401.

Perhaps the most impressive study advocating shiftability of the corporation tax was done by Marian Krzyzaniak and Richard Musgrave.[10] Their basic approach was to formulate an econometric model based on firm behavior. The variables included were supposed to be those to which the firm responds. One model, for example, hypothesized that the gross rate of return resulting from changes in taxes $Y_{g,t}$ is a function of the following variables:

$$Y_{g,t} = A_0 + A_1 \Delta C_{t-1} + A_2 V_{t-1} + A_3 J_t + A_4 X_t + A_5 G_t + A_6 X_{t-1} + U_t$$

where ΔC is the change in consumption, V is the inventory-to-sales ratio for all manufacturing, J is the tax variable for taxes other than corporation tax, G is federal purchases, and X_t and X_{t-1} are the present and preceding year's corporate tax variables. Using data from the period 1935–1959 and multiple regression techniques, Musgrave and Krzyzaniak sought to isolate the effect of the tax on the firm's response. The rather startling result was *short-run forward shifting* by 134 percent!

As part of their explanation of how corporations had accomplished forward shifting, Krzyzaniak and Musgrave stated that despite the theoretical models of economists, businessmen regard the tax as a cost and make adjustments accordingly:

The businessman . . . has been skeptical regarding the entire approach of marginal cost pricing. His position has been that taxes are treated as a cost when determining prices, be it as part of a " full-cost-pricing " rule, by application of a conventional mark-up rate defined net of tax, or by pricing to meet a net of tax target rate of return. According to these formulas, a change in tax rate leads to an adjustment in price. The profits tax becomes a quasi sales tax. The fact that such a price policy is not consistent with the usual concepts of profit maximization does not disprove its existence.[11]

While portions of this statement are borne out by our discussion in Chapter 11, the implication that such behavior on the part of firms can *successfully sustain and even raise profit ratios* is quite another thing. What is necessary is substantial pretax unrealized profits throughout the economy. There is reason to believe, in fact, that the markup conventions, profit targets, and so on used in most markets do not reflect the most profitable price-quantity relationship. We may, of course, expect to find oligopoly situations where various inhibitions to collusion have left room for successful shifting. Carl Shoup has argued that the magnitude and extent of such shifting is limited.[12]

Other recent studies[13] lend support to the shifting hypothesis, but it is the Musgrave-Krzyzaniak analysis which has elicited the most response. It is appropriate for us to turn to the other side of the argument and then offer a critical examination of their conclusions.

STUDIES INDICATING NO SHIFTING

In addition to the traditional theoretical arguments, several empirical studies, using quite different approaches, have arrived at the conclusion that little, if any, forward shifting is possible.

M. A. Adelman compared a period of low corporate taxes (1922–1929) and a period of high corporate taxes (1945–1955) to ascertain whether *before-tax* corporate profits had increased.[14] If no such increase could be found, the hypothesis of no forward shifting would be supported. Finding the before-tax ratios of profits to GNP to be almost identical,[15] Adelman concluded that forward shifting had not occurred.

Similar conclusions were reached by Challis Hall, Jr., in a study of relative income shares received by labor and capital over the period 1919–1959.[16] Hall employed the Cobb–Douglas production function and the assumption of neutral technological change to investigate the effect

---

[10] M. Krzyzaniak and R. Musgrave, *The Shifting of the Corporation Income Tax* (Baltimore, Md.: Johns Hopkins Press, 1963).

[11] *Ibid.*, pp. 2, 3.

[12] Carl Shoup, "Some Considerations on the Incidence of the Corporation Income Tax," *Journal of Finance*, vol. 6, no. 2 (June 1951).

[13] The forward-shifting hypothesis was also tested and supported by Robert W. Kilpatrick in a study relating profit ratios and concentration in certain industries during the Korean war: "The Forward Shifting of the Corporate Income Tax," *Yale Economic Essays*, vol. 5 (Fall 1965), pp. 355–422. In addition, Karl Roskamp applied the Musgrave–Krzyzaniak models to West German data and found substantial shifting: "The Shifting of Taxes on Business Income: The Case of the West German Corporation," *National Tax Journal*, vol. 18 (September 1965), pp. 247–257.

[14] M. A. Adelman, "The Corporate Income Tax in the Long Run," *Journal of Political Economy*, vol. 65 (April 1957), pp. 151–157.

[15] For 1922–1929 the average was 23 percent; for 1946–1955 the average was 23.23 percent.

[16] Challis Hall, Jr., "Direct Shifting and the Taxation of Corporate Profits in Manufacturing, 1919–1959," *Proceedings of the American Economic Association for 1963*, pp. 258–271.

of the corporation income tax on input usage and income shares.[17] Since he was able to "fit" his data to a model fashioned within this framework (and incorporating the hypothesis of no shifting), he concluded that the stockholders necessarily bear the incidence of the tax.

In response to the Krzyzaniak–Musgrave study, John Cragg, Arnold Harberger, and Peter Mieszkowski contend that during the period studied (1935–1942 and 1948–1959) there exists "a spurious correlation between the corporation tax rate and the gross-of-tax rate of return on corporate capital in manufacturing."[18] Although some account of this had been taken, the correction was inadequate.[19] They utilized the Krzyzaniak–Musgrave econometric model but added two variables—one a dummy to account for high profits and taxes during war years (1941, 1942, 1950, 1951, and 1952) and another, the employment rate, to account for low tax rates and profit rates during the Depression and the 1949, 1954, and 1958 recessions. They contend that the data do not in fact support the shifting hypothesis but, instead, the "plausible range for capital's share of total burden of the corporation income tax lies between 90 and 120 percent."[20]

A more recent econometric model by R. J. Gordon, which more closely exemplifies the markup behavior of firms described in the preceding chapter, likewise supports the no-shifting hypothesis.[21] Once again an attempt is made to determine what *might* have happened without the tax and then compare that with what did happen. One of the more important variables included in the model is the productivity of capital, which has risen rapidly. Consequently, while Gordon finds that the profit rate has remained relatively stable, he claims it would have risen without the increase in the corporation income tax rate. The results follow the conclusions previously drawn from our theoretical analysis. In competitive markets, even though markup conventions may exist, these usually represent the normal return to capital, and there are no unrealized profits. Thus, no shifting can occur. Correspondingly, the Gordon study indicates partial shifting in oligopoly markets where unrealized profits exist, because the profit target reflects "satisficing" or because of a fear of the Attorney General or retaliation by other firms.

NONNEUTRAL ALLOCATIONAL EFFECTS UNDER LIMITED SHIFTING

EFFECTS OF INCIDENCE ON STOCKHOLDER CAPITAL

In view of the complexities we foresaw in the preceding section, we are not surprised that the incidence issue remains unresolved. Nevertheless, certain suggestions will be made.

In many markets businessmen *attempt* in the short run to pass on rate changes by marking up prices. While they may be unsuccessful, the immediate influence on prices is inflationary.[22] If the monetary authorities *allow* the supply and velocity of money to grow, the long-run " apparent " incidence can be passed on to the consumer. The long-run incidence of the tax is difficult to discern, since income shares depend on other factors as well. Yet the theoretical argument that the tax places a wedge between capital cost and the return to capital is difficult to refute and leads us to reaffirm the hypothesis that little successful long-run forward shifting can be accomplished.

Consequently, let us continue under the assumption that although there are opportunities for shifting in certain industries, the general incidence is on stockholder capital. The basic function of the tax is to reduce the purchasing power of the private sector—and this tax in particular is aimed at reducing the effective demand for " capital " resources. One of two purposes may prompt an increase in the tax: (1) to shift purchasing power to the public sector so that more public goods relative to private goods may be produced, or (2) to reduce private sector spending (without an increase in public sector spending), thereby easing inflationary pressures. If the tax is increased for the second purpose and inflationary

[17] The Cobb–Douglas function is a homogeneous function (usually linear) with the important characteristic that the elasticity of substitution between inputs is always unitary. Hence, a relative change in the ratios of inputs is exactly matched by a relative change in the ratios of their marginal products. If we assume wages and the rate of return to be directly related to the marginal products of labor and capital, we find that any change in the relative quantities of labor and capital will be accompanied by a relative change in wages and returns such that the aggregate income shares remain the same. Moreover, if technological change is neutral, shifts in the production function will not disturb this relationship between marginal products. The student desiring further explanation of these concepts is again referred to a text in microeconomic theory.

[18] John Cragg, Arnold Harberger, and Peter Mieszkowski, " Empirical Evidence on the Incidence of the Corporation Income Tax," *Journal of Political Economy*, vol. 75 (December 1967), pp. 811–821.

[19] A related criticism bears on the direction of causation. Should we assume that firms are raising pretax profits in response to higher tax rates; or is it perhaps the higher profit rates experienced during " boom " periods which encourage higher tax rates?

[20] *Ibid.*, p. 821. They contend these results agree with those of an earlier study of Harberger using yet another approach—a general equilibrium model of two sectors (corporate and noncorporate), in which the corporate income tax was viewed as a tax on the use of capital in the corporate sector. Harberger, " The Incidence of the Corporation Income Tax," *Journal of Political Economy*, vol. 70 (June 1962).

[21] R. J. Gordon, " The Incidence of the Corporation Income Tax in U.S. Manufacturing, 1925–1962," *American Economic Review*, vol. 57 (September 1967), pp. 731–758.

[22] The Krzyzaniak–Musgrave study indicated a " ratchet " effect on prices; when tax rates are reduced, there is no reciprocating reduction in profit targets.

pressures have been assessed correctly, the use of the tax need not create "nonneutral" changes between private and public goods. To the extent that a change in the tax rate is precipitated by the first purpose, we expect resource allocation between private and public sector investment to change; however, if voter priorities have been assessed correctly the shift improves inter-sector resource allocation.

A second and more subtle aspect of nonneutrality which may occur is the encouragement of labor-intensive versus capital-intensive industries. If the tax alters the price ratio between labor and capital—capital being made more expensive—there is a substitution effect from capital to labor. Businessmen who seek to equate the price of each input with its marginal revenue product will substitute labor for capital. Moreover, the aggregate consumption of output shifts towards products of industries which are labor intensive. Here, again, evidence of this tendency is scarce. There have been significant shifts in the composition of output, but changes in technology and tastes have been so influential in these shifts that the influence of the corporation tax is difficult to quantify.

A third aspect of tax incidence on stockholder capital is the tendency to favor those firms and industries which are in a position to borrow from banks or other financial intermediaries as opposed to those who must borrow by issuing stock. Since interest paid on borrowed funds is deductible while dividends paid to stockholders are not, firms who can more easily shift to the former type of borrowing are favored. The issuance of stock usually allows a greater flexibility in the assumption of risks between firms. However, since interest rates do not share this flexibility, firms with high risks find it difficult to borrow extensively. Supposedly, then, the tax has a tendency to inhibit growth of high-risk firms.

A fourth possibility of tax incidence, if it falls on capital, is a tendency to favor noncorporate types of firms. Presumably, the imposition of the tax lowers the after-tax rate of return to corporations. As a result, capital will flow to unincorporated firms until the effective rates of return are equalized. Here, again, the evidence does not show significant changes resulting from tax incidence. The corporate form of business has been growing in importance (accounting for 58 percent of business sector income in 1929 and 67 percent in 1964). The advantages of the corporate form in the raising of capital, the spreading of liability, indefinite longevity and specialized management apparently outweigh any disadvantage the corporation income tax may impose.

Finally, state and local corporation income taxes may affect the location of industrial activity. Obviously, other things equal, management would choose to build in an area with lower taxes; however, other considerations are usually important. For example, a locality may use funds from the tax to provide services not offered in localities without the tax. Alternatively, other localities may be imposing other taxes, such as property tax, which also have disincentive effects. Most studies show that occasional factors such as proximity to markets and input sources are much more important than corporation income tax.

NONNEUTRAL EFFECTS OF CERTAIN PROVISIONS

If the IRS definition of depreciation for tax purposes differs from actual (physical) depreciation several important nonneutral effects occur. Let us consider a shift from an " efficient " rate structure where the IRS rates exactly match actual rates to situations where they do not match. If the shift is to IRS rates which allow faster write-offs (" accelerated " depreciation) the shift lowers the price of capital and thus encourages substitution of capital for labor. If the shift is to IRS rates which allow slower write-offs the shift encourages substitution of labor for capital. If the economy had previously accomplished some "ideal" resource allocation either shift would involve *negative nonneutrality*. If we are not at the "ideal" position then a nonneutral shift might be in the direction of a second-best allocation. In recent years changes in IRS depreciation rates have lowered the cost of capital by accelerated depreciation and defining service lives as being shorter.

The investment tax credit has been used on several occasions as a macroeconomic policy tool. The credit as it has been used allows corporations to deduct 7 percent of the cost of capital equipment (with service lives of eight years or more) directly from their tax liability (not their taxable income). The nonneutrality is "positive " or " negative " depending on the influence of other tax provisions and many other variables. If the existing allowances are inefficient with respect to the timing and amount of returns from new assets, accelerated depreciation will have positive nonneutrality.[23]

An additional question involves the composition of output fostered by the tax credit. Obviously, the tax credit favors those firms with a high

[23] For an argument to this effect see Richard Goode, "Accelerated Depreciation Allowances as a Stimulus to Investment," *Quarterly Journal of Economics*, vol. 69, no. 2 (May 1955).

turnover of capital. In addition, those firms whose growth is capital intensive are favored over those whose growth is labor intensive. Consequently, this aspect of the tax may have a nonneutral effect on the long-run composition of output.

The composition of industry is affected in a similar way by accelerated depreciation rates. The advantages of quicker write-offs favor those firms with a high and continuous rate of investment in capital goods which may be depreciated.

The carry-over loss. The provisions which allow firms to average incomes over time also provide that firms with losses can carry these over when merging with other firms. This encourages firms with substantial profits to reduce their tax base by merging with firms temporarily experiencing losses. This may not, of course, be the only reason a particular merger is undertaken, but the carry-over loss encourages increased concentration within industries. The net effect of this tendency is hard to evaluate. Mergers of this type may well make for greater overall efficiency, since the new firm has the advantage of the technology and management skill of the more profitable firm. If, however, there are few such " economies of scale," the merger may not be so justified. The efficiency gained by concentration may well be offset by the loss of competition.

Exemptions and preferential treatment. For various reasons, many types of " nonprofit" organizations are exempted from paying taxes. Some religious, educational, and civic organizations seem to qualify on " merit " grounds. Others, such as labor unions and professional organizations, seem to be businesses which offer services. Often the dividing line is quite thin.

Agricultural cooperatives and enterprises operated by state and local governments also escape the federal tax. Such treatment, of course, means that these types of firms have a distinct advantage over their competitors. Since cooperatives have an advantage over competitors in the retail grocery and farm equipment fields, these institutions can be less efficient than their counterparts and still survive. The same situation occurs in the case of public utilities, where state and local governments enjoy tax advantages over private companies. Thus, we expect that more utilities are publicly owned and operated than would be economically feasible without the provision for exemption.

NONNEUTRALITY AND INCOME DISTRIBUTION

To the extent that the incidence of the tax falls on the income of stockholders, their income relative to that of other individuals is reduced. In general, the tax is progressive, since those individuals with large holdings of stock tend to be in the upper income groups.

But if in fact the tax is completely shifted forward, its influence on income distribution is regressive. This is because the poor, who spend more on consumption, bear more of the burden as prices are raised.

We have opted for the hypothesis that the stockholders bear most of the burden and thus have their income diminished. The special cases where the burden *is* shifted experience nonneutral price effects, and in turn affect the real income of various individuals. Consumers who spend a large proportion of their income on commodities whose prices increase are hurt relatively. An important feature of the federal tax is its generality—a feature which makes for an even impact on all corporate income. Stockholders of those firms able to pass on the burden will benefit relative to other investors. In passing, however, we once again note that the generality of the tax limits the ability of either investor or consumer to avoid it.

NONNEUTRALITY AND MACROECONOMIC POLICY

The basic function of the tax—reducing private sector purchasing power—serves the purpose of anti-inflationary fiscal policy. The relationships among the major components of aggregate demand will be examined more closely in Part IV. We simply observe now that an increase in the corporation income tax with no change in government expenditures or the money supply must eventually reduce aggregate demand and hence stem inflation. This assumes, of course, that "demand-pull" rather than "cost-push" inflation is the culprit. In the "inflationary psychology" of a cost-push situation the response of many firms to higher taxes could well be to raise prices.

Previously we noted that in order for the corporation income tax to be "passed on," replacement of spending power is required. We assume that the monetary authorities, like the fiscal authorities, would be exercising restraint in periods of inflation. We note, however, that the monetary authorities have not always been willing or able to exercise the kind of control necessary to change the money supply in the desired direction. Several factors may thwart monetary policy. Consumers may reduce their savings and borrow heavily in order to maintain their level of spending. Similarly, firms may reduce their holdings in government securities or borrow in order to finance new projects. In recent years we have observed that "slack" exists in credit creation in the forms of excess bank reserves and resort to intermediary credit institutions, so that the money supply may actually expand under a policy of restraint. The firm's demand for investment funds is often said to be inelastic to the rate of interest—depending more on such things as expectations of expanding sales. In such cases an increase in the corporation income tax rate may not suffice to limit investment spending if funds are available—even though the interest rate may be high.

A decrease in the tax rate may be employed when more aggregate spending is desired. Here, again, fiscal and monetary policy may be thwarted if businessmen's expectations do not agree. A lower tax rate may provide more internal funds for investment, but if prospects are bleak there may be no subsequent increase in real investment.

Two of the tax's special provisions which may be used to affect investment spending are investment tax credit and accelerated depreciation. It is difficult to tell exactly the impact of a change in one of these provisions, since many other factors enter into investment decisions. However, Hall and Jorgenson, using econometric models of firm behavior, have attempted to isolate their effects.[24] The effects should be of the following forms: (1) an initial surge of investment spending as firms take advantage of additional funds available to them and, with respect to the investment tax credit, the greater profitability of marginal investment opportunities, (2) a permanent increase in investment, owing to annual replacement of a larger capital stock, and (3) secondary increases in investment opportunities and spending, owing to increased consumption spending generated by the initial surge in investment. Hall and Jorgenson found a substantial initial surge resulting from the 1954 change to accelerated depreciation methods. The peak effect occurred in 1955 and accounted for 70.8 percent ($680 million in 1954 dollars) of net investment in manufacturing equipment and 28.9 percent ($434 million) of net investment in manufacturing structures. Over the 1954–1963 period about 20 percent of net investment may be attributed to the change in depreciation.

Hall and Jorgenson also found substantial effects on investment from the revised depreciation guidelines introduced in 1962, though the impact was not as great as from the 1954 changes. The peak effect occurring in 1963 was 14.8 percent of the net investment in manufacturing equipment.

The impact of the 7 percent investment tax credit was found by Hall and Jorgenson to be "quite startling." They stated: "Fully 40.9 percent of the net investment in manufacturing equipment in 1963 can be attributed to the investment tax credit."[25]

In a later article Hall and Jorgenson attempted to evaluate two more recent attempts to influence investment spending via changes in the corporation income tax. The tax cut of 1964 included not only a change in rates in personal and corporation rates (the latter from 52 to 48 percent) but deletion of the requirement that firms reduce their tax base for depreciation by the amount of the investment credit. In a later period (October 1966 to March 1967) the investment tax credit and certain types of accelerated depreciation were removed. In both cases impacts of these fiscal actions were found to be substantial.[26]

Not surprisingly, Hall and Jorgenson have encountered detractors who question their methodology and conclusion.[27] Econometric studies which attempt to compare what happened to what might have happened will invariably be open to controversy. We will reserve final evaluation until completion of our examination of macroeconomic analysis. At that time we will pay additional attention to the interplay and feedback between investment and consumption, a subject inadequately accounted for in the Hall–Jorgenson model. Our brief comments on the use of tax incentives to influence investment have demonstrated that fiscal authorities at least *think* tax incentives are important fiscal policy tools, even though precise measurement of their impact is impossible.

SUMMARY AND CONCLUSIONS

The federal corporation income tax scores fairly well on the tax criteria. Since the impact of the tax is on the fixed factors, the possibility of *negative nonneutrality* is small, at least in the short run. The major problem in terms of the public choice efficiency criteria is one of *visibility*. The tax is a very important source of federal revenue, yet the average individual has only indirect contact with it. Consequently, his awareness of the tax as a "marginal cost" is quite vague. Of course, the actual impact of the

[24] Robert E. Hall and Dale W. Jorgenson, "Tax Policy and Investment Behavior," *American Economic Review*, vol. 57 (June 1967), pp. 391–414.
[25] *Ibid.*, p. 410.
[26] Robert E. Hall and Dale W. Jorgenson, "Tax Policy and Investment Behavior: Reply and Further Results," *American Economic Revirew*, vol. 59 (June 1969), pp. 388–401.
[27] See Robert M. Coen, "Tax Policy and Investment Behavior: Comment," *American Economic Review*, vol. 59 (June 1969), pp. 370–379; and Robert Eisner, "Tax Policy and Investment Behavior: Comment," *American Economic Review*, vol. 59 (June 1969), pp. 379–388.

federal program on resource allocation only occurs *if and when* such revenues are used by government to purchase resources or output from the private sector. However, since government expenditures are usually fairly close to revenues, the individual could better judge the marginal costs of fiscal activity if all taxes were highly visible.

While recognizing that the tax is relatively neutral, we have introduced certain reservations of varying importance. The most important concerns the inclusion of the normal return of stockholders in the tax base. The tax thereby is imposed not only on abnormal profits but also on an input, stockholder capital. There is probably little shifting in the short run because the amount of investment capital employed is relatively fixed and cannot immediately change in response to tax changes. In the long run, however, the smaller return on stockholder capital could possibly reduce saving and investment. Here, again, the generality of the tax tends to somewhat offset this "nonneutral" effect. Moreover, the relationship between planned savings and planned investment is somewhat indirect. If people tend to save less than otherwise because of the tax, monetary and fiscal policies designed to influence investment spending might well offset the tax's impact on the composition of spending.

Other possible "nonneutral" effects owing to specific exemptions and deductions were also noted. Both investment tax credit and depreciation write-off formulas have been used to affect investment spending. These provisions, however, may also have unintended nonneutral influences on the allocation of resources among goods in the private sector. Further analysis would be required to determine whether these nonneutral influences are positive or negative. Another question of nonneutrality with respect to the composition of output arises because of the liberality of present depletion allowances. If, as many argue, depletion allowances are exorbitant, their influence can be seen as increasing the flow of productive factors to the extractive industries and the industries dependent on them. Finally, exemptions of certain religious, education, and charitable organizations can also be seen to influence the composition of output. Since the goods and services of the organizations qualify as "merit" goods and since the exemptions have been designed to encourage their production, these nonneutral results are not necessarily negative.

13

THE TAXES ON SALES, PROPERTY, ESTATES, AND SOCIAL SECURITY

We now turn to the microeconomic effects of the taxes on sales, property, estates and social security. The sales and property taxes are the primary sources of revenue for the states and localities respectively. In recent years sales taxes have furnished slightly over half the revenue from state sources, while the property tax has provided slightly over half the revenue from locality sources. Social insurance taxes and contributions account for over one-fourth of federal revenue. What effects do these taxes have on economic behavior?

THE SALES TAXES

There are two basic types of sales taxes, and their economic effects are quite different. The general sales tax covers price transactions on all commodities. The excise tax is directed at a particular commodity or class of commodities. The nature of the excise tax may be *specific* or *ad valorem*. That is, the tax may be stated as a certain amount per unit of output, such as 5 cents per pack of cigarettes, or it may be stated as a percent of the selling price, e.g., 5 percent of the price of liquor. Because of the nature of the excise tax we would expect some forward shifting. By definition its nature is not general; it increases marginal costs and it causes output prices to be raised. In fact, legislatures typically assume that excise taxes will be completely shifted forward. Moreover, it is usually assumed that the general sales tax will likewise be shifted forward. The veracity of these assumptions will be subsequently examined. First, however, we shall outline the development and current structure of excise and general sales taxes.

DEVELOPMENT OF EXCISE TAXES

As outlined in Part II, excise taxes have been an important source of revenue since the first years of our government. The federal government initially relied almost entirely on tariff excises but in recent years it has left excise taxation primarily to the states and localities.

Until World War I excise taxes on foreign exchange were the main sources of federal revenue. Internal excise taxes were also applied— especially during war years. The most prominent internal taxes were those placed on tobacco and alcohol. Usually these taxes were increased at the beginning and then reduced at the end of the particular emergency. The period after World War I was no exception; during the 1920s most excise taxes were repealed.

With the Depression and the repeal of prohibition, the excise taxes on alcohol and tobacco again rose in importance. Moreover, the federal excise tax on gasoline was enacted in 1932 and has remained an important source of revenue. Excise taxes were further raised as part of the overall increase in taxes during World War II.

The period after World War II has witnessed a reduction in federal excise taxes. Tax legislation enacted in 1954, 1965, and 1971 substantially reduced both rates and the number of items taxed.[1] This trend can be expected to continue when inflationary pressures abate.

Excise taxation at state and local levels has become important only in the last 50 years. During the 1920s states and localities greatly expanded their services and necessarily their taxes. In 1919, Oregon adopted a successful excise tax on gasoline. Other states quickly followed suit, and by the late 1920s all states had gasoline taxes. In fiscal year 1927, state tax collections from motor vehicle fuel sales were $259 million or 16 percent of all state revenue. By 1932 this proportion was even larger; the $527 million collected by states from gasoline sales taxes in 1932 represented 28 percent of all state revenue.

States further increased their revenue during the twenties and thirties by adopting excise taxes on sales of tobacco products and alcoholic beverages. State collections from these two sources had been practically nonexistent as late as 1927. However, in 1932, states collected $19 million from taxes on sales of tobacco products and $1 million from sales of alcohol beverages. By 1940, states were collecting $97 million from tobacco excises and $255 million from taxes on alcoholic beverages. Now all fifty states impose excises on alcoholic beverages and tobacco and collect over $1.5 billion and $2.5 billion, respectively.

Some localities tax gasoline, alcohol, cigarettes, amusements, and public utilities; however, their importance in terms of total revenue is small. Sales taxes supplied $3 billion or only 5 percent of the $60 billion in total revenue localities collected from their own sources in 1970.

THE SHIFTING AND INCIDENCE OF EXCISE TAXATION

Whether the form of an excise tax is *specific* or *ad valorem*, it represents an *increase in cost per unit of output* to the firm. Hence marginal costs shift, and part of the tax will be shifted forward. The degree of shifting depends importantly on the nature of the market in which the product is produced and sold. The mechanics of shifting in various market situations were discussed in Chapter 11.

We will not attempt to trace through the shifting and incidence of each tax in each market situation. It is, however, useful to recall the importance of the elasticity of demand and supply to the degree of shifting. In short, the *more inelastic* market demand, the greater the forward shifting; the *more elastic* market supply, the greater the forward shifting. Figures 13.1 and 13.2 are useful in illustrating these remarks. In part (a) of 13.1 the market demand curve is relatively inelastic. Consequently, an excise tax, which shifts the supply curve through its effect on marginal costs, will cause a relatively large degree of forward shifting. This can be seen in the price change from P to P'. Part (b), however, illustrates that a similar tax would result in a smaller degree of forward shifting if the market demand curve were more elastic. Figure 13.2 illustrates the effects of an excise tax under different elasticities of market supply. When market supply is relatively inelastic, it is difficult for inputs to move to other occupations and thus escape the tax; consequently, price and quantity change little. When market supply is relatively elastic as in part (b), however, there is more forward shifting. It is important to note that the more elastic supply also results in a greater change in quantity. In the long run, supply is much more elastic since inputs have ample time to flow to other industries. Consequently, less of the tax can be shifted backward onto the resource owners, and more is shifted forward.

From the standpoint of *neutrality* the excise tax scores poorly. Marginal costs are affected directly, and much of the tax is shifted forward. Price ratios between commodities are changed, and consumers can be expected to change their composition of purchases. Resource allocation is affected, presenting the question of whether the new allocation is closer to or further from the "welfare maximum."

---

[1] The 1965 reduction in federal excise taxation was significant with respect to the number of taxes repealed and the overall reduction in rates. Among the important retail taxes repealed were the 10 percent excise taxes on luxuries such as furs, jewelry, luggage, handbags, cosmetics, room air conditioners, business machines, musical instruments, radio and television sets, and sporting goods.

In addition, federal excise taxes on admissions, private phone lines, and electric light bulbs were repealed. Also repealed were the 5 percent manufacturers' excise taxes on household appliances such as refrigerators and freezers.

The 10 percent excise taxes on telephone service and on automobiles and several other miscellaneous taxes were reduced but were not phased out as planned because of inflationary pressures in the late 1960s. The automobile excise tax which had been reduced to 7 percent was finally removed in 1971 as an anti-recession move.

FIGURE 13–1

Excise taxes under different
elasticities of demand

Relatively inelastic demand

Relatively elastic demand

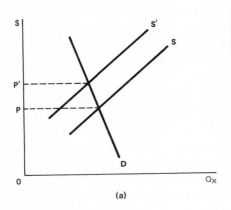

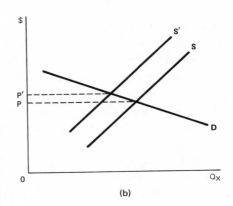

(a)

(b)

FIGURE 13–2

Excise taxes under different
elasticities of supply

Relatively inelastic supply

Relatively elastic supply

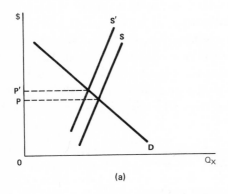

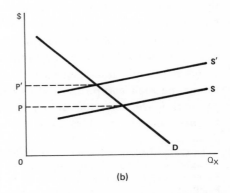

(a)

(b)

The recognition that part of the excise tax is shifted forward is not lost
upon those who legislate our taxes. Indeed, it is usually assumed that the
entire amount of the tax is passed forward to the consumer. Significantly,
excise taxes are usually imposed on commodities for which the demand is
relatively inelastic. This is apparent upon reconsideration of the outline of
excise taxes above. Consumers show little propensity to substitute other

goods for automobile transportation, tobacco products, liquor, and public utilities. Moreover, the market supply of these goods is relatively elastic—especially in the long run. Although most of the tax is shifted forward, resource allocation may not be affected as greatly as it would seem. The imposition of the excise tax causes both income and substitution effects. This imposition on a good whose demand is relatively inelastic does not substantially change the quantity produced and sold; hence, the substitution effect may be said to be small. It may be that there is little change in the composition of goods purchased by the consumer. Since the higher price of the taxed good reduces the consumer's income, he must reduce his number of purchases. He may not greatly change the composition of purchases however. In such cases the final result of the excise tax is similar to that of the income tax—or, more precisely, the general sales tax. The allocation of resources within the economy may not be altered significantly—barring complications arising from inadequate aggregate spending—unless the public sector uses the tax receipts to purchase goods or resources from the private sector.

These considerations suggest that nonneutrality of excise taxes may not be as great as at first suspected. The fact that these taxes are primarily on goods whose demand is relatively inelastic reduces the impact on resource allocation.

To the extent, however, that the consumer does substitute in response to the change in prices, resource allocation will be affected; consumption and production of the taxed good will be reduced, and employment of labor and capital will flow to other industries. There is no reason to believe that the new resource allocation will be less " efficient " in terms of the way a firm uses inputs. The nonneutrality affects the price of the taxed good relative to others, and unless its production has higher opportunity costs (of using resources to produce this good instead of others) which are now correctly reflected by the higher price, the nonneutrality will be negative.

SUMPTUARY AND REGULATORY TAXES

The assumption that pretax prices correctly reflect the real opportunity costs of production may not hold. It may be that the new prices will lead to improved resource allocation. Those excise taxes which are intentionally *aimed* at reducing the consumption of goods with negative externalities are called *sumptuary* taxes. Obviously, taxes on alcoholic beverages and cigarettes derive part of their justification from this reasoning. Many members of the population desire to discourage consumption of these products. Often implicit in their reasoning is one of two assumptions: either the average person does not know what is best for him, or he recognizes a need for this type of restraint to be imposed upon him.

Another rationale for imposing these taxes concerns the *neighborhood effects* of drinking and smoking. It can be argued that increased use of alcoholic beverages increases crime, broken homes, loss of working time, and other effects which injure not only the alcoholic but other members of society. Cigarette smoking causes forest fires, pollutes the air at cocktail parties, burns holes in carpets, and increases the costs of the Medicare program. Taxes which reduce consumption of these products will benefit society. In addition, revenue from the tax may be used to pay for the external diseconomies created by their users.

Taxes may also be imposed for regulatory purposes. Taxes imposed on narcotics, gambling, and alcohol are used for these reasons. Federal agents breaking up moonshine stills derive their authority from the tax law with which the moonshiner has not complied.

Two equity considerations should be mentioned in passing. The excise tax structure as it exists is quite regressive. That is, taxes on alcohol, cigarettes, and gasoline impose a relatively heavier burden on low-income groups. Excise taxes on luxuries only partially offset this tendency. To the extent that voters do not take this effect into consideration, their assessment of the redistributive effect of the tax system is inaccurate. Second, the tax does not provide horizontal equity. That is, it does not treat equally families of equal income and family situation but whose consumption patterns differ with regard to the taxed product. Of course, to the extent that the tax is sumptuary, this differentiation is intended. Even so, where the taxes on alcohol and cigarettes bring real hardships to, say, the children of an already destitute family, the equity of the tax may be brought into question.[2]

SOME EMPIRICAL STUDIES OF EXCISE TAX INCIDENCE

Changes in excise taxes have provided opportunity to observe the firm's response. A rather basic approach is to observe prices before and after a change in taxes. It is important, of course, to account for all other factors which might influence prices—such as a general inflation—so as to isolate the incidence of the tax itself.

Studies have been directed toward the excise reductions of 1954 and 1965. In both cases, substantial reaction on the part of firms was observed. A study by Harry Johnson of the 1954 reductions revealed that the response was often a greater percentage change in price than the change in the tax.[3] His study shows the percentage by which prices declined for 676 appliance models in response to the tax reduction. Although most (78.1 percent) prices declined in most of the 676 models he studied, there was a wide variety in the response. In the major appliance category 76.1 percent of the prices were reduced; whereas the percent of the suggested price accounted for by the tax reduction ranged between 2 and 3 percent, a large number of the reductions, 58.2 percent, were greater than 3 percent. In other words, firms responded to the tax reduction by lowering suggested prices by more than the tax. The proportion responding in the smaller appliance group was larger, 91.3 percent; however, most were in the 2 to 3 percent reduction or lower categories.

Johnson goes on to relate the greater-than-tax response to monopoly power. For example, he compares average price reduction to concentration ratios for the appliance groups. Within appliance groups the leading firms were found to be those whose response was to change price by a greater percentage than the tax reduction. Johnson does not say why it is that monopoly power should evoke such a response; but examination of demand factors during that period provides some explanation. Our static models suggest a ready explanation for tax shifting. Since marginal costs are affected, firms change price in response to a change in the tax. The markets in question fall under the oligopoly category, and various types of interdependence exist. It is reasonable to assume that in the

[2] For examples of studies of the distribution of excise (and other) taxes in particular states see William H. Hickman, "Distribution of the Burden of California Sales and other Excise Taxes" (Sacramento: State Board of Equalization, 1958); Gerhard N. Rostvold, "Distribution of Property, Retail Sales, and Personal Income Tax Burdens in California: An Empirical Analysis of Inequity in Taxation," *National Tax Journal*, vol. 19 (March 1966), pp. 38–47; David G. Davies, "Commodity Taxation and Equity," *Journal of Finance*, December 1961, pp. 581–590; and K. B. Marx, "Tobacco, Alcoholic Beverage, and Pari-Mutuel Taxes," *Report of the Commission of Revenue*, State of Illinois (Springfield: The Commission, 1963), pp. 702–759.

[3] "Tax Pyramiding and the Manufacturer's Excise Tax Reduction of 1954," *National Tax Journal*, vol. 17 (1964), pp. 297–302. An earlier but less complete (274 appliance models) study by John F. Due led to much the same conclusions, except that according to Due the shift in price was somewhat greater than in the Johnson study. Due, "The Effect of the 1954 Reduction in the Federal Excise Taxes upon the List Prices of Electrical Appliances—A Case Study," *National Tax Journal*, September 1954.

1953–1954 recession the firms in more competitive situations had adjusted prices to compensate for the sluggish growth in aggregate demand. In those markets where more direct retaliation was feared, however, firms were slow to adjust. The tax reductions acted as a signal for the interdependent firms to reduce prices by a greater percent than that of the tax cuts.

The response to the 1965 reductions in excise taxes offers an interesting contrast to that in 1954. A study by Oswald Brownlee and George Perry again bore out our simple models of shifting of excise taxes.[4] The firms immediately lowered prices, and the reductions were quite close to the reductions in taxes. In a few cases, prices were reduced by more than the tax. Again, a probable explanation can be found by examining the nature of demand. The economy was in a period of expansion with ample aggregate demand but with sufficient capacity to allow for increased output and sales. As Brownlee and Perry observed:

We believe that for most of the commodities whose prices were studied, the price elasticities of demand were sufficiently small and supply was still sufficiently elastic that the resulting price changes would approximately equal the amount of the tax reduction. The results we obtained for most commodities are consistent with this belief.[5]

EXCISE TAXES AS USER PRICES

Economists continually argue for the extension of user charges on quasicollective goods which are publicly produced. When feasible, it is argued, a charge should be made for that portion of the benefits derived from a quasicollective good which are divisible. For example, a public park area benefits an entire community both directly and indirectly. It may be feasible and appropriate to help defray park expenses by charging those who use certain park facilities. Similarly, while many people benefit from a new bridge, charging a toll creates user prices for some of the benefits. The excise taxes on motor fuels and automobile parts and tires also serve this purpose. The more a motorist uses highways, the more tax he pays; thus, costs are roughly connected with benefits. In many states and localities funds from the excise taxes on gasoline and the license fees on automobiles and trucks are earmarked for highway and street improvement. The Federal Highway Trust Fund established in 1956 serves a similar purpose for the interstate highway system.

In additional to the Highway Trust Fund the federal government in 1970 established the Airport and Airway Trust Fund. However, much broader use of user charges has been advocated and supported by the administrative branch. Presidents in recent years have asked Congress to expand user charges for a wide range of benefits to include air and inland waterway facilities, parks, and other recreation facilities. More important, it may be desirable to incorporate user charges into broad programs to curb air and water pollution. As might be predicted, the decision-making processes in Congress have been the stumbling blocks for most such proposals. It is there the interest groups which would have to pay can most easily find sufficient support.

THE GENERAL SALES TAX

General sales taxes can be classified by the stage of production to which they are applicable. The tax with which we are most familiar is applied at the final or retail stage. The tax can, however, be applied to another stage or to all stages. In Canada and Britain, for example, the tax is applied at the manufacturing stage. The tax may also be applied at every stage involving a price transaction; so applied, the sales tax is termed a "turnover tax." Predictably, the turnover tax encourages vertical integration among firms, since by a merger firms can reduce the number of price transactions involved in the production process. The "value-added" tax is similar to the turnover tax but is based only on the *net value added* at each stage of production; consequently, it avoids encouraging vertical integration.

In the United States the general sales tax is collected at the retail level. The federal government has left this revenue source to the states and localities, who depend upon it heavily. The state and local taxes are usually coordinated. Quite often the locality will receive a percentage credited by the state. The states' dependence on the general sales tax has increased over threefold in each of the past three decades. It furnished $451 million in 1939; $1,670 million in 1950; $4,302 million in 1960 and $14,127 million in 1970. It also has been growing in relative importance and now accounts for about 30 percent of state revenue.

[4] Brownlee and Perry, "The Effects of the 1965 Federal Excise Tax Reduction on Price," *National Tax Journal*, vol. 20 (September 1967), pp. 235–249.
[5] *Ibid.*, p. 236.

THE INCIDENCE OF THE GENERAL SALES TAX

Extending the analysis of the excise tax on specific goods, we might conclude that the general excise tax also tends to be shifted forward to the consumer. Indeed, most legislators and consumers tend to accept this reasoning as self-evident. But the *generality* of the general sales tax requires that we analyze its effects in terms of general rather than partial equilibrium analysis—a procedure that yields some interesting insights.

The shifting and incidence of the tax depend importantly on what is assumed about the flexibility of prices and monetary policy. Let us consider three alternative sets of assumptions—or rather three different "models." First let us assume that prices are flexible in both directions. This corresponds to the classical model of "laissez faire" capitalism. In this model a reduction in the money supply simply causes proportional decreases in prices, and the economy remains at *full* employment. Assume now that a general sales tax is imposed. In the absence of monetary activity, the money supply will not allow the same volume of purchases at the old prices plus the tax. Let us assume that no compensatory monetary policy is forthcoming. The *sales tax cannot be passed on to the consumer*, since consumers simply do not have enough money to buy all of the goods and services at the higher prices; hence, *the tax must be shifted backward to owners of inputs*. The retailer, the wholesaler, the blue collar worker, the executive, the lender of capital, and so on must receive lower remuneration. The incidence of the tax immediately falls on owners of inputs. Thus, the incidence of the tax is identical to that of *a proportional income tax*.

The astute student has no doubt already questioned the accuracy of the assumptions used in the preceding analysis. As consumers in the 1930s observed, output prices do not readily fall and input owners do not readily agree to lower rates of remuneration. Moreover, firms often formulate their prices in terms of certain profit targets. Their initial response to a general sales tax would be to raise prices by the full amount of the tax, especially if the legislature expected and encouraged them to do so. Let us assume that retailers attempt to pass the tax to consumers by raising prices. The assumption about monetary policy now becomes crucial. If no compensatory monetary activity occurs, aggregate effective demand will be inadequate at the higher price level. Surpluses will pile up, and unemployment of both labor and capital will increase. The growth potential of the economy will not be realized.

In recent years monetary and fiscal authorities have become more aware of their capabilities and responsibilities for providing adequate aggregate spending. *It has become more realistic to assume that compensatory action will be taken in response to a change in aggregate demand.* Assuming that adequate money is pumped into the model, merchants will be able to raise prices by the amount of the tax, and consumers will be able to purchase all goods produced; hence, the incidence will be passed on to consumers. Once again the nature of the incidence of the tax is similar to that of a proportional income tax. The major difference between this and the first model (where the tax was shifted backward to resource owners) is that the invidual can now partially escape the tax by saving.[6]

The most plausible model includes the assumption that the government will increase *expenditures* by the amount of the tax. This seems quite realistic, since we are considering state and local finance. If public expenditures are expanded as private expenditures increase, no problem arises with respect to change in aggregate demand; consequently, the burden will be passed on to the consumer. The input owners, as such, will not suffer, since the public activities will be bidding for their services. Consumers will be forced to reduce consumption, and they will adjust the composition of goods purchased according to the marginal utility they receive relative to price. There are no primary nonneutral effects on prices of commodities or inputs. Some secondary effects may result from the composition of the new public spending, the technology and resource allocation in those industries, and so on.

The net effect the tax and expenditure has on consumers and input owners depends on whether the expansion of this particular public activity is a move towards more efficient resource allocation. If the tax is shifted forward, it is proportional with respect to consumption; *with respect to income, however, the tax now becomes regressive,* since the upper income levels save more (and thus pay tax on a smaller proportion of

---

[6] One aspect of the tax on consumption may be that relatively more resources are devoted to the production of capital goods; thus, one nonneutral effect of the general sales tax involves a change in the growth path of the economy. At the same time, such changes in the composition of production may present difficulties to the monetary and fiscal authorities attempting to predict future levels of production and spending. Assuming that these difficulties are resolved, subsequent periods will reflect a higher growth rate than would otherwise have occurred. This result may involve a nonneutral benefit rather than burden if the existing growth pattern did not reflect collective preferences.

their income). If we assume that the "proper" income distribution had been attained prior to the imposition of the tax, the nature of the non-neutrality is contrary to society's distribution goal.[7]

As in the income tax case, the general sales tax can be escaped by devoting more time to leisure. By consuming goods which do not involve a price transaction, one also escapes the tax. Certain other nonneutral effects occur because of the particular structure of the different sales taxes. No states have sales taxes so general that they cover consumption of all goods and services. Accordingly, relative prices will favor those goods and services which do not fall under the tax. These include such services as those of the physician, the lawyer, and certain other professionals, as well as in some states such goods as food, medicine, and clothing.

Having noted possible nonneutral effects of the tax on income distribution and consumption, let us return to the central question: Upon whom does the major incidence of the general sales tax fall? We have noted that this depends on flexibility of prices and monetary policy. We have tentatively concluded that the assumptions which allowed the tax to be passed on to consumers through price increases and the necessary monetary activity seem to be the most plausible. However, let us consider the nature of the incidence which results from this shifting. It is quite different from that found in the partial equilibrium model used when examining the specific excise tax. Now the price rise is accompanied by an increase in money income, which allows the consumer to buy the same amount of goods; thus, the real income of the consumer remains unchanged. *It turns out that there is no real burden to the imposition of the general sales tax.*

The solution to this paradox is not hard to find. It rests in the assumption implicit in our model that no government expenditure takes place as a direct result of the imposition of the general sales tax. If no resources are withdrawn from private sector use and full employment prevails, it is obvious that the consumption of private goods will not be curtailed. It is, of course, highly likely that increases in government expenditure will accompany an increase in taxes. Judgments as to the net benefit or burden of such taxes can only be made in terms of changes in both marginal benefits and costs occurring as a result of the new allocation of resources. Since this approach has been presented and utilized at several other places in the text, there is no need to pursue it at length here. We simply note that when a truly general tax is considered, a simple analysis of shifting and incidence does not completely answer the question of where the real burden or benefit of the tax falls.

The behavior of firms in response to current sales taxes, however, is relatively easy to observe. Firms add full tax to the advertised price of each item.[8] The consumer is aware beforehand that the tax will be added when payment is made. The reaction of firms to subsequent reductions in sales, if any, resulting from passing on the tax, does not appear to be significant. In view of the various other factors influencing aggregate demand discussed above, it would be difficult to isolate secondary effects of the firm's apparent practice of adding the tax to existing prices.

The generality of the tax enhances its neutrality. In most states the tax applies to all retail sales of tangible personal property and specified services. Fourteen states exempt purchases of medicine and eleven exempt purchases of food. Thus partial escape can be found by shifting purchases to those goods, or to other goods and services which involve no price transaction at the retail level.

Since the sales tax is not imposed in all states, one may escape by traveling out of the state to purchase goods. Usually, however, the opportunity costs of the transportation involved are too high except for those persons living near state borders. City taxes are more susceptible to evasion of this nature. All states with general sales taxes have "use" taxes which require that taxes be paid on items purchased outside the state. The main purpose of the "use" tax laws is to furnish a basis for prosecuting flagrant violators of the general sales tax. It would be difficult and expensive to enforce the "use" tax laws vigorously. Automobile purchases subject to the "use" tax are an exception, however, since enforcement of the law is, in this case, facilitated by the title registration requirements of the states involved.

---

[7] For examples of empirical studies of the effect of the sales tax on income distribution see D. G. Davies, "An Empirical Test of Sales Tax Regressivity," *Journal of Political Economy*, vol. 67 (February 1959), pp. 72–78; Hickman, "Distribution of the Burden of California Sales and Other Excise Taxes"; and *Maryland Tax Study* (College Park: Bureau of Business and Economic Research, University of Maryland, 1965).

[8] An early study by R. M. Haig and C. S. Shoup revealed mixed reactions of firms to retail sales taxes in New York, Illinois, and Michigan. At that time, however, the sales tax was not widely used, and separate quotation of the tax was not universally practiced. Haig and Shoup, *The Sales Tax in the American States* (New York: Columbia University Press, 1934).

THE VALUE ADDED TAX

There has been considerable interest recently in the value added tax (VAT) due to its growing use in other countries (especially the Common Market countries) and consideration by the Nixon Administration and some states.

As noted, it differs from other sales taxes in that its base is not the gross value of the retail sale but rather the *net* value added at each stage of production. The production process of most goods features a multitude of stages performed by different firms. The liability of each firm is based on the difference between the prices it has to pay for materials and its own selling prices. Theoretically each firm could figure its tax bill by subtracting all its costs of materials from its selling prices and applying the tax rate. In practice each firm is required to account for the value added taxes paid by firms at previous stages. It must *credit* these amounts against the taxes owed on the entire selling price it charges. This technique allows for double checking by tax authorities and discourages evasion.

If a country adopts the value added tax one question which must be answered is how each firm is to account for its capital costs. Obviously, a firm which uses a machine in its production process will "use up" part of the machine's value. Moreover, taxes on value added have been paid during the production process of the machine itself. But when does the firm use the machine as a "cost"? When it buys the machine, or each year as the machine depreciates? If the firm is allowed to deduct entire credit when the capital equipment is *purchased*, the system is termed a *consumption VAT*. If the firm is allowed to deduct the credit as the equipment *depreciates* over time, the system is termed an *income VAT*.

In symbolic terms the tax base of the consumption variety is sales, S, minus materials, M, minus purchases of capital assets, C:

$$VAT_C = S - M - C.$$

Similarly the tax base of the income variety is sales, S, minus materials M, minus depreciation, D:

$$VAT_I = S - M - D.$$

A third system would not allow firms to deduct *any* tax paid on capital equipment. Under this variety, termed *product VAT*, the tax base is basically GNP (the total value of all consumption and production goods and services. From the firms' view it would be sales, S, minus only materials, M:

$$VAT_P = S - M$$

The consumption variety has the advantage of simplicity since the firm can deduct the entire tax paid on durable goods when purchased. Moreover the system has fewer disincentive effects for investment since all producer's goods are exempted. It is essentially a tax on all retail sales and must cope with the problem of defining when a good is sold for *use* in production or consumption.

The income variety is more complex for the firm since it must account for tax credit on the basis of the equipment's service life. The tax base is more equivalent to personal *income* since it is the income flow *less depreciation* for the year which is being taxed.

THE INCIDENCE OF THE VALUE ADDED TAX

It is usually assumed that the value added tax, like the sales tax, is fully shifted forward to the consumer. The value added tax features separate quotation of tax credit which supposedly makes the tax visible and more easily shifted. However, the mechanics of the general sales tax seems more amenable to shifting since it occurs only at one stage of production and is tabulated at the end of the sale. As we have seen, there is no guarantee that even the general sales tax is fully shifted. Certainly farmers and other firms in very competitive markets would have difficulty shifting the tax in the short run. For the most part, however, the incidence of the consumption variety of the value added tax is the same as the general sales tax (which excludes producers' goods). The income and product varieties feature relatively more incidence on firms and owners of capital.

SHOULD WE ADOPT THE VALUE ADDED TAX?

The growing use of the value added tax in European and other countries has led to interest in its use as a federal tax for the United States. In most of the European countries the tax has been used to replace the turnover tax whose disadvantages have been outlined. In the United States it has been suggested as a source for revenue sharing to localities (thereby easing the burden of the property tax), or to replace the corporation income tax.

The effect of either change is difficult to assess. The VAT_C is regressive in the same way as a general sales tax. If we assume that a substantial part of the corporation income tax falls on the owners, the net effect of a shift away from it to a VAT_C would be regressive (a shift to VAT_I or VAT_P would less be regressive). If, however, we assume that the coroporation income tax is fully shifted forward, the change to VAT_C would have no effect on income distribution.

As noted, the incidence of the property tax is difficult to assess. It seems to differ according to such variables as the nature of the real estate market, the property's geographical location, and so on. It appears to fall heavily on the poor who rent. Consequently the shift from property taxes to VAT_C, VAT_I, or VAT_P may well decrease regressivity.

The value added tax has several disadvantages relative to the general sales tax. Its administration is more complicated due to the bookkeeping small firms must do if tax credits are used. It is less adaptable to exemptions such as food, medicine, and so on which some states now employ. It involves difficulties in differentiating " use in production " if producers' goods are to be exempted. In summary, the VAT_C is essentially a tax on consumption and must be considered as an alternative to the general sales tax. In the United States at least it would seem more sensible to increase the use of the general sales tax than shift to VAT. One final argument should be noted. It is argued that reliance on the corporation income tax instead of VAT places our firms at a disadvantage relative to the European countries. Since the VAT features a refund on exports, a shift in that direction would in fact subsidize our exports. It is uncertain, however, that our present system is less favorable to exports than the European systems since they feature corporation taxes as well. Our retail sales taxes are not applicable to exports.[9]

THE PROPERTY TAX

HISTORY AND CONCEPTS OF PROPERTY TAXATION

The history of taxation of property is a long one, going back practically as far as records of financing by government. The manner and scope of property taxation have changed through the ages with changing forms of government, structures of property rights, and so on. It would be too time-consuming to trace that history here. Instead, we will examine some of the more important economic ideas and their impact on property taxation.

The theoretical argument for a tax on property began with the Physiocrats, a group of French "economists" of the eighteenth century. François Quesnay, a physician and the leader of the school, viewed the economic system as a circular flow of income—perhaps derived from the notion of the flow of blood through the human body. From observing the flow of income through the agricultural, manufacturing, and land-owning sectors, he concluded that only the agricultural sector added real income to this circular flow—the other sectors being sterile. This net product occurred when seeds were planted and later yielded not only enough grain and so on to plant next year's crop but a surplus as well. The Physiocrats concluded that the only logical base for taxation was land. Moreover, while taxing any other sector would disrupt production, taxing land would not—because land, whether taxed or not, is always available for use.

The English classical economist David Ricardo also perceived the economy as a system within which questions of production and distribution of income are simultaneously settled. While Ricardo's perspective differed in many ways from that of the Physiocrats, he also concluded that land was the most appropriate factor of production to tax. Ricardo started from the proposition that all value was created by labor. A return to capital was made possible because capital was "labor-embodied"—its value having been imparted to it by the labor used in its (the capital good's) production. The return to land, however, could only be seen as a residual. As the population increased and more marginal land was put into use, the return to more fertile and better-situated land increased. Ricardo reasoned that this surplus accruing to landlords did not represent a real cost of production, since no sacrifice on the part of the landlord was required; consequently, it should be taxed away.

From time to time since Ricardo, various groups have advocated a single tax on land as a method for solving the public sector's need for revenue and society's goal of redistributing wealth. This movement

[9] For additonal arguments on the advantages and disadvantages of value added taxes see Clara Sullivan, *The Tax on Value Added* (New York: Columbia University Press, 1965); A. A. Tait, *Value Added Tax* (London: McGraw-Hill U.K. Ltd., 1972); and *The Value Added Tax*, Hearings before the Joint Economic Committee, Congress of the United States, March 1972, (Washington: 1972).

gained strong support in America under the leadership of Henry George in the 1870s. George adhered to the Ricardian notion that the return to land was a rent. Further, he reasoned that since the supply of land is fixed, a tax on this surplus could not be shifted and thus could not disturb the allocation of resources. That part of the value of land which represented improvements to its original state was not to be taxed. However, the increase in the value of the *pure rent* brought about by a growing economy was seen as a social surplus produced by the society as a whole; thus rightfully it should be taxed.

The major flaw in the Ricardian and Georgian theory of value is that it is based on " sacrifice " (or alternatively " utility ") while making no attempt to account for scarcity. Yet the pricing mechanism accounts for both of these elements when communicating the prices of factors to potential users. If the " surplus " accruing to land were all taxed away, the extra opportunity costs of not employing land in its most efficient use would be removed.

A second flaw in the reasoning of Ricardo and George is that their definition of rent applies only to land. Today rent, or more precisely *economic rent*, is defined as the return to *any* factor of production over and above that which the factor could receive in its next best employment. If land can be used only to produce scrub pine, then practically *any* payment for its use is an *economic rent*. If a professional football player's next best opportunity is digging ditches, any amount he is paid over the ditch digger's salary is a surplus—and could be taxed away without causing him to change occupations. Such a surplus, economic rent, may accrue to any factor of production.

Henry George's plan would encounter a third difficulty in differentiating between the value of land representing an economic rent and that accruing because of improvements. Changes such as the clearing, draining, and irrigating of land are examples of investment, not economic rent.

The single tax proposal was never adopted and has little support today. This historical background does, however, help to explain the importance of land in property taxation and some of the special provisions in various local and state tax structures.

THE PRESENT STRUCTURE OF PROPERTY TAXES

As outlined previously, the property tax is the most important source of revenue for localities. The percentage it makes up of revenue raised by localities has decreased slowly over the years but still remains at 56 percent. In recent years the federal and state governments have chosen to leave this source of revenue to localities. The relative dependence localities place on the tax varies considerably from region to region, as does the per capita collection.

There is also wide diversity in the *method* of property taxation. One difference stems from the definition of the tax base. In general, the property tax is imposed on assets. Assets of different types are often taxed at different rates. A tax on real property, if consistent, would be on *all* tangible property. All *intangible* property (such as stocks, bonds, cash, deposits, mortgages) merely representing claims against real property would be exempted. The tax base, defined as all real property, would necessarily include tangible personal property such as furniture, jewelry, automobiles, washing machines, and so on.

Although the definition of real property is quite straightforward, none of the widely diverse property tax structures uses this definition as its tax base. Some localities attempt to tax tangible and nontangible assets, yet the difficulty of taxing personally owned nontangibles has led to their being exempt in the localities of most states and subject to low rates in others. Present systems usually lie somewhere between the extremes of a tax only on land and a tax based on all real property.

Generally, little differentiation is made according to ownership of the property. Some types of personal property have proven difficult to tax. In Delaware, Hawaii, New York, and Pennsylvania all personal property is exempted; in many other states different types of personal property are exempted. Only sixteen states attempt a rather general taxation of personal property. Several of the most important exemptions based on ownership are those for property owned by the federal government, certain nonprofit educational, charitable, and religious institutions, and, in some cases, owner-occupied residences.

DIFFERENCES BETWEEN ASSESSED AND REAL VALUES

Customarily, assessed value is stated as some percentage of real value when assets are assessed for tax purposes. Of course, initial evaluation can only be made in terms of actual market values. On a national average, assessed values usually represent about 30 percent of real values, but they vary widely.

There is little logical foundation for this practice. Obviously, a property owner's tax bill is not different if he is taxed 6 percent on an assessed value representing 50 percent of the real value than it would be if he were taxed 3 percent on the full value. Moreover, amounts required by the government in question remain the same regardless of the method used.

Localities and counties often encourage low assessed values because one of the criteria for determining state property tax liability in the locality is *total assessed valuation*. Counties compete to lower the assessment rate and thereby lower their relative share of the tax burden. Recently states have begun to require more consistency and equalization of assessed and real valuation.

THE SHIFTING AND INCIDENCE OF THE PROPERTY TAX

Capital values arise because certain physical goods have the capacity to generate income or services over time. For certain machines, buildings, and so on the generated service may extend over long periods. Value of the asset depends, then, on the value of services generated and the length of time these services will be generated. Income or services to be available at some future date must be discounted in order to ascertain their present value. Summing the values of income generated in this and future periods (appropriately discounted) gives the present value of a capital asset. Theoretically, one should be able to arrive at capital values by discounting anticipated income flow by the current rate of interest, since the current rate of interest is what one must now pay for obtaining expected future income. Within this theoretical context it can be seen that a tax on capital value is the same thing as a tax on income from capital.

Although the two are theoretically identical, there are basic differences in the taxation of capital and of income from capital. Under the present income tax structure, capital gains income receives preferential treatment. Property taxation, however, when accompanied by periodic reassessment of property values, typically allows no such special treatment.

There is another important difference between tax on income and tax on capital. The income tax allows depreciation of *capital assets* to be counted as costs, thereby reducing the tax bill. No such costs are allowed for depreciation of the *human body* or any " embodied " investment; hence, labor income and investment in humans such as education, technical training, and health programs are discriminated against. On the other hand, property taxation uses only capital as its base, and investment in humans and the resultant remuneration escapes the tax. Therefore, property tax favors investment in humans. The net effect of these two taxes is difficult to estimate. Obviously, the tendency of each is to offset the other with respect to the amount of resources devoted to human and capital investment. It is not necessary, however, to be precise in order to come to a policy conclusion. A "judgment" can be made on a marginal basis. In other words, society through Congress and the Executive can express its opinion of whether we have "too little" or "too much" investment in humans or capital and act accordingly. On the expenditure side of the budget, expenditures on public education promote human capital. We will not attempt to make a "judgment" about the net effect of the budget; we simply point out that one broad economic effect of the property tax is to shift resources into investment in humans rather than capital goods.

A related effect of the property tax is to reduce the rate of return on capital investment. With an increase in the property tax, consumption becomes relatively more attractive than investment in property. This might tend to reduce saving, investment, and economic growth. Two observations should be made in this connection. With respect to consumers there is an indirect relationship between amount of saving and availability of capital to investing firms. The rate of interest is controlled to a great extent by monetary authorities. A reduction in consumer saving does not automatically mean less investment and slower economic growth. Second, businesses do not usually have a choice between consumption and investment but merely among alternative investments. If we assume that the government keeps aggregate demand high, the overall attractiveness of investment should also remain high. We might even assume that monetary authorities reduce the rate of interest, so that the net rate of return remains unchanged. Perhaps this is carrying our chain of logic a mite too far; yet the assumption that monetary and fiscal authorities will compensate for shifts in aggregate demand is not so farfetched.

Using this general perspective allows us once again to observe an important point: In order to make a final evaluation of most taxes it is necessary to know if and how the revenue is used. If we assume that a new property tax is imposed but no resources are withdrawn from the private sector, compensatory action by the monetary and fiscal authorities may minimize any effect on the composition of spending.

Several empirical studies have attempted to trace the incidence of the tax and its effects on income distribution.[10] These studies typically show

[10] For a survey of these studies see D. Netzer, *Economics of the Property Tax* (Washington, D.C.: Brookings, 1966), chap. 3.

the tax to be highly regressive. Where only homeowners are considered, regression stems from the fact that the proportion of income spent on housing falls as income rises. If no shifting of owner to tenant is accounted for, the regressivity observed is smaller (and in some cases progression seems to hold). However, the important question relative to income distribution is whether property taxes are passed on to low-income tenants. In many low-income housing markets the alternatives open to the tenant are few, owing to his lack of mobility and lack of access to credit. These market imperfections suggest that the tax is shifted to tenants in such situations, thus adding to the regressivity of the tax. It is difficult to measure the incidence precisely.

Studies attempting to ascertain and measure the incidence of property tax on businesses suffer similar difficulties. For the most part a general property tax on all businesses will be passed on to consumers according to the elasticity of the market demand curve. Assuming adequate aggregate demand, the tax is roughly equivalent to a general sales tax. To the extent that the property-labor ratio between firms differs, the labor-intensive firms are favored. When the actual provisions of business property taxes are studied, it is evident that the practice of taxing different types of property at different rates creates considerable non-neutrality with respect to both input and output prices.

CAPITALIZATION OF THE PROPERTY TAX

It is often held that little shifting from person to person can take place in response to the imposition of a property tax. In other words, the full burden of the tax is usually assumed to remain with the person owning the property when the property is first taxed. Although this view is generally held, legislators imposing the tax probably assume that somehow future property owners will also pay the tax. Property tax "capitalization" means that the whole burden rests on the current property holder. Since the net income flow through time from the taxed property is reduced by the amount of the tax, future purchasers will buy only if the expected return from their investment is as high as other alternatives. Consequently, the owner of the taxed property can sell his property only if he reduces its price to the new capitalized value of the expected income flow. The purchaser will pay only an amount equal to the reduced capital value and will thus escape the tax.

The probable assumption of most legislators enacting a property tax is

---

that its burden will fall on property owners through time in relation to the income earned.

The actual result is somewhere between these two positions. If the tax is *general* and applies to all capital, the purchaser has no alternative except to purchase taxed capital. Consequently, he cannot escape the tax. The current owner bears the burden only to the extent that the net income stream is reduced during the period of his ownership. *No tax capitalization takes place.*

Few of the existing property taxes are completely general; to the extent that the tax is less than general, part of the tax will be capitalized. At the state level the sale of taxed property must compete with the alternatives of purchasing bonds, stocks, and other instruments of firms outside the state. At the local level even more alternatives are available. Real estate purchasers, for example, may simply purchase property outside the boundaries of the locality and thus escape the tax. In such cases it is difficult for the present owner to escape tax capitalization.

Yet one important qualification should be mentioned. A new property tax will probably be accompanied by increased public services to members of the locality in question. This would tend to increase the value of the property and offset the capitalization of the property tax. Here, again, consideration not only of costs imposed by a tax but also of benefits deriving from related public expenditures is necessary if the effect on welfare is to be adequately evaluated.

DEATH AND GIFT TAXES

When compared to other tax sources, death and gift taxes yield quite a modest revenue, amounting to less than one and one-half percent of all governmental revenue. As we shall see, however, these taxes have important effects on the allocation of resources and the distribution of wealth and income.

There are two main types of death taxes: the *estate tax*, whose base is all property of the deceased, and the *inheritance tax*, whose base is the property received by a particular individual.

FEDERAL ESTATE TAX

The federal estate tax has a progressive rate structure ranging from 3 to 77 percent. It makes no allowance for differences in the *number* of beneficiaries to which the estate is transferred; however, certain exemptions and deductions are granted. All estates valued at $60,000 or less are entirely exempt. Consequently, only about 2 percent of all deaths result in transfers of property which incur federal estate tax liability. Property passing to the decedent's wife or husband is allowed a deduction equal to one-half of its value. Administrative and funeral expenses as well as debt claims upon the estate also are deductible.

Certain tax credits are allowed against the tax bill. The most important is a credit for death taxes paid to states. This credit, which can offset up to 80 percent of the federal estate tax liability,[11] has been quite important in influencing the structure of state death tax laws.

STATE DEATH TAXES

Prior to 1926, when the provision for federal credit for state taxes was adopted, states had widely varying death tax structures. Some states competed with each other in attracting wealthy elderly citizens by lowering their death tax rates. The Revenue Act of 1926 put limits upon this competition, since revenue within the 80 percent credit would be collected either at the federal or state level. Many states with low estate taxes changed their laws to insure that this revenue was paid to state coffers. Only Nevada has chosen to impose no death taxes and thus forego such revenue. While only five states now have " pick-up " taxes designed to impose a tax just equal to the federal credit, forty others have clauses which " pick up " this revenue if its collection is not otherwise provided for in their tax law. Thirty-six states rely on inheritance taxes rather than estate taxes; however, all but three of these have estate taxes to assure collection of the federal credit.

The states' preference for inheritance taxes dates from the first death tax enacted by Pennsylvania in 1825. Other states have enacted similar taxes, but these early experiments were of no lasting effect; the modern inheritance tax is modeled after that imposed by Wisconsin in 1903. The most notable feature of the state taxes is their diversity. Tax liability for similar estates or inheritances is quite different among states. Certain types of heirs are totally exempt in some states, while others may have no exemptions. The inheritance tax rates are usually progressive, but they usually differ according to the type of heir. For example, the rate may range from 1 to 4 percent for spouse, child, or parent; from 3 to 12 percent for brother or sister; and from 5 to 20 percent for nonrelatives. The estate taxes are also progressive, ranging from .8 to 23 percent. Only 13 states incorporate gift taxes into their tax law.

GIFT TAXES

The federal gift tax complements the estate tax. Just as the estate is the tax base at death, the gift tax is imposed on the giver. The tax is cumulative. The liability for a particular year is figured by subtracting from the tax on all gifts (since 1932 when the law was enacted) the amount of tax liability (already paid) on gifts up to the current year. The gift tax rate is 75 percent of the estate tax rate; thus, the individual can partially escape the estate tax by giving before he dies. Certain exemptions and deductions further encourage giving. An amount of $3000 can be excluded from the gift tax base annually (for the married couples this amounts to $6000). An *additional* $30,000 exemption on gifts may be taken at any time (for the estate of a married couple this exemption is $60,000). The gifts from spouse to spouse also receive special treatment, being taxed at half their value in a fashion similar to the estate tax. Finally, there are exemptions for gifts donated to certain nonprofit charitable, religious, and educational institutions.

Since the primary function of the gift tax is to complement the estate tax, it is not needed when inheritance rather than estate taxes are imposed.

DEATH TAXES, WELFARE, AND EFFICIENCY

Welfare maximization involves the wedding of society's priorities with the economy's production possibilities. Thus, welfare criteria involve society's basic notions of equity, individual freedom and opportunity, and a " proper " distribution of income as well as the specific question of whether individual material wants are met by efficient allocation of resources.

DEATH TAXES AND CONCEPTS OF EQUITY

Individuals within our society take different views of the equity of the estate and inheritance taxes. Some question whether it is equitable when certain persons, through no effort of their own, inherit great wealth while other persons are not so benefited. Those who voice such reservations usually argue that our economic system should offer each citizen equal *opportunity* and that the right of some to receive a large inheritance conflicts with this goal. On the other hand, some feel that one of the rights

---

[11] The allowable credit is based on the value of the estate and is stated as a table of graduated rates on taxable estates exceeding $40,000.

which goes along with the freedom to acquire, own, and transfer property is the right to decide who shall receive it upon death.

Such opinions are obviously value judgments and as such are not open to economic analysis—just as in the case of deciding the "proper" distribution of income.

DEATH TAXES AND DISTRIBUTION OF WEALTH AND INCOME

Can we view our estate and inheritance taxes as part of society's income distribution goal? Presumably political institutions within a democratic society allow individuals and groups to implement a tax system roughly in accord with their wishes. There is, in fact, general consensus in favor of the tax; however, much of the consensus derives from the fact that only 2 percent must pay. We are aware that judging the tax strictly in terms of a social goal would involve value judgments we are not prepared to make. The fundamental reason for considering the "redistribution goal" is to provide a point of departure for examining the efficiency of the institution used to implement the public sector's redistribution function. While the redistribution which takes place under the federal estate tax does not seem to circumvent the redistribution function, it seems less efficient than would an inheritance tax. The redistribution goal is most easily stated in terms of the distribution of wealth among individuals rather than estates.

The federal and most state taxes are highly progressive, the marginal rate ranging from 3 to 77 percent. Generally speaking, the tax hits hardest at the very wealthy. The vast majority of estates escape the federal tax, and almost half of the revenue collected comes from estates valued at $1 million or more.

Another distributive effect of death and gift taxes stems from the exemption of transfers to charitable and education institutions. Although indirect, this provision has significant long-run redistributive effects. Presumably the benefited charitable and educational institutions give services to many who otherwise could not afford them. Moreover, services of educational institutions enhance the income earning capacity of the recipients.

THE ALLOCATION OF RESOURCES AMONG INSTITUTIONS

The exemption of death transfers to charitable and educational institutions also affects allocation of society's resources. We can assume that more resources are devoted to these institutions and their services than would be the case without the tax. However, to the extent that the services provided by the recipient institutions would otherwise have been provided by government, the present system features less decision making on the part of government and more on the part of private nonprofit institutions.

THE ALLOCATION OF RESOURCES: CHOICE BETWEEN WORK AND LEISURE

Death taxes, like income taxes, change the relative prices of work and leisure—work becoming relatively less remunerative. This implies a non-neutral effect on choices individuals make between work and leisure. At the immediate microeconomic level the imposition of the tax not only reduces an individual's welfare by reducing income but also arbitrarily changes the price ratio. The latter observation *presumes* that the "correct" price ratio between work and leisure existed before the tax.

A possible deterrent to the individual's substitution of leisure for work comes from the "income effect" of the tax. As in the case of the personal income tax, the "income effect" reduces work income and may reduce or offset the substitution effect. The net effect on work effort is hard to predict. The imposition of the tax may cause the individual to work harder in order to provide his heirs with the inheritance he had originally planned; or he may react by working less because leisure has become relatively cheaper. The importance of this income effect is hard to predict; however, it would seem to be less than that of the "income effect" in the personal income tax situation. Moreover, since income and substitution effects tend to offset each other, it seems likely that empirical observation of the net effect could accompany only a relatively large change in the tax structure. To date no empirical evidence has been presented which substantiates a large nonneutral effect on the individual's choice between work and leisure.

The death tax is essentially an excise tax on the transfer of property between individuals—the special condition being that one of the individuals is no longer alive. As such, the death tax by itself is obviously not general. The individual may escape the tax either by not acquiring property in the first place or by transferring his property to someone else *prior* to death. The gift tax, then, is an appropriate complement to the death tax by increasing its *certainty*. The federal estate and gift tax rates are generally biased towards giving; hence, one may partially escape the estate tax by giving. Other built-in escapes are the exemptions of wealth transferred to certain charitable, religious, and educational institutions. The individual may also take advantage of various trust fund devices. Finally, the individual may escape the tax by consuming rather than saving or by substituting leisure for work and income. One condition of the tax is quite certain—that all estate owners will eventually die.

THE ALLOCATION OF RESOURCES: CONCENTRATION IN INDUSTRY

The allocation of resources may also be affected by the need for highly liquid assets within the estate to pay the estate inheritance tax. If the estate were entirely in the form of closely held stocks for which there was a small market, the necessity to sell at death might result in substantial losses. If death occurs when money is tight, the loss may be even greater. It has been hypothesized that individuals, anticipating such possibilities, attempt to structure their estate so that it contains enough liquid assets to pay the tax liability. The tax may then be said to have nonneutral effects on relative prices of liquid vs. less easily marketable assets. Potentially this effect could have substantial influence on the allocation of the economy's resources. It would follow that industries financed by typically more liquid assets would more easily obtain credit and thus grow more than they would without the tax.

The need for liquidity might also influence resource allocation by encouraging mergers. Assume again that the estate is in the form of closely held securities. The possibility of a liquidity crisis at death might lead the owner to sell or to merge the firm with a larger firm. In the latter case, the merger could be accomplished by exchanging securities, and no capital gains tax need be paid. After the merger, the estate would contain more liquid assets: the stock of the larger firm.

While both these factors probably have some effect on individual behavior, their overall significance is probably small. In the first place, most large estates would include an adequate amount of liquid assets to pay the tax anyway. Moreover, since the tax applies only to a small portion of assets held at any one time, the overall impact on resource allocation is probably quite small. Of the two, the influence toward mergers is probably the more significant, but the overall impact would be difficult to discern.

THE ALLOCATION OF RESOURCES BETWEEN CONSUMPTION AND INVESTMENT

Death and gift taxes, like income taxes, may influence decisions between consuming and saving and, in turn, the allocation of resources between consumption and investment. The argument is similar to the work-vs.-

leisure argument. The death tax reduces the effectiveness of income left to the individual's benefactors. The tax increases the price of leaving income to one's heirs; the individual will *substitute* consumption for saving. We have noted that there is a rather tenuous link between saving and real investment, since different people make the two types of decisions. The link becomes more tenuous if we assume that the monetary authorities can and do influence the interest rate and the availability of credit to encourage " adequate " investment spending. We can probably assume, however, that a significant increase in consumption over savings would encourage resources to flow towards consumption-oriented industries and to flow away from the capital goods industries.

A further reservation to the hypothesis that death taxes reduce investment comes from the influence of the " income effect." The " substitution effect " occurs as a result of the change in relative prices in favor of consumption. The " income effect " results from taxes' lowering the individual's real income. The tax lowers the effectiveness of the estate's wealth. If the individual has the welfare of his estate's recipients at heart, the tax's imposition may cause him to increase rather than decrease his savings plans. In other words, the " income effect " may be more powerful than the " substitution effect." In such a case the income and substitution effects are in opposite directions, so that they at least partially offset each other. The net result is quite hard to predict, and empirical evidence is hard to come by. Most researchers have concluded that the effect of the death tax on investment via savings decisions is insignificant.

SOCIAL SECURITY TAXES

Although the social security tax is a direct tax on income we did not consider it with the personal income tax because the functions of the two are fundamentally different. The dual function of the personal income tax is to furnish general revenue and provide for income redistribution. The function of the social security tax is to finance a social insurance program. Although elements of redistribution are present the tax is basically a user charge for insurance produced by the public sector. Other differences are the types of income included and the fact that part of the social security tax is paid by the employer.

As outlined in Chapter 7 the social security programs began as part of the New Deal in the 1930s. They have been greatly expanded since that time. During the years 1937–1949 the maximum taxable base was $3000,

TABLE 13–1	Year	Trust fund in billions of dollars
Assets of old-age and	1937	0.3
survivors insurance trust	1939	1.2
fund, selected years	1941	2.4
1937–1974	1943	4.3
	1945	6.6
	1947	8.8
	1949	11.3
	1951	14.7
	1953	18.4
	1955	21.1
	1957	23.0
	1959	21.5
	1961	20.9
	1963	19.0
	1965	20.2
	1967	23.5
	1969	28.2
	1970	32.7
	1972	37.9
	1974	51.5

and the employer and employee each were taxed at a 1 percent rate for a maximum of $60 per employee. Since 1950 the taxable base and the rate have been raised frequently until the base is now $10,800 and the combined rate is 11.7 percent. The expected contributions to the program have risen from $2.1 billion in 1939, $5.7 billion in 1949 to about $78.2 billion in 1974.

EVALUATING SOCIAL INSURANCE TAXES

Our evaluation of the social insurance taxes depends importantly on the perspective used. Should we view the social insurance program as a private good provided by the public sector? If so, it is appropriate to view the social security taxes simply as " user-charges " to those insured.

Much of our earlier discussion differentiating between the Ability-to-Pay and the Benefit perspectives of taxation are relevant here. If we judge the tax under ability-to-pay norms it fares poorly. The proportional rate applied to a maximum base makes the tax quite regressive. Consequently the tax stands condemned under the " equal sacrifice " criteria under almost any assumption as to how rapidly the marginal utility of income diminishes.

Viewed from the Benefit perspective, the regressivity of the tax is less onerous since payments to the program are directly associated with benefits in a manner similar to insurance programs in the private sector.

DEBATE TOPIC: SHOULD THE PROGRAM BE ACTUARIALLY SOUND?

At its inception as part of the New Deal, the social security program was seen primarily from the Benefit perspective. A trust fund was set up to receive revenues from the social security taxes, to invest the funds, and to make payments to the insuree (or his survivors) at his retirement (or death or disability). The usual criteria of actuarial soundness for such a fund hold that the contributions by the individual and his employer plus the returns on investment should equal the probable payment to the individual (or his beneficiaries) upon retirement (or death or disability). Moreover the rationale in setting up the trust fund would be that the fund should be able to cover any obligations already incurred, were the program discontinued at any point in time. This approach would require that when benefits were increased for a particular person, his payments be increased accordingly.

Table 13.1 shows the way the social security trust fund has grown over the years. The trend of growth reflects the changing attitude of Congress towards the necessity of keeping the program "actuarially sound." Although the program has never been "sound" on strict actuarial criteria, in its early years the trust fund was expanded sufficiently to roughly meet future obligations. But over the years benefits have been expanded regularly without compensating increases in taxes. Indeed, starting in 1958, benefit payments have approximated and even slightly surpassed the yearly revenue. Therefore, while obligations have been greatly expanded, the trust fund has not kept pace. Although Congress has not explicitly debated the issue, an important *public choice* is inherent in the shift from treating the social insurance program on a roughly actuarial basis to one which merely balances yearly expenditures and revenues. Thus we must ask who benefits and who loses from the shift in policy? Before answering let us consider the other perspectives for evaluating gains and losses.

If we use the Ability-to-Pay perspective the trust fund is not required at all. The obligations to those insured are taken "as given"—essentially a transfer payment—and the question becomes: How should the burden of the tax be apportioned? Presumably we should work from a norm such

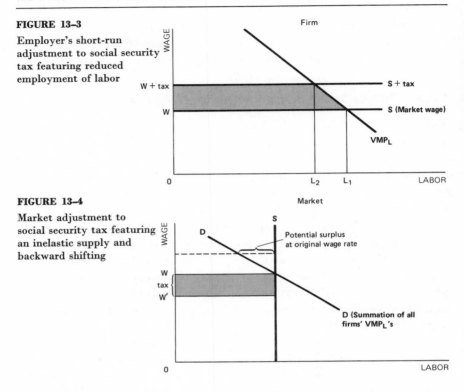

FIGURE 13–3

Employer's short-run adjustment to social security tax featuring reduced employment of labor

FIGURE 13–4

Market adjustment to social security tax featuring an inelastic supply and backward shifting

as " equal sacrifice " so as to minimize the burden of the tax. As noted the regressivity of the social security taxes receives low marks under this criteria.

A third alternative is to view social insurance from the Benefit approach but to see it as a continuing social contract. If the program is continual, all that is required for solvency is that revenues keep pace with current outlays. The basic observation is that current taxpayers support the current group of retirees (and survivors) with the understanding that they will be supported similarly when their time comes. Yet inherent in this social contract are several important factors which change as succeeding generations participate in the program. In the first place both population and personal income may be expected to grow so that the current tax base (or ability-to-pay) is always ahead of the current obligations. Thus the current taxpaying group benefits from previous growth. Secondly, benefits will probably be expanded over time. Part of the increase in benefits may be seen simply as compensation for rising costs of living and thus no real gain for the recipients. But periodic benefit expansion also creates real gains for those who receive more benefits than promised when they were taxpayers. The latter "bonus" is an *intergenerational transfer* from the current to the former taxpayer.

After considering the question of who actually pays the social insurance taxes, we will return to the problem of relating costs to benefits.

WHO PAYS?

The question of who pays the social security taxes is another instance where the opinion of economists differs from that of most Americans. For example, most Americans assume that they pay only the 5.8 percent tax levied on their taxable base. But traditional economic theory holds that the amount the employer pays is also shifted directly to the employee.

The traditional argument relies on the model of a rational employer choosing input combinations based on the value of the input's marginal product, VMP. The employer's part of the social security tax is directly tied to how much labor he hires. The tax increases the cost of employing labor as an input. If we depict the adjustment in terms of the familiar equi-marginal rule, we see that the employer has incentive to hire less labor and more capital until the ratios of VMP to cost are once again equal:

$$\frac{VMP_L \uparrow}{w + t_x \uparrow} = \frac{VMP_K \downarrow}{r}$$

(where $w + t_x$ is wage rate plus tax and r is the interest rate or rather the cost of capital). The solid arrow shows the initial change in labor costs while the dash arrows show the adjustment towards less labor (thus raising VMP_L) and more capital (thus lowering VMP_K). Figure 13.3 shows the short-run adjustment the employer would attempt to make if labor were the only variable.

Backward shifting is insured if the market supply of labor is inelastic as shown in Figure 13.4. This is probable since the social security tax is so general (it covers most types of work) and the tax's income effect may well offset the substitution effect of the work-leisure choice.

As the firms attempt to readjust their input composition, a surplus of marginal workers appears. This surplus forces the market wage downward until in the final equilibrium the tax is completely shifted to labor.

As a final "clincher" the traditional argument notes that since no increase in the money supply is assumed it follows that the tax cannot be shifted forward since at higher prices there would not be sufficient spending to clear the market. Actually this observation is not quite as straightforward as it seems. Once the macroeconomic question is broached another layer of complexity is revealed.[12]

An alternative assumption about employer behavior is that instead of reducing employment he attempts to pass the tax burden on to the consumer in the form of higher output prices. In classical theory featuring perfect competition this is not possible. But in the "real world" of imperfect knowledge, labor union power to resist wage reductions, and "cost-plus" pricing by firms, we might well expect employers to raise output prices (which may or may not lead eventually to reduced sales and employment).

As with other taxes the response we may expect from a particular firm depends on the competitiveness of its market, its accepted rules of pricing and employment, and the current state of economic growth. If the economy is in the first stages of expansion and the firm's sales are expanding, it can readily pass increased taxes on to the consumer; and, in fact, since shortages of labor are occurring, wages may well be increasing. Subsequent expansion of the economy will lead to higher prices of both outputs and inputs, but since the tax now acts as a wedge between the wage rate and the input's value of marginal product, the wage rate will not rise as much as output prices and the return to capital.

To summarize, regardless of the nature of competition and macroeconomic situation posed, the theoretical analysis leads to the conclusion that *labor bears both the employee and employer parts of the tax.* The time it takes for the backward shift however differs according to the situation. If the tax is raised during the downswing when surplus labor is already abundant, backward shifting will occur with little delay. If the tax is raised during the period of rapidly expanding consumer spending, the tax may initially be passed on to the consumer. An increase in the tax may even accentuate a "cost-push" situation. As outlined earlier, rational price setting for both inputs and outputs is not possible in the prisoner's dilemma imposed by the cost-push phenomenon. Although individual labor unions, wholesalers, retailers, etc. may be aware that their mutual actions will lead to inflation, they are each caught up in the competition to push their own wages and prices in order to maintain their relative position.

Since the tax is so general and since so many other factors have affected the relative shares of labor and capital through time, it would be impossible to prove conclusively that the tax's burden rests solely on labor. A recent study comparing real wages in countries with varying employment taxes lends support to the hypothesis that the employer's part is fully shifted backward. John A. Brittain ran cross-section regression analyses of aggregative data for 64 countries.[13] Various sophisticated techniques were employed in an attempt to isolate the long-run impact of the employer's part of the taxes on real wage rates. Brittain's calculations suggested that differences in wage rates and tax rates could be "explained" quite well under the full backward-shifting hypothesis.

Some would agree that the employer tax causes a long-run substitution of capital for labor. This supposedly follows because the tax makes labor more costly. But if the burden is fully shifted backward as theory and Brittain's study suggest, this long-run substitution is slight. Thus the tax does little to curtail job opportunities. As indicated previously, the backward-shifting result depends importantly on an *inelastic* supply curve for labor. There are several reasons we expect labor supply to be inelastic. First the tax is general and most job opportunities are covered. Secondly there are few good substitutes for the income earned from being employed. Finally while the shifted tax is a cost to the employee, *there are also benefits* forthcoming from his participating in the social security program. Consequently, even if it were possible to shift to a job with slightly higher wages but no social security coverage, the individual might well choose to remain.

[12] We have already encountered the difficulties involved in various assumptions about what macroeconomic policy will accompany a change in a specific tax. We have found the assumption that the government will not replenish aggregate spending power somewhat strained. Such an assumption is even more awkward when analyzing the social security tax, since the link between tax and expenditure is direct.

[13] John A. Brittain, "The Incidence of Social Security Payroll Taxes," *American Economic Review*, March 1971, pp. 110–125.

14

TAXES AND EXPENDITURES: SOME CONCLUSIONS AND SUGGESTIONS

THE BUDGET AND INDIVIDUAL WELFARE RECONSIDERED

We conclude our microeconomic analysis of taxes and expenditures by shifting once again to the general perspective. First we return briefly to the question of the impact of individual taxes and expenditures and the overall effect of the budget as a whole. This review introduces the question of how taxes are interrelated with respect to our fiscal goals. Then, finally, we will consider suggestions for improving our taxes and expenditures.

One obvious conclusion from our survey of the budget's microeconomic effects is that there are a myriad of ways the various taxes and expenditures affect individual welfare and behavior. We have found it difficult to trace the incidence of several of our major taxes. Thus it seems unlikely that we can estimate the net impact of the budget on an individual's welfare with any precision.

Our previous analysis has revealed the impossibility of measuring the welfare of individuals and relating it to the public sector budget. A major problem is the measurement of welfare. Even if an appropriate standard could be found, summing up costs and benefits would involve interpersonal welfare comparisons and necessary value judgments. Another dimension of the problem is added by the nature of public goods which, by *requiring joint consumption*, requires also that we evaluate their *collective* benefits. It turns out that it is impossible to make an evaluation of public expenditures even in dollar terms without making assumptions about how the well-being of different individuals and groups is affected. Can we, for example, simply assume that everyone benefits equally from a public good such as defense?

Measuring welfare lost via the individual's tax bill has also proven difficult. In the preceding chapters, we have attempted to trace the incidence of the various taxes making up our present system. We have encountered serious difficulty arriving at monetary calculations of incidence. Even if we could successfully make such monetary calculations they would not necessarily be a consistent measure of the taxes' effects on the *welfare* of different individuals.

Once again we observe that two major difficulties arise in measuring the benefits or costs of public expenditures and taxes in terms of individual welfare. The first difficulty is tracing the incidence . . . who benefits and who pays? The second difficulty occurs because individual preferences differ and the monetary incidence may not reflect the change in an individual's welfare.

448

LINKING EXPENDITURES AND TAXES

A recurrent theme in our attempt to evaluate the public budget has been to *link* expenditures and taxes so as to generalize in terms of marginal benefits and costs. The directness of links between expenditures and taxes varies.

Since the federal personal income tax and defense spending are of approximately equal size and are the largest items in the budget, it is possible to tenuously link the two. Since both are so visible it follows that many individuals evaluate the two together. That is, they ask the question: "Am I willing to pay more income tax for more defense?"

On the other hand there are many other federal expenditures which the individual may link with his tax dollar. And the individual may also reason that these other activities are "marginal" in the sense that Congress would curtail them first if the income tax were lowered. Consider the conservative who favors more defense spending but passionately objects to federal aid to families with dependent children. His resistance to tax increases will depend on his estimate of their impact on expenditures. Which will be expanded: defense expenditures or welfare? His estimate depends on his assessment of the attitudes of the Administration and Congress.

In summary the individual's assessment of the "opportunity costs" inherent in the income tax depends importantly on where he thinks the additional increments would be spent.

Other taxes and expenditures have more direct connections. Federal and state gasoline taxes are often earmarked for highway construction. The price of gasoline does not *exactly* reflect the opportunity costs—due to oil import quotas, differentials in traffic congestion and other hidden costs and benefits. Even so, the price of gasoline to the individual includes a rough approximation of the costs of highway building and maintenance. Thus the costs he faces when adjusting his use of the public highways (relative to other private expenditures) encourage adjustment roughly conforming to the equi-marginal rule. In describing the incidence of gasoline taxes it would hardly be appropriate to castigate their "nonneutrality" on the grounds that they cause individuals to substitute other activities for driving. Indeed, one purpose of making the tax a "user charge" is to encourage such behavior.

We have also noted a direct link between social security taxes and social insurance received by the individual. Although the program produces external benefits to society, most of the benefits go directly to the individual. Consequently taxation of the insured individuals is based on the benefits received.[1] Since participation is compulsory, the "user" cannot adjust the quantity purchased as in the case of highway usage. Consequently a marginal benefit-marginal cost adjustment by each individual is not possible. On the other hand there is a highly visible link between insurance benefits and the tax. The voters and their representatives are well aware that increased benefits will probably mean increased taxes. Thus it is not difficult for voters to assess the program in terms of marginal costs and benefits, and to the extent that our budgetary process is responsive to our collective decisions, the quantities of resources devoted to the program are in accord with our resource allocation criteria.

Similar considerations hold for the link between the services offered by localities and the local property tax. The "nonneutrality" of a higher property tax increases the attractiveness of untaxed property. But the accompanying public services such as police and fire protection, streets, sidewalks, and lighting will tend to offset the former effect.

Within the context of this overview, we conclude that the visible links among several of our most important expenditures and taxes encourage welfare maximizing behavior by individual voters and consumers. Yet we have also noted that several other of our most important expenditures and taxes do not seem to lend themselves to this argument. We have noted that the link between defense spending and the federal personal income tax is tenuous at best. What can we say about the corporation income tax? Can we argue that the corporate tax is complementary to the tax on personal income so that both are evaluated in terms of the benefits from defense spending? Or would it be more appropriate to link all of the public aids to business (such as the patent system, foreign trade policy, public support of research and transportation and direct subsidies to business) to the corporation tax? Either approach would further strain our argument. In any event visibility of the tax is not sufficient for the average voter to make benefit-cost comparisons.

Another "poor fit" between expenditure and tax is the relationship between education and the sales and property taxes. The question of how to finance education is a crucial one and will be a center of controversy in the next few years. It appears that the states will feel obliged to make changes in the revenue systems now in use. Currently there are important differences among states in their roles in educational finance relative to the roles played by their localities. In some states most of the revenue for education is funneled through the state government and dispersed according to some formula of the "needs" of the localities (such as the number of pupils on the locality's roles). In other states the state government plays a smaller role and the education expenditure depends more on the preferences *and resources* of the locality. On the average, states furnish about 40 percent of the revenue for public elementary and secondary schools. Thus the major part must be borne by the locality which must rely on the property tax. Since property wealth differs greatly from locality to locality, there are great differences in expenditure per pupil. The public choice question here is not so much whether individual voters can assess benefits and costs. From one perspective it would seem that placing the education decision at the local level would enhance resource allocation—especially since increased expenditures often require a local referendum linking taxes and spending. But another important question revolves around whether voters view educational opportunity from a local, state or national perspective. Since localities differ widely in ability-to-pay, a broader perspective suggests that a broader tax base be used.

Our observations have brought us back to a fundamental feature of public and quasi-public goods which must be accounted for in evaluating expenditures and taxes in terms of public choice efficiency. Our general equilibrium models infer that efficiency is enhanced if individuals are free to make adjustments according to their own preferences. It would seem also that allowing localities to differ in the composition of public services offered would enhance efficiency, especially since individuals are free to move to that community offering the budget they prefer. But where benefits are collective, and abilities to pay are inconsistent with the scope and nature of the benefits, the advantages of diversity may not hold.

SOME GENERALIZATIONS ABOUT COLLECTIVE BENEFITS

As we have seen, the nature of the *benefits* is crucial in any attempt to link expenditures with taxes. One reason individuals fail to link defense expenditures with their own income tax bill is that the benefits from defense are collective. The "free rider" is at work here. While he may

[1] We discussed alternative approaches for linking social security taxes and benefits in Chapter 13.

make a connection between defense spending and *income taxes in general*, he may not make a connection between defense spending and his own tax bill.

In other cases the benefits are more direct so that a connection between taxes and expenditures is more easily seen. We have observed that benefits produced by gasoline taxes and social security taxes are fairly direct. Thus it is hardly pertinent to argue that the nonneutrality of the gasoline tax causes people to substitute other activities for driving. We must also consider that expenditures on highway construction make driving more attractive. Similarly the effect of imposing a property tax would be to influence prospective buyers to buy elsewhere. But the accompanying public services (such as police and fire protection, and street lighting) will tend to offset the former effect. Where the link between costs and benefits is fairly close citizens should, and usually do, evaluate the two together.

Another important aspect of tax and expenditure interrelatedness concerns the benefits consumed by individuals of various tastes and income levels. The benefits of a pure public goods such as defense are indivisible, and sometimes said to be enjoyed *equally* by all. But it certainly cannot be said that all persons receive equal *satisfaction* from defense expenditures. Without sufficient knowledge of individual preference patterns we cannot of course assess the benefits precisely. If, as supposed in Chapter 9, a positive income effect applies to most public as well as to most private goods, we can expect that the marginal benefits derived from a given expenditure on defense are relatively greater, the higher an individual's income. It follows that taxes associated with expenditures of this type should increase with the income of the individual. Benefits from public goods may increase with income for reasons other than simply a positive "income effect." An early benefit approach argument for progressive taxation, we recall, was that the services of the state protect and enhance the productivity of wealth; consequently, the wealthy should pay more taxes. Defense expenditures (to include police and fire protection) tend to make the current distribution of wealth more secure. Similarly expenditures (such as foreign aid, trade missions, and basic research) which enhance the productivity of capital would seem to call for taxes on the owners of capital.

On the other hand certain types of expenditures directly benefit the lower income groups. Aid to families with dependent children, aid for the blind, old-age assistance, and federal housing, are in fact specifically designed for that purpose. Justification for funding these expenditures from a progressive income tax must come from the income distribution goal rather than the goal of linking taxes and direct benefits.

Instead of being able to trace benefits and costs (and income redistribution) with some precision as in our imaginary Fiscal Department model, we find it difficult to make even a rough estimate of the impact of taxes and expenditures on individual welfare. Indeed estimation of the net incidence of the budget even on *monetary income* is hazardous.

THE BUDGET AND INDIVIDUAL INCOME RECONSIDERED

Can we decipher society's distribution goal from that inherent in the budget? The most visible rate structure is that of the personal income tax. But most people are aware that many other taxes and expenditures affect distribution. At the same time few people have good insight as to the net redistribution caused by the budget. It is also doubtful that the public knows the differences between nominal and actual rates of the income tax. Individuals of the same income level pay widely different taxes. Some of these differences are the result of exemptions and deductions designed to treat " unequals " unequally. Thus they reflect rational tax policy. But other differences seem to thwart the goal of equal treatment among equals.

A related problem is that special provisions allow the actual progression in rates to depart substantially from the nominal progression. If society actually wants a rate structure with only small progression (especially at the very top) then why does not the actual rate structure reflect this? One possible answer is that the preferences of society in general are thwarted by special interest groups gaining special provisions. A factor encouraging such behavior is the complexity of tax legislation. This creates a " fiscal illusion " which inhibits the public from distinguishing the actual from the nominal rates.

In previous chapters the incidence of various taxes has been examined. The personal income tax was found to be much less progressive than the marginal rates would suggest due to considerable erosion of the tax base through exemptions. We found the effect of the corporation income tax on individual income also hard to measure due to the difficulty in tracing the shifting and incidence of the tax. If fully shifted, the tax acts as a sales tax and as such is regressive since the lower income groups save at a lower rate. If the tax falls on the stockholder, it is progressive since upper

FIGURE 14–1

Overall tax burden by
income class (1954)

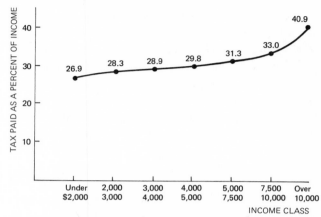

Source: Richard A. Musgrave, "The Incidence of the Tax
Structure and the Effects on Consumption," in Joint
Committee on the Economic Report, *Federal Tax Policy
for Economic Growth and Stability* (Washington, D.C.;
U.S. Government Printing Office, 1955), p. 98.

TABLE 14–1

Estimated tax rates as a
percent of family income

Family income level (1)	Federal taxes (2)	State and local taxes (3)	All taxes, or (2) + (3) (4)
Under $2,000	13.0%	15.1%	28.1%
$2,000–2,999	14.0	12.7	26.7
$3,000–3,999	17.1	12.6	29.7
$4,000–4,999	17.3	11.8	29.1
$5,000–5,999	17.9	11.5	29.4
$6,000–7,499	17.8	10.8	28.5
$7,500–9,999	18.4	10.1	28.5
$10,000–14,999	21.1	9.6	30.6
$15,000 and over	34.9	9.1	44.0

Source: *Allocating Tax Burdens and Government Benefits
by Income Class* (New York: Tax Foundation, 1967), p. 7.
Data for 1965.

income groups hold wealth in that form. We (or rather the author) opted
for the latter arguments but with the provision that partial shifting may
take place where monopoly positions have not previously been exploited.

The general sales tax was found to be regressive but less so if food is
exempted. Property tax incidence turns out to be highly regressive for
low-income tenants and homeowners and nearly proportional for other
income categories. If tenants are included and no shifting allowed for,

the tax appears to be slightly progressive for middle income groups. With shifting, which is particularly evident in housing for the poor, the tax is seen to be regressive. Excise taxes have various effects but most are highly regressive. The tax on cigarettes is perhaps our most regressive tax; however, the tax on liquor is slightly progressive.

What is the net effect of these taxes taken together on the distribution of income? A study by Musgrave and others for 1954 estimated the overall tax burden at that time to be roughly *proportional for the middle income levels accounting for the great majority of families.* The results, illustrated in Figure 14.1, showed progression at low-income and high-income levels. Similar results were obtained by the Tax Foundation in a 1967 study. Their estimate shows the combined rates to be roughly proportional with regression at the low incomes and progression at the high incomes. As Table 14.1 shows, both the federal system and the combined state and local systems are roughly proportional in the middle income ranges. And taken together the tax rate is remarkably proportional from the income level under $2000 (28.1 percent) all the way to the $7000–$9999 level (28.5 percent). Federal taxes are progressive at the extremes; the combined state and local systems are regressive.

Expenditures, if taken in strictly monetary terms, seem to be highly progressive, although the distribution of benefits from specific taxes such as the property tax and the gasoline tax may not be so.[2] In earlier studies[3] as well as a more recent one,[4] benefits are shown to be roughly proportional to costs for the middle income groups. However at the extremities substantial redistribution occurs. Irvin Gillispie's estimates, given in Figure 14.2, are interesting in that they show taxes to have a mixed effect and in fact to be quite regressive in the upper-middle income groups. Expenditures, however, if considered primarily in monetary terms, cause the *net* pattern of income redistribution to be progressive.

---

[2] With regard to the property tax see D. Netzer, *Economics of the Property Tax* (Washington, D.C.: Brookings, 1966), pp. 59–62.

[3] Under the 1946–1947 budgets John Adler found the lowest income groups (under $1000) had real income increased by 73 percent while the highest group (over $7500) had theirs reduced by 22 percent. See Adler's Chapter 8 in Kenyon E. Poole, ed., *Fiscal Policies and the American Economy* (Englewood Cliffs, N.J.: Prentice-Hall, 1951).

[4] W. Irvin Gillispie, "Effects of Public Expenditures on the Distribution of Income," in R. A. Musgrave, ed., *Essays in Fiscal Federalism* (Washington, D.C.: Brookings, 1966), pp. 122–186.

TABLE 14-2

Budgetary incidence as a percentage of total income for all families by income class, 1965

	Under $2000	$2000 to 2999	$3000 to 3999	$4000 to 4999	$5000 to 5999	$6000 to 7499	$7500 to 9999	$10000 to 14999	$15000 and over	Total
Taxes										
Personal	2.9	3.8	5.2	6.9	7.2	7.9	9.1	10.7	28.2	9.6
Corporate	1.2	2.1	4.3	1.7	2.3	1.7	2.0	5.4	15.5	3.8
Social insurance	4.1	4.2	4.5	4.8	4.6	4.4	4.2	3.9	2.1	4.2
Consumption	9.8	8.5	8.6	7.9	7.5	7.0	6.4	5.9	4.4	6.9
Property	7.1	5.3	4.5	3.7	3.4	3.1	3.1	3.4	6.3	3.8
Total taxes	25.1	23.9	27.1	25.0	25.0	24.1	24.8	29.3	56.5	28.3
Expenditures										
General benefit	46.2	26.7	21.2	17.9	16.0	14.3	12.8	11.3	9.3	15.6
Defense and international	26.2	15.1	12.0	10.1	9.0	8.1	7.2	6.4	5.3	8.8
Other	20.0	11.6	9.2	7.8	7.0	6.2	5.6	4.9	4.0	6.9
Nongeneral benefits	62.8	38.3	24.8	15.8	13.4	11.1	9.3	8.7	6.9	14.3
Total expenditures	109.0	65.0	46.0	33.7	29.5	25.4	22.1	20.0	16.3	29.9
Total	83.9	41.1	18.9	8.7	4.5	1.3	-2.7	-9.3	-40.2	1.6

Source: Lester C. Thurow, *The Impact of Taxes on the American Economy* (New York: Praeger, 1971) Table 4-1, p. 73. Calculated by modifying the results of *Tax Burdens and Government Expenditures by Income Class, 1961 and 1965* (New York: Tax Foundation, 1961, 1967).

457

FIGURE 14–2

Redistribution from
taxes and expenditures
by income class (1960)

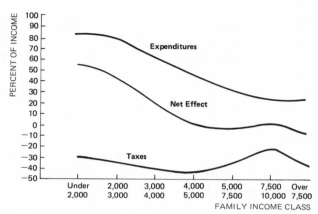

Source: W. Irwin Gillispie, "Effect of Public Expenditure on the Distribution of Income," in R. A. Musgrave, ed. *Essays in Fiscal Federation* (Washington, D.C.: Brookings, 1966), p. 165.

An analysis by Thurow also indicates that the net impact of the budget is progressive.[5] By his estimation of tax incidence by income class, he finds a proportional effect on incomes until the level $10,000 (see Table 14.2). The system becomes progressive for higher incomes due to the burdens imposed on owners of capital. Thurow sees personal taxes as slightly progressive while corporation taxes are generally proportional except for high-income levels. His estimates of regression in the social security and general sales taxes follow our earlier analysis. As Table 14.2 shows, property taxes are regressive for lower income levels but progressive for higher income levels. This is because he assumes that one-half of the property tax is passed on to the consumer and the other half is borne by property owners. Under this assumption the tax would be highly progressive for incomes higher than $15,000 because of the higher concentration of property ownership.

Thurow's estimates show an inverse relationship between benefits and income. He assumes that half of the benefits from general expenditures are distributed by population and half on the basis of income. Even so, he estimates that general benefits are progressively distributed (they fall with income). Nongeneral benefits (that is, those easily traced to a specific beneficiary) are, as we would expect, even more progressively distributed.

---

[5] Lester C. Thurow, *The Impact of Taxes on the American Economy* (New York: Praeger, 1971), chap. 4.

An examination of the budget quickly reveals why most studies show expenditures to be progressive. Those pure public goods such as defense are usually assumed to benefit all income groups equally. More readily measurable are expenditures specifically designed to give direct benefit to the lower income groups. There are, of course, important *indirect* economic effects of the budget which aid the various income groups. For example, there are many indirect benefits to the lower income groups created by public education and the enforcement of civil rights. On the other hand, many indirect benefits accrue to upper income groups through government aids to commerce and transportation, foreign trade policies, and other aids to business.

That these studies should be taken with caution is only too obvious in light of our examination of the incidence of expenditures and taxes in previous chapters. As we have demonstrated, different assumptions in tax shifting models could lead to significantly different estimates of the overall effect.

An attempt to consider the net effect of the budget in terms of individual welfare would be even more adventurous. However, the monetary perspective used in the studies mentioned above may itself be quite misleading. If we accept the argument that public wants (and satisfaction) increase with income, the "benefits" accruing to higher income individuals from such pure public goods as defense should be assigned greater values. If in addition we assume that the marginal utility of income declines as income rises, the estimates of redistribution of income in real (rather than money) terms would be quite different from those shown above.

THE BUDGET AND THE SUPPLIES OF CAPITAL AND LABOR

How do taxes and expenditures affect the supplies and allocation of productive inputs? First we recall that every major tax creates both income and substitution effects. Since the income effect may well be in the opposite direction from the substitution effect, it is impossible to predict how the supplies of the factors will be affected without prior knowledge of the relative strengths of these opposing effects.

Secondly we recall that the way in which taxes are levied determines their impact. *Taxes may or may not affect the producer's marginal costs of employing a certain input. Similarly, taxes may or may not affect the consumer's marginal costs of consuming a certain input. Finally, taxes may or may not affect the input owner's marginal costs (or marginal dis-utility) of employing his input in a certain employment.* In our survey of taxes we have observed numerous ways in which nonneutrality may lead to misallocation of resources. On the other hand we have demonstrated that when taxes are levied as user charges they *enhance* resource allocation. Taken collectively, users adjust both their use and the amount of the public good produced according to the equi-marginal rule. Making the user charge a part of each user's marginal cost makes for better allocation. If the good were produced by the public sector and supplied as a *free good* to users, there would be overuse (either overcrowding or overproduction). Even with our present system of using gasoline taxes as a user charge for highways, many of the costs are not included and thus we have overuse in many geographical areas.

In general when the public sector supplies goods which have direct benefits and are financed from general taxes, there will be overuse and probably overproduction. There are two aspects to the " free rider " problem here. On the benefit side, if certain groups benefit *more than others* they will use their influence to increase the good's production while funding it from general funds. On the cost side, the use of general taxes often means that certain groups pay less than others. The groups that pay less will advocate greater spending.

Public expenditures, of course, directly alter resource allocation by using up resources to produce public and quasi-public goods. We began our study by demonstrating that misallocation would occur if the private sector were left the responsibility of producing goods whose benefits are public. Whether the public sector produces the *optimum* amounts of public and quasi-public goods is a question which depends on the responsiveness of budget institutions to the preferences of the individuals within our society.

Public expenditures may also create complementary and substitute effects on private sector production. These effects may not be easy to trace. Hence in making a choice to produce a certain public good we may inadvertently be affecting resource allocation in ways we do not expect.

THE WORK-LEISURE CHOICE

The long-run trend in the U.S. towards greater leisure could theoretically be interpreted as a response to higher taxes; but probably other factors are more important in this long-run collective decision. Most likely the major factor is the *income effect* of a long-term upward trend in personal income. Leisure is a normal good with a positive income effect. Consequently as income has increased, the long-run changes in work customs and institutions have reflected a public choice for greater leisure. The substitution effect of a tax on work income will favor leisure both in the short and long run. The income effect may also favor leisure in the short and long run. The income effect can be positive or negative in either the short or the long run. We have assumed that the long-run influence of increasing income has been to favor more leisure. But since the substitution effect also has favored leisure, we cannot tell which effect is more powerful.

The short-run response to a tax increase could be quite different since, after all, the long-run effects reflected changes in tastes and work and leisure institutions. Moreover while after-tax income has increased over time the short-run effect of a tax will be to reduce income. Given the individual's resistance to lower his spending level, the short-run income effect for most tax increases will probably be in the direction of more work effort. If, in addition, the income effect is stronger than the substitution effect an increase in taxes would bring forth more work effort.

THE TAX BASE AND WORK EFFORT

In order to evaluate how different taxes may effect work effort it is useful to compare them in terms of their tax base. In the preceding chapters we observed that the individual's spending power could be taxed (1) according to its *income-earning potential* (a *wealth* tax), (2) as income is spent on consumption (a *sales* tax), or (3) as income is earned (an *income* tax). From either perspective the tax base is essentially the same thing: the individual's ability to control the use of commodities or factors of production. If taxes placed at either of these three stages were completely general they would not create substitution effects—and by our criteria of nonneutrality would be efficient.

But, as we have noted, each tax has various omissions in terms of generality. If we presume the property tax to be a tax on wealth, we immediately see glaring omissions such as human capital and several other types of "intangible" property. Similarly, the income tax treats income from certain types of wealth more favorably than others; and certain types of income (such as the services of the housewife) are not covered at all. Moreover, the tax on consumption exempts savings.

An increase in either tax will create both income and substitution effects. For those with savings targets, the response to an increase in either the property tax or the income tax will be to work harder; a shift to greater reliance on consumption taxes will produce the opposite effect. For those with consumption targets a shift to greater reliance on consumption taxes will increase work effort while a shift towards either income or property taxation will reduce it. It would be precarious to predict the net effect of such responses on work effort. One aspect of the income tax, however, bears attention. Any unfavorable effect on work effort from the income tax would derive primarily from the progressivity of the tax rates. A shift from the income tax base with progressive rates to either of the other bases would naturally favor the higher income groups and would reduce any disincentive which may exist. We have noted earlier that a shift to the *negative income tax* would reinforce any disincentive effect of the progressivity of the present income tax structure. Owing to the necessity for having an adequate minimum income and a feasible break-even income, the marginal tax rates must be quite high. Any adverse effects on work effort shifting from sales and property taxes to income taxes would be intensified under the negative income tax scheme. We should recognize, however, that shift from the present system of welfare payments to the negative income tax may increase work incentives.

THE TAX BASE AND THE FIRM'S CHOICE BETWEEN LABOR AND CAPITAL

The tax on property discriminates against the use of capital and encourages short- and long-run substitution of labor for capital. If the tax were truly general, all productive capacity would be included in the base. The lack of generality of the property tax creates several types of non-neutrality, a major one being the favoritism given investment in human capital. The trend over the years towards greater reliance on income and sales taxation has somewhat reduced this favoritism—especially since under the income tax, most educational expenditures and depreciation of humans are not considered costs in arriving at the tax base. This is not to say, of course, that the net effect of the budget is to encourage "too much" or "too little" investment in human capital. After all, voters may voice their preferences for more education by voting for greater expenditures on public education. Still it is useful to analyze the influences taxes have on private and public decision-making processes.

THE BUDGET AND INTERSECTOR RESOURCE ALLOCATION

In our survey of taxes and expenditures we considered the impact of
each on savings and investment. Our discussion recognized that one
cannot assume that saving automatically becomes investment. There
are different types of savings and investment decisions. Firms may be
thought of as saving (for their stockholders) when they retain earnings.
They may or may not be responsive to stockholders' desires for dividends.
Individuals may "invest" in either monetary assets (such as stocks
and bonds) or in real assets (such as residential housing). There is a
tenuous link between the savings plans of individuals and the investment
plans of firms.

Our models have emphasized that the public sector also "invests."
Thus it is appropriate to think of government as saving when it with-
holds funds from public sector consumption projects and devotes it
instead to public investment projects.

When we consider the impact of the whole budget, it is appropriate to
compare the marginal propensity to save (and invest) of the private
sector (individuals and firms) with the marginal propensity to save
(and invest) of the public sector. For a given increase in the budget,
what are the various characteristics of private and public sector *decision
making* which will influence the consumption-investment ratio?

If we take the *average* propensity to invest as an indication of the
marginal propensity, we find that roughly 20 percent of all government
revenues go to capital investment under a strict classification, while
roughly 40 percent go to investment under a more liberal classification
(which includes investment in human capital such as education and
health care). Investment, under a strict classification, accounts for only
18 percent of all private sector expenditures and 28 percent under the
more liberal classification including human capital investment.

Our immediate observation is that a shift in resource allocation to the
public sector would increase investment. But such speculation is not too
useful. The alternative *choices* we are interested in concern *changes* in
specific expenditures and taxes, and these differ considerably in their
impact on the consumption-investment ratio. Consider, for example,
an increase in defense expenditures financed by increasing our public
debt. If the debt is financed in such a way as to reduce private sector
investment and the defense expenditures soon become "used up" or
obsolete, the combined impact will be to reduce aggregate investment.
By contrast the combined impact of an increase in hospital construction

accompanied by a shift in revenues towards the consumption tax would favor aggregate investment over consumption.

The effect on investment of increased public expenditure financed by increased use of the property tax is difficult to predict. If we assume the incidence to fall heavily on the very poor and the very rich, the influences on savings would be in opposite directions. A shift from the personal income tax to the property tax would have mixed effects owing to the lack of generality of each. For example a reduction in the personal income tax would favor saving by helping the high-income groups; however, increased property taxes would lower the after-tax return and thus decrease the incentive to invest.

Our survey revealed several other ways in which taxes affect the consumption-investment decision. The impact of the corporation income tax depends on its incidence. If paid by the firm (or rather its stockholders), the tax either reduces the earnings from which the firm might invest or it reduces dividends to stockholders (who themselves have high savings rates). The savings-investment linkage is of course stronger for earnings that stay within the firm. Firms average from 45 to 50 percent payout of dividends from earnings. Thus if the corporation income is borne by the firm and stockholder, it reduces internal investment and dividends (where stockholder savings *may* in turn help finance investment) by the above percentage.

If, on the other hand, the tax is passed on to the consumer, the impact on savings (but not necessarily investment) would be the same as the general sales tax. The impact on savings would be less than the income tax since those who save more can avoid the incidence.

Although the incidence of the social security tax is much easier to trace it also creates a complex set of influences on the flow of investment funds. First, social security is an insurance and annuity program featuring required saving by the employee. Obviously it *substitutes* for saving the individual would otherwise perform. Thus we can predict that more private sector saving (and investment) would occur in the absence of the program. No doubt, however, the aggregate saving would be less since many of those who " save " in this way would not do so unless required. We noted that the federal government keeps a much smaller reserve against future obligations than would private sector insurance companies. This means that the government is providing the individual a monetary investment that is not backed up with as much real investment as would otherwise be the case. Put another way, individuals are not required to reduce consumption as much to get the same amount of insurance. This influence somewhat is in the opposite direction of that mentioned above which " forces " increased savings.

Another relevant question is how the trust funds are used. Not only are the corresponding reserves of private insurance companies larger (relative to future obligation) but the funds are invested primarily in private sector activities (rather than in public sector activities as are the public trust funds). This last aspect of the shift to public insurance tends to lower the supply of investment funds to the private sector.

A final crucial factor is the impact of government macroeconomic policy. We have frequently dealt with the question of how the inter-sector resource allocation goal and the macroeconomic goals are inter-related. Determining the amounts of private investment and consumption is a necessary part of the choice of macroeconomic tools to be used to influence aggregate spending. Of interest from the public choice perspective is how the macroeconomic tools affect the ability of voters and their representatives to effectively voice their preferences. The policy decision to manipulate aggregate demand must reflect individual and collective priorities among investment and consumption alternatives.

The shift from one tax base to another also influences the *composition* of investment spending. The income tax discriminates against investment in human capital since it does not allow the costs of education or depreciation to be counted against income. Taxes using consumption as a base favor investment in human capital to the same extent that they favor investment in general. The property tax, however, also discriminates among investment alternatives. It favors investment in human capital both because it raises the firm's after-tax price of real capital and because it lowers the tax bill of the individual who invests in human as opposed to real capital.

Here again a change in the budget may have reinforcing effects. Suppose for example an increase in public education expenditure was financed by increased property taxes. Both the expenditures and the revenue sides of the budget would combine to favor increased investment in human capital. The net effect on the aggregate investment-consumption ratio would be difficult to predict since part of the shift would involve a substitution among investment alternatives.

In general, however, the tax system is biased in favor of investment in physical as opposed to human capital. The depreciation allowances for physical capital under the income taxes make the tax rate on human capital relatively higher. The average rates of return reflect this. The rate of return to manufacturing investment averages around 20 percent after personal income taxes while the rate of return on investment in a college education is about 9 percent. If the rate of return were the only consideration we would expect a shift in funds away from human capital into physical capital which would tend to bring the two rates closer. The fact that the two rates differ indicates that the " consumption " aspects of education and other investment in human capital tend to offset the favoritism given by the tax system. Finally if we are trying to analyze the impact of the whole budget on individual and collective choices, we must consider the influences inherent in the public expenditures as well. For example, our collective choice to distribute education as a free good contains a bias favoring over-use owing to the substantial direct benefits inherent in this quasi-public good.

PUBLIC SECTOR EXPENDITURES AND OPPORTUNITY COSTS

Obviously when the *public sector* produces goods it uses up resources that could be used in the private sector to produce private goods. The " opportunity costs " of the public exhaustive expenditures are the resources used. We have demonstrated that for the most part these costs are not hidden but in fact are made explicit by the price mechanism. That is, the prices of resources used represent their real cost (the value of their marginal product in the production of other goods). Therefore the amount spent on a public activity shows us in dollar terms the value of goods foregone. While our models have shown this to be true as a general rule we have also observed many exceptions. Economies of scale, externalities, complementary and substitute effects occur which often make it difficult to measure the marginal social costs of a public activity. It is the task of cost-benefit analysis to take these hidden costs and benefits into account.

The impact a change in government expenditures has on the affected input markets depends importantly on the mobility of the inputs. It also depends on the proportion of the demand the public sector furnishes in the specific industry. For example the public sector accounts for 90 percent of the demands for ordnance. Moreover inputs used in the industry are highly specialized; thus, a major reduction in ordnance spending, instead of making additional resources immediately available to other industries, would create unemployment and unused resources. On the other hand a reduction in the Army's demand for clothing would not have the same effect since the public sector represents a small percent

(2 percent) of the demand in the apparel industries and the machines and labor so used could be employed to produce for the private sector.

The impact of a shift in government expenditure also depends importantly on macroeconomic conditions. If the economy is expanding, the unused resources are much more likely to find employment. If however the economy is sluggish, the reduction in a government activity will not "save" as many resources as it would seem. For example when the government cut back on certain aero-space projects during the recession-inflation of the early 1970s the result was widespread unemployment of those factors of production—including even a group of usually highly mobile resources: engineers.

Government expenditures are not the only measure of the opportunity costs of government. The public sector can influence microeconomic behavior simply by passing new laws. Alternatively, tax incentives and disincentives can be used to encourage certain behavior. When taxes are used in this way, however, they must be subjected not only to the resource allocation criteria but to the income distribution and macroeconomic policy criteria as well. Tax deductions for gifts to nonprofit organizations do mischief to voter assessment of the income redistribution function even though they fare well under the resource allocation criteria. Usually anything that can be accomplished through special tax provisions can also be accomplished through direct subsidies. The term *tax expenditures* may be used for those tax provisions giving favorable treatment to certain ways of earning or spending income. Tax expenditures are quite substantial in current budgets. One of the largest tax expenditures is special treatment given health and welfare expenditures. Also important are special tax provisions for community development and housing and transportation. Two tax expenditures which tend to circumvent our income distribution goal are the favoritism given interest on state and local bonds (which presumably improves efficiency in resource allocation by helping the states and localities) and the capital gains treatment which presumably favors economic growth by encouraging savings and investment.

FROM MICRO TO MACRO

In assessing the microeconomic effects of different taxes and public expenditures we have found it impossible to abstract from their macroeconomic effects. In some instances we have assumed that *full employ-*

ment prevails before and after a tax is imposed. On occasion our analysis has implicitly assumed flexible prices and perfect mobility of inputs. When focusing on particular taxes we have often attempted to ignore expenditures. This practice, however, leaves open the question of how the necessary spending power is generated. Do we assume that spending power is replenished by government expenditure; or is private investment increased (via an increase in the money supply); or is private consumption increased (via transfers or a tax cut)? This latter alternative amounts to substituting one tax for another. All of these options affect not only resource allocation but the level of employment as well.

Federal macroeconomic policy has made frequent use of the personal income tax and the corporation income tax to influence aggregate demand. The effect of changes in the corporation tax is sometimes difficult to predict. When the goal is to change investment by changing the tax rate, giving a tax credit for investment, or changing depreciation schedules, the hoped-for effect may be offset by changes in expectations and shifts in the demand for investment.

The major attribute of the personal income tax for macroeconomic policy is that it allows widespread changes in purchasing power to be instituted rapidly. Neither the sales tax nor the property tax as presently constructed have this advantage. However, if the sales tax were general among the states it could be used more effectively than the income tax owing to its immediate connection with consumption expenditures. As presently constituted the personal income tax is the best suited for most macroeconomic policies. However the use of this and other taxes along with different types of expenditures creates a myriad of important macroeconomic effects.

In Parts I and II we made use of the imaginary Fiscal Department model to analyze the relationships among basic public sector functions and the tools available for implementing them. In the very simple model we demonstrated how, theoretically at least, one goal could be pursued in such a way as to be neutral towards the others. As we have proceeded to further examine the mechanics of the expenditures and taxes themselves, we have gained an appreciation for their various microeconomic effects and their impact on individual and social priorities. And we have found that instead of being neatly separable (as in the model), the macroeconomic policy decisions have important influence on the incidence of taxes and public expenditures and, in turn, on the behavior of individuals and firms.

IV
MACROECONOMICS AND THE PUBLIC SECTOR

15

INTRODUCTION TO FISCAL POLICY: THE BASIC CLASSICAL AND KEYNESIAN MODELS

PUBLIC CHOICES AND THE MACROECONOMIC POLICY FUNCTION

In starting our more extensive study of macroeconomic policy it is appropriate to recall our familiar Fiscal Department model with its three branches: The Public Goods Branch, the Income Distribution Branch and the Macroeconomic Policy Branch. As we have noted on several occasions, these imaginary branches are useful in describing the various methods used by the public sector to accomplish the three broad social goals: "welfare-maximizing" resource allocation, "proper" income distribution and "full-employment-with-stable-prices" macroeconomic policy. This essentially normative frame of reference has also been useful for analyzing public sector functions from a public choice perspective. We have noted, for example, that the methods used in accomplishing one function often affects the accomplishment of another. Moreover the use of certain tools affects the ability of decision makers (for example, voters and their representatives) to assess results of public activities. One of our tasks in these chapters, as we examine the macroeconomic policy tools, will be to ask how the use of a particular tool affects decision making on income distribution and intersector (private and public) resource allocation.

Within the context of the simple Fiscal Department model developed in Chapter 4, we were able to show how with an appropriate mix of taxes, transfers and expenditures we could isolate the three broad functions and accomplish them simultaneously. But in the "real world," difficulties of specifying the goals, plus rigidities, bottlenecks, and other imperfections in the decision-making process obviate a neat, simultaneous solution and require that we analyze the complex relationships among methods and preferences.

In addition to the tradeoffs among the three broad economic goals, the implementation of macroeconomic policy involves many other public choices as well. And as we examine the effect of the various fiscal and monetary tools we will consider as well the public choices inherent in using one combination of tools as opposed to another.

Our first task is to increase our understanding of the mechanics of the fiscal and monetary tools. This, we should be forewarned, will be no easy task. For in recent years the widespread acceptance among economists of traditional Keynesian prescriptions has been shaken on the one hand by arguments regarding the impact of various policies—especially monetary policies—and on the other hand by recent economic events—especially the cost-push phenomenon of 1969–1973.

FIGURE 15–1

The circular flow model

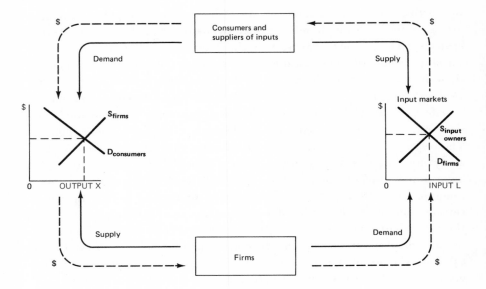

A fundamental assumption behind the Keynesian prescriptions is that the economy can be regulated by manipulating *aggregate demand*. But in a cost-push situation, this assumption no longer holds. Thus as we begin our examination of the simple Keynesian model, it is important for us to be forewarned that the model is severely limited by its exclusion of the factors influencing *aggregate supply*. We will attempt to build a more complete analysis in subsequent chapters.

THE CLASSICAL ECONOMISTS' MODEL REVIEWED

Let us once more use the circular flow model of the classical economists as a starting point.

It is, of course, only for expositional purposes that we impute the circular flow model to the "classical economists." Adam Smith and David Ricardo certainly had the notion of competitive forces working for equilibrium in commodity and resource markets in the economy (as did the Physiocrat Quesnay); however, many refinements have been added to the notion of competitive equilibrium through the years. And the

---

" Keynesian Revolution " itself was simply a further extension of this development. Keynes in his *General Theory* merely pointed out several ways in which the forces making for equilibrium at full employment may be circumvented so that equilibrium is reached at less than full employment.

General equilibrium in the circular flow model, we recall, is built around the assumption of perfect competition in all markets. Figure 15.1 shows the model in its simplest form. Money flows through input and output markets. Competitive forces insure that demand equals supply in the markets for each kind of output and each kind of input. The profit motive encourages each owner of resources and each firm to employ resources in their most efficient capacity. The price mechanism acts as a communications system through which these signals become known. Owners of the resources are paid, and in turn they use these funds to purchase goods and services in output markets.

We can see how full employment is assured under the assumption of perfect competition within the model. Prices adjust in both the input and commodity markets so that no surpluses appear. In the input markets for labor, wages adjust so that demand equals the supply of workers with various skills. In the input markets for investment funds, the prices (or rather the interest rates) adjust so that demand and supply are equated. Changes in the quantity of money within the system will not effect the full employment equilibrium since prices adjust accordingly.

THE EQUATION OF EXCHANGE AND THE QUANTITY THEORY OF MONEY

The familiar equation of exchange model illustrates the classical assumption that the competitive forces operating within the economy will balance demand and supply in each market. Competition also insures that aggregate demand equals aggregate supply, so that all resources are fully employed. One of the earlier classical economists, Jean Baptiste Say, stated this proposition formally in a concept which became known as Say's law. The argument starts from the assumption that people produce goods only because they anticipate earning income in order to buy other goods. Thus there will always be a sufficient aggregate demand. More importantly, Ricardo pointed out that people's wants are insatiable and that, since prices in each market adjust to where supply equals demand, there

FIGURE 15-2

Aggregate demand and
supply in the classical
model

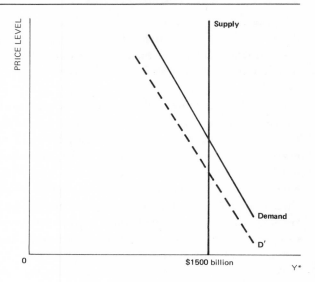

is no danger that temporary hoarding of money will result in long-run surpluses and unemployment. Consequently, full employment is assured for two reasons: (1) Owners of resources are motivated to hire out their services only in order to buy output with the proceeds. They estimate how much they will work on the basis of the money needed to purchase desired goods. Thus, aggregate demand should be roughly equal to aggregate supply. (2) Even supposing there be some leakage in the circular flow of money—such as excessive hoarding of money for speculative reasons—prices will adjust to make surpluses impossible. Flexible prices (to include the interest rate) allow for the constant adjustment of demand to supply at full employment.

The aggregate supply curve appears as a vertical line at the appropriate full employment level (as shown in Figure 15.2). The implication is that regardless of changes in the price level, real output, Y^*, will stay at the full employment level. In the case illustrated in Figure 15.2 output remains at $1500 billion even though aggregate demand falls to D'.

The classical assumptions about aggregate demand can best be illustrated by using the so-called "equation of exchange." Of the several similar versions of this relationship, the one most suited to our investigation is

$$MV = PY^*$$

---

where M is the money supply, V is the velocity of the money supply (how many times money changes hands within the given time period), P is the price level, and Y^* is the quantity of output in real terms.

One way of viewing the equation is as an identity: Say's identity. As such, the equation simply states that the amount of money used in purchasing national output times the number of times it was used (velocity) is the same as the value of national output in money terms (the price level times real output). But the classical economists, as we have noted, implied more. Short-run " gluts " and business depressions could occur, but they soon would be dispelled by the self-correcting nature of the system. In the more basic version of the model it is assumed that no one would hoard money for speculative purposes. Even if such hoarding occurred, however, prices would adjust so that full employment would continue.

Thus the classical economists' equation of exchange model is capable of coping with the problem of leakage in the circular flow caused by people's hoarding money as a store of value and thus causing a temporary excess supply of goods. If consumers oversave and do not divert all of their income to either buying commodities or lending to business (which in turn would spend), the price and interest mechanism will adjust so as to compensate for the new quantity of money in circulation.

We may state these relationships in a simple version of the so-called *quantity theory of money*. We assume that velocity V, is constant. This follows from the observation that the rate at which money turns over depends on rather stable institutional arrangements within our economy. Some people are paid by the week, some by the month; some bills are paid when purchases are made while others are paid monthly, semiannually, and so on. But unless unusual institutional changes occur, the velocity of these payments remains fairly stable.

Since Y^* is stable at full employment and velocity is constant, we are left with only two variables in our equation of exchange. We denote this by putting bars over V and Y^* in the equation below.

$$M\bar{V} = P\bar{Y}^*$$

Under the classical assumptions, *if the supply of money in circulation decreases, there will be a compensating change in the price level.*

$$\downarrow M\bar{V} = \downarrow P\bar{Y}^*$$

FIGURE 15–3

The circular flow with government

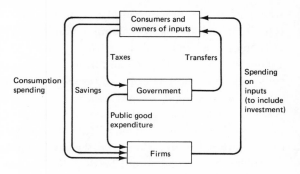

Similarly, if the money supply increases, the price level will rise accordingly.

$$\uparrow M\overline{V} = \uparrow P\overline{Y}*$$

The determination of aggregate output, Y^*, depends only on the supply of resources and technology. While these may change over time (resulting in a shift in the aggregate supply curve), they are fixed in the short run.

On the other hand, there is a direct relationship between the money supply and the price level. The prices of commodities adjust so as to make underconsumption impossible, and the interest rate adjusts so as to make "oversaving" impossible. Consequently the savings "leakage" in the circular flow cannot cause less aggregate spending and unemployment. Of course, commodity prices and the interest rate are factors in the decisions of consumers to spend or save (and invest). Yet unless there is a change in the demand for money as a store of value (hoarding), the interest rate will adjust so that any change in the amount spent for consumption will become investment. In Figure 15.3 we see that if the amount saved (savings) is equal to that amount demanded (for investment), then there is no real leakage in the circular flow. Instead of consumers spending, businesses borrow and spend.

Figure 15.3 also includes another "leakage" from consumer spending in the form of taxes collected from resource owners and spent by the government. Again, *no interruption in the circular flow need occur if the budget is balanced.* The classical model leads us to conclude that all macroeconomic policy requires is a stable money supply (so as to avoid inflation or deflation) and a balanced public sector budget.

KEYNES VERSUS THE CLASSICAL MODEL

Although logically consistent, the classical model of perfect competition is an unsatisfactory description of our economy. This became painfully obvious during the 1930s. The Keynesian critique of the classical model points out some of the important discrepancies.

In the first place, savings plans are not necessarily equal to investment plans *ex ante*. Moreover, the investment behavior of businessmen is somewhat unresponsive to changes in the rate of interest.

Second, the money market is certainly not perfectly competitive. Hence, the interest rate may not adjust so as to equate savings (as planned by suppliers of funds) with investment (as planned by businessmen). As we shall see, savings will equal investment *ex poste* but not necessarily at the full employment level.

Third, when the interest rate reaches what people assume to be its lowest level, people will hoard all additional money. This phenomenon, which Keynes termed the "liquidity trap," arises because the lower interest rate makes hoarding money less costly and because people anticipate future increases. Therefore, they hoard in order to loan at higher rates in the future. This puts a "floor" on the interest rate. Once the interest rate has reached this floor, increases in the money supply cannot be effective in lowering the rate of interest and increasing the quantity invested.

Finally, Keynes noted that prices in the commodity and labor markets are sluggish in their downward adjustment. Casual observation of our economy supports this contention. Producers of "name brands" are reluctant to reduce prices. There are even "fair trade" laws which make it illegal to do so. Likewise, unions resist wage cuts even though the danger of less employment may be quite real. And, for the economy as a whole, even if prices of inputs (to include wages) *were* cut, the aggregate demand originating from these owners of resources would also be cut. So commodity prices would have to be cut further. Then another round of input price cuts would be in order, and the deflationary spiral would continue without reducing unemployment.

Given these imperfections, it is easy to see that the economic system does not insure equilibrium at full employment. We may illustrate this in terms of the equation of exchange by saying that a decrease in M is more likely to be reflected in a decrease in real output than an adjustment in price level:

$$\downarrow M \overline{V} = \overline{P} Y* \downarrow$$

FIGURE 15-4

Aggregate demand and
supply under the Keynesian
assumptions

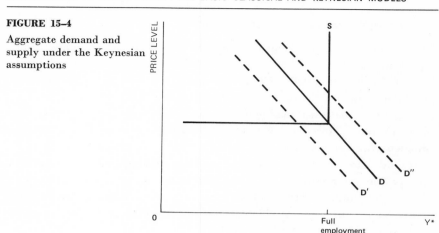

Moreover, under conditions of less than full employment, an increase in effective demand would result in an increase in $Y*$.[1]

$$\uparrow M \overline{V} = \overline{P} Y* \uparrow$$

Additional insight can be gained by comparing the classical and Keynesian positions in terms of aggregate demand and supply. The classical position, which features a vertical supply curve, was shown in Figure 15.1. The Keynesian position is shown in Figure 15.4. If demand is insufficient, D', the price level does not adjust, and output is less than the full employment level. If demand increases beyond "capacity," however, prices adjust upward.

If we assume the aggregate supply curve of our economy to be shaped like that in Figure 15.4, the problem for fiscal policy becomes one of adjusting aggregate demand. If we know the full employment limit, we will attempt to adjust aggregate demand so as to reach that point. But if we shift aggregate demand too far to the right, we will experience inflation.

The first problem at hand is that of insuring adequate demand to reach full employment. Consequently, when we use the term Y, we refer to aggregate demand or spending. We will assume, however, that when we increase Y, we are moving toward a known target of full employment. Under these assumptions, which will be relaxed later, we can devote our full attention to the problem of manipulating aggregate demand.

A SIMPLE KEYNESIAN MODEL OF AGGREGATE DEMAND

We now have the background for a closer look at the position of aggregate spending. Consider the simple "circular flow" model as depicted in Figure 15.3. First assume that taxes are zero and that consumers either spend on commodities or save. We will, however, give the government the ability to spend even though it levies no taxes.

Given: $Y =$ national income

$C =$ consumption expenditures

$I =$ investment expenditures

$G =$ government expenditures (for goods and services)

$S =$ saving

We know that individual consumers may apportion their income to either consumption or saving. Aggregate spending, however, will be made up of C and I and G. Thus, we can look at national income from two perspectives:

$$Y = C + S$$

or

$$Y = C + I + G$$

Suppose we cannot reach the full-employment level because at that level we would have too much savings relative to investment. In order to "soak up" the savings "leakage" we must increase government spending. An illustration will be useful. Suppose our *full employment* level of national income is $1500 billion, as shown in Table 15.1. It is obvious that the equilibrium level of aggregate spending is at $1500 billion also. For at $1500 billion, $S = I + G$ and there is no "leakage" in the circular flow. Notice that C changes with income (and, of course, S changes accordingly). For the moment, however, we assume that I and G spending decisions *are not directly influenced* by changing Y. Consequently, we call them "exogenous," since they are determined by something outside our model.

---

[1] Recall that the classical interpretation of the equation of exchange would assume that $Y*$ remained at full employment always, so that

$$\uparrow M \overline{V} = \uparrow P \overline{Y}*$$

and

$$\downarrow M \overline{V} = \downarrow P \overline{Y}*$$

FIGURE 15–5

The consumption function and equilibrium of aggregate spending

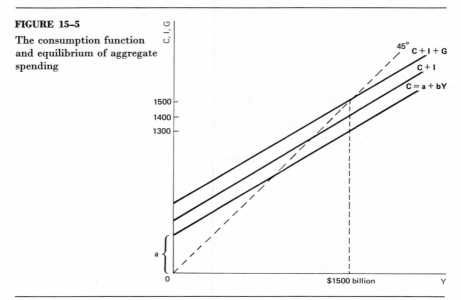

TABLE 15–1

Hypothetical equilibrium of aggregate spending (in billions of dollars)

National income (Y)	Con-sumption (C)	Planned saving (S)	Investment (I)	Government spending (G)	Generated aggregate spending (C + I + G)	Movement
1800	1540	260	100	100	1740	↓
1700	1460	240	100	100	1660	↓
1600	1380	220	100	100	1580	↓
1500	1300	200	100	100	1500	equilibrium (Y = C + I + G)
1400	1220	180	100	100	1420	↑
1300	1140	160	100	100	1340	↑
1200	1060	140	100	100	1260	↑
1100	980	120	100	100	1188	↑
1000	900	100	100	100	1100	↑
900	820	80	100	100	1020	↑

Now it is obvious that a level of $1600 billion *cannot be supported*, since $C + I + G$ will generate only $1580 billion of aggregate spending for the next " cycle " of the circular flow. Businessmen will receive back less than they paid out while producing national income. The S leakage will be greater than I plus G. Consequently, the movement will be downward towards the $1500 billion level (from which there will be no tendency to move).

The table also depicts the tendency to move from lower levels upward to the $1500 billion equilibrium. If Y in the first period were $1200 billion, then $1060 billion of consumption would be generated, which (along with $I = \$100$ billion and $G = \$100$ billion) would result in businessmen's receiving $1260 billion in spending. Assuming the full employment level has not been reached, businessmen will expand output. This process will continue until the $1500 billion level is reached.

Now assume that the government does not spend. The equilibrium level will be where $S = I$, or at the $1000 billion level. At that level $C + I$ (or $900 + 100$) will equal $C + S$ (or $900 + 100$) and there will be no leakage in the circular flow. On the other hand, this may be at a level of national income far below that possible with full employment of resources.

We can illustrate the equilibrium solution to Table 15.1 in graphical form as well. First let us state our relationships in the form of equations.

$$Y = C + I + G \tag{1}$$
$$C = a + bY \tag{2}$$
$$I = I_0 \tag{3}$$
$$G = G_0 \tag{4}$$

Equation (1) gives the definition of national income as the summation of aggregate spending. Equation (2) shows consumption as a function of income. Equations (3) and (4) simply designate investment and government spending as exogenous to our model.[2]

---

[2] Note that we assume the consumption function to be a straight line. The value of a is nothing more than the intercept of the line with the vertical axis (see Figure 15.5). The a value simply determines the *position* of the consumption function. What is more important to us is the *slope* of the line—how *consumption is related to income*. This is given by the value b. A simple illustration will prove that changes in C are entirely dependent on b.

We know that

$$C = a + bY$$

And we desire to know how a change in C, ΔC, is related to a change in Y, ΔY. Therefore we write the following equation:

$$C + \Delta C = a + b(Y + \Delta Y)$$

This gives us

$$C + \Delta C = a + bY + b\,\Delta Y$$

In order to look only at the changes involved, we subtract $C = a + bY$ from both sides of our equation. Thus, we find that

$$\Delta C = b\,\Delta Y$$

The value b is called the marginal propensity to consume. It is the percentage of an increase in income, Y, that will be spent for consumption, C.

FIGURE 15–6

The multiplier effect

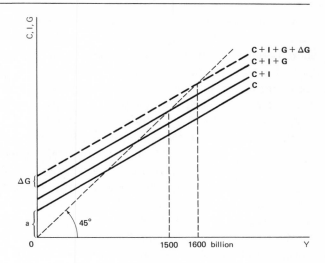

A GRAPHICAL INTERPRETATION OF EQUILIBRIUM AGGREGATE SPENDING

Now consider the solution to the hypothetical income data in Table 15.1. We assume that the equilibrium income is

$$Y = C + I + G \qquad \text{or} \qquad 1500 = 1300 + 100 + 100$$

Also

$$C = a + bY \qquad \text{or} \qquad 1300 = 100 + .8(1500)$$

Here the marginal propensity to consume is .8. This implies that the consumer spends 80 percent out of new additions to his income.

Figure 15.5 shows the solution to the equations and the data in Table 15.1. On the vertical axis we show $C + I + G$. At the equilibrium level (where $Y = C + I + G$) C is 1300, I is 100, and G is 100.

The slope of the consumption function shows how consumption changes with income. Since MPC (the marginal propensity to consume) is less than one (.8 in this example), the savings leakage grows as Y increases. Thus if higher equilibrium levels are to be reached, $I + G$ must grow to compensate for the increase in S. Assume that instead of $1500 billion our full employment level is $1600 billion. Consumption will account for only $1380 billion of this. And since saving, S, is $220 billion at the $1600 billion level, either I or G must increase to fill the gap. If G increases by $20 billion to $120 billion, the new equilibrium Y will be at the desired

---

$1600 billion (an increase of $100 billion). Figure 15.6 graphs the relationship between ΔG and ΔY. Notice how the Y resulting from a vertical shift in G (to $G + \Delta G$) depends on the slope, b, of the consumption function.

THE MULTIPLIER

The relationship between changes in G (or I) and Y is called the "multiplier." In order to isolate the "multiplier," let us return to the formal equations themselves. Recall that in the equation (1):

$$Y = C + I + G$$

Substituting equations (2), (3), and (4) into the righthand side gives us

$$Y = (a + bY) + I_0 + G_0 \tag{5}$$

We now subtract bY from both sides

$$Y - bY = a + I_0 + G_0 \tag{6}$$

and then divide both sides by $1 - b$:

$$Y = \frac{1}{1 - b}(a + I_0 + G_0) \tag{7}$$

Using this equation to examine the change in Y resulting from a change in G, we find that

$$Y + \Delta Y = \frac{1}{1 - b}(a + I_0 + G_0) + \frac{1}{1 - b}\Delta G$$

and subtracting equation (7) from both sides we see that the

$$\Delta Y = \frac{1}{1 - b}\Delta G$$

or

$$K_G = \frac{1}{1 - b} = \frac{\Delta Y}{\Delta G}$$

We are not surprised to find that the increase in government spending in the economy has a multiplier effect that depends on the marginal propensity to consume. In other words, as the impact of increased government spending spreads throughout the economy, it spawns more spending each time it passes through an income earner's hands. But the magnitude of this impact depends on how much each person spends from the new income he receives. In the case illustrated by Table 15.1 the marginal propensity to consume, b, was .8 and thus the multiplier was 5. If G were changed from $100 billion to $120 billion, the equilibrium $(Y = C + I + G)$ would change from $1500 billion to $1600 billion. Thus the $20 billion change in G causes a $100 billion change in Y.

The multiplier effect is evident in Figure 15.6. When G is increased by ΔG, the $C + I + G$ line shifts upward to $C + I + G + \Delta G$. Assuming the ΔG to be $20 billion and the multiplier to be 5, the equilibrium changes from $1500 billion to $1600 billion. The dependence of the multiplier on the slope of the consumption function (the marginal propensity to consume) is apparent. The greater the slope, the greater the effect on aggregate spending a given change in G or I will have. The reverse is also true. If, for example the marginal propensity to consume (which is the slope of the consumption function) were .6, then the multiplier (K_G) would be $1/(1 - .6)$ or 2.5. Consequently, if ΔG were $10 billion, the ΔY would be only $25 billion.[3]

We might say that equations (1)–(7) and Figure 15.6 are a " model," since they are a simplified representation of certain important economic *relationships* in our economy. The example used in demonstrating the government spending multiplier indicates the usefulness of the " model " to an organization such as the Council of Economic Advisers. If studies indicate that potential Y in the coming year is $1500 billion (as in the example above) and investment is not changing enough to compensate for the savings " leakage," then an additional change in $C + I + G$, effected through fiscal policy (such as a tax cut, increased government spending, investment tax credits, or increased transfer payments), will be necessary.

As we can see from Figures 15.5 and 15.6, the consumption function is the base upon which the Keynesian system is built. Let us digress briefly to consider whether reliable estimates of consumption habits can be made.

EMPIRICAL SUPPORT FOR THE CONSUMPTION FUNCTION MODEL

Keynes provided little statistical evidence to support his argument. He was, as noted, aware of the budget studies which had been made over the years. The studies invariably reveal a consumption function much like that postulated by Keynes. The lower income groups typically dissave and the higher income groups typically save. The marginal propensity to consume is positive, less than one, and changes very little from income group to income group.[4] Almost all studies indicate that the marginal propensity to consume in the United States is between .6 and .8.

But do these relationships hold when we speak of how *aggregate consumption changes with aggregate income*? It was not until 1942 that adequate data for appropriate statistical investigation of such questions became available. When economists first ran regressions on the time series data from 1929 to 1941, they found extremely close relationships between consumption and income. Moreover, the fit was so precise that it seemed that *all other factors* influencing consumption could be *ignored*. Keynes's " guesses " seemed to be verified by the data. The tests indicated that the consumption function for this period was approximately

$$C = 25 + .75\,Y$$

---

[3] Perhaps some numerical examples would help demonstrate the effect on aggregate spending that new government or investment expenditures have as they travel from person (or firm) to person (or firm) through the economy.

Example 1. Assume the marginal propensity to consume is .8 and government spending increases by $10.00.

Expenditure	Amount	Recipient
Initial change in G	$10.00	Income to A
Consumption by A	8.00	Income to B
Consumption by B	6.40	Income to C
Consumption by C	5.12	Income to D
Consumption by D	4.10	Income to E
Consumption by E	3.28	Income to F
Consumption by F	2.62	Income to G
Consumption by G	2.10	Income to H
Consumption by H	1.68	

$43.30—eventually $50.00

Thus our multiplier is $1/(1 - .8)$ or 5.

Example 2. Assume the marginal propensity to consume is .6 and government spending increases by $10.00.

Expenditure	Amount	Recipient
Initial change in G	$10.00	Income to A
Consumption by A	6.00	Income to B
Consumption by B	3.60	Income to C
Consumption by C	2.16	Income to D
Consumption by D	1.30	Income to E
Consumption by E	.78	Income to F
Consumption by F	.47	Income to G
Consumption by G	.28	

$24.59—eventually $25.00

Thus our multiplier is $1/(1 - .6)$ or 2.5.

A comparison of the two examples reveals that the major portion of the impact on spending is worked out in the initial exchanges. Also, the lower the MPC the faster the multiplier effect works itself out.

[4] It declines only slightly as income rises.

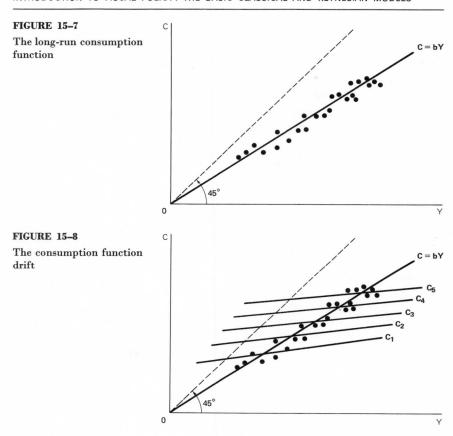

FIGURE 15–7

The long-run consumption function

FIGURE 15–8

The consumption function drift

Consumption was determined in part by an amount ($25 billion) which was independent of income and in part by a tendency of each group to consume three-fourths of their income. The marginal propensity to consume was positive, less than one, and showed little tendency to decline with rising income. Needless to say, economists were enthusiastic about what seemed to be a very reliable tool for predicting aggregate spending. With knowledge of what consumption would be and with estimates of investment spending, it would be a simple matter to predict the appropriate amount of government expenditures necessary to equate forthcoming aggregate spending (demand) with forthcoming aggregate production (supply).

It is hard to imagine that economists could believe that the consumption-income relationship could be linear, nonproportional, and yet stable over long periods of time. Yet some of them did—until later statistical studies produced conflicting data. Two significant studies, published in 1946 by Simon Kuznets of the National Bureau of Economic Research, indicated that the long-run relationship between consumption and income was *proportional* rather than nonproportional.[5] Kuznets' estimates, arrived at by overlapping decades from 1869 to 1938, indicated a stable MPC of between .84 and .89. Since the relationship was proportional (i.e., MPC and APC were equal), the consumption function would appear as in Figure 15.7. Kuznets' and subsequent studies ended the euphoria some economists had experienced from the notion that the consumption function could be nonproportional over the long run. It became crucial to reconcile the new long-run estimates with the short-run estimates previously obtained.

Arthur Smithies offered an explanation by proposing that the consumption function had been slowly drifting upward.[6] Over a short period of time, the consumption function would appear to be nonproportional (shown by C_1 through C_5 in Figure 15.8), but when averages were taken for longer periods this nonproportionality would necessarily disappear. Smithies was able to reconcile his approximation of the consumption function with Kuznets' data quite nicely. However, there have been, and continue to be, further developments which do not coincide with Smithies' conclusions.

More recently it has been argued that instead of a steady drift upward the consumption function *shifts* up rapidly on occasions when factors other than income change the consumption-income relationship. The theory of the usually stable function which periodically shifts agrees with the findings of short-run nonproportional functions and a long-run proportional function.

Other economists such as James Duesenberry[7] and Milton Friedman[8] propose to reconcile the figures in an entirely different way. They would emphasize that consumption is basically a *proportional* function of income

[5] Simon Kuznets, *National Product Since 1869* (New York: National Bureau of Economic Research, 1946) and *National Income: A Summary of Findings* (New York: National Bureau of Economic Research, 1946).

[6] Arthur Smithies, "Forecasting Postwar Demand: I," *Econometrica*, vol. 13 (January 1945).

[7] James Duesenberry, *Income, Saving, and the Theory of Consumer Behavior* (Cambridge Mass.: Harvard University Press, 1949).

[8] Milton Friedman, *A Theory of the Consumption Function* (Princeton, N.J.: Princeton University Press, 1957).

FIGURE 15–9

The Duesenberry "ratchet" effect

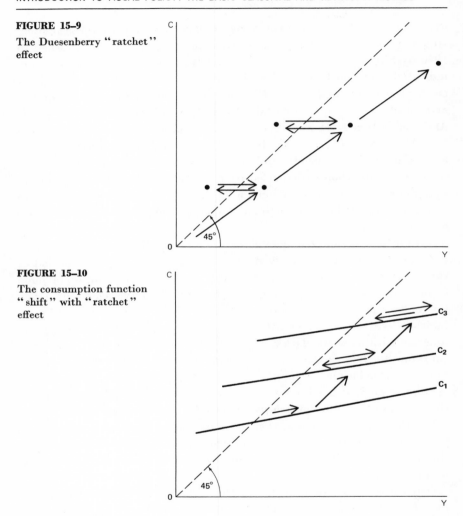

FIGURE 15–10

The consumption function "shift" with "ratchet" effect

whereas the short-run nonproportionality must be explained by changes in factors other than income. Duesenberry argues that the short-run non-proportionality results from the uneven pace of economic growth. In periods of sustained growth consumption grows at the proportional rate. However, in periods of recession consumers resist cutting expenditures back at the same proportional rate. This sequence of events is depicted in Figure 15.9. During periods of sustained expansion, consumption expenditures increase along the steeper proportional arrows. During short-run recessions consumers reduce consumption as shown by the horizontal arrows. Once recovery is begun, consumers increase spending at a non-proportional rate (horizontal arrows) until they restore savings to their previous level. Once they again reach their *previous peak income*, however, they return to the higher, proportional, consumption rate. This is because they are attaining higher levels of income and feel less obliged to save and more confident of the future.

Friedman's explanation of how the proportional consumption-income relationship may be disturbed is known as the *permanent-income hypothesis*. Let us consider a simplified outline of one of its several versions.

The basic premise is that most individuals have a good idea of their long-term earning capacity. The long-term proportional consumption function reflects these expectations. Yet in the short run the individual is subject to fluctuations in income in the form of, say, overtime pay in periods of boom and shortened hours (or unemployment) in recession. Friedman hypothesizes that individuals rightly consider these income fluctuations as *transitory* and base spending more on their permanent, proportional rate. In general the individual's propensity to increase or reduce consumption from transitory income changes is less than his propensity to consume from permanent income.

The permanent income hypothesis is consistent with the observations that the short-run MPC is less than the long-run MPC (which is proportional and thus the same as APC). One difficulty in using the hypothesis for predictions is that we must anticipate whether individuals will regard income changes as transitory or permanent.

There may be one or more factors which combine to shift the consumers' level of spending. The *stock of durable goods* accumulated (or " used up ") by consumers in previous periods may cause a shift in consumer spending. Likewise the *stock of monetary assets* held by consumers may influence their willingness to spend. *Tastes and habits* may also change. One notable characteristic of tastes is that they tend to harden. Once a family becomes used to consuming certain goods, these goods tend to be thought of as *necessities*. If a temporary reduction in income occurs they will dissave rather than reduce consumption expenditures.

Keynes speculated that the high level of spending in the 1920s may be partially explained by the increase in the *stock of monetary assets* resulting from the large capital gains accruing in the stock market.

A " ratchet " effect is consistent with all of the theories presented. Figure 15.10 illustrates the " ratchet " effect inherent in the theory that the consumption function shifts. Suppose that a shift in the consumption function occurs at the end of a boom period. If a recession follows the consumption function would act as a "ratchet"; consumption would not be reduced at a rate proportional to the previous increase.

Although the several competing theories are similar in several ways they differ significantly in terms of their implications for the use of fiscal policy.

IMPLICATIONS FOR FISCAL POLICY

The assumptions held by policy makers are important in their assessment of what the fiscal policy tools will do. For examples the expected impact may differ according to (1) whether tastes are changing (and perhaps shifting the consumption function), (2) whether the policy leads to new or previous income peaks, or (3) whether the policy increases income in such a way that it is regarded as "transitory" rather than "permanent."

As outlined above several of the consumption theories are consistent with a "ratchet" effect during periods of recession. It follows that policy prescriptions from each would be similar since all would assume a low MPC for additional income.

For fiscal policies designed to increase aggregate spending to levels not previously reached, however, estimates of the multiplier effects would differ substantially. Let us compare the different approaches with reference to a tax cut: Under the assumptions of the simple Keynesian model we would expect a stable consumption function and we would expect to be able to accurately predict the multiplier effect. Under the more sophisticated Keynesian approaches we would entertain the possibility of *shifts* occurring in the consumption function (due to changes in such factors as tastes, the stock of durable goods, the stock of monetary assets, or the distribution of income). Such shifts would of course affect the mechanics of the tax multiplier.

Under our simple version of Duesenberry's "ratchet effect" we would predict different results according to the relationship of the multiplier effect and the previous income peak. If most individuals are below their previous income peaks we would expect MPC and the tax multiplier to be relatively low. If most individuals are currently enjoying their highest income levels, the appropriate MPC would be the higher long-run proportional MPC. Thus the tax multiplier would be greater. Quite conceivably the proposed tax cut would have a mixed multiplier effect which in its first stages brought individuals to their previous income peaks and then beyond.

Under our simple version of the permanent income hypothesis we would predict different results according to whether the individuals consider the tax cut temporary or permanent. The assumptions of the hypothesis seem to indicate that a tax cut would usually be treated as a *transitory* change in income. The expected multiplier effect might be substantially lower than that expected in certain conditions under the Duesenberry model.

Further elaboration would be required to contrast the precise differences between the different approaches. Our brief outline has been sufficient to demonstrate that the assumptions concerning the nature of the consumption function are crucial to predicting the effects of fiscal policy.

THE MECHANICS OF THE SIMPLE CONSUMPTION FUNCTION MODEL

A CHANGE IN GOVERNMENT SPENDING

The impact of changes in government spending have been illustrated above. Quite simply, it is assumed that the impact is direct—that is, government spending directly augments aggregate demand through the multiplier. This effect was shown in Figure 15.6, the ΔY being related to ΔG according to the marginal propensity to consume (the slope of C).

An inherent assumption of the model is that the consumption function remains stable during the period in question. If this holds true, the multiplier effect holds for government spending *reductions* as well as increases. Suppose, for example, aggregate spending for the next year were predicted to be \$1600 billion, composed of $C = \$1380$ billion, $I = \$100$ billion, and $G = \$120$ billion. Further suppose that the full employment level of national income, Y, is \$1500 billion. A curtailment of government expenditure by \$20 billion would, through the multiplier effect[9], reduce aggregate spending to \$1500 billion. Figure 15.11 depicts this process. The $C + I + G$ function shifts downward to $C + I + G - \Delta G$ and a new equilibrium at \$1500 billion.

We will not evaluate the consumption model until the other fiscal tools have been introduced. Several crucial assumptions, however, should be mentioned in passing. First, we note that the consumption function was

---

[9] We still assume $MPC = .8$, so that the multiplier is 5.

FIGURE 15–11

The multiplier effect of a reduction in government spending

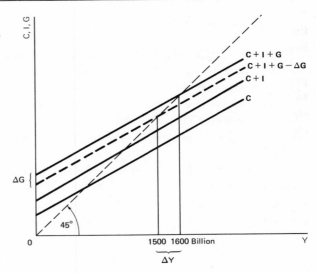

stable for both increases and decreases in public spending. Thus, we must assume that the additional expenditures would not generate a change in the spending habits of individuals. Alternatively, the nature of the reduction in consumption (and ratchet effect if any) accompanying the reduction in G is assumed to be known. Second, we assume that investment spending, I, is stable. The ΔG is assumed to occasion no change in businessmen's expectations, nor does investment change in response to a change in the rate of interest. We necessarily assume that the monetary authorities manipulate the money supply so that the rate of interest will remain stable even with a change in the number of transactions.

Finally, we assume that the tax and transfer system would not impede the multiplier effect on spending. But if taxes increase with income (and transfers decrease), we cannot expect the full multiplier effect.

A CHANGE IN INVESTMENT SPENDING

Under the simplifying assumptions just outlined a change in investment spending has the same effect as a change in government spending. In the example in point, where the consumption function is assumed to have a slope of .8, the investment multiplier (K_I) is 5. Therefore, a change of $20 billion in investment spending would shift the $C + I + G$ function in Figure 15.11 in the same manner as the $20 billion change in government spending.

But the process by which fiscal policy may effect changes in investment spending is much more indirect than in the case of government spending. Since investment spending originates from firms in the private sector, fiscal policy, if it is to be effective in this area, must change businessmen's expectations and investment costs. The government may affect investment decisions by several means: through investment tax credits, through changes in depreciation rates, or through changing the corporation income tax rate itself.

The impact of these government fiscal policies on investment is quite difficult to predict. Moreover, opinions conflict as to the significance and even the direction of government activities in this area. Since the question is of some importance, we shall examine it in some detail in Chapter 16. For the moment we will assume that the estimates of our economic advisors are sufficiently accurate to enable us to use fiscal policy to effectively influence investment and aggregate spending.

A CHANGE IN PERSONAL TAXES OR TRANSFERS

The massive tax cut of 1964 was a bold step into government use of Keynesian fiscal policy. To most laymen the idea that production could be increased (and even the tax yield increased) by a tax cut was suspect, to say the least. Today most people accept, even if they do not fully understand, the efficacy of Keynesian fiscal policy.

The simple consumption function model lends itself well to the presentation of the relationship between taxes, transfers, and aggregate demand. But first it is necessary to modify the model slightly to explicitly include taxes and transfers. Initially, we consider personal income taxes and transfers simply as direct monetary grants to individuals. Their impact on aggregate spending is by way of the change in consumers' disposable income. The model becomes

$$Y = C + I_0 + G_0 \tag{1}$$

$$C = a + b Y_d \tag{2}$$

$$Y_d = Y - T_x + T_r \tag{3}$$

$$I = I_0 \tag{4}$$

$$G = G_0 \tag{5}$$

$$T_x = T_{x0} \tag{6}$$

$$T_r = T_{r0} \tag{7}$$

FIGURE 15–12

The multiplier effect of a
tax reduction

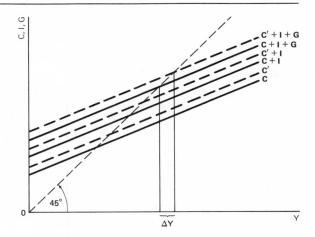

Since taxes and transfers affect aggregate demand *through* affecting
consumption rather than directly as with changes in G, we expect their
multiplier effect to be different. In Figure 15.12 the change in C appears
not as a vertical shift by the amount of the tax cut but as a horizontal
shift. *With a reduction in taxes, more consumption is forthcoming at every
level of Y.* In other words, a given amount of C will be associated with a
lower level of Y. Thus the shift for a tax cut is to the left.

The nature of the multiplier effect is shown in Figure 15.12. Consumption shifts, and since G and I are assumed to be stable, the shift in the
$C + I + G$ function (to $C' + I + G$) is directly proportional. Obviously,
the tax and transfer multipliers will be smaller than K_G and K_I. The
tax multiplier (K_{T_x}) can be derived from our model's system of equations
in the same way as K_G.

Given:

$$Y = C + I + G \tag{1}$$

$$C = a + bY_d \tag{2}$$

$$Y_d = Y - T_x + T_r \tag{3}$$

$$I = I_0 \tag{4}$$

$$G = G_0 \tag{5}$$

$$T_x = T_{x0} \tag{6}$$

$$T_r = T_{r0} \tag{7}$$

We substitute equation (3) into equation (2) and then equation (2) into equation (1) to get

$$Y = a + b(Y - T_x + T_r) + I + G$$

Removing the parentheses, we get

$$Y = a + bY - bT_x + bT_r + I + G$$

Now, solving for Y, we bring all Ys to the lefthand member:

$$Y - bY = a - bT_x + bT_r + I + G$$

and obtain

$$Y = \frac{1}{1-b}(a - bT_x + bT_r + I + G) \tag{8}$$

Introducing a change in tax and a corresponding change in Y, we get

$$Y + \Delta Y = \frac{1}{1-b}[a - b(T_x + \Delta T_x) + bT_r + I + G]$$

which gives

$$Y + \Delta Y = \frac{1}{1-b}[a - bT_x - b\Delta T_x + bT_r + I + G]$$

or

$$Y + \Delta Y = \frac{1}{1-b}(a - bT_x + bT_r + I + G) + \frac{1}{1-b}(-b\Delta T_x) \tag{9}$$

Now, in order to focus attention only on the changes, we subtract equation (8) from equation (9) to get

$$\Delta Y = \frac{1}{1-b}(-b\Delta T_x) = -\frac{b}{1-b}\Delta T_x$$

Thus the tax multiplier is

$$K_{T_x} = \frac{\Delta Y}{\Delta T_x} = -\frac{b}{1-b}$$

Similar derivation shows that the transfer multiplier is

$$K_{T_r} = \frac{\Delta Y}{\Delta T_r} = \frac{b}{1-b}$$

TABLE 15-2

Hypothetical equilibrium of
aggregate spending (in billions of
dollars)

National income (Y)	Consumption (after taxes) (C)	Taxes (T_x)	Investment (I)	Government spending (G)	Generated aggregate spending (C + I + G)	Movement
1800	1460	100	200	100	1760	↓
1700	1380	100	200	100	1680	↓
1600	1300	100	200	100	1600	equilibrium
1500	1220	100	200	100	1520	↑
1400	1140	100	200	100	1440	↑
1300	1060	100	200	100	1360	↑
1200	980	100	200	100	1280	↑

And, of course, the multiplier for a *tax cut* would be the same as the transfer multiplier. In the hypothetical case where $b = .8$,

$$K_{T_x} = -\frac{b}{1-b} = -\frac{.8}{1-.8} = -\frac{.8}{.2} = -4$$

and

$$K_{T_r} = \frac{b}{1-b} = \frac{.8}{1-.8} = \frac{.8}{.2} = 4$$

These are one less than the K_G and K_I.[10]

This can be explained intuitively. When an increase in G occurs, the immediate effect is an increase in spending. For example, the government buys typewriters or paper clips or a firm purchases a steam shovel. The initial transaction involves the purchase of real goods or services. This new spending is then subject to the multiplier effect as each recipient, in turn, spends. When a change in taxes or transfers occurs, the effect of aggregate spending is through C via a change in Y_d. The first step in the multiplier process is skipped. This was the step where, for K_G, the change in G was matched by a change in Y. Thus K_{T_x} and K_{T_r} are always one unit less than K_G and K_I.

A NUMERICAL EXAMPLE OF A TAX CUT

Consider the hypothetical data in Table 15.2. Suppose that full employment output for next year is predicted to be $1700 billion. However, at the present level of T_x, I, and G the aggregate spending generated will only be \$1600 billion. How great a tax reduction is needed if the consumption function is

$$C = a + b(Y - T_x)$$

or rather

$$C = 100 + .8(1600 - 100)$$
$$= 1300$$

Since the marginal propensity to consume is .8, the tax multiplier, K_{T_x}, is 4. Therefore, a \$25 billion tax cut is necessary to raise Y by \$100 billion. After-tax consumption and savings are different at every level of Y. At the \$1700 billion level $C = \$1400$ billion, $I = \$200$ billion, and $G = \$100$ billion.

SOME MORE SOPHISTICATED TAX AND TRANSFER MODELS: TAXES AND TRANSFERS AS A FUNCTION OF INCOME

An important feature of our tax and transfer systems derives from the fact that both are tied to income. Thus when income, Y, changes, taxes and transfers change. In order to introduce this characteristic into our system of equations, we must make both taxes and transfers a function of income:

The model becomes

$$Y = C + I + G \tag{1}$$
$$C = a + bY_d \tag{2}$$
$$Y_d = Y - T_x + T_r \tag{3}$$
$$I = I_0 \tag{4}$$
$$G = G_0 \tag{5}$$
$$T_x = l + mY \tag{6}$$
$$T_r = n - pY \tag{7}$$

Taxes now increase and transfers decrease with income. Intuitively, we can see that such a system will cushion or dampen the multiplier effects of a change in government or investment spending. Moreover, it is obvious that the significance of this dampening effect depends on m and p, the rates at which taxes and transfers change as income, Y, changes.

---

[10] If $b = .6$, then $K_{T_x} = -1.5$ and $K_{T_r} = 1.5$, where we have noted that $K_G = 2.5$ and $K_I = 2.5$.

In order to see this relationship more directly, let us derive the new multiplier by the same sort of reasoning used before.

First, let us substitute equations (6) and (7) into equation (3) to get

$$Y_d = Y - l - m\,Y + n - p\,Y$$

We substitute this equation into the consumption function to get

$$C = a + b(Y - l - m\,Y + n - p\,Y)$$

which we then substitute into equation (1) to get

$$Y = a + bY - bl - bmY + bn - bpY + I + G$$

Solving for Y, we bring all Ys to the lefthand member:

$$Y - bY + bmY + bpY = a - bl + bn + I + G$$

and obtain

$$Y(1 - b + bm + bp) = a - bl + bn + I + G.$$

$$Y = \frac{1}{1 - b(1 - m - p)}[a - bl + bn + I + G] \tag{8}$$

We can now use equation (8) to examine the relationship between changes in I or G and changes in Y. Let us consider a change in G:

$$Y + \Delta Y = \frac{1}{1 - b(1 - m - p)}[a - bl + bn + I + G + \Delta G]$$

or

$$Y + \Delta Y = \frac{1}{1 - b(1 - m - p)}[a - bl + bn + I + G]$$
$$+ \frac{1}{1 - b(1 - m - p)}[\Delta G]$$

Subtracting equation (8), we find the relationship between changes in G and Y to be

$$\Delta Y = \frac{1}{1 - b(1 - m - p)}[\Delta G] \tag{9}$$

Thus the modified multiplier is:

$$K_G = \frac{\Delta Y}{\Delta G} = \frac{1}{1 - b(1 - m - p)}$$

The modified multiplier clearly illustrates how the marginal rate of taxation, the marginal rate of transfer payments and the marginal propensity to consume are directly related in determining the multiplier. We can see that both personal taxes and transfers tend to make the multiplier smaller.[11]

---

[11] The calculus can be used to obtain the same results and provide some additional insights. We start with the model outlined above:

$$Y = C + I_0 + G_0$$
$$C = a + b(Y - T_z + T_r) \qquad (a > 0; \ 0 < b < 1)$$
$$T_z = l + mY \qquad\qquad\quad (l > 0; \ 0 < m < 1)$$
$$T_r = n - pY \qquad\qquad\quad (n > 0; \ 0 < p < 1)$$

Substituting we get the equation:

$$Y = \frac{1}{1 - b(1 - m - p)} \, (a - bl + bn + I_0 + G_0)$$

The partial derivatives reveal the familiar government spending multiplier

$$\frac{\partial Y}{\partial G} = \frac{1}{1 - b + bm + bp} > 0$$

and the multipliers associated with different elements of the tax and transfer functions

$$\frac{\partial Y}{\partial l} = \frac{-b}{1 - b + bm + bp} < 0$$

$$\frac{\partial Y}{\partial m} = \frac{-b(a - bl + bn + I_0 + G_0)}{(1 - b + bm + bp)^2} \gtreqless 0 \quad \text{as} \quad bl \gtreqless a + I_0 + G_0$$

$$\frac{\partial Y}{\partial n} = \frac{+b}{1 - b + bm + bp} > 0$$

$$\frac{\partial Y}{\partial p} = \frac{-b(a - bl + bn + I_0 + G_0)}{(1 - b + bm + bp)^2} \gtreqless 0 \quad \text{as} \quad bn \gtreqless a + I_0 + G_0$$

The derivatives for l and n may be termed *nonincome* tax and transfer multipliers since those elements of the functions are not connected with income. They show the multiplier when taxes (or transfers) are changed in such a way that the income tax (or transfer) rate is not affected. As expected an increase in taxes has a negative multiplier on Y and an increase in transfers has a positive effect.

Changes in m and p, the income tax and transfer rates, are more difficult to assess. Each of these multipliers has an indeterminate sign. The denominator will be positive since it is a square. The income-tax-rate multiplier will be *negative* if bl is less than $a + I_0 + G_0$; the result we would expect. The *income-transfer-rate multiplier* will be *positive* if bn is less than $a + I_0 + G_0$; again the result we would expect.

AN APPLICATION

An example is in order. Suppose the tax function is:

$$T_x = l + mY$$
$$T_x = 50 + .08Y$$

In other words, part of each year's personal income tax intake ($50 billion) is *independent of income*. The tax intake is, however, a positive function of income, and the rate at which it changes with income is .08.

The function which relates changing transfer payments to income is

$$T_r = n - pY$$
$$T_r = 20 - .02Y$$

Transfer payments of $20 billion are not related to income. However, a certain part of transfer payments are negatively related to income. As national income increases in the short run, transfer payments decline at the rate of $.02Y$.

If we use a marginal propensity to consume of .8, our government spending multiplier now becomes

$$\frac{1}{1 - b(1 - m - p)} = \frac{1}{1 - .8(1 - .08 - .02)} = \frac{1}{1 - .72} = \frac{1}{.28} = 3.6.$$

Without the dampening effect of the automatic stabilizers, however, the multiplier would have to be

$$\frac{1}{1 - b} = \frac{1}{1 - .8} = \frac{1}{.2} = 5.$$

Obviously the effect of the automatic stabilizers can be considerable.[12] Such effects are quite useful when, for some reason, aggregate spending drops off sharply or investment spending increases too rapidly. In such cases the fluctuations are less severe than they would be if taxes and transfers were not a function of Y. Suppose, for example, that the full employment level has been reached but firms become overly optimistic and invest an additional $10 billion of excess spending. If automatic stabilizers are of the degree of those in the hypothetical case, the additional aggregate spending is only $36 million instead of the $50 billion. This is because as spending and income increased, taxes also increased and transfer payments decreased.

On the other hand, it is notable that the effectiveness of government spending as a fiscal tool is decreased by the automatic stabilizers in the same way the investment spending multiplier is decreased. To an extent, the same thing can be said about the tax and transfer multipliers. Yet there is a distinct difference. Consider again the case of the 1964 tax cut. Not only were taxes cut but the marginal rate of taxation was also lowered. This meant not only a change in the quantity of tax revenues, but also a change in the tax multiplier itself.

THE NET EFFECT OF BUDGET CHANGES

In a growing economy, changes in the public budget are inevitable. We expect both expenditures and taxes to increase, the latter perhaps automatically, owing to the increase in income. In formulating fiscal policy it is necessary to consider the net effect of budget changes on aggregate spending.

Suppose it appears that aggregate spending will be sufficient in the forthcoming period. Is a " balanced budget " the appropriate fiscal policy? Will an increase in personal income taxes by the same amount as the increase in expenditures produce a neutral effect on aggregate spending? Obviously not, since the government spending multiplier is not the same as the tax multiplier.

In the simple consumption function model, application of a " balanced " budget change produces an interesting result. The impact of such a change on aggregate spending is always the exact amount of the change in the budget itself. This phenomenon occurs because the government spending multiplier is always one greater than the tax multiplier in the simple model. Consequently, the net effect of an equal change in G and T_x will be an increase in the level of aggregate spending by the amount of the change in the budget. The change in income is the sum of the changes brought about by the change in G and T_x.

$$\Delta Y = K_G \, \Delta G + K_{T_x} \, \Delta T_x$$

---

[12] If both the marginal rate of taxation and the marginal rate of transfer payments were higher, of course the effect on the multiplier would be greater. If, for example, m were 15 percent and p were 5 percent, the multiplier would be reduced to:

$$\frac{1}{1 - .8(1 - .15 - .05)} = \frac{1}{1 - .8(.8)} = \frac{1}{1 - .64} = \frac{1}{.36} = 2.8.$$

or

$$\Delta Y = \frac{1}{1-b} \Delta G + \left(-\frac{b}{1-b}\right) \Delta T_x$$

Now if the change in G is equal to the change in T_x, both can be designated by B:

$$\Delta G = \Delta T_x = \Delta B$$

Thus we can write:

$$\Delta Y = \frac{1}{1-b} \Delta B - \frac{b}{1-b} \Delta B$$

$$= \frac{1-b}{1-b} \Delta B$$

$$\Delta Y = \Delta B$$

Thus, the change in aggregate spending (or Y) is always equal to the change in the budget, regardless of the multiplier. For example if the marginal propensity is .8, $K_G = 5$ and $K_{T_x} = 4$. For an increase of $10 billion in taxes and expenditures the net multiplier effect of the $K_G \cdot \Delta G$ of $50 billion and $K_{T_x} \cdot \Delta T_x$ of $40 is $10 billion. Similarly with an MPC of .6 and $K_G = 2.5$ and $K_{T_x} = 1.5$, the net effect of a $10 billion change would be $25 billion minus $15 billion, or $10 billion.

If we take account of the link between taxes and income, the results are not so straightforward. Both the government spending and the tax multiplier are smaller, owing to the dampening effect of taxes on consumption as income changes. Even so, the net effect of the budget change on aggregate spending will be a multiplier of one.[13]

If the change in taxes involves a change in the marginal rate of taxation m, again both K_G and K_{T_x} are affected. Consequently, an increase in the budget (with taxes and expenditures increased equally) which is accompanied by an increase in m will have reduced both K_G and K_{T_x}. After account is taken of these qualifications the net multiplier effect is still likely to be close to unity.[14]

We have of course used the multiplier-of-one example only for expositional purposes.

Assuming one knows the next period's full-employment Y and the planned increase in G, how does one arrive at the appropriate tax? The answer depends on whether the rate of the tax is to be changed in addition to the amount of revenue. Recall the equations:

$$T_x = l + mY \qquad T_r = n - pY$$

Which gives us a multiplier for both taxes and transfers combined of:

$$K_{T_{xr}} = -\frac{b(1 - m_2 - p_2)}{1 - b(1 - m_2 - p_2)}$$

and a government spending multiplier of

$$K_G = \frac{1}{1 - b(1 - m_2 - p_2)}$$

For any desired ΔY, when ΔG is known, the ΔT_{xr} is simply

$$\Delta Y = \Delta G \cdot K_G - \Delta T_{xr} \cdot K_{T_{xr}}$$

---

[13]Assume as in the application above $b = .8$, $m = .08$ and $p = .02$. The government spending multiplier is:

$$K_G = \frac{1}{1 - b(1 - m - p)} = \frac{1}{1 - .8(1 - .08 - .02)} = \frac{1}{.28} = 3.6$$

It follows that the tax and transfer multiplier is:

$$K_{T_{xr}} = -\frac{b(1 - m - p)}{1 - b(1 - m - p)} = -\frac{.8(1 - .08 - .02)}{1 - .8(1 - .02 - .02)} = -2.6$$

Consequently if the change in the budget involves no change in the tax or transfer rates but only the amounts, the net multiplier is one. For an increase in the budget of $10 billion, $\Delta G \cdot K_G = \$36$ billion and $\Delta T_{xr} \cdot K_{T_{xr}} = \$26$ billion for a net effect of $10 billion.

[14] Let m_1 and p_1 be the old marginal rates of taxation and transfer, respectively, and let m_2 and p_2 be the new rates. If we are to arrive at a balanced budget, we must know just how to change the rates to achieve a ΔT_{xr} that equals ΔG. The new multipliers will be

$$K_G = \frac{1}{1 - b(1 - m_2 - p_2)}, \qquad K_{T_{xr}} = -\frac{b(1 - m_2 - p_2)}{1 - b(1 - m_2 - p_2)}$$

Suppose that the new marginal rate of taxation is .10 and the new marginal rate of transfer is .01. The multipliers become

$$K_G = \frac{1}{1 - .8(1 - .10 - .01)} = 3.45$$

$$K_{T_{xr}} = -\frac{.8(1 - .10 - .01)}{1 - .8(1 - .10 - .01)} = -2.45$$

Again the difference between the multipliers is one.

or

$$\Delta T_{xr} = \frac{\Delta Y - \Delta G \cdot K_G}{K_{T_{xr}}}$$

The appropriate mix of macroeconomic tools will depend on the particular situation and will not necessarily call for a balanced budget. Moreover, as we shall see, various conditions in the money market may dampen the balanced budget multiplier.[15]

In a hypothetical situation where the desired ΔY is $20 billion, the planned ΔG is $10 billion, K_G is 3.5 and $K_{T_{xr}}$ is 2.5 the solution is as follows:

$$\Delta T_{xr} = \frac{20 - 10(3.5)}{2.5}$$

$\Delta T_{xr} = \$6$ billion

The required change in T_{xr} is less than the planned change in government expenditures, ΔG, because the budget is being used to increase aggregate spending by more than the simple balanced budget multiplier-of-one.

Suppose we wish to find the tax and transfer *rate* changes necessary to produce the appropriate change in aggregate spending. Let us simplify by combining m and p so that the tax-transfer multiplier becomes

$$K_{T_{xr}} = -\frac{b(1-t)}{1-b(1-t)}$$

and the government spending multiplier becomes

$$K_G = \frac{1}{1-b(1-t)}$$

We again start from the equation:

$$\Delta Y = \Delta G \cdot K_G - \Delta T_{xr} \cdot K_{T_{xr}}$$

If there is to be no change in the amount of T_{xr} the $\Delta T_{xr} \cdot K_{T_{xr}}$ drops out and we solve for

$$\Delta Y = \Delta G \cdot \frac{1}{1-b(1-t)}$$

as follows:

$$\Delta Y = \Delta G \cdot \frac{1}{1 - b - bt}$$

$$\Delta Y(1 - b - bt) = \Delta G$$

$$\Delta Y - \Delta Yb - \Delta Ybt = \Delta G$$

$$-\Delta Ybt = \Delta G - \Delta Y + \Delta Yb$$

$$t = \frac{-G\Delta + \Delta Y - \Delta Yb}{\Delta Yb}$$

Since the desired change in aggregate spending, ΔY, the planned change in government spending, ΔG, and the marginal propensity to consume, b, are all known, it is not difficult to find the required tax rate.

The choice of t is not as simple as we have intimated in our simple model. In the first place we note that our equations

$$T_x = l + mY$$

$$T_r = n - pY$$

represent a tax and transfer rate structure which is progressive, proportional, or regressive depending on the values of l, m, n, and p. If we wish to change taxes and remain "neutral" towards our income distribution goal it would be rather complicated even in our simple model; and we would undoubtedly have to change l and n as well as m and p. In reality, our tax rate structure is not a simple linear function, but instead the marginal rates are different for different levels of income. This would seem to complicate the rate-change decision even further but an excellent expedient is available: the tax surcharge. This is essentially the procedure we used in our simple "Fiscal Department" model presented in Chapter 4. The procedure employed was to first use taxes and transfers to accomplish the income distribution goal; then if taxes were needed for stabilization purposes, the Macroeconomic Policy Branch manager would tax each

---

[15] In Chapter 16 we will expand the Keynesian model to demonstrate how a stable money supply dampens the multiplier effects via changes in the rate of interest. More sophisticated models which account for the availability of credit in special situations may even produce a *negative* balanced budget multiplier. See, for example, Roger W. Spencer and William P. Yohe, "The 'Crowding Out' of Public Expenditures by Fiscal Policy Actions," Federal Reserve Board of St. Louis, *Review*, vol. 52, no. 10 (October 1970), pp. 12–24.

individual the same percentage of his remaining income. In " real world " implementation of the tax surcharge, the regular rate schedule is used—in which the distribution goal is inherent—and then a certain percentage is added to each person's tax bill. Thus *relative* income positions remain unchanged, and it can be argued that the tax surcharge is neutral with respect to the income distribution goal.

The tax surcharge has attributes which enhance its " neutrality " with respect to intersector resource allocation as well. The high visibility of the tax helps remind citizens that it is a temporary macroeconomic policy measure and thus does not necessarily constitute real opportunity costs (private sector benefits lost through withdrawal of resources from private sector to public sector) but is instead a reduction of inflationary pressures.

16

KEYNESIANISM, MONETARISM, AND
DIRECT WAGE AND PRICE CONTROLS

In the last chapter we introduced the basic Quantity-Theory-of-Money and Keynesian models. It is now appropriate to elaborate on these models and to discuss the assumptions, value judgments, and trade-offs inherent in the choice of a given macroeconomic policy. It is also appropriate that we consider the resort to Direct Wage and Price Controls as an alternative to either a Keynesian or Monetarist approach. As we shall see, each approach contains quite different judgments about the effectiveness of market adjustments and of the various policy tools. One basic difference, we have observed, is that the Keynesian and Monetarist approaches rely on *indirect* tools to influence the level of aggregate spending. Thus they put far fewer constraints on the economic choices made by individuals and firms than do the Direct Wage and Price Controls.

Let us proceed by first expanding the Keynesian model.

INVESTMENT AS A FUNCTION OF THE RATE OF INTEREST

Up to now we have included investment in our model as an exogenous variable—that is, we have focused attention on other variables while taking investment as "given." It is obvious, however, from our discussion of the simple investment model and from casual observation that investment spending is an important determinant of aggregate spending and growth. It is equally obvious from our examination of individual and firm behavior in Chapters 9 and 11 that *predicting investment response to fiscal activity is difficult.*

We begin by reviewing the factors which businessmen consider when making investment decisions. These factors, as outlined in Figure 16.1, are best demonstrated with reference to a hypothetical investment decision:

Suppose you run an airline and you are considering an additional jet airliner. In the process of determining the profitability of the purchase, your first step is to make an estimate of the revenue you expect in the form of fees from your customers. Against this you consider operating costs such as gas, oil, maintenance, and the wages of the pilots, engineers, and hostesses. The difference between these totals is "expected net returns." The "profitability" of a project is determined by subtracting the present cost of the airplane from the expected net revenue.

Once the profitability of an investment project has been determined, one compares this with the cost of investment funds (i.e., the rate of interest) and decides whether or not to undertake the project. For example, if the profitability of the additional jet airliner turns out to be

FIGURE 16–1

The determinants
of investment

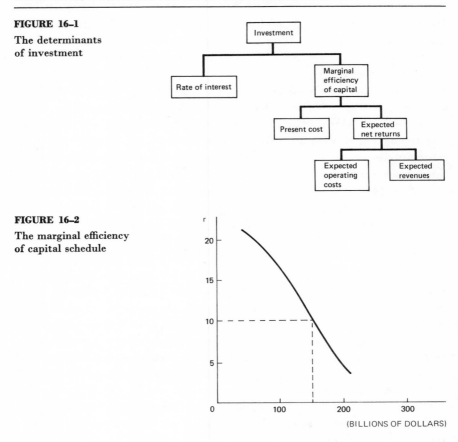

FIGURE 16–2

The marginal efficiency
of capital schedule

more than the going rate of interest, it is to your advantage to undertake the project. This is true whether you finance it with internally generated funds or borrow from the capital market. On the other hand, if the interest rate is higher than the profitability of the project, it is best not to undertake it even if funds are available within the firm. You could put funds to better use by lending them at the going interest rate.

Most firms are able to expand or contract in the short run according to the profitability of various alternative plans or projects. The marginal efficiency of capital (*MEC*) schedule is simply the summation of the profitability of all alternatives available to firms in the economy. The schedule shows how much investment will be forthcoming at each rate of interest. Obviously, firms will invest in all projects whose profitability

(or efficiency) is greater than the rate of interest. In fact, firms will invest
in all projects out to the point where they can just break even; i.e.,
where the *MEC* $= r$. When the rate of interest falls, additional projects
become feasible; consequently, more investment takes place. This is
consistent with the *MEC* schedule as shown in Figure 16.2. Since businessmen will invest according to the profitability of projects available
to them, we can consider the *MEC* schedule a *demand schedule* for
investment funds.

There are two rather serious drawbacks to using the marginal efficiency
of capital schedule for predicting forthcoming investment. In the first
place, the schedule itself *shifts* frequently. In our brief analysis of investment, we noted several things which affect it. If the *MEC* schedule
shifts, one of the variables we have assumed stable has changed. For
example, we assumed that businessmen's *expectations* about business
conditions and the profitability of alternative projects would be stable.
When, however, businessmen's expectations change (and they frequently
do), their whole outlook on the marginal efficiency of capital changes.
Moreover, we have assumed that technology does not change. If, however, technology changes in such a way as to increase the number of
profitable investment opportunities, the schedule shifts to the right.
Alternatively, the initial or operating costs of certain undertakings might
increase (or decrease). If costs go up—say, as a result of rising wages—
the MEC schedule would shift to the left. Fewer projects would be
profitable at a given rate of interest.

And, of course, government fiscal policy can have an effect on the
MEC schedule. For example, an investment tax credit essentially lowers
the initial costs of investment projects, shifting the *MEC* to the right.

A second drawback concerns the elasticity of the function. Most
studies indicate that businessmen's investment decisions are somewhat unresponsive to changes in the rate of interest. They seem reluctant
to change investment decisions simply on the basis of a change in the
rate of interest—partly, no doubt, because uncertainty plays such a
large role in investment planning.

These two characteristics of the MEC make it somewhat unreliable as a
predictive tool. Anyone familiar with statistics can appreciate the
difficulties involved in working with a function which is inelastic and
which often shifts. The problem is that one does not know whether a
change in investment is due solely to a corresponding change in r or
whether it is partly due to a shift in the function.

FIGURE 16–3

The commodity market
showing a change in
investment

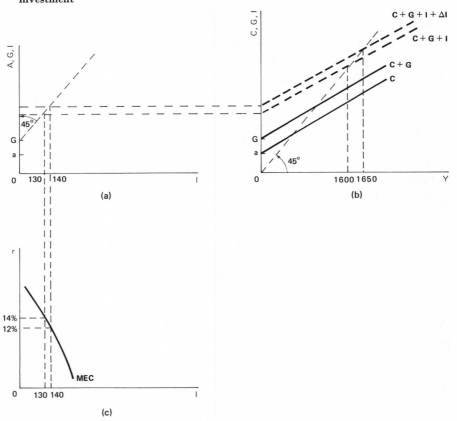

Since we must use the MEC schedule with caution, we use a general function to represent the relationship:

$$I = f(r)$$

With the inclusion of investment as a function of r, our simple model becomes

$$Y = C + I + G \tag{1}$$

$$C = a + bY \tag{2}$$

$$I = f(r) \tag{3}$$

$$G = G_0 \tag{4}$$

Equation (4) reveals that we are still considering G an exogenous variable (determined outside the model). Now let us trace through a hypothetical example to see how businessmen respond to a change in the rate of interest and how the resultant change in investment affects aggregate spending via the multiplier.

Suppose that Y is $1600 billion, that the interest rate falls from 14 to 12 percent, and that this results in $10 billion of investment spending. Suppose also that the marginal propensity to consume, b, is .8 giving us an investment multiplier of 5. The new equilibrium spending level is $50 billion greater, or $1650 billion.

Figure 16.3 illustrates the case just described. As the interest rate falls from 14 to 12 percent, investment increases from $130 billion to $140 billion.[1]

When the change in investment is reflected onto diagram (b), the familiar consumption function, a new equilibrium income of $1650 billion is indicated where $Y = C + I + G$. The multiplier effect is shown by the new dotted line, which follows the slope of the consumption function (the slope being the marginal propensity to consume) and relates the change in investment to the new equilibrium level of spending (Y).

$$\Delta Y = K_I \cdot \Delta I$$

Since different equilibrium levels of spending, Y, are associated with different rates of interest, r, we may use diagrams (a), (b), (c) to derive a schedule showing this relationship. This schedule, known as the IS function, is shown in diagram (d) of Figure 16.4. It simply states that at lower rates of interest we have more aggregate spending, Y. The reason for greater Y at lower rates of interest is inherent in the related diagrams: at a lower rate of interest we have more I which via the multiplier (which is inherent in diagram 2) gives us more Y. We will make use of the IS function shortly.

---

[1] Diagram (a) is simply a mechanical device for reflecting the amount of investment [diagram (c)] onto the consumption function diagram. This is done by drawing a 45-degree line so as to reflect equal amounts of investment on each of the axes. Since we desire to have I reflected onto the consumption function at the proper level, we add a and G to I before transferring it to diagram (b). This is done by adding a and G to the vertical axis of diagram (a) and moving the 45-degree angle up accordingly.

Thus, it will be necessary to shift G and a in both diagrams (a) and (b) any time we have a change in G or a shift in the consumption function.

FIGURE 16-4

The commodity market
showing the derivation of
the I-S function

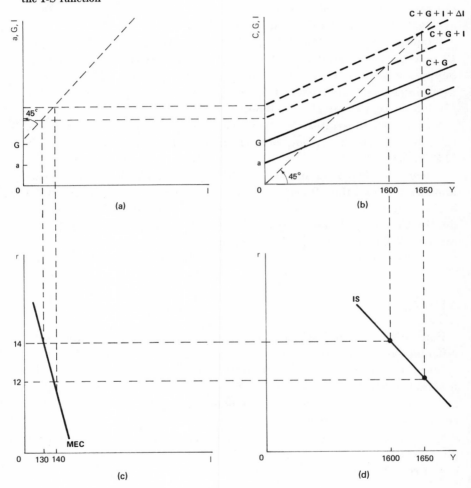

INVESTMENT AS A FUNCTION OF INCOME

Since businessmen's expectations of future earnings depend importantly
on what is happening to aggregate spending, it is often helpful to consider
investment as a function of Y:

$$I = f(Y)$$

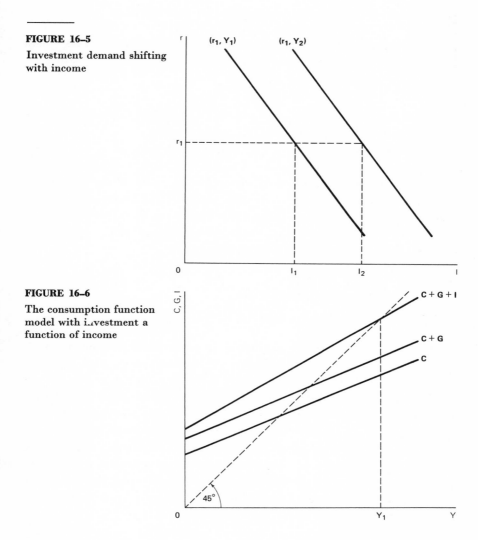

FIGURE 16–5

Investment demand shifting
with income

FIGURE 16–6

The consumption function
model with investment a
function of income

In periods when Y is increasing rapidly, businessmen's expectations
are likely to become more optimisitic. The demand for investment funds,
MEC, may shift to the right, as shown in Figure 16.5. As Y increases
from Y_1 to Y_2, investment increases from I_1 to I_2, even with no change
in the interest rate. Figure 16.6 depicts the relationship in terms of the
consumption function diagram. Since investment increases with income,
the slope of $C + G + I$ is steeper than that of the C function. For any
change such as ΔG, ΔT_x, ΔT_r, or ΔI the multiplier effect is augmented

by the change in investment induced by the change in Y. This effect, known as the "acceleration principle," is more precisely written as

$$I = f(\Delta Y)$$

Stated in this way, investment is seen to be related to how fast income is growing rather than simply the level it has reached.

As we shall see later, the effect of the accelerator is more complex than our simple depiction implies. The accelerator, it turns out, is more powerful in some situations than others. For example, at the start of an upturn when firms already have excess capacity, the accelerator is weak since few firms need new plants and machinery. On the other hand when firms are already approaching capacity, increased sales will induce them to invest in new plants and machinery.

FISCAL ACTIVITY AND INVESTMENT

EXPENDITURES AND INVESTMENT

The simple multiplier effect of a change in government spending depends on an increase in consumption. Unless the acceleration principle is operative, no investment will be induced by the change in Y.

The *nature* of government spending, however, is crucial to the response of businessmen. Government expenditures may take the form of public investment in roads, flood control, ports, communication facilities, education, and other things. Such expenditures enhance the productivity of private capital and tend to encourage private investment. In addition, government promotion of basic research in fields such as the space program, agriculture, and health is likely to spawn private sector innovation and investment.

On the other hand, certain types of government expenditures may retard private investment. This is especially likely in industries where governmental services are *substitutes* for those produced in the private sector—for example, in communications, power, and education.

Transfer expenditures also have a multiplier effect, which, as we know, involves a shift in the consumption function (plus an increase in consumption in response to increased Y). Obviously, use of this technique to increase Y will have the effect of increasing the proportion of C relative to I. In addition, certain types of transfer payments create a substitution effect which reduces private saving and possibly investment.

Expansion of programs such as social security, Medicare, and unemployment compensation, which meet the needs "target savers" had been saving for, will reduce savings effort—not only by partially meeting savings goals (such as old-age retirement) but by reducing uncertainty about possible costs of unemployment, hospitalization, and other misfortunes.

Finally, if fiscal policy is successful in sustaining nearly full employment over a long period, individuals will change their estimates of the amounts required to be set aside for possible unemployment. In terms of the simple consumption function model, the result of these influences is to increase consumption and the marginal propensity to consume. The latter result, of course, increases each of the multipliers.

TAXES AND INVESTMENT

The primary effect of an increase in the tax on personal income is a reduction in consumption, which through the tax multiplier reduces Y. In the event that businessmen's expectations become less optimistic, they reduce investment; consequently, the curtailment of aggregate spending is accelerated. Possibly, of course, businessmen, convinced that the tax increase is needed, will be encouraged by such evidence of " sound " fiscal policy and will invest more rather than less.

Another effect of increased personal income taxes is to reduce the ability to save, thereby reducing the funds available for investment. This effect may be limited by savers with particular savings goals and by monetary authorities who act to insure availability of credit. Firms which obtain funds for investment internally will certainly not be affected. Moreover, an increase in personal income taxes increases the attractiveness of income from capital gains rather than dividends, and this may well encourage stockholders to allow firms to retain a greater percentage of funds for investment purposes.

Fiscal policy may involve the choice between regressive taxes such as the payroll taxes and progressive taxes such as the personal income tax. A popular argument is that, since the upper income groups save more, progressive taxes will reduce the funds available for investment; so, accordingly, investment and economic growth will be reduced. But we have noted on several occasions that the marginal propensity to consume falls only slightly as income rises. While the lower income groups may still dissave, the tax relief from a shift to a more progressive tax structure

FIGURE 16–7

Investment demand shift
due to investment tax
credit

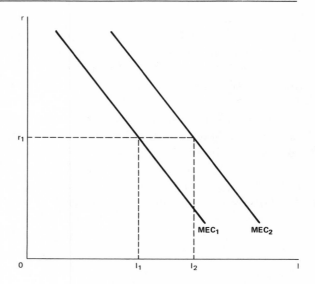

may bring about a reduction in their debt. The argument that increasing tax progressivity reduces investment is further discredited when we recall our previous discussions (Chapters 9 and 10) of the tenuous link between saving and real investment.

An increase in the corporation income tax reduces corporation income and hence the base for investment from internal funds. Some firms will be in a position to pass the tax on to consumers, while others will reduce dividends to stockholders; otherwise, investment will necessarily be reduced. We recall from our discussion of the behavioral models of corporations that a relatively independent management with certain sales goals may resist reducing investment if it is also able to pay the tax and keep stockholders satisfied with reduced dividends.

Changes in depreciation rates and tax credits for investment have been used aggressively in recent years to influence investment spending. Accelerated depreciation rates allow companies to recoup investment spending more rapidly and thus have it available for more investment. For a steadily expanding firm this initial bonus continues indefinitely. The investment tax credit directly lowers the present cost of investment projects and encourages the undertaking of previously marginal projects. In both cases the demand for investment funds *shifts* to the right, as pictured in Figure 16.7, and more investment is undertaken at the current rate of interest. This additional investment spending is, of course, subject to the multiplier effect and the acceleration principle (if operative).

MONEY IN THE KEYNESIAN MODEL

The primary connection between the functional relationships summed up in the *IS* function and the money market is the rate of interest—and this connection, as we have seen, is somewhat tenuous. According to the elasticity of the MEC schedule, a change in *r* will result in a change in *I*, which, through the multiplier effect, will change *Y*.

THE SUPPLY OF MONEY

Demand deposits are the most important portion of the money supply, accounting for three-fourths of the total. Our examination of the Federal Reserve's role in macroeconomic policy will focus on its influence on the demand deposits held in the bank system.

There are three primary monetary tools at the disposal of the "Fed." The most important is its ability to buy and sell government securities on the open market, thus increasing or decreasing the amount of lending power left in the private sector. The Fed also has the power to raise or lower the percentage of money banks must hold as legal reserve against deposits, thereby increasing or decreasing the base upon which credit can be extended. The Fed also on occasion loans money to private banks. Consequently, by lowering or raising the rate on the loans (the "rediscount rate") the Fed can increase or decrease the money supply.

The impact of these three operations is magnified by the *credit multiplier*, the process by which banks, having only to hold a fraction of new deposits as reserves, can collectively expand the money supply by a multiple of the original increase. Let us assume that the Open Market Committee of the Fed decides that expansion of the money supply is desirable. The Fed *buys* securities, thus placing money (instead of securities) in the private sector. Typically, the Fed buys securities, say Treasury bills, from a dealer in New York, who then deposits the check into his firm's account in a commercial bank. Now if the bank's legal reserve requirement is only 15 percent, the other 85 percent of the deposit may be used for loans. These loans become demand deposits for customers, who use them to pay other firms or persons, who in turn deposit this amount in their respective banks. For each bank receiving this second round of deposits, "excess reserves" are created upon which more loans

FIGURE 16–8

The transactions demand
for money

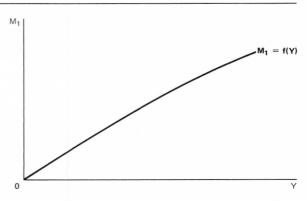

can be made. If the process continues without leakage, the 15 percent
requirement allows credit to be multiplied by $6\frac{2}{3}$ times the original injection of money by the Fed.[2]

In periods of expansion and high expectations, banks try to stay
"loaned up" by keeping available reserves at work. The rediscount
privilege allows them to borrow from the Fed when they are running
the danger of a temporary shortage of deposits backing up their loans.
When the Fed raises the rediscount rate and requires more stringent
guidelines for its loans, banks respond by tightening credit, thus reducing the money supply. Since actual member bank borrowing from the
Fed is small, the primary use of the rediscount rate is as an "announcement effect." That is, the Fed raises or lowers the rate to let banks and
businesses know that it is going to follow a policy of tight or easy money.

Changing the reserve requirement for member banks influences the
money supply in two ways. First, it changes the reserve position of the
bank. A decrease in the reserve requirement creates "excess" reserves,
which may be used to expand credit. The credit multiplier is also changed,
so that as these additional loans become deposits in other banks, a
smaller proportion of them is needed to fulfill the reserve requirement.
The effectiveness of a change in the reserve requirement depends on the
reserve position of the bank. In periods when expectations are high and
the bank is "loaned up," an increase in the reserve requirement will
effectively tighten credit. However, commercial banks have a precau-
tionary demand for money and when expectations are low their *effective*
reserve ratio may be higher than the *actual* requirement. According to the
situation a very small percentage change in the requirement can generate
large changes in the money supply. Consequently the Fed uses the reserve requirement to meet the economy's long-term needs for more

money. Thus the tool the Fed primarily relies on for short-run macroeconomic adjustments is open market operations.

There are, of course, limitations to the Fed's ability to control the money supply. Initially, however, we will assume that the Fed can control the money supply, M, and we introduce it as an exogenous variable to our model:

$$M = M_0$$

THE TWO DEMANDS FOR MONEY

There are two basic reasons people and firms demand money: as a medium of exchange and as a store of value. Businesses and individuals need a certain amount to carry on transactions: payments for labor, materials, groceries, and so on. The amount of money required to carry on these transactions depends for the most part on institutional arrangements, such as billing procedures and the frequency of paydays. These arrangements may change over time, and such changes should be accounted for in macroeconomic analysis. What is important in the short run is the amount of money required for transactions at different levels of business activity. Consequently, we state the transactions requirement as a positive function of income:

$$M_1 = f(Y)$$

and represent it graphically as in Figure 16.8.

The recognition of the demand for money as a store of value was an important part of the Keynesian argument. Keynes noted that people's expectations about price fluctuation have a significant effect on their willingness to hold money. At any given time the amount they wish to hold is inversely proportional to what they can earn by loaning it out. When interest rates seem relatively high, people are anxious to invest and will hold very little money for liquidity purposes. Conversely, when interest rates seem relatively low, people will hold larger amounts, since they anticipate that the rates will soon go up. At very low rates Keynes predicted that people will hold practically all additional money they

---

[2] It turns out that the credit multiplier is the reciprocal of the reserve requirement. For 15 percent the multiplier is $\frac{1}{.15} = 6\frac{2}{3}$. Thus, for an injection of \$1,000,000 the possible expansion of the money supply is \$6,666,667. In the case of a 20 percent requirement the credit multiplier is $\frac{1}{.20}$ (or 5), and an injection of \$1,000,000 could lead to an increase in the money supply of \$5,000,000.

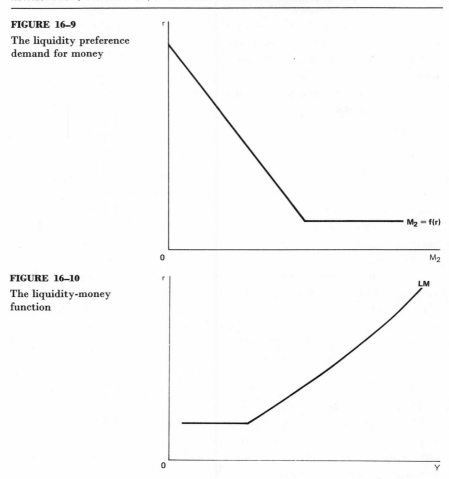

FIGURE 16–9

The liquidity preference demand for money

FIGURE 16–10

The liquidity-money function

receive rather than invest any. If they were to invest it at a low rate, it would be tied up in the event of a rate increase. As Keynes conceived it, the function is an inverse relationship between money and the rate of interest:

$$M_2 = f(r)$$

and can be represented as in Figure 16.9. Note the floor on the interest rate at which further additions of money are held and do not reduce the rate. Since this demand is highly dependent on people's expectations, a change in people's attitudes toward the economy may shift the function significantly.

Our simple model has been expanded to include the following functions:

$$Y = C + I + G \tag{1}$$

$$C = a + bY \tag{2}$$

$$I = f(r) \tag{3}$$

$$G = G_0 \tag{4}$$

$$M = M_0 \tag{5}$$

$$M_1 = f(Y) \tag{6}$$

$$M_2 = f(r) \tag{7}$$

$$M = M_1 + M_2 \tag{8}$$

Let us consider the relationships between the supply and the two demands for money. Assume the money supply, M, is predetermined by the Federal Reserve. At a particular level of income, Y, a certain amount of money, M_1, is required for transactions. The part of M that is left to fulfill liquidity demand, M_2, *is associated with a particular rate of interest, r*. At a higher level of Y more of the money supply is required for transactions; thus, a lower M_2 is associated with a higher r. At a lower level of Y less of the money supply is required for transactions; thus, a lower M_2 is associated with a lower r. The relationships are inherent in the liquidity-money function shown in Figure 16.10.

FISCAL AND MONETARY POLICY IN THE COMPLETE KEYNESIAN MODEL

The relationship between the variables in the commodity and money markets can now be demonstrated more clearly. An equilibrium may attain, as shown in Figure 16.11. At the rate of interest r_1 and level of income Y_1, $IS = LM$. What this means in terms of the commodity market is that at r_1 a certain level of I is made and that given the consumption function and G, a certain level of spending, Y_1, takes place. In terms of the money market we know that at Y_1 a certain amount of money is tied up in transactions, M_1, and given the money supply the liquidity demand for money makes for a certain rate of interest, r_1.

Fiscal and monetary policy may influence Y in the following ways:

1. *A change in government spending.* We recall that a change in government spending changes Y through the multiplier effect, the latter depending on MPC, the slope of the consumption function. With an MPC of .8

FIGURE 16–11

Equilibrium between the commodity and money markets

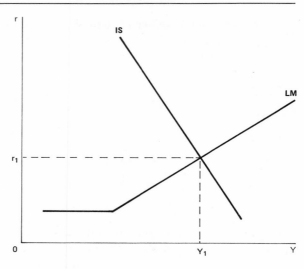

FIGURE 16–12

A shift in the IS function

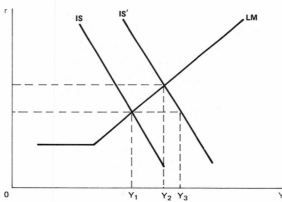

FIGURE 16–13

A shift in the LM function

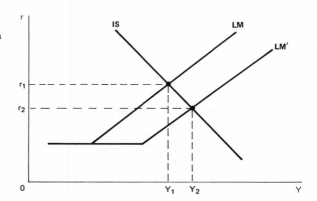

---

the multiplier is $1/(1 - .8) = 5$. An increase in G shifts $C + I + G$ upward and the IS function to the right. Realizing that taxes and transfers are a function of Y, we know that they exert a dampening effect on the increase in Y.

The money market *cushions* the multiplier effect of a ΔG on Y. As Y increases, more M_1 is required, and given the liquidity demand, a higher r occurs. The multiplier effect is cushioned by the decrease in I associated with the rise in r. The relationships are summarized in the IS-LM diagram (Figure 16.12). The horizontal shift in IS (from Y_1 to Y_3) at the original r shows the full multiplier effect. However, since r rises as Y increases, the final equilibrium is at Y_2. A decrease in G would have the opposite effect. The reduction in Y would be cushioned by the money market. The lower rate of interest would make for a partially offsetting increase in I and Y.

2. *A change in depreciation rates or the investment tax credit.* A more liberal investment tax credit (or accelerated depreciation) will shift MEC to the right and raise $C + G + I$. The corresponding shift in IS is like that shown in Figure 16.12. Moreover, the cushioning effect of the money market is the same as that described above. In both cases we are assuming that the Fed is holding M constant.

Reduction in the investment tax credit (or in depreciation allowances) will shift MEC to the left and lower $C + G + I$. The corresponding shift to the left in IS will be accompanied by a reduction in r and a somewhat offsetting influence on I.

3. *A change in taxes and/or transfers.* A change in taxes or transfers shifts the consumption function and hence $C + G + I$. A tax cut shifts $C + G + I$ upward and IS to the right; the multiplier is cushioned by the money market. The multiplier effect of a tax increase is depicted as a lower $C + G + I$ and a shift to the left in IS, and it also is cushioned by a lower r.

4. *A change in the money supply.* Monetary policy affects Y by changing r. An increase in M will leave more money available to satisfy liquidity demand. As r decreases, businessmen will increase investment. This makes for a greater Y through the multiplier effect. In terms of the IS-LM diagram (Figure 16.13) the LM shifts to the right and now crosses IS at a point where Y is greater, Y_2.

We have now outlined the basic mechanics of the complete Keynesian model. The important differences in the IS-LM model and the simple Consumption Function model are that we have made I a function of r and have included the money market.

FIGURE 16–14

Inelastic IS function

FIGURE 16–15

The liquidity trap

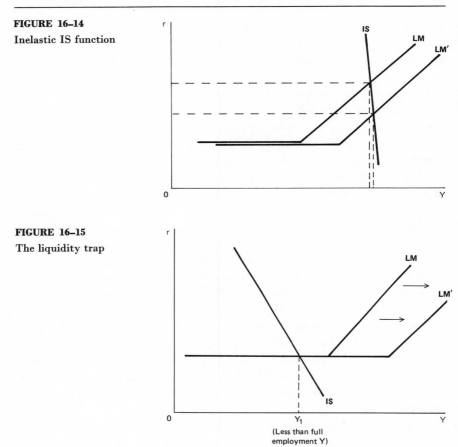

In our discussion of investment spending we observed that it is an important variable, but one that is very difficult to predict or control. Not only must we estimate how businessmen's expectations will change their willingness to invest, but we must estimate the impact of the accelerator.

In outlining the mechanics of the multiplier effects we noted *two types of cushions* that will become important in later discussions. First we noted that taxes and transfers are a function of income. Indeed, the personal income tax is a *progressive* function of income. Thus, as aggregate spending moves one way, changes in taxes and transfers *shifts the consumption function* so as to partially offset the multiplier effect. These and related effects, popularly known as the "automatic stabilizers," must be accounted for in macroeconomic policy.

The money market also *cushions* any multiplier effect in the complete Keynesian model. In tracing through the mechanics of the government spending, investment, and tax-transfer multipliers we assumed that the Fed was holding the money supply constant. The result, according to Keynes, is that any movement in aggregate spending occasions a change in the rate of interest which, by affecting investment spending, dampens that movement. Thus in effect the money market also acts as an automatic stabilizer.

The *IS-LM* model also demonstrates the mechanics by which monetary policy can play a more central role. According to Keynes the sequence of causation goes

$$M \to r \to I \to Y.$$

The usual Keynesian prescription would feature a *coordinated* fiscal and monetary policy mix. In general though, monetary policy is not as crucial in the Keynesian system as it is in the Quantity Theory of Money. In fact in special circumstances the Keynesian system implies that monetary policy can have very little effect. These special circumstances are confined to a deep depression. Two diagrams, the *MEC* function and the liquidity preference demand function, are useful in illustrating these effects. Suppose that businessmen's expectations are pessimistic and that a lower rate of interest will not induce any substantial increase in investment. In terms of the *MEC* diagram this means that the *MEC* function is *inelastic*. If the *MEC* function is inelastic it follows that the *IS* function is also inelastic. Consequently a shift in the *LM* function, as depicted in Figure 16.14, would have little effect on *Y*.

Another special circumstance which may reduce the effectiveness of monetary policy in the Keynesian model is when the liquidity preference demand is situated so that an increase in money will not lower the rate of interest. From our discussion of liquidity preference we recall that the amount of money people wish to hold for speculative purposes is usually inversely related to the reward they get for loaning it out, *r*. However at some very low rate (that people feel will eventually rise), all additional money people receive will be held rather than tied up in securities, etc.

This floor to the interest rate is called the "liquidity trap." Assume that the economy is in the throes of a deep depression. The usual monetary policy prescription is to boost aggregate spending by increasing *M*, reducing *r*, and increasing *I*. But if *r* is already so low that people hold all additions to the money supply, monetary policy can no longer be effective. This situation is depicted in Figure 16.15. The increase in the money supply causes more money to be left for liquidity preferences. However this does not lower the rate of interest because of the horizontal portion of the liquidity preference schedule (see Figure 16.9) which is reflected in the *LM* function. As *LM* shifts to the right the new equilibrium of *IS-LM* is at approximately the same level of aggregate spending, Y_1. This is because no new investment spending has been generated by monetary policy. According to Keynes, it is possible for the economy to be caught in such a situation in times of depression. On such occasions only massive fiscal policy—say massive doses of government spending—can provide adequate aggregate spending.

Except for these special cases, the Keynesian model suggests coordinated monetary and fiscal policies based on the relationships outlined previously. Before contrasting the Keynesian and Quantity Theory prescriptions, let us examine the latter in more detail.

MORE ON THE QUANTITY THEORY OF MONEY

We have already considered the classical argument that the money supply directly affects the price level. In terms of the equation of exchange we observed that the "crude quantity theory" implied that velocity, V, and real output, Q, were stable so that an increase in the money supply caused an increase in the price level

$$\uparrow M \bar{V} = \uparrow P \bar{V}$$

and a decrease in the money supply caused a decrease in the price level.

$$\downarrow M \bar{V} = \downarrow P \bar{Q}$$

A modern exponent of the quantity theory of money, Professor Milton Friedman, expounds an approach which, although more sophisticated, builds upon the "crude theory." The essence of his argument is that the policy makers—especially the Federal Reserve—can do considerable mischief to the self-regulating mechanics of the competitive system.

According to Friedman the Fed generally *over-compensates* when it attempts to use monetary policy to regulate economic activity. Moreover there are both short-run and long-run "feedback" effects on economic activity which the Fed cannot foresee. Consequently its policies have often been in error both in terms of direction and magnitude.

In recent years both Keynesians and Monetarists alike have changed their views on the relationship of money and velocity. According to the crude quantity theory, velocity was an institutional datum which would not change. Historically, however, there have been changes in V. For many years before 1939, V exhibited a downward trend. Since that time there has been a gradual rise in V. There are also small short-run changes in V which generally have a positive relationship with changes in output.

The modern Quantity Theorists do not regard V as a constant. Instead they argue that if M is controlled, changes in V will be so small or so predictable that *in general* the effect of M on P and Q will be favorable.

It is useful to ask just how the modern quantity theory differs from the crude theory. Instead of the straightforward relationship between M and P (with V constant and Q always at the full employment level), the modern quantity theory allows that (1) velocity may vary and (2) the economy may not always tend towards the full-employment level.

To the extent that modern Quantity Theories admit that velocity may vary and output be at less-than-full-employment, they are closer to the Keynesian perspective. Moreover *both approaches come to the conclusion that it is difficult to predict how changes in M will effect output.* We recall that in the Keynesian system we have a rather tenuous link between M and Y: M affects r, r affects I, and I (through the multiplier) affects Y. Moreover the relationships between these variables vary according to circumstances. For examples (1) liquidity preference may circumvent the change in r and (2) changing expectations may shift MEC thus altering the effect of r on I.[3]

---

[3] Some recent studies suggest that V may be much less stable than either the Keynesian or modern Quantity Theory hold. In the Keynesian theory money is seen not only as a medium of exchange but as an asset, which, along with bonds may be held as a " store of wealth." According to Keynesian theory there is a rather predictable demand for money to hold for liquidity purposes. However, as outlined in the model, it is only in a depression that the liquidity demand for money circumvents monetary policy. More recently, attention has been focused on the role of other liquid money substitutes such as time deposits, savings and loan shares, and Treasury bills which also play a part in satiating liquidity demand. Supposedly the presence of these substitutes may circumvent monetary policy by shifting the liquidity preference schedule to offset changes in the money supply. For two different approaches which both suggest substantial changes in V see England, Treasury, Committee on the Working of the Monetary System [Chairman, Lord Radcliffe] *Report of the Committee on the Working of the Monetary System* (London, 1959), and J. G. Gurley and E. S. Shaw, *Money in a Theory of Finance*, (Washington, D.C.: Brookings, 1960).

The modern quantity theorists argue that, although complicated time lags and feedback effects inherent in monetary adjustments make it difficult to predict the exact relationship between M and Y, it is still a more accurate predictor than the Keynesian approach. To bolster this argument they cite studies which suggest that the velocity of money is more stable in behavior than the investment multplier.[4] Of course the Keynesians do not simply rely on their ability to predict " autonomous " investment as a means for claiming to be able to regulate the economy. They have taken considerable pride in their predictions about consumption and saving and have great faith in the effectiveness of fiscal policy (to include methods of influencing investment spending). Even so, if the Quantity Theorists could explain changes in Y simply by looking at M, their theory would certainly be the more useful. Unfortunately Quantity Theorists readily warn that their analyses are not sufficiently accurate to provide a basis for aggressive monetary policy.

Indeed according to the Quantity Theorists, the most frequent error of the monetary authorities has been overreaction. What the Fed has tended to think of as " fine tuning " has, in Friedman's words, amounted to " drastic and erratic changes in direction." The problem, of course, is that the Fed is not aware of the disequilibrating effects, the time lags, and the feedback effects, of changes in the money supply. Consequently it turns out that monetary policy *itself* is a major source of economic maladjustment.

Yet the Quantity Theorists do not advocate an entirely passive policy. If there have been obvious, major disturbances in the economy, they would advocate appropriate monetary policy to help mitigate them. If, for example, the federal budget had been allowed to be excessively expansionary, monetary restraint in the form of a *slower-than-normal rate of growth* in the money supply would help curb inflation. Alternatively, a drastic budget shift in the opposite direction—say at the end of a war—would call for an increase in the money supply at a slightly quicker pace than the optimum stable rate.

But according to Friedman:

The potentiality of monetary policy in offsetting other forces making for instability is far more limited than is commonly believed. We simply do not know enough to be able to recognize minor disturbances when they occur or to be able to predict either what their effects will be with any precision or what monetary policy is required to offset their effects.[5]

DIRECT WAGE AND PRICE CONTROLS

The cost-push inflation experienced during the Nixon Administration was not a new phenomenon. During the Eisenhower Administration recessions of 1953–1954 and 1957–1958 prices not only failed to decline but continued to advance at an inflationary pace. This phenomenon is inconsistent with the orthodox demand-pull explanations inherent in both the Keynesian and Quantity Theory models.

The term " cost-push " inflation is usually used to place the " blame " on strong, "monopolistic " unions. Sometimes large, "monopolistic " corporations are added to the list of culprits. Economists have often pointed out that a general price increase can hardly be blamed on a few unions or a few corporations even though it is recognized that they play an important part in our economy. In order to demonstrate how the " cost-push " phenomenon can spread so as to be pervasive in practically all markets, we will resort to a concept we have used frequently: the " prisoner's dilemma." The " prisoner's dilemma " involved in the " cost-push " phenomenon can become effective under a situation which we term: "inflationary psychology."

It is conceivable but not probable that a " cost-push " inflation could begin without being preceded by a " demand-pull " inflation. The process could be begun by powerful unions and firms gaining increases in wages and prices which other sectors of the economy seek to emulate. What makes it more likely that significant " cost-push " pressures occur only *after* a " demand-pull " inflation, is that a general " cost-push " phenomenon can occur in the more competitive sectors of the economy *only after a rather widespread " inflationary psychology " has set in.* This seems possible only after a relatively long period of inflation which could only be sustained by strong " demand-pull " pressure.

Let us once again examine the prisoner's dilemma involved in the cost-push phenomenon. The dilemma arises because the *combined* effect

---

[4] See for example Milton Friedman and David Meiselman, " The Relative Stability of Monetary Velocity and the Investment Multiplier in the United States, 1897–1958," *Stabilization Policies*, Commission on Money and Credit Series, (Englewood Cliffs, N.J.: Prentice-Hall, 1963). For critiques and a rebuttal see Albert Ando and Franco Modigliani, "The Relative Stability of Monetary Velocity and the Investment Multiplier," Michael De Prano and Thomas Mayer, "Tests of the Relative Importance of Autonomous Expenditures and Money," plus a reply by Friedman and Meiselman and rejoinders, all in the *American Economic Review*, vol. 55 (September 1965).

[5] "The Role of Monetary Policy," *American Economic Review*, vol. 58 (March 1968), pp. 1–17.

FIGURE 16–16

Cost-push inflation

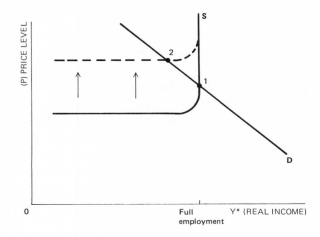

of firms (acting to promote their own individual interests) results in an inflationary spiral of rising wages and prices.

Consider the behavior of unions and firms in an oligopoly market. If the union were only able to raise wages at one firm, it is doubtful that the firm could raise prices to compensate for higher costs. However if all of the oligopoly firms are to be included, the increased costs can be passed on in the form of higher prices. That is, if all of the firms raise prices simultaneously, the loss in sales will depend only on the elasticity of *market demand*. All that is necessary is that each oligopolist think his competitors will be raising their prices as well.

The process of price increases just described for the oligopoly market could also occur in markets with larger numbers of firms *if each firm can assume his competitors will also be passing all cost increases along in the form of higher prices*. This assumption cannot be made in the traditional models of competitive markets. It is much more likely to hold, however, in "real world" situations where imperfect knowledge and other "imperfections" have resulted in *cost-plus pricing policies*. Moreover after a long period of inflation it becomes widely observed that both wages and prices are continually being raised. In the latter context it becomes *rational profit-maximizing behavior* for wage earners and firms to press for higher wages and salaries. It would be irrational for the individual wage earner or firm to "hold the line" since his individual effort would do little to stem the inflationary spiral.

THE REQUIREMENTS OF ANTI-COST-PUSH POLICY

Now let us use our description of the cost-push phenomenon to derive certain requirements for a policy cure. First it is necessary to differentiate between and to determine the strengths of the demand-pull and the cost-push forces at work. Consider Figure 16.16. We see that in terms of the original supply curve (solid line) there is excess aggregate *demand* at position 1. Proper macroeconomic policy would provide restraint by the usual indirect fiscal and monetary prescriptions. If, however, cost-push factors force up the aggregate supply curve (as shown by the dotted line) we may reach a new equilibrium at position 2 which features a higher price level and a less-than-full employment level of real income. Obviously it would be a mistake to assume that fiscal and/or monetary tools aimed at restraining aggregate demand would have their usual effect. Indeed, in Figure 16.16, rising prices have already cut purchasing power below that necessary for full employment at the new price level. Further restraint of aggregate spending would cause demand to shift to the left to a new equilibrium at an even lower level of national income. Moreover there is no guarantee that curtailing demand would stop the upward shift of the supply curve. Indeed, if monetary restraint is used, it would not only reduce aggregate spending; but by increasing the rate of interest, it would be raising *costs* for many types of businesses.

Persuasion and communication by public officials may have some limited effect *in the first stages* of a cost-push phenomenon. This is because in those stages inflationary psychology may not be widespread. The large unions and firms may be directly confronted by government. Moreover the public sector usually has direct economic ties (such as large contracts, favorable import or tax laws) which may be used as leverage with the large firms. However, once the cost-push phenomenon is widespread, appeals to the general public can have only limited effect. The nature of the prisoner's dilemma in question is not simply a communications problem. It will not help to tell each person attempting to raise his wage or price that if everyone does the same inflation will make everyone worse off. He may already know this. But whether he does or not, it still may be to his *individual advantage* to raise his wage or price at a pace at least equal to the general increase in prices.[6]

---

[6] There will remain, of course, many markets in which it is to the advantage of the individual firm to keep his prices down and thus gain a larger share of the market. This becomes even more tempting after a period in which rising prices for the market have begun to produce fewer sales.

The force and persistency of the "cost-push" phenomenon depends not only on the actions of a few large unions and corporations, but on the number of markets in which raising prices faster than productivity has become the accepted (and perhaps for the individual firm, the most profitable) pattern of behavior. If there is a widespread tendency for wage earners and firms to attempt to offset their eroding purchasing power and profits by continually pushing up wages and prices, they will not immediately desist in the face of macroeconomic policies causing further erosion. The attempt to fight inflation with restrictive monetary policy during the 1969–1972 recession lends support to the argument that a relatively severe recession would have been required to break the "inflationary psychology."

RULES FOR DIRECT WAGE AND PRICE CONTROLS

The "rules" a regulatory body should use to regulate wages and prices and combat cost-push inflation are not as obvious as they would seem. Here again the tendency is to think of price regulation in the more familiar terms of either regulating public utilities or combating demand-pull inflation. With public utility regulation it is appropriate to raise prices to preserve a "fair return" in the face of increasing costs. With demand-pull inflation it is appropriate to disallow any price increase where the industry is already operating at "capacity." Neither of these rules are appropriate for "cost-push" price regulation.

The appropriate rules are as follows:

Rule 1. No wage increase should be allowed which prevents full employment in a specific labor market.

Rule 2. No price increase should be allowed which allows quantity demanded to be less than the "capacity" output level.

Rule 3. Monetary and fiscal policy should maintain adequate aggregate demand. If the situation is similar to that depicted in position 2 of Figure 16.16, this would require an *increase* in aggregate spending.

Rule 4. A target level of "acceptable" inflation should be set—say 1 or 2 percent—and an estimate should be made of the expected increase in productivity. These two figures can then be used to set standards for price and wage increase.

Rule 5. A general guideline should be published for price increases. The price guideline should be based on the target level of "acceptable" inflation, say 1 or 2 percent.

Rule 6. A general guideline should be published for wage increases. The wage guideline should be based on the inflation target and allow for increases in *productivity* as well. If productivity were expected to increase by 3 percent, the wage guideline could be 4 or 5 percent.

Rule 7. Price increases exceeding the general guideline should be allowed for markets where output and sales were already at " capacity."

Rule 8. Price reductions would be required for markets where output and sales were substantially below " capacity."

Rule 9. Wage increases exceeding the general guideline would be allowed where the labor market was " tight " and where the higher wages could be expected to attract more workers.

Rule 10. Wage increases in markets where unemployment was high would, if allowed at all, be smaller than that allowed by the general guideline.

These "rules" are useful in highlighting the differences between macroeconomic policy designed to combat cost-push inflation and those designed to combat demand-pull inflation. Remedies for the cost-push problem must deal with widespread behavioral patterns which make private and social goals deviate. They must also deal with underemployment and misallocation of resources. Even though prices are rising it may be appropriate to stimulate aggregate demand. In addition, they must supplement the price mechanism in its function of setting prices so as to efficiently allocate resources.

The simplicity of the above "rules" belies the tremendous organizational and political difficulties of their implementation. The organizational difficulties include the assumed task of policing the activities of all regulated markets, processing all inquiries, and adjudicating all accused violations. Obviously wage and price controls could never be successfully implemented without the voluntary support of those regulated. Of course since the self-interests of buyers are involved we could expect them to aid in reporting violations by sellers. On the other hand, a strike threat by a powerful union cannot be taken lightly by the regulatory authorities even if the union's demands exceed established guidelines.

The necessity of having broad support for imposing direct wage and price controls means that they cannot be used in the early stages of inflation as *preventive* policy. In addition these direct controls, like the fiscal tools, need to run the gamut of the legislative process. In 1971 this did not prove to be a problem. Congress had given President Nixon the necessary emergency powers to impose direct wage and price controls long before he chose to implement them. But if he had attempted to impose controls at an earlier stage of the inflationary spiral, the lack of support by the public and Congress might have been an impediment.

The question of whether the policy makers will have the necessary support and authority for timely policy implementation brings us back to the more basic question: What is timely implementation? Our outline of the mechanics of demand-pull and cost-push inflation provides some insight. We noted that there are different assumptions about the economy inherent in the Keynesian, Quantity Theory and cost-push models. In general, the Keynesian and Quantity Theory approaches do not allow for the behavior by wage earners and firms which would be necessary for cost-push inflation. In our presentation of cost-push inflation we have opted for an *eclectic* approach. We have assumed that in most situations the indirect tools will suffice but that the special conditions of the cost-push situation call for direct controls.

We note that the Keynesian model we presented was eclectic in the same sense; that is, some tools were considered more effective in some situations than in others. In the special situation of depression in the Keynesian model the liquidity trap and pessimistic businessmen's expectations make ineffective those fiscal and monetary tools aimed at increasing investment spending. Moreover, cuts in income taxes are less effective since the incomes of many are either low or nonexistent. In this situation government spending and transfers are the only effective tools.

THE KEYNESIAN MODEL AND COST-PUSH

It is not difficult to expand our "complete" Keynesian model to include the cost-push situation. We note that the shape of the aggregate supply curve in Figure 16.4 has the Keynesian feature that prices (and wages) are sticky downward. It is this horizontal portion of the curve that creates under-employment as the curve is pushed upward by costs.

In terms of the choice of tools and the timing of macroeconomic policy the eclectic approach is made more feasible if demand-pull and cost-push situations can be clearly distinguished. Let us describe one hypothetical sequence of events in which the policy prescriptions are readily apparent. Suppose that the economy is at a full employment equilibrium with stable prices. Then there is a rapid increase in defense spending with no offsetting increase in taxes. The excess demand creates demand-pull

---

inflation. At this point the use of the traditional Keynesian tools, such as increased taxes and removal of the investment tax credit, would be appropriate. If on the other hand, adequate adjustments were not made, inflation might enter into a second stage with demand-pull inflation fostering a beginning of the cost-push phenomenon. During this stage it would be difficult to designate which price and wage increases could be attributed to "demand-pull" and which to "cost-push." We have hypothesized that the cost-push phenomenon originates in the less competitive markets where for some reason (such as public pressure, imperfect knowledge or traditional pricing policies) firms and unions had not fully exploited their monopoly power. If this is the situation, the appropriate policy mix would be to use the traditional tools (such as an increase in taxes) to restrict aggregate demand while at the same time using *selective price and wage controls* in those industries where increased prices (1) cause the costs of other industries to increase, (2) are creating an inflationary *demonstration effect* for others to follow, and yet (3) cannot be justified in terms of the industry having reached "capacity." The major benefit of using selective controls at this stage is not the immediate relief afforded from cost-push forces. More importantly, selective controls provide a demonstration effect of their own discouraging further spread of an "inflationary psychology."

In the absence of appropriate macroeconomic policy in the second stage of inflation yet a third stage may develop in which the cost-push phenomenon becomes widespread in the economy. This stage (as outlined previously), features continued inflation and high unemployment as well. Now more extensive controls on prices and wages are required.

CONCLUDING COMMENTS

In this chapter we have continued our examination of the mechanics of the fiscal and monetary tools. We have expanded the Keynesian and Quantity Theory models and contrasted them with the direct controls which may be required to combat cost-push inflation. We have asked whether an eclectic theory might be developed which includes both indirect and direct macroeconomic tools. In a very cursory way we outlined assumptions and mechanics of an eclectic model incorporating the Keynesian system with direct controls for the special case of cost-push. Theoretically we could build an eclectic model to incorporate the Quantity Theory with direct controls used only for the special case of

FIGURE 16A-1

The money market

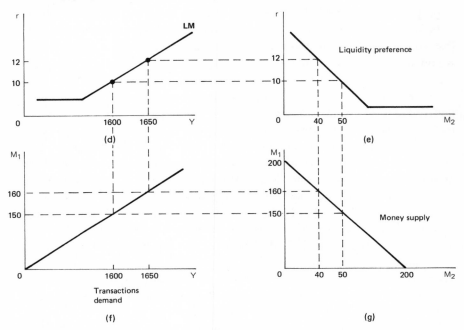

cost-push. This marriage would be less complementary than the former for obvious reasons. The Quantity Theory differs with the Keynesian model on two basic assumptions, the first concerning the *competitiveness* of the economy and the second concerning the feasibility and efficiency of aggressively manipulating the economy. Since the Quantity Theorist is more prone to rely on competitive forces to restore the economy to equilibrium, he would be inclined to resort to direct controls only in a severe emergency. The resort to controls on occasions that did not really warrant them might, in fact, weaken the effect of the economy's self-regulating forces.

The Quantity Theorist would also question the ability of the policy makers to accurately predict the timing and magnitude of direct controls which would be required in a cost-push situation. It is no simple task to determine that a given price increase is a result of cost-push rather than demand-pull forces. Consequently with demand-pull inflation, the tendency of policy makers to overreact might itself become a disequilibrating influence.

In the process of examining the various theories as to the effects of the macroeconomic tools we have necessarily encountered "public choice" questions inherent in the assumptions of the specific models. In the next chapter we will attempt to deal with these "public choice" questions more explicitly.

APPENDIX ONE TO CHAPTER 16:

A DIAGRAMMATIC MODEL OF THE COMPLETE KEYNESIAN MODEL

This appendix provides a more thorough development of the relationships outlined in the previous chapters.

We have already derived the I-S function, showing how different rates of interest are associated with different amounts of I and (through the multiplier) different levels of Y.

Figure 16A.1 demonstrates the derivation of the LM function. These relationships have been presented previously. Diagrams (e) and (f) show the liquidity preference and transactions demands for money. Diagram (g), which incorporates the money supply, has some mechanical features which should be noted. The money supply is measured on both the vertical and horizontal axes. The triangle made by the line connecting these points has the property that the values on one axis will be *mirrored* on the other. Thus, of the $200 billion in the money supply, the $160 billion required for transactions is measured from the origin on the vertical axis while the $40 billion left for liquidity preferences is measured from the origin on the horizontal axis.

Let us trace through the derivation starting with diagram (f). At a Y of $1600 billion, $150 billion is required for transactions. The amount of money left, $50 billion, is mirrored onto the horizontal axis of diagram (g) and can be traced up to diagram (e). The liquidity preference schedule shows us that with $50 billion M_2, the interest rate will be 10 percent. Thus, when Y is $1600 billion, r must be 10 percent, given these hypothetical relationships in the money market. The student is encouraged to trace through the derivation of other points on the LM function.

Figure 16A.2 shows the shift in the LM function which takes place when the money supply increases. M, as measured on both axes of diagram (e), is increased to $205 billion, leaving more M_2 available at any level of income. Consequently, LM shifts to the right.

FIGURE 16A–2

The money market
showing a shift in the money
supply

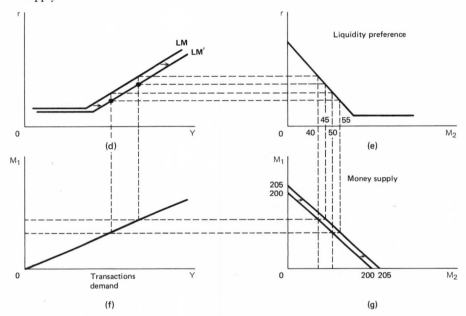

Figure 16A.3 shows the unique equilibrium solution satisfying the relationships in both markets. The unique solution is at a Y of \$1650 billion and an r of 12 percent. It is also possible to read off values for C, I, G, M, M_1, and M_2.

Now let us trace through the changes wrought by the use of fiscal and monetary tools as outlined previously.

An increase in government spending. A change in G shifts up $C + G$ and $C + G + I$ (see Figure 16A.4). The 45-degree line in diagram (a) must also be shifted so as to reflect the new value of G.[1] The multiplier effect is, of course, implicit in diagram (b) and is reflected in the shift of IS.

Nothing in the money market shifts, but the cushioning effect of higher interest rates is evident. As Y rises, more M_1 is required for transactions [diagram (f)] and less is left for liquidity preference [diagram (g)], which results in a higher rate of interest [diagrams (e) and (d)]. The cushioning effect of the money market, we recall, is felt in the commodity market through the higher rate of interest, which reduces investment. This is

539

FIGURE 16A–3

Equilibrium in the
commodity and money
markets

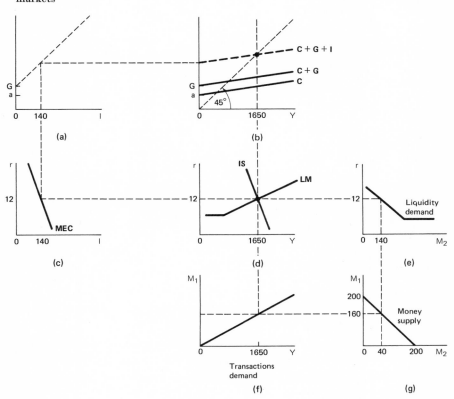

demonstrated by starting with the higher rate of interest and tracing
through diagrams (c), (a), and (b) in that order.

---

[1] The necessity to shift the 45 degree line in diagram (a) is a rather awkward feature of
our model. The sole purpose of diagram (a) is to reflect I onto diagram (b) at the appropriate level—namely stacked on top of the $C + G$ function. It performs this task by the
45 degree line which reflects what is on the horizontal axis (the I determined in the
MEC diagram) to the vertical axis.

In order that I be at the right level we must add to it a (the consumption function
intercept) and G.

Thus if a or G change on diagram (b), it is necessary to shift the 45-degree line in
diagram (a) so that I can still be traced onto diagram (b) at the proper level (stacked on
top of a and G).

FIGURE 16A–4

The government spending
multiplier (an increase in
government spending)

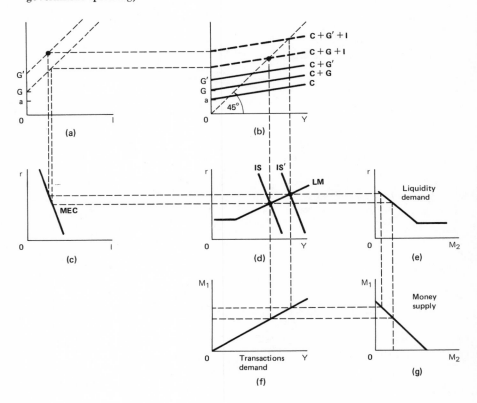

An increase in the personal income tax. The multiplier effect of an
increase in taxes is shown in Figure 16A.5. Starting with diagram (b),
observe that the c shifts downward. This, of course, shifts $C + G$ and
$C + G + I$, so that a new equilibrium will occur where $Y = C + I + G$.

Once again the money market cushions the multiplier effect of fiscal
policy. As the IS curve shifts to the left, the rate of interest falls and
investment increases slightly; consequently, the decrease in aggregate
spending is less than predicted in our simple consumption function
model. In following through the effect of higher interest rates in diagrams
(c), (a), and (b), we again note the mechanics of diagram (a), which now
account for the smaller value of a.

541

FIGURE 16A-5

The tax multiplier (an increase in the personal income tax)

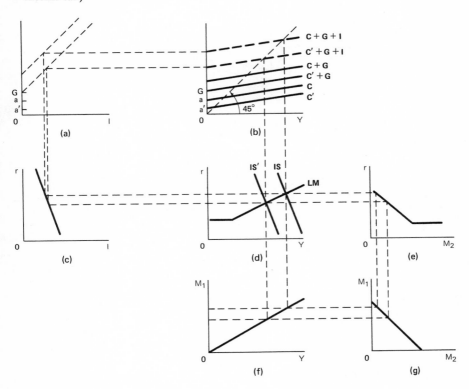

The student is encouraged to draw the model several times and work through the effects of tax cuts (with or without a change in tax rates).

A change in the investment tax credit. An increase in the tax credit given businesses for investment lowers the present cost of investing and shifts the *MEC* to the right, as shown in diagram (c) of Figure 16A.6. The increase in *I* traced through to diagram (b) demonstrates the multiplier effect inherent in the consumption function model.

As the *IS* curve shifts to the right, the new equilibrium of *IS* and *LM* again shows the cushioning effect of the money market. If the money supply is held constant, the increase in *r* causes the increase in *I* to be smaller than it would have been at the original *r*.

FIGURE 16A–6

An increase in the investment
tax credit

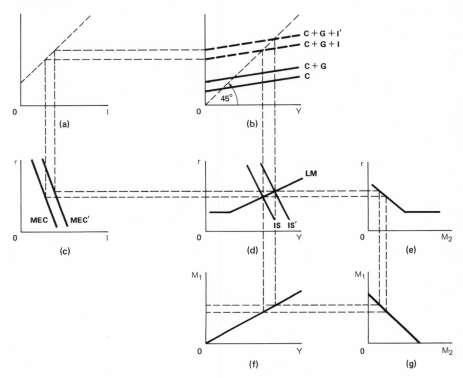

A change in the investment tax credit in the other direction would have opposite effects. Once more the student is encouraged to trace through these relationships to the new equilibrium.

A change in the money supply. We have already seen how an increase in the money supply [in diagram (g)] shifts the *LM* function in diagram (d) to the right. Now let us consider the case of monetary constraint on the entire model.

As the Fed reduces the money supply, the line in diagram (g) of Figure 16A.7 shifts toward the origin. With less money available to satisfy liquidity preference the *LM* shifts to the left—the former level of spending could only be supported at a higher rate of interest.

None of the functions in the commodity market shifts. However, at the higher rate of interest, *I* is reduced. The final $C + G + I'$ is consistent with the equilibrium of *IS* and *LM'* at a higher *r* and *lower Y*.

543

FIGURE 16A–7

A decrease in the money
supply

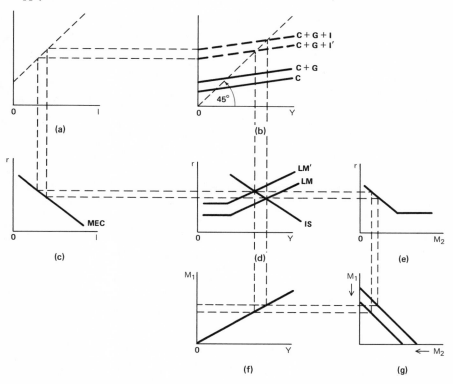

APPENDIX TWO TO CHAPTER 16:

FISCAL POLICY AND ECONOMIC GROWTH

We have already begun to discuss the various ways fiscal policy influences economic growth. It is therefore appropriate to digress and consider some of the perspectives and "models" economists use to analyze growth.

First, we might consider whether the phenomenon can be rigorously defined. The usual measure is to compare GNP through time. Account must be taken, of course, of changes in the price level which distort comparisons of real GNP. Account must also be taken of the changing quality of goods produced. Similarly, the proportion of goods produced that are not included in GNP (such as the services of housewives) may change through time. Also important to consider, though difficult to quantify, is the increase in leisure and in the "quality" of life over time. Moreover, for some purposes *per capita* income is more important than aggregate GNP totals, which furnish only a rough indication of the change in well-being over time.

THE RATIONALE FOR PUBLIC SECTOR GROWTH POLICY

We can best consider the requirements of fiscal growth policy by restating the rationale for public sector activity in this area. Originally we posited a *laissez faire* model, where all resource allocation was accomplished by the private sector. Both the full employment and growth goals were shown to be accomplished smoothly if all the conditions of the perfectly competitive model were met. This model has been useful to us in demonstrating how certain types of public sector activity may be required when certain of the model's conditions do not hold. Essentially the same prescriptions appropriate for price stability and full employment are also appropriate for the goal of economic growth. Hence, the use of taxes, transfers, and expenditures to manipulate aggregate demand is essential to the growth goal. The waste which attends unemployment is compounded over time.

A question unique to growth policy is how society's preferences for growth may be revealed. In the classical model, growth follows from the savings habits of individuals and from firms' investment in innovation. Self-interest is at work in both cases. Individuals save because they have certain future spending goals and also because they are rewarded for saving. Firms invest and pursue research in order to gain future profits.[1] If full employment prevails, the abstinence of consumers determines investment and hence growth. Some rather basic value judgments about the process of decision making are required. We recall that such judgments were preconditions if the forthcoming resource allocation were to be deemed "optimal." Similarly, the legitimacy of the forthcoming decisions on saving, investment, and growth depend on our judgment as to whether the process adequately reflects the preferences of the individuals making up the society. If we wished to demonstrate how an "acceptable" growth goal for society might be meted out in a mixed economy, we would necessarily include judgments about the part played by competitive markets and the political process as well. We could make the judgment, for example, that our democratic political process adequately relays individual preferences concerning national growth to the representatives who are responsible for fiscal policy. The resultant fiscal policy presumably reflects not only the appropriate *amount* of aggregate spending but the appropriate composition of investment relative to consumption.

Since, in fact, our economic system differs substantially from the theoretical model presented in the beginning chapters, we must ask whether the savings, investment, and growth forthcoming from the private sector adequately reflect individual and community preferences for growth. There seem to be a number of important reasons for not likening the real world to the "ideal" model. Our experience demonstrates that, with or without aggressive macroeconomic policy, full employment with stable prices is difficult to attain. And, generally speaking, full employment is a "necessary condition" for achieving the growth goal. In the absence of appropriate fiscal policy there is no guarantee that savings preferences of consumers will be reconciled with the investment decisions of firms. The familiar "paradox of thrift" is pertinent here: If most consumers become more "thrifty," their savings goals may not be realized, since inadequate aggregate consumption may dampen aggregate spending and growth. Yet, if fiscal policy is used to manipulate C, S, and I, then the resultant growth path certainly cannot be said to accord with that dictated by the market.

There are other reasons why public sector activity is necessary if an "optimum" growth policy is to be achieved. Recall the assumptions of

---

[1] The various factors influencing the investment decisions of individuals and firms were considered in some detail in Chapters 9 and 11.

perfect mobility, a large number of competitors in each market, and perfect knowledge. Where one of these is missing, public activity may be called for if growth possibilities are to be realized. Public training programs, antitrust legislation, employment agencies, and other measures designed to remedy these imperfections certainly enhance growth.

It is also useful to distinguish several types of externality that relate public activity and growth. The benefits created by basic research are often insufficiently divisible and assignable to be accounted for by the market price system. Public support in the form of patent laws, research grants, and public research programs and facilities is therefore in order. Long-run benefits to society from investment in human beings such as education and health programs are also important to growth and may require public financing.

PERSPECTIVES AND MODELS OF ECONOMIC GROWTH

Broadly defined, theories of economic growth can be derived from theories of history—of which there are many. Some view history as predictable, and economic growth has been likened to the growth of a healthy biological plant. Others would focus on the " great men " or " great ideas " that have changed the course of history and economic growth. Alternatively, growth can be seen as occurring in stages, each dependent on a particular set of institutions and economic and social variables.

The approach of some economists—sometimes termed the Institutional School—is to view the stages of economic growth as dependent on a multitude of variables and institutions. They argue persuasively that no one theory of growth will suffice to explain growth at different periods of time or in dissimilar economies. A variant of this approach, the " genetic " method, seeks to explain economic development in terms of cumulative causation.[2]

The tension between emphasis on institutional studies and model building is natural, since growth cannot usually be analyzed within the context of a single set of institutions. As we shall see, certain simple models can give insight within a particular institutional setting; however, these models are highly restrictive and their predictive use is limited. A more general perspective is required if long-run predictions are to include not only changes in national income but changes in the political and economic institutions as well. Adam Smith's bright view of the growing wealth of nations was based on faith in specialization within a free enterprise system. Thomas Malthus, however, rejected the idea that nations were headed toward wealth. A growing population employed with a fixed quantity of natural resources must evoke diminishing returns and lead to a subsistence level of per capital income. Although "Parson" Malthus allowed that discretion as to family size might ease the inexorable burden of diminishing returns, long-run growth was not foreseeable. David Ricardo developed the concept of diminishing returns in more precise terms and demonstrated how income distribution is effected as the economy expands. The institution of private property insured that the returns to the fixed factor, land, go to the landowners. And as more labor is applied to each unit of land, the marginal product of land and hence the return to landowners will increase.

Karl Marx's analysis of economic growth relied heavily on Ricardian economics; however, Marx saw the returns diverted from labor to the owners of capital instead of the owners of land. According to Marx's predictions the resultant shifts in income distribution would cause maladjustments in aggregate demand, fluctuations, increasing unemployment, and finally revolt. Marx's predictions have never really been tested. The capitalistic systems he described have been modified substantially.[3]

The discussion above leads us to three conclusions: (1) Theories of economic growth must be consistent with the institutional context within which they are formulated. Their use in another institutional context is hazardous. (2) A complete analysis of growth potential must include possible political and sociological as well as economic variables. (3) All three perspectives must be used when the analysis extends over time or over geographical boundaries.

We will consider models couched in the political and sociological setting of the Western democracies. Whereas the focus in developed countries is on adjusting the composition of aggregate spending, the focus in many developing countries is on the Malthusian race between population and scarce resources.

---

[2] For examples of the use of this approach to explain the rise of capitalism in Western democracies see Werner Sombart, *Der moderne Kapitalismus* (Leipzig: Duncker and Humbolt, 1902–1927), and R. H. Tawney, *Religion and the Rise of Capitalism* (New York: Harcourt Brace Jovanovich, 1926).

[3] Though some countries have turned to communism through violent revolution, none of these was at an advanced stage of capitalism at the time.

Many variables determine economic growth: the supply of resources, technology, the institutional structure, the tastes, moods, and habits of the citizenry, and so on. The analyst attempts to focus on the relationships which are most critical and to incorporate them into models from which hypotheses can be made and tested. Ideally, the model includes only a small number of *quantifiable* relationships, and all other variables can be assumed constant; however, economists have not had a great deal of success in explaining growth with such models or "theories." The other alternative is to include all of the important variables, whether quantifiable in pecuniary terms or not. This approach necessarily leads us beyond the realm of what many would call economics. The most important growth variable in the classical model was population size, which was dependent on the wage rate (or rather the size of the wages fund). The accumulation of capital depended on profits, which were a residual after rent was paid landlords. When profits were positive and wages were higher than subsistence, output and population would increase. However, this growth process would end in a "stationary state," where diminishing returns (land being fixed) eliminated profits and reduced wages to the subsistence level.

With the exception of Marx, few economists after Mill paid much attention to growth theory until the 1930s, even though by that time other aspects of classical economics had been substantially changed and refined. It was still generally held that the system was self-equilibrating —the price mechanism insuring full employment—while growth was determined by the saving and investment decisions of individuals and firms.

Joseph Schumpeter (1883–1950), like Marx, explored the question of economic fluctuation and growth through time. He also concluded that the capitalistic system bore the seeds of its own destruction but for reasons other than those put forward by Marx. The process went as follows: Innovational change originated growth. Innovations induced changes in organizational and psychological setting, engendering other innovations. Eventually, change was carried too far as imitators in succeeding periods made poor judgments. Moreover, the imitators were borrowing when credit is tight, so they had less room for error. The forthcoming depression chastized those who had made mistakes and provided a breathing space during which new innovations would be developed.

Changes in the institutional structure of capitalism, however, seemed to Schumpeter to be leading in a direction not conducive to further innovation and growth. The concentration of industry, the growth of corporations, and the transfer of decision making from the owner-entrepreneur to professional management would purge the system of the individual freedom and possibility of rewards so necessary for innovation.

John Maynard Keynes' presentation was essentially a static, short-run prescription for reaching full employment. Much of contemporary growth theory is primarily an attempt to make the Keynesian models dynamic. The problem at hand in the 1930s was that of stimulating income and aggregate demand so as to adequately utilize the capital stock. Extrapolating over time, the problem one visualizes is the *balance* between investment, the capital stock, consumption, and saving. Will the income generated be sufficient to fully absorb the production forthcoming from a growing capital stock? And, in turn, will demand each period be such that it furnishes the incentive for an appropriate addition to the capital stock?

SIMPLE DYNAMIC PROCESSES

Simple equations may be used to illustrate the various types of growth which may occur through time. Jan Tinbergen, one of several Dutch contributors to growth theory, pioneered in the use of simple difference equations to describe various dynamic patterns.[4]

Consider the following equation:

$$Y_t = \beta Y_{t-1}$$

where Y_t is national income at a particular time period, and β is some constant growth factor. If we are given a starting point, Y_0, we see that in each period Y is dependent on the Y of the preceding period, $t-1$. Let $\beta = 1.04$ and $Y_0 = \$800$ billion. Thus we have

$$Y_t = 1.04 Y_{t-1}, \qquad Y_0 = \$800 \text{ billion}$$

which gives rise to the following system:

$Y_1 = (1.04) \cdot (800) = \$832$ billion
$Y_2 = (1.04) \cdot (832) = \$865$ billion
$Y_3 = (1.04) \cdot (865) = \$901$ billion
$Y_4 = (1.04) \cdot (901) = \$937$ billion
$Y_5 = (1.04) \cdot (937) = \$970$ billion
$Y_6 = (1.04) \cdot (970) = \$1009$ billion

---

[4] See, for example, Jan Tinbergen, "Ein Schiffbauzyklus," *Wirtshaftliches Archiv*, 1931.

FIGURE 16A–8

Behavior of $Y_t = A\beta^t$ where $\beta > 1$

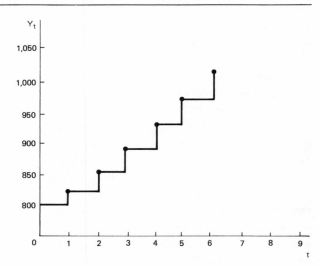

FIGURE 16A–9

Behavior of $Y_t = A\beta^t$ where $0 < \beta < 1$

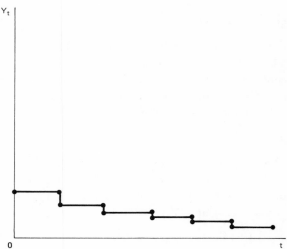

and so on. It turns out that another way of writing the equation is

$$Y_t = (1.04)^t \cdot (800)$$

or, in general terms,

$$Y_t = A\beta^t, \qquad \text{where } A \text{ is the } Y_0 \text{ value}$$

Several patterns are possible, depending on the value of β.

If $\beta > 1$ and $A > 0$, as in our example, the pattern is explosive and would appear as in Figure 16A.8. The larger the value of β, the faster the rate of explosion. If $\beta > 1$ and $A < 0$, the Y_t explodes in the negative direction.

Another pattern of possible interest shows a declining influence through time—say, the declining influence of an injection of investment. A simple difference function with $0 < \beta < 1$ may be used to illustrate this phenomenon. The time path of Y_t in this case would gradually decline towards the stationary value zero (Figure 16A.9).

Other patterns of interest are those which oscillate. The introduction of time lags allows us to include variables which may have cyclical influence. Where expectations are involved, "too much" of something in one period might encourage "too little" in the following, which in turn might make for "too much" in the next, and so on. If $\beta < 0$, the Y_t will oscillate. If $-1 < \beta < 0$, then the oscillation will gradually decline towards zero, as in Figure 16A.10. If $\beta < -1$, then the pattern of Y_t will be both oscillatory and explosive, as shown in Figure 16A.11.[5]

---

[5] We have thus far considered only the homogeneous system. If

$$Y_t = \beta Y_{t-1} + C$$

and

$$Y_0 = \alpha$$

A general solution, if $\beta \neq 1$, may be written

$$Y_t = \beta^t \alpha + C \left(\frac{1 - \beta^t}{1 - \beta} \right)$$

or

$$Y_t = \frac{C}{1 - \beta} + \alpha \left(\frac{C}{1 - \beta} \right)(\beta)^t$$

which may be simplified by letting

$$\gamma_0 = \frac{C}{1 - \beta} \quad \text{and} \quad \gamma_1 = \alpha - \frac{C}{1 - \beta}$$

and reduced to

$$Y_t = \gamma_0 + \gamma_1(\beta)_t$$

The pattern of the function again depends on the value of β. The major difference is that a nonhomogeneous system can be used to show convergence on a particular value other than zero. Thus if $0 < \beta < 1$, then $(\beta)^t$ approaches zero as t increases, and Y_t approaches the constant value γ_0. Alternatively, if $-1 < \beta < 0$, then $(\beta)^t$ oscillates and converges to zero while Y_t oscillates and converges on γ_0.

FIGURE 16A–10

Behavior of $Y_t = A\beta^t$
where $-1 < \beta < 0$

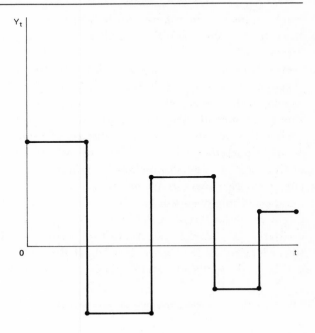

FIGURE 16A–11

Behavior of $Y_t = A\beta$
where $\beta < -1$

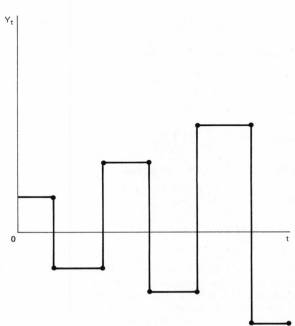

THE SAMUELSON MULTIPLIER-ACCELERATOR MODEL

Paul Samuelson of MIT was one of the first to express the Keynesian model in dynamic terms. His model attempts to explain the possible effects of an injection of investment. The first obvious question is whether a change in investment is a one-shot phenomenon or whether it is sustained over time. A second question is whether investment decisions are affected as income and consumption change. In other words, when a ΔI makes for a ΔY, then what secondary effect does the forthcoming ΔC have for I? As we noted in the last chapter, Samuelson claimed that the multiplier effect was in fact augmented by this secondary investment effect, which he termed the "acceleration" principle. We are now in a position to appreciate more fully his description of their interaction over time.

Samuelson used a second-order homogeneous system to describe the Keynesian model.[6] Starting with the simple model

$$Y_t = C_t + I_t$$

he made C a function of the preceding period's income:

$$C_t = b Y_{t-1} \qquad (0 < b < 1)$$

This period's investment is *induced* and depends on the change in consumption and the acceleration coefficient a:

$$I_t = a(C_t - C_{t-1}) \qquad (a > 0)$$

This can be expressed

$$I_t = ab Y_{t-1} - ab Y_{t-2}$$

By substituting C_t and I_t, we can express the Y_t equation as a second-order difference equation:

$$Y_t = b(1 + a) Y_{t-1} - ab Y_{t-2}$$

As in the case of first-order difference equations, it is appropriate to examine the possible solutions to such a system in order to shed light on the workings of the multiplier-accelerator model. We first form an auxiliary equation

$$Y_t = r^t$$

---

[6] Second- and higher-order difference equations are defined as differences between lower-order equations. Y_t in the equation above is the difference between first-order equations Y_{t-1} and Y_{t-2}.

TABLE 16A–1

Multiplier-accelerator model,
$MPC = .5$, accelerator $= 2$

System:

$$Y_t = b(1 + a)Y_{t-1} - abY_{t-2} + G$$

Given:

$$Y_{t-1} = 20, \quad Y_{t-2} = 20, \quad G = 10$$

Equilibrium income for Y_t would be

$$1.5_{Y-1} - Y_{t-2} + 10 = Y_t$$
$$1.5(20) - 20 + 10 = 20$$

But now introduce a change in G of 1

$$1.5(20) - 20 + 11 = 21$$

and the multiplier-accelerator interaction proceeds as follows

$$
\begin{aligned}
Y_{t+1} &= 1.5(21) &- 20 &+ 11 = 22.5 \\
Y_{t+2} &= 1.5(22.5) - 21 &&+ 11 = 23.8 \\
Y_{t+3} &= 1.5(23.8) - 22.5 &&+ 11 = 23.2 \\
Y_{t+4} &= 1.5(23.2) - 23.8 &&+ 11 = 22.0 \\
Y_{t+5} &= 1.5(22.0) - 23.2 &&+ 11 = 20.8 \\
Y_{t+6} &= 1.5(20.8) - 22.0 &&+ 11 = 20.2 \\
Y_{t+7} &= 1.5(20.2) - 20.8 &&+ 11 = 20.5 \\
Y_{t+8} &= 1.5(20.5) - 20.2 &&+ 11 = 21.6 \\
Y_{t+9} &= 1.5(21.6) - 20.5 &&+ 11 = 22.9 \\
Y_{t+10} &= 1.5(22.9) - 21.6 &&+ 11 = 23.8 \\
Y_{t+11} &= 1.5(23.8) - 22.9 &&+ 11 = 23.8 \\
Y_{t+12} &= 1.5(23.8) - 23.8 &&+ 11 = 22.9
\end{aligned}
$$

TABLE 16A–2

Multiplier-accelerator model,
$MPC = .5$, accelerator $= .2$

System:

$$Y_t = b(1 + a)Y_{t-1} - abY_{t-2} + G$$
$$= .6Y_{t-1} - .1Y_{t-2} + G$$

Given:

$$Y_{t-1} = 20, \quad Y_{t-2} = 20, \quad G = 10$$

Equilibrium income for Y_t would be

$$Y_t = (.6)(20) - .1(20) + 10 = 20$$

Now change G to 11; since the multiplier is 2, the new equilibrium is at $Y = 22$.

$$Y_t = (.6)(20) - .1(20) + 11 = 21$$

The multiplier-accelerator interaction proceeds as follows:

$$
\begin{aligned}
Y_{t+1} &= (.6)(21.00) &- .1(20.00) &+ 11 = 21.60 \\
Y_{t+2} &= (.6)(21.60) &- .1(21.00) &+ 11 = 21.86 \\
Y_{t+3} &= (.6)(21.86) &- .1(21.60) &+ 11 = 21.96 \\
Y_{t+4} &= (.6)(21.96) &- .1(21.86) &+ 11 = 21.99 \\
Y_{t+5} &= (.6)(21.99) &- .1(21.96) &+ 11 = 21.998 \\
Y_{t+6} &= (.6)(21.998) - .1(21.99) &&+ 11 = 22.000 \\
Y_{t+7} &= (.6)(22.000) - .1(21.998) &&+ 11 = 22.001 \\
Y_{t+8} &= (.6)(22.001) - .1(22.000) &&+ 11 = 22.000
\end{aligned}
$$

---

and substitute in its lagged equivalents to form the equation:

$$r^t = b(1 + a)r^{t-1} - abr^{t-2}$$

which can be reduced to the quadratic equation by rewriting

$$r^t - b(1 - a)r^{t-1} + abr^{t-2} = 0$$

and dividing through by r^{t-2}:

$$r^2 - b(1 + a)r + ab = 0$$

We find that we may have (1) real and equal roots, (2) real and unequal roots, or (3) complex and imaginary roots, depending on the outcome of the familiar quadratic formula.

Once the roots are found, we can proceed to find the general solution:

$$Y_t = \mu r_1 t + \lambda r_2 t$$

Such a solution is not difficult to obtain, since in formulating the model we have at least two observations of Y_t which allow us to solve for the unknowns μ and λ.

Our primary interest in this inquiry is to speculate as to the plausible path of multiplier-accelerator interaction over time. Since this time path depends on r_1 and r_2, and these in turn depend on a and b, let us consider the possible time paths for different values of a and b. The outcome depends importantly on whether ab is greater, equal to, or less than unity. In general, we may say that if $ab > 1$ and the roots are complex, there is an explosive oscillation; if $ab < 1$ with complex roots, there is a damped oscillation. If $ab > 1$ with distinct real roots, there is an unstable nonfluctuating time path; if $ab < 1$ with equal real roots, there is a stable nonfluctuating time path. Finally, if $ab = 1$, it turns out that the roots are real and equal and the time path will fluctuate regularly.

Now suppose the marginal propensity to consume is .5 and the accelerator is 2. What kind of time path does this make for? Consider Table 16A.1. With no accelerator and a multiplier of $1/(1 - .5) = 2$ an increase in G of 1 would raise Y from 20 to 22. Interaction with the accelerator, however, causes a steady fluctuation around the value 22. A fluctuation of stable amplitude is insured because $ab = (.5)(2) = 1$. Suppose $MPC = .5$ and the accelerator $= .2$. Under the assumptions shown in Table 16A.2

FIGURE 16A–12

Comparison of
growth paths

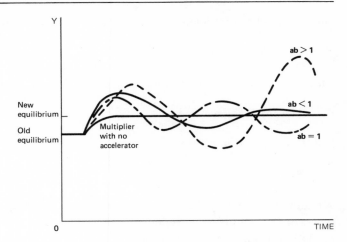

a change in G would start the time path towards an equilibrium of Y at 22.0 (since the multiplier is 2). Thus:

$$Y_t = b(1 + a)Y_{t-1} - abY_{t-2} + G$$
$$Y = (.6 \times 22) - .1(22) + 11 = 22$$

The multiplier effect moves Y directly to $Y = 22$, as described in Chapter 15. Interaction with the accelerator in this case (where $ab < 1$) causes Y to approach 22 through damped oscillation. The student may wish to test a situation where $ab > 1$ (say, where $MPC = .8$ and $a = 4$). An accelerator of this value implies that businessmen are highly responsive to changes in consumption, and their changes in investment would cause Y to oscillate and explode.

Figure 16A.12 is useful for comparing the three cases: $ab > 1$, $ab = 1$, and $ab < 1$.

The case where $ab < 1$ is the most appealing, since the time path generated is not explosive—and this *seems* true of most of our business fluctuations. Alvin Hansen, among others, argues that the values of a and b are in this range (although close to the condition where $ab = 1$). The marginal propensity to consume, b, has been shown, he argues, to be about .5 when the effects of taxes are considered. He asserts that the value of the accelerator is less than but near 2, since it is based on the *marginal* efficiency of adding new capital. Broad estimates of the capital-output ratio usually place it near 3; however, much of the capital stock is relatively fixed, and what we wish to know is the *marginal* rather than the average capital-output ratio, and this technical relationship is nearer to 2.

To attempt to explain the accelerator as a relationship primarily dependent on the technological constraints is somewhat problematical. In the first place, we must ponder just how one arrives at the figure 2 (or any figure) for the accelerator. If one associates it with the capital-output ratio, the time period involved is one year. But in order to be compatible with the model it must be expressed in terms of the consumption lag:

$$I_t = a(C_t - C_{t-1})$$

The consumption lag, however, is certainly less than a year and is closer to a quarter, in which case the value of a would have to be 8 rather than 2. By this reasoning the model would be unrealistically explosive.

A related inconsistency in the model tends to explain why the "real world" time path of Y is more stable than the model would imply. This is the built-in assumption that the change in consumption calls forth a change in investment to be completed in the same period. In reality, investment decisions in response to changes in consumption are implemented in the following period. The more realistic approach is to *lag* the accelerator effect:

$$I = a(C_{t-1} - C_{t-2})$$

which will make for greater stability in the model.

The basic fallacy of assuming that the accelerator depends on a technological relationship—i.e., the marginal capital-output ratio—is that it does not account for businessmen's expectations of *sales relative to capacity*. If the change in demand comes at a time when the firm has excess capacity, the firm simply increases its variable costs and output and may not change its investment plans. But if the change in demand comes when the firm has little excess capacity, the firm must resort to increasing output through overtime, using marginal equipment, and so on; and if the increase in demand is expected to persist, new real investment will be undertaken. Richard Goodwin,[7] John R. Hicks[8] and others

[7] See Goodwin, *Econometrica*, vol. 19 (1951), pp. 1–17, and in A. H. Hansen, *Business Cycles and National Income* (New York: Norton, 1951).

[8] Hicks, *A Contribution to the Theory of the Trade Cycle* (London: Oxford University Press, 1950), as well as James Duesenberry, "Hicks on the Trade Cycle," *Quarterly Journal of Economics*, vol. 64 (August, 1950), pp. 464–476.

have developed modified accelerator models which have constraints in the forms of full employment "ceilings" or rising cost schedules. As we shall see below, these models depict a fluctuation between recession and the full employment ceiling.

An important variable, according to Keynes, is the *rate of capital accumulation*. An inherent danger to growth over time is the oversaturation of capital. Expressed in terms of the static model in the preceding chapter, such a situation might occur when an overabundance of capital depressed the expected marginal return from additional investment. Even at very low interest rates the equilibrium (between *IS* and *LM*) would be at less than full employment. Couched in dynamic terms, the problem becomes one of how income (and investment opportunities) grow relative to the capital stock. Keynes was pessimistic in this regard. He reasoned that if the capital stock grew faster than the labor supply, it was inevitable that eventually the marginal return to capital would be pushed down.

THE GROWTH MODELS OF DOMAR AND HARROD

But it is not inevitable that new productive capacity discourages investment in the next period. If demand in the next period is sufficient, the capital stock will be fully utilized and adequate incentive will be provided for continued investment and growth.

By what *rate* must demand grow in order to fully utilize capital and provide the appropriate incentive so that the rate of investment (and growth) can be continued at a stable rate? As income grows, a certain amount of consumption demand will be generated according to the marginal propensity to consume. If the *MPC* is known, the crucial question becomes the demand for investment. Professor Evsey Domar outlines the problem in the following way: Suppose we know the marginal propensity to consume and its complement, the marginal propensity to save, *s*. Suppose also that the productivity of new capital is known, σ. New investment has a dual role affecting both income and production. More precisely, the rate of new investment must provide an increase in income sufficient to absorb savings and new productive capacity. The growth equation is [9]

$$\frac{\Delta I}{I} = \sigma s$$

Domar's formulation of the growth "problem" succinctly reveals another dimension of fiscal policy. It is not enough that the savings "leakage" be offset by investment (or government spending). National income must grow at the correct rate: a rate which increases demand sufficiently to account both for savings and the productivity of new capital.

Fiscal policy can take any one of several tacks according to the desired "solution" of the growth "problem." Our previous examination revealed that the composition of spending in each period could be adjusted so as to provide for full employment. A policy incorporating a growth *target* requires more sophisticated analysis. The growth "problem" obviously depends on the marginal propensity to save and the productivity of new capital. Both of these variables can be affected by fiscal policy. Changes in s may be accomplished simply by changing the tax rate (this change need not affect the distribution of income). Changes in σ are more difficult, since the problem here involves both expectations and technology. Over the long run, research financed through the public sector may enhance the productivity of capital and, theoretically, may encourage either labor-using or capital-using technological change. More importantly, fiscal policies such as the investment tax credit and accelerated depreciation rates can be used to change expectations as to the profitability of investment. Here, again, the effort is not simply to provide enough aggregate spending but (1) to adjust the *composition* of spending to provide for the desired amount of real investment, and (2) to recognize the productivity of this investment and *the requirements it will impose on fiscal and monetary policy in succeeding periods.*

While Domar's formulation is useful for visualizing fiscal policy in a growth perspective, it does not attempt to show how certain types of

---

[9] For example, if national income is $1000 billion and the marginal propensity to save is 10 percent, full employment requires that $.10 \times 1000 = 100$ be invested. At the same time this increases productive capacity by the amount invested, 100, times the productivity ratio σ, which for this example is .40; therefore, $(.40)(100) = 40$. The productive capacity of the economy will rise by

$$1000(.10)(.40) = 40 \text{ billion}$$

and the rise in income must be the same. In relative terms national income must rise each year by

$$\frac{1000(\sigma s)}{1000} = \frac{1040}{1000} = 4 \text{ percent}$$

economic behavior make for a tendency toward or away from an equilibrium growth path. Other models by Samuelson, Goodwin, and Hicks include the assumption that investment is related to changes in consumption. A model by Roy F. Harrod offers a model of investment behavior which explains the tendency towards equilibrium growth and how divergencies may occur. The crucial behavioral assumption is that investment is primarily a function of expectations and that, if expectations are realized in the present and preceding periods, they will tend to be perpetuated. In the absence of evidence to the contrary businessmen will repeat outlays so that the *rate of growth* in the previous period will be maintained. The "warranted rate of growth" is defined as that which will allow all firms to realize their expectations of the preceding period and thus expect continued success in the future. We may express this concept as

$$G_w = \frac{s}{c}$$

where G_w is the warranted rate of growth, $\Delta Y/Y$; s is the marginal propensity to save, and c is the ratio of induced investment to changes in income. The similarity between the models of Harrod and Domar becomes more evident when one notes that Harrod's c is close kin to the reciprocal of the σ in Domar's model, the latter being the productivity of new capital.[10]

If in one period optimism causes investment to exceed the warranted rate, the increase in demand will exceed the increase in output, and shortages will appear. Even greater optimism will create even greater shortages in subsequent periods. Alternatively, pessimism will create ever-growing surpluses and unemployment. Hence, the system will either explode or break down if it ever diverges from the equilibrium path. If it explodes in an upward direction, it will eventually run into a "ceiling" imposed by the quantity of resources and the state of technology (the "natural rate of growth"). The latter possibility allows for fluctuations. In essence, however, the system is quite volatile and incorporates no corrective forces.

HICKS' MODEL OF FLUCTUATING GROWTH

J. R. Hicks criticizes the inherent instability of the Harrod model, which derives primarily from the absence of a time lag in the investment function. In Hicks's view the nature and effects of induced changes in investment are better explained by a time lag than by the assumption of concurrent changes in I and Y.

In Hicks's model, autonomous I and Y grow at a fairly constant rate, while the accelerator and multiplier change induced investment in such a way as to make actual growth oscillate around a stable time path. He incorporates a time lag for both investment and consumption. The accelerator turns out to be strong enough to cause Y to diverge from the path, but certain constraints set limits to the oscillation. Any reduction in I would not fall below zero; thus, reductions in Y will cease and the accelerator will effect an increase in the next period. Any upward movement is limited by the full employment constraint set by autonomous investment.

The Hicks model can "explain" how a stable business cycle is built upon a stable growth path. Yet we might question whether our economic system is self-regulating in this manner. In other words: is the accelerator sufficiently high to insure recovery?[11] We have already noted Alvin Hansen's argument that the accelerator is lower than that proposed by Hicks and generates damped oscillation. According to Hansen, without government intervention, expansions will not reach the "growth ceiling" before petering out. He argues, however, that shifts in autonomous investment—caused by changes in population, technology, and so on—may in turn cause fluctuations which are accentuated by the accelerator but are damped in character.

SOME CRITICISMS AND FURTHER COMMENTS

Our discussion leads us to suspect that while certain insights may be gained from the simple models of Harrod, Hicks, Hansen, and others, a more general explanation is needed. Specifically, observation leads us to conclude that on occasion inflation occurs in the manner Hicks predicted when the growth "ceiling" is reached. On other occasions—as in

[10] The basic difference between the Domar and Harrod models is with respect to the time treatment. While Domar expresses his model in discrete terms (a difference equation), Harrod expresses similar relationships in continuous terms (a differential equation). Thus, while the two say essentially the same thing, the difference in time treatment is important, as explained below.

[11] This question is put by James Duesenberry in his article, "Hicks on the Trade Cycle." Earlier, Jan Tinbergen offered empirical evidence suggesting that the accelerator is not large: "Statistical Evidence on the Acceleration Principle," *Economica*, vol. 5, N.S., (May 1938).

the 1930s—the system seems not to have demonstrated built-in forces insuring growth. A more sophisticated view is required, which, instead of assuming the accelerator to be a fixed technological constant, examines the variables which change the accelerator. One requirement is a model of firm investment behavior. One must ask what important variables are at work on the firm's profit expectations and hence on the firm's willingness to increase investment. As these variables change, what happens to the value of the accelerator?

James Duesenberry has developed an accelerator-multiplier model in which the accelerator is dependent on changing firm investment behavior. According to Duesenberry, the firm maximizes profit by equating the marginal efficiency of investment to the marginal cost of raising capital. The latter is not simply the rate of interest; instead, the marginal cost of capital schedule is upward sloping, increasing from the cost of internally generated funds to costlier funds outside the firm. These rising costs make for a lower multiplier and accelerator than found in most models. However, each may change according to variables such as retained earnings, dividend rates, and the like. Long-term growth, according to Duesenberry, is dependent on structural changes which in turn affect the rate of growth in the capital stock and the rate of growth of income. Booms and recessions may result from shocks to the system and may, as in the Hicks model, reach and rebound from the " ceiling." On the other hand, if capacity tends to rise faster than demand (as Hansen anticipated), a long-term depression may set in with no guarantee of growth.

Another objection to the usual accelerator-multiplier model is that a fixed capital-output ratio is assumed. As argued above, the *nature* of technical change is important. The rise in prices and the " ceiling " depend not only on the " slack " in the economy but on whether technical change is capital-using or labor-using. On certain occasions the " ceiling " might be due to labor shortages; on others, to capital shortages. In either event the " substitutability " of labor and capital is important. To the extent that input quantities and *input prices* are flexible, the model takes on a neoclassical rather than a Keynesian character. Samuelson, Robert Solow, James Meade, and others have included neoclassical assumptions in their models. As Solow demonstrates, the flexibility introduced by allowing some input substitutability makes for models which do not require the delicate balance between capital accumulation and income necessary in the Harrod-Domar-Hicks models.[12]

The perspectives we have examined in our short discourse on growth theory will be useful to us in the next chapter. They will add to our ability to analyze effects of fiscal policy through time.

[12] Solow, "A Contribution to the Theory of Economic Growth," *Quarterly Journal of Economics*, vol. 70 (February 1956).

17

MACROECONOMIC POLICIES AND PUBLIC CHOICES 1920–PRESENT

What are some of the judgments inherent in the choice between various macroeconomic tools? In the process of our study we have observed that any economic model (and any policies predicated on it) is necessarily built upon a set of assumptions and value judgments about the economy. We must also deal with value judgments when examining the "appropriate" functions of the public sector. One way of dealing with the latter question is to assume that individual and social preferences can be taken as "given." The possibility of approaching the resource allocation question this way led us to examine the concept of a unique welfare-maximizing allocation of resources. We also used the imaginary Fiscal Department model to demonstrate that with a given set of priorities, several goals can *theoretically* be pursued at once. In the "real world" we cannot assume that preferences are known. Preferences are revealed within the context of the budget process and other institutions which implement the various functions of the public sector. Since we cannot be certain as to the composition of social preferences, and since any one government activity may affect several of society's goals, we, as economists, cannot make final judgments on its desirability. Instead we attempt to examine policies in such a way as to reveal the public choices involved as well as the mechanics of the policy's economic effects. To summarize, it is not always obvious whether a particular policy-mix is *best* from either the perspectives of *efficiency* or the perspectives of *welfare maximization*. When this is true it is the economist's responsibility not only to comment on the relative effectiveness of different policies but also on how they affect the decisions or "choices" made by individuals and groups within society.

Let us now survey the macroeconomic disturbances and policies from the years just prior to the "Keynesian revolution." In our survey we will examine the policy-mix not only in terms of its effectiveness but in terms of the inherent choices made between other social priorities.

MACROECONOMIC POLICIES AND CHOICES SINCE 1920

In previous chapters we have examined the different macroeconomic tools on the basis of how they work in a given model with a given set of assumptions. It is appropriate for us to make a critique of fiscal policies with reference to historical events.

564

565

Our discussions of how consumption and investment functions may
shift during periods of prosperity offer good starting points for the macroeconomic events of the 1920s.[1] More specifically the growth in aggregate
spending can be explained as interaction between the accelerator and the
multiplier. The base for the boom was provided by large and sustained
capital expenditures by businessmen. There was great demand for investment goods, in part as a result of the World War I drain on capital
equipment, but primarily because of the creation of new products and
investment opportunities. Several major industries arose as certain products were marketed on a massive scale for the first time. These were
commodities such as the automobile, the telephone, the radio, and
electrical appliances such as stoves, refrigerators and washing machines.
The markets grew not only because the commodities were new ones but
because the new techniques of mass production lowered their costs. The
effects of these new techniques are reflected in the downward trend of the
consumer price index which fell from 69.8 percent in 1920 (using the
1957–1958 base of 100) to 59.7 percent in 1929. In addition, expanded
aggregate spending was augmented by a residential housing boom and
other needs of increasing urbanization.

The 1920s boom cannot be explained as a product of enlightened fiscal
policy. The rule for fiscal policy in the 1920s was that the budget should
be balanced and should not be used as a weapon for fostering full employment. "Sound" fiscal responsibility was assumed to be achieved only
when expenditures were equal to tax receipts over the fiscal year. Although
deficits had been accepted in times of war, the rule for normal years was
the balanced budget.

Economic policy, instead of relying on fiscal tools, relied primarily on
the corrective devices of the competitive system: flexible prices and
wages in the commodity market and a flexible interest rate in the money
market. On the other hand it was widely accepted that if any contingency

---

[1] The Hicksian growth model presented in Appendix Two to Chapter 16 is also useful in
portraying the nature of fluctuations in the 1920s. The World War I years had been ones
of increasing GNP, the war spending furnishing ample aggregate demand. The end of the
war and the cutback in expenditure occasioned a brief slump in 1919, a quick rebound in
1920, and a rather severe recession in 1921. From here the oscillations increased in size.
Except for brief employment slumps in 1924 and 1927, the economy expanded vigorously
until the theoretical "ceiling" was reached in 1929 causing a violent downward movement.

arose, monetary action would be adequate. Although monetary policy during the 1920s could not be called aggressive, it furnished conditions conducive to growth. The growth of commercial banks was encouraged and as the value of land, building, and stock increased, additional collateral was created for further borrowing.

THE GREAT CRASH AND THE 1930s

In October of 1929 the stock market collapsed, triggering a sharp cutback in business activity. GNP fell from its $204 billion level in 1929 (in 1958 dollars) to a low of $141 billion in 1933. Investment spending fell from about $43 billion (in 1958 dollars) to less than $5 billion during the same period.

Several factors combined to make the depression severe. With the stock market crash, optimism and speculation turned to pessimism and caution. The monetary value of assets fell rapidly. From 1929 to 1933 almost 10,000 of the 24,500 banks in operation failed. Businessmen's expectations changed dramatically. In Keynesian terminology the marginal efficiency of capital schedule shifted to the left. The strong multiplier-accelerator effect of the late 1920s turned into a strong downward multiplier-accelerator effect.

The high level of consumer spending of the 1920s had suddenly come to an end. The expansion of consumer debt had leveled off as greater proportions of consumers' incomes were obligated to periodic payments. The residential housing market had also become saturated. Moreover, as consumer assets fell in value, this acted as a restraint on the consumption function.

Monetary policy. The faith put in the efficacy of monetary policy was soon dispelled. Actually, aggressive monetary policy as we think of it today was not used. But the Federal Reserve failed even in the limited mission the Friedmanists would require—keeping the supply of money stable. During the 1920s and the early 1930s the Fed relied primarily on discount rate changes to effect monetary policy. During that period there were frequent rate changes and heavy bank borrowing. The rate was raised a full percentage point in July 1929 but was progressively lowered until 1931 when it was raised for balance-of-payments purposes ... *long before the depression hit bottom in 1933*. The Fed's use of other monetary tools had even less impact. The Fed did not have the authority to change the required reserve ratio in 1929 and it remained constant. Open market operations were used and in the right direction; however, the scale of these operations was small relative to today's transactions. During the 1920s the holdings of the Fed averaged around $250 million. The Fed did not significantly increase its holdings until 1932 when they were increased to about $2500 million, remaining at that level until the war. There is some question as to whether the Fed did all it could. In any event what it did was not enough. From 1929 to 1933 the money supply contracted from $26.4 million to $19.8 billion.

If we interpret these events in terms of the familiar equation of exchange we see that the naive assumption of flexible prices certainly did not hold. While prices were reduced in some cases the major response to the contraction of M was unemployment and reduced Y^*:

$$\downarrow M \bar{V} = \bar{P} Y^* \downarrow$$

Fiscal policy. Even though the effectiveness of monetary policy and the self-regulating mechanics of the market were noticeably absent, many economists clung to the classical prescriptions for economic recovery. When President Roosevelt came into office in 1933, he promised to restore "fiscal responsibility." Balanced budgets had also been the aim of the Hoover Administration, but deficits had occurred due to the reduced tax yield. Roosevelt continued to cling to this goal for some time to come although he later acquiesced in the face of mounting deficits and the advice of some of his economic advisors.

It is difficult to evaluate the effectiveness of fiscal policy in the early 1930s. In 1931, 1932, and 1933 there were deficits but primarily because of lower tax receipts, which fell from $4.1 billion in 1930 to $1.9 billion in 1932 and $2.0 billion in 1933. The framers of the New Deal, regardless of their preference for a balanced budget, realized the need for government programs designed to increase employment. Accordingly, government expenditures were increased from $4.6 billion in 1933 to $6.6 billion in 1934. The necessary consequence of falling revenues and increasing expenditures was that aggregate demand was stimulated through deficit financing. The 1934 deficit was $3.6 billion. Gross national product began climbing back up. The increase of GNP from 1933 to 1936 was from $55.6 billion to $90.4 billion in then-current dollars. In terms of the 1958 index, the increase was from $141.5 billion to $203.2 billion.

In 1936 Lord Keynes's *General Theory of Employment, Interest and Money* appeared. By this time several influential economists were in agreement with his prognosis that massive government spending would

FIGURE 17–1

The liquidity trap

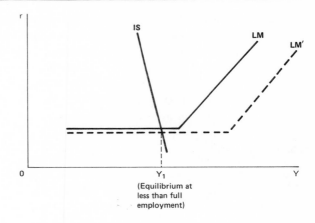

(Equilibrium at
less than full
employment)

be needed to pull the economy completely out of depression. Unemployment, which had reached a high of 24.9 percent in 1933, was still 14.3 percent in 1937.

After another slump occurred in 1937 and 1938, several economists within the New Deal administration accepted the argument that deficit financing was a positive fiscal tool. From a GNP of $90.4 billion in current dollars ($203.2 in 1958 dollars) in 1937 there had been a decline to $84.7 billion ($192.9 billion in 1958 dollars) in 1938. Government spending, reduced in 1937 and 1938, was finally increased to $8.8 billion in 1939.

The period following 1937 offers some support for the "liquidity trap" case we discussed in the context of the Keynesian model. For in that period there was an attempt by the monetary authorities to increase aggregate spending by expanding the money supply. In the Keynesian model, we recall, the liquidity trap can occur when people hold money rather than bid down the rate of interest. An interest rate "floor" shows up as the horizontal portion of the LM curve in Figure 17.1. Even if we are successful in shifting the LM curve to LM' there is no change in Y. This is because the increase in M has not lowered r and thus there is no increase in I with its attendant multiplier effect.

Economists did not gain much experience during the Great Depression in using the Keynesian perspective to "fine tune" the economy. The deficit financing of the early 1930s was an accident due in part to "make work" programs and falling revenues. The slump in 1937 did offer evidence that sustained governmental support for aggregate spending was required; but before the new approach was fully implemented[2] in the late

1930s, war expenditures provided a more-than-adequate boost. No "fine tuning" was possible because aggregate demand quickly overshot the area where a *choice* is required between price stability and lower unemployment.

THE SECOND WORLD WAR

Mobilization for World War II temporarily made moot the question of how much government expenditure was required to adequately stimulate the economy. The budget became not only expansionary but inflationary. The new question was: How could war mobilization be financed while keeping inflationary pressures within limits? Federal expenditures increased from $9055 million in 1940 to $98,303 million in 1945 while national defense expenditures rose from $1498 million to $81,216 million. The economy responded vigorously to this stimulation. Unemployment, which was still as high as 14.9 percent in 1940, dropped to 4.7 percent by 1942 and hit a low of 1.2 percent in 1944. Gross national product rose from $99.7 billion in 1940 to $211.9 billion in 1945.[3] This increase in government spending necessarily generated large amounts of spending power in the hands of consumers. Disposable income doubled in the period from 1940 to 1945. Without regulated prices and rationing, galloping inflation would have resulted.

Under such conditions the methods used to finance the war seem subject to critical examination. In the first place the decision was made to finance the war primarily through raising the debt rather than by reducing consumer spending through taxation. This decision seems excusable in the initial stages of the war when an immediate and drastic change in tax rates might have had disruptive effects on an economy undergoing rapid adjustment. But the argument is less valid for periods after the initial stage. The spending power consumers retained as a consequence of financing the war through debt was to create great inflationary pressures later.

Another questionable aspect of the financing was the decision to allow

---

[2] The Hansen growth model presented in Appendix Two of the preceding chapter provides a useful description of the action of the accelerator during the 1930s. According to Hansen the accelerator is not sufficient to generate sustained expansion. Unless substantial autonomous investment or government spending occurs, any expansion will damp out and reach an equilibrium at a less-than-full employment of spending.

[3] In terms of the 1958 index the increase from 1940 to 1945 was from $227.2 billion to $355.2 billion.

FIGURE 17–2

The savings leakage

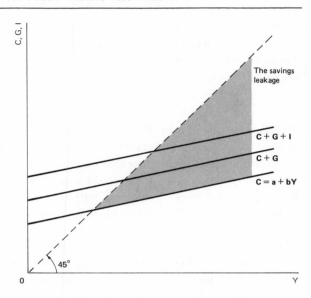

the banking system to purchase government securities when the demand of individuals was insufficient. During the first " bond drives " of the war the banking system purchased substantial amounts of securities. This, of course, added to the lending capability of banks and increased inflationary pressures. Bonds owned by the commercial banks could be resold to the Fed, thus increasing revenues and, through the credit multiplier, the money supply. Unsuccessful attempts were made to limit purchases by banks in subsequent drives. By the end of the war commercial bank holdings of government securities had risen from $16.1 billion in 1940 to $84.2 billion. This source of credit expansion added significantly to inflationary pressures in the postwar years.

In deference to the Treasury, the Federal Reserve agreed to " peg " the prices of government securities by buying when the prices dropped to certain levels. During World War II the Fed bought nearly a third of the securities issued by the government. More important, this practice, until finally dropped in 1951, seriously curtailed the flexibility of monetary policy.

The public's conception of the federal government's responsibility *vis-à-vis* the economy had changed during the depression and war years. This assessment was legislated into the Employment Act of 1946. The Act made it clear that it was the duty of the government to use both fiscal and monetary tools to achieve stable full employment. The Council of Economic Advisers was created to aid the President in economic planning. For the most part, however, fiscal and monetary policy in the immediate postwar era failed to stem the inflationary pressures built up during the war.

One reason fiscal policy makers were slow to curtail postwar inflationary spending was the persuasive argument of some economists who predicted a serious shortage of aggregate demand.

PUBLIC CHOICE AND THE MYTH OF THE STAGNATIONISTS

The experience of the Great Depression and World War II led to a disturbing interpretation of the Keynesian model. Several economists—who became known as the Stagnationists—argued that the only cure for an otherwise stagnant economy was massive doses of government spending. If this were the case it would make for a serious conflict between macroeconomic policy goals on the one hand and the goal of intersector resource allocation on the other. If massive government expenditures were required for macroeconomic policy, the cost-benefit considerations allocating resources to the production of certain quantities of public goods, quasi-public goods, and private goods would have to be ignored.

Let us consider the Stagnationist argument: If the consumption function was stable and relatively flat—as it was thought to be—the amount of savings generated by long-term increases in aggregate spending would be very large (see Figure 17.2). The lower the marginal propensity to consume, the greater the amount of income that would be diverted from the flow of spending. Unless investment or government spending increased enough to compensate for this leakage, economic growth would be curtailed by inadequate spending. The economy would "stagnate."

The Stagnationists held little hope that private investment spending would keep pace with the increase in savings. No new "seminal" innovations seemed in the offing, and population growth was declining. A natural extension of the Keynesian concept of investment was that the MEC schedule was stable and inelastic. Consequently, as the stock of capital grew through investment, there would be fewer and fewer investment opportunities.

The Stagnationists' prescription for filling the gap between income generated and income spent (the savings leakage) was massive doses of government spending. Taxes, of course, would not be raised by a corresponding amount since this would reduce consumer spending. The long-run fiscal policy deriving from the Stagnationists' position would feature large and continuous deficit financing.

The Stagnationists have been proven wrong on several counts. In the first place the cross-sectional view of the consumption function is not stable over long periods of time—as discussed at length in Chapter 15. This means that the long-run average and marginal propensities to consume are not as low as the stagnationists assumed, and the savings-leakage-gap is not as large as anticipated. Also the rapid change in technology has continued to produce new uses for capital. The population has grown in the post-World War II years as a result of both high birth rates and low death rates.

Some public choice aspects of the Stagnationist argument are still with us. We have had large increases in government expenditure since the short-run cutback following World War II. It is still popular to argue that without large expenditures on defense, the economy would suffer. In our survey of the macroeconomic tools, however, we have presented a rather convincing argument that the public sector can use such tools as tax cuts and monetary ease to stimulate private sector demand if that choice is made. Consequently it is not ordinarily necessary that macroeconomic policy be *nonneutral* with respect to the intersector resource allocation goal.[4]

THE COMPOSITION OF SPENDING IN THE LATE 1940s

After averaging $73 billion during the war years, federal spending dropped to $38.9 billion in 1947 and stayed around $40 billion from 1948 to 1951. Private investment and consumption rose to more than compensate. The postwar "accelerator" had changed considerably as a result of several factors which raised businessmen's expectations of profit. The war had introduced new techniques and products which were yet to be exploited by the private sector (the marginal efficiency of capital schedule had shifted to the right). Finally, predictions of consumer spending, based on consumer habits in the 1930s, were also too low. Owing to the depletion of durable goods during the war, increased monetary assets, and perhaps also a change in "tastes," *the consumption function had shifted upward.*

Other factors adding heat to the expansionary fire were an increase in residential housing and a high level of exports resulting from war damage in Europe and American loans and grants. Gross national product increased from $208.5 billion in 1946 to $257.6 billion in 1948. The expansion in terms of the 1958 index, however, was only from $312.6

billion to \$323.7 billion. The consumer price index (using the 1958 base) had risen from 62.7 percent in 1945 to 83.8 percent in 1948.

In 1948 the government finally had a surplus of net receipts (\$41.4 billion) over net expenditures (\$33.0 billion) of \$8.4 billion. Moreover, the President asked for a \$4 billion surplus in 1949. But, alas, this did not materialize. In the last quarter of 1948 the economy embarked on its first post-World War II recession.

The record of the monetary and fiscal authorities during the 1949 recession was again dubious. The rediscount rate, which had been raised twice in 1948, was held constant throughout the recession. The required reserve ratio, which also had been raised in 1948, was not lowered until May of 1949. From that time on, however, it was lowered several times during the remainder of the recession. The open market operations of the Fed, still constrained to " peg " bond prices, were decidedly *procyclical*. The Fed should have been buying securities in order to place money into the commercial banking system and thus lower the rate of interest and increase investment spending. Instead, the Fed's holdings of government securities fell from about \$23 billion in late 1948 to below \$18 billion in 1950.

The fiscal activity of the government, although perhaps no more enlightened, was at least in the right direction. Owing to a tax cut which had been approved in 1948 (though not with the recession in mind) and the automatic stabilizers, net receipts fell by \$3.7 billion to \$37.7 billion in 1949. At the same time federal expenditures rose by \$6.5 billion to \$39.5 billion, owing to increases in transfer payments and defense expenditures. This shift in the budget provided needed spending power to the economic system.

---

[4] One exception should be noted. In the deep depression situation, the Stagnationist argument may hold. This is because most of the other tools may become ineffective. We have noted that monetary policy may be ineffective due to the liquidity trap and the pessimistic expectations of businessmen. For the latter reason an investment tax credit would have no effect. Finally a personal income tax cut would have little effect if incomes were quite low anyway. It may be that the Stagnationist prescription (a massive dose of *G*) would be the only available remedy.

Even in this situation, however, there is an alternative to depending solely on government expenditures. Obviously, increases in transfers would have the effect of shifting the consumption function and providing needed aggregate spending. As we know, the present system does this to a certain extent automatically. If and when the negative income tax concept is built into the personal income tax structure the automatic change in consumption expenditure should be much stronger.

In 1950 the economy reacted favorably, and it was soon beset by the expansionary and inflationary pressures of the Korean war.

THE UPS AND DOWNS OF THE 1950s

The economy fluctuated between inflation and recession in the 1950s, with fiscal and monetary policy often serving as the cause rather than the cure. From 1950 to 1953 the economy expanded vigorously, the GNP rising from a 1949 level of $324.1 billion (in terms of the 1958 index) to $412.8 billion. Government expenditures rose from $39.5 billion in 1950 to $74.1 billion in 1953.

The 1954 recession was due, in part, to the military cutback but also to overoptimism on the part of businessmen, who based their growth rate on the expansion of the 1951–1952 period. The multiplier-accelerator, spurred by government spending, had pushed growth to its " ceiling." Consequently, bottlenecks occurred and inventories began piling up in 1953. When defense spending was cut back in 1954 with no compensating fiscal policy, the result was a recession in business activity. Once the recession was underway, monetary and fiscal activity helped to reverse the trend. Federal Reserve authorities increased the supply of money and credit by lowering the discount rate, by lowering the required reserve ratio, and by buying securities on the open market. Fiscal policy was also in the right direction. Fortuitously, a tax cut had been legislated, although once again the tax cut had not been instigated as part of planned countercyclical fiscal policy. The automatic stabilizers also played a part in mitigating the recession. In addition, private long-term investment held up well, owing to technological advances, population growth, and continued demand for residential housing.

The economic growth during the 1955–1957 period has been called the durable goods boom. The greatest part of the expansion came in 1955, when GNP increased from $364.8 billion to $398.0 billion in current prices or from $407.0 billion to $438.0 billion in terms of the 1958 price index. In 1956 and 1957 consumer spending on residential housing and automobiles was weak in an otherwise expanding economy. Banks continued to expand their loans, and business expenditures for new plant and equipment increased from $28.7 billion in 1954 to $37.0 billion in 1957. The consumer price index (using the 1957–1959 base) remained relatively steady during the first part of the expansion but rose from 94.7 to 98.0 percent during 1957.

The 1957–1958 recession, although short, was severe. GNP, rising slightly in terms of current dollars (from $441.1 billion to $447.3 billion), fell in terms of the 1958 price index by $5.2 billion (from $452.5 billion to $447.3 billion). Businesses cut back investment spending from $37 billion to $30.5 billion, and unemployment rose to its highest postwar level, 6.8 percent.

The action of the monetary authorities before and during the recession had the effect of curtailing investment and consumer spending and increasing the severity of the recession. The monetary situation finally was eased in the latter part of the recession by reduction of reserve requirements and the rediscount rate.

Although there was no aggressive fiscal policy, the automatic stabilizers were very responsive, producing budget deficits of $2.8 billion in 1958 and $12.4 billion in 1959. During 1959, GNP rose from $447.3 billion to $483.7 billion.

THE "NEW ECONOMICS" OF THE SIXTIES

In the summer of 1960 yet another recession was born, again with the help of monetary and fiscal policy makers. The Federal Reserve had quickly returned to a policy of constraint and had actually reduced the money supply from $144.9 billion in 1959 to $143.8 billion in 1960. The fiscal activity of the Federal government was also restrictive. The budget deficit of fiscal year 1959 of $12.4 billion suddenly became a large surplus as expenditures were reduced and the automatic rise in taxes continued.

Although the 1960 recession was mild, it was an occasion for a critical look at the economy by economists and the general public. Coming on the heels of the 1957–1958 recession, it made explicit the continuing problem of preserving a stable growth rate. Unemployment, which had usually remained between 2 and 3 percent in the postwar years, had generally ranged from 4 to 5 percent after 1958. The average growth rate during the decade from 1947 to 1959 of almost 4 percent had faded to 2.5 percent from 1957 to 1960.

In 1960 President Kennedy was elected not only on the basis of his superior deportment on television but for his promise to " get the economy moving." Very little was new about the " new economics " implemented in the early 1960s. But for the first time the United States had a President willing to attempt aggressive fiscal policy as conceived within the framework of Keynesian economic analysis. During the late 1950s economists had begun to argue their case in terms of " potential " versus " realized "

FIGURE 17–3

The full-employment
GNP gap

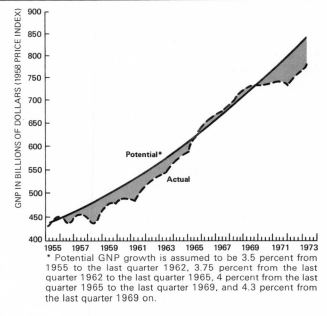

* Potential GNP growth is assumed to be 3.5 percent from
1955 to the last quarter 1962, 3.75 percent from the last
quarter 1962 to the last quarter 1965, 4 percent from the last
quarter 1965 to the last quarter 1969, and 4.3 percent from
the last quarter 1969 on.

FIGURE 17–4

Actual versus full-
employment budgets

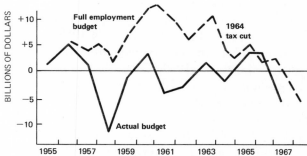

growth rates. A necessary condition for reaching the " potential " rate is
that sufficient aggregate spending takes place each year.

Several factors, however, worked against the aggressive use of fiscal
policy. First, of course, were the notions of the public and Congress of
fiscal "responsibility." Second, the economy was slowly expanding in
1961 and there was already a deficit. Since expansion was identified with
"prosperity" more aggressive fiscal policy did. not seem needed. A
common fallacy among some economists at that time was that a business
cycle of predictable expansion and contraction was almost inevitable.
Thus the proper role of macroeconomic policy was to cushion the swings

of the cycle. Using a rather naive countercyclical perspective, one could argue that deficits may occur in recession but surpluses should occur in expansion. Finally it was becoming widely accepted that the high rates of unemployment the economy had been experiencing were resulting from basic structural changes within the economy. If so, fiscal actions designed to reduce unemployment below 5 or 6 percent would only result in inflation.

Of major importance to the introduction of Keynesian economic analysis into federal fiscal policy was the sympathetic hearing given economists by both Presidents Kennedy and Johnson. Without a massive program of publicity and education by their administrations, the necessary acquiescence of the public and Congress could not have been achieved. President Kennedy introduced the concept of the production gap—the gap between actual and potential GNP—into the political arena. And it was on the basis of this concept that the distinction between countercyclical and growth-oriented fiscal policy could best be made. To Kennedy's Council of Economic Advisers the " gap " could be roughly estimated as the difference between the existing GNP and growth rate and that which could be achieved *if unemployment could be lowered to 4 percent*. Thus the potential " full employment " GNP was estimated on the basis of only 4 percent unemployment. Figures 17.3 and 17.4 demonstrate the differences between " potential " and " actual " growth and between the " full-employment " and " actual " budgets. Potential GNP is an estimate of the GNP forthcoming if unemployment were lowered to only 4 percent. The " full employment " budget is based on what spending power would be required to bring spending to the full employment level (again assuming it to be with only 4 percent unemployment).

The shift from the countercyclical to the growth-oriented perspective was well stated in the Council's January 1962 *Annual Report*: " The mandate of the Employment Act renews itself perpetually as maximum levels of production, employment, and purchasing power rise through time. The weapons of stabilization policy—the budget, the tax system, control of the supply of money and credit—must be aimed anew, for their target is moving."[5]

This new orientation meant that fiscal policy would be formulated in different terms—most notably in terms of the " production " or " performance " gap. The countercyclical view can easily fall prey to the notion

[5] *Annual Report* (January 1962), p. 142.

that when the economy is expanding, fiscal constraints should be applied in early stages lest the economy become overheated. To a certain extent this is true; and in the past we seem to have suffered from not enough rather than too much fiscal activity. But emphasis on "leaning against the cycle" can lead to recoveries which never reach their potential—as in 1959.

FISCAL DRAG AND FULL EMPLOYMENT BUDGET SURPLUS

Moreover, the role of the automatic stabilizers can be misunderstood if the countercyclical perspective is the only one used. The automatic stabilizers which dampen the short-run cyclical swings can also dampen the long-run growth rate. Unless the automatic rise in tax receipts is offset, the tax-transfer structure acts as a "fiscal drag" on economic growth. This is especially crucial in view of the progressivity of the personal income tax.

The most important aspect of the "fiscal drag" notion is the way it relates to the "potential" GNP. In the early 1960s economists, and especially those on the Council of Economic Advisers, cast their estimates of the stimulus or drag of the budget in terms of its surplus or deficit *at the potential GNP.*[6]

As illustrated in Figure 17.4, the actual budget deficit in fiscal year 1961 was $3.9 billion. But had potential GNP been accomplished (assuming an unemployment figure of 4 percent), the budget would have shown a *surplus* of $10 billion. *From this perspective a strong fiscal drag was being exerted on the economy.* Thus, fiscal policy featuring much more stimulation was in order.

The 1964 tax cut, the largest and most dramatic example of current fiscal policy, rightly deserves much of our attention. But some of the other fiscal actions are also important and quite relevant to the question of consumption vs. investment spending.

The initial plunge of the Kennedy administration into Keynesian growth economics took the form of tax incentives to business investment, proposed in 1961 and enacted in 1962. These incentives offered an investment tax credit of 7 percent on new capital equipment and more liberal depreciation schedules, allowing companies to "write off" a greater percentage of the cost of newly purchased equipment in the early years of its use. Since businesses could count off more depreciation costs against their tax bill, they could retain funds longer and use them for investment purposes. The mechanics of this fiscal policy in terms of the Keynesian model were outlined in the last chapter. The present costs of investment projects are lowered, shifting the *MEC* schedule to the right. This in turn shifts the *IS* curve to the right, since more investment spending will be forthcoming at a given rate of interest.

The business sector responded vigorously to the stimulus of the investment tax credit. Business expenditures for new plant and equipment jumped from $34.4 billion in 1961 to $37.3 billion in 1962. As outlined previously, this increase in investment spending generated an increase in consumption spending through the multiplier effect. Personal consumption expenditures increased from $338.0 billion to $356.8 billion. During the same period (from calendar year 1961 to 1962) GNP rose from $518.7 billion to $556.2 billion—an increase of over 7 percent. Other government policies contributed to this expansion. Purchases of goods and services by the federal government increased from $57.0 to $62.9 billion. Several training and educational programs were instituted in 1961, and the activities of the employment service systems were expanded in an effort to increase the mobility of labor. Monetary policy was one of relative ease, although there was only a small increase in the supply of money. As mentioned in the last chapter, the Federal Reserve attempted to lower long-term interest rates, thus encouraging investment by business, while raising short-term rates to encourage retention of foreign funds for balance-of-payments purposes. This latter policy was continued throughout the expansion, until the Fed became alarmed at the growing government expenditures on Vietnam and in December of 1965 sought to tighten credit by raising the rediscount rate.

The wage-price guidelines introduced in early 1962 no doubt played a part in restraining inflationary pressures during this period of expanding spending. However, their effectiveness is difficult to judge, especially since they were only one aspect of economic policy.

The growth during 1962 was successful in terms of the Council of Economic Advisers "production" gap criterion. The gap between

---

[6] See Walter Heller, *New Dimensions of Political Economy* (New York: Norton, 1967), especially pp. 64–70. Heller notes that Charles L. Schultze presented the concept of the full employment deficit or surplus in "Current Economic Situation and Short-Run Outlook," *Hearings before the Joint Economic Committee*, 86th Congress, 2nd Session, December 7 and 8, 1960 (Washington, D.C.: U.S. Government Printing Office, 1960), pp. 114–122. Heller also notes that the concept was analyzed in detail in the Council's January 1962 *Annual Report* (pp. 78–84) and later in testimony before the Subcommittee on Fiscal Policy of the Joint Economic Committee, July 20, 1965.

realized and potential GNP was reduced from $50 billion in early 1961 to $30 billion in 1962. But the " gap " held stubbornly at that level—unemployment had dropped from 6.7 percent to 5.6 percent but was still 5.7 in 1963 and 5.2 in 1964. In view of the fiscal drag being exerted and the remaining gap between realized and potential GNP, the decision to ask for a massive tax cut was made by President Kennedy in 1962. It was realized, however, that such a bold leap into Keynesian economic policy would require a large educational offensive, especially in view of continuing economic growth and an already large deficit. It was not, in fact, until 1964 that the tax cut proposal was passed under President Johnson; and the great majority of the public was skeptical even then.

This skepticism faded in light of the exceptional success of the tax cut, whose impact on the economy followed closely the path predicted by economists. Gross national product rose from $612.0 billion in fiscal year 1964 to $651.8 billion in 1965 to $712.0 billion in 1966 and to $769.8 billion in 1967. These more recent expansions were due in part to a 1965 cut in excise taxes of some $5 billion and increased defense expenditures, which rose from $96.5 billion in fiscal year 1965 to $106.9 in 1966 to $112.8 billion in 1967. Moreover, unemployment dropped to under 4 percent by 1966. In addition, until the intervention of the massive Vietnam expenditures, we were indeed headed for the *balanced budget at full employment*—the theoretical abstraction upon which the magnitude of fiscal actions had been based. As Walter Heller points out, by the first half of 1965 the federal budget was in *surplus*.[7] In the absence of the Vietnam crisis further income tax cuts to reduce fiscal drag would have been in order, even with greatly expanded programs under the War on Poverty.

The expansion of the war in Vietnam changed the fiscal outlook practically overnight and brought new challenges to monetary and fiscal policy makers. At first the attempt was made to stem the inflationary pressures brought on by increased Vietnam expenditures by monetary action alone. In the view of many economists, a combined fiscal and monetary approach would have been more successful. As early as December of 1965, the Federal Reserve turned from its policy of monetary ease to restraint. When the rediscount rate was raised and borrowing from the Fed curtailed, commercial banks quite obligingly, if not eagerly, raised interest rates. The experience during and after that time revealed some of the difficulties of relying heavily on monetary policy to stem inflationary pressures in a high-employment economy.

In the first place, the impact of the rise in interest rates is uneven. Since consumer demands remain high, those industries which use primarily internally generated funds for expansion have not been affected as much as those who depend on funds from the capital market. Moreover, the constraint of rising interest rates on some industries not in danger of overexpansion is uncalled for. When the Fed tightened money sharply in 1966, the economy responded quickly and inflation temporarily slowed. After "ease" was introduced, however, inflation continued. The Fed encouraged banks to raise interest rates and they again were most patriotic; however, the money supply was allowed to grow, thus accentuating the inflationary spiral. Corporations, having been forewarned, quickly changed the composition of their investment portfolios so as to have credit available. The increase in interest rates in 1967 and 1968 only served to boost prices elsewhere. When the credit squeeze finally was felt in 1969, states, localities, small businesses, and consumers still managed to obtain credit.

Several fiscal measures to reduce spending were introduced in early 1966. Some of the Great Society programs were reduced; planned cuts in excise taxes on telephones and automobiles were discontinued; and the rate of corporate income tax payments was speeded up. But the proposal for a surtax was not acted upon. There were several reasons for the delay. It still remained to be seen whether this was indeed the "full employment" level or whether unemployment could be cut to 3 or 2 percent without serious inflation. Second, it was (rightly) feared that if a cutback was required, political necessity would dictate a further cut in the poverty programs. These programs, however, were the main basis of hope that the unemployment could be cut to 2 or 3 percent without inflation, since for the most part they were attempts to increase the quality and mobility of labor. Moreover, economists, aware of the annual increase in *fiscal drag*, assumed that this in itself would eventually retard inflation.

Few economists realized the enormity of the inflationary pressures building up at that time; consequently, few advised the stringent measures that would have been required to nip inflation in the bud. In retrospect their failure stems from two factors. First, few people were aware of the rapid increase in expenditures on Vietnam. Even the Council of Economic Advisers was not informed of the vast amounts of spending power being injected into the economy. Second, economists misjudged the marginal

[7] *New Dimensions of Political Economy* (New York: Norton, 1967), pp. 72–73.

FIGURE 17-5

Shifts in aggregate demand
and supply functions

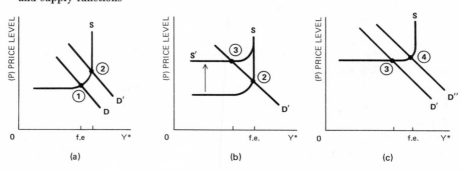

(a)   (b)   (c)

propensity to consume and the accelerator. The consumption function, it turns out, shifted considerably in the sixties. For several reasons consumers spent much more freely than anticipated. A long period of prosperity plus more adequate public insurance programs increased the marginal propensity to consume. As incomes continued to rise luxuries quickly became necessities. As sales continued to grow, businessmen's expectations became more optimistic. The value of the accelerator increased accordingly.

As inflationary pressures became more obvious in 1967, economists became more insistent in their demands for aggressive anti-inflationary policy. A surtax, first suggested in 1966, was advocated more strongly, but it was not to be implemented by Congress until mid-1968. Continued increases in war expenditures and the delay of the surtax were to have serious repercussions in the late sixties and early seventies as demand-pull inflation finally induced a full-fledged cost-push inflation.

One reason for the delay of the surtax legislation is interesting to us because it is another example of how effective macroeconomic policy can be circumvented by a disagreement over priorities between the private and public sectors. As we know from our study of the budgetary process, the chairman of the House Ways and Means Committee has virtual veto power over any legislation involving taxes. On the occasion of President Johnson's surtax proposal, Chairman Wilbur Mills chose to exercise his veto power by refusing to introduce the necessary legislation until the Administration promised to cut back various expenditure programs. More specifically some of the Great Society programs did not fit in with Mills' idea of the proper allocation of resources between the private and public sectors. The resulting conflict between Johnson and Mills over social priorities was not resolved until an inflationary spiral had begun.

POLICY SHIFTS UNDER THE NIXON ADMINISTRATION

The first stages of cost-push inflation were already evident when the Nixon Administration unfolded its economic " game plan " after the 1968 election. The plan was to rely on monetary policy to gradually cool down the economy. In retrospect it is obvious that stringent fiscal policy and " moral suasion " (to include selective wage and price controls) should also have been employed. Instead the Nixon Administration announced that it would not resort to controls of any sort. Moreover it used the unfortunate term " gradualism " to describe its policy prescription.

As cost-push inflation increased in severity over the next three years only perfunctory steps were taken to use " moral suasion " to limit price and wage increases. The argument was accepted that inflationary psychology could only be broken by a sustained period of high unemployment. The result was a long and painful recession but little relief from rising prices. Unemployment, which was 3.4 percent in January of 1969 rose rapidly and stayed around 6 percent.

The aggregate demand and supply curves in Figure 17.5 are useful in depicting the chain of economic events which occurred during the late 1960s and early 1970s. The large and continued spending on the Indo China war, plus a substantial accelerator effect, shifted the aggregate demand curve to the demand-pull position 2 in diagram (a). The belated passage of the income surtax was insufficient to restrain this shift in demand. Later, however, the automatic stabilizers and a tight monetary policy were successful in restraining demand. In the meantime, unfortunately, the cost-push forces had become widespread.

As outlined in the preceding chapter, the cost-push phenomenon can create both rising unemployment and prices. The strength of the cost-push phenomenon was amply demonstrated during the years that the Nixon Administration maintained its policy of " gradualism." Prices continued to rise in the face of increasing *fiscal drag*, monetary restraint and rising unemployment. Demand-pull inflation is partially restrained by the fiscal drag of reduced unemployment and welfare payments and progressively increasing revenues. But if unemployment is high and corporate profits down, the automatic stabilizers have less impact on reducing spending power. Actually under cost-push inflation it may not be desirable to cut back aggregate spending via fiscal drag.

As noted previously the cost-push phenomenon cannot be combated by the traditional monetary and fiscal tools. The traditional tools used to adjust aggregate demand can be effective in combating *either* rising prices *or* unemployment. The cost-push phenomenon, as depicted in diagram (b), is a double-faceted problem: Action must be taken to stop the upward shift of the supply function and, if full employment is to be reached, aggregate demand must be increased as in diagram (c).

PHASE I

On August 15, 1971, President Nixon used national television to announce a dramatic shift from his policy of gradualism to a program of direct wage and price controls. The pressures to make such a policy shift had been building for some time due to the obvious failure of his former approach. The immediate crisis which led to the shift was not so much the effect of the cost-push phenomenon on the domestic economy but the rapidly deteriorating position of the dollar relative to other currencies. During the years since World War II the U.S. had stabilized the price of gold and allowed for fixed exchange rates among currencies. However, serious maladjustment in exchange rates occurred from time to time due to the rising productivity of the formerly war-torn nations—especially West Germany and Japan. This long-term maladjustment plus the domestic inflation-recession produced a large balance-of-payments deficit in 1971 and severe pressure on the dollar.

Nixon's new program contained a number of provisions—some of which conflicted. The two most radical provisions were a 90-day *freeze* on all wages, prices, and rents and termination of our practice of buying gold at $35 an ounce.

The 90-day freeze was administered by a newly appointed Cost-of-Living Council which worked through the Office of Emergency Preparedness. Due to the immensity of the regulatory task the freeze necessarily depended on voluntary support. Of course voluntary support could readily be expected from consumers who did not wish their prices to be raised and firms who did not wish to raise wages and the prices paid their suppliers. Moreover the plan had the simplicity that it froze essentially *all* wages, prices and rents—even those increases previously contracted.

Since the currency exchange rates were directly tied to our support of the price of gold, reevaluation of exchange rates became necessary upon our abrupt discontinuance of that support. Another protectionist measure in the new plan was a 10 percent tariff on all imports not already covered by specific quotas or agreements. These measures created considerable disruption in world finance until exchange ratios and our continued support of gold were reestablished. This process required considerable bargaining, the " devaluation " of the dollar in terms of gold, and the upward adjustment of other currencies in terms of the dollar.

President Nixon's August 15 message included additional aid to our automobile industry in the form of a proposal to end the 7 percent excise tax on automobiles. Thus the incentives to the consumer to buy an American automobile included frozen prices at the 1971 model level, a 10 percent tariff on foreign makes, and the 7 percent tax reduction which was generally passed on to the consumer.

Two additional proposals to spur aggregate demand were reinstatement of the investment tax credit and stepping up the schedule for increased personal exemptions on the income tax.

Strangely enough, the President also promised budget cuts and the postponement of certain new spending proposals. The latter steps were obviously an attempt to appease those who still believed that demand-pull inflation was the problem and that " fiscal responsibility " was the proper solution.

POLITICS AND PUBLIC CHOICES IN PHASE II WAGE-PRICE CONTROLS

The decision-making organizations in Phase II of the Nixon wage-price controls are interesting to us not only as macroeconomic policy tools but as examples of how and why it is politically advantageous to delegate difficult public choices to organizations with varied representation.

There were two organizational aspects which were significant. First, the decisions on wages were delegated to one board and the decisions on prices to a separate board. This feature had the effect of diminishing one important element of the cost-push phenomenon: that increases in wages were automatically passed on in the form of high prices. Now when a union appeared before the Pay Board with a contract featuring large wage gains, the firms in question could have no assurances that corresponding price increases would be approved by the Price Board. To reinforce these doubts the Price Board declared that unwarranted wage increases could not be used as a justification when firms applied for price increases.

A second significant organizational feature was that the Board's membership, instead of being made up of Administration officials, was appointed from recognized experts (in the case of the Price Board) and from the major interest groups (labor, industry and the "public" in the case of the Pay Board). In both cases the delegation of responsibility helped to reduce the Administration's identification with the unpopular decisions.

In general the implementation of the two boards' responsibilities followed the outline in Chapter 16. The Pay Board set a guideline maximum of 5.5 percent wage increase and the Price Board set a guideline of 2.5 percent. Large wage contracts and price increases for large firms were required to be submitted to the respective board regardless of whether they fell within the guidelines or not. Investigation of complaints and answers to inquiries were carried out by a rapidly organized force from the Office of Emergency Preparedness and the Internal Revenue Service. This force was augmented by voluntary and often aggressive hordes of housewives and other types of buyers who had been chaffing for several years at what seemed to be arbitrary increases in prices. To aid in this process the Price Commission required all sellers to post lists of their prices and any changes.

The record of the two boards in the fourteen months of regulation was quite good. Moreover the implementation of controls was accomplished without the large bureaucracy that many experts had predicted would be required.

The differences in the decisions made by the two boards are interesting in light of the differences in the nature of membership. The Price Board was composed of seven "experts" who were supposed to control prices in the interests of the "public." The Pay Board was tripartite in form with fifteen members representing three distinct interests: labor, business, and the public.

A major reason for use of the tripartite form was that labor leaders had insisted on representation. Their participation had several advantages from the point of view of the Administration. First, the "blame" for wage decisions could be shifted away from the Administration. Secondly, it was more likely that unions would accept the decisions if some form of labor representation had participated. Thirdly, their participation along with that of management would provide informative input into the complex decisions. Finally, assuming that the Board's labor representatives accepted the results, there would be considerable pressure on the union in question to refrain from using the strike.

Predictably, the decisions of the Pay Board often reflected the pressures of the interests groups at the expense of consistency. By "consistency" we mean conformance to the general rules outlined in Chapter 16. These rules, we recall, were derived from the broad social priorities for macroeconomic policy, intersector resource allocation, and income distribution. The latter consideration turned out to be a source of considerable conflict especially in the Board's early decisions. The Board members were concerned to make adjustments according to "equity"; that is, to keep one group—say electricians—in their "accepted" position relative to other occupations—such as plumbers and carpenters.

In an early decision the Pay Board allowed for a "catch-up" increase of 15 percent in wages in the soft-coal industry. "Equity" considerations were thus judged more important by the big labor and big business representatives than the goals of price stability and efficient resource allocation. Virgil Day of General Electric, the Chairman of the Board's business members, justified their support of the decision as being "not inconsistent with other recent settlements, such as the steel industry." Due to considerable public pressure, the Pay Board's resistance stiffened when confronted by contracts calling for large increases in the aerospace industry. But here again precedents set in pre-controls contracts were considered important. The aerospace contracts were closely adapted to pre-control agreements in the automobile and steel industries. Day described the contract as one of "the last cows that must be gotten through the (Pay Board) gate, although possibly slimmed down some."[8] The Pay Board required labor and management to renegotiate. The final aerospace wage settlement was 8 percent for the first year. Although this may be scored as a victory, in that the Pay Board did not acquiesce to a powerful union, the result was much more liberal than envisioned by the criteria suggested in Chapter 16. In general the aerospace industry, like the soft-coal industry, was depressed and unemployment was very high. In subsequent decisions consensus among representatives of big labor on the one hand and management and the public on the other became increasingly difficult. This was in part because it was impossible for the labor representatives to behave in such a way as to satisfy their

[8] *Business Week*, December 11, 1971, p. 34.

constituency and the Board's purpose. In addition the inflation-recession was continuing to undercut the worker's buying power while the profits of certain industries were breaking records. Citing the latter inequities the labor representatives resigned in March of 1972, and President Nixon reorganized the Pay Board with only seven members all of whom were to represent the "public." The decisions of the second Pay Board, while more rational in terms of the controls criteria, still had to contend with the power of certain unions to disrupt the economy.

Decision making by the Price Board contrasted sharply with the tripartite Pay Board. Under the leadership of C. Jackson Grayson the Price Board generally followed the controls criteria. Moreover, the Price Board was more consistent and stringent in its policies than the first Pay Board. It is difficult to tell what factors explain the differences. One factor is simply the power of big labor as evidenced first by its representation on the Pay Board and secondly by the Board's decisions. But another factor was certainly the decision-making process itself. With conflicting interest groups represented, we would expect a shifting majority and more varied results than with a homogeneous group of decision makers.

A CRITIQUE OF PHASES I, II, AND III

Except for its obvious tardiness, the most important criticism of President Nixon's economic package of August 1971 was that it contained poorly timed boosts to aggregate spending. As our rather simplistic diagrams of aggregate demand and supply illustrate, the cost-push phenomenon may be accompanied by a substantial shortage of spending. Moreover, one potential weapon against the inflationary spiral is the excess capacity firms are enjoying. If this excess capacity is utilized, gains in productivity and real income can be won. This might have been accomplished had aggregate demand been given a greater boost while the wage-price freeze was in effect. The Nixon Administration had hoped its incentives for investment would encourage businessmen to expand, but existing excess capacity and dim expectations restrained their response. Unfortunately, the tax breaks for consumers were not effective until April of the next year. The timing of monetary policy was similarly unfortunate. The original "game plan" of the Nixon Administration of a stable increase in the money supply had been abandoned in the summer of 1971. Instead of a policy of "ease," the expansion of the money supply was held to a 1 percent annual rate from July through December 1971. Then in the first half of 1972 the money supply was expanded at an annual rate of almost 10 percent. As it turned out, the Price and Pay Boards began easing their controls just as the pressure of new spending power was being fully realized. Moreover, omissions in the Price Board coverage had allowed for resumption of inflation in certain key areas of the economy—most notably food prices, an area dear to the heart of the housewife and highly visible to everyone. This sequence of events would seem more conducive than necessary to a renewal of the " catch up " psychology of cost-push inflation.

On January 12, 1973, President Nixon abruptly lifted the mandatory wage and price controls of Phase II and inaugurated Phase III, a system of quasi-voluntary controls. The Price and Pay Boards were abolished; however, the Cost-of-Living Council was expanded and the Administration retained the right to "step in" to any wage or price increases which were out of line with the general guidelines. Treasury Secretary George P. Shultz explained that the government was retaining "an ability to bring the stick out of the closet" to enforce acceptable behavior. The wage-increase standard remained at 5.5 percent; however, the price and profits guidelines were eased. Under Phase II, companies that had raised prices were not permitted to raise their profit margin above an average of the best two of three years prior to controls. Under Phase III, companies could also use any fiscal year since controls.

The change in policy seemed dubious in light of continuing unemployment and residual " cost-push " in some industries coupled with " demand-pull " factors (particularly new investment) in other industries. Indeed, the appropriate policy would have been to readjust the controls according to the changing economic environment using the criteria outlined in Chapter 16, at the same time making more vigorous efforts to *increase productivity* in those industries where supply was lagging.

The response to Phase III was immediate. Prices soared at record rates in February, March, and April. A second international monetary crisis occurred which abolished existing exchange rates, forced the " floating " of all major currencies, and allowed the dollar to be devalued once more. The initial action of the Nixon Administration to soaring food prices was to place ceilings on meat prices at the retail, wholesale, and processing levels. As other prices continued to rise, pressure for renewed controls was increased. It remains to be seen whether or not the

Administration will utilize the appropriate combination of macroeconomic tools (to include both direct and indirect controls and incentives). The record to date does not inspire confidence.

A FINAL NOTE

A major theme of this study has been the interplay of individual and social preferences within our myriad of decision-making institutions. One of our basic models demonstrated how, under ideal circumstances, our public choices concerning resource allocation (between private and public goods), income distribution, and macroeconomic policy could each be pursued in ways not affecting the other goals. However, we have outlined recent "budget battles" between the President and Congress in which resource allocation choices (say between defense and urban renewal) were purposely linked with macroeconomic choices. Similarly, we have outlined the dilemma of Congress in trying to set overall budget and debt ceilings while at the same time allocating resources effectively among public needs.

Other perspectives featured voting and budgeting models with which to analyze the interplay of interest groups at the federal, state, and local levels. The continuing conflicts and tradeoffs among public needs such as defense, education, job opportunity, the "energy crisis," the environment, transportation, and poverty, promise to furnish ample opportunity for the student to apply the many concepts, perspectives, and models we have presented.

INDEX